Contents

Peterson's

College Guide

for

Visual Arts Majors

2007

PETERSON'S

A ⓝelnet. COMPANY

PETERSON'S

A (n)elnet. COMPANY

About Peterson's, a Nelnet company

Peterson's (www.petersons.com) is a leading provider of education information and advice, with books and online resources focusing on education search, test preparation, and financial aid. Its Web site offers searchable databases and interactive tools for contacting educational institutions, online practice tests and instruction, and planning tools for securing financial aid. Peterson's serves 110 million education consumers annually.

For more information, contact Peterson's, 2000 Lenox Drive, Lawrenceville, NJ 08648; 800-338-3282; or find us on the World Wide Web at www.petersons.com/about.

Editor: Linda Seghers; Production Editor: Teresina Jonkoski; Copy Editors: Bret Bollmann and Pam Sullivan; Research Project Manager: Jennifer Fishberg; Programmer: Alex Lin; Manufacturing Manager: Ivona Skibicki; Composition Manager: Gary Rozmierski; Interior Design: Katie Cordisco; Client Relations Representatives: Danielle Groncki, Mimi Kaufman, Karen Mount, and Eric Wallace.

ISBN-13: 978-0-7689-2172-4
ISBN-10: 0-7689-2172-4
ISSN 1552-7751

Printed in the United States of America

10 9 8 7 6 5 4 3 2 1   08 07 06

Twelfth Edition

Foreword

There's a certain myth about the creative process that many high school students and aspiring artists have heard: Artists usually work best in unstructured, independent environments and without formal education in the arts.

This couldn't be farther from the truth. A college or university that specializes in the arts can offer a number of benefits to students—by helping them grow creatively, providing them with access to state-of-the-art equipment and facilities, and ultimately preparing them for successful arts-related careers. As members of a creative community, art students receive inspiration, encouragement, and feedback from peers, professors, and visiting artists—all of whom form a valuable network of creative and professional contacts.

Members of colleges and universities that specialize in arts education often make up a community that inspires and nourishes creativity. Students interact with peers who share a love of the arts and grow along with their classmates, who can provide critiques, offer tips, and share opportunities for collaboration, both within major programs and across disciplines. International students also add diversity and global perspectives to the community. A student body that collectively embraces difference, promotes curiosity, and explores questions permits aspiring artists to not only hone their specific craft, but to develop an overall concept of the world and their place within it.

Faculty members at arts-related institutions serve as an invaluable resource to their students. These professors may be practicing artists or authors, curators, scholars, or theorists. The credentials they carry to the classroom—education and career experience, including publications, exhibitions, collaborations, and professional affiliations—impact their students, who benefit from knowledgeable critiques, answers to technical questions, and contacts in their field of study. To ensure that they choose an institution where they will receive maximum support from faculty members, prospective students may want to speak with both current students and professors. Office hours, availability outside the classroom, willingness to provide recommendations for internships or employment, and overall commitment to students all are important considerations. In addition, a combination of new and long-term faculty members often signals a mix of fresh ideas and seasoned professionalism.

Visual Arts

Effective arts colleges and universities offer their students ample opportunities to learn from guest speakers and artists. Whether they serve as artists-in-residence for a term, spend a few days providing individual critiques, or deliver a lecture or demonstration, professional artists share technical insight, innovative ideas, and market awareness through their communications with students.

In addition to the opportunities to interact with an array of artists, arts-centered colleges and universities offer students access to media, equipment, and facilities that individual artists may not be able to afford. The level of support for these resources varies from institution to institution, and prospective students may want to research whether and how this commitment affects opportunities in their area of interest. For example, a school that offers technology-dependent programs, such as animation, sound design, and visual effects, should regularly update software and hardware. Labs for disciplines such as metals and jewelry and industrial design should adhere to safety standards.

At an arts college or university, students also learn about potential areas of specialization that they might not otherwise have discovered. At Savannah College of Art and Design, for example, a student interested in computer art has the opportunity to explore a variety of focused majors, including animation, broadcast design and motion graphics, interactive design and game development, and visual effects, as well as sound design and film and television.

While students at many institutions of higher learning can experience off-campus programs and internships, at an arts-focused school, these opportunities are geared toward students' artistic growth and development. Internships help students get a foot in the door of their chosen industry, whether that means working at a high-end interior design firm or studying with a noted freelance artist. Professors, visiting artists, and even peers can prove valuable sources of internship leads, and schools also offer career services departments devoted to publicizing job openings for artists. Off-campus programs focused on arts can provide inspiration, motivation, and comprehensive understanding of creative industries. Arts-focused schools offer fashion students trips to New York during fashion week; offer art history students visits to Milan, Rome, and Venice; and offer painting and historic preservation students art history programs abroad, all of which let students experience diverse settings and explore other cultures, enhancing both the college experience and an artist's vision.

Ultimately, artists communicate through their work. They express their ideas, their dreams, their perspectives and their personal stories in forms that may endure for generations and speak to millions. An arts-centered educational community enables students to explore their talents and learn how best to articulate their unique perceptions to the world.

Sandra Reed
Dean of Graduate Studies
Savannah College of Art and Design

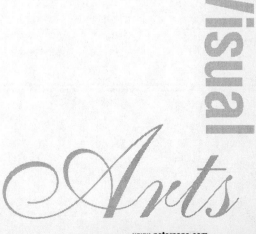

A Note from the Peterson's Editors

As a prospective art major, you probably know where your talent lies and can see yourself becoming a graphic designer, a photographer, a filmmaker, or maybe an art teacher one day. You are one of the lucky college-bound students who already know what they want to study and have one foot solidly on their career path. That part might have been easy.

But what's usually not easy is choosing a school and a program. You have some of the same considerations as all college-bound students: Do I want to be at a large school or a small school, in a busy city or on a quiet rural campus, 5 hours away from home by plane or 20 minutes away by car? But as an art student, you also have to decide if you want to attend a specialized art college or a liberal arts college or university and choose between a professional degree (B.F.A.) program and a liberal arts (B.A.) program. That's a lot to decide.

Peterson's College Guide for Visual Arts Majors will help you make the right decisions.

The first three sections of the guide, **The Right Program for You, Applying and Getting In,** and **You're In! What's Next?,** give you invaluable advice to help you assess your educational needs, discover what options are out there, navigate the admissions process, and learn what it's really like to be a serious art student. You'll learn the differences between B.F.A. and B.A. programs and what to expect at a specialized art college versus majoring in art at a liberal arts college. If you're in the early stages of college prep, you'll gain invaluable insight into how to prepare a portfolio—perhaps the most important part of the whole application process. Admissions directors at six top art colleges across the country reveal what they look for when reviewing students' portfolios. You'll also get advice from current art majors and a glimpse into what a typical day in art school is like. There are practical tips on making the most of your college visits and interviews and covering your college costs and a checklist to help you make sure you've found the right program for you. Finally, "Up Close and Personal with Professional Artists" gives you a look at some careers in the art field and what working artists say about art education.

Visual Arts

When it's the nitty-gritty details you need, the **Profiles of Visual Arts Programs** section contains comprehensive, detailed descriptions of professional degree programs in art arranged alphabetically by name of school. Each profile provides all the need-to-know information on accredited art programs throughout the U.S. and Canada. Some schools have provided even more information about their facilities, faculty, alumni, and special programs in *More About the School* at the end of their profile. There isn't an easier or more efficient way to explore art programs. To get the most out of the **Profiles,** just turn to "How to Use This Guide." It provides in-depth explanations about each data element found in the **Profiles.**

For those who already have specifics in mind, the **Quick-Reference Chart** lists schools by state and lets you compare programs at a glance. The **Appendixes** include additional resources, including listings of summer programs and scholarships. The **Indexes** let you locate schools by their majors or concentrations or alphabetically by name.

Peterson's publishes a full line of resources to help guide you and your family through the private secondary school admission process. Peterson's publications can be found at your local bookstore, library, and high school guidance office, and you can access us online at www.petersons.com.

We welcome any comments or suggestions you may have about this publication and invite you to complete our online survey at www.petersons.com/booksurvey. Or you can fill out the survey at the back of this book, tear it out, and mail it to us at:

Publishing Department
Peterson's
2000 Lenox Drive
Lawrenceville, NJ 08648

Your feedback will help us to provide personalized solutions for your educational advancement.

Remember, there is no "best" school—only the best school for you. Start examining your goals, your interests, your personality, your talents; and by all means, talk with your teachers and guidance counselors. The editors at Peterson's wish you the best of luck in your art school search!

Visual

Arts

The Right Program for You

Finding the right college art program is a challenge. What makes a program right for one person might make it very wrong for someone else. In order to find the perfect fit, you need to consider your needs, talents, and goals and then begin to explore your options.

Liberal Arts Education vs. Specialized Education

Jon Fraser

If you are planning to major in art, it's important to choose the college art program that's right for you and an environment that nurtures you as an artist. That's what a good school can do for you: develop and nurture the talent you may already have and prepare you, in some cases, for a professional career.

The difference between a liberal arts education and a specialized education is significant. A specialized school usually awards a Bachelor of Fine Arts degree and offers intense training in your art form, with little emphasis on other subjects. A liberal arts education offers you a broad training that attempts to make you a well-rounded, well-educated member of society. Some programs offer a specialized approach in a liberal arts environment, where you'll study other subjects while receiving intense training in your art form. And some programs are highly specialized and preprofessional. Which one is best for you?

B.A./B.F.A./B.S.

Colleges offer three types of degrees in the visual arts: a general degree, called a Bachelor of Arts (B.A.), a preprofessional degree called a Bachelor of Fine Arts (B.F.A.), and a Bachelor of Science (B.S.) for areas such as art therapy. The main difference between the types of degree programs is the number of classes you will be required to take in your major. The goals of these various types of degrees are also different.

B.F.A. programs allow students to focus most of their studies in art—up to 70 percent of all course work—and don't usually permit as many electives in areas outside the major as B.A. programs. These programs are meant for those who intend to pursue a professional career in their field of study. The B.F.A. program in the visual arts at a university will be rigorous and professional, typically offering a broad range of courses and electives. Universities vary, though, as to whether or not areas for specialization are available.

The Right Program for You

The B.A. program is meant for those who want a broad-based education with plenty of room for electives and who may not be sure what they want to do after they graduate.

The B.S. is generally a more technically oriented degree in a subject like art therapy, where the career is related to art but requires other skills.

Some schools offer two or three degrees in the same subject and let you choose which program to pursue. Other schools have stricter entrance requirements for the B.F.A. or B.S. degree programs than for the B.A. program.

As a general rule of thumb, if you're not sure or you have to ask, it's probably best to pursue a B.A. degree. If you feel you have no choice, that your art form is what you must do for the rest of your life, the B.F.A. or B.S. is probably the right choice. Another thing to keep in mind is that in many schools with several degree programs, you may switch from one to the other once you get there.

LIBERAL ARTS COLLEGE OR SPECIALIZED COLLEGE

Once you've decided on a degree program, you need to decide which type of school is right for you. The choice between attending a liberal arts college and a specialized college is highly individual. It is not about which one will make you successful. Both types of school may or may not help you to become a success at what you do. You don't get a "better" education at one or the other. What you get is a different sort of education that may or may not serve your needs.

Competition within a specialized school tends to be more intense than in a liberal arts environment. Moreover, liberal arts schools may have a minimum grade point average requirement for staying in their programs. So, a word of warning: If you're planning on majoring in the arts, plan on working hard!

As someone who has worked for a liberal arts institution (Long Island University's C.W. Post Campus) for many years, I have my prejudice about which one you should choose. For most people, I feel that a liberal arts education makes a better artist, in the holistic sense that any art form is more than simply good technique. It requires intelligent inquiry and critical thinking about the world around you. A good liberal arts undergraduate education in the arts should develop not only your artistic skills and talent, but your intellectual and critical skills as well. Usually offered outside the department or school of art, liberal arts programs offer a wide range of electives from many disciplines, including business, languages, literature, and sciences. Art students interested in developing in-depth study in a liberal arts subject can often do so through the options of minors or dual majors.

In addition, keep in mind that graduate school is where there is plenty of time to focus your energies on developing career-related skills in your specific art form. Getting a Master of Fine Arts (M.F.A.) degree may be part of your future plans, and it won't matter so much where you went to undergraduate school, but how well you did as evidenced not only by grades, but by your portfolio.

That being said, the rule of thumb here is: If you have to ask or are not sure, go to the liberal arts school. If you have no doubt about your future, if art is the only thing you want to do, consider a specialized college. And remember, if you find yourself at the wrong school, you can always transfer.

Jon Fraser is Acting Dean of the School of Visual and Performing Arts at C.W. Post Campus, Long Island University.

The Right Program for You

Choosing a Specialized School

Kimberly Stogner

Many people refer to college as the best time of their lives. But you may be wondering how you can achieve that experience if you enroll in a specialized school. What should you look for to make sure you get both a specialized education and the college experience you've always dreamed of?

MAKE SURE IT'S WHAT YOU LOVE

It may seem obvious, but before you commit to a specialized school, make sure you are really interested in that subject area. In other words, if you choose an art college and then decide you actually want to be a biomedical engineer, you will have to transfer to another college. However, if you love art, the more time spent in those courses, the better. And some specialized schools offer a wide range of majors and minors, allowing flexibility and cross-disciplinary study. So do your research on curriculum to know how limited or how broad a college's choices are.

VERIFY ACCREDITATION

Like money, you don't realize how important it is unless you don't have it. Accreditation is your thumbs up that a college's curriculum, faculty, facilities, and resources are on par with other institutions and professionals in the field. In other words, accreditation is what qualifies a college to confer degrees. There are two basic types of accreditation: regional (such as the Southern Association of Colleges and Schools) and programmatic (like the National Architectural Accrediting Board). Lack of accreditation can keep you from transferring credits to other universities and becoming licensed in your field. When visiting colleges, ask them about their accreditation, talk to professionals in your intended field, and look online for licensure requirements. If you just want a certificate and some training and experience, you may not need to worry so much about accreditation. But make sure you know what you're paying for ahead of time.

CHECK REPUTATION

Once you know your college has the appropriate accreditation, you also want to look into its reputation in your field. What have the faculty members accomplished? What are alumni doing? Will potential employers recognize your school? Do companies actively recruit graduates? What are job placement rates? Is there a career placement office to assist with employment opportunities? Since you know the field you want to pursue, you can take a very close look at the faculty in that area. Your professors should have terminal degrees in their field (the highest degree possible), and they should have recent work experience. Equipment, software, and procedures are constantly changing in every industry, and you want the most updated knowledge and experience. You also want professors with contacts in your field. These are the people who will write recommendations for your internship and job applications, so the better their contacts, the better your odds of securing the job you want.

SHOW ME THE MONEY

Another important consideration, of course, is the cost. Don't be shy about asking for financial assistance. Apply for federal aid online at www.fafsa.ed.gov and check with your guidance counselor for local or state funding sources. Ask the college admission department about scholarships and need-based aid, as well as alternative loans, work-study assistance, and part-time jobs. A college education gets more expensive every year, but let's face it: You probably can't make a better investment in your future.

DON'T SACRIFICE STUDENT INVOLVEMENT

While the art program and academics are obviously your top priorities in choosing a college, the fun you have outside class may be the most important influence in keeping you there until you graduate. Maybe the swim team is your thing, or writing for the student newspaper. Whatever your interests, you are more than your major, and your college should recognize and encourage that. Ask about special events, clubs, and competitions, and if there aren't enough, ask if you can start your own. See if there are study-abroad opportunities. Look for a student body with the size and diversity to foster your needs and interests.

Other services may also be important to you, such as disability and counseling resources, career planning and placement, security, dining and residence life, health and fitness, learning assistance, religious organizations, and transportation and parking. All these should be available to the degree that you desire.

VISIT

Take a tour. Talk to students. See how far it really is from the residence hall to the grocery store. Sit in on a class. Go to a soccer game. See if you like the climate, the neighborhood, the feeling you get walking around the campus. Visiting your top-choice schools is the best way to find a college that's right for you.

Kimberly Stogner is an admission representative at the Savannah College of Art and Design.

Making the Most of Your Campus Visit

Dawn B. Sova, Ph.D.

The campus visit should not be a passive activity for you and your parents. You will see many important indicators during your visit that will tell you a lot about the true character of the college and its students. Most organized campus visits include tours of such campus facilities as dorms, dining halls, libraries, student activity and recreation centers, and the health and student services centers. Some may only be pointed out, while you will walk through others. As an art student, you will of course be interested in seeing the facilities that pertain to your particular major, and those might be a major factor when considering a school. However, the general environment of the campus is important as well and merits close attention. Colleges do not train their tour guides to deceive prospective students, but they do caution guides to avoid unflattering topics and campus sites. Does this mean that you are condemned to see only a sugarcoated version of life on a particular college campus? Not at all—especially if you are observant.

VISITOR CENTER/ADMISSIONS OFFICE

Your first stop on a campus visit is the visitor center or admissions office. Begin your investigation with the visitor center staff members. As a student's first official contact with the college, they should make every effort to welcome prospective students and to project a friendly image.

- How do they treat you and other prospective students who are waiting? Are they friendly and willing to speak with you, or do they try their hardest to avoid eye contact and conversation?

- Are they friendly with each other and with students who enter the office, or are they curt and unwilling to help?

If the visitor center staff members seem indifferent to *prospective* students, there is little reason to believe that they will be warm and welcoming to current students.

SCHOOL NEWSPAPER

If time permits, look through several copies of the school newspaper, which should reflect the major concerns and interests of the students. The paper is also a good way to learn about the campus social life.

- Does the paper contain a mix of national and local news?

- What products or services are advertised?

- How assertive are the editorials?

- With what topics are the columnists concerned?

- Are movies and concerts that meet your tastes advertised or reviewed?

- What types of ads appear in the classified section?

The newspaper should be a public forum for students, and, as such, should reflect the character of the campus and of the student body. A paper that deals only with seemingly safe and well-edited topics on the editorial page and in regular feature columns might indicate administrative censorship. A lack of ads for restaurants might indicate either a lack of good places to eat or that area restaurants do not welcome student business. A limited mention of movies, concerts, or other entertainment might reveal a severely limited campus social life. Even if ads and reviews are included, you can also learn a lot about how such activities reflect your tastes.

BULLETIN BOARDS

Bulletin boards in the dorms and student centers contain a wealth of information about campus activities, student concerns, and campus groups. Read the posters, notices, and messages to learn what _really_ interests students. Unlike ads in the school newspaper, posters put up by students advertise both on- and off-campus events, so they will give you an idea of what is also available in the surrounding community. Art exhibits, poetry readings, jam sessions, writers' groups, and other activities may be announced and show diversity of student interests on that campus. Even the brief bulletin board messages offering objects for sale and noting objects that people want to purchase reveal a lot about a campus. Are most of the items computer related? Or do the messages specify compact discs, audio equipment, or musical instruments? Don't ignore the "ride wanted" messages. Students who want to share rides home during a break may specify widely diverse geographical locations. If so, then you know that the student body is not limited to only the immediate area or one locale.

BUILDINGS

As you walk through various buildings, examine their condition carefully.

- Is the paint peeling, and do the exteriors look worn?

- Are the exteriors and interiors of the building clean?

- Do they look well maintained?

- Is the equipment in the classrooms up-to-date?

As an art major, you will of course be most interested in their art facilities. Check out as many of the studios and as much of the equipment as you can. Is the equipment up-to-date? Is there independent studio space for painting majors? What sort of computer equipment do they have? No matter what you're planning to major in, all disciplines overlap at some point—painters and sculptors may need photo equipment for slides, filmmakers may need access to costume design or model building facilities. Having access to state-of-the-art equipment is important.

Pay particular attention to the dorms, especially to factors that might affect your safety. Ask about the security measures in and around the dorms.

- Are the dorms noisy or quiet?

- Do they seem crowded?

- How good is the lighting?

- Are the dorms spread throughout the campus or are they clustered in one main area?

- Who has access to the dorms in addition to students?

- How secure are the means by which students enter and leave the dorm?

CAMPUS SAFETY

While you are on the subject of dorm safety, you should also ask about campus safety. Don't expect that the guide will rattle off a list of crimes that have been committed in the past year. To obtain that information, access the recent issues of the *Chronicle of Higher Education* and locate its yearly report on campus crime. Also ask the guide about safety measures that the campus police take and those that students have initiated.

- Can students request escorts to their residences late at night?

- Do campus shuttle buses run at frequent intervals all night?

- Are "blue-light" telephones liberally placed throughout the campus for students to use to call for help?

- Do the campus police patrol the campus regularly?

If the guide does not answer your questions satisfactorily, wait until after the tour to contact the campus police or traffic office for answers.

HEALTH SERVICES

Campus tours usually just point out the health services center without taking the time to walk through. Even if you don't see the inside of the building, you should take a close look at the location of the health services center and ask the guide questions about services.

- How far is the health center from the dorms?

- Is a doctor always on call?

- Does the campus transport sick students from their dormitories or must they walk?

- What are the operating hours of the health center?

- Does the health center refer students to the town hospital?

If the guide can't answer your questions, visit the health center later and ask someone there.

ACTIVITIES CENTERS

Most campus tours seem to take pride in showing students their activities centers, which may contain snack bars, game rooms, workout facilities, and other means of entertainment. Should you scrutinize this building as carefully as the rest? Of course. Outdated and poorly maintained activity equipment contributes to your total impression of the college. You should also ask about the hours, availability, and cost (no, the activities are usually *not* free) of using the bowling alleys, pool tables, air hockey tables, and other items.

STUDENTS

As you walk through campus with the tour, look carefully at the appearance of the students you pass. The way they act and dress communicate a lot more than any guidebook can. If everyone seems to conform to the same look, you might feel that you would be uncomfortable at the college, however nonconformist that look might be. On the other hand, you might not feel comfortable on a campus that stresses diversity of dress and behavior, and your observations now can save you discomfort later.

- Does every student seem to wear a sorority or fraternity t-shirt or jacket?

- Does everyone seem to be wearing expensive name-brand clothes?

- Do most of the students seem to be working hard to look outrageous in regard to clothing, hair color, and body art?

- Would you feel uncomfortable in a room full of these students?

Is appearance important to you? If it is, then you should consider very seriously if you answer *yes* to any of the above questions. You don't have to be the same as everyone else on campus, but standing out too much may make you unhappy.

As you observe the physical appearance of the students, also listen to their conversations. What are they talking about? How are they speaking? Are their voices and accents all the same, or do you hear diversity in their speech? Are you offended by their language? Think how you will feel if surrounded by these students for four years.

The Right Program for You

WHERE SHOULD YOU VISIT ON YOUR OWN?

Your campus visit is not over when the tour ends because you will probably have many questions yet to be answered and many places still to be seen. If you haven't seen any residential hall, health and student services center, gym or fitness center, dining hall, the library, or recreational center, visit them on your own and ask questions of the students and staff members you meet.

Eat lunch in one of the dining halls. Most will allow visitors to pay cash to experience a typical student meal. Food may not be important to you now while you are living at home and can simply take anything you want from the refrigerator at any time, but it will be when you are away at college with a meal ticket to feed you.

- How clean is the dining hall? Consider serving tables, floors, and seating.

- What is the quality of the food?

- How big are the portions?

- How much variety do students have at each meal?

- How healthy are the food choices?

While you are eating, try to strike up a conversation with students and tell them that you are considering attending their college. Their reactions and advice can be eye-opening. Ask them questions about the academic atmosphere and the professors.

- Are the classes large or small?

- Do the majority of the professors only lecture, or are tutorials and seminars common?

- Is the emphasis of the faculty career-oriented or abstract?

- Do they find the teaching methods innovative and stimulating or boring and dull?

- Is the academic atmosphere pressured, lax, or somewhere in between?

- Which are the strong majors? Which are the weak majors?

- Is the emphasis on grades or social life or a mix of both?

- How hard do students have to work to receive high grades?

Current students can also give you the inside line—the true highs and lows of campus life. Ask them about drug use, partying, dating, drinking, and anything else that may affect your life as a student.

- Which are the most popular club activities?

- What do students do on weekends? Do most go home?

- How frequently do concerts occur on campus? Ask them to name groups that have recently performed.

- How can you become involved in specific activities (name them)?

- How strictly are campus rules enforced and how severe are penalties?

- What counseling services are available?

- Are academic tutoring services available?

- Do they feel that the faculty really cares about students, especially freshmen?

You will receive the most valuable information from current students, but you will only be able to speak with them after the tour is over. And you might have to risk rejection as you try to initiate conversations with students who might not want to reveal how they feel about the school.

SURROUNDING COMMUNITY

Make a point of at least driving through the community surrounding the college, because you will be spending time there shopping, dining, working in a part-time job, or attending events. Even the largest and best-stocked campus will not meet all of your social and personal needs. If you can spare the time, stop in several stores to see if they welcome college students.

The Right Program for You

- Is the surrounding community suburban, urban, or rural?

- Does the community offer stores of interest, such as bookstores, craft shops, and boutiques?

- Do the businesses employ college students?

- Does the community have a movie or stage theater?

- Are there several types of interesting restaurants?

- Do there seem to be any clubs that court a college clientele?

- Is the center of activity easy to walk to, or do you need a car or other transportation?

REVIEW YOUR NOTES

You might feel that a day is not enough to answer all of your questions, but even answering some questions will provide you with a stronger basis for choosing a college. Many students visit a college campus several times before making their decision. Keep in mind that not only will you spend the next four years of your life at a college, but for the rest of your life you will be associated with that college. The effort of spending several days to collect information to make your decision is worthwhile.

FOLLOWING UP

Your connection with a college does not end when you return home, no matter what your impression might be. Whether or not you wish to attend the school, you should take the time to follow up. Write a letter to thank people specifically for taking the time to meet with you. Beyond common courtesy, this also leaves the college officials with a positive view of you, and the letter will most likely be placed in your file. Will it make the difference between being accepted or rejected? No one can say. Write to the visitor center to thank counselors for their time, even if your experience was less than pleasant. You may have contact with them in the future and there is no reason not to leave them with a good impression.

Dawn B. Sova is a former newspaper reporter and columnist who teaches creative and research writing as well as scientific and technical writing, newswriting, and journalism.

Searching for Art Programs and Scholarships Online

Choosing a college art program involves a serious commitment of time and resources. Therefore, it is important to have the most up-to-date information about institutions and their programs at your fingertips. The Internet can be a great tool for gathering that information, and one of the best sites to visit during the college selection process is Peterson's Visual & Performing Arts (VPA) channel at www.petersons.com.

PETERSON'S VISUAL & PERFORMING ARTS CHANNEL

The VPA channel at Petersons.com is a one-stop source of information on college art programs in the U.S. and Canada. Just click on Visual & Performing Arts to access Peterson's comprehensive database of arts programs. If you know what area of art you're interested in, you can locate a school or program by clicking on "Art" on the Program Search pull-down menu, which gives you a list of art majors or concentrations. Simply click one of these and you will get a list of schools that offer a degree program in that field. Or, if you'd like to search by location, you can access lists of schools offering art programs in any state or in Canada. Finally, if you have a particular school in mind and want to see what art programs it offers, you can do an alphabetical search on the school's name and get information about their programs.

You can also request information from some schools by clicking on "Get Free Info." Within minutes, the school will receive your message and mail a catalog, an application, or information on financial aid to you. If you find the perfect school for a friend, you can even send the page to him or her with a message. There also are links to the school's Web site.

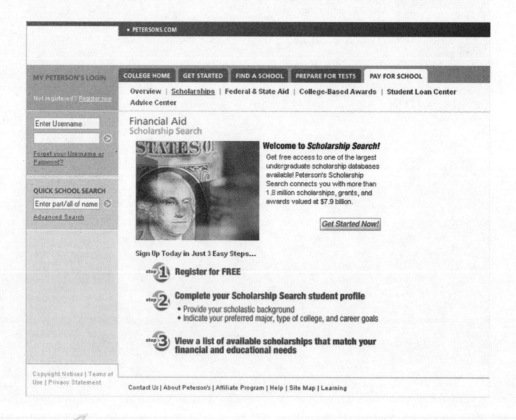

PETERSON'S FREE SCHOLARSHIP SEARCH

Petersons.com is a great site for any college-bound student. There is a wealth of information on undergraduate, graduate, online learning, and study-abroad programs and also some of the best financial aid advice available.

With Peterson's free Scholarship Search on the financial aid channel of Petersons.com (www.petersons.com/finaid), you can explore more than 1.7 million scholarships, grants, and prizes totaling nearly $8 billion and do an individualized search for awards that match your financial and educational needs. In just three easy steps, you can register; complete a customized profile indicating your scholastic and personal background, including intended major, work experience, and a host of other criteria that will allow you to access a list of scholarships that match your needs. Each scholarship is described in detail with eligibility and application requirements, contact information, and links to its e-mail address and Web site. Finding money for college couldn't be easier.

So, what are you waiting for? Log on to Petersons.com and let us help you with your college planning!

The Right Program for You

Covering Your College Costs

A college education is expensive: more than $150,000 for four years at some of the higher-priced colleges and universities and more than $50,000 at many lower-cost, state-supported colleges. Figuring out how you and your family will come up with the necessary funds to pay for your education requires planning, perseverance, and learning as much as you can about the options available.

For most families, paying the total cost of a student's college education out of savings is not possible. Clearly, the more your family has saved, the better off you will be and the less you will need to earn and borrow. But paying for college should not be looked at merely as a four-year financial commitment. While some of the money you need will likely come from funds that you and your parents have managed to save, some will come from a portion of your or your parents' current income. The rest will come from future earnings, through loans you or your parents will pay off later.

If your family has not saved the total amount or does not have sufficient current income to cover the costs, you can still attend college. That's where financial aid comes in. The amount you and your family will be expected to contribute toward your college expenses will be based upon your and your family's income and assets. But if this is not enough, the rest of the expenses can be met through various financial aid programs.

FINANCIAL AID BASICS: HOW FINANCIAL AID IS AWARDED

When you apply for aid, your family's financial situation is analyzed using a government-approved formula called the Federal Methodology. The result of this is the amount you and your family are expected to contribute toward your college expenses, called your Expected Family Contribution or EFC. If this is equal to or more than the cost of attendance at a particular college, then you do not demonstrate "financial need." However, even if you don't have financial need, you may still qualify for aid since there are many grants, scholarships, and loans that are not based on financial need.

If the cost of education is greater than your EFC, then you will be eligible for "need-based" assistance. The calculation of "financial need" is very simple:

Total Cost of Attendance
− Expected Family Contribution
Financial Need

Visual Arts

The total aid you are awarded by any one college will likely differ from the amount offered by other colleges you may be applying to because, among other things, the costs of attendance are different. Secondly, not all colleges have the same amount of funds available to offer their needy students. But, your EFC should remain about the same regardless of which college you attend. It is the goal of every financial aid office to meet the financial needs of its students and help all families find the information they need to finance the tuition, fees, room and board, and other costs.

SOURCES OF FINANCIAL AID

The largest single source of aid is the federal government, which awarded over $90 billion during 2004–05. More than 14 million people apply for financial aid each year. But the federal government is not the only source of financial aid. The colleges and universities themselves are the next-largest source of financial aid. Institutions award an estimated $24 billion to students each year. Some of this aid is awarded to students who have a demonstrated need based on either the Federal Methodology or another formula, the Institutional Methodology, which is used by some colleges to award their own funds in conjunction with other aid. Some aid is not based on need and is called merit aid. Merit-based aid is usually awarded based on a student's academic performance or specific talents or abilities, or to students the institutions most want to attract.

Another source of financial aid is from state governments, awarding more than $6 billion per year. All fifty states offer grant and/or scholarship aid, most of which is need-based, but some of which is merit-based. Most state programs award aid only to state residents attending college in their home state, although a few do allow their state aid to be "portable" from state to state.

Other sources of financial aid include private agencies, foundations, corporations, clubs, fraternal and service organizations, civic associations, unions, and religious groups that award grants, scholarships, and low-interest loans. Some employers provide tuition reimbursement benefits for employees and their families.

More information about these different sources of aid is available from high school guidance offices, public libraries, college financial aid offices, and directly from the sponsoring organizations. In addition, Peterson's offers an excellent source of scholarship leads at www.petersons.com.

APPLYING FOR FINANCIAL AID

Every student must complete the Free Application for Federal Student Aid (FAFSA) to be considered for federal aid. The FAFSA is available in your high school guidance office and many public libraries, or directly from the U.S. Department of Education. Students are encouraged to apply for aid on the Web by using the electronic FAFSA, which can be accessed at www.fafsa.ed.gov. If you apply online, you and one parent will need to obtain an electronic signature before filing. To get your Personal Identification Number or PIN, go to www.pin.ed.gov.

To award their own funds, many schools require a second application, the Financial Aid PROFILE®. The PROFILE® asks supplemental questions that some colleges and awarding agencies feel provide a more accurate assessment of the family's ability to pay for college. It is up to the college to decide whether it will use only the FAFSA or both the FAFSA and the Financial Aid PROFILE®.

The first thing you will have to do is determine whether you will need to fill out only the FAFSA or whether you will also have to complete the PROFILE®. The listings later in this book will tell you what forms are required. You should also read the schools' brochures, or speak to someone in the financial aid office to be sure. The PROFILE® contains a list of schools and agencies that require the form.

If Every College You're Applying to in 2007 Requires Just the FAFSA

This scenario is pretty simple: Complete the FAFSA sometime after January 1, 2007, being certain to send it in before any college-imposed deadlines. (You are not permitted to send in the 2007–2008 FAFSA before January 1, 2007, which should not pose a problem because most college application deadlines are in February or March.) It is best if you wait until you have all your financial records for the previous year available, but if that is not possible, you can use estimated figures. It is critical to file by the published filing deadline. Filing late can mean the loss of thousands of dollars in assistance.

After you send in your FAFSA, either on paper or electronically, you'll receive a Student Aid Report (SAR) that includes all of the information you reported and shows your EFC. The SAR will be sent to you electronically if you provided an e-mail address. Otherwise, you will receive a paper-copy SAR in the mail. Be sure to review the SAR, checking to see if the information you reported is correct. If you used estimated numbers to complete the FAFSA, you may have to resubmit the SAR with any corrections to the data. The college(s) you have designated on the FAFSA will receive the information you reported and will use that data to make their decision. In many instances, the colleges you've applied to will ask you to send copies of your and your parents' federal income tax returns for 2006 plus any other documents needed to verify the information you reported.

If a College Requires the PROFILE®

Step 1: Register for the Financial Aid PROFILE® in the fall of your senior year in high school.

You can apply for the PROFILE® online at http://profileonline.collegeboard.com/index/jsp.

Registration information with a list of the schools requiring the PROFILE® is available in most high school guidance offices.

There is a fee for using the Financial Aid PROFILE® application ($23 for the first college and $18 for each additional college). You must pay for the service by credit card when you register. If you do not have a credit card, you will be billed.

Step 2: Fill out your customized Financial Aid PROFILE®.

Once you register, your application will be immediately available online and

- will have questions that must be completed by you and your parents (unless you are considered independent and the colleges or programs selected do not require parent information).

- *may* have supplemental questions needed by one or more of your schools or programs. If required, those will be found in Section Q of the application.

In addition to the PROFILE® application, which you complete online, you may be required to complete a Business/Farm Supplement in a traditional paper format. Completion of this form is not part of the "online" process. Instead, instructions about how to download and print the supplemental form are provided if it is required.

If your biological or adoptive parents are separated or divorced and your colleges and programs require it, your noncustodial parent may be asked to complete the Noncustodial PROFILE®.

Once you complete and submit your PROFILE® application, your information is processed and sent directly to the colleges and programs that you requested.

FINANCIAL AID AWARDS

After you've submitted your financial aid application and usually after you've been accepted for admission, each college will send you a letter containing your financial aid award. Most award letters show the college's budget, how much you and your family are expected to contribute, and the amount and types of aid awarded. Most students who are eligible for aid are awarded aid from a combination of sources and programs; hence your award is often called a "package." For first-year students, award letters are often sent with, or soon after, the letter of admission.

FINANCIAL AID PROGRAMS

There are three types of financial aid: scholarships (also known as grants or gift aid), loans, and student employment. Scholarships and grants are outright gifts and do not have to be repaid. Loans must be repaid, usually after graduation; the amount you have to pay back is the total you've borrowed plus an interest charge. Student employment is a job arranged for you during the academic year. Loans and student employment programs are generally referred to as self-help aid.

The federal government has two large grant programs, the Federal Pell Grant and the Federal Supplemental Educational Opportunity Grant; a student employment program called the Federal Work-Study Program; and several loan programs, including one for parents of undergraduate students. Students who are Pell Grant eligible and have completed a rigorous high school program may be eligible for the Academic Competitiveness Grant. Additional information on this new federal grant program is available from your college's financial aid office or high school guidance office.

The Subsidized Direct Stafford Student Loan, the Subsidized FFEL Stafford Student Loan, and the Federal Perkins Loan are all need-based, government-subsidized loans. Students who borrow under these programs do not have to pay interest on the loan until after they graduate or leave school. The Unsubsidized Direct Stafford Loan, the Unsubsidized FFEL Stafford Student Loan, and the Parent Loan (PLUS) program are not based on need, and these loans accrue interest while the student is in school.

There are also a number of federal tax–based programs that help families with incomes up to $107,000. Additional information about the Hope Scholarship and Lifetime Learning tax credits is available from the IRS. You should consult a tax adviser for other educational tax deductions.

IF YOU DON'T QUALIFY FOR NEED-BASED AID

If you are not eligible for need-based aid, or the aid you have been awarded is not sufficient, you should look into three other funding sources.

First is the search for merit scholarships, which you can start during your junior year of high school at the initial stages of the aid application process. Merit-based awards are becoming an increasingly important part of college financing plans, and many colleges award these grants to students they especially want to attract. As a result, applying to a school at which your qualifications put you at the top of the entering class may be a good idea since you may receive a merit award. It is also a good idea to look for private scholarships and grants, especially from local service and community groups.

The second source of aid is employment, during both the summer and the academic year. The student employment office at your college should be able to help you locate a job in the area, either on or off campus.

The third source is borrowing through the Unsubsidized FFEL Stafford Student Loan or the Unsubsidized Direct Stafford Student Loan, both of which are open to all students. The terms and conditions are similar to the subsidized loans. The biggest difference is that the borrower is responsible for the interest while still in college, although most lenders permit students to delay paying the interest right away and add the accrued interest to the total amount owed.

After you've secured what you can through scholarships, work, and loans, your parents will have to figure out how they will meet the balance of the college bill. Most colleges offer monthly payment plans that spread the cost out over the academic year. For many parents, the monthly payments still turn out to be more than they can afford, so they can borrow through the Federal Parent Loan for Undergraduate Students (PLUS) program, through one of the many private education loan programs available, or through home equity loans and lines of credit. This spreads the cost out over a longer time period and makes the monthly payments more manageable. The college financial aid office usually has a list of preferred programs that offer the best terms for students and their families.

Students and parents who are interested in more information about financing a college education and in learning more about the financial aid application process should read *Peterson's College Money Handbook.*

How Do You Know It's the Right Program for You?

Putting together a list of eight or ten schools to apply to is the easy part. Waiting to hear if you've gotten in can be nerve-racking. But being admitted to more than one school and choosing the right one to attend can often be the hardest part of the college admissions process.

What makes an art program right for one person might make it very wrong for someone else. Here is a list of things to think about for each school you're considering:

- Are you happiest in a big school or small school? Do you prefer a big city or a small town? What is the overall environment of the school?

- How many people are majoring in the program you are interested in?

- What is the student-faculty ratio in your area of study? In the arts, you really shouldn't have studio classes with more than 15 or so students in the class. While the history of art, theater, or film may be taught in large sections, classes in, say, painting, photography, and film editing should have limited numbers of students.

- Where do the students in the program come from? Is this a regional school of commuting students, or does it attract students from all over the region—or country? What is the age group?

- Tour the facilities and ask which ones are available to you. Is there independent studio space for painting majors? Is there a foundry for sculptors? What kind of computer equipment does the school have?

- How many courses are offered in your area of interest?

- Try to attend a student exhibition. Is this the kind of work you hope to achieve?

Visual

Arts

- What opportunities will you have for professional exposure? Are there exhibition opportunities on or off campus? Are there student memberships in professional organizations? Are there opportunities for reality-based course work, such as designing a poster for a community group?

- Does the program feature visiting artists or critics so you can meet practicing professionals and learn the latest theories and techniques? Who are they? How many come each semester? Do they lecture in an auditorium, or do they come into the studios and talk and work with students?

- Does the program arrange job internships? Internships are one of the best tickets to a job following graduation. You'll want to have examples of recently awarded internships and find out with whom the students worked, as well as whether academic credit was given.

- Check the faculty biographies in the college catalog or on the school's Web site to see what degrees faculty members have and from which institutions. Look for a high percentage of M.F.A.s or equivalent degrees as well as at their professional experience in terms of awards and exhibitions. Often, professional artists will have their own personal Web sites as well. And don't forget to check out the liberal arts faculty; liberal arts are part of the B.F.A.

- A good B.F.A. program should have a career development center that helps students in both placement and assessment. Are the opportunities local and/or national? Does the center help students assess their abilities, skills, and interests early on and assist them in putting together their programs of study?

- Try to find recent graduates of the program. Are they working in their chosen field? What kind of entry-level jobs did they get? What internships helped them? What aspects of their college curriculum helped them?

Later, you can use a pros and cons list and compare schools to see which one matches your needs, talents, interests, and goals the best. But don't forget to trust your first impressions—often a school just "feels" like home right away. When it's the right fit, you know it.

The Right Program for You

Applying and Getting In

Colleges and universities all compete for students, so don't let the college admissions process intimidate you. Develop the best portfolio you can, choose five to eight schools, and pay close attention to your applications. You might find that the hardest part of the process will be choosing which offer of admission to accept!

The College Admissions Process

THE APPLICATION

When you have finally narrowed your list to the eight to ten schools to which you have decided to apply, it is time to approach the applications. Application forms have several components. When you decide to apply to a school, do not go immediately to the school's Web site, fill out the application online, and submit it quickly. Rather, either download a copy and sit down with the print-out of the application, or if you cannot get the entire document downloaded, start to fill it out as a DRAFT and save as you go along, but do NOT hit "submit" until you have truly reviewed the entire document for completeness. (Note that many colleges now strongly prefer that you use the online application, and in recent times more than half of all applicants have applied online.)

If you are applying with hard copy and via "snail mail," first, read the application carefully. Then make a photocopy of the application and fill it out as your draft. It is important that applications be neat and legible, either typed or printed in black or blue ink. Never submit an application that has been filled out in pencil or an odd color ink or that has been scribbled in haste. Fill out the informational section first and then think about the essay questions, if required.

If you do apply electronically, be sure to do a spell check and to print out your draft to proofread before transmitting it. Always print and save a hard copy for yourself. Some schools will ask you also to send a hard copy with the application fee.

Academic Profile

Colleges will require a copy of your high school transcript(s). Be sure that you have checked your transcript for accuracy before it is sent by your high school. Many schools will also require college entrance examination scores. Some schools use standardized test scores for placement, and some use them as another indicator in the academic profile. If you plan to apply to schools that require SAT, ACT Assessment, or SAT Subject Tests and have not received scores that you think are truly representative of your ability, you should consider doing some test preparation and retaking the test to raise your score.

In analyzing your scholastic record, colleges are trying to decide if you will be able to withstand the academic rigor of their environment. If you are applying to a specialized school, your academic profile is secondary in consideration to your demonstrated talent, but at liberal arts colleges and for joint programs, the academic profile is more important in establishing the match. If you want to leave all options open for college, the most prudent approach is to take the most challenging assortment of academic courses, including math, science, and foreign language electives. However, if you absolutely know that you are applying to an art college, taking an extra year of something in which you are not strong is probably not going to have any effect on an admissions decision, and by not taking it you may have more time to take an art course that could help you prepare material for your portfolio. Be sure to speak to your guidance counselor about this and, if necessary, to call a few admissions officers for opinions.

Personal Profile

The personal profile that a college gathers on you consists largely of information that is entirely in your control. This includes your list of extracurricular activities, your recommendations, essays, and any appropriate supplementary materials you send. Let's consider each of these.

Extracurricular Activities

This term refers to any activity outside of the classroom. Many colleges will ask you to put this information in a table, showing the activity, any position of leadership, hours spent in the activity, etc.

As an artist, you may not have joined many clubs in your high school, focusing all your time on artistic endeavors. That's great! Do not hesitate to acknowledge such dedication. If you have participated in many activities, draft a list including school activities, any jobs you've held, hobbies, community or volunteer activities, church groups, honors, and awards. The point is to make the list comprehensive, but not exhaustive. Depth in one activity is important, so don't try to pad the list.

Recommendations

Many colleges request teacher recommendations as well as the guidance counselor report. You should choose teachers who know you well as a student and as a person, who like you, and who write well. You should also choose teachers who will add balance and another dimension to your application. For instance, if you plan on majoring in photography, consider asking your language arts teacher for a recommendation. When you ask a teacher to write a letter of recommendation, remember to:

- ask politely;

- give the teacher the forms, with the top part filled out with your name, etc., well before the deadline;

- provide the teacher with stamped envelopes addressed to the colleges; and

- include a cover letter to the teacher that gives the deadlines for each school, a list of your extracurricular activities, or anything else that might be helpful to the teacher in writing your recommendation.

Guidance counselors are often also asked to fill out a counselor recommendation form that may include a checklist and narrative. If you attend a large school where the counselors have many responsibilities other than college advising, you would do well to establish a relationship with your guidance counselor. Schedule meetings, stop by the office to ask quick questions, and, in general, make yourself known to him or her. Additional letters of recommendation from a non–high school teacher or from a boss can be helpful.

Essays

While most admissions representatives say that an essay will not make or break an application, there have been applicants who essentially "wrote" themselves into acceptance. The essay is another opportunity for the admissions committee to get to know you better. Even if the essay is optional, it's a good idea to provide one. A well-written essay will make your application more memorable and distinctive.

You must plan to write several drafts of your college essay. Ask your parents, a trusted friend, your college counselor, and/or a teacher to read it and give their reactions. While some editorial help is not out of line, never allow anyone else to write your essay. Admissions counselors know when you have not submitted your own work. Also, do not allow someone to edit so much that the tone becomes stale or stilted. Do have someone proofread your final draft, however.

The best essays resonate with the personal voice of the applicant, describing ideas in very specific, reflective ways that may reveal fears, fantasies, or insecurities but are always thoughtful, fresh, and spontaneous. The worst essays present a factual, often chronological version of an experience—the art history class's tour to Europe, for example—in a way that is totally lacking in creativity or individuality. The trip to Europe essay that simply describes arriving in Paris, visiting the Louvre, and then taking a bus to the next place is hardly riveting. The same essay telling how you got lost on the Metro and how you dealt with that situation becomes specific and says something about you.

There is no "right" essay, but there are several approaches that you should avoid. For example, do not submit a poem as an essay. If you also have talent as a poet, consider submitting a few select samples of your poetry as supplementary material. Also, do not use the essay as a moment to make excuses for something in your background. If you have a special situation, consider writing about it in a separate letter or asking a teacher or your guidance counselor to mention it in his or her letter of recommendation. Do not repeat information from other parts of your application, and avoid writing about trendy topics, your religious beliefs, relationships, drugs, sex, alcohol, or the importance of a college education. Do not try to impress an admissions committee with your vocabulary, revealing that you have thumbed through the thesaurus. Rather, write simply about something you really care about in a personally specific manner.

Try to limit yourself to the space provided, or type your essay on separate sheets and write, "See essay attached." In general, it is the quality, not the quantity, that counts.

Personal Statement

Many colleges require students applying for their art programs to submit a "Personal Statement" or "Statement of Intent" in addition to, or instead of, the admissions essay. The schools usually ask you to write about why you are applying to their program, what you hope to gain from the program, and what your career plans are. Be honest and try to mention something about the particular school—but be original. Don't, for instance, go on about New York being the center of the creative universe, which they no doubt have read thousands of times. Above all, make sure your statement is personal and revealing and shows that you have a passion for your art.

Interviews and Portfolios

When you read the catalog, note whether an interview is optional or required. Because of staff restrictions, travel difficulties, and financial constraints, very few colleges make the interview mandatory. If you do decide to have an interview, never drop in; be sure to make the arrangements well in advance. Often, specialized colleges do not hold interviews but just require that you send in your portfolio. At liberal arts colleges the interview is usually with an admissions representative, who might ask you briefly about your work but does not see your portfolio, which is submitted directly to the appropriate art department or school of art for evaluation. For advice on having a successful college interview, see "Acing Your College Interview" in this guide.

When evaluating portfolios, liberal arts universities usually use faculty members from the department or school of art. Art colleges use trained admissions staff members who are usually artists themselves, as well as faculty members. Portfolio evaluators at the more selective art colleges and universities are looking for more than raw talent. They are looking for a particular level of competency and technical skill as well as conceptual ability. The emphasis placed on conceptual ability versus skill varies from college to college because each has a different philosophy of education and programmatic thrust and looks for students who are a good match for that institution. What all colleges look for, however, are students who demonstrate through their artwork that they are creative, intellectually curious, and seriously invested and committed—even compelled—to make art. For more in-depth advice on preparing a portfolio, see "Developing an Undergraduate Visual Portfolio" and "Portfolio Advice from Admissions Directors" in this guide.

Deadlines

You can do yourself and the admissions office a favor by submitting your application before it is actually due. Remember to proofread your application before you mail or transmit it and to keep a copy of it for your files. If sent by standard "snail mail," it is a good idea to include a postcard saying, "College X has received the application from Mary Jones. Signed by admissions: Date:" Also, watch for a canceled check or check the statement of the credit card you used. Things do get lost in "snail" and electronic mail, and you want to be sure that your application does not go astray. And, if you are using e-mail or otherwise filing electronically, remember to print out a hard copy of whatever you transmit to save for your files, too.

Refer to the College Admissions Timetable on pages 41–46 and use it as a guideline for the admission process.

ADMISSIONS OUTCOMES

After the application and portfolio review, admissions committees meet to determine whether to admit you, reject you, or place your name on a waiting list. Beware that the weight of the letter or size of the envelope does not necessarily indicate the admissions decision.

If you are admitted to more than one school, weigh the pros and cons of each institution, perhaps visit again, ask lots of questions, and try to respond to the Office of Admissions in plenty of time, before their acceptance deadline. Most institutions comply with the guidelines established by the National Association of College Admissions Counselors (NACAC) and the College Board, which set the Candidate's Reply Deadline (CRD) as May 1. If a school requires you to make a decision before that deadline or before you have heard from all of your schools, you have every right to question that institution. If, in order to make an informed decision about your college choice, you need more information, or if your financial aid package has not arrived in time to meet the deadline, call the college and request an extension of the deadline. If you do not contact the college at all by the college's deadline, the admissions staff may assume that you have decided to attend another institution and offer your place to someone on the waiting list. Be certain to contact your college by the deadline stipulated.

The wait list is a positive place to be. It means that a college realized your strengths, but due to a limited number of openings was not able to offer you admission at this time. Your initial response will probably be disappointment and irritation, but wait a few days before you do anything. Then you will be more able to make a rational decision about whether to remain active on a wait list or to accept the offer of another college that admitted you.

If you want to be considered from the wait list, now is the time to be even more proactive in demonstrating your desire to attend. Call, send an e-mail, and/or write to the college to say that you want to be considered from the wait list. Include any new information about yourself since the review of your application. If it is true, let a college know that if taken off the wait list, you will enroll. Talk to your guidance counselor about any further steps you should take and then be patient. You should probably submit a deposit to your second-choice school to protect yourself, in the event that the first choice does not take anyone from the wait list. If you are admitted from the waiting list, however, and intend to accept the offer of admission and enroll, be sure to immediately contact the school where you gave your deposit so that they may possibly offer your place to someone else. You should never make a deposit at more than one school, as multiple deposits are considered unethical in college admissions.

If You Want To Defer Admission

Often, a student who has been admitted will want to take a year off to travel or work. Many colleges and universities are pleased to grant a deferral of a year. They may give you guidelines about what they will allow you to do with the year. For instance, attending another college usually is not allowed, and they may give a new deadline for committing to enrollment. Some schools may ask for an account of what you have done with your time off.

INTERNATIONAL STUDENTS' CHECKLIST

Any student who is not a citizen or permanent resident of the United States is usually considered an "international" or "foreign" student (the term varies at schools). Many schools recruit abroad and most schools welcome students from abroad. The admissions procedures at most schools are the same for international students as for U.S. applicants. However, there are a few additional aspects international students should take into account.

- Begin your search extra early. International mail takes additional time and catalogs cannot be faxed at this point.

- Take advantage of the Internet and e-mail in expediting your questions, but always print a hard copy for yourself.

- Determine from each college or university whether you must take the TOEFL (Test of English as a Foreign Language), if English is not your native language. Arrange to take the test, if necessary, so that your scores can be submitted at the required time. Contact www.TOEFL.org or ETS at 609-771-7760.

- Be sure to study English intensively. There are many good English as a Second Language (ESL) programs both in the United States and abroad and many summer programs in the United States. An Internet search should help you to discover ESL programs available to you.

- Investigate the visa process early. Many conservatories or colleges will issue you a letter to present to a consulate in order to obtain a B-2 Prospective Student Visa. An I-20 will be issued to admitted students only. Everything regarding visas does take time, so plan ahead.

- Determine a school's policy on financial aid for international students. Government or state loans are not available to students from abroad, and many schools reserve their limited scholarship funds for domestic students. Some schools will not admit a qualified international student who has applied for financial aid. Be sure to ask for the current policy, and do not hesitate to ask for clarification of the policy if you are in doubt.

- Find out whether the school requires a guarantee of financial support in advance.

- Ask about tape or application pre-screening or regional auditions in your country.

- Complete the application on your own, especially the essays. If your English is not good enough to write an acceptable essay, you probably won't be able to understand the lectures or complete the assignments at a U.S. school.

- Be sure that schools know about your academic history in terms of the grading and overall educational system in your country. For instance, if no one from your high school has ever applied to schools in the United States before, you should send a prospectus or profile of your school.

- Some colleges and universities may require that your official transcript be reviewed or translated by the World Education Service (WES). Ask about the requirements of the specific schools. The Web address for WES is www.wes.org.

- Find out whether it is possible for international students to work while attending the program.

- Ask whether there are quotas on the number of students from a certain country or on foreign students in general.

- Find out about advisers and other support services for students from abroad.

- Find out if the program is authorized to grant Practical Training status to international students.

FINANCIAL AID

Many art students considering postsecondary education need some form of financial aid. Do not eliminate a school from your list just because of the school's cost. Often, the most expensive schools have the largest endowments and are able to be particularly generous in financial aid. In order to qualify for financial aid, you must apply for it. Many middle-income families, in particular, assume that financial assistance is not available to them; this may not be true. Read the catalog and any financial aid information very carefully, and be sure to speak to a financial aid officer at the college to which you are applying. Ask questions about the financial aid process and find out exactly what forms you will need. It is essential that you submit all the required forms and documents and meet deadlines in applying for financial aid. For safety's sake, keep photocopies of every form you send, whether you file these via regular mail or electronically.

Aside from scholarships, there are a variety of grants, loans, and work-study opportunities to help you finance your education. The Foundation Center, www.Fdncenter.org; 79 Fifth Avenue, New York, NY 10003 (212-620-4230), is an excellent resource and has regional branches in the United States. There are also many helpful financial aid guides at libraries and in guidance offices. Do not overlook religious organizations, community and civic organizations, or state programs in your quest for funding. There are also many fine Web sites, such as Petersons.com, College-Scholarships.com, or Collegetoolkit.com that have fine information about funding higher education, but beware of those Internet sites that advertise and request a fee for finding you funds. Ask your parents to check if they work for a company or belong to an association or union that sponsors children for scholarships.

Here are some questions that you will want to ask about financial aid:

- Are scholarships based on merit? On need? On a combination of both?

- Are financial aid decisions made separately from admissions decisions?

- What percentage of students receives scholarships? Other financial aid?

- What are the most common mistakes people make in filling out financial aid forms?

- Should I assume that if my parents make (some dollar amount) as their income I would not be eligible for any aid?

- Do you have payment plans?

- What happens if I do not meet deadlines in filing forms for financial aid?

- Do you give financial aid to applicants admitted from the waiting list?

- Do I have a better chance of obtaining financial aid if I audition during the earliest auditions?

Deadlines are very important when applying for financial aid. It is critical that the FAFSA (Free Application for Federal Student Aid) be completed and mailed to the College Scholarship Service (CSS) as early as possible. Many colleges have January and February deadlines for submission of this form. If parents have not completed their income tax returns by February, estimate income as accurately as possible, and submit corrections later in the process.

If the financial aid package you are offered is not adequate, or if your first-choice school offers less than a second or third choice, call the admissions or financial aid office of your first-choice school and discuss this with them. Schools may reconsider their original financial aid offer. They may ask you to send a copy of the other school's offer and then make you a counter-offer. In general, there is a great deal more comparative shopping and negotiating in financial aid these days.

College Admissions Timetable

Below is a general outline of how to proceed and pace yourself in the college admissions process. Your actual timetable may differ slightly, depending on the deadlines at the schools you have chosen. Keep an up-to-date spreadsheet with deadlines and use this as a list of guideposts.

SOPHOMORE YEAR (TENTH GRADE)

September–October

- Make learning and your education a priority, along with developing your art. Aim for balance.

- Take a practice PSAT in October. This is good practice for junior year, when PSAT scores count toward National Merit® Scholarships. (National Merit Scholarships are based on the scores you achieve on this test when you take it in your junior year.) Note that many schools require that sophomores take a practice PSAT, some make it optional to take, and other schools do not offer it to tenth-graders at all. It can be a useful exercise to take it in tenth grade, and you should inquire in September about taking it if your guidance counselor does not have everyone register.

December

- Obtain your PSAT results. Review the answer sheet. Talk to your guidance counselor about the advisability of taking a test-preparation course.

January–April

- Begin your review of Web sites for colleges and universities.

- Write for college catalogs. Read them, noting portfolio requirements.

- Obtain a social security number if you do not already have one.

- Investigate the National Foundation for Advancement in the Arts (NFAA) or ARTS annual scholarship competition and National Portfolio Days.

- Meet with your guidance counselor. Discuss course plans—APs, honors, or additional art—and other plans for your future.

- Research taking and registering for any SAT Subject Tests in a course in which you have done well and which may be required by the school you're interested in attending. Speak to your teacher first.

- Start researching financial aid and scholarship opportunities.

- Keep a file of various documents. Keep reviews, copies of art exhibit programs, photos, and any papers you have written about art and received good comments and grades on.

- Attend college fairs. Find out all you can about schools you are considering.

- Plan your summer to expand your experience in art. Participate in a summer art program. Remember to ask for letters of recommendation.

JUNIOR YEAR (ELEVENTH GRADE)

September

- Meet with your guidance counselor or college adviser to renew or establish your acquaintance. Review plans; register for the PSAT.

- Do well in your classes this year.

October

- Take the PSAT (again). Remember that this time it counts for National Merit Scholarships.

- Obtain information. Surf the Internet and get catalogs and applications from all the schools you are considering.

- Continue to investigate financial aid opportunities.

- Keep your spreadsheet up-to-date.

December

- Review PSAT results. PSAT scores indicate what areas you need to strengthen for the SAT.

- Register for the SAT or ACT Assessment. Also consider SAT Subject Tests and the TOEFL, if appropriate. Prepare on your own or take a review course.

March–June

- Meet with your guidance counselor and parents/guardians to discuss college plans, your testing schedule, course selections for your senior year, college application essay topics, and any other related matters.

- Start your college visits.

- Take the SAT, ACT Assessment, TOEFL, and any SAT Subject Tests, if necessary.

- Attend college fairs.

- Plan another enriching summer.

July–August

- Continue your college visits and interviews over the summer.

- Continue to surf the Internet, send for applications, visit colleges, and interview.

- Work on your portfolio.

SENIOR YEAR (TWELFTH GRADE)

September–October

- Continue your college visits and interviews. Keep notes of your impressions.

- Meet with your guidance counselor or college adviser. Discuss your college list and try to narrow it down.

- Consider applying Early Decision to your top-choice school. Check deadlines. November 1 and November 15 are common dates.

Applying and Getting In

- Get letters of recommendation from teachers and former employers.

- Apply for the ARTS recognition scholarship through NFAA. (National Foundation for Advancement in the Arts, 444 Brickell Avenue, Miami, FL 33131; 305-377-1140; www.artsawards.org.)

- Be sure you have all application forms. Start drafting college application essays.

- Attend or make plans to attend National Portfolio Days.

November

- Meet Early Decision deadline, if appropriate.

- Fill out college application forms. Continue to revise and perfect your essays.

- Take any additional tests: SAT, ACT, TOEFL, or SAT Subject Tests.

- Complete and submit your applications. Proofread them thoroughly and photocopy them before mailing.

- Request that ETS or ACT send your test results to the colleges that require them.

- Continue developing your portfolio.

December–January

- Early Decision results are mailed. Celebrate if you were admitted and meet all deadlines for enrollment deposits. If you were deferred or rejected, submit other applications and move on.

- Obtain the FAFSA, if you are applying for Financial Aid. Start filling out financial aid forms and be aware of deadlines.

- Finalize your portfolio.

- Forward transcripts and test scores. Be sure to have your guidance counselor or college adviser send transcripts and test scores to the schools you've chosen.

- Last chance to take the SAT and ACT Assessment.

February–March

- Check to make sure that all your financial aid documents are in order.

April

- Make your decision. Consider with your parents and adviser the pros and cons of each institution.

- Revisit any college if your decision to attend is not crystal clear.

- Notify colleges of your decision by May 1. If a school asks for a decision response before May 1, you have a right to request an extension until the May 1 Candidate's Reply Deadline (CRD).

May

- Be sure to notify all colleges by May 1, even if you are on the waiting list.

- Take any AP exams, if applicable.

Applying and Getting In

COLLEGE ADMISSIONS CHECKLIST

Use this convenient checklist to remind yourself of individual college admissions requirements and to record the progress of your application procedures.

College Name								
College Address								
Application Deadline								
Application Fee								
Required Tests:	Registration Deadline	Testing Date	Registration Deadline	Testing Date	Registration Deadline	Testing Date	Registration Deadline	Testing Date
PSAT/NMSQT								
SAT								
ACT Assessment								
Others								
Course Requirements Fulfilled								
Personal Interview Required								
Interview Date								
Portfolio Required								
Portfolio Date								
Applications Requested								
References Required								
Names/Addresses of References								
References Completed								
Application Filed								
Transcript Forwarded								
College Reply Date								
Financial Interview Required								
Required Financial Forms:								
CSS Financial Statement								
ACT Financial Statement								
Others								
Housing Deadline								
Housing Fee								
Housing Application Mailed								

Visual

Arts

Acing Your College Interview

A college interview is your opportunity to be more than just a stack of papers in the admissions office; it's your chance to personalize the process. Interviews do not usually make or break admissions decisions, but you should try to have an interview at those schools that are of real interest to you and are realistic choices.

TIMING OF INTERVIEWS

If you are prepared, plan your interviews as part of your campus visit. Don't schedule your first interview to be at your first-choice school; you'll do better after you've had some experience in an interview situation. Also, try to avoid making your first-choice school your last interview, as you want to remain fresh and spontaneous in your responses.

Practice interviews are helpful to some students. Ask your college counselor to conduct a mock interview with you or have a family friend role-play with you.

Schedule all interviews well in advance. And, if you cannot attend an interview appointment, be sure to call and cancel. A cancelation will not be held against you, but a missed appointment probably will be. If you get hopelessly lost en route to an interview and are running late, be sure to call.

GETTING READY

Preparing for an interview is important. Be sure to read the school's catalog and write down a list of questions that you want to ask. Take time to think about your strengths and weaknesses, and be prepared to speak about them in a positive way. College interviews are not the time for modesty and monosyllabic answers. At the same time, you do not want to sound boastful or arrogant.

Take stock of the extracurricular activities in which you have participated, your hobbies, volunteer work, and other ways that you spend your time. If there are special circumstances in your life that have affected your academic record, you may want to bring them up at an interview. For instance, if you missed a great deal of school because your family went through a particularly grueling year, with divorce, unemployment, or sickness, you may want to talk about it with your interviewer. Be careful not to sound as though you are making excuses for yourself, but rather adding to the college's understanding of who you are.

And above all, be prepared to talk about art in general and your artwork in particular in an intelligent and meaningful way, whether you are interviewing with someone who sees your portfolio or someone who never sees it at all.

WHAT TO WEAR

Just as there are costumes for performances, there are interview "costumes." For women, a nice skirt (not too short) or pants and a blouse, possibly with a blazer, or a simple dress is recommended, worn with low to medium heels. Men should wear nice pants with a shirt, jacket, and tie, or a turtleneck or shirt with a collar. Be neat and clean.

TYPICAL INTERVIEW QUESTIONS

Every interviewer has his or her favorite questions, but there are some common areas that are covered in most interviews. These include:

- Your high school experience

- Your personal traits, relationships with others, and family background

- Your interests outside the classroom—hobbies, extracurricular activities, summer vacations, movies you've seen, etc.

- Your values and goals, and how you view the world around you

- Your impressions of the college you are visiting

- Answering your questions

You might anticipate questions like these:

- Tell me about your high school. How long have you attended? What are the students like? Do you like your high school? What would you preserve or change about it?

- Which courses have you liked most? Which least? Which have been the most challenging?

- How well do you think your school has prepared you for your future study?

- How would you describe yourself as a student?

- Do you know what you want to major in?

- What has been your most stimulating intellectual experience?

- What extracurricular activity have you been most involved in? How much time do you devote to it?

- Do you have hobbies or special interests?

- After a long, hard day, what do you enjoy doing most? What do you do for fun?

- How have you spent your summer vacations? Why did you decide to spend them that way?

- How would you describe yourself in five adjectives?

- What is your family like? Describe your upbringing. How has your environment influenced your way of thinking?

- How would your friends describe you?

- Which relationships are most important to you? Why?

- Have you ever encountered people who thought and acted differently from you? What viewpoints or actions challenged you the most? How did you respond? What did you learn about yourself?

- What do your friends and family expect of you? What pressures have you felt?

- If you had a year to go anywhere and do whatever you wanted, how would you spend that year?

- What magazines or newspapers do you read regularly?

- What books have you read recently? Are there any authors you particularly like?

Applying and Getting In

- What movie have you seen recently and what did you think of it?

- Who are your favorite artists? Why?

- How did you choose your particular area of art? Why do you want to pursue this art form?

- Who has been your most memorable teacher? Why?

- Why do you want to go to college?

- Why have you chosen this college to investigate? What first brought us to your attention?

- What do you picture yourself doing ten years from now?

- What do you think of the National Endowment for the Arts (or some current affair in the arts)?

- What distresses you most about the world around you? If you had the opportunity to change the world, where would you start?

- Are there any outside circumstances that have interfered with your performance in school? An after-school job? Long commute back and forth to school? Home responsibilities or difficulties? Illness? Parental pressure? English not spoken at home? Problems with course scheduling?

- What more do you want to know about us?

This last question is your opening to ask your questions. Do not be shy about taking out your list; no one expects you to memorize a list of questions, and you want to be sure that you are learning all that you can during your visit to make the decision as to whether or not this is a campus where you could be happy. Many of the questions regarding campus life were probably answered by your tour guide or student host. Here are some other general questions you may want to ask.

- Who teaches freshmen? Transfers?

- How does registration work? Is it easy to get the classes I want to take?

- What is the advising system like? What are its strengths and weaknesses?

- Are there any changes anticipated in the curriculum?

- Are there any departments that might be cut or discontinued? What departments have been discontinued in the past two years?

- Are there any planned cutbacks in faculty? Any new appointments scheduled?

- Are there any new programs being contemplated? What are they?

- What percentage of students receive financial aid?

- Are there jobs on campus for students? What is a typical work/study job? Are there jobs in the community?

- Are there any opportunities for internships? Study abroad?

- Are financial aid decisions made separately from admissions decisions? Will applying for financial aid influence admissions decisions?

- Do you have any merit-based scholarships?

- What is your policy on fee waivers, if I cannot afford the application fee?

- What is the overall financial security of the school? Is tuition increased annually? What additional fees might I anticipate?

- What is most important in admissions decisions?

WHAT NOT TO DO AT YOUR INTERVIEW

Here are some things you should *not* do at an interview:

- Smoke

- Chew gum

- Complain or make excuses

- Swear or use language that it too colloquial

- Exhibit a negative attitude (bored, arrogant, etc.)

- Answer in monosyllables or one-sentence answers

- Ask questions if you have no interest in the response

- Ask for an evaluation of another school you are considering

- Bring your scrapbook of reviews, articles, or term papers for the interviewer to read

- Dress in an inappropriate fashion

- Twitch, fidget, or slump in your seat

- Pretend to be someone you are not. Be yourself!

AFTER YOUR INTERVIEW

Be sure to write down your impressions of the interview for future reference. And, most important, write the interviewer a thank-you note. Mention something specific that came up in the conversation. Three lines on nice stationery or even a postcard should be sufficient.

Developing an Undergraduate Visual Portfolio

Heidi Vee Metcalf

WHAT IS AN UNDERGRADUATE VISUAL PORTFOLIO?

A visual portfolio can mean many things to many colleges, and you should always consult directly with the colleges to which you are applying to determine what you should include in your visual portfolio as well as how you should submit it—whether in slide form, in person, as prints, etc. However, there are standard things that most colleges require in an admission portfolio. Therefore, for the purpose of this article, a visual portfolio is defined as any collection of works that appeal to the sense of sight, including but not limited to the following: drawings, paintings, films, photography, computer imagery, ceramics, sculpture, and printmaking.

WHAT ROLE DOES CREATIVITY PLAY IN THE VISUAL PORTFOLIO?

A college entrance portfolio is a collection of your artwork; it should be personal and creative by nature. We all see the world differently, and what you choose to draw, say, from a given still life is not likely to be what your classmates draw. There will be common elements but your work will be infused with your touch, vision, and interpretation. Your portfolio should reflect you. It should show off your skill set at this particular time in your life and expression of the world. Therefore, creativity is important to the makeup of your portfolio and can be expressed in something as simple as an angle, position, subject, proportion, etc.

WHEN SHOULD YOU START DEVELOPING YOUR PORTFOLIO?

Developing a visual portfolio for college entrance typically begins in your sophomore or junior year of high school. Creating art is like playing an instrument. It takes time and practice. In music, you need to master the notes, and in art, you need to master the mark making. Every work you create, be it good or bad, will bring you closer to a finished body of work. The more time and energy you put into developing your skills, the better your chances will be of producing a college-level entrance visual portfolio.

Applying and Getting In

WHY DRAW FROM OBSERVATION?

Once you start the process of looking at specialty art schools or programs, you most likely will begin to hear the phrase, "drawing from observation." In other words, you need to create works that are derived by observing. You look at an object or objects and you create a drawing, painting, sculpture, etc., from this direct observation. Those students who have been trained in high school to draw from observation know the importance of showing this concept in their portfolio. Observational work is an important part of a portfolio.

Most specialty schools do not encourage or will even not permit drawings done from two-dimensional photographs, magazine pictures, etc. The reason for this is quite simple: the physical process of reproducing a two-dimensional image to a two-dimensional surface is easy, but the physical process of translating the three-dimensional world (still life, landscape, people, etc.) onto a two-dimensional surface (your paper, canvas, etc.) is complex and requires really paying attention to how the components in your still life, landscape, etc. relate to each other, particularly how these components intersect.

How can you improve your drawing skills?

If you started late, you may need to improve or develop your drawing skills before you start putting together your portfolio. Or perhaps you started early but feel like you could use some help getting a new perspective on your skill level. We recommend taking a pre-college or college class while you are still in high school to both develop your skills and also assess your own level of commitment to art. Pre-college classes are offered at numerous specialized art schools and vary from once-a-week courses that run for several weeks to intensive summer programs that run five days a week for a month. These programs can kick-start a portfolio in your sophomore or junior year, often offer different majors or subjects, and give you an opportunity to sample a particular major.

Another option is teaching yourself, which is a bit more challenging but can be done with some good reference books. We recommend picking up a few "how to" books from your school library or local bookstore. Two good "how to draw" books are *Keys to Drawing* by Bert Dodson and *Drawing on the Right Side of the Brain* by Betty Edwards. If you need some help with color theory, check out *Color Theory* by Jose M. Parramon. And finally, if you want to teach yourself to improve or develop your drawing skills, master the "blind contours," drawing without looking at the paper.

WHAT SIZE SHOULD MY WORKS BE? WHAT SUBJECT MATTER SHOULD I INCLUDE IN MY PORTFOLIO?

Size is important to your portfolio, and concentrating on the larger rather than smaller work is always recommended in portfolio development. You want to experience drawing objects life-size or larger. You can learn faster and show off your skills more readily if your work is not too small to see. Schools usually don't make you stick to a particular size, but 18 × 24 is a good place to begin—working up and down from that size.

Many schools recommend or require a self-portrait and a pencil rendering of a still life. If you are stuck for ideas, here are a few tried-and-true drawing subjects for you to tackle.

Self-Portrait: Draw yourself from a mirror and do it often. Try different mediums and sizes. Life-size is always a good place to start.

Footwear: Footwear is a great subject. It's not only fun to draw but can have a great deal of character because shoes, boots, slippers, ice skates, sneakers, etc., take on the character of their owner's foot. Be creative and try to come at footwear from a different direction.

Glass/Bottle/Cups/Vases: Translucent, transparent, or just a plain reflective surface, glass of any kind is challenging to draw and is a good way to flex your drawing muscles.

Metallic Objects/Pots/Pans/Chrome: If you really take a look at a metal teapot or cooking pan, you will understand the challenges that are to be found in reflective surfaces such as metal. At first glance it's just shiny, but through further investigation everything in the room including you is now twisted and distorted across the metal surface.

Fabric: Michelangelo created an abundance of fabric studies in his day in order to master the flow of fabric over the human form. Fabric is metamorphic. It has its own texture and reflects light accordingly but it's malleable and can contour to form its subject.

Paper Bags: Angular and crisp, paper bags seem easy enough to draw, but try getting your drawing to look, feel, and sound like paper.

Hard-boiled Eggs: Light is a beautiful subject and watching light float across white hard-boiled eggs is eye-opening.

Objects in Nature: Nature is a good place to go searching for subjects to draw. Whether it's flowers, bugs, fruits, or plants, there is always something in nature that can add color, texture, and design to your portfolio.

Landscapes/Cityscapes: Pull up a piece of grass or slab of concrete; drawing the land or cityscapes around you can demonstrate your ability to create perspective on a grander scale than the common still life, pushing houses, buildings, and lines further into the page.

WHAT ABOUT SKETCHBOOKS AND UNFINISHED WORKS?

Most colleges accept and even want to see your sketchbook and unfinished works as part of your portfolio as long as you have enough other work to demonstrate the full range of your skills. A word to the wise: If you do have a sketchbook, make sure there is enough work in it to make it worth showing. Additionally, if you have unfinished artwork or work in progress, make sure there is a reason for showing it. Perhaps the unfinished work is a great idea or is just coming out extremely well. Make an active choice to include or exclude works.

HOW MANY WORKS SHOULD BE INCLUDED IN A VISUAL PORTFOLIO?

The number of pieces required will vary from school to school, and you should research your prospective school(s) by looking at their admissions Web sites. Typically, however, you should have at least eight to twenty pieces in your portfolio. The majority of schools will require ten to eighteen works, and most will not accept more than twenty. A word of advice: Don't include the weak pieces just to have more work in your portfolio. Less truly can be more. If the school requires twelve and you have twelve strong pieces, stick with the twelve. Don't add works that are weak to reach the maximum number of works. Weak pieces can pull down the overall quality of your portfolio and should not be included if they are not required.

HOW CAN I GET SOME ADVICE ON MY WORK?

A preliminary review is important in order to understand what needs to be done to create a quality portfolio. You should take advantage of the many National Portfolio Days throughout the United States and Canada. For more information about the National Portfolio Day Association (NPDA), go to www.npda.org. These events are designed to help students understand what is required in a college entrance portfolio. Even if you only bring a few pieces, it is better to know up front what needs to be done in order to meet the portfolio requirement. If you wait until you are a senior to show someone your portfolio, you could be creating an unnecessary problem for yourself. So start early, and do your research at least in the beginning of your junior year.

WHAT MEDIA SHOULD I INCLUDE IN MY PORTFOLIO?

Most schools do not require you to present particular media. However, most do expect you to have a number of works in pencil and a few works done in other media. The most common media are pencil, charcoal (soft or hard), pastels (oil or dry), paint (oil, acrylic, watercolor, or colored inks or dyes), photography, computer-generated work, printmaking (block, etching, silk screen, or lithography), and collage. You are not required to have all, and the most important aspect of the media you choose is that you use them well and the works are strong. If possible, your portfolio should have works in black & white, color, and a few three-dimensional works. Variety and quality are the key points when deciding on media. If you cannot seem to master a particular medium, don't include it. Quality should not be compromised for variety.

WHAT IS A HOME EXAM/HOME TEST?

A home exam or home test is required at some college(s) in addition to the general portfolio. These home exams/tests give you a particular problem to solve and typically ask for this problem to be solved in particular dimensions. Some schools require that the original home exam/test work be mailed to them directly, and in some cases you cannot have this work back. Therefore, it is important that you document all of your work so that you have a record of your early works. You should check with all your potential school(s) to find out what requirements they may have for the home exam/test. These home exams/tests can get very detailed in terms of the particular requirements such as size, medium, etc. Pay close attention to the fine print.

HOW CAN I EDIT MY VISUAL PORTFOLIO?

When it comes to editing your work, there are many ways to get the job done. The first and most obvious way of editing your work is to have your high school art teacher help you out. The second way is to have a classmate or family member help you critique your work and edit using this information. The third way is to have a pre-review by one of your potential colleges. (See "How can I get some advice on my work?") The fourth way is to make sure you are not keeping works in your portfolio that are weak just because they have sentimental value. If you did a work in seventh grade and everyone thought it was the greatest work ever done, don't assume it's still great. You have grown, and hopefully your work has grown too. Finally, the most important aspect of editing your work is you. After you have collected all necessary opinions, remember you have the final word on what stays in and what is left out.

HOW DO I PRESENT OR SUBMIT MY VISUAL PORTFOLIO?

Each school has its own requirements in regards to how you should and how you can submit work. Most schools do not require your work to be matted or framed and some even encourage you not to do so. Some schools will review your work in person and grade your portfolio and require no other reproductions. Other schools may review your work in person but also require reproductions to be sent with your applications. Still other schools may not offer personal interviews and may require all applicants to submit reproductions. Therefore, you need to get the details of what your potential school(s) requires. Don't wait to find out this information in your senior year. Do your research early and learn what will be expected of you.

However, no matter what the requirements of your potential school(s), it is recommended that you take slides of your visual work to keep as a visual record of your artwork history. To this day, I still have my slides from high school and I am grateful to my high school art teacher for stressing the importance of visual documentation. Most schools will accept slides and some even require them. However, some schools will accept images of your work either on a VHS, CD-ROM, DVD, via the Internet, or printed out, typically in an 8 × 10 format. It is extremely important that you find out the format required and/or accepted by your potential school(s). There may be size requirements and program requirements that are critical to the application process. At Pratt, we often receive CDs and DVDs with files that cannot be opened, and I am sure we are not alone.

Reproducing your work

35-mm Slides

You can take your own slides easily, provided you have or can borrow a 35-mm camera, a tripod, and daylight 200-slide film. Most high schools that offer photography have a 35-mm camera and tripod that you may be able to borrow or use at the school to take your slides. Even if your school doesn't have a photography department, you may want to talk to your art teacher or guidance counselor to see if there is any assistance or equipment available at your school.

Once you have your 35-mm camera, tripod, and daylight 200-slide film, the rest is pretty easy. First set your 35-mm camera according to the instructions on the film. Then select a room that is evenly flooded with natural light. Do not use inside lighting, spot lights, etc. Use natural light only and not direct natural light. Then select a flat wall and place a large piece of black felt or board on the wall in an area larger than your largest two-dimensional works. Place each piece in the center of this black field individually, move in tightly on each image (close enough not to have too much excess space and not too close as to cut off part of your image) and take the number of slides you need of each work. Duplicates generally cost more than developing the slide directly from the film, and therefore, you should take multiple slides of the same artwork.

Three-dimensional works are shot by draping a piece of black felt or velvet over a box on a table. The goal here is to have the three-dimensional image completely surrounded by the black field.

Digital Images to Slides

With today's technology, it is possible to have digital images of your work converted into 35-mm slides. Generally, you will need to make sure you take the digital images using a similar ratio as the 35-mm slide film such as 2 × 3 or 3 × 2 depending on the direction of your work. This translates into a pixels size of 1,200 × 1,800 or 1,800 × 1,200. Most companies that convert these images into slides accept the standard tif or jpeg files. You should also note that we don't recommend that you take images using a pixel size smaller than 600 × 900 as this will produce blurry results.

Digital Images on VHS, Photo Paper, CDs, DVDs, or Web Sites

No matter how you want to present your digital work, it is critical that you check with your potential schools for their requirements and restrictions.

Although stressful at times, creating your portfolio should be an enjoyable endeavor. The process alone should help your artwork improve and develop. Specialty schools require hard work once you're in, and getting into most of these schools requires putting the necessary time and energy into your portfolio.

Reprinted with permission of Heidi Vee Metcalf, Director of Admissions at Pratt Institute, Brooklyn, New York.

Applying and Getting In

Portfolio Advice from Admissions Directors

Here is what some admissions directors at top art colleges across the country say about portfolios.

JANET SCHIPPER
Assistant Director of Admissions Operations
Otis College of Art and Design

One of the most important elements of the admission process is the portfolio. It demonstrates a student's artistic experience, education, and talent and helps us identify creative, talented students who will work hard at Otis and be successful.

What we look for in an admission portfolio is a balance between technical skills and creativity.

The B.F.A. program at Otis begins with the Foundation Year, during which students take four studio art classes: drawing and composition, figure drawing, second design, and third design along with their academic classes, such as English, art history, and social science. The idea is that studying basic drawing, design, and creative thinking will prepare students to enter any of Otis's seven majors.

Students applying to Otis directly from high school are applying to Foundation. Because of the Foundation Year emphasis on drawing, we like to see examples of "observational drawing," which is drawing by looking at a real object, person, or scene. A still life drawing with fruit and other small objects is a familiar kind of observational drawing. Other kinds of artwork, such as photographs, paintings, sculptures, digital prints, PowerPoint presentations, animations, etc., can be important in the admission portfolio and show different kinds of technical skills. For creativity, we suggest students submit the work they think is their best. It should show their ideas, personal expression, and passions.

For students who wish to transfer to Otis at sophomore or junior level, the portfolio needs to show a higher level of experience—the same level and quality of skills that we expect from students who have attended Otis from Foundation Year.

Students who are interested in Otis are always encouraged to visit the campus and bring their artwork. An admissions counselor can give feedback and suggestions for how to make the portfolio fit the criteria we use in making admission decisions.

JULIE HINGELBERG
Dean of Enrollment Services
College for Creative Studies

An acceptable portfolio is one that exhibits technical and conceptual preparation for college-level work at the College of Creative Studies. All portfolios must include a minimum of ten pieces representing your selected major or areas of strength.

General Guidelines

- **Edit your work.** Quality is more important than quantity. Ten great pieces are better than twenty that are inconsistent. Work completed within the last two years is usually the strongest.

- **Neatness counts.** Present your drawings and other work neatly on paper. Matted or mounted work is preferable, but not required.

- **Drawings.** If drawings are included in the portfolio, draw from observation of objects, scenes and people. Include good descriptive or representational drawings. Include accurate line drawings and good examples of fully-rendered compositions using a complete range of light, middle, and dark values. If possible, include figure drawings or partial-figure drawings (hands, feet, etc.) or portraiture.

- **Be original.** We would like to see work that expresses your ideas and feelings about a subject.

- **Consider the entire picture surface.** Try not to isolate one object in the center of the page.

For the following majors, portfolios should include:

- *Advertising Design:* A combination of conceptual or observational drawings, 2D design (traditional or digital), short films or videos, software exploration (Photoshop, Illustrator, etc.), photography, lettering samples, and creative writing or any other conceptual thinking.

- *Animation and Digital Media:* A combination of photographs, 2D design in either traditional or digital forms, live-action short films or animations, drawing, creative writing, or any 3D work.

- *Crafts:* A combination of work from the following list: ceramics, glass, metals, fiber, painting, sculpture, prints, photography, video or digital, or drawings.

- *Fine Arts:* Five drawings of any kind. The remainder should represent solid examples of your best creative efforts in any medium; they may include, but are not limited to, painting, sculpture, prints, photography, crafts, video, or digital.

- *Graphic Design:* A combination of work from the following list: photographs, collages, software exploration (Photoshop, Illustrator, etc.), printmaking, lettering samples, drawing, creative writing, or any 3D work.

- *Illustration:* At least five drawings from direct observation. The remainder can represent your selected major or areas of interest.

- *Industrial Design (includes Product and Transportation Design):* At least five drawings from direct observation. The remainder can represent your selected major or areas of interest.

- *Interior Design:* At least five drawings from direct observation. The remainder can represent your selected major or areas of interest.

- *Photography:* A combination of photographs and other forms of 2D or 3D design that expresses your creative potential.

- *Undeclared:* At least five drawings from direct observation. The remainder can represent your areas of interest.

THERESA BEDOYA
Director of Admissions
Maryland Institute, College of Art

Each art college has expectations and academic requirements particular to the program of study you choose. For most professional colleges, the evaluation of your portfolio will supersede the review of all other criteria for admission. The term "competitive" will have a different meaning if you are applying to a professional college specializing in art. The goal of the selective art colleges is to admit students of extraordinary talent. Many visual arts colleges even prescreen potential applicants through review of the portfolio prior to application in order to determine eligibility for admission.

In contrast, most comprehensive colleges and universities offering majors in art rely on academic criteria to make an admission decision. The portfolio, if required, plays a secondary role. You should take these factors into consideration when deciding whether or not to apply to a specialized art college.

That said, you should gain as much studio experience as possible in order to develop a strong portfolio. Take full advantage of your high school art program and enroll in extra Saturday or summer classes. Exhibit your artwork when the opportunity is provided. Become better informed as an artist by studying art history and the works of contemporary artists.

JON FRASER
Acting Dean
School of Visual and Performing Arts
C.W. Post Campus, Long Island University

No school is expecting you to be Pablo Picasso when you walk in the door for a portfolio review. What they are all looking for is potential and talent. There are no standard portfolio requirements. They vary from school to school. Make sure that you know what each school is looking for, and adhere strictly to its requirements. It could be that one style of portfolio presentation will work for several schools, but be prepared to change and alter your portfolio to match a specific school's requirements. To find out what an individual school may want, check the Web site, or call directly to the department. If you call, simply tell the person answering the phone that you'd like to speak to someone about portfolio requirements. Then, ask them the questions below, along with any other questions you may have.

Your portfolio should be as professional as possible. It should also show you to your best abilities. Try to choose material that shows who you are as an individual. Make brave choices. Remember that the people viewing your work are seeing hundreds of potential students, so you need to stand out (in a good way) to be recognized.

How various schools look at your portfolio is entirely subjective. One school may love you and offer you a scholarship based on your portfolio; the next school will reject you entirely based on that same portfolio. There's no way to make sense of it, so just do the best you can. Try to maintain a positive attitude and make sure you know:

- How many pieces should be included

- Whether the school will accept slides, photographs, or CD-ROMs of your work

- What media the school is interested in seeing

- How to talk about your work intelligently

RITA GAGLIANO
Executive Director of Admission
Savannah College of Art and Design

Before formally submitting your portfolio for review, you will want to be sure you are clear regarding the submission formats required by each institution. Generally, traditional visual artwork is submitted in slide format. If slides are required, determine whether they must be included in a plastic slide sheet for viewing or whether they may be submitted in a box for later transference to a slide carousel. In any case, slides should always be properly cropped using film tape (available at most photo shops). Label each slide with your name and the title of the work. Give some indication of the orientation of the piece if it's unclear which side should face up.

More recently, some colleges are allowing students to submit visual artwork on CD-ROM. If submitting traditional work on CD-ROM, be sure to check your disk on a number of computers to be sure you have saved your work properly and that it can be easily opened by others. Most files should be saved as high-resolution JPEG files to allow for easy viewing on most computers.

Students submitting computer-generated artwork may submit the work in digital format on CD-ROM, DVD, or VHS videotape. If submitting a VHS tape, be sure it is NTSC formatted. Generally, all 2D and 3D images should be saved as high-resolution JPEG files, Adobe pdf files, or digital portfolios created in PowerPoint, Director, Flash, or HTML. Again, be sure you check for submission format specifications as required by the college to which you are applying.

Real-time animations and work with multimedia content may be submitted on DVD or in formats compatible with Quicktime, RealTime, or Windows Mediaplayer. Film and video work, along with performing arts auditions, may be submitted on VHS tape or DVD. Be sure these types of pieces are acceptable by the institution to which you are applying. If a college or university will accept your online portfolio, be sure to include all letters in the URL address and that the site is working. Have friends try it out from their home computers and get their feedback on ease of navigability. Keep in mind that schools receive a significant number of portfolio submissions each year and rely on your efforts to move efficiently during the review process.

Some colleges accept work in a wide variety of media, including photography, sound design, performing arts, and architectural viewbooks, among others. Be sure the various media are welcomed by the college and then ascertain the submission format requirements.

Regardless of format, all students should include an inventory sheet. The inventory sheet provides the opportunity to identify each piece by title or project, medium (or software/materials used), size, and date of completion. Some students include a description of the work and an explanation of the inspiration for the piece. This is a nice touch and allows the reviewer a glimpse of the artist's motivation and passion.

Applying and Getting In

National Events That Can Help You Prepare

NATIONAL PORTFOLIO DAYS

Each year, members of the National Portfolio Day Association sponsor National Portfolio Days in thirty-five cities across the nation and in Canada. These events provide an opportunity for students interested in pursuing undergraduate or graduate study in the visual arts to meet with representatives from some of the most outstanding colleges, universities, and independent schools that teach art and design. Attendees have their portfolio of artwork reviewed and gain guidance about their future artistic development. Participating institutions also provide information about programs of study, careers in art, admission requirements, financial aid, and scholarships.

Posters announcing dates and locations are mailed in September to high school art departments. You can also visit www.npda.org for more information.

ARTS RECOGNITION AND TALENT SEARCH PROGRAM (ARTS)

ARTS is a national program designed to identify, recognize, and encourage high school seniors and other 17- and 18-year-old artists who demonstrate excellence in dance, film and video, classical instrumental music, jazz music, voice, theater, visual arts, photography, and writing. ARTS is a program of the National Foundation for Advancement in the Arts (NFAA), an independent, nongovernmental institution dedicated to the support of young artists.

NFAA offers an award package of more than $1 million for ARTS applicants whose work has been judged as outstanding by a national panel of experts. Students selected for recognition share cash awards totaling more than $500,000, with individual awards ranging up to $10,000 each. Each January, up to 160 students are invited to participate in an all-expenses-paid ARTS Week in Miami. ARTS Week consists of master classes, performances, exhibitions, workshops, and final live adjudications. In addition, through the Scholarship List Service, NFAA provides the names of all ARTS applicants who are seniors in high school

Visual

Arts

to colleges, universities, and professional institutions that are actively recruiting students in the creative and performing arts.

NFAA is also the exclusive agent for nominating selected ARTS winners to the Commission on Presidential Scholars, which names the Presidential Scholars in the Arts. For an application form and more information, contact the NFAA at 1-800-970-ARTS or apply online at www.NFAA.org.

PERFORMING AND VISUAL ARTS COLLEGE FAIRS

The NACAC (National Association for College Admission Counseling) Performing and Visual Arts College Fairs are events for college and college-bound students interested in pursuing undergraduate and graduate programs of study in the areas of music, dance, theatre, visual arts, graphic design, and other related disciplines. Attendees learn about educational opportunities, admission and financial aid, portfolio days, audition and entrance requirements, and much more by meeting with representatives from colleges, universities, conservatories, festivals, and other educational institutions with specialized programs in the visual and performing arts.

For information about NACAC's Performing and Visual Arts College Fairs, call the national office at 1-800-822-6285. For a schedule, visit www.nacac.com.

Applying and Getting In

You're In! What's Next?

You have followed your dream and it has paid off. What will your life be like as a full-time art major? And what lies ahead for you if you decide to become a professional artist? Find out from those in the know.

The Importance of Foundation Studies

Maureen Garvin

Foundation studies programs are an integral part of a visual arts education. These programs are a series of studio classes taken during the first year of study in an art college or program. The primary function of foundation programs is to prepare all students to be successful in their major programs.

The names of the foundation programs are variations on the terms "Visual Fundamentals" and "Preliminary Courses," which were used to describe the first year in the Bauhaus, a design school founded in Germany that migrated to Chicago in 1937. The structure and content of many of today's foundation programs developed from traditions established in the Bauhaus: material exploration and an understanding of form, color, and composition. More contemporary terms such as "Core Studio Practice" and the more common "Foundation Studies" are used to describe a sequence of classes that teach both the technical and conceptual skills needed to pursue any area of art and design.

LEARNING THE VISUAL LANGUAGE

While the sequence and titles of the foundation courses vary from college to college, the common goal is to teach visual literacy. Visual literacy is about understanding the language used in art and design. In the same manner that one learns French or Italian, one can learn about the elements of visual language: line, shape, value, color, and how to manipulate and compose these elements to visually communicate ideas. Georgia O' Keeffe said, "I found I could say things with color and shapes that I couldn't say any other way."

The elements and the principles of design are the language students use in their majors. In these first-year studio classes, students learn to handle a variety of media that can range from the traditional—charcoal, graphite, and gouache—to digital versions of these traditional tools. Foundation programs teach how to develop ideas, how to understand the terminology of visual language, and how to evaluate or critique the work. Most programs include drawing classes to train a student's eye and hand to see and translate information out in the real world into a visual representation or response. Learning to draw has been used as a method to train artists since the Renaissance.

Students often perceive foundation courses as something to get through to move on to "real" courses in the major. It can be a struggle to see the purpose of taking courses that appear unrelated to a major. The reality is that the visual language and skills learned in foundation courses are the common denominator in all the fields. Designing an ad, creating visual effects for a film, constructing a garment, and designing a building all begin with knowing how to manipulate visual language to relay content, an idea.

NEW WAYS OF SEEING

As a result of your foundation classes, you literally will begin to see in different ways. You will start to understand how artists and designers think, how one thought, sketch, doodle leads to another and another and to a series of ideas that generate new designs or images. Another frequent outcome of taking foundation classes is that students accomplish what they never believed they could do. An example would be the drawing-phobic student who slowly realizes that he or she can actually draw and even reach a point where he or she wants to draw and enjoys the process of drawing. You will begin to make connections between the design principles you learn: balance, repetition, rhythm, emphasis, and why an image can look calm, boring, or comforting. You will look at an artist's work and understand what he or she was aiming to accomplish and how he or she went about it. (This can impress and amaze relatives.) New ideas will occur when looking at familiar objects. You might think, "The chair could be more comfortable and better-looking if the back was a different shape."

ADVANTAGES OF TAKING FOUNDATION COURSES

One advantage of beginning your career with the foundation courses is that you can picture yourself pursuing a variety of careers. You will be in classes with students who are interested in architecture, fashion, animation, furniture design, painting, and maybe a few majors you have never even heard of, such as sound design, broadcast design, or information architecture. Most first-year programs include the opportunity to take several electives to try out different areas of interest. Some students arrive with the desire to be a graphic designer and after taking an elective in ceramics or glass begin to see an entirely new future for themselves.

A second advantage of that first-year program is that you learn how to be disciplined, that good art and design come from practice and perseverance, and that creativity occurs with the willingness to go beyond what is obvious, to see, to visualize in new ways. Mary Stewart is a noted artist and author of a text frequently used in foundation studies courses, titled *Launching the Imagination: A Comprehensive Guide to Basic Design.* She writes about the seven characteristics of thinking: receptivity, curiosity, a wide range of interests, attentiveness, connection seeking, conviction, and complexity. Throughout the sequence of foundation courses, you will learn not only the mechanics—the tools, techniques, and concepts— but how to think and see in new ways. You will be developing the ability to be a creative thinker.

A third advantage to foundation studies is that you will start to see the common language used in all the fields you could choose as a major. The edges of an architectural detail will remind you of lines in a drawing and a pattern on a fabric. This brings into play some of the characteristics to which Mary Stewart refers: connection seeking, curiosity and attentiveness.

SUMMING IT UP

- The primary function of foundation programs is to prepare all students to be successful in their major programs.

- The common goal is to teach visual literacy.

- Foundation programs teach how to develop ideas, understand the terminology of visual language, and how to evaluate or critique the work.

- "You are not only learning to draw but to see."

- One result of foundation classes is that you will begin to literally see in different ways.

- You will accomplish what you never believed you could do.

- A student can arrive with the desire to be a graphic designer and after taking an elective in ceramics or glass begin to see an entirely new future for themselves.

- You will be acclimated to hard work and confident in your ability to learn. You will be ready.

Maureen Garvin is Dean of the School of Fine Art, Savannah College of Art and Design

Typical First-Year Schedules

While all schools differ in their degree requirements, the following samples of first-year schedules for various B.F.A. programs at a typical specialized college give you an idea of what a week in the life of an art major is like.

Computer Graphics

Mon	Survey of World Art	12:00–2:50
Tues	Imaging Techniques	9:00–11:50
Wed	Drawing	9:00–2:50
Thurs	Language and Literature	9:00–11:50
Fri	Introduction to Animation	2:00–6:50

Fine Arts

Mon	Painting	9:00–2:50
Tues	Sculpture	12:00–5:50
Wed	Drawing	9:00–2:50
Thurs	Free	
Fri	Survey of World Art	12:00–2:50
	Language and Literature	3:00–5:50

Photography

Mon	Free	
Tues	Digital Imaging	9:00–11:50
	History of Photography	3:00–5:30
Wed	Language and Literature	9:00–11:50
Thurs	Photo Workshop	9:00–2:50
	Studio Workshop	6:30–9:20
Fri	Free	

Visual Arts

Current Art Majors Tell All

ED MOORMAN
Comic Art
Minneapolis College of Art and Design

If you want to major in art, it's obvious to make sure that your portfolio is your focus; you want to have a variety of work and you want to make sure that it's about something. Art is how you communicate, and you want to have something to communicate. The more specific your work is to you and the way that you feel, the more you'll stand out to admissions officers. Also, do as much work as you can outside of school and just push yourself. Sequester yourself in your room with your materials and follow all the ridiculous ideas you might have. Study history and artists that interest you and/or work within your chosen field. Trust your obsessions. Read, watch films, listen to music, and go to museums as much as you can. Everything you take in will feed and inform what you're doing.

When you go to Portfolio Days, pay attention to what the admissions officers are looking for. If, for example, they're looking to see if your proportions are dead-on or that you have included a landscape, a figure, etc., that says something about what the school cares about, because they're instructing their employees to find people who have these things. I went to a Portfolio Day and a popular school that shall remain nameless focused on those things alone while quickly sifting through my stuff. I went to the table for the Minneapolis College of Art and Design and the admissions officer talked with me for a long time about my intentions and what I was doing, laughed at my comics, commented on my line quality, and generally seemed to be in tune with caring about me and how I was growing and would grow as an artist—instead of staunch criteria that has nothing to do with how a piece will affect the viewer. Lo and behold, MCAD is a great school.

As for once you're in school: I could advise you to learn how to manage your time, but you will learn through experience and stupidity (as we all do) that sleeping and eating are not negotiable enterprises.

Pay very close attention to selecting your teachers. Art school can cost your mortal soul in debts and there's no reason you shouldn't have all fantastic instructors.

Watch out for debts! Don't pay for school on credit cards. There is a teacher at my school who lives part of the time in Ireland because he has been running from credit card bills ever since he left college.

If you're going to a good school, you will be amazed how easy it is to make friends, no matter how alienated or awkward you may have felt beforehand. As it always is, your friends will be your saving grace in art school, and what's more, they'll be your artistic peers. I always know that if I have trouble with a project and I need an objective viewpoint, there are certain friends of mine whose opinion I respect to the highest degree who will help out.

I'm majoring in comic art and will try my hand with independent publishers after college for awhile. Then, at some point, I'll go to graduate school and get a master's in art education, since I really want to be an art teacher.

As an artist, you may never make a great deal of money. You must make peace with this idea. My sculpture teacher talks about the janitors who are great novelists, the art museum guards who are great painters, etc., and there is always the possibility that that will be you. But if you think that your passion for art can drive you through school and life, you're blessed, because you will always have that and you will always be okay because of it.

DANIELLE SMITH
Film and Television, with a Minor in Sound Design
Savannah College of Art and Design

Visiting my sister who was attending a large university while I was still in high school allowed me to experience college life at an early age. I went to parties, football games, and sat in on a few of her classes—in an auditorium with hundreds of other students she barely knew. I can remember thinking, "Is something wrong with me or is this just not that appealing?" I mean, the only thing she did for fun was go to parties and sporting events. Right then and there, I promised myself I would make a different college decision—not for my parents, not for my friends, but for my future.

I requested catalogs from several different colleges with good film programs. I had decided I wanted to study film and that was that. By chance, I went with my video production club on a tour of the Savannah College of Art and Design and the rest is history. I brought my dad back for a visit and I remember thinking about it being the best college visit we had had out of the many colleges we visited up and down the East Coast. I applied, got in, and have never regretted my decision.

When I arrived at SCAD, I didn't know anyone. But that was a good thing. I knew that if I had gone to any of the other in-state colleges, I'd basically be living a rerun from high school. I knew that to grow I would need to expand my horizons by leaving my comfort zone. I can remember calling my friend during my first year of college to see how she was enjoying the new college life. The conversation went a little something like this:

"Hey, Jerry, what's going on? What are you up to?"

"Nothing much," she replied. "I'm just studying for this stupid science test I have tomorrow. What are you up to?"

"Oh, nothing really. I'm on a film shoot right now, so that's really cool. I got to work on a graduate student's film just yesterday too."

I wasn't trying to brag but I couldn't help but to express my excitement. She was amazed that I was already working in my major too.

At SCAD, it's like everyone is passionate about something. We love going to class and getting the chance to work with our favorite media. The best part about it is that our classmates love their work too, and they're excited to share it with you. It's never just busy work either. Every little thing you do can contribute to your portfolio if you want it to, and that makes students work even harder.

The networking possibilities are endless from the day you get here. From meeting graphic designers, architects, textile designers, and Hollywood directors, we experience it all. And we make connections with students in other majors. For instance, when I need an actor, I ask media and performing arts students. When they need headshots, they work with their photography friends. When photography students need to jazz up photos a little, they go to their graphic design friends.

I could seriously go on and on about how there's a tremendous networking cycle. I shot a music video for my senior project. If there's one thing you learn at SCAD, it's how to work in teams effectively. My roommate, who studies fashion, oversaw all of my costume design. A production design student was able to receive credit for being my art director. She took care of all my set design and worked closely with my production team and even had an assistant from the industrial design department help with the construction of the sets just because he was interested in helping. A metals and jewelry sophomore made a beautiful necklace with matching earrings for the singer to wear, and a sound design student came in to take care of the music playback. I couldn't have done it without them, not to mention the additional 11 film students who helped out in so many other ways.

A day in the life of an art student varies depending on the current projects on which he or she is working. The best advice I can provide is to make sure you're passionate about what you do. If you find yourself saying, "Well I guess that would be cool," then take a step back and really take into consideration what you enjoy doing and what you're good at. As a film and sound design student at SCAD, a typical day for me may start out attending an art history course, leaving there to grab a bite to eat, then going to recording studio class where I get to mix a film soundtrack. I might end my day as assistant director of a classmate's film project. That doesn't include my part-time job, studying, completing homework assignments, helping on other projects, and attending a Bahamian party or two. Yes, we party too! The next day could be completely different though. You need time management skills to survive.

My time is consumed by my passion for what I'm doing. I'm surrounded by people who love what they do, and that's important. It's never about making a grade. It's about producing my best work. With two internships under my belt, I feel even closer to the perfect career path: a job at an entertainment company in the music and television industry.

JOHN RENAUD
Fashion Design
Pratt Institute

It's 2:00 a.m. and I'm still in the studio, sewing machine buzzing away, and I have two more garments to make. I have been here since 9:00 a.m. Luckily, I have access to a 24-hour supply of coffee or I surely would be asleep on one of the cutting tables by now. I have to finish this collection; the fashion show is tomorrow. Some may think I have put myself in a dreadful situation, but I couldn't be happier. I am in bliss. I am creating. The hard work and long hours are worth the end result. The wave of relief and accomplishment that will come over me as my final model walks down the runway will be worth all the effort.

Many people think fashion design students sit around and draw pretty pictures all day. This is a common misconception. The truth is that fashion design, while it is my passion and I could never see myself doing anything else and being happy, is a tough, challenging, and very time-consuming major. At Pratt, fashion design students are constantly broadening their horizons through the many different classes they take. Classes in sportswear, knitwear, menswear, childrenswear, lingerie, tailoring, and numerous other subjects allow students to graduate with a more diverse knowledge of the multi-billion dollar fashion industry than any other school.

The required liberal arts classes give all art and design students the well-rounded education they need to get to the top of our fields. We are encouraged to expand our knowledge by taking our art electives in other departments. The professors in Pratt's fashion design department are fashion industry veterans. Many own their own lines, many have been head designers at major design companies, and all of them love teaching. Getting to work one-on-one with our teachers is a very important advantage we have over the larger, less-selective fashion design schools.

As I cut the final thread of the blouse I have been sewing, I glance at the clock. It's 3:34 a.m. I feel proud that I have finished this piece. It has taken all day. I then look to the cutting table at a pile of fabric and pattern paper. I still have two more to go.

KRISTEN SEGHERS
Art History
Rutgers University

Like a lot of students, I kind of fell into my major. I'd always had an appreciation for art and a critical eye, but I'd been planning on majoring in journalism in college. When it came time to register for spring classes during my freshman year I needed another course, and my adviser suggested I take art history. Luckily, I was on the crew team at the time and got to register early because art history courses usually fill up quickly; it's hard for a freshman to get in. It turned out to be my favorite class. So I took two more art history courses sophomore year and then knew I had found what I wanted to major in.

As I said, most introductory art history classes are popular and crowded. Some people think it's an easy way to satisfy a history requirement but later see they were mistaken. The large Intro to Art History lectures consist of those with an interest in art sitting in the front and those just trying to pass a history course in the back. So always try to sit with others who are engaged in the material and not just taking advantage of the dim lights (needed to view the slides) to catch up on sleep. And, as practically all my professors say, drink coffee: it's cheap and legal and will help combat the sleepiness that somehow befalls you in the dark. Or, take morning classes.

Most courses require you to go to a museum and write a paper on a selected work. While the papers may be required to be rather long, most professors are positive about any interpretation or response as long as you can back it up. Art is really about how you feel about something, and the trick is trying to find words to describe what you think the artist felt. Papers usually aren't a huge sweat, as there are ample resources available on all topics in art. The study of art history includes discussion of not only the art created in a period, but the history of when it was created, the philosophy of the people of the time, and the psychology behind an artist's work. You are rarely strapped for information. The hard part is fitting it together coherently.

I am extremely lucky to have the access to New York City that Rutgers offers. New York provides the perfect setting of world-class museums surrounded by an artistic culture. Any school in proximity to a major museum provides the best opportunity for special tours, internships, and other programs. Honestly, any art history professor will tell you that art needs to be experienced and seen up close and personal. The feeling you get knowing that there is only that one painting in the entire world and you are standing right in front of it, as the artist once did, is truly amazing. And check out a school's study-abroad programs. They should take you right to the source and offer something more than just a tour that any person could take. I am planning to do Rutgers' Summer in Paris program next year, where I'll be exploring the museums and architecture of Paris and its surrounding cities.

At this point, I am open to all career paths. I would like to work at a museum or a gallery and also further my interest in the developing field of art therapy. I would truly like to help change the world with my degree and reintroduce art as an important part of our culture. I remember that when I was growing up, art class was never considered as important as math or science class, and I think we need a serious overhaul of our values—especially in this country. I feel that many Americans take art (like everything else) for granted and really lack appreciation for it. I'd like to help bring some prestige and appreciation back to the art world in this country.

Up Close and Personal with Professional Artists

SUSAN WHITE
Art Conservator

Susan White, owner of White Conservation Services—a New York–based art conservation business—received her B.A. in chemistry and art history from Duke University in 1982. As an undergraduate, White was interested in pursuing a career in medicine, but she longed to be involved in the visual arts as well. Unable to decide whether to choose a career in science or one dedicated to art, White elected to combine her interests by going into the then young field of fine art conservation. She attended graduate school at the University of Delaware/ Winterthur Program, receiving an M.S. in fine art conservation with a specialty in objects restoration in 1985. She then went on to do internships at the National Gallery of Art, the National Museum of American History, and the Metropolitan Museum of Art. While she was at the Met, she published research in the study of ancient Egyptian goldworking technology in addition to working as a conservator for other museums, private dealers, and collectors in New York City.

In 1987, she visited China on a fellowship from the Met in order to learn more about restoration techniques used in that country. In 1988, she moved to Boston to study sculpture at the School of the Museum of Fine Arts, receiving a diploma in 1991. She subsequently attended the Massachusetts College of Art and received her M.F.A. in sculpture. After teaching at the college level and serving as artist-in-residence at a Boston-area private high school, she returned to New York City in 1997, where she now runs a private art conservation business.

White has worked on a wide variety of objects, from ancient Greek and Roman ceramics to contemporary sculpture. She works on porcelain, glass, stone, ivory, and wood—anything three-dimensional. She's repaired baby carriages for network executive wives and Outsider Art for Soho dealers. When asked what is the most interesting piece she has worked on, she says it's difficult to say. Was it the ninth-century life-size gold Buddha riddled with bullet holes that a dealer smuggled out of Nepal? Or perhaps the "ancient Chinese bronze" stork that turned out to be made from a collection of modern parts, including a toilet buoy and a brass dog bowl? White says that whatever crosses her bench presents new challenges, which is what she most loves about her work.

However, it's not only the art that White finds fascinating. She says that one of the most interesting aspects of her work are her clients, who range from modest, work-a-day folks to the powerful elite of the world of museums and collectors. She's particularly intrigued by the way some people attach to their works of art and says that many of her clients see their objects as "perfect reflections of themselves." When one of those objects breaks, she says, she has to "repair not only the object but the owner as well." She finds these to be the most interesting and the most challenging of jobs.

Owning her own business allows White unusual flexibility and freedom and is one of the great benefits of having chosen this field. "The work is not always steady, but when it comes, it is lucrative and interesting." And between jobs she is able to pursue her two creative loves: making art and writing. She is currently working on a manuscript about her work as a private art conservator, entitled *Objects and Their People*.

JEANNIE FRIEDMAN
Owner and President, Design Firm; Graphic Designer

Jeannie Friedman, owner and president of New York City–based graphic design firm Design Five, graduated from The Cooper Union School of Art with a degree in graphic design. Under Friedman's direction, the award-winning 15-person company produces classroom materials from pre-kindergarten through college for major U.S. educational publishers.

Having begun her college career as a painting major at the University of Chicago, Friedman's interests diversified once she arrived at Cooper. "I quickly discovered the silkscreen lab, the photography lab, and the typography lab," she says, and "that really turned me on to graphic design." Her interest in painting never waned, however, and one of the things she most enjoys about her current career is that "I'm still a painter and I'm financially supported by the work that I do as a graphic designer."

Friedman credits her real-world work experience with helping her to succeed both in school and in her field.

"I worked my way through school and I really recommend this to kids thinking of going to art school," says Friedman. "I was the art editor for a small magazine. This was how I supported myself while attending school. It was some of the best training I've ever had. I really learned how to put together a magazine from start to finish."

"Now that I'm the owner," Friedman says, "while I don't do the hands-on work, I'm still using the visual skills I learned at Cooper."

LILI BERNARD FERGUSON
Painter
www.homagehues.com

The arts played an integral role in my familial, native-Cuban upbringing. Fine art, music, and theater thrived in our household. When I was just a toddler, my family emigrated to the United States. In our little Brooklyn brownstone my mother gave me my first lesson in drawing. I was four years old. With great focus and joyful seriousness she showed me how to arrange circles and triangles to create a beautiful bird. I delighted at the complex simplicity of my mother's design. That moment was pivotal in my decision to become an artist. I was utterly fascinated by the living form that my mother was able to create, via the combination of two mere shapes.

Since I can remember, my mother used to always say that she knew I was going to grow up to be a famous artist one day. She and my father instilled in my siblings and me the knowledge that we could achieve any and every goal. My father, an electrical engineer, used to bring home discarded blueprints. My brothers and sisters and I squealed euphorically as he unrolled the huge papers on the kitchen table and spilled crayons on top of them. For hours we drew and colored on the back of those discarded blueprints. My father categorically saved our childhood drawings for each one of us to enjoy in our adulthood. I spent most of my time growing up in New Jersey. However, in the beginning of my junior year of high school, my family relocated to Tokyo, where I graduated from the American School in Japan. My art teachers in both New Jersey and Tokyo nourished my artistic capabilities. The uplifting nature of my teachers, coupled with the self-sacrificing love of my parents and their wonderful lessons in art, propelled me to study fine arts at Cornell University.

A visiting professor of painting at Cornell University named Patrick Webb taught me invaluable lessons on the derivation and arrangement of colors. Today, in my painting, I continue to incorporate many of the methods that I learned from Professor Webb as well as from many of the dynamic art professors at Cornell University. Along with fine arts, I also studied the sciences and acting at Cornell. My theater professor, Bruce Levitt, encouraged me to consider pursuing a career in acting and recommended that I study in New York City. After three years at Cornell, I left and started a successful acting career in New York, where I studied theater for three years, under the tutelage of Sonia Moore. My fine art continued to develop, alongside my thespian life. I used to come home from rehearsals and performances and paint. At my parents urging and with their support, I completed my bachelor's degree at the City University of New York.

My college education has been instrumental in my career as an artist, both in theater and in fine arts. It has given me the knowledge, skill, and fortitude necessary to forge through my occupation as an artist. Today, as a wife and a mother of five young boys, my vocational focus is more on fine arts. I paint prolifically while my children slumber or attend school. When they are home, they delight in watching me paint, often offering invaluable criticism and support. They boast about my art shows to their teachers and peers. My children tangibly benefit from my college education; I impart to them many of the invaluable lessons in art that I gained as a college student. Clearly, my college education has enriched my life, not only as an artist, but also as a mother.

My studio is a very well lit room in the upstairs of our Los Angeles home. We call it the "mirror room" because there are wall-to-wall mirrors on one side, fantastically reflecting the abundant, southern-exposure sunlight. Upon the mirrors, taped in random order, are inspirational photographs and words, most smudged with paint and charcoal. The hardwood floors beneath my easels are splattered in paint. There is always music playing in the background that relates to the subject I am painting. I often dance when I paint and sometimes speak to the canvas, as if it has a life of its own. Painting is always a joy-filled experience. One of my goals is to share with viewers a small portion of the joy I am blessed to feel, all within the process of creating art.

The subjects of my paintings range from the spiritual, through the natural, to the ancestral. I paint in oils, sans thinning agents. One of the most time-consuming and yet therapeutic aspects in my painting is the mixing of colors on the pallet. I tend to derive hues that are brightly colored, which reflect, rather than absorb, light.

It is always rewarding to see how positively my paintings impact people. This is most evident at the opening of an art show. I measure the success of a painting by the length of time people stand in front of it and stare or by the questions they ask, regarding the work. My acting career has helped me with the Questions & Answers portion of art show openings when I have had to stand before more than 100 people and speak about my inspiration and creative process.

I look at every venue to display and sell my work as an utter blessing. This is particularly true in the context of relatively few women and people of color being represented in the art world. One of my most gratifying experiences as an artist is being able to commune with other artists, of all types. I enjoy the soul connection that invariably exists between artists and benefit from listening to the reflections and insights of artists who are more experienced in the professional world of art than I am.

In the eve of a career as a professional fine artist, my plans for the future involve applying to graduate school so that I may pursue a Master of Fine Arts (M.F.A.) for my own personal edification and fortification. I look forward to benefiting from the relationships I will form with other graduate students as well as with professors who themselves are experienced artists. Being equipped with an M.F.A. will also give me the option to pursue a career as an instructor of art at the college level, should I so desire. My other plans for the future involve my forming a collaborative of artists who are typically underrepresented in the art world, namely women and people of color.

You're In! What's Next?

How to Use This Guide

Peterson's College Guide for Visual Arts Majors offers detailed information on professional degree programs in art offered at institutions in the U.S., its territories, and Canada. The guide should be used as a first step toward identifying potential programs; students are encouraged to consult with their school counselors and arts teachers for additional guidance.

ART PROGRAMS AT-A-GLANCE

If you want to find out quickly which professional degrees are offered by a specific school, turn to the **Quick-Reference Chart.** Organized geographically, the chart provides the most basic information about each school in this guide, including:

- *Institution name and location*

- *Professional degrees offered in art*

- *Total enrollment*

- *Tuition and fees for the 2006–07 or 2005–06 academic year*

- *Profile page reference*

PROFILES OF VISUAL ARTS PROGRAMS

This guide profiles professional degree programs only. The **Profiles of Visual Arts Programs** section is organized alphabetically by institution name.

Each profile consists of the following elements:

Institutional control: Private institutions are designated as *independent* (nonprofit), *independent/religious* (sponsored by or affiliated with a religious group or having a non-denominational or interdenominational religious orientation), or *proprietary* (profit-making). Public institutions are designated by their primary source of support, such as *federal, state, commonwealth* (Puerto Rico), *territory* (U.S. territories), *county, district* (an administrative unit of public education, often having boundaries different from units of local government), *city, state, and local* ("local" refers to county, district, or city), or *state-related* (funded primarily by the state but administered autonomously).

Student body type: Categories are *men* (100 percent of student body), *primarily men*, *women* (100 percent of student body), *primarily women*, and *coed*.

Campus setting: Setting is designated as *urban, suburban, small town*, or *rural*.

Degrees: Many of the degrees listed (both undergraduate and graduate) are purely professional in scope and definition. Institutions may also offer B.A., B.S., M.A., and M.S. degrees that are considered "professional" based upon the prescribed curriculum and course load within the discipline. In a professional degree program, the majority of the curriculum is made up of course work within the particular arts field, while the rest of the program involves traditional liberal arts course work. A professional degree program allows students to focus most of their studies in art and emphasizes professional training and acquiring professional skills.

Enrollment: This data element cites the number of matriculated undergraduate and (if applicable) graduate students at the institution, both full-time and part-time, as of fall 2005.

Student profile: Whole-figure percentages are given for the total program enrollment broken down into the following categories: *minorities, female, male, international*.

Faculty: Numbers are given for undergraduate and (if applicable) graduate faculty members teaching full-time and part-time in the respective area of study. The percentage of full-time faculty members who have appropriate terminal degrees in their field is listed, as is the ratio of undergraduate students to faculty members teaching undergraduate courses. Finally, mention is made if graduate students teach undergraduate courses in the program.

Student life: This section lists program-related organizations and campus activities in which visual arts students may participate. The availability of housing opportunities designated solely for visual arts students is mentioned here as well.

Expenses: Figures are given for the 2006–07 academic year (actual or estimated) or for the 2005–06 academic year if more recent figures were

Visual Arts

not yet available at the time of data collection. Annual expenses may be expressed as a *comprehensive fee* (this includes full-time tuition, mandatory fees, and college room and board) or as separate figures for full-time *tuition, mandatory fees, college room and board*, or *college room only*. For public institutions where tuition differs according to residence, separate figures are given for area and/or state residents and for out-of-state residents. The tuition structure at some institutions is complex in that freshmen and sophomores may be charged a different rate from that for juniors and seniors, or a professional or vocational division may have a different fee structure than the liberal arts division of the same institution. In such cases, the lowest tuition appears in the profile, followed by the notation minimum. Also, in instances where colleges report room and board costs that vary depending on the type of accommodation and meal plan, the figures given are either for the most common room arrangement and a full meal plan or for the lowest figures, followed by the notation minimum. If the institution charges special program-related fees for students in the visual and performing arts, these are listed as well.

Financial aid: This section provides information regarding any college-administered award opportunities dedicated exclusively for undergraduate students in the program. Keep in mind that while these awards are only for students in the program, program students may qualify for other financial aid opportunities at the institution as well.

Application procedures: This section indicates if students are admitted directly into the professional program when they enroll for the freshman year or if they must apply for admission into the professional program at some point during their undergraduate career. Admission application deadlines and dates for notification of acceptance or rejection into the program are given either as specific dates or as *continuous* for freshmen and transfers. Continuous means that applications are processed as they are received, and qualified students are accepted as long as there are openings. Continuous notification means that applicants are notified of acceptance or rejection as applications are processed up until the date indicated or until the actual beginning of classes. Application requirements are grouped into either *required* or *recommended*. In addition to these requirements, an institution may indicate if *portfolio reviews* are held and where they are held (on or off campus).

Contact: Information includes the name, title, mailing address, phone number, fax number, and e-mail address of the person to contact for further information. Where applicable, a graduate contact is listed as well.

More About the School: A **Special Message** may be included for schools that wish to place additional emphasis on some aspect of their program offerings.

APPENDIXES

The **Summer Programs in Art** appendix lists names and contact information for summer programs that can help high school students develop their talent and skills and build their portfolio.

Scholarships for Artists contains a partial listing of private scholarships, grants, and prizes awarded to college-bound art students. The awards are based on data collected between January and April 2006 through survey mailings and phone interviews. Every effort has been made to provide up-to-date information. However, changes in particular program information may occur after this book is published. To make sure that you have the most current information, always contact the sponsors directly.

The **Additional Resources** appendix provide readers with lists of various art education organizations and resources that provide support to students in the arts.

INDEXES

The **Majors and Concentrations** index presents 152 major fields of study. The majors are listed alphabetically. The terms used for the majors are the most widely used. However, many institutions use different terms for the same or similar areas. In addition, while the term "major" is used in this guide, some schools may use other terms such as concentration, program of study, or field.

The **Alphabetical Listing of Schools** index lists every professional degree-granting institution in the guide alphabetically and gives the page number(s) on which its profile can be found.

DATA COLLECTION PROCEDURES

The data contained in the quick-reference chart, profiles, and indexes were collected through *Peterson's Survey of Professional Degree Programs in the Visual & Performing Arts*. Questionnaires were sent to the more than 1,100 programs that meet the criteria for inclusion outlined below. All data included in this edition have been submitted by officials (usually program directors, department heads, or admissions personnel) at the institutions themselves. In addition, the great majority of institutions that submitted data were contacted directly by Peterson's editorial staff to verify unusual figures, resolve discrepancies, and obtain additional data. All usable information received in time for publication has been included. The omission of any items from an index or profile listing signifies either that the data were not applicable to that institution or that data were not available. Institutions that did not return a survey are listed with an abbreviated profile in order to ensure a comprehensive reference product. We have every reason to believe that the information presented in this guide is accurate. However, students should check with a specific college or university to verify such figures as tuition and fees, which may have changed since the publication of this volume.

CRITERIA FOR INCLUSION IN THIS BOOK

Peterson's College Guide for Visual Arts Majors covers accredited baccalaureate-degree-granting institutions in the United States, U.S. territories, and Canada. Institutions have full accreditation or candidate-for-accreditation (preaccreditation) status granted by an institutional or specialized accrediting body recognized by the U.S. Department of Education or Council for Higher Education Accreditation. Recognized institutional accrediting bodies, which consider each institution as a whole, are the following: the six regional associations of schools and colleges (Middle States, New England, North Central, Northwest, Southern, and Western), each of which is responsible for a specified portion of the United States and its territories; the Association for Biblical Higher Education (ABHE); the Accrediting Council for Independent Colleges and Schools (ACICS); the Accrediting Commission of Career Schools and Colleges of Technology (ACCSCT); the Distance Education and Training Council (DETC); the American Academy for Liberal Education (AALE); the Council on Occupational Education; and the Transnational Association of Christian Colleges and Schools (TRACS). Program registration by the New York State Board of Regents is considered to be the equivalent of institutional accreditation, since the Board requires that all programs offered by an institution meet its standards before recognition is granted. A Canadian institution must be chartered and authorized to grant degrees by the provincial government, affiliated with a chartered institution, or accredited by a recognized U.S. accrediting body. There are recognized specialized accrediting bodies in more than forty different fields, each of which is authorized to accredit specific programs in its particular field. This can serve as the equivalent of institutional accreditation for specialized institutions that offer programs in one field only (schools of art, music, optometry, theology, etc.).

In addition, a profiled institution must grant one or more of the following undergraduate professional degrees in art, dance, music, or theater:

Artist's Diploma
Associate in Occupational
    Studies
Bachelor of Architecture
Bachelor of Art Education
Bachelor of Arts
Bachelor of Arts/Bachelor
    of Education
Bachelor of Arts/Bachelor
    of Fine Arts
Bachelor of Arts/Bachelor
    of Science
Bachelor of Design
Bachelor of Education
Bachelor of Fashion Design
    and Merchandising
Bachelor of Fine Arts

Bachelor of Fine Arts/
    Master of Arts
Bachelor of Fine Arts/
    Master of Architecture
Bachelor of Fine Arts/
    Master of Art Teaching
Bachelor of Graphic Design
    and Advertising
Bachelor of Industrial
    Design
Bachelor of Interior
    Architecture
Bachelor of Interior Design
Bachelor of Science
Bachelor of Science in
    Education
Bachelor of Science/
    Bachelor of Fine Arts

Many of these institutions also offer advanced degrees at the master's or doctoral level:

Doctor of Education
Honors Bachelor of Arts
Honors Bachelor of Music
Master of Architecture
Master of Art Education
Master of Art in Art
    Education
Master of Arts
Master of Arts/Doctor of
    Philosophy
Master of Arts/Master of
    Fine Arts
Master of Arts/Master of
    Science
Master of Arts in Education
Master of Arts in Teaching
Master of Design
Master of Education
Master of Fine Arts

Master of Humanities
Master of Industrial Design
Master of Interior
    Architecture
Master of Interior Design
Master of Landscape
    Architecture
Master of Professional
    Studies
Master of Public Art
    Studies
Master of Science
Master of Science in
    Education
Master of Science in
    Teaching
Doctor of Arts
Doctor of Education
Doctor of Philosophy

Quick-Reference Chart

Art Programs At-a-Glance

	Art	Enrollment	Tuition and Fees	Summer Programs	Page
Alabama					
Auburn University		23,333	$5516**		129
Birmingham-Southern College	BFA	1,411	$21,055*		133
Jacksonville State University	BFA	9,110	$4040*	Art	188
The University of Alabama	BFA, MFA	21,835	$4864*		285
University of Montevallo		2,999	$5664*		309
University of North Alabama	BFA	6,415	$4366*		310
University of South Alabama		13,122	$4502*		316
Alaska					
University of Alaska Anchorage		16,261	$3465*		286
Arizona					
The Art Institute of Phoenix	BA	1,114	$18,144*	Art	129
Collins College: A School of Design and Technology	BA	1,828	$13,875*		155
The University of Arizona	BFA, MA, MFA, PhD	37,036	$4498*		286
Arkansas					
Arkansas State University	BFA	10,414	$5440*		122
Harding University		5,744	$11,200*		178
University of Arkansas	BFA, MFA	17,821	$5494*		287
University of Central Arkansas	BFA	11,375	$5664*		289
Williams Baptist College	BFA	653	NR		338
California					
Academy of Art University	BFA, MFA	8,270	$14,480**	Art	113
Art Center College of Design	BFA, BS, MA, MFA, MS	1,642	$28,000*		124

* Expenses for 2005–2006. ** Estimated expenses for 2006–2007. NR = Not reported.

	Art	Enrollment	Tuition and Fees	Summer Programs	Page
California—*continued*					
The Art Institute of California–San Francisco	BFA, BS	1,347	NR	Art	128
California College of the Arts	BA, BARC, BFA, MA, MARC, MFA	1,616	$26,100*	Art	138
California Institute of the Arts	BFA, BFA, MFA, MFA	1,327	$27,725*		140,142
California State University, Chico	BFA, MFA	15,919	$3370*		142
California State University, Fullerton	BFA, MA, MFA	35,040	$2990*		143
California State University, Long Beach	BFA, MFA	1,344	$2864**	Art	144
La Sierra University	BA, BFA	1,941	$20,634**		195
Notre Dame de Namur University	BA, BFA	1,588	$23,850**		230
Otis College of Art and Design	BFA, MFA	1,098	$27,546**	Art	234
San Francisco Art Institute	BA, BFA, MA, MFA	595	$27,400**	Art	258
San Jose State University	BFA, BS, MA, MFA	29,975	$13,462*		260
Sonoma State University	BFA	7,749	$3616*		270
University of Southern California	BFA, MFA, MPAS	32,836	$32,008*	Art	317
University of the Pacific	BFA	6,196	$26,088*		322
Colorado					
Colorado State University	BFA, MFA	27,133	$4562*		155
Metropolitan State College of Denver	BFA	20,761	$2859*	Art	211
Rocky Mountain College of Art & Design	BFA	448	$17,880*	Art	255
University of Colorado at Boulder	BA, BFA, MA, MFA	31,068	$5372*		291
University of Denver	BFA, MA, MFA	10,374	$28,410*		293
Connecticut					
Albertus Magnus College	BFA, MA	2,230	$17,310*		116
Lyme Academy College of Fine Arts	BFA		$16,916*	Art	199
University of Bridgeport	BA, BFA, BS	3,626	$20,595*		287
University of Connecticut	BFA, MFA	23,185	$8362**		292

* Expenses for 2005–2006.   ** Estimated expenses for 2006–2007.   NR = Not reported.

	Art	Enrollment	Tuition and Fees	Summer Programs	Page
Connecticut—*continued*					
University of Hartford	BFA, MFA	7,260	$25,766**	Art	296
Delaware					
University of Delaware		20,373	$7318*		293
District of Columbia					
American University	BFA, MFA	11,279	$29,701**	Art	118
Corcoran College of Art and Design	BFA, BFA/ MAT, MA	590	$22,800*	Art	161
Howard University		10,623	$12,295*		179
Florida					
Florida Atlantic University	BA, BFA, MAT, MFA	25,704	$3259*		174
Florida International University	BA, BFA, MFA	36,904	$3314*		175
Florida State University	BFA, MFA	39,146	$3208*		176
International Academy of Design & Technology	BFA	2,405	NR		185
Jacksonville University	BFA	2,948	$19,970*		188
Miami International University of Art & Design	BA, BFA, MFA	1,406	$18,960**	Art	211
New World School of the Arts	BFA	371	$12,000*		224
Ringling School of Art and Design	BFA	1,088	$21,400*	Art	253
University of Central Florida	BFA, MFA	44,953	$3339*		290
University of Florida	BA, BFA, MA, MFA	49,693	$3094*		294
University of Miami		15,674	$29,020*		305
University of North Florida	BFA	15,234	$3269*		313
University of West Florida	BA, BFA	9,632	$3197*		324
Georgia					
Augusta State University	BFA	6,312	$2920*		130
Brenau University	BFA	743	$16,440*	Art	136
Georgia Southern University		16,646	$3462*		177

* Expenses for 2005–2006.   ** Estimated expenses for 2006–2007.   NR = Not reported.

Visual Arts

	Art	Enrollment	Tuition and Fees	Summer Programs	Page
Georgia—*continued*					
Georgia State University		25,945	$4464*		177
Savannah College of Art and Design	BFA, MA, MArch, MFA	7,356	$23,450**	Art	260
Shorter College		967	$13,500*		269
University of Georgia	BFA, MA, MFA, PhD	33,660	$4628*		295
University of West Georgia		10,155	$3270*		324
Valdosta State University	BFA, MAE	10,503	$3278*		328
Hawaii					
University of Hawaii at Manoa		20,644	$4513*		296
Idaho					
Idaho State University	BFA, MFA	13,977	$11,700**		180
University of Idaho		12,476	$3968*		297
Illinois					
American Academy of Art	BFA, MFA	410	$20,930**	Art	118
Bradley University	BA, BFA, BS, MA, MFA	6,154	$18,830*	Art	135
Columbia College Chicago	BA, BA, BA, BFA, BFA, MFA, MFA, MFA	10,842	$16,788**	Art	156,158, 159
Harrington College of Design	BFA	1,563	$7510*	Art	178
The Illinois Institute of Art–Chicago	BA, BFA	2,588	$19,020**		180
Illinois State University	BFA, MA/MS, MFA	20,653	$7091*		182
Illinois Wesleyan University		2,146	$29,076**		183
International Academy of Design & Technology	BA, BFA	2,768	$23,000**		186
Millikin University	BFA	2,641	$21,121*	Art	214
Northern Illinois University	BA, BFA, BS, MA, MFA, MSEd	25,208	$6439*		228
Quincy University	BFA	1,359	$19,010**		250

* Expenses for 2005–2006.   ** Estimated expenses for 2006–2007.   NR = Not reported.

	Art	Enrollment	Tuition and Fees	Summer Programs	Page
Illinois—*continued*					
School of the Art Institute of Chicago	BA, BFA, BIA, MA, MArch, MDes, MFA, MIA, MS	2,679	$29,200**		261
Southern Illinois University Carbondale	BFA, MFA	21,441	$6831*		271
Southern Illinois University Edwardsville		13,460	$5179*		272
University of Illinois at Chicago	BFA, MFA	24,812	$8302*		297
University of Illinois at Urbana–Champaign	BFA, EdD, MA, MFA, PhD	41,938	$8624*		298
Western Illinois University		13,404	$6899*		335
Indiana					
Ball State University	BFA, MA	20,351	$6458*		130
Indiana State University	BFA, BS, MFA	10,679	$5864*	Art	183
Indiana University Bloomington	BFA, MA, MAT, MFA, PhD	37,958	$7112*		183
Indiana University–Purdue University Fort Wayne		11,795	$5067*		184
Indiana University–Purdue University Indianapolis	BAE, BFA, MAE	29,933	$6219*	Art	184
Saint Mary's College	BA/BFA	1,397	$25,580**		257
University of Evansville	BFA	2,836	$21,660*		294
University of Indianapolis	BFA	4,462	$17,980*		299
University of Notre Dame	BFA, MA, MFA	11,417	$33,442**		314
Iowa					
Clarke College	BFA	1,246	$18,945*		148
Drake University	BA, BFA	5,277	$21,462*		167
Iowa State University of Science and Technology	BFA, MFA	25,741	$5634*		186
Maharishi University of Management	BFA	741	$24,430**		200
The University of Iowa	BFA, MA, MFA, PhD	28,426	$5935**		299
University of Northern Iowa	BFA, MA	12,622	$5602*		313

* Expenses for 2005–2006.   ** Estimated expenses for 2006–2007.   NR = Not reported.

	Art	Enrollment	Tuition and Fees	Summer Programs	Page
Kansas					
Emporia State University	BFA, BSEd	6,288	$3306*		171
Pittsburg State University	BFA, BSEd, MA	6,628	$3562*		243
University of Kansas	BFA, MFA	28,949	$5413*		300
Washburn University	BFA	7,261	$4982*		331
Kentucky					
Murray State University	BFA	10,266	$4428*	Art	222
Northern Kentucky University	BFA	13,908	$4968*		228
University of Louisville	BFA, MA, MAT, PhD	20,734	$5532*		301
Western Kentucky University		18,634	$5316*		336
Louisiana					
Louisiana State University and Agricultural and Mechanical College	BFA, MFA	31,264	$4419*		197
Louisiana Tech University	BFA, MFA	11,691	$4375*		198
Loyola University New Orleans	BA, BFA	5,423	$25,246*		198
Northwestern State University of Louisiana	BFA, BS	9,847	$3393*	Art	229
University of Louisiana at Lafayette	BIRD	17,075	$3324*	Art	300
Maine					
Maine College of Art	BFA, MFA	490	$25,320**	Art	201
University of Southern Maine	BFA	10,944	$5,906*	Art	317
Maryland					
Maryland Institute College of Art	BFA, BFA/MA, BFA/MAT, MA, MFA	1,717	$26,920*	Art	204
Massachusetts					
Anna Maria College	BA, BFA	1,042	$21,880*		119
The Art Institute of Boston at Lesley University	BFA, BFA/MA, BFA/MEd, MFA	6,521	$19,600*	Art	126
Boston University	BFA, MFA	30,957	$31,966*	Art	133

* Expenses for 2005–2006.   ** Estimated expenses for 2006–2007.   NR = Not reported.

	Art	Enrollment	Tuition and Fees	Summer Programs	Page
Massachusetts—_continued_					
Emmanuel College	BFA	2,296	$22,300*		170
Massachusetts College of Art	BFA, MFA, MS	2,130	$6850*	Art	209
Montserrat College of Art	BFA	308	$20,679*	Art	218
School of the Museum of Fine Arts, Boston	BA/BFA, MAT, MFA	773	$24,760*	Art	265
Suffolk University	BFA, MA	8,474	$21,220*	Art	276
122496University of Massachusetts Amherst	BFA, MA, MArch, MFA, MS	25,093	$9595**		302
University of Massachusetts Dartmouth	BA, BFA, MAE, MFA	8,549	$8036*		302
University of Massachusetts Lowell	BFA	10,666	$8166*		304
Michigan					
Adrian College	BFA	1,013	$18,630*	Art	115
Albion College	BFA	1,979	$24,296*		116
Aquinas College		2,193	$17,926*		121
Central Michigan University	BFA, MA, MFA	27,221	$5868*		147
College for Creative Studies	BFA	1,291	$24,635**	Art	150
Grand Valley State University	BFA	22,565	$6220*		177
Hope College	BA	3,141	$21,540*		179
Kendall College of Art and Design of Ferris State University	BFA, BS, MFA	942	NR		192
Lawrence Technological University	BFA, BIA, MIntD	4,122	$19,443**	Art	195
Michigan State University	BFA, MFA	45,166	$7587*		213
University of Michigan	BFA, MFA	39,993	$9400*		305
Wayne State University	BA, BFA, BS, MA, MFA	33,137	$6439*		332
Western Michigan University	BFA, MA, MFA	26,239	$6478*		336
Minnesota					
College of Visual Arts	BFA	202	$18,040*		154

* Expenses for 2005–2006.   ** Estimated expenses for 2006–2007.   NR = Not reported.

Visual Arts

	Art	Enrollment	Tuition and Fees	Summer Programs	Page
Minnesota—*continued*					
Minneapolis College of Art and Design	BFA, BS, MFA	722	$25,040*	Art	216
Minnesota State University Mankato	BFA, MA	14,335	$5846*		216
St. Cloud State University		15,964	$5322*		257
University of Minnesota, Duluth	BFA, MFA	10,496	$8928*		305
University of Minnesota, Twin Cities Campus	BFA, MFA	51,175	$8622*		306
Mississippi					
Delta State University		3,998	$4252*		167
Mississippi University for Women	BFA	2,328	NR		217
University of Mississippi	BFA, MA, MFA	14,901	$4320*		307
Missouri					
Central Missouri State University	BFA, BSEd	10,604	$5835**		147
Columbia College	BFA	1,149	$11,995*		156
Culver-Stockton College	BFA	840	$15,250**		166
Fontbonne University	BFA, MA/ MFA	2,836	$17,440**		176
Kansas City Art Institute	BFA	588	$22,392*	Art	189
Lindenwood University	BA, BFA, MA, MFA	9,076	$12,240**		196
Maryville University of Saint Louis	BA, BFA	3,223	$17,320*		207
Missouri State University	BFA, BS, BSEd, MS	18,928	$5454**	Art	218
Stephens College	BFA	824	$20,500**	Art	276
Truman State University	BFA, MAE	5,803	$5812*		283
University of Missouri–Columbia	BFA, MFA	27,985	$7745*		307
Washington University in St. Louis	BFA, MFA	13,383	$33,788**		332
Webster University	BA, BFA, MA	7,327	$17,210*		334
Montana					
The University of Montana–Missoula	BFA, MA, MFA	13,602	$5030**		308

* Expenses for 2005–2006.   ** Estimated expenses for 2006–2007.   NR = Not reported.

	Art	Enrollment	Tuition and Fees	Summer Programs	Page
Nebraska					
Concordia University	BFA	1,317	$17,724*		160
University of Nebraska–Lincoln	BFA, MFA	21,675	$5540*		309
New Hampshire					
University of New Hampshire		14,564	$10,401**		309
New Jersey					
Centenary College	BFA	2,472	$20,870*		146
The College of New Jersey	BA, BFA	6,768	$9707*		152
Rutgers, The State University of New Jersey, Mason Gross School of the Arts	BFA, MFA		NR		208
Seton Hall University	BA, BS, MA	9,637	$24,720**	Art	268
New Mexico					
College of Santa Fe	BFA	1,661	$22,276*		153
New Mexico State University	BFA, MA, MFA	16,072	$3918*		223
University of New Mexico	BFA, MA, MFA, PhD	26,172	$4108*		309
New York					
Alfred University	BFA, MFA	2,235	$20,960*	Art	117
Brooklyn College of the City University of New York	BFA, MA, MFA	15,281	$4375**		137
Cazenovia College	BFA	1,124	$18,940*		146
The College of New Rochelle	BFA, BS	2,306	$20,596*	Art	152
The College of Saint Rose	BFA, BS, MS	5,149	$17,954*		153
Cornell University	BFA, MFA	19,447	$31,467*		163
Daemen College	BFA	2,315	$16,800*		166
Fashion Institute of Technology	BFA, MA	10,381	$4770**		171
Hunter College of the City University of New York		20,843	$4349**		180
Ithaca College	BA, BFA, BFA	6,412	$25,194*		187
Long Island University, C.W. Post Campus		8,472	$23,230*		196
New York Institute of Technology	BFA	11,141	$19,236*	Art	224

* Expenses for 2005–2006.   ** Estimated expenses for 2006–2007.   NR = Not reported.

	Art	Enrollment	Tuition and Fees	Summer Programs	Page
New York—*continued*					
New York School of Interior Design	BFA, MFA	739	$18,820**		225
New York University	BFA, BFA, MA, MFA, PhD	40,004	$31,690*	Art	226,227
Parsons The New School for Design	BBA, BFA, MA, MFA, MRCH	3,502	$29,180*	Art	237
Pratt Institute	BARC, BFA, BID, BS, MARC, MFA, MID, MPS, MS	4,588	$29,230**	Art	245
Purchase College, State University of New York	BFA, MFA	3,826	$5608**	Art	248
Russell Sage College	BA	838	$23,520*		257
School of Visual Arts	BFA, MAT, MFA, MPS	3,575	$21,080*	Art	266
State University of New York at Buffalo	BFA, MFA	27,220	$6068*		273
State University of New York at Plattsburgh	BFA	6,044	$5296**		274
State University of New York, Fredonia	BFA	5,432	$5441*		274
Syracuse University	BFA, BID, BS, MFA, MID	17,266	$28,285*	Art	277
North Carolina					
Appalachian State University		14,653	$3918**		121
Barton College	BFA, BS	1,189	$16,670*	Art	131
East Carolina University		23,164	$3627*		170
Guilford College	BFA	2,682	$23,020**		178
North Carolina School of the Arts	BFA, MFA	827	$4306*	Art	227
The University of North Carolina at Charlotte	BFA	20,772	$3549*		311
The University of North Carolina at Greensboro	BA, BFA, MFA	16,060	$3813**		311
Western Carolina University	BFA, MAEd, MAT, MFA	8,665	NR		335
North Dakota					
University of North Dakota	BFA, MFA	12,954	$5327*		312

* Expenses for 2005–2006.   ** Estimated expenses for 2006–2007.   NR = Not reported.

	Art	Enrollment	Tuition and Fees	Summer Programs	Page
Ohio					
Art Academy of Cincinnati	BFA, MA		$19,600**	Art	122
Bowling Green State University	BFA, MA, MFA	19,016	$8560*		135
Capital University	BFA	3,901	$24,100*		144
The Cleveland Institute of Art	BFA, MFA	610	$27,177*	Art	148
Columbus College of Art & Design	BFA	1,455	$20,278*	Art	159
Kent State University	BA, BFA, MA, MFA	23,622	$7954*		193
Miami University	BFA, BS, MA, MFA	16,338	$21,487*	Art	212
Ohio Northern University	BFA	3,542	$28,260**		231
The Ohio State University	BFA, MFA	50,504	$8082*		231
Ohio University		20,396	$8235*		232
Ohio Wesleyan University		1,976	$28,280*		232
The University of Akron	BA, BFA	21,049	$7958*	Art	284
University of Cincinnati	BFA, MA, MFA	27,932	$8883*		290
University of Dayton	BFA	10,572	$22,846*		292
Wright State University	BFA	16,207	$7278**		338
Youngstown State University	BA, BFA, BS	12,809	$6333*		340
Oklahoma					
Oklahoma Baptist University	BFA	1,883	$13,846*		232
Oklahoma State University	BFA	23,461	$4365*		233
University of Oklahoma		26,968	$4408*		314
Oregon					
Marylhurst University	BFA	1,268	$14,220*		207
Oregon College of Art & Craft	BFA		$17,882**	Art	234
Pacific Northwest College of Art	BFA	293	$18,172**	Art	237
Southern Oregon University	BFA	4,977	$4986**		272
University of Oregon	BFA, MFA	20,347	$5613*		314

* Expenses for 2005–2006.   ** Estimated expenses for 2006–2007.   NR = Not reported.

	Art	Enrollment	Tuition and Fees	Summer Programs	Page
Pennsylvania					
Arcadia University	BA, BFA	3,403	$25,990**	Art	121
Carnegie Mellon University	BFA, MFA	10,017	$34,578**	Art	145
Drexel University	BARC, BS, MARC, MS	18,466	$24,280*	Art	168
Kutztown University of Pennsylvania	BFA, BS, MEd	9,864	$6425*		193
Moore College of Art & Design	BFA	491	$23,602**	Art	220
Pennsylvania Academy of the Fine Arts	BFA, MFA		NR	Art	239
Pennsylvania College of Art & Design	BFA	225	$14,057**	Art	241
The Pennsylvania State University University Park Campus	BFA, BS, MFA	40,709	$11,508*		243
Point Park University	BA	3,407	$16,740*	Art	244
Seton Hill University	BFA, MA	1,863	$21,990*		268
Slippery Rock University of Pennsylvania		8,105	$6275**		270
Temple University	BARC, BFA, MA, MEd, MFA, PhD	33,693	$9640*	Art	283
The University of the Arts	BFA, BS, MA, MAT, MFA, MID	2,277	$25,680**	Art	320
West Chester University of Pennsylvania	BA, BFA	12,988	$6147**		334
La Roche College	BS	1,707	$17,380*		194
Rhode Island					
Rhode Island College	BA, BFA, BS, MAT	8,871	$4676*	Art	250
Rhode Island School of Design	BFA, BGD, BID, MA, MARC, MAT, MFA, MIARC, MID, MLARC	2,258	$31,380**	Art	251
Roger Williams University	BA	5,214	$24,066**		256
South Carolina					
Converse College		2,176	$22,234**		161
University of South Carolina	BFA, MFA	27,065	$6914*		316
South Dakota					
The University of South Dakota		8,641	$4829*		316

* Expenses for 2005–2006.   ** Estimated expenses for 2006–2007.   NR = Not reported.

	Art	Enrollment	Tuition and Fees	Summer Programs	Page
Tennessee					
Appalachian Center for Craft, Tennessee Tech University	BFA	9,313	$4660**		119
Belmont University	BFA	4,319	$17,260*		132
East Tennessee State University		11,894	$4662**		170
Memphis College of Art	BFA, MFA	326	$17,460*	Art	209
Middle Tennessee State University		22,554	$4600*		213
O'More College of Design	BFA		NR		233
University of Memphis		20,465	$5084*		304
The University of Tennessee	BFA, MFA	31,157	$5626*		318
The University of Tennessee at Chattanooga		8,656	$5400*		318
Texas					
Abilene Christian University		4,685	$15,160*		113
Baylor University	BFA	13,975	$22,814**		131
Midwestern State University	BFA	6,279	$4566**	Art	214
Rice University		5,258	$23,746*		253
Sam Houston State University		15,000	$3822*		258
Southern Methodist University	BFA, MFA	11,152	$28,630**		272
Stephen F. Austin State University	BFA, MFA	11,435	$4718*		275
Sul Ross State University	BFA, MA, MEd	1,954	NR		277
Texas A&M University–Commerce	BA, BFA, BS, MFA	8,787	$4824*		279
Texas A&M University–Corpus Christi	BFA, MFA	8,227	$4516*		280
Texas Christian University		8,749	$21,320*		281
Texas State University-San Marcos	BFA	27,129	$5252*		281
Texas Tech University	BFA, MFA, DA	28,001	$6152*	Art	281
Texas Woman's University	BFA, MA, MFA	11,344	$5010**		282
University of Houston	BFA, MFA	35,344	$6486*		297
The University of Texas at Austin	BFA, MFA	49,696	$6972*		319

* Expenses for 2005–2006.   ** Estimated expenses for 2006–2007.   NR = Not reported.

Visual Arts

	Art	Enrollment	Tuition and Fees	Summer Programs	Page
Texas—*continued*					
The University of Texas at El Paso	BFA	19,268	$5064*		319
The University of Texas at San Antonio		27,337	$5858*		320
West Texas A&M University	BFA, MA, MFA	8,667	$3756*		336
Utah					
Brigham Young University	BA, BFA, MFA	34,067	$5116*	Art	136
University of Utah	BFA, MFA	29,012	$4342*		323
Utah State University	BFA, MFA	14,458	$3672*	Art	328
Weber State University	BFA	18,142	$3138*		333
Vermont					
Johnson State College		1,866	$6906**		189
Virginia					
James Madison University		16,938	$5886*		189
Longwood University	BFA	4,289	$7020*		197
Radford University		9,552	$5130*		250
Virginia Commonwealth University	BA, BFA, MAE, MFA, PhD	29,349	$5385*	Art	329
Virginia Intermont College	BFA	1,138	$16,450*		331
Washington					
Cornish College of the Arts	BFA, BFA	768	$21,500*	Art	164
Pacific Lutheran University		3,680	$22,040*		237
University of Washington	BFA, MFA	39,251	$5532*		323
West Virginia					
Marshall University	BFA, MA	13,988	$3932*		203
Shepherd University	BFA	3,901	$4046*		269
West Virginia University	BFA, MA, MFA	26,051	$4164*	Art	337
Wisconsin					
Milwaukee Institute of Art and Design	BFA	645	$23,400**	Art	214

* Expenses for 2005–2006.   ** Estimated expenses for 2006–2007.   NR = Not reported.

	Art	Enrollment	Tuition and Fees	Summer Programs	Page
Wisconsin—*continued*					
University of Wisconsin–Madison	BFA, BS, MA, MFA	41,480	$6617*		325
University of Wisconsin–Milwaukee		27,502	$6224*		325
University of Wisconsin–Oshkosh	BFA	10,997	$4981*		325
University of Wisconsin–Stevens Point	BFA	8,577	$5062*		326
University of Wisconsin–Stout	BFA, BS	7,891	$6592*		326
University of Wisconsin–Superior	BFA, BS, MA	2,872	$5,188*		327
University of Wisconsin–Whitewater		10,750	$5080*		328

* Expenses for 2005–2006.   ** Estimated expenses for 2006–2007.   NR = Not reported.

Visual Arts

Profiles of Visual Arts Programs

Abilene Christian University

Abilene, Texas

Independent, coed. Urban campus. Total enrollment: 4,685. Art program established 1906.

Academy of Art University

San Francisco, California

Proprietary, coed. Urban campus. Total enrollment: 8,270. Art program established 1929.

Degrees Bachelor of Fine Arts in the areas of advertising, animation/visual effects, computer arts/new media, fashion, fine art, graphic design, illustration, industrial design, interior architecture and design, motion pictures & television, photography. Majors and concentrations: acting, advertising design, animation, computer art, fashion design and technology, film and video production, graphic design, illustration, industrial design, interior architecture, motion graphics, painting/drawing, photography, printmaking, sculpture, transportation design, visual effects. Graduate degrees offered: Master of Fine Arts in the areas of advertising, animation/visual effects, architecture, computer arts/new media, fashion, fine art, graphic design, illustration, industrial design, interior architecture and design, motion pictures & television, photography. Program accredited by NASAD, FIDER.

Enrollment 8,262 total; 6,596 undergraduate, 1,666 graduate.

Art Student Profile 51% females, 49% males, 35% minorities, 20% international.

Art Faculty 135 total (full-time), 540 total (part-time). 17% of full-time faculty have terminal degrees. Graduate students do not teach undergraduate courses. Undergraduate student–faculty ratio: 12:1.

Student Life Student groups/activities include American Society of Interior Designers, Western Art Directors Club, Society of Illustrators.

Expenses for 2006–2007 Application fee: $100. Comprehensive fee: $26,480 includes full-time tuition ($14,400), mandatory fees ($80), and college room and board ($12,000). College room only: $8400. Special program-related fees: $45–$400 per semester for lab fees; vary depending on major.

Financial Aid Program-specific awards available.

Application Procedures Students admitted directly into the professional program freshman year. Deadline for freshmen and transfers: continuous. Required: high school transcript, college transcript(s) for transfer students, high school diploma/GED. Recommended: interview.

Web Site http://www.academyart.edu

Undergraduate Contact Mr. John Meurer, Vice President, Admissions, Academy of Art University, 79 New Montgomery Street, San Francisco, California 94105; 800-544-ARTS ext. 2219, fax: 415-263-4130, e-mail address: admissions@academyart.edu

Graduate Contact Mr. John Meurer, Vice President of Admissions, Graduate School, Academy of Art University, 79 New Montgomery Street, San Francisco, California 94105; 800-544-ARTS ext. 2219, fax: 415-263-4130, e-mail address: info@academyart.edu

More About the Academy

Founded in 1929, Academy of Art University (AAU) has steadily grown to become the largest private, accredited art and design school in the nation. The campus now encompasses more than twenty buildings in and around downtown San Francisco with more than 8,500 students from twenty-five countries. The Academy's mission is to provide aspiring artists and designers with career preparation, combined with academic excellence for the A.A., B.F.A., M.F.A. degrees and nondegree personal enrichment classes in the areas of art and design. Courses can be taken on campus and online.

Visual Arts

Academic of Art University (continued)

Campus and Surroundings The city of San Francisco is one of the great cultural centers of the world—a melting pot of diversity and creativity that has spawned major museums and galleries, world-class performing arts, film production, and technological innovation. The climate is moderate and offers kaleidoscopic blends of sunshine and fog nine months of the year. The Academy's classrooms, studios, galleries, and dormitories are located in such areas as the world famous Fisherman's Wharf, historic Union Square, the Financial District, and the South of Market Area (SOMA). A private fleet of Academy buses, which are scheduled around classes and lab times, connect all campus facilities.

Program Facilities Academy of Art University is one of the leading schools in the country for providing students with the latest in technological advances, utilizing constantly updated, industry-professional equipment. AAU provides students with a number of facilities, including an eight-story Digital Arts Center with numerous computer workstations, software, and equipment that includes the Power Mac G5, G4, and G3; HP Desktops; and Silicon Graphics workstations, to name a few.

The Motion Picture and Television/Acting Department has multiple Final Cut Pro stations, Media 100, Avid Xpress, and Avid nonlinear editing stations and linear tape-to-tape suites, including a Bosch Telecine and several KEM flatbeds for celluloid linear editing; Arri cameras, fluid head tripods, magazines, changing bags/tents, and acrylic/timecode slates. Also available for student use are 16mm and 35mm film cameras, Beta SP, Sony 3-chip DV cameras, Canon 1-chip and 3-chip DV cameras, Panasonic SVHS video cameras, and an extensive inventory of lighting and sound grip equipment as well as a green screen studio and a newly constructed 150-seat theater.

The Fine Art Department houses three nonprofit galleries for students to display their work in San Francisco's downtown gallery district. The 50,000-square-foot Sculpture Center includes a 25-foot-high ceiling equipped with cranes that include scanners directly linked to the Computer Education Center.

Computer Arts/New Media and Animation & Visual Effects have an advanced facility, including a digital photography studio, G5, G4, and G3 Macintosh computers, Wacom Digitizing Tablets, CD/DVD burners complete with FireWire/USB connections, scanners (reflective and slide), Epson inkjet printers, Fiery printers, digital audio workstations, two flame and smoke suites, and industry software, such as Alias Maya, Illustrator, Flash, Fireworks, Dreamweaver, and DVD Studio Pro.

Academy of Art University also offers a very active schedule of events and activities throughout the year. Campus Affairs & Student Events (CASE) organizes a variety of student activities including mixers, San Francisco Bay boat tours, ski trips, camping trips, and more. Student groups and activities include the American Society of Interior Designers (ASID), Western Art Directors Club, Society of Illustrators, soccer, and rowing to name a few.

Student Performance/Exhibit Opportunities

More than eighty student shows are exhibited each year in the three main galleries. Each May, the Spring Show takes over five to eight floors of the Digital Arts Center for three weeks. The annual AAU Fashion Show highlights senior and M.F.A. collections in a runway show in which international designers such as Burberry and Oscar de la Renta have been guests of honor.

Faculty, Resident Artists, and Alumni Students of the Academy have the rare opportunity to learn from professionals at the top of their field from the biggest art and design companies in the industry. This allows students to learn the most sought-after techniques, in addition to making the contacts they need to obtain positions with such companies as Warner Brothers, Pixar, LucasFilm, Electronic Arts, and Escada, who are known for recruiting AAU students. The Academy averages 450 instructors in the spring and fall semesters, 90 percent of whom are full-time art and design professionals and part-time teachers. The student to teacher ratio for undergraduate classes is about 18:1; for graduate students, it is 15:1. Internationally known artists also lecture and show their work in Academy galleries throughout the year.

Career Placement Services and Opportunities

Academy graduates embark upon successful careers in the art and design industry. Eighty percent of Academy of Art University's graduates are working in the art and design industry. Alumni have been hired by prestigious companies all over the world, including Walt Disney, Sega, Donna Karan, Apple, Industrial Light + Magic, Hewlett-Packard, and Electronic Arts.

The Academy does a great deal to give exposure to students' work, including job fairs and the Annual Spring show, which attracts recruiters for the industry's top professions. Students' work is also constantly shown in many publications, the Academy's e-gallery at http://www.academyartgallery.com, and the Academy's three storefront art galleries located centrally in San Francisco. These galleries and the e-gallery allow the students to showcase their fine art work and gain firsthand knowledge of how to become working artists.

Adrian College

Adrian, Michigan

Independent, coed. Small town campus. Total enrollment: 1,013. Art program established 1962.

Degrees Bachelor of Fine Arts in the areas of art, interior design, art education. Majors and concentrations: art education, art/fine arts, arts management, interior design, pre-architecture, pre-art therapy. Cross-registration with Siena Heights University, Fashion Institute of Technology, Center for Creative Studies-College of Art and Design, The American College (London, Los Angeles, Atlanta).

Enrollment 110 total; all undergraduate.

Art Student Profile 69% females, 31% males, 7% minorities, 2% international.

Art Faculty 5 undergraduate (full-time), 6 undergraduate (part-time). 100% of full-time faculty have terminal degrees. Graduate students do not teach undergraduate courses. Undergraduate student–faculty ratio: 14:1.

Student Life Student groups/activities include American Society of Interior Designers, Art Club.

Expenses for 2005–2006 Application fee: $20. Comprehensive fee: $24,900 includes full-time tuition ($18,530), mandatory fees ($100), and college room and board ($6270). College room only: $2880. Room and board charges vary according to board plan.

Financial Aid Program-specific awards: 55 studio art scholarships for program majors and minors ($3000–$8000).

Application Procedures Students admitted directly into the professional program freshman year. Deadline for freshmen and transfers: August 15. Required: high school transcript, college transcript(s) for transfer students, minimum 2.0 high school GPA, SAT I or ACT test scores (minimum composite ACT score of 16), portfolio for scholarship consideration. Recommended: essay, minimum 3.0 high school GPA, 2 letters of recommendation, portfolio. Portfolio reviews held numerous times on campus; the submission of slides may be substituted for portfolios when distance is prohibitive or scheduling is difficult.

Web Site http://www.adrian.edu

Undergraduate Contact Ms. Caroline Quinlan, Director of Admissions (Acting), Adrian College, 110 South Madison Street, Adrian, Michigan 49221; 800-877-2246, fax: 517-264-3331, e-mail address: admissions@adrian.edu

Alberta College of Art & Design

Calgary, Alberta, Canada

Province-supported, coed. Urban campus. Total enrollment: 1,093.

Degrees Bachelor of Design in the area of visual communications design; Bachelor of Fine Arts in the areas of ceramics, drawing, glass, jewelry and metals, painting, print media, sculpture, fibre, photography, media arts and digital technologies. Majors and concentrations: ceramic art and design, fibers, glass, jewelry and metalsmithing, media arts and digital technology, multidisciplinary studies, painting/drawing, photography, printmaking, sculpture, visual communication design. Cross-registration with University of Calgary, Mount Royal College.

Enrollment 1,086 total; all undergraduate.

Art Student Profile 67% females, 33% males, 4% international.

Art Faculty 45 undergraduate (full-time), 60 undergraduate (part-time). 25% of full-time faculty have terminal degrees. Graduate students teach a few undergraduate courses. Undergraduate student–faculty ratio: 9:1.

Student Life Student groups/activities include gallery exhibitions, visiting artist talks, public design projects.

Expenses for 2005–2006 Application fee: $50 Canadian dollars. Tuition, fee, and room and board charges are reported in Canadian dollars. Province resident tuition: $4,490 full-time. Mandatory fees: $674 full-time. Full-time tuition and fees vary according to course load. College room and board: $7000. College room only: $4000. International student tuition: $11,943 full-time. Room and board is available at the Southern Alberta Institute of Technology. Special program-related fees: $7–$25 per credit for supplemental materials.

Visual

Arts

Alberta College of Art & Design (continued)

Financial Aid Program-specific awards: 214 general scholarships for program students, 3 international entrance scholarships for international program students ($2000).

Application Procedures Students apply for admission into the professional program by junior year. Deadline for freshmen and transfers: April 1. Notification date for freshmen and transfers: June 1. Required: essay, high school transcript, college transcript(s) for transfer students, minimum 2.0 high school GPA, portfolio, 60% average GPA on 4 grade-12 subjects. Recommended: minimum 3.0 high school GPA. Portfolio reviews held twice on campus; the submission of slides may be substituted for portfolios for large works of art, three-dimensional pieces, or when distance is prohibitive.

Undergraduate Contact Joy Borman, Associate Director of Admissions, Student Services, Alberta College of Art & Design, 1407-14 Avenue NW, Calgary, Alberta T2N 4R3, Canada; 800-284-7689, fax: 403-284-7644, e-mail address: joy.borman@acad.ca

Albertus Magnus College

New Haven, Connecticut

Independent Roman Catholic, coed. Suburban campus. Total enrollment: 2,230. Art program established 1976.

Degrees Bachelor of Fine Arts in the area of art. Majors and concentrations: art history, graphic design, photography, studio art. Graduate degrees offered: Master of Arts in the area of art therapy.

Enrollment 61 total; 15 undergraduate, 46 graduate.

Art Student Profile 66% females, 34% males, 28% minorities.

Art Faculty 2 undergraduate (full-time), 2 undergraduate (part-time), 2 graduate (full-time), 6 graduate (part-time). 100% of full-time faculty have terminal degrees. Graduate students do not teach undergraduate courses. Undergraduate student–faculty ratio: 12:1.

Expenses for 2005–2006 Application fee: $35. Comprehensive fee: $24,860 includes full-time tuition ($16,600), mandatory fees ($710), and college room and board ($7550). Full-time

tuition and fees vary according to class time and program. Special program-related fees: $40–$50 per course for expendable art supplies.

Financial Aid Program-specific awards available.

Application Procedures Students apply for admission into the professional program by freshman year. Deadline for freshmen and transfers: continuous. Required: high school transcript, college transcript(s) for transfer students, minimum 2.0 high school GPA, 2 letters of recommendation, SAT I or ACT test scores. Recommended: interview.

Web Site http://www.albertus.edu

Undergraduate Contact Mr. Richard Lolatte, Dean of Admissions, Albertus Magnus College, 700 Prospect Street, New Haven, Connecticut 06511; 203-773-8501, fax: 203-773-5248, e-mail address: admissions@albertus.edu

Graduate Contact Dr. William More, Director, Master of Arts in Art Therapy Program, Albertus Magnus College, 700 Prospect Street, New Haven, Connecticut 06511; 203-773-8903, e-mail address: more@albertus.edu

Albion College

Albion, Michigan

Independent Methodist, coed. Small town campus. Total enrollment: 1,979. Art program established 1977.

Degrees Bachelor of Fine Arts. Majors and concentrations: art history, visual arts.

Enrollment 60 total; 10 undergraduate, 50 nonprofessional degree.

Art Student Profile 66% females, 34% males, 5% minorities, 1% international.

Art Faculty 7 undergraduate (full-time). 100% of full-time faculty have terminal degrees. Graduate students do not teach undergraduate courses. Undergraduate student–faculty ratio: 5:1.

Student Life Student groups/activities include Art Club, senior exhibition, New York Arts program.

Expenses for 2005–2006 Application fee: $20. Comprehensive fee: $31,224 includes full-time tuition ($24,012), mandatory fees ($284), and college room and board ($6928). College room

only: $3388. Room and board charges vary according to housing facility.

Financial Aid Program-specific awards: 25 Fine Arts Scholarships for freshmen ($500–$1000), 10 Janson Scholarships for program majors ($200–$1000), 1 Taup Scholarship for program majors ($2000), 1 Geoffrey Morris Scholarship for program majors ($1800), 1 J. Gregory Scholarship for program majors ($1200), 1 Harmon Scholarship for art education majors ($2000).

Application Procedures Students apply for admission into the professional program by sophomore, junior year. Deadline for freshmen: May 1; transfers: continuous. Required: high school transcript, college transcript(s) for transfer students, SAT I or ACT test scores, portfolio for scholarship consideration. Recommended: essay, minimum 2.0 high school GPA, interview. Portfolio reviews held on routine basis until March on campus; the submission of slides may be substituted for portfolios.

Web Site http://www.albion.edu

Undergraduate Contact Director of Admissions, Albion College, 616 East Michigan, Albion, Michigan 49224; 517-629-0321, fax: 517-629-0509.

Alfred University

Alfred, New York

Independent, coed. Rural campus. Total enrollment: 2,235. Art program established 1900.

Degrees Bachelor of Fine Arts in the areas of ceramics, graphic design, two-dimensional studies and electronic art, three-dimensional studies. Majors and concentrations: art education, ceramics, glass, graphic design, metals, neon, painting/drawing, photography, pre-art therapy, print media, sculpture, video and sonic arts, wood design. Graduate degrees offered: Master of Fine Arts in the areas of ceramics, glass, sculpture, electronic integrated arts. Cross-registration with State University of New York College of Technology at Alfred, Houghton College, RAC Consortium (Rochester Area Colleges). Program accredited by NASAD.

Enrollment 537 total; 492 undergraduate, 35 graduate, 10 nonprofessional degree.

Art Student Profile 63% females, 37% males, 6% minorities, 4% international.

Art Faculty 33 total (full-time), 10 total (part-time). 99% of full-time faculty have terminal degrees. Graduate students do not teach undergraduate courses. Undergraduate student–faculty ratio: 12:1.

Student Life Student groups/activities include The Robert Turner Student Gallery exhibitions, Alternative Cinema/Alternative Space Festival, Annual Outdoor Light Exhibition. Special housing available for art students.

Expenses for 2005–2006 Application fee: $40. Comprehensive fee: $30,706 includes full-time tuition ($20,150), mandatory fees ($810), and college room and board ($9746). College room only: $5076. Full-time tuition and fees vary according to student level. Room and board charges vary according to board plan and housing facility. Special program-related fees: $11–$77 per credit hour for material fees.

Financial Aid Program-specific awards: portfolio scholarships Art Portfolio Review Scholarship for students with an exceptional portfolio ($6500–$8500), art and design grants Alfred University Dean's Scholarship for students with exceptional high school grades/test scores ($5000–$7000), Scholastic Art Awards Alfred University Presidential Scholarship for students with exceptional high school grades/test scores ($6500–$8500), Jonathan Allen Leadership Award for demonstrated leaders with volunteer/service work experience ($3500–$5000).

Application Procedures Students admitted directly into the professional program freshman year. Deadline for freshmen: February 1; transfers: April 1. Notification date for freshmen: March 15; transfers: April 15. Required: essay, high school transcript, college transcript(s) for transfer students, minimum 2.0 high school GPA, letter of recommendation, portfolio, SAT I or ACT test scores, slides of portfolio, transfer students having completed fewer than 24 studio art credits must apply by freshman deadline. Recommended: minimum 3.0 high school GPA, interview. Portfolio reviews held numerous times depending on the number of applicants (all portfolios are reviewed by a committee of Art and Design Faculty) on campus; the submission of slides may be substituted for portfolios.

Web Site http://art.alfred.edu

Undergraduate Contact Ms. Lindsay Stern, Art Recruitment Specialist, Admissions, Alfred University, 1 Saxon Drive, Alfred, New York 14802;

Alfred University (continued)

607-871-2115, fax: 607-871-2198, e-mail address: admwww@alfred.edu

Graduate Contact Mrs. Cathleen Johnson, Coordinator of Graduate Admissions, Admissions, Alfred University, 1 Saxon Drive, Alfred, New York 14802; 607-871-2141, fax: 607-871-2198, e-mail address: gradinquiry@alfred.edu

Allen R. Hite Art Institute

See University of Louisville

American Academy of Art

Chicago, Illinois

Proprietary, coed. Urban campus. Total enrollment: 410. Art program established 1923.

Degrees Bachelor of Fine Arts. Majors and concentrations: art/fine arts, commercial art. Graduate degrees offered: Master of Fine Arts in the areas of painting and drawing, digital media and design.

Enrollment 301 total; all undergraduate.

Art Student Profile 32% females, 68% males, 38% minorities, 1% international.

Art Faculty 24 total (full-time), 5 total (part-time). 76% of full-time faculty have terminal degrees. Graduate students do not teach undergraduate courses. Undergraduate student–faculty ratio: 10:1.

Student Life Student groups/activities include student juried competitions, Ravinia Poster Competition, teaching assistants at Gallery 37.

Expenses for 2006–2007 Application fee: $25. Tuition: $20,680 full-time. Mandatory fees: $250 full-time. Special program-related fees: $400 per course for computer lab access fee.

Financial Aid Program-specific awards: 8 High School Scholarship Competition Awards for high school seniors ($3340).

Application Procedures Required: high school transcript, college transcript(s) for transfer students, interview. Recommended: essay, minimum 2.0 high school GPA.

Web Site http://www.aaart.edu

Undergraduate Contact Stuart Rosenbloom, Admissions Director, American Academy of Art, 332 South Michigan Avenue, Suite 300, Chicago, Illinois 60604; 312-461-0600, fax: 312-294-9570, e-mail address: aaart@interaccess.com

Graduate Contact Stuart Rosenbloom, Admissions Director, American Academy of Art, 332 South Michigan Avenue, Suite 300, Chicago, Illinois 60604; 312-461-0600, fax: 312-294-9570, e-mail address: aaart@interaccess.com

American InterContinental University

Los Angeles, California

Proprietary, coed. Urban campus. Total enrollment: 1,405 (2004). Art program established 1970.

American InterContinental University

Atlanta, Georgia

Proprietary, coed. Urban campus. Total enrollment: 1,732. Art program established 1970.

American University

Washington, District of Columbia

Independent Methodist, coed. Suburban campus. Total enrollment: 11,279. Art program established 1942.

Degrees Bachelor of Fine Arts in the area of studio art. Majors and concentrations: art/fine arts, graphic arts, painting/drawing, printmaking, sculpture, studio art. Graduate degrees offered: Master of Fine Arts in the areas of painting, printmaking, sculpture; also offers 2-year MFA program in Italy. Cross-registration with Consortium of Universities of the Washington Metropolitan Area.

Enrollment 335 total; 200 undergraduate, 35 graduate, 100 nonprofessional degree.

Art Student Profile 50% females, 50% males, 8% minorities, 20% international.

Art Faculty 14 total (full-time), 15 total (part-time). 100% of full-time faculty have terminal degrees. Graduate students do not teach undergraduate courses. Undergraduate student–faculty ratio: 12:1.

Student Life Student groups/activities include Thursday Night Artist on Art Lecture Series, Visiting Artists Programs, semester in Italy.

Expenses for 2006–2007 Application fee: $45. Comprehensive fee: $41,043 includes full-time tuition ($29,205), mandatory fees ($496), and college room and board ($11,342). College room only: $7197. Special program-related fees: $400 for studio program in Italy.

Financial Aid Program-specific awards available.

Application Procedures Required: high school transcript, college transcript(s) for transfer students, minimum 2.0 high school GPA, 2 letters of recommendation, SAT I test score only. Recommended: minimum 3.0 high school GPA, interview, portfolio.

Web Site http://www.american.edu/academic.depts/cas/art

Contact Ms. Glenna Haynie, Administrator, Department of Art, American University, 4400 Massachusetts Avenue, NW, Washington, District of Columbia 20016; 202-885-1670, fax: 202-885-1132.

Anna Maria College

Paxton, Massachusetts

Independent Roman Catholic, coed. Rural campus. Total enrollment: 1,042. Art program established 1947.

Degrees Bachelor of Arts in the areas of art education, art therapy, art and business, art, graphic design; Bachelor of Fine Arts in the area of studio art. Majors and concentrations: art, art and business, art education, art therapy, graphic design. Cross-registration with Worcester Consortium.

Enrollment 30 total; all undergraduate.

Art Student Profile 66% females, 34% males, 3% international.

Art Faculty 1 undergraduate (full-time), 6 undergraduate (part-time). Graduate students do not teach undergraduate courses. Undergraduate student–faculty ratio: 4:1.

Student Life Student groups/activities include senior art exhibit, student/teacher exhibit, gallery sitting.

Expenses for 2005–2006 Application fee: $40. Comprehensive fee: $29,815 includes full-time tuition ($19,900), mandatory fees ($1980), and college room and board ($7935). Special program-related fees: $25 per credit for model fee, $40 per 3-credit course for studio fee, $130 per 3-credit course for practicum/internship fee.

Application Procedures Students admitted directly into the professional program freshman year. Deadline for freshmen and transfers: continuous. Required: essay, high school transcript, college transcript(s) for transfer students, minimum 2.0 high school GPA, 3 letters of recommendation, portfolio, SAT I or ACT test scores. Recommended: interview. Portfolio reviews held by appointment on campus; the submission of slides may be substituted for portfolios when distance is prohibitive.

Web Site http://www.annamaria.edu

Undergraduate Contact Ms. Julie Mitchell, Director of Undergraduate Admissions, Anna Maria College, Box U, Paxton, Massachusetts 01612-1198; 508-849-3365, fax: 508-849-3362.

Tennessee Technological University
Appalachian Center for Craft

Cookeville, Tennessee

State-supported, coed. Small town campus. Total enrollment: 9,313. Art program established 1980.

Degrees Bachelor of Fine Arts in the areas of clay, fibers, glass, metals, wood, painting, art education. Majors and concentrations: art education, ceramics, clay, fibers, glass, jewelry and metalsmithing, metals, painting, surface design, textile arts, weaving and fibers, wood, woodworking design. Program accredited by NASAD.

Enrollment 130 total; all undergraduate.

Art Student Profile 50% females, 50% males, 7% minorities, 5% international.

Art Faculty 10 undergraduate (full-time). 100% of full-time faculty have terminal degrees. Graduate students do not teach undergraduate courses. Undergraduate student–faculty ratio: 12:1.

Student Life Student groups/activities include Visual Art Society, Annual Celebration of Craft. Special housing available for art students.

Appalachian Center for Craft (continued)

Expenses for 2006–2007 Application fee: $15. State resident tuition: $4660 full-time. Nonresident tuition: $14,620 full-time. College room and board: $6650. College room only: $3096. Special program-related fees: $60–$120 per credit hour for studio fees (in clay, fibers, glass, metals and wood).

Financial Aid Program-specific awards: 4 Bacchanal Scholarships for program majors ($1000).

Application Procedures Students admitted directly into the professional program freshman year. Deadline for freshmen and transfers: August 1. Required: high school transcript, college transcript(s) for transfer students, ACT test score only.

Web Site http://www.tntech.edu/craftcenter/

Undergraduate Contact Mr. Ward Doubet, Director, Appalachian Center for Craft, Tennessee Technological University, 1560 Craft Center Drive, Smithville, Tennessee 37166; 615-597-6801, fax: 615-597-6803, e-mail address: craftcenter@tntech.edu

More About the Craft Center and the University

The Appalachian Center for Craft, a satellite campus of Tennessee Tech University (TTU), promotes excellence in American craft by teaching tradition and innovation in technique, concept, and design. The Craft Center provides access to the highest quality craft education, professional artists, and career opportunities. The school offers students the option of five Bachelor of Fine Arts (B.F.A.) degree or nondegree Craft Certificate concentrations in fine craft: clay, fibers, glass, metals, and wood. The B.F.A. degree is accredited by the National Association of Schools of Art and Design and the Southern Association of Colleges and Schools.

The B.F.A. degree program features a contemporary approach to fine craft built on traditional techniques. Students become proficient in the materials, processes, and techniques used by professional craft artists and develop confidence in the use of tools and equipment in a studio environment. The measure of accomplishment is the B.F.A. senior thesis exhibition, requiring high standards of professionalism in preparation, design, and execution. The ultimate reflection of accomplishment is the students' consistent record of success beyond graduation. Craft Center students continue to raise the bar in contemporary craft innovation, winning national and

regional awards, participating in prestigious shows and exhibitions, and receiving grants, scholarships, and artist residencies.

The nondegree Craft Certificate programs allow students to develop or enhance the professional skills necessary to embark on a career in craft. The certificate is conferred as a formal recognition by the Craft Center faculty of a level of studio knowledge and accomplishment at an emerging professional level.

Located on more than 500 wooded acres overlooking Center Hill Lake in Middle Tennessee, the Craft Center's facilities are among the finest in the nation. The facility exceeds 87,000 square feet, including 50,000 square feet of spacious studios, a library, a large conference room, two audiovisual/lecture rooms, more than 4,000 square feet of exhibition and gallery space, student housing, administrative offices, and a café.

In addition to the outstanding facilities and studio equipment, the Craft Center offers an experienced tenured faculty of nationally renowned craft artists; individual attention; and a private art school experience at a public school price. Students attend general education and art foundation courses on the main campus of Tennessee Tech University in Cookeville (approximately 25 minutes east of the Craft Center; free shuttle service is available).

The Craft Center's 5 full-time faculty members are nationally and internationally renowned and respected craft artists in the fields of clay (Vince Pitelka), fibers (Jeanne Brady), glass (Curtiss Brock), metals (Robert Coogan), and wood (Graham Campbell). All faculty members have Master of Fine Arts degrees in their respective fields and are extremely active in exhibitions, teaching workshops, publishing, and professional craft organizations, in addition to their teaching and studio work.

The Craft Center also offers an Artist-in-Residence program, which is a one- to three-year competitive program allowing emerging professional artists to work in the intensive studio environment of the Craft Center. Each studio has a resident artist with a B.F.A., M.F.A., or professional equivalent in his or her field. The residents come from all over the country and abroad to study, teach, and further develop their work at the Craft Center. They are invaluable to all programs of the Craft Center, providing additional expertise and experiences to the students.

The clay studio includes a variety of firing options from raku, bonfire, salt, soda, and wood to electric and gas kilns; tons of space for handbuilding and wheel work; and glaze and clay mixing rooms. The fibers studio, focused on surface design and weaving, has a large loom room, a dye kitchen, and fully equipped surface design facilities. The glass studio emphasizes the technical skills of glassblowing and has one of the best equipped hot- and cold-working shops in the nation. The metals department has studios for fine jewelry, large-scale sculptural work, and blacksmithing. The wood studio, focusing on studio furniture design and production, has bench rooms for work with hand and power tools, a large fully-equipped machine room, and a spray room.

The Craft Center is located approximately 60 miles east of Nashville and 120 miles west of Knoxville off Interstate-40, near the town of Smithville. The main campus of Tennessee Tech University is located in Cookeville, approximately 25 minutes east of the Craft Center, off I-40. The Craft Center offers free shuttle service from the Craft Center to TTU and return service in order to provide easy access to classes on the main campus and at the Craft Center. TTU also offers two other B.F.A. concentrations, art education and painting, on TTU's main campus. The studios of TTU's Bryan Fine Arts Building have been recently renovated to provide more work space for these programs as well as improved ventilation, lighting, and storage.

For more information about the Craft Center, students should call 615-597-6801, e-mail craftcenter@ tntech.edu, or visit http://www.tntech.edu/craftcenter. For more general information about TTU and main campus art programs, students should visit http://www. tntech.edu.

Appalachian State University

Boone, North Carolina

State-supported, coed. Small town campus. Total enrollment: 14,653. Art program established 1937.

Aquinas College

Grand Rapids, Michigan

Independent Roman Catholic, coed. Suburban campus. Total enrollment: 2,193. Art program established 1965.

Arcadia University

Glenside, Pennsylvania

Independent, coed. Suburban campus. Total enrollment: 3,403. Art program established 1925.

Degrees Bachelor of Arts in the areas of scientific illustration, art therapy, art history; Bachelor of Fine Arts in the areas of graphic design, interior design, painting, printmaking, ceramics, metals and jewelry, photography, art education. Majors and concentrations: art education, art history, art/fine arts, ceramic art and design, graphic design, interior design, jewelry and metalsmithing, painting/drawing, photography, pre-art therapy, printmaking, scientific illustration, studio art. Program accredited by NASAD.

Enrollment 200 total; all undergraduate.

Art Student Profile 60% females, 40% males, 15% minorities, 3% international.

Art Faculty 9 undergraduate (full-time), 15 undergraduate (part-time). 89% of full-time faculty have terminal degrees. Graduate students do not teach undergraduate courses. Undergraduate student–faculty ratio: 12:1.

Student Life Student groups/activities include Arcadia Association of Fine Arts, Arcadia University Art Gallery.

Expenses for 2006–2007 Application fee: $30. Comprehensive fee: $35,650 includes full-time tuition ($25,650), mandatory fees ($340), and college room and board ($9660). Special program-related fees: $25–$100 per course for lab supplies.

Financial Aid Program-specific awards: 5–10 achievement awards for program majors ($1000–$5000).

Application Procedures Students admitted directly into the professional program freshman year. Deadline for freshmen and transfers: continuous. Required: essay, high school transcript, college transcript(s) for transfer students, minimum 2.0 high school GPA, 2 letters

Arcadia University (continued)

of recommendation, portfolio, SAT I or ACT test scores. Recommended: minimum 3.0 high school GPA, interview. Portfolio reviews held 6 times on campus; the submission of slides may be substituted for portfolios if a campus visit is impossible.

Web Site http://www.arcadia.edu

Undergraduate Contact Office of Enrollment Management, Arcadia University, 450 South Easton Road, Glenside, Pennsylvania 19038-3295; 877-272-2342, fax: 215-572-4049, e-mail address: admiss@arcadia.edu

Arizona State University

Tempe, Arizona

State-supported, coed. Suburban campus. Total enrollment: 51,612.

Arkansas State University

State University, Arkansas

State-supported, coed. Small town campus. Total enrollment: 10,414. Art program established 1936.

Degrees Bachelor of Fine Arts in the areas of studio art, art education, graphic design. Majors and concentrations: art education, ceramics, graphic design, painting/drawing, photography, printmaking, sculpture, studio art. Program accredited by NASAD.

Enrollment 154 total; 112 undergraduate, 42 nonprofessional degree.

Art Student Profile 48% females, 52% males, 8% minorities, 3% international.

Art Faculty 12 total (full-time), 1 total (part-time). 100% of full-time faculty have terminal degrees. Graduate students do not teach undergraduate courses. Undergraduate student–faculty ratio: 12:1.

Expenses for 2005–2006 Application fee: $15. State resident tuition: $4260 full-time. Nonresident tuition: $10,965 full-time. Mandatory fees: $1180 full-time. Full-time tuition and fees vary according to course load, location, and program. College room and board: $4190. Room and board charges vary according to board plan and housing facility.

Financial Aid Program-specific awards: 5 art scholarships for art majors ($1900–$2000).

Application Procedures Students apply for admission into the professional program by sophomore year. Deadline for freshmen and transfers: continuous. Required: high school transcript, portfolio, SAT I or ACT test scores, minimum 2.0 college GPA for transfer students. Portfolio reviews held 3 times on campus and off campus in Little Rock, AR; the submission of slides may be substituted for portfolios for three-dimensional work.

Web Site http://www.clt.astate.edu/art/

Undergraduate Contact Mr. Curtis Steele, Chair, Department of Art, Arkansas State University, PO Box 1920, State University, Arkansas 72467; 870-972-3050, fax: 870-972-3932, e-mail address: csteele@astate.edu

Graduate Contact Dean of the Graduate School, Graduate School, Arkansas State University, PO Box 60, State University, Arkansas 72467; 870-972-3029, fax: 870-972-3857, e-mail address: gradsch@astate.edu

Art Academy of Cincinnati

Cincinnati, Ohio

Independent, coed. Urban campus. Art program established 1869.

Degrees Bachelor of Fine Arts in the areas of fine art, communication arts, studio with an emphasis in art history/museum studies. Majors and concentrations: art history, digital design, digital media, drawing, graphic design, illustration, painting, photo design, photography, printmaking, sculpture. Graduate degrees offered: Master of Arts in the area of art education. Cross-registration with members of the Greater Cincinnati Consortium of Colleges and Universities. Program accredited by NASAD.

Enrollment 216 total; 188 undergraduate, 28 graduate.

Art Student Profile 49% females, 51% males, 6% minorities, 2% international.

Art Faculty 17 total (full-time), 40 total (part-time). 98% of full-time faculty have terminal degrees. Graduate students do not teach undergraduate courses. Undergraduate student–faculty ratio: 12:1.

Student Life Special housing available for art students.

Expenses for 2006–2007 Application fee: $25. Tuition: $19,250 full-time. Mandatory fees: $350 full-time. Special program-related fees: $350 per year for student activities.

Financial Aid Program-specific awards: 20–30 entrance scholarships for incoming students ($1500–$12,000).

Application Procedures Students admitted directly into the professional program freshman year. Deadline for freshmen and transfers: continuous. Notification date for freshmen and transfers: August 1. Required: essay, high school transcript, college transcript(s) for transfer students, minimum 2.0 high school GPA, letter of recommendation, interview, portfolio, SAT I or ACT test scores (minimum combined SAT I score of 950, minimum composite ACT score of 19). Recommended: minimum 3.0 high school GPA. Portfolio reviews held continuously on campus and off campus in 20 cities on National Portfolio Days; the submission of slides may be substituted for portfolios when distance is prohibitive.

Web Site http://www.artacademy.edu

Contact Joseph L. Fisher, Acting Director of Admissions, Art Academy of Cincinnati, 1212 Jackson Street, Cincinnati, Ohio 45202; 800-323-5692, fax: 513-562-8778, e-mail address: admissions@artacademy.edu

More About the Academy

The Art Academy of Cincinnati is a small, independent college of art for students seeking a superior education in the creation and understanding of art. The Art Academy's origins reach back to the early nineteenth century, when individual artists offered classes in Cincinnati. In 1869 the school was established as the McMicken School of Art and Design. When the Cincinnati Museum Association was established in 1885, the school's founder suggested affiliating the art school with the museum. In November 1887, the Art Academy moved to Eden Park, where it existed until August 2005 when it moved into a newly renovated facility in Over-the-Rhine, just north of downtown Cincinnati.

Students are attracted to the Academy for several reasons, particularly the closeness of the community of 200 full-time students. The Academy has an intimate atmosphere conducive to learning, experimenting, questioning, and producing. Faculty members are familiar with each student's talents and needs, and there is a focus on the visual arts that only a professional art college can offer.

The Art Academy offers four-year programs leading to the Bachelor of Fine Arts degree in three areas: fine arts, with emphases in painting, printmaking, photography, digital media, drawing, and sculpture; communication arts, with emphases in digital multimedia, graphic design, photo design, and illustration; and art history. A five-semester Associate of Science degree in graphic design is available through an intensive, career-focused, accelerated program of study.

In completing the Bachelor of Fine Arts degree, a student is exposed to an integration of studio work, liberal studies, and art history, supporting the Academy's philosophy that the artist's strongest imagery and most effective visual statements come from a broad and rich mind. Fine arts students select a major area of emphasis and supplement their education with electives. The curriculum supports the understanding and benefits of the interrelationships of the various media, broadens students' visual concerns, and expands their self-expression. The Fine Arts Program is augmented by guest lecture series, seminars, workshops, visits to private collections, and field trips to museums and galleries in Cincinnati as well as to institutions in Chicago, Cleveland, Columbus, Detroit, Indianapolis, New York, and Washington, D.C.

The Communication Arts Program offers professional, career–oriented instruction that integrates conceptual processes, media skills, technical methods, problem-solving theory, and social/historical references to applied design and gives students practical experience that helps them to move easily into business opportunities after graduation. Students are introduced during their first year to the use of computers for solving problems and creating ideas. Hands-on experiences in the profession are provided through internships, an in-house design service, and client-based assignments.

Campus and Surroundings Greater Cincinnati is a center for social, cultural, sports, and educational activities. There is something for everyone, including major league sports teams, amusement parks, and restaurants of every kind. The Art Academy itself is located blocks from where the nationally acclaimed Symphony Orchestra, Cincinnati Ballet Company, Cincinnati Opera, and May Festival Chorus perform. The Contemporary Arts Center, Taft Museum, Historical Society, Cincinnati Zoo, and Museum of Natural History are all a quick ride from the campus.

Program Facilities The Art Academy's main facility is a newly renovated space of 120,000 square feet, with state-of-the-art equipment and expanded classrooms and labs. There are studio spaces available to

Art Academy of Cincinnati (continued)

every junior and senior student. Three gallery spaces have changing exhibitions throughout the year. Students have 24-hour access to studios and classrooms during the academic year. Several blocks from the Art Academy's main building is River City Works, a 6,500-square-foot sculpture studio. This space is equipped with a woodshop and metalworking and hot-glass facilities as well as individual studios for sculptors.

Faculty, Resident Artists, and Alumni The faculty of professional artists, designers, and scholars is committed to challenging students intellectually, conceptually, and aesthetically. There are 17 full-time faculty members; 16 have received a master's degree or its equivalent as their highest earned degree, and 1 has a doctorate. The Academy has 35 part-time faculty members. The student-faculty ratio is 12:1.

Each year the Art Academy invites outstanding professional artists to lecture and to teach. A number of visitors spend a day or two as artists-in-residence, working with students in the studios and conducting critiques. The Art Academy regularly collaborates with the Cincinnati Art Museum, the Contemporary Arts Center, and Lightborne Communications in visiting artist programs. In addition, the American Institute of Graphic Arts (AIGA) hosts a major lecture series each year, bringing a roster of well-known designers and illustrators.

Art Center College of Design

Pasadena, California

Independent, coed. Suburban campus. Total enrollment: 1,642. Art program established 1930.

Degrees Bachelor of Fine Arts in the areas of advertising, illustration, graphic design, photography, fine arts, film; Bachelor of Science in the areas of environmental design, product and transportation design. Majors and concentrations: advertising design and communication, art/fine arts, environmental design, film studies, graphic design, illustration, industrial design, photography, product design, transportation design. Graduate degrees offered: Master of Arts in the area of art theory and criticism; Master of Fine Arts in the areas of media design, fine arts, film; Master of Science in the areas of product design, environmental

design. Cross-registration with Occidental College, California Institute of Technology. Program accredited by NASAD.

Enrollment 1,642 total; 1,512 undergraduate, 130 graduate.

Art Student Profile 40% females, 60% males, 51% minorities, 23% international.

Art Faculty 66 undergraduate (full-time), 320 undergraduate (part-time), 4 graduate (full-time), 30 graduate (part-time). Graduate students do not teach undergraduate courses. Undergraduate student–faculty ratio: 9:1.

Student Life Student groups/activities include Contraste (Latino student group), Chroma (African-American student group), Industrial Design Society of America Student Chapter.

Expenses for 2005–2006 Application fee: $45. Tuition: $27,800 full-time. Mandatory fees: $200 full-time. Special program-related fees: $200 per semester for universal studio usage fee.

Financial Aid Program-specific awards: 300 Art Center Scholarships for program majors ($1000–$6500), 100 entering grants for program majors ($5000), 12 Art Center Outreach Grants for Latino, African-American, Native American students ($6200), 1 Nike Grant for Latino, African-American graphics designers, female product designers ($3000), 1 Knapp Grant for Latino and African-American fine arts majors ($12,400).

Application Procedures Students admitted directly into the professional program freshman year. Deadline for freshmen and transfers: continuous. Notification date for freshmen and transfers: continuous. Required: essay, high school transcript, college transcript(s) for transfer students, portfolio, SAT I or ACT test scores, minimum TOEFL score of 550 for international students. Recommended: minimum 3.0 high school GPA, interview. Portfolio reviews held continuously on campus.

Web Site http://www.artcenter.edu

Contact Ms. Kit Baron, Vice President, Admissions, Art Center College of Design, 1700 Lida Street, Pasadena, California 91103; 626-396-2373, fax: 626-795-0578.

More About the College

Art Center College of Design was founded in 1930 in downtown Los Angeles with a single purpose—to educate students for careers of achievement in the visual arts professions. The founder, Tink Adams, vowed to work closely with the leaders of industry to prepare professionals for meaningful careers. This tradition of close industry relationships continues today at the Pasadena campus.

Art Center attracts attention from firms throughout the world. Companies, such as Nike, Honda, Sony, The Gap, Nokia, and Universal Studios, have decided to sponsor special student research projects at the College. Students have the opportunity to work with real clients on futuristic and conceptual projects.

In addition to visiting industry guests, the College features a faculty of practicing professionals who reinforce this tradition of real-world influence. Most are part-time faculty members who maintain their own distinctive client lists.

Fine arts students have an opportunity to work with some of the most provocative artists and painters working today, such as Mike Kelley, Liz Larner, and Jeremy Gilbert-Rolfe.

Art Center acknowledges and encourages the dissolution of boundaries between disciplines, and, although students apply to and study within specific majors, there are opportunities for new kinds of art making, based on digital and other technologies. Students are exposed to projects that focus on social and humanitarian issues within the global community. The College's mission is to lead the way for the industry in exploring new roles for design, photography, and film.

The average freshman at Art Center is 23 years old. All students must declare a major before entering the College, and this has resulted in a mature and focused student body. Campus life, too, is influenced by the maturity of the students. There is currently no on-campus housing. Students choose from an abundance of housing within the Pasadena and Los Angeles area.

Art Center's graduates have made significant marks in the world of art and design, and alumni return to the campus to recruit for their own employment needs. The high demand for Art Center graduates is attributable to the degree of specialization and professionalism required of the students. In excess of 200 firms visit the College to interview graduating students each year, and job listings are printed regularly for the use of students and alumni. Some of the firms that have recruited on campus are Harcourt Brace & Co., Capitol Records, The Walt Disney Company, Ford Motor Company, General Motors Corporation, Pentagram, Virgin Records, Landor Associates, Honda, Nike, MCA-Universal Studios, Neiman Marcus Direct, TBWA/Chiat/Day, Daimler-Chrysler, Industrial Light and Magic, DreamWorks SKG, and Mattel Toys.

With two campuses in suburban Pasadena, Art Center offers a physically beautiful environment juxtaposed with the internationalism of Los Angeles and the Pacific Rim. Art Center encourages a diverse population of students and faculty members. The goal in bringing together a community of students from throughout the United States and the world is to develop new solutions to design issues and to promote the importance of design within the world communities. It is within this context that students receive highly individualized and rigorous programs of study. Critical thinking, as well as development of technical skills, is emphasized.

Facilities Art Center is an acknowledged leader in providing new technologies and state-of-the-art facilities to its students. Features include a distinctive contemporary campus in the hills overlooking Pasadena's Rose Bowl; a 215,000-square-foot glass and steel building designed by Craig Ellwood; an 11,000-square-foot computer graphics lab with 220 Macintosh stations, sixty-two Silicon Graphic workstations, thirty-one SGI/NT 320 workstations, and one of the world's largest computer-aided industrial design (CAID) networks as well as a vast array of software to introduce students to the newest digital technologies; a professional recording studio; photography areas with black-and-white labs with seventy-five enlargers, a color lab with a 20-inch fully automated E-6 processor, a 20-inch fully automated cibachrome processor, and a 20-inch RA4 fully automated processor; two 4,600-square-foot shooting stages that provide twenty-six shooting stages equipped with seamless background colors, including one 15 × 30 flying flat; and digital-imaging facilities, including Kodak XL 7700 thermal printer, RFS 2035 film scanners, H-P Paint Jet printer, 840 AV workstation, a Microtech 4 × 5 film scanner, and an

visual

Arts

Art Center College of Design (continued)

Agfa flatbed transparency scanner. A second campus, also in Pasadena, houses graduate and public education programs.

Special Programs The College encourages a global and international approach to design education. Art Center facilitates a wide variety of internship opportunities with major corporations and firms, such as Ford, Toyota Motor Corporation, Electronic Arts, Nike, and Wieden & Kennedy. Students may also accept paid mentorship positions or enroll in a mentorship class to assist local Pasadena high school students.

The Art Institute of Colorado

Denver, Colorado

Proprietary, coed. Total enrollment: 2,886. Art program established 1952.

The Art Institute of Atlanta

Atlanta, Georgia

Proprietary, coed. Suburban campus. Total enrollment: 2,651. Art program established 1949.

The Art Institute of Boston at Lesley University

Boston, Massachusetts

Independent, coed. Urban campus. Total enrollment: 6,521. Art program established 1912.

Degrees Bachelor of Fine Arts in the areas of fine arts, illustration, graphic design, fine arts/illustration, illustration/design, photography, illustration, animation, art history; Bachelor of Fine Arts/Master of Arts in the area of art/expressive therapies; Bachelor of Fine Arts/Master of Education in the area of art education. Majors and concentrations: advertising illustration, animation, art history, art/fine arts, book illustration, commercial photography, documentary photography, drawing, editorial illustration, graphic design, illustration, multimedia design, painting, photography, printmaking, sculpture, Web design. Graduate degrees offered: Master of Fine Arts in the area of visual arts. Program accredited by NASAD.

Enrollment 553 total; 540 undergraduate, 13 graduate.

Art Student Profile 58% females, 42% males, 11% minorities, 12% international.

Art Faculty 25 total (full-time), 80 total (part-time). 90% of full-time faculty have terminal degrees. Graduate students do not teach undergraduate courses. Undergraduate student–faculty ratio: 10:1.

Student Life Student groups/activities include student exhibitions in galleries and sites around Boston, Graphic Artists Guild student membership (AIGA). Special housing available for art students.

Expenses for 2005–2006 Application fee: $40. Comprehensive fee: $29,550 includes full-time tuition ($19,600) and college room and board ($9950). College room only: $6100. Full-time tuition varies according to program. Room and board charges vary according to housing facility. Special program-related fees: $475 per year for department fees.

Financial Aid Program-specific awards: 50 AIB Scholarships for incoming students ($5000), 1 Presidential Scholarship for incoming students, 160 Art Institute of Boston Grants for those demonstrating need ($500–$3500), 10–20 Community College Transfer Scholarships for incoming students with AA degree ($4000), 1–2 ACCESS Scholarships for incoming African, Latino, Asian, or Native American students, 50 Deans Scholarships for incoming students ($7000).

Application Procedures Students admitted directly into the professional program freshman year. Deadline for freshmen and transfers: continuous. Required: essay, high school transcript, college transcript(s) for transfer students, interview, portfolio, SAT I or ACT test scores, resume/list of accomplishments, awards. Recommended: minimum 3.0 high school GPA, 2 letters of recommendation. Portfolio reviews held as needed on campus and off campus at National Portfolio Days; the submission of slides may be substituted for portfolios if a campus visit or National Portfolio Day review is not possible to arrange.

Web Site http://www.aiboston.edu

Undergraduate Contact Office of Admissions, The Art Institute of Boston at Lesley University, 700 Beacon Street, Boston, Massachusetts 02215; 617-585-6710, fax: 617-585-6720, e-mail address: admissions@aiboston.edu

Graduate Contact Graduate Office of Admissions, The Art Institute of Boston at Lesley University, 29 Everett Street, Cambridge, Massachusetts 02138; 617-349-8300, e-mail address: info@lesley.edu

More About the Institute

The Art Institute of Boston (AIB) at Lesley University is a professional college of art that was founded in 1912. Its programs are studio intensive, integrating liberal arts courses specifically designed to broaden students' intellectual and artistic perceptions. The Art Institute of Boston at Lesley University provides a supportive environment to enable students to succeed in their careers—the atmosphere is both challenging and nurturing, helping to maximize personal growth, intellectual growth, and artistic potential. The Art Institute of Boston at Lesley University is one of the four colleges within Lesley University. AIB's strengths as a professional college of the visual arts are combined with the resources of a university, providing expanded educational opportunities for students not usually found at most independent colleges of art yet preserving the character of a small private college of art.

The AIB community is small and close-knit, and most students and faculty members know each other by the end of the first semester. The Art Institute of Boston at Lesley University has an exceptional faculty, many of whom are well-known practicing artists, designers, illustrators, and photographers.

Some of AIB's faculty members include Professor in the Foundation Department, Nathan Goldstein, a recognized authority on art education, lecturer and artist; Christopher James, Professor and Chair of the Photography Department, an internationally renowned photographer who has won numerous awards and fellowships and whose work is in museum collections around the world; Jane Tuckerman, Associate Professor of Photography, a widely-exhibited photographer and recipient of an NEA fellowship and other prestigious grants and fellowships; and Anthony Apesos, Professor of Visual Arts, who is an accomplished painter, lecturer, and art critic.

The faculty members at AIB serve as mentors to their students and are very accessible to them. Students at AIB benefit from lectures, exhibitions, and the visiting artists who contribute to the positive energy of studio critiques and workshops. Activities and opportunities for growth and learning at AIB include student on- and off-campus exhibitions, lectures, workshops, field trips to galleries in New York and New England, and a visiting artist program. Acclaimed artists, such as Chuck Close, Duane Michals, Edward Sorel, Milton Glaser, Roy DeCarava, Luis Gonzalez Palma, and Andres Serrano have recently been guest lecturers at the college.

Education at AIB is not confined to the studios and galleries of the college. Students benefit from the talent and experience of the faculty members and the extensive connections to the Boston art and business communities that the college has nurtured. Boston is a thriving cultural and commercial center, home to countless museums and galleries, symphonies, and theaters and renowned for its medical centers, financial institutions, and universities. These communities provide venues for a wealth of internships and full-time employment. In addition to continuing exhibitions of student work throughout the University, students exhibit at numerous galleries around Boston. Students are encouraged to show their work long before graduation, gaining valuable life experiences outside the classroom.

The practical aspect of developing a career in art is part of the formal curriculum at AIB. By the time students graduate, they are well prepared for their professions through course work devoted to professional development, such as presentation and portfolio building, and learning to make contacts in their fields. AIB graduates cite the practical skills and the encouragement they received as key factors in building the confidence needed to succeed in their careers.

Visual Arts

The Art Institute of Boston at Lesley University (continued)

Program Facilities The Art Institute of Boston's facilities include five state-of-the-art Macintosh computer laboratories, an animation lab, an updated photography lab with color and black-and-white printers, a digital photography lab, a printmaking lab with etching and lithography presses, a wood shop, and a clay lab with kilns. Senior fine arts students have their own individual studios in which to create.

The Art Institute of Boston was selected to join the New Media Centers Program, a consortium of higher education institutions and digital technology companies dedicated to advancing learning through new media. AIB has newly expanded multimedia programs that use state-of-the-art technology and equipment.

The AIB library collection is devoted principally to the visual arts and contains more than 10,000 books, seventy-five serial titles, 45,000 slides, a video-viewing room, and more than 500 art-related videos, and it subscribes to AMICO, the image database. The library has the National Gallery of Art's American Art Collection on videodisc, a visual reference of more than 26,000 images spanning three centuries.

In addition, the Eleanor De Wolfe Ludcke Library at Lesley provides a state-of-the-art multimedia resource center and a collection of 100,000 books, 700 current periodicals, 2,200 computer software and CD-ROM titles, 650 film and video titles, media material, and circulating media equipment. Students have borrowing privileges at six additional libraries through the Fenway Library Online.

The Art Institute of Boston sponsors a full program of exhibitions and lectures by visiting artists. The gallery presents major exhibitions of contemporary and historical work by established and emerging artists, including the alumni of the Art Institute of Boston. Students have the opportunity to assist in mounting exhibitions and to personally meet visiting artists. A student gallery and reserved areas show student work year-round. Gallery South exhibits the work of student photographers throughout the year, including group and senior exhibitions.

Special Programs The duPont Lecture Series brings the work of accomplished artists of color to the college; frequent visits to the college by known artists; a collaboration with Maine Photographic Workshop; study-abroad programs in France and at the Art Institute of Florence, Lorenzo de Medici; internships at art galleries, design and animation studios, and advertising agencies; freelance and placement listings through artists' resources, counsel-

ing, guidance, and tutoring services. Master's degree programs in art education and expressive therapies are offered in conjunction with Lesley University. Precollege classes give high school students an opportunity to earn college credit and develop portfolios.

The Art Institute of California–San Francisco

San Francisco, California

Proprietary, coed. Urban campus. Total enrollment: 1,347. Art program established 1939.

Degrees Bachelor of Fine Arts in the area of fashion design; Bachelor of Science in the areas of graphic design, media arts and animation, interactive media design, game and art design, visual and game programming, interior design, advertising, fashion marketing and management. Majors and concentrations: advertising, computer animation, fashion design, fashion marketing and management, game art and design, graphic design, interior design, multimedia/ web design, visual and game programming.

Enrollment 1,347 total; all undergraduate.

Art Student Profile 40% females, 60% males, 5% international.

Art Faculty 22 undergraduate (full-time), 86 undergraduate (part-time). Graduate students do not teach undergraduate courses. Undergraduate student–faculty ratio: 16:1.

Student Life Student groups/activities include student newsletter, internal design projects, community design projects.

Financial Aid Program-specific awards: 10–25 scholarship competitions for high school seniors ($4400–$13,200), merit scholarships for students with GPA above 2.5 and demonstrated need.

Application Procedures Students admitted directly into the professional program freshman year. Deadline for freshmen and transfers: continuous. Required: essay, high school transcript, college transcript(s) for transfer students, interview. Recommended: minimum 2.0 high school GPA, letter of recommendation.

Web Site http://www.aicasf.aii.edu

Undergraduate Contact Admissions Department, The Art Institute of California–San Francisco, 1170 Market, San Francisco, California 94102; 415-865-0198, fax: 415-863-6344, e-mail address: aisfadm@aii.edu

The Art Institute of Fort Lauderdale

Fort Lauderdale, Florida

Proprietary, coed. Urban campus. Total enrollment: 3,500.

The Art Institute of Phoenix

Phoenix, Arizona

Proprietary, coed. Suburban campus. Art program established 1995.

Degrees Bachelor of Arts. Majors and concentrations: advertising, digital media production, fashion marketing, game art and design, graphic design, interactive media, interior design, media arts/animation, visual and game programming, visual effects and motion graphics.

Enrollment 1,219 total; 1,182 undergraduate, 37 nonprofessional degree.

Art Student Profile 41% females, 59% males, 30% minorities, 1% international.

Art Faculty 49 undergraduate (full-time), 52 undergraduate (part-time). 10% of full-time faculty have terminal degrees. Graduate students do not teach undergraduate courses. Undergraduate student–faculty ratio: 20:1.

Student Life Student groups/activities include American Institute of Graphic Design Student Chapter, Siggraph Student Chapter, American Society of Interior Designers. Special housing available for art students.

Expenses for 2005–2006 Application fee: $50. One-time mandatory fee: $100. Tuition: $18,144 full-time. Full-time tuition varies according to course load. College room only: $5217. Special program-related fees: $430–$495 for program fees.

Financial Aid Program-specific awards: 1 Evelyn Keedey-Reed Scholarship for high school seniors, 1 Karen Swan Memorial Scholarship for high school seniors in Arizona, California, or Texas, 16 IBA Scholarships for high school seniors, 1 Catherine Yoder Award for female

students, 3 US Congressional District Art Competition for high school students, 1 National Art Honor Society Award for high school seniors who are members of National Art Honor Society, 10 Arizona Private School Association Awards for high school seniors.

Application Procedures Students admitted directly into the professional program freshman year. Notification date for freshmen and transfers: continuous. Required: essay, high school transcript, college transcript(s) for transfer students, minimum 2.0 high school GPA, interview, minimum 2.5 high school GPA for game art/design majors. Recommended: 2 letters of recommendation, portfolio, SAT I or ACT test scores. Portfolio reviews held 4 times on campus.

Web Site http://www.aipx.edu

Undergraduate Contact Jerry Driskill, Director of Admissions, The Art Institute of Phoenix, 2233 West Dunlap Avenue, Phoenix, Arizona 85021; 602-331-7500 ext. 7502, fax: 602-331-5301, e-mail address: aipxadmit@aii.edu

The Art Institute of Portland

Portland, Oregon

Proprietary, coed. Urban campus. Total enrollment: 1,583. Art program established 1963.

The Art Institute of Washington

Arlington, Virginia

Proprietary, coed. Urban campus. Total enrollment: 1,200.

Auburn University

Auburn University, Alabama

State-supported, coed. Small town campus. Total enrollment: 23,333. Art program established 1927.

Augusta State University

Augusta, Georgia

State-supported, coed. Urban campus. Total enrollment: 6,312. Art program established 1958.

Degrees Bachelor of Fine Arts in the area of art. Majors and concentrations: art/fine arts, ceramics, drawing, medical illustration, painting, printmaking, studio art. Program accredited by NASAD.

Enrollment 78 total; 66 undergraduate, 12 nonprofessional degree.

Art Student Profile 70% females, 30% males, 30% minorities, 3% international.

Art Faculty 7 undergraduate (full-time), 8 undergraduate (part-time). 100% of full-time faculty have terminal degrees. Graduate students do not teach undergraduate courses. Undergraduate student–faculty ratio: 15:1.

Student Life Student groups/activities include Student Art Organization.

Expenses for 2005–2006 Application fee: $20. State resident tuition: $2438 full-time. Nonresident tuition: $9754 full-time. Mandatory fees: $482 full-time. College room only: $4920. Special program-related fees: $75 per course for studio lab fee.

Financial Aid Program-specific awards: 1 departmental scholarship for program majors ($500), 1 Mary Byrd Scholarship for graduates of local Georgia high schools ($1500), 1 Nathan Bindler Award for artistically talented program majors ($500), 2–4 Pamplin Scholarships for program majors ($500).

Application Procedures Students admitted directly into the professional program freshman year. Deadline for freshmen and transfers: July 18. Required: high school transcript, college transcript(s) for transfer students, minimum 2.0 high school GPA, 2 letters of recommendation, SAT I or ACT test scores. Recommended: portfolio. Portfolio reviews held once on campus; the submission of slides may be substituted for portfolios when distance is prohibitive.

Web Site http://www.aug.edu

Undergraduate Contact Dr. Angela Morgan, Chair, Fine Arts Department, Augusta State University, 2500 Walton Way, Augusta, Georgia 30904-2200; 706-737-1453, fax: 706-667-4937, e-mail address: amorgan@aug.edu

Austin Peay State University

Clarksville, Tennessee

State-supported, coed. Suburban campus. Total enrollment: 8,813.

Ball State University

Muncie, Indiana

State-supported, coed. Suburban campus. Total enrollment: 20,351.

Degrees Bachelor of Fine Arts in the area of art. Majors and concentrations: animation, ceramic art and design, drawing, electronic arts, jewelry and metalsmithing, painting, photography, printmaking, sculpture, visual communication. Graduate degrees offered: Master of Arts in the area of art. Program accredited by NASAD.

Enrollment 599 total; 425 undergraduate, 6 graduate, 168 nonprofessional degree.

Art Student Profile 55% females, 45% males, 3% minorities, 2% international.

Art Faculty 28 total (full-time), 4 total (part-time). 100% of full-time faculty have terminal degrees. Graduate students do not teach undergraduate courses. Undergraduate student–faculty ratio: 15:1.

Student Life Student groups/activities include National Art Education Association Student Chapter, Fine Arts League, Crafts Guild.

Expenses for 2005–2006 Application fee: $25. State resident tuition: $6030 full-time. Nonresident tuition: $15,790 full-time. Mandatory fees: $428 full-time. College room and board: $6680.

Financial Aid Program-specific awards: 4–6 freshmen scholarship awards for outstanding freshmen program applicants ($1000), 8 Fine Art Scholarships for outstanding freshmen program applicants ($1000), 5 Ruth Swain Scholarships for outstanding sophomores, juniors, or seniors ($1000), 2 Roberta Law Scholarships for outstanding sophomores, juniors, seniors ($1000), 1 Dorotha Stock Scholarship for outstanding sophomores, juniors, or seniors ($500), 1 Alice Nichols Scholarship for outstanding art education students ($360), 1

Visual

Arts

Indiana Arts and Craftsman Scholarship for outstanding art majors ($250).

Application Procedures Students admitted directly into the professional program freshman year. Deadline for freshmen: April 1; transfers: continuous. Notification date for freshmen: May 1. Required: high school transcript, college transcript(s) for transfer students, portfolio, SAT I or ACT test scores (minimum combined SAT I score of 1000, minimum composite ACT score of 21). Recommended: minimum 2.0 high school GPA. Portfolio reviews held once on campus; the submission of slides may be substituted for portfolios if a campus visit is impossible.

Web Site http://www.bsu.edu/art/

Undergraduate Contact Ms. Barbara Giorgio-Booher, Primary Department Advisor, Department of Art, Ball State University, Muncie, Indiana 47306-0405; 765-285-5841, fax: 765-285-5838, e-mail address: bgiorgio@bsu.edu

Graduate Contact Prof. Kenton Hall, Graduate Director, Department of Art, Ball State University, Muncie, Indiana 47306-0405; 765-285-5838, fax: 765-285-5838, e-mail address: khall@bsu.edu

Barry University

Miami Shores, Florida

Independent Roman Catholic, coed. Suburban campus. Total enrollment: 9,207. Art program established 1951.

Barton College

Wilson, North Carolina

Independent, coed. Small town campus. Total enrollment: 1,189.

Degrees Bachelor of Fine Arts in the areas of graphic design, ceramics, painting, photography; Bachelor of Science in the area of art education K-12. Majors and concentrations: art education, ceramics, graphic design, painting, photography.

Enrollment 92 total; 72 undergraduate, 20 nonprofessional degree.

Art Student Profile 60% females, 40% males, 15% minorities, 1% international.

Art Faculty 4 undergraduate (full-time), 4 undergraduate (part-time). 100% of full-time

faculty have terminal degrees. Graduate students do not teach undergraduate courses. Undergraduate student–faculty ratio: 16:1.

Expenses for 2005–2006 Application fee: $25. Comprehensive fee: $22,470 includes full-time tuition ($15,390), mandatory fees ($1280), and college room and board ($5800). College room only: $2774. Full-time tuition and fees vary according to course load and program. Room and board charges vary according to housing facility. Special program-related fees: $43 per studio for supplies, $110 for photography supplies.

Financial Aid Program-specific awards: 1 Bessie Massengill Award for sophomores and juniors, 1 TEAM Award for sophomores and juniors ($1000), 1 National Scholastic Award for freshmen ($1000), 1 Art Faculty Scholarship for sophomores, juniors, seniors ($750), 1 Triangle East Advertising and Marketing Association Scholarship for sophomores, juniors, seniors ($1000), 1 Stuart Walston Scholarship for those with minimum 2.5 GPA ($500).

Application Procedures Students admitted directly into the professional program freshman year. Deadline for freshmen and transfers: continuous. Required: high school transcript, college transcript(s) for transfer students, letter of recommendation, SAT I or ACT test scores. Recommended: minimum 2.0 high school GPA, interview, portfolio. Portfolio reviews held by appointment on campus; the submission of slides may be substituted for portfolios.

Web Site http://www.barton.edu/

Undergraduate Contact Ms. Susan B. Fecho, Chair, Art Department, Barton College, PO Box 5000, Wilson, North Carolina 27893-7000; 252-399-6480, fax: 252-399-6571.

Baylor University

Waco, Texas

Independent Baptist, coed. Urban campus. Total enrollment: 13,975.

Degrees Bachelor of Fine Arts in the areas of painting, printmaking, graphic design, ceramics, sculpture, photography, fabric design. Majors and concentrations: ceramic art and design, fabric design, graphic design, painting, photography, printmaking, sculpture.

Baylor University (continued)

Enrollment 245 total; 186 undergraduate, 59 nonprofessional degree.

Art Student Profile 75% females, 25% males, 12% minorities, 7% international.

Art Faculty 16 undergraduate (full-time), 4 undergraduate (part-time). 100% of full-time faculty have terminal degrees. Graduate students do not teach undergraduate courses. Undergraduate student–faculty ratio: 18:1.

Student Life Student groups/activities include Art Club, Advertising Club of Baylor.

Expenses for 2006–2007 Application fee: $50. Comprehensive fee: $29,939 includes full-time tuition ($20,574), mandatory fees ($2240), and college room and board ($7125). College room only: $3600. Special program-related fees: $50 per course for studio lab fees.

Financial Aid Program-specific awards: 1 Friends of Baylor Fine Arts Award for continuing students ($2940), 4 Patricia Johnston Scholarships for continuing students ($8900), 1 C. C. and Helen Reid Scholarship for continuing students ($350), 2 freshmen art scholarships for freshmen ($6600), 2–3 Allbritton Art History Awards for continuing students ($5900), 1 Adrienne J. Barna Memorial Scholarship for continuing students ($3650), 1 Erica Cummings Memorial Scholarship for continuing students ($1050), 5 Dodson Memorial Awards for continuing students ($5600).

Application Procedures Students admitted directly into the professional program freshman year. Deadline for freshmen and transfers: April 15. Required: high school transcript, college transcript(s) for transfer students, minimum 2.0 high school GPA, SAT I or ACT test scores. Recommended: minimum 3.0 high school GPA, letter of recommendation.

Undergraduate Contact Mr. John D. McClanahan, Chair, Department of Art, Baylor University, PO Box 97263, Waco, Texas 76798-7263; 254-710-1867, fax: 254-710-1566, e-mail address: john_mcclanahan@baylor.edu

Bellevue University

Bellevue, Nebraska

Independent, coed. Suburban campus. Total enrollment: 5,929. Art program established 1966.

Belmont University

Nashville, Tennessee

Independent Baptist, coed. Urban campus. Total enrollment: 4,319. Art program established 1984.

Degrees Bachelor of Fine Arts in the areas of studio, art education, design communications. Majors and concentrations: art education, design communication, studio art. Cross-registration with O'More College. Program accredited by NASAD.

Enrollment 80 total; all undergraduate.

Art Student Profile 70% females, 30% males, 10% minorities, 1% international.

Art Faculty 6 total (full-time), 6 total (part-time). 100% of full-time faculty have terminal degrees. Graduate students do not teach undergraduate courses. Undergraduate student–faculty ratio: 14:1.

Student Life Student groups/activities include Art Association, Blvd Gallery and Design (student-run, on-campus business).

Expenses for 2005–2006 Application fee: $35. Comprehensive fee: $25,910 includes full-time tuition ($16,360), mandatory fees ($900), and college room and board ($8650). College room only: $5300. Full-time tuition and fees vary according to class time and course load. Room and board charges vary according to board plan, housing facility, and location. Special program-related fees: $100 per semester for design communication courses, $100 per semester for photography lab fee, $100 per semester for model fees, materials fee.

Financial Aid Program-specific awards: 4 Leu Art Scholarships for freshmen art majors ($2000), 4 art supply scholarships for those demonstrating need ($250), 1 rising senior award ($1000), 1 Hatch Showprint Scholarship for rising seniors ($4000).

Application Procedures Students admitted directly into the professional program freshman year. Deadline for freshmen and transfers: continuous. Required: high school transcript, college transcript(s) for transfer students, minimum 2.0 high school GPA, letter of recommendation, portfolio, SAT I or ACT test scores. Recommended: interview. Portfolio reviews held by arrangement on campus; the submission of slides may be substituted for portfolios whenever needed.

Web Site http://www.belmont.edu/art/
Undergraduate Contact David Ribar, Interim Chair, Department of Art, Belmont University, 1900 Belmont Boulevard, Nashville, Tennessee 37212-3537; 615-460-6773, fax: 615-460-6757.

Bemidji State University

Bemidji, Minnesota

State-supported, coed. Small town campus. Total enrollment: 4,893.

Birmingham-Southern College

Birmingham, Alabama

Independent Methodist, coed. Urban campus. Total enrollment: 1,411. Art program established 1946.

Degrees Bachelor of Fine Arts in the area of studio art. Majors and concentrations: art history, painting, photography, printmaking, sculpture. Cross-registration with University of Alabama at Birmingham. Program accredited by NASAD.

Enrollment 350 total; 190 undergraduate, 160 nonprofessional degree.

Art Student Profile 60% females, 40% males, 10% minorities, 5% international.

Art Faculty 5 undergraduate (full-time), 4 undergraduate (part-time). 100% of full-time faculty have terminal degrees. Graduate students do not teach undergraduate courses. Undergraduate student–faculty ratio: 15:1.

Student Life Student groups/activities include Art Students League.

Expenses for 2005–2006 Application fee: $25. Comprehensive fee: $28,135 includes full-time tuition ($20,425), mandatory fees ($630), and college room and board ($7080). College room only: $5000. Special program-related fees: $30–$50 per unit for materials.

Financial Aid Program-specific awards: 10 art scholarships for art majors ($1300–$8000).

Application Procedures Students admitted directly into the professional program freshman year. Notification date for freshmen and transfers: continuous. Required: essay, high school transcript, college transcript(s) for transfer students, minimum 2.0 high school GPA, SAT I or ACT test scores (minimum combined SAT I score of 870, minimum composite ACT score of 21), interview for scholarship consideration. Recommended: 2 letters of recommendation, interview, portfolio. Portfolio reviews held once on campus; the submission of slides may be substituted for portfolios when distance is prohibitive.

Web Site http://www.bsc.edu
Undergraduate Contact Ms. Sheri Salmon, Associate Vice President of Admissions, Birmingham-Southern College, 900 Arkadelphia Road, Box 549008, Birmingham, Alabama 35254; 205-226-4696, fax: 205-226-3074.

Boston Architectural College

Boston, Massachusetts

Independent, coed. Urban campus. Total enrollment: 910. Art program established 1889.

Boston University

Boston, Massachusetts

Independent, coed. Urban campus. Total enrollment: 30,957. Art program established 1954.

Degrees Bachelor of Fine Arts. Majors and concentrations: art education, graphic design, painting, sculpture. Graduate degrees offered: Master of Fine Arts in the areas of painting, sculpture, graphic design, art education, studio teaching. Cross-registration with Boston College, Brandeis University, Tufts University.

Enrollment 306 total; 230 undergraduate, 65 graduate, 11 nonprofessional degree.

Art Student Profile 60% females, 40% males, 10% minorities.

Art Faculty 21 total (full-time), 10 total (part-time). 100% of full-time faculty have terminal degrees. Graduate students do not teach undergraduate courses. Undergraduate student–faculty ratio: 16:1.

Student Life Student groups/activities include American Institute of Graphic Arts, Copley Society, Boston University Art League. Special housing available for art students.

Visual Arts

Boston University (continued)

Expenses for 2005–2006 Application fee: $70. Comprehensive fee: $42,046 includes full-time tuition ($31,530), mandatory fees ($436), and college room and board ($10,080). College room only: $6450. Full-time tuition and fees vary according to class time and degree level. Room and board charges vary according to board plan and housing facility. Special program-related fees: $35–$50 for lab fee, $100 for studio fee for painting majors.

Financial Aid Program-specific awards: 160 grants-need/performance awards for enrolled program students ($17,000).

Application Procedures Students admitted directly into the professional program freshman year. Deadline for freshmen: January 15; transfers: April 1. Notification date for freshmen: April 15; transfers: May 30. Required: essay, high school transcript, college transcript(s) for transfer students, portfolio, SAT I or ACT test scores. Recommended: minimum 3.0 high school GPA, 3 letters of recommendation. Portfolio reviews held continuously on campus; the submission of slides may be substituted for portfolios.

Web Site http://www.bu.edu/cfa/visual

Contact Jeannette Guillemin, Assistant Director, School of Visual Arts, College of Fine Arts, Boston University, 855 Commonwealth Avenue, Boston, Massachusetts 02215; 617-353-3371, fax: 617-353-7217, e-mail address: visuarts@bu.edu

More About the University

Boston University College of Fine Arts (CFA) is a small, conservatory-style school within a major university, offering outstanding professional training in music, the theater, and visual arts. The College was founded as the College of Music in 1873 and has a long and distinguished history of training artists. The Division of Applied Arts, now known as the School of Visual Arts, was added in 1919, and it currently enrolls approximately 250 students.

The student painters, sculptors, graphic designers, and art educators at the School of Visual Arts prepare for leading positions in the art world by engaging in its present and understanding its past. With a faculty composed of practicing professional artists, the School offers an intensive program of studio training combined with liberal arts studies leading to the Bachelor of Fine Arts (B.F.A.) and Master of Fine Arts (M.F.A.).

Campus Surroundings Boston University—independent, coeducational, nonsectarian—is an internationally recognized center of higher education and research. The University is located in the heart of Boston, along the banks of the Charles River and adjacent to the historic Back Bay district of Boston. Boston University is perfectly situated to enjoy both the charm and beauty of the city and its cultural and recreational attractions. School of Visual Arts students benefit from the many major museums and galleries as well as the theaters and musical organizations that make Boston a rich and varied environment for the art student.

Program Facilities The School of Visual Arts offers painting, drawing, and sculpture studios; a welding and wood shop; computer labs; photography and printmaking studios; a book and slide library; and exhibition spaces, including the Boston University Art Gallery, the 808 Showroom Gallery, the Sherman Gallery, and the Commonwealth Gallery.

Faculty, Resident Artists, and Alumni The faculty of dedicated teachers includes some of the finest painters, sculptors, graphic designers, and art educators in the country. Distinguished faculty members include John Walker, painter; Judith Simpson, art educator; Alston Purvis, graphic designer; and Isabel McIlvain, sculptor. Visiting artists include Vincent Desiderio, painter; Greg Amenoff, painter; William Tucker, sculptor; William Bailey, painter; Rackstraw Downes, printmaker; Mags Harries, sculptor, Jonathan Shahn, painter; Pat Steir, painter; Tim Rollins, educator; Al Leslie, painter; and Suzanne Coffey, painter. Alumni include the distinguished American artists Pat Steir and Brice Martin; designer Ira Yoffe, Vice President and Creative Director for *Parade Magazine;* Penelope Zencks, sculptor; and Richard Heinrichs, sculpture and production/set designer, whose credits include *Planet of the Apes, Fargo,* and *Pirates of the Carribean.*

Exhibition Opportunities Each year, the School of Visual Arts exhibits student work in its spring show. Additional exhibition opportunities exist throughout the year for students, faculty members, and alumni in the Boston University Art Gallery, the Sherman Gallery, the 808 Gallery, and the Commonwealth Gallery.

Special Programs Through the Boston University Collaborative Degree Program (BUCOP), students may obtain a dual degree in the College of Fine Arts and another of the University's schools or colleges. Students may minor in liberal arts, business, or communications. Painting and graphic design students are encouraged to study abroad at the Scuola Internazionale di Graphica in Venice, Italy. A five-year B.F.A./M.F.A. is available to students interested in majoring in a studio area along with art education.

Bowling Green State University

Bowling Green, Ohio

State-supported, coed. Small town campus. Total enrollment: 19,016.

Degrees Bachelor of Fine Arts. Majors and concentrations: art education, ceramics, computer art, digital art, drawing, fibers, glassworking, graphic design, jewelry and metalsmithing, painting, photography, printmaking, sculpture, three-dimensional studies, two-dimensional studies. Graduate degrees offered: Master of Arts in the area of art history; Master of Fine Arts in the areas of digital arts, three-dimensional studies, two-dimensional studies. Cross-registration with University of Toledo. Program accredited by NASAD.

Enrollment 900 total; 750 undergraduate, 30 graduate, 120 nonprofessional degree.

Art Faculty 46 total (full-time), 13 total (part-time). 100% of full-time faculty have terminal degrees. Graduate students teach a few undergraduate courses. Undergraduate student–faculty ratio: 13:1.

Student Life Student groups/activities include Student Art Education Association, Computer Art Club, 2-D Design Club.

Expenses for 2005–2006 Application fee: $35. State resident tuition: $7314 full-time. Nonresident tuition: $14,622 full-time. Mandatory fees: $1246 full-time. College room and board: $6434. College room only: $3934. Room and board charges vary according to board plan and housing facility. Special program-related fees: $5–$125 per course for lab fees.

Financial Aid Program-specific awards: 60 art scholarships for outstanding studio art majors ($500–$1000).

Application Procedures Students admitted directly into the professional program freshman year. Deadline for freshmen: March 25; transfers: July 11. Required: high school transcript, college transcript(s) for transfer students, minimum 2.0 high school GPA, portfolio, SAT I or ACT test scores. Recommended: interview.

Portfolio reviews held 5 times on campus; the submission of slides may be substituted for portfolios when distance is prohibitive.

Web Site http://www.bgsu.edu/departments/art

Undergraduate Contact Sue Weisshaar, Coordinator of Fine Arts Admissions, School of Art, Bowling Green State University, Bowling Green, Ohio 43403-0211; 419-372-0107, fax: 419-372-2544.

Graduate Contact Mille Guldbeck, Graduate Coordinator, School of Art, Bowling Green State University, Bowling Green, Ohio 43403-0211; 419-372-9319, fax: 419-372-2544.

Bradley University

Peoria, Illinois

Independent, coed. Urban campus. Total enrollment: 6,154.

Degrees Bachelor of Arts in the areas of studio art, art education, art history; Bachelor of Fine Arts in the area of studio art; Bachelor of Science in the areas of studio art, art education. Majors and concentrations: art education, art history, studio art. Graduate degrees offered: Master of Arts in the area of studio art; Master of Fine Arts in the area of studio art. Program accredited by NASAD.

Enrollment 225 total; 8 undergraduate, 10 graduate, 207 nonprofessional degree.

Art Student Profile 51% females, 49% males, 8% minorities, 3% international.

Art Faculty 10 total (full-time), 18 total (part-time). 100% of full-time faculty have terminal degrees. Graduate students teach a few undergraduate courses. Undergraduate student–faculty ratio: 11:1.

Student Life Student groups/activities include Spectrum, American Institute of Graphic Arts (AIGA), Potters Guild, Art History Club, National Art Education Association Students (NAEAS).

Expenses for 2005–2006 Application fee: $35. Comprehensive fee: $25,280 includes full-time tuition ($18,700), mandatory fees ($130), and college room and board ($6450). College room only: $3700. Full-time tuition and fees vary according to program. Room and board charges vary according to board plan. Special program-related fees: $25 per credit hour for supplies.

Visual *Arts*

Bradley University (continued)

Financial Aid Program-specific awards: 30 art scholarships for art majors ($1221).

Application Procedures Students apply for admission into the professional program by sophomore year. Deadline for freshmen and transfers: continuous. Required: high school transcript, college transcript(s) for transfer students, minimum 2.0 high school GPA, portfolio, SAT I or ACT test scores. Recommended: 2 letters of recommendation. Portfolio reviews held 3 times on campus; the submission of slides may be substituted for portfolios (slides preferred for scholarship decisions).

Web Site http://gcc.bradley.edu/art/

Undergraduate Contact Ms. Nickie Roberson, Director of Admissions, Office of Undergraduate Admissions, Bradley University, Swords Hall, Peoria, Illinois 61625; 800-447-6460, fax: 309-677-2797, e-mail address: admissions@bradley.edu

Graduate Contact Janet Lange, Executive Director of Graduate Enrollment Management, Graduate School, Bradley University, 1501 West Bradley Avenue, Peoria, Illinois 61625; 309-677-2375.

Brenau University

Gainesville, Georgia

Independent, Small town campus. Total enrollment: 743. Art program established 1973.

Degrees Bachelor of Fine Arts. Majors and concentrations: art education, arts management, ceramics, fashion merchandising, graphic design, interior design, painting/drawing, sculpture. Program accredited by FIDER.

Enrollment 110 total; all undergraduate.

Art Student Profile 78% females, 22% males, 19% minorities, 2% international.

Art Faculty 7 undergraduate (full-time), 8 undergraduate (part-time). 86% of full-time faculty have terminal degrees. Graduate students do not teach undergraduate courses. Undergraduate student–faculty ratio: 8:1.

Student Life Student groups/activities include American Society of Interior Designers, Fashion Merchandising Club, Kappa Pi Art Honorary Society.

Expenses for 2005–2006 Application fee: $35. Comprehensive fee: $24,990 includes full-time tuition ($16,440) and college room and board ($8550). Full-time tuition varies according to class time, location, and program. Room and board charges vary according to housing facility. Special program-related fees: $25–$90 per course for lab equipment fees.

Financial Aid Program-specific awards: 20 art scholarships for program majors ($1000–$5000).

Application Procedures Students admitted directly into the professional program freshman year. Deadline for freshmen and transfers: continuous. Required: high school transcript, college transcript(s) for transfer students, minimum 2.0 high school GPA, letter of recommendation, SAT I or ACT test scores (minimum combined SAT I score of 900, minimum composite ACT score of 19). Recommended: interview, portfolio. Portfolio reviews held 3 times on campus; the submission of slides may be substituted for portfolios if a campus visit is impossible.

Web Site http://www.brenau.edu/sfah/arts

Undergraduate Contact Christina White, Coordinator of Admission, Brenau University, 500 Washington Street, SE, Gainesville, Georgia 30501; 800-252-5119 ext. 5320, fax: 770-538-4306, e-mail address: cwhite@lib.brenau.edu

Brigham Young University

Provo, Utah

Independent, coed. Suburban campus. Total enrollment: 34,067. Art program established 1925.

Degrees Bachelor of Arts in the areas of art history, art education; Bachelor of Fine Arts in the areas of studio art, graphic design, photography, illustration, animation. Majors and concentrations: animation, art education, art history, ceramics, graphic design, illustration, painting/drawing, photography, printmaking, sculpture, studio art. Graduate degrees offered: Master of Fine Arts in the area of studio art. Program accredited by NASAD.

Enrollment 448 total; 403 undergraduate, 45 graduate.

Art Student Profile 58% females, 42% males.

Art Faculty 33 total (full-time), 30 total (part-time). 78% of full-time faculty have terminal degrees. Graduate students teach more than half of undergraduate courses.

Student Life Student groups/activities include Art History Student Association, National Art Education Association Student Chapter.

Expenses for 2005–2006 Application fee: $30. Comprehensive fee: $10,906 includes full-time tuition ($5116) and college room and board ($5790). Full-time tuition varies according to reciprocity agreements. Room and board charges vary according to board plan and housing facility. Special program-related fees: $200 per semester for supplies.

Financial Aid Program-specific awards: 150 talent awards for program majors ($200–$1000), 1–5 J. Roman Andrus Printmaking Award for printmaking majors ($200–$300), 5 Demery Scholarships for program majors ($200–$300), 5 Anna F. Sommers Scholarships for program majors ($200–$400), 25 Olena K. and George K. Lewis Scholarships for painting majors ($200–$400), 15 Betty M. and Paul J. Boshard Scholarships for program majors ($200–$300), 15 Cory Nathan Belleau Scholarships for program majors ($200–$700), 1–5 Max Dickson and Ruth Kimball Weaver Scholarship for ceramics majors ($200–$300).

Application Procedures Students apply for admission into the professional program by freshman, sophomore year. Deadline for freshmen: February 15; transfers: March 15. Notification date for freshmen: April 15; transfers: May 1. Required: essay, high school transcript, college transcript(s) for transfer students, minimum 3.0 high school GPA, letter of recommendation, portfolio, ACT test score only (minimum composite ACT score of 25), 10 pieces of best work, creative exercise. Portfolio reviews held 3 times on campus.

Web Site http://www.byu.edu/visualarts/home.html

Undergraduate Contact Aliesha Cook, Department Secretary, Department of Visual Arts, Brigham Young University, Provo, Utah 84602; 801-422-8773, fax: 801-422-0695, e-mail address: aliesha_cook@byu.edu

Graduate Contact Ms. Sharon Heelis, Secretary to Chair, Department of Visual Arts, Brigham Young University, E-509 HFAC, Provo, Utah 84602; 801-422-4429, fax: 801-422-0695, e-mail address: sharon_heelis@byu.edu

Brooklyn College of the City University of New York

Brooklyn, New York

State and locally supported, coed. Urban campus. Total enrollment: 15,281. Art program established 1967.

Degrees Bachelor of Fine Arts in the area of art. Majors and concentrations: computer art, painting/drawing, photography, printmaking, sculpture. Graduate degrees offered: Master of Arts in the area of art education (K-12); Master of Fine Arts in the area of art. Cross-registration with City University of New York System.

Enrollment 75 total; 20 undergraduate, 25 graduate, 30 nonprofessional degree.

Art Student Profile 55% females, 45% males, 25% minorities, 15% international.

Art Faculty 17 total (full-time), 9 total (part-time). 100% of full-time faculty have terminal degrees. Graduate students teach a few undergraduate courses. Undergraduate student–faculty ratio: 16:1.

Student Life Student groups/activities include Art Group, Graduate Art Student Union.

Expenses for 2006–2007 Application fee: $65. State resident tuition: $4000 full-time. Nonresident tuition: $8640 full-time. Mandatory fees: $375 full-time. Special program-related fees: $15–$20 per course for supplies and model fees.

Financial Aid Program-specific awards: 10–20 Charles G. Shaw Memorial Awards for studio art majors ($400–$1000), 2–3 Bernard Horlick Awards for program majors ($500–$750), 1–2 Jerome J. Viola Memorial Scholarships for program majors ($350–$500), 1–2 Bernard Cole Memorial Scholarships for photography majors ($150–$250), 1 Thomas S. Buechner Award for program majors ($500), 2 Diana and Lewis Sills Memorial Scholarships for program majors ($500).

Application Procedures Students apply for admission into the professional program by sophomore year. Deadline for freshmen and transfers: continuous. Notification date for freshmen and transfers: continuous. Required: high school transcript, college transcript(s) for

Brooklyn College of the City University of New York (continued)

transfer students, portfolio, minimum 2.8 high school GPA. Recommended: interview, SAT I or ACT test scores. Portfolio reviews held twice on campus; the submission of slides may be substituted for portfolios for large works of art.

Web Site http://depthome.brooklyn.cuny.edu/art/

Undergraduate Contact Prof. Michael Mallory, Chair, Department of Art, Brooklyn College of the City University of New York, 2900 Bedford Avenue, Brooklyn, New York 11210-2889; 718-951-5181, fax: 718-951-4728, e-mail address: mmallory@brooklyn.cuny.edu

Graduate Contact Prof. Jennifer McCoy, Deputy Chair, Department of Art, Brooklyn College of the City University of New York, 2900 Bedford Avenue, Brooklyn, New York 11210-2889; 718-951-5181, fax: 718-951-4728, e-mail address: artmfa@brooklyn.cuny.edu

Brooks Institute of Photography

Santa Barbara, California

Proprietary, coed. Suburban campus. Total enrollment: 1,507 (2003). Art program established 1945.

Caldwell College

Caldwell, New Jersey

Independent Roman Catholic, coed. Suburban campus. Total enrollment: 2,229. Art program established 1972.

California College of the Arts

San Francisco, California

Independent, coed. Urban campus. Total enrollment: 1,616. Art program established 1907.

Degrees Bachelor of Arts in the area of writing and literature; Bachelor of Architecture; Bachelor of Fine Arts in the areas of furniture, glass, ceramics, sculpture, painting, drawing,

printmaking, photography, textiles, jewelry/metal arts, graphic design, illustration, industrial design, fashion design, media arts, community arts, interior design, visual studies. Majors and concentrations: architecture, ceramic art and design, creative writing, fashion design, furniture design, glass, graphic design, illustration, industrial design, interior design, jewelry and metalsmithing, media arts, painting/drawing, photography, printmaking, public art studies, sculpture, textile arts, visual studies. Graduate degrees offered: Master of Arts in the areas of visual criticism, curatorial practice; Master of Architecture; Master of Fine Arts in the areas of design, writing, fine arts. Cross-registration with Mills College, Holy Names College. Program accredited by NAAB, NASAD, FIDER.

Enrollment 1,616 total; 1,312 undergraduate, 304 graduate.

Art Student Profile 59% females, 41% males, 23% minorities, 7% international.

Art Faculty 42 undergraduate (full-time), 328 undergraduate (part-time), 14 graduate (full-time), 119 graduate (part-time). 64% of full-time faculty have terminal degrees. Graduate students do not teach undergraduate courses. Undergraduate student–faculty ratio: 14:1.

Student Life Student groups/activities include American Institute of Graphic Arts, American Institute of Architects, American Society of Interior Designers. Special housing available for art students.

Expenses for 2005–2006 Application fee: $50. Comprehensive fee: $34,530 includes full-time tuition ($25,810), mandatory fees ($290), and college room and board ($8430). Full-time tuition and fees vary according to course load. Room and board charges vary according to housing facility. Special program-related fees: $50–$275 per year for lab fees, $60 for student activity fee, $230 per year for registration fee.

Financial Aid Program-specific awards: 118 Creative Achievement Awards for freshmen ($5175), 37 Faculty Honors Awards for transfer students ($5270), 948 CCA Scholarships for students demonstrating need ($6812), 165 named scholarships for those demonstrating need ($5005), 29 diversity scholarships for under-represented populations ($4068).

Application Procedures Students admitted directly into the professional program freshman

year. Deadline for freshmen and transfers: continuous. Required: essay, high school transcript, college transcript(s) for transfer students, minimum 2.0 high school GPA, 2 letters of recommendation, portfolio, minimum TOEFL score of 550 (paper-based) or 213 (computer-based) for international applicants. Recommended: interview, SAT I or ACT test scores. Portfolio reviews held continuously on campus and off campus at National Portfolio Days; the submission of slides may be substituted for portfolios (slides preferred).

Web Site http://www.cca.edu

Undergraduate Contact Ms. Robynne Royster, Director of Undergraduate Admission, California College of the Arts, 1111 Eighth Street, San Francisco, California 94107; 415-703-9532, fax: 415-703-9539, e-mail address: enroll@cca.edu

Graduate Contact Ms. Kathryn Ward, Assistant Director of Graduate Admission, California College of the Arts, 1111 Eighth Street, San Francisco, California 94107; 415-703-9593, fax: 415-703-9539, e-mail address: graduateprograms@cca.edu

More About the College

Founded in 1907, California College of the Arts (CCA) is the largest regionally accredited, independent school of art and design in the western United States. CCA offers twenty undergraduate majors in the areas of architecture, art, design, and

writing. In 2007, the College will introduce a new Bachelor of Fine Arts (B.F.A.) program in animation.

At CCA, students make art that makes a difference. CCA programs emphasize creative expression, self-discipline, intellectual and artistic exploration, and technical mastery. Students are encouraged to collaborate within and across disciplines. This interdisciplinary approach to art-making provides fertile ground for emerging sensibilities. CCA undergraduates regularly win major recognition in their fields; in 2005, twelve graphic design students had work in the *Graphis New Talent Design Annual*, and in 2006, products by industrial design students were shown at the Milan Furniture Fair.

In CCA's intimate private-college environment, students have the opportunity to work closely in the studio with well-known faculty members, find support for personal goals, and prepare for professional achievement. CCA has strong connections to the arts community and helps students make the transition from school to career through internships.

CCA's Bay Area location offers exceptional access to world-class museums, galleries, theaters, film festivals, and diverse exhibition and performance spaces. Visiting artists and scholars bring fresh perspectives to the campus through stimulating lectures and studio visits. A wide range of approaches ensures a lively exchange of ideas in an environment where excellence is the standard.

Undergraduates begin in a Core program, emphasizing skill building, experimentation, problem solving, and critical skills through exposure to a variety of media, processes, principles, and imaginative strategies. After the first year, students move into their selected programs for in-depth exploration of a discipline, while grounding that work in a larger context. Studio course work includes traditional and technology-based art-making techniques. CCA encourages students to find their own voices, explore various media, and consider how theory and practice converge.

Program Facilities The Oakland campus is home to the B.A. programs and first-year and fine arts studios, including the spacious Treadwell Ceramic Arts Center; Simpson Sculpture Studio (featuring one of the largest working college foundries); Blattner Print Studio; silkscreen, papermaking, and drawing/painting studios; and facilities for glass, jewelry/metal arts, textiles, and media arts (film/video production and an innovative hybrid lab for interactive media). In San Francisco, CCA's light-filled main building houses the Boyce Fashion Design Studio (facilities for cutting, draping, and sewing), Wornick Wood and Furniture Studios (bench room, machine

California College of the Arts (continued)

room, spray booth, upholstery shop), and spacious architecture and design studios. Both campuses offer computer labs and individual studio spaces. Facilities are open to students from 16 to 24 hours daily.

San Francisco campus galleries include the CCA Wattis Institute for Contemporary Arts, presenting international exhibitions, and PlaySpace, which is run by an interdisciplinary group of graduate students. On the Oakland campus, faculty and alumni shows appear at the Oliver Art Center.

Faculty, Resident Artists, and Alumni Faculty members' work is in the Museum of Modern Art, Whitney Museum, Smithsonian, and other major collections. Architecture and design faculty members are recognized internationally. Noted alumni include painters Raymond Saunders and Squeak Carnwath; ceramicists Robert Arneson and Peter Voulkos; filmmaker Wayne Wang; and designers Lucille Tenazas and Michael Vanderbyl. The Wattis Institute's Capp Street Project residency program brings acclaimed artists to campus each year. Visiting artists also teach in selected programs.

Student Exhibitions The undergraduate exhibition program presents shows throughout the year in galleries dedicated to student work, including the Isabelle Percy West Gallery, Irwin Student Center Gallery, and North/South Galleries in Oakland and Bruce Galleries in San Francisco. The annual Baccalaureate Exhibition is held in Oakland; the Graduate Exhibition is held in San Francisco.

Special Programs CCA students may enrich their studies through the AICAD mobility program (allowing study at another art college) or by cross registration at Mills College and Holy Names College in Oakland. Through study abroad, students can experience different ways of seeing, making, and communicating about art at top art schools in Canada, Mexico, Europe, and Asia. CCA also offers its own summer study-abroad courses.

A teaching concentration, open to students in all majors, satisfies prerequisites for application to postgraduate art teacher credential programs. Through the College's Center for Art and Public Life, students serve as teaching assistants in public schools, mentor young artists, participate in Alternative Spring Break, and create their own community art projects. Through internships, students gain practical experience and make professional connections while earning academic credit. Internship sites include design and architecture firms, galleries, museums, nonprofit organizations, publishing houses, and others. Internships are required for architecture, community arts, graphic design, and interior design students and are encouraged for all upper-division students.

California Institute of the Arts
Valencia, California

Independent, coed. Total enrollment: 1,327. Art program established 1971.

Degrees Bachelor of Fine Arts in the areas of art, graphic design, photography. Majors and concentrations: art/fine arts, graphic design, photography. Graduate degrees offered: Master of Fine Arts in the areas of art, graphic design, photography. Program accredited by NASAD.

Enrollment 289 total; 198 undergraduate, 91 graduate.

Art Student Profile 53% females, 47% males, 34% minorities, 4% international.

Art Faculty 30 total (full-time), 15 total (part-time). 90% of full-time faculty have terminal degrees. Graduate students do not teach undergraduate courses. Undergraduate student–faculty ratio: 8:1.

Student Life Student groups/activities include Community Arts Partnership (CAP), Integrated Media Program, interdisciplinary project. Special housing available for art students.

Expenses for 2005–2006 Application fee: $65. Comprehensive fee: $35,422 includes full-time tuition ($27,260), mandatory fees ($465), and college room and board ($7697). College room only: $4095. Full-time tuition and fees vary according to course load. Room and board charges vary according to board plan, housing facility, and location. Special program-related fees: $475 per year for technology fee.

Financial Aid Program-specific awards: 120 CalArts Scholarships for those demonstrating merit ($4000–$8000), 6 CalArts Minority Scholarships for minority students ($4000–$8000).

Application Procedures Students admitted directly into the professional program freshman year. Deadline for freshmen and transfers: January 5. Required: essay, high school transcript, college transcript(s) for transfer students, portfolio, personal statement. Recommended: 2 letters of recommendation, video (if applicable). Portfolio reviews held continuously on campus and off campus at National

Portfolio Days; the submission of slides may be substituted for portfolios (slides preferred).

Web Site http://www.calarts.edu

Contact Ms. Taryn Wolf, Assistant Director of Admissions, California Institute of the Arts, 24700 McBean Parkway, Valencia, California 91355; 661-255-1050, fax: 661-253-7710, e-mail address: twolf@calarts.edu

More About the Institute

The School of Art at California Institute of the Arts (CalArts) offers undergraduate and graduate programs in the areas of art, graphic design, and photography and media. The undergraduate programs lead to a Bachelor of Fine Arts (B.F.A.) degree and the graduate programs to a Master of Fine Arts (M.F.A.) degree.

Faculty, Resident Artists, and Alumni The School's faculty is made up of innovators and leaders in contemporary art practice. Since all faculty members are working artists with an abundance of real-world experience, they prepare students for the creative and professional demands of contemporary art and design.

A faculty mentor serves as each student's artistic and academic adviser, guiding them through the program and assisting the student in customizing a curriculum to fit their personal interests and artistic goals. The School of Art regularly invites a wide range of visiting artists, designers, photographers, performers, writers, and theorists to share their experience and vision with students to supplement the expertise of the faculty members. The School of Art alumni are prominent in the art and design communities at the local, national, and international levels, and can often be found on faculty rosters of some of the most esteemed colleges.

Programs of Study Encompassing both studio practice and theory, The Program in Art offers instruction in a wide range of media, including painting, drawing, printmaking, photography, digital imaging, sculpture, installation, video, film, writing, and performance. The program does not require students to concentrate on a particular medium; instead, it relies on a flexible structure of individualized instruction and mentoring to emphasize the articulation of ideas.

The four-year B.F.A. curriculum begins with a selection of foundation course options, along with critical studies, where students investigate various media, art-historical traditions, and theoretical positions. Additional course work includes a combination of seminars, group critique classes, technical work-

shops, and independent studies. By the third year in residence, undergraduates are expected to pursue independent projects.

The Program in Graphic Design prepares students for a wide range of professional options—from Web design and motion graphics to editorial design and environmental graphics, from film title and broadcast design to exhibitions and careers in education. The program emphasizes both practical and conceptual skills and enables each designer to integrate a command of visual language with imagination, theory, and new technology. The highly structured B.F.A. curriculum begins with courses covering basic design principles, imagemaking, typography, history, and theory.

The Program in Photography and Media is committed to educating independent artists in a world where photographic imagery and new media representations and strategies are omnipresent. The program encourages debate and experimentation, and students are encouraged to challenge conventions in a genre that includes many new practices.

The B.F.A. curriculum begins with a year of intensive photographic foundation work, followed by a mixture of courses that includes classes on specific issues in photography, video and Internet practice, the histories of photography and film, media theories and semiotics, as well as critique classes, technical workshops, and independent studies. Students are welcome to work in darkroom photography, digital-and/or time-based formats, and beyond.

Program Facilities The MacLab is used for creating digital and print-based work, including drawing, painting, photo manipulation, editorial design, type design, 3-D rendering, motion graphics, sound design and Web, and CD and DVD authoring.

The Photography and Media Lab includes high-capacity black-and-white and color processors, a 16-inch capacity Cibachrome color processor, black-and-white printing bays, and individual color darkrooms, including an 8-by-10 inch color mural enlarger. The digital photography and video lab is equipped with 4 Final Cut Pro Stations, digital imaging software, a negative scanner, and two large Epson digital photographic printers.

The Print and Media Lab is used for producing multiples through silk-screening, etching, lithography, or letterpress. It contains light tables, work tables, paper cutters, an exposure unit, various presses, and a digital imaging lab with a large output capacity printer and a vinyl cutter.

The Super Shop is the Institute's main sculpture studio and features work areas and equipment for

Visual Arts

California Institute of the Arts (continued)

woodworking, metalworking, machining, sandblasting, spraying, and mold making.

The Video Lab offers an assortment of high-quality equipment for time-based media production and post-production, as well as facilities for classroom instruction and student use. Digital video and Hi-8 cameras, tripods, microphones, lighting kits, mini-disc sound recorders, and other production equipment are available for checkout.

Undergraduates in the Programs in Art and Photography and Media share studios, while most upper-level undergraduates work in individual studios. Graphic design students have individual workspace cubicles in larger studios that have adjoining critique rooms.

Student Performance/Exhibit Opportunities

School of Art students exhibit their work in seven on-campus galleries, and in various unconventional or informal settings around campus. First- and second-year undergraduates participate in several group shows, while upper-level undergraduates are required to mount solo exhibitions. Shows are often accompanied by opening receptions and parties, which are organized by students and open to the public as well as the CalArts community.

California Institute of the Arts

Valencia, California

Independent, coed. Total enrollment: 1,327. Art program established 1961.

Degrees Bachelor of Fine Arts in the areas of character animation, experimental animation, film/video. Majors and concentrations: animation, film and video production. Graduate degrees offered: Master of Fine Arts in the areas of experimental animation, film/video, film directing.

Enrollment 365 total; 239 undergraduate, 126 graduate.

Art Student Profile 34% females, 66% males, 33% minorities, 21% international.

Art Faculty 31 total (full-time), 40 total (part-time). 80% of full-time faculty have terminal degrees. Graduate students do not teach undergraduate courses. Undergraduate student–faculty ratio: 6:1.

Student Life Student groups/activities include Community Arts Partnership. Special housing available for art students.

Expenses for 2005–2006 Application fee: $65. Comprehensive fee: $35,422 includes full-time tuition ($27,260), mandatory fees ($465), and college room and board ($7697). College room only: $4095. Full-time tuition and fees vary according to course load. Room and board charges vary according to board plan, housing facility, and location. Special program-related fees: $475 per year for technology fee.

Financial Aid Program-specific awards: CalArts Scholarships for students demonstrating talent and need ($1000–$10,000).

Application Procedures Students admitted directly into the professional program freshman year. Deadline for freshmen and transfers: January 6. Required: essay, high school transcript, college transcript(s) for transfer students, 2 letters of recommendation, portfolio. Portfolio reviews held at National Portfolio Days.

Web Site http://www.calarts.edu

Contact Libby Hux, Admissions Counselor, California Institute of the Arts, 24700 McBean Parkway, Valencia, California 91355; 661-255-1050 ext. 7884, fax: 661-253-7710, e-mail address: lhux@calarts.edu

California State University, Chico

Chico, California

State-supported, coed. Small town campus. Total enrollment: 15,919.

Degrees Bachelor of Fine Arts in the areas of studio art, interior design, electronic arts. Majors and concentrations: ceramic art and design, electronic arts, glass, interior design, painting/drawing, printmaking, sculpture, weaving and fibers. Graduate degrees offered: Master of Fine Arts in the area of studio art. Cross-registration with California State University System. Program accredited by NASAD.

Enrollment 399 total; 25 undergraduate, 9 graduate, 365 nonprofessional degree.

Art Faculty 20 undergraduate (full-time), 7 undergraduate (part-time). 100% of full-time faculty have terminal degrees. Graduate students teach a few undergraduate courses. Undergraduate student–faculty ratio: 19:1.

Student Life Student groups/activities include General Student Art Club, Ceramics Student Art Club, Glass Art Club.

Expenses for 2005–2006 Application fee: $55. State resident tuition: $0 full-time. Nonresident tuition: $12,690 full-time. Mandatory fees: $3370 full-time. College room and board: $7993. College room only: $5550. Room and board charges vary according to board plan and housing facility. Special program-related fees: $10–$100 per course for materials fee.

Financial Aid Program-specific awards: academic and performance awards for incoming freshmen.

Application Procedures Students apply for admission into the professional program by junior year. Deadline for freshmen: November 30. Notification date for freshmen: continuous. Required: high school transcript, college transcript(s) for transfer students, minimum 3.0 high school GPA, 2 letters of recommendation, portfolio, SAT I or ACT test scores, minimum 3.0 college GPA in art for entry into BFA program. Portfolio reviews held twice on campus; the submission of slides may be substituted for portfolios whenever necessary.

Web Site http://www.csuchico.edu

Undergraduate Contact Mr. Tom Patton, Chairman, Department of Art and Art History, California State University, Chico, Chico, California 95929-0820; 530-898-5331, e-mail address: tpatton@csuchico.edu

Graduate Contact Michael Bishop, Professor, Department of Art and Art History, California State University, Chico, Chico, California 95929-0820; 530-898-5331, e-mail address: mbishop@csuchico.edu

California State University, Fullerton

Fullerton, California

State-supported, coed. Urban campus. Total enrollment: 35,040. Art program established 1962.

Degrees Bachelor of Fine Arts in the areas of entertainment art/animation, drawing/painting, printmaking, sculpture, crafts, ceramics and glass, graphic design, illustration, creative photography. Majors and concentrations: ceramics, crafts, entertainment art/animation, glass, graphic design, illustration, jewelry and metalsmithing, painting/drawing, photography, printmaking, sculpture. Graduate degrees offered: Master of Arts in the areas of drawing/painting, printmaking, sculpture, ceramics and glass, graphic design, creative photography, illustration, jewelry and metalsmithing, exhibition design, art history, crafts; Master of Fine Arts in the areas of drawing/painting, printmaking, sculpture, ceramics and glass, crafts, graphic design, creative photography, illustration, jewelry and metalsmithing, exhibition design. Cross-registration with California State University System. Program accredited by NASAD.

Enrollment 1,559 total; 1,448 undergraduate, 111 graduate.

Art Student Profile 57% females, 43% males, 34% minorities, 5% international.

Art Faculty 32 total (full-time), 66 total (part-time). 76% of full-time faculty have terminal degrees. Graduate students teach a few undergraduate courses. Undergraduate student–faculty ratio: 19:1.

Student Life Student groups/activities include Pencil Mileage Club, The Art Network, Graphic Design Club. Special housing available for art students.

Expenses for 2005–2006 Application fee: $55. State resident tuition: $0 full-time. Nonresident tuition: $10,170 full-time. Mandatory fees: $2990 full-time. Full-time tuition and fees vary according to course load. College room only: $4504. Special program-related fees: $10 per course for ceramic glaze fee, $10–$16 per course for lab fees.

Financial Aid Program-specific awards: 2 Mert Purkiss Awards for incoming freshmen ($1000), 2–4 Florence Arnold Awards for continuing students ($500), 1–3 John Olson Awards for design/crafts majors ($700), 2–3 Tribute Fund Awards for transfer students ($750), 1 California China Painters Association Award for traditional/descriptive art majors ($1000), 2 Costa Mesa Art League Awards for juniors or seniors ($500), 1 Jeff and Rosalie Bacon Award for incoming students ($2000), 2 Orange County Fine Arts Awards for new and continuing students ($500), 2 Art Alliance Scholarships for transfer students from community colleges ($1000).

California State University, Fullerton (continued)

Application Procedures Students apply for admission into the professional program by sophomore year. Deadline for freshmen and transfers: continuous. Required: high school transcript, college transcript(s) for transfer students, minimum 2.0 high school GPA, SAT I test score only.

Web Site http://www.art.fullerton.edu/

Undergraduate Contact Ms. Heather D. Guzman, Undergraduate Secretary, Department of Visual Arts, California State University, Fullerton, PO Box 6850, Fullerton, California 92834-6850; 714-278-3471, fax: 714-278-2390.

Graduate Contact Ms. Jackie Reynolds, Graduate Secretary, Department of Visual Arts, California State University, Fullerton, PO Box 6850, Fullerton, California 92834-6850; 714-278-3471, fax: 714-278-2390.

California State University, Long Beach

Long Beach, California

State-supported, coed. Suburban campus. Total unit enrollment: 34,547. Art program established 1949.

Degrees Bachelor of Fine Arts in the area of art. Majors and concentrations: art education, art history, ceramics, fibers, graphic arts, illustration, intermedia, jewelry and metalsmithing, museum studies, painting/drawing, photography, printmaking, sculpture, wood. Graduate degrees offered: Master of Fine Arts in the area of art. Cross-registration with California State University System. Program accredited by NASAD.

Enrollment 2,050 total; 300 undergraduate, 150 graduate, 1,600 nonprofessional degree.

Art Student Profile 55% females, 45% males, 55% minorities, 10% international.

Art Faculty 40 total (full-time), 59 total (part-time). 95% of full-time faculty have terminal degrees. Graduate students teach a few undergraduate courses. Undergraduate student–faculty ratio: 15:1.

Student Life Student groups/activities include Student Art Association.

Expenses for 2006–2007 Application fee: $55. State resident tuition: $0 full-time. Nonresi-

dent tuition: $10,170 full-time. Mandatory fees: $2864 full-time. College room and board: $6648. Special program-related fees: $58 per class for model fees.

Financial Aid Program-specific awards: 40 art scholarships for program majors ($1500).

Application Procedures Students apply for admission into the professional program by sophomore, junior year. Deadline for freshmen and transfers: November 30. Required: high school transcript, college transcript(s) for transfer students, SAT I or ACT test scores, minimum 2.75 GPA on initial 56 units at undergraduate level. Recommended: portfolio. Portfolio reviews held twice and as needed on campus; the submission of slides may be substituted for portfolios for out-of-state applicants.

Web Site http://www.csulb.edu

Undergraduate Contact Mr. John Snidecor, Undergraduate Advisor, Department of Art, California State University, Long Beach, 1250 Bellflower Boulevard, Long Beach, California 90840-0119; 562-985-4376, fax: 562-985-1885.

Graduate Contact Mr. Jay Kvapil, Graduate Advisor, Department of Art, California State University, Long Beach, 1250 Bellflower Boulevard, Long Beach, California 90840-0119; 562-985-4376, fax: 562-985-1885.

Capital University

Columbus, Ohio

Independent, coed. Suburban campus. Total enrollment: 3,901.

Degrees Bachelor of Fine Arts. Majors and concentrations: art education, art therapy. Cross-registration with Higher Education Council of Columbus .

Enrollment 62 total; all undergraduate.

Art Faculty 3 undergraduate (full-time), 4 undergraduate (part-time). 100% of full-time faculty have terminal degrees. Graduate students do not teach undergraduate courses. Undergraduate student–faculty ratio: 9:1.

Student Life Student groups/activities include Capital University Student Art Therapy Association, Phi Beta.

Expenses for 2005–2006 Application fee: $25. Comprehensive fee: $30,444 includes full-time tuition ($24,100) and college room and board

($6344). Full-time tuition varies according to course load, degree level, program, and student level. Room and board charges vary according to board plan and housing facility.

Financial Aid Program-specific awards: Special Talent Awards for students who participate in Ohio Governor's Youth Art Exhibit ($1000).

Application Procedures Students admitted directly into the professional program freshman year. Deadline for freshmen and transfers: continuous. Required: high school transcript, college transcript(s) for transfer students, letter of recommendation, SAT I or ACT test scores (minimum combined SAT I score of 900, minimum composite ACT score of 18), minimum 2.6 high school GPA, minimum 2.25 cumulative college GPA for transfer students, college report form for transfer students. Recommended: interview, portfolio. Portfolio reviews held as needed on campus; the submission of slides may be substituted for portfolios for large works of art.

Web Site http://www.capital.edu

Undergraduate Contact Ms. Lisa McKitrick, Associate Director of Admission, Capital University, 1 College and Main, Columbus, Ohio 43209; 614-236-6101, fax: 614-236-6926, e-mail address: admissions@capital.edu

Cardinal Stritch University

Milwaukee, Wisconsin

Independent Roman Catholic, coed. Suburban campus. Total enrollment: 6,785.

Carnegie Mellon University

Pittsburgh, Pennsylvania

Independent, coed. Urban campus. Total enrollment: 10,017. Art program established 1910.

Degrees Bachelor of Fine Arts. Majors and concentrations: art. Graduate degrees offered: Master of Fine Arts in the area of art. Cross-registration with Chatham College, University of Pittsburgh, Duquesne University, Carlow College, Point Park College, Robert Morris College, Community College of Allegheny County, Pittsburgh Theological Seminary, LaRoche College. Program accredited by NASAD.

Enrollment 198 total; 180 undergraduate, 18 graduate.

Art Student Profile 60% females, 40% males, 34% minorities, 9% international.

Art Faculty 9 undergraduate (part-time), 22 total (full-time). 100% of full-time faculty have terminal degrees. Graduate students do not teach undergraduate courses. Undergraduate student–faculty ratio: 8:1.

Student Life Student groups/activities include weekly exhibitions, student-managed gallery exhibitions, Surg (undergraduate research grant projects).

Expenses for 2006–2007 Application fee: $60. Comprehensive fee: $43,858 includes full-time tuition ($34,180), mandatory fees ($398), and college room and board ($9280). College room only: $5440. Special program-related fees: $20–$215 per 10 units for materials fees for various courses.

Financial Aid Program-specific awards: Jacques and Natasha Gelman Scholarships, Scholastic Art Awards, Ethel Murdock Kirk Awards, Eleanor Zygler Awards for junior and senior painting majors.

Application Procedures Students admitted directly into the professional program freshman year. Deadline for freshmen: October 1; transfers: December 1. Notification date for freshmen: continuous; transfers: April 15. Required: essay, high school transcript, college transcript(s) for transfer students, 3 letters of recommendation, portfolio, SAT I or ACT test scores. Recommended: minimum 3.0 high school GPA, interview. Portfolio reviews held 11 times on campus and off campus at National Portfolio Day Associations locations; the submission of slides may be substituted for portfolios.

Web Site http://artserver.cfa.cmu.edu

Undergraduate Contact Michael Steidel, Director of Admission, Warner Hall 212, Carnegie Mellon University, 5000 Forbes Avenue, Pittsburgh, Pennsylvania 15213-3890; 412-268-2082.

Graduate Contact Ms. Cynthia Lammert, Facilities and Project Manager, School of Art, Carnegie Mellon University, College of Fine Arts Building, Room 300, 5000 Forbes Avenue,

Carnegie Mellon University (continued)

Pittsburgh, Pennsylvania 15213-3890; 412-268-6707, fax: 412-268-7817, e-mail address: cl2w@andrew.cmu.edu

Cazenovia College

Cazenovia, New York

Independent, coed. Small town campus. Total enrollment: 1,124. Art program established 1982.

Degrees Bachelor of Fine Arts in the areas of interior design, studio art, visual communications. Majors and concentrations: fashion design, interior design, photography, studio art, visual communication.

Enrollment 261 total; all undergraduate.

Art Student Profile 79% females, 21% males, 7% minorities, 1% international.

Art Faculty 13 undergraduate (full-time), 20 undergraduate (part-time). 79% of full-time faculty have terminal degrees. Graduate students do not teach undergraduate courses. Undergraduate student–faculty ratio: 13:1.

Student Life Student groups/activities include Art Club, Fashion Design Club, New York State Eleven Albany Conference (Interior Design).

Expenses for 2005–2006 Application fee: $30. Comprehensive fee: $26,450 includes full-time tuition ($18,940) and college room and board ($7510). College room only: $4200. Full-time tuition varies according to course load. Room and board charges vary according to board plan. Special program-related fees: $75 per semester for required fee.

Financial Aid Program-specific awards: merit scholarships for art majors ($500), 1 Lettergraphics Scholarship for advertising designers ($1000), 1 Morgan Scholarship for interior designers ($500).

Application Procedures Students admitted directly into the professional program freshman year. Deadline for freshmen and transfers: August 25. Notification date for freshmen and transfers: November 1. Required: high school transcript, college transcript(s) for transfer students, minimum 2.0 high school GPA. Recommended: essay, minimum 3.0 high school GPA, 2 letters of recommendation, portfolio, SAT I or ACT test scores. Portfolio reviews held as needed on campus and off campus in Lake Placid, NY and at least one other location; the submission of slides may be substituted for portfolios when distance is prohibitive or if scheduling is difficult.

Web Site http://www.cazenovia.edu

Undergraduate Contact Robert Croot, Dean for Enrollment Management, Admissions and Financial Aid, Cazenovia College, 13 Nickerson Street, Cazenovia, New York 13035; 315-655-7208, fax: 315-655-4486, e-mail address: rcroot@cazenovia.edu

Centenary College

Hackettstown, New Jersey

Independent, coed. Suburban campus. Total enrollment: 2,472.

Degrees Bachelor of Fine Arts. Majors and concentrations: art and design, fashion design, graphic design, multimedia.

Enrollment 113 total; all undergraduate.

Art Student Profile 80% females, 20% males, 15% minorities, 3% international.

Art Faculty 5 undergraduate (full-time), 7 undergraduate (part-time). 67% of full-time faculty have terminal degrees. Graduate students do not teach undergraduate courses. Undergraduate student–faculty ratio: 13:1.

Student Life Student groups/activities include Art Guild, Performing Arts Guild.

Expenses for 2005–2006 Application fee: $30. Comprehensive fee: $28,770 includes full-time tuition ($19,840), mandatory fees ($1030), and college room and board ($7900). Full-time tuition and fees vary according to location and program.

Application Procedures Students admitted directly into the professional program freshman year. Deadline for freshmen and transfers: continuous. Notification date for freshmen and transfers: continuous. Required: essay, high school transcript, college transcript(s) for transfer students, portfolio, SAT I or ACT test scores (minimum combined SAT I score of 850, minimum composite ACT score of 18), TOEFL for international students. Recommended: minimum 2.0 high school GPA, 2 letters of recommendation, interview. Portfolio reviews held as needed on campus; the submission of slides may be substituted for portfolios when distance is prohibitive.

Web Site http://www.centenarycollege.edu

Undergraduate Contact Diane Finnan, Vice President for Enrollment Management, Admissions Office, Centenary College, 400 Jefferson Street, Hackettstown, New Jersey 07840; 800-236-8679 ext. 2217, fax: 908-852-3454, e-mail address: finnan@centenarycollege.edu

Central Michigan University

Mount Pleasant, Michigan

State-supported, coed. Small town campus. Total enrollment: 27,221. Art program established 1971.

Degrees Bachelor of Fine Arts in the areas of two-dimensional studies, three-dimensional studies, graphic design. Majors and concentrations: art education, ceramics, fibers, graphic design, painting/drawing, photography, printmaking, sculpture. Graduate degrees offered: Master of Arts in the area of studio art; Master of Fine Arts in the area of studio art.

Enrollment 351 total; 35 undergraduate, 9 graduate, 307 nonprofessional degree.

Art Student Profile 60% females, 40% males, 3% minorities, 2% international.

Art Faculty 17 total (full-time), 15 total (part-time). 100% of full-time faculty have terminal degrees. Graduate students teach a few undergraduate courses. Undergraduate student–faculty ratio: 20:1.

Student Life Student groups/activities include Photography Club, Students in Design, Student Art League.

Expenses for 2005–2006 Application fee: $35. State resident tuition: $5868 full-time. Nonresident tuition: $13,632 full-time. Full-time tuition varies according to student level. College room and board: $6376. College room only: $3188. Room and board charges vary according to board plan, housing facility, and location. Special program-related fees: $15–$35 per course for supplies.

Financial Aid Program-specific awards: 4 art scholarships for art majors ($1000), 4 scholarships for Native American art students ($2000).

Application Procedures Students apply for admission into the professional program by sophomore year. Deadline for freshmen and transfers: continuous. Required: high school

transcript, college transcript(s) for transfer students, SAT I or ACT test scores, portfolio and artist's statement for entry into BFA program, portfolio and test for entry BFA in graphic design. Portfolio reviews held twice on campus.

Web Site http://www.ccfa.cmich.edu/

Contact Mr. David Stairs, Chair, Art Department, Central Michigan University, 132 Wightman Hall, Mount Pleasant, Michigan 48859; 989-774-3025, fax: 989-774-2278.

Central Missouri State University

Warrensburg, Missouri

State-supported, coed. Small town campus. Total enrollment: 10,604. Art program established 1871.

Degrees Bachelor of Fine Arts in the areas of commercial art, interior design, studio art; Bachelor of Science in Education in the area of art education. Majors and concentrations: art education, commercial art, graphic design, illustration, interior design, studio art. Program accredited by NASAD.

Enrollment 480 total; all undergraduate.

Art Student Profile 55% females, 45% males, 5% minorities, 5% international.

Art Faculty 14 undergraduate (full-time), 10 undergraduate (part-time). 100% of full-time faculty have terminal degrees. Graduate students do not teach undergraduate courses. Undergraduate student–faculty ratio: 20:1.

Student Life Special housing available for art students.

Expenses for 2006–2007 Application fee: $30. State resident tuition: $5835 full-time. Nonresident tuition: $11,250 full-time. College room and board: $5109. College room only: $3406. Special program-related fees: $5–$45 per course for expendable supplies (when applicable).

Financial Aid Program-specific awards: 20–30 art achievement awards for incoming freshmen ($200–$1000).

Application Procedures Students admitted directly into the professional program freshman year. Deadline for freshmen and transfers: continuous. Required: high school transcript, college transcript(s) for transfer students, ACT

Central Missouri State University (continued)

test score only (minimum composite ACT score of 20). Recommended: standing in top 67% of graduating class, completion of high school core curriculum.

Web Site http://www.cmsu.edu

Undergraduate Contact Mr. Paul Orscheln, Director of Admissions, Central Missouri State University, WDE 1422, Warrensburg, Missouri 64093; 660-543-4290, fax: 660-543-8517.

Central State University
Wilberforce, Ohio

State-supported, coed. Rural campus. Total enrollment: 1,623.

Chowan University
Murfreesboro, North Carolina

Clarion University of Pennsylvania
Clarion, Pennsylvania

State-supported, coed. Rural campus. Total enrollment: 6,338. Art program established 1980.

Clarke College
Dubuque, Iowa

Independent Roman Catholic, coed. Urban campus. Total enrollment: 1,246. Art program established 1843.

Degrees Bachelor of Fine Arts in the areas of studio art, graphic design. Majors and concentrations: art history, ceramics, drawing, graphic design, painting, printmaking, sculpture. Cross-registration with Loras College, University of Dubuque.

Enrollment 60 total; 35 undergraduate, 25 nonprofessional degree.

Art Student Profile 65% females, 35% males, 3% minorities, 3% international.

Art Faculty 5 undergraduate (full-time), 2 undergraduate (part-time). 80% of full-time

faculty have terminal degrees. Graduate students do not teach undergraduate courses. Undergraduate student–faculty ratio: 12:1.

Expenses for 2005–2006 Application fee: $25. Comprehensive fee: $25,390 includes full-time tuition ($18,360), mandatory fees ($585), and college room and board ($6445). College room only: $3135. Full-time tuition and fees vary according to class time. Room and board charges vary according to board plan and housing facility. Special program-related fees: $20–$50 per course for lab fees.

Financial Aid Program-specific awards: 12–15 art scholarships for art students (renewable) ($1000–$3000).

Application Procedures Students apply for admission into the professional program by sophomore year. Deadline for freshmen and transfers: continuous. Required: high school transcript, college transcript(s) for transfer students, minimum 2.0 high school GPA, letter of recommendation, portfolio, SAT I or ACT test scores (minimum combined SAT I score of 1015, minimum composite ACT score of 21). Recommended: essay, interview. Portfolio reviews held by appointment from January to April on campus and off campus in Chicago, IL; St. Louis, MO; Minneapolis, MN; the submission of slides may be substituted for portfolios when distance is prohibitive.

Web Site http://www.clarke.edu

Undergraduate Contact Sharon Lyons, Director, Office of Admissions, Clarke College, 1550 Clarke Avenue, Dubuque, Iowa 52001; 563-588-6366, fax: 563-588-6789, e-mail address: slyons@clarke.edu

The Cleveland Institute of Art
Cleveland, Ohio

Independent, coed. Urban campus. Total enrollment: 610. Art program established 1882.

Degrees Bachelor of Fine Arts. Majors and concentrations: ceramics, digital art, drawing, enameling, fibers, glass, graphic design, illustration, industrial design, interior design, medical illustration, metals, painting, photography, printmaking, sculpture. Graduate degrees offered: Master of Fine Arts in the area of medical illustration and digital arts. Cross-registration with members of the Northeast Ohio Council on Higher Education. Program accredited by NASAD.

Enrollment 548 total; 536 undergraduate, 8 graduate, 4 nonprofessional degree.

Art Student Profile 52% females, 48% males, 11% minorities, 3% international.

Art Faculty 47 undergraduate (full-time), 54 undergraduate (part-time). 80% of full-time faculty have terminal degrees. Graduate students do not teach undergraduate courses. Undergraduate student–faculty ratio: 8:1.

Student Life Student groups/activities include Industrial Design Society of America. Special housing available for art students.

Expenses for 2005–2006 Application fee: $30. Comprehensive fee: $36,313 includes full-time tuition ($24,917), mandatory fees ($2260), and college room and board ($9136). College room only: $5480. Room and board charges vary according to board plan and housing facility. Special program-related fees: $40 per credit hour for lab fees (under 12 credit hours), $50 per credit hour for technology fee (under 12 credit hours), $275–$525 per semester for technology fee (depending on major), $275 per semester for lab fees (12-15 credit hours).

Financial Aid Program-specific awards: portfolio scholarships and grants for freshmen ($4000–$19,745), 100 portfolio grants ($2000–$5000), 18 transfer portfolio grants for transfer students ($2000–$5000).

Application Procedures Students admitted directly into the professional program freshman year. Deadline for freshmen and transfers: continuous. Required: essay, high school transcript, college transcript(s) for transfer students, minimum 2.0 high school GPA, 2 letters of recommendation, SAT I or ACT test scores, slides or CD of portfolio. Recommended: interview. Portfolio reviews held bi-monthly on campus.

Web Site http://www.cia.edu

Undergraduate Contact Ms. Catherine Redhead, Director of Admissions, The Cleveland Institute of Art, 11141 East Boulevard, Cleveland, Ohio 44106; 216-421-7422, fax: 216-754-3634, e-mail address: credhead@cia.edu

Graduate Contact Dr. Gary Sampson, Director of Graduate Studies, The Cleveland Institute of Art, 11141 East Boulevard, Cleveland, Ohio 44106; 216-421-7369, fax: 216-421-7438, e-mail address: gsampson@cia.edu

More About the Institute

The Cleveland Institute of Art (CIA) offers one of America's most comprehensive educational programs in the visual arts.

Drawing, color, design, art history, literature, and digital art classes make up the core curriculum of the Foundation. Both traditional and conceptual approaches to drawing and painting are emphasized. Composition, design theory, and the organization of 2-D and 3-D space are the focus of design classes. Art history includes the Paleolithic era through contemporary works of the late twentieth to early twenty-first centuries, which are discussed in the last semester of study. The contemporary writings of each era are studied in the literature classes, which encompass composition and critical analysis of those works. Digital art courses are required and serve as an introduction to both the Macintosh platform and the use of graphics software as a tool for art and design. Foundation students may take open studio electives. Majors offer elective classes that help students make informed decisions, based on experience, regarding which major they wish to study during the later years of their education.

The Cleveland Institute of Art (continued)

Each major at CIA is categorized into one of three environments—visual art and technology, design and material culture, or integrated media. Cross-discipline study is an integral part of the curriculum. Regardless of their major, all students take courses outside their discipline, and everyone graduates with a Bachelor of Fine Arts (B.F.A.) degree.

Liberal arts electives continue to play an important role in a student's development as a professional artist during the later years of study. An array of subjects in the humanities and social sciences are offered each term. The structure of the program ensures a broad distribution by requiring students to pursue advanced studies across six areas.

The culmination point of the program is the B.F.A. thesis exhibition and review. During this requirement for graduation, the candidates present their work throughout the school and receive formal critique by peers and faculty members. Much of the final year is spent independently preparing for this review, much the same way that one would prepare work for an agency or develop a body of work for a gallery show.

Program Facilities Individual studio spaces are provided for all majors. The facilities at the Cleveland Institute of Art include big, bright, professional art and design studios. Available to students are high-output printers; woodshops; darkrooms; a foundry; Macintosh, Silicon Graphics, and IBM computer labs; printmaking equipment; glass furnaces; metal lathes; milling machines; kilns; critique spaces; and the Jessica Gund Memorial Library.

Faculty, Resident Artists, and Alumni Studio faculty members are practicing artists and designers. Their work can be found in national and international, public and private collections, including the Hirshhorn Museum; the Corcoran Gallery; the Library of Congress; the Smithsonian Institution of Washington, D.C.; the Metropolitan Museum of Art; the Museum of Modern Photography in New York City; the Cleveland Museum of Art; and the Victoria and Albert Museum in London. Liberal arts faculty members are historians, poets, and researchers. The Visiting Artist program offers learning through the firsthand experiences of prominent artists. Alumni work in a variety of art fields at distinguished institutions and industry leaders, including Fisher Price, General Electric, Disney, Yale University, Rubbermaid, Mattel, the Metropolitan Museum of Art, General Motors, and American Greetings.

Student Performance and Exhibit Opportunities The Cleveland Institute of Art offers generous student gallery space, library gallery space, the annual Student Independent Exhibition, and various local restaurants, coffeehouses, and galleries.

Special Programs Students attending the Cleveland Institute of Art have the opportunity to participate in the New York Studio program, extensive internship opportunities, cross-registration with other colleges and universities, intensive summer workshops, and liberal arts tutoring. Biomedical art students work with the medical and dental schools of Case Western Reserve University, University Hospitals, and the Cleveland Clinic Foundation. A wide range of study-abroad opportunities are available.

College for Creative Studies

Detroit, Michigan

Independent, coed. Urban campus. Total enrollment: 1,291. Art program established 1906.

Degrees Bachelor of Fine Arts in the areas of fine arts, crafts, photography, communication design/illustration, industrial design, interior design, animation/digital media. Majors and concentrations: advertising design, animation, art/fine arts, ceramic art and design, crafts, furniture design, glass, graphic design, illustration, industrial design, interior design, jewelry and metalsmithing, painting/drawing, photography, printmaking, product design, sculpture, studio art, textile arts, transportation design. Cross-registration with Association of Independent Colleges of Art and Design. Program accredited by NASAD.

Enrollment 1,265 total; all undergraduate.

Art Student Profile 41% females, 59% males, 11% minorities, 6% international.

Art Faculty 43 undergraduate (full-time), 183 undergraduate (part-time). Graduate students do not teach undergraduate courses. Undergraduate student–faculty ratio: 10:1.

Student Life Student groups/activities include Student Government, Black Artists Researching Trends, Industrial Design Society of America. Special housing available for art students.

Expenses for 2006–2007 Application fee: $35. Tuition: $23,490 full-time. Mandatory fees: $1145 full-time. College room only: $3900. Special program-related fees: $400–$900 per year for lab/material fees.

Financial Aid Program-specific awards: 1 Award of Excellence for entering students ($21,990),

12 Walter B. Ford Scholarships for entering students ($12,000), 15 President's Scholarships for entering students ($10,000), CCS Scholarships for entering students ($2500–$5500).

Application Procedures Students admitted directly into the professional program freshman year. Deadline for freshmen and transfers: continuous. Notification date for freshmen and transfers: August 15. Required: high school transcript, college transcript(s) for transfer students, portfolio, SAT I or ACT test scores, minimum 2.5 high school GPA, minimum 2.0 college GPA for transfer students. Recommended: essay, 2 letters of recommendation. Portfolio reviews held throughout the year on campus; the submission of slides may be substituted for portfolios.

Web Site http://www.ccscad.edu

Undergraduate Contact Julie Hingelberg, Dean of Enrollment Services, Admissions Office, College for Creative Studies, 201 East Kirby Street, Detroit, Michigan 48202; 800-952-ARTS, fax: 313-872-2739, e-mail address: admissions@ccscad.edu

More About the College

The College for Creative Studies (CCS) is among the nation's leading colleges of art and design. Students can pursue a Bachelor of Fine Arts degree in the following majors: advertising design, animation and digital media, art education, crafts, fine arts, graphic design, illustration, interior design, photography, product design, and transportation design.

At the College for Creative Studies, first-year students can enter their chosen department and concentrate their studies in one area or spend their first semester "undeclared" and take an orientation class to learn about the eleven studio majors. While students are immersed in their chosen area of study immediately upon entering CCS, they are also encouraged to take classes outside of their major to broaden their skills.

Each department emphasizes four distinct components of a visual arts education: technical skill, aesthetic sensibility, conceptual ability, and practical experience, combining studio and academic classes with more individualized instruction. Upper-level students have the opportunity to begin working independently in private and semiprivate studio settings. While these students have the freedom to cultivate their own personal vision and style, they are regularly visited by faculty members for critiques and guidance. Internships give students an opportunity to work side by side with art and design professionals.

CCS' faculty consists of professional artists and designers who are also working and exhibiting in their fields of expertise. They provide students with an immediate connection to the real world by bringing new trends, practical insights, and networking opportunities to the College, shedding a realistic light on theoretical classroom exercises. Students are assigned a faculty academic adviser in their department upon entering the school.

Studies at CCS are also fully supported by state-of-the-art facilities. The College has woodworking, metalsmithing, and hot glass studios; a foundry; a clay modeling studio; a Thermwood 5-axis CNC milling machine; a rapid prototyping studio for creating 3-D color models from computer-generated designs; an AutoCad lab for interior design; a digital photography lab; advanced audio-video editing suites; and a film production studio. There is also a visual arts library with a large collection of art and design publications. An on-site imaging center offers color and wide-format printing and a campuswide network provides Internet access in all dorm rooms and e-mail for all students and faculty members.

Computer facilities are constantly updated to adapt to rapidly changing technology. Currently, there are approximately 400 Macintosh and Windows 2000 computer workstations running 3D Studio Max; Alias/Wavefront Studio Tools; AutoCad; After Effects; Final Cut Pro; Illustrator; Macromedia Dreamweaver, Flash, Fireworks, and Director; Maya; Photoshop; Premiere; and InDesign software. Students can take computer-based courses in animation, interactive media, Web page design, publishing, illustration, and digital imaging, among others.

The Academic Advising Center helps with general advising questions regarding scheduling, transfer credits, and the College's mobility program. The center also provides personal counseling. Students in need of academic assistance have access to the Student Success Center, where trained professionals help students develop study and time management skills. The center also helps students improve their language, reading, and writing abilities. A career counselor is available to assist current students with internships and summer jobs as well as to help graduating seniors or CCS alumni secure jobs.

CCS students have many opportunities to exhibit their work publicly. Work is displayed in the U245 Student Gallery and at such events as the Detroit Festival of the Arts and numerous gallery exhibitions. The annual Student Exhibition, held in conjunction with commencement, is a major public event that draws thousands of people to view and purchase student artwork.

College for Creative Studies (continued)

CCS' location is a valuable resource in itself. The campus is situated in Detroit's Cultural Center. It is within walking distance of a number of educational institutions and museums, including the Detroit Institute of Arts (the nation's fifth-largest museum), the Charles H. Wright Museum of African-American History, the Detroit Public Library, and Wayne State University. The surrounding metropolitan area is also inspiring to art students, with theaters and cafés, eclectic neighborhoods, and galleries displaying the work of emerging and established artists.

Professional opportunities abound in the Detroit area. Automotive manufacturing and supply industries have a constant need for creative industrial designers, and because Detroit is the fourth-largest producer of advertising in the U.S., creative professionals are in constant demand.

For a visual arts education that stresses the personal development of style and vision and the practical experience needed to succeed in the real world, the College for Creative Studies is an excellent educational option.

The College of New Jersey

Ewing, New Jersey

State-supported, coed. Suburban campus. Total enrollment: 6,768.

Degrees Bachelor of Arts in the area of art education; Bachelor of Fine Arts in the areas of fine arts, graphic design. Majors and concentrations: art education, art history, art/fine arts, digital art, graphic design.

Enrollment 228 undergraduate.

Art Faculty 14 undergraduate (full-time), 15 undergraduate (part-time). 100% of full-time faculty have terminal degrees. Graduate students do not teach undergraduate courses.

Student Life Student groups/activities include Art Directors Club of New Jersey, National Art Education Association, International Sculpture Center, AIGA.

Expenses for 2005–2006 Application fee: $50. State resident tuition: $7051 full-time. Nonresident tuition: $12,314 full-time. Mandatory fees: $2656 full-time. College room and board: $8458. College room only: $6090. Room and board charges vary according to board plan.

Special program-related fees: $10–$25 per semester for supplemental materials.

Application Procedures Students admitted directly into the professional program freshman year. Deadline for freshmen and transfers: March 1. Notification date for freshmen and transfers: April 1. Required: essay, high school transcript, college transcript(s) for transfer students, portfolio, SAT I test score only. Recommended: minimum 3.0 high school GPA, letter of recommendation. Portfolio reviews held 5 times on campus; the submission of slides may be substituted for portfolios (slides preferred).

Undergraduate Contact Office of Admissions, The College of New Jersey, PO Box 7718, Ewing, New Jersey 08628; 609-771-2131.

The College of New Rochelle

New Rochelle, New York

Independent, coed, primarily women. Suburban campus. Total enrollment: 2,306. Art program established 1929.

Degrees Bachelor of Fine Arts in the areas of studio art, art therapy, art education; Bachelor of Science in the areas of art therapy, art education. Majors and concentrations: art education, art therapy, art/fine arts, computer graphics, graphic design, painting, printmaking, sculpture, studio art.

Enrollment 55 total; 50 undergraduate, 5 nonprofessional degree.

Art Student Profile 100% females, 20% minorities, 3% international.

Art Faculty 5 undergraduate (full-time), 4 undergraduate (part-time). 100% of full-time faculty have terminal degrees. Graduate students do not teach undergraduate courses. Undergraduate student–faculty ratio: 10:1.

Student Life Student groups/activities include Artists Anonymous, Phoenix Literary & Art Magazine, Student Theater Ensemble. Special housing available for art students.

Expenses for 2005–2006 Application fee: $20. Comprehensive fee: $28,476 includes full-time tuition ($20,246), mandatory fees ($350), and college room and board ($7880). Full-time tuition and fees vary according to course load and program. Room and board charges vary according to housing facility.

Financial Aid Program-specific awards: 7–10 art scholarships for program majors ($2000–$5000).

Application Procedures Students admitted directly into the professional program freshman year. Deadline for freshmen and transfers: continuous. Required: high school transcript, college transcript(s) for transfer students, SAT I or ACT test scores, minimum 2.5 high school GPA, portfolio for BFA applicants. Recommended: essay, letter of recommendation, interview, portfolio. Portfolio reviews held continuously on campus; the submission of slides may be substituted for portfolios if a campus visit is impossible.

Web Site http://www.cnr.edu

Undergraduate Contact Ms. Cristina de Gennaro, Chair, Art Department, School of Arts and Sciences, The College of New Rochelle, 29 Castle Place, New Rochelle, New York 10805; 914-654-5856, fax: 914-654-5290, e-mail address: cdegennaro@cnr.edu

The College of Saint Rose

Albany, New York

Independent, coed. Urban campus. Total enrollment: 5,149. Art program established 1995.

Degrees Bachelor of Fine Arts in the areas of studio arts, graphic design; Bachelor of Science in the area of art education. Majors and concentrations: art education, graphic design, painting, photography, printmaking, sculpture, studio art. Graduate degrees offered: Master of Science in the area of art education. Cross-registration with State University of New York at Albany, Rensselaer Polytechnic Institute, Skidmore College. Program accredited by NASAD.

Enrollment 278 total; 180 undergraduate, 38 graduate, 60 nonprofessional degree.

Art Student Profile 75% females, 25% males, 4% minorities, 1% international.

Art Faculty 12 undergraduate (full-time), 9 undergraduate (part-time), 7 graduate (full-time), 2 graduate (part-time). 100% of full-time faculty have terminal degrees. Graduate students do not teach undergraduate courses. Undergraduate student–faculty ratio: 16:1.

Student Life Student groups/activities include New York State Art Teachers Association, National Association of Schools of Art and Design, College Art Association.

Expenses for 2005–2006 Application fee: $35. Comprehensive fee: $25,770 includes full-time tuition ($17,368), mandatory fees ($586), and college room and board ($7816). College room only: $3684. Full-time tuition and fees vary according to course load and program. Room and board charges vary according to board plan. Special program-related fees: $30–$100 per semester for material fees for some studio classes.

Financial Aid Program-specific awards: 32 art scholarships for incoming freshmen ($2000–$7000).

Application Procedures Students apply for admission into the professional program by sophomore year. Deadline for freshmen and transfers: continuous. Notification date for freshmen: May 1; transfers: June 1. Required: essay, high school transcript, college transcript(s) for transfer students, 2 letters of recommendation, portfolio, SAT I or ACT test scores (minimum combined SAT I score of 1030), minimum 2.5 high school GPA. Recommended: interview. Portfolio reviews held 4-5 times on campus and off campus in Boston, MA; Syracuse, NY; Hartford, CT; Philadelphia, PA; New York, NY on National Portfolio Days; the submission of slides may be substituted for portfolios if original work is not available.

Web Site http://academic.strose.edu/Academic/Art/

Undergraduate Contact Ms. Mary Grondahl, Dean of Admissions, The College of Saint Rose, 432 Western Avenue, Albany, New York 12203; 518-454-5150.

Graduate Contact Ms. Karene Tarquin Faul, Chair, Art Department, The College of Saint Rose, 432 Western Avenue, Albany, New York 12203; 518-485-3900, fax: 518-485-3920, e-mail address: faulk@rosnet.strose.edu

College of Santa Fe

Santa Fe, New Mexico

Independent, coed. Suburban campus. Total enrollment: 1,661. Art program established 1984.

Visual Arts

College of Santa Fe (continued)

Degrees Bachelor of Fine Arts in the area of studio art. Majors and concentrations: intermedia, painting, photography, printmaking, sculpture.

Enrollment 199 total; 47 undergraduate, 152 nonprofessional degree.

Art Student Profile 70% females, 30% males, 26% minorities.

Art Faculty 13 undergraduate (full-time), 15 undergraduate (part-time). 86% of full-time faculty have terminal degrees. Graduate students do not teach undergraduate courses. Undergraduate student–faculty ratio: 8:1.

Expenses for 2005–2006 Application fee: $35. Comprehensive fee: $28,978 includes full-time tuition ($21,530), mandatory fees ($746), and college room and board ($6702). College room only: $3204. Room and board charges vary according to board plan and housing facility. Special program-related fees: $30–$155 per course for studio fee.

Application Procedures Students apply for admission into the professional program by sophomore year. Deadline for freshmen and transfers: continuous. Required: essay, high school transcript, college transcript(s) for transfer students, minimum 2.0 high school GPA, 2 letters of recommendation, interview, SAT I or ACT test scores. Recommended: minimum 3.0 high school GPA, portfolio, campus visit. Portfolio reviews held 2 times on campus; the submission of slides may be substituted for portfolios (slides preferred, 20 or less).

Web Site http://www.csf.edu

Undergraduate Contact Mr. Jeff Miller, Dean of Enrollment, College of Santa Fe, 1600 Saint Michael's Drive, Santa Fe, New Mexico 87505; 505-473-6133, fax: 505-473-6129, e-mail address: admissions@csf.edu

College of Visual Arts

St. Paul, Minnesota

Independent, coed. Urban campus. Total enrollment: 202. Art program established 1924.

Degrees Bachelor of Fine Arts in the areas of visual communication, fine arts, visual studies. Majors and concentrations: art, communication design, drawing, illustration, painting, photography, printmaking, sculpture, visual studies.

Enrollment 199 total; all undergraduate.

Art Student Profile 56% females, 44% males, 8% minorities, 1% international.

Art Faculty 9 undergraduate (full-time), 52 undergraduate (part-time). 85% of full-time faculty have terminal degrees. Graduate students do not teach undergraduate courses. Undergraduate student–faculty ratio: 8:1.

Student Life Student groups/activities include College of Visual Arts Design Group-AIGA Student Chapter, The Sculpture Posse, Chasing the Sublime: A Journal of the College of Visual Arts.

Expenses for 2005–2006 Application fee: $40. Tuition: $17,510 full-time. Mandatory fees: $530 full-time. Full-time tuition and fees vary according to course load. Special program-related fees: $53 per course for lab fees.

Financial Aid Program-specific awards: 59 merit scholarships for continuing and incoming students ($1580), 96 College of Visual Arts Grants for those demonstrating need ($1025).

Application Procedures Students admitted directly into the professional program freshman year. Deadline for freshmen and transfers: continuous. Notification date for freshmen and transfers: continuous. Required: essay, high school transcript, college transcript(s) for transfer students, minimum 2.0 high school GPA, interview, portfolio, SAT I or ACT test scores, portfolio home exam as explained in the college catalog. Recommended: minimum 3.0 high school GPA, 2 letters of recommendation. Portfolio reviews held continuously on campus; the submission of slides may be substituted for portfolios for large works of art, three-dimensional pieces, or when distance is prohibitive.

Web Site http://www.cva.edu

Undergraduate Contact Ms. Jane Nordhorn, Director of Admissions, College of Visual Arts, 344 Summit Avenue, St. Paul, Minnesota 55102-2124; 800-224-1536, fax: 651-224-8854, e-mail address: jnordhorn@cva.edu

Collins College: A School of Design and Technology

Tempe, Arizona

Proprietary, coed. Urban campus. Total enrollment: 1,828. Art program established 1978.

Degrees Bachelor of Arts in the areas of visual communication, animation, media arts. Majors and concentrations: animation, film and television, game art and design, graphic design, interior design, motion graphics, multimedia, visual effects.

Enrollment 1,497 total; all undergraduate.

Art Student Profile 40% females, 60% males, 40% minorities, 4% international.

Art Faculty 86 undergraduate (full-time), 5 undergraduate (part-time). 5% of full-time faculty have terminal degrees. Graduate students do not teach undergraduate courses. Undergraduate student–faculty ratio: 17:1.

Student Life Student groups/activities include IIDA-International Interior Design Association, AIGA-American Institute of Graphic Arts, IGDA-International Game Designers Association.

Expenses for 2005–2006 Application fee: 50. Tuition: $13,875 full-time. Full-time tuition varies according to class time, course level, course load, degree level, location, program, reciprocity agreements, and student level. College room only: $2970.

Financial Aid Program-specific awards: 102 scholarships for enrolled students ($1000).

Application Procedures Students admitted directly into the professional program freshman year. Deadline for freshmen and transfers: continuous. Required: essay, high school transcript, college transcript(s) for transfer students, interview. Recommended: portfolio. Portfolio reviews held continuously by appointment on campus.

Web Site http://www.collinscollege.edu

Undergraduate Contact Toby Craver, Senior Director of Admissions, Collins College: A School of Design and Technology, 1140 South Priest Drive, Tempe, Arizona 85281; 480-946-1204, fax: 480-829-0183, e-mail address: tcraver@collinscollege.edu

Colorado State University

Fort Collins, Colorado

State-supported, coed. Urban campus. Total enrollment: 27,133.

Degrees Bachelor of Fine Arts in the area of art. Majors and concentrations: drawing, fibers, graphic design, metals, painting, photography, pottery, printmaking, sculpture. Graduate degrees offered: Master of Fine Arts in the areas of metalsmithing, fibers, sculpture, printmaking, graphic design, drawing, painting.

Enrollment 580 total; 550 undergraduate, 30 graduate.

Art Student Profile 59% females, 41% males, 10% minorities, 1% international.

Art Faculty 23 total (full-time), 15 total (part-time). 96% of full-time faculty have terminal degrees. Graduate students teach a few undergraduate courses. Undergraduate student–faculty ratio: 20:1.

Student Life Student groups/activities include Student Organization for the Visual Arts. Special housing available for art students.

Expenses for 2005–2006 Application fee: $50. State resident tuition: $3381 full-time. Nonresident tuition: $14,343 full-time. Mandatory fees: $1181 full-time. College room and board: $6316. College room only: $2852. Room and board charges vary according to board plan and housing facility. Special program-related fees: $50 per semester for technology fee.

Financial Aid Program-specific awards: 40 Creative and Performing Arts Awards for program students ($1000), 4 Founding Faculty Awards for program students ($1000), 2 Anna Lawton Printmaking Awards for printmakers ($1000), 1 Tracie Noah Memorial Scholarship for painters ($1000), 1 Bob Coonts Scholarship for graphic designers ($350), 1 Northern Colorado Artists Association Award for studio majors ($750), 1 Melanie Metz Memorial Scholarship for graphic designers ($500), 1 Evalyn Prouty Hickman Scholarship for program students ($1000).

Application Procedures Students admitted directly into the professional program freshman year. Deadline for freshmen and transfers: continuous. Notification date for freshmen and transfers: continuous. Required: high school transcript, college transcript(s) for trans-

Colorado State University (continued)

fer students, minimum 3.0 high school GPA, 3 letters of recommendation, SAT I or ACT test scores, portfolio for transfer students. Portfolio reviews held as needed on campus.

Web Site http://www.colostate.edu/Depts/Art/

Undergraduate Contact Ms. Julia Morrigan, Administrative Assistant II, Art Department, Colorado State University, Fort Collins, Colorado 80523-1770; 970-491-6774, fax: 970-491-0505, e-mail address: morrigan@lamar.colostate.edu

Graduate Contact Kathy Chynoweth, Graduate Coordinator, Art Department, Colorado State University, Fort Collins, Colorado 80523-1770; 970-491-6775, fax: 970-491-0505, e-mail address: kchynowe@lamar.colostate.edu

Columbia College

Columbia, Missouri

Independent, coed. Small town campus. Total enrollment: 1,149. Art program established 1858.

Degrees Bachelor of Fine Arts in the area of art. Majors and concentrations: art education, art history, art/fine arts, ceramics, commercial art, computer graphics, graphic design, illustration, painting/drawing, photography. Cross-registration with University of Missouri, Stephens College, William Woods University, Lincoln University, Westminster College.

Enrollment 80 total; 25 undergraduate, 55 nonprofessional degree.

Art Student Profile 66% females, 34% males, 21% minorities, 8% international.

Art Faculty 5 undergraduate (full-time), 1 undergraduate (part-time). 100% of full-time faculty have terminal degrees. Graduate students do not teach undergraduate courses. Undergraduate student–faculty ratio: 5:1.

Student Life Student groups/activities include C.A.L.M. Club.

Expenses for 2005–2006 Application fee: $25. Comprehensive fee: $17,006 includes full-time tuition ($11,995) and college room and board ($5011). College room only: $3152. Full-time tuition varies according to class time and course load. Room and board charges vary

according to board plan. Special program-related fees: $20 per course for model fees, lab fees.

Financial Aid Program-specific awards: 33 talent awards for program majors ($1038), 2 Louis Blosser Scholarships for program majors ($1050), 3 Vivian Sloan Fiske Scholarships for program majors ($750), 1 Elizabeth Estes Gentry Scholarship for program majors ($550), 4 Lucinda Van Meter Haynie Awards for art students ($125), 2 Mary Robinson Art Scholarships for program majors ($100), 1 Hurst John Scholarship for art students ($450), 1 Margaret Courter Memorial Scholarship for program majors ($100), 1 Sidney Larson Student Art Award for program majors ($500).

Application Procedures Students apply for admission into the professional program by sophomore year. Deadline for freshmen and transfers: continuous. Required: high school transcript, college transcript(s) for transfer students, minimum 2.0 high school GPA, SAT I or ACT test scores, portfolio for scholarship consideration. Portfolio reviews held as needed on campus; the submission of slides may be substituted for portfolios when distance is prohibitive.

Web Site http://www.ccis.edu/academics/depinfo.asp?Art

Undergraduate Contact Ms. Regina Morin, Director of Admissions, Columbia College, 1001 Rogers Street, Columbia, Missouri 65216; 573-875-7352, fax: 573-875-8765, e-mail address: admissions@ccis.edu

Columbia College Chicago

Chicago, Illinois

Independent, coed. Urban campus. Total enrollment: 10,842. Art program established 1967.

Degrees Bachelor of Arts in the area of film/video. Majors and concentrations: alternative forms, audio recording technology, cinematography, computer animation, critical studies, directing, documentary, editing, production, screenwriting, traditional animation. Graduate degrees offered: Master of Fine Arts in the area of film/video.

Enrollment 2,052 total; 1,994 undergraduate, 58 graduate.

Art Student Profile 51% females, 49% males, 30% minorities, 2% international.

Art Faculty 33 total (full-time), 125 total (part-time). Graduate students do not teach undergraduate courses. Undergraduate student–faculty ratio: 12:1.

Student Life Student groups/activities include Documentary Film Group, Japanese Animation Club, Sunrayz Film Society.

Expenses for 2006–2007 Application fee: $35. Comprehensive fee: $26,553 includes full-time tuition ($16,328), mandatory fees ($460), and college room and board ($9765). College room only: $8265. Special program-related fees: $20–$415 per course for class fee.

Application Procedures Students admitted directly into the professional program freshman year. Deadline for freshmen and transfers: continuous. Notification date for freshmen and transfers: continuous. Required: essay, high school transcript, college transcript(s) for transfer students, letter of recommendation, students with less than a 2.0 GPA may be required to see an admissions counselor for a personal interview and may be required to attend an intensive remediation program, portfolio for transfer students. Recommended: minimum 2.0 high school GPA, interview, SAT I or ACT test scores. Portfolio reviews held on campus.

Web Site http://www.colum.edu

Undergraduate Contact Mr. Murphy Monroe, Director, Office of Admissions, Columbia College Chicago, 600 South Michigan Avenue, Chicago, Illinois 60605; 312-344-7133, fax: 312-344-8024, e-mail address: admissions@ colum.edu

Graduate Contact Keith Cleveland, Dean, Graduate School, Graduate School Admissions, Columbia College Chicago, 600 South Michigan Avenue, Chicago, Illinois 60605; 312-344-7261, fax: 312-344-8047, e-mail address: kcleveland@ colum.edu

More About the College

Columbia College Chicago is the nation's largest and most diverse arts and media college. Located in the heart of downtown Chicago, Columbia sits at the heart of the Midwest's arts and communications industries. Columbia's faculty and student body comprise a widely diverse mix of cultures and

backgrounds, creating a stimulating environment ideally suited to the pursuit of creative innovation. Intimate class settings facilitate personal attention and practical mentoring with a faculty of working professionals.

Columbia College takes a "hands-on, minds-on approach to learning that encourages students to fully explore their chosen field of interest in the arts and communications. A required core series of liberal arts classes provide a broad and enriching academic foundation, and elective credit hours allow students to investigate a wide variety of different disciplines throughout the College.

Campus and Surroundings Located in the middle of the South Loop, Chicago's liveliest downtown district, students enjoy direct access to major theaters, museums, concert halls, restaurants, clubs, parks, galleries, recreational facilities, and Lake Michigan.

Columbia sits right in the middle of Chicago's professional community, easily connecting students to the city's major corporations, ad agencies, television and radio stations, public relations firms, production houses, recording facilities, theaters, galleries, museums, design studios, and dance companies. Even before they graduate, students can explore all of the nuances of their future careers through internships and professional networking opportunities.

Faculty The faculty members at Columbia College Chicago are actively engaged in the subjects that they

Columbia College Chicago (continued)

teach and are uniquely qualified to share their expertise in the classroom. As working professionals who are accomplished in their fields, Columbia's faculty members bring insight on industry-current aesthetics, techniques, and viewpoints to the classroom. Students at Columbia learn from Pulitzer Prize-winning journalists, Emmy Award-winning producers, and nationally recognized artists; in short, faculty members who do what they teach. In turn, students are inspired to work hard, get their hands dirty, take risks, and push themselves and their ideas to the fullest. Together, these ingredients combine to create an extraordinary academic environment that transcends the traditional collegiate classroom experience.

Student Performance/Exhibit Opportunities When they are not showing at campus galleries, publishing in award-winning magazines, or freestyling at poetry slams, Columbia students take an active role in Chicago's arts community. The influence of Columbia's young talent can be felt in theaters, bookstores, and radio stations throughout the city. And every spring, students return the favor by inviting Chicago to their doorstep for Manifest, the city's largest student arts exhibition.

Special Programs Academic and social assistance programs include the Conaway Achievement Project (services for students with disabilities), Comprehensive Academic and Career Advising Center, Bridge Program, Mentorship Programs, ESL, Portfolio Center, and Student Counseling Services. Off-campus study includes an immersion experience on site at the CBS studio lot in Los Angeles. Students can also elect to participate in affiliated study-abroad programs. The most common destinations are England, Mexico, Russia, Czech Republic, and Italy. The High School Summer Institute is an opportunity for motivated high school juniors and seniors to experience college life and earn academic credit.

Cooperative Agreements Columbia College Chicago maintains a variety of articulation agreements with academic institutions both in and out of Illinois. Other affiliations include the Office of Community Arts Partnerships, Museum of Contemporary Photography, Center for Black Music Research, Chicago Jazz Ensemble, Chicago Center for Arts Policy, Institute for Science Education, and Science Communication.

Columbia College Chicago

Chicago, Illinois

Independent, coed. Urban campus. Total enrollment: 10,842. Art program established 1970.

Degrees Bachelor of Arts in the area of art and design; Bachelor of Fine Arts. Majors and concentrations: advertising art direction, art and design, art/fine arts, fashion design, graphic design, illustration, interior design, product design. Graduate degrees offered: Master of Fine Arts in the areas of architectural studies, interior design.

Enrollment 1,403 total; 1,382 undergraduate, 21 graduate.

Art Student Profile 64% females, 36% males, 30% minorities, 5% international.

Art Faculty 31 total (full-time), 120 total (part-time). 43% of full-time faculty have terminal degrees. Graduate students do not teach undergraduate courses. Undergraduate student–faculty ratio: 9:1.

Student Life Student groups/activities include Arts Community, Columbia College Fashion Association, Columbia Advertising Federation.

Expenses for 2006–2007 Application fee: $35. Comprehensive fee: $26,553 includes full-time tuition ($16,328), mandatory fees ($460), and college room and board ($9765). College room only: $8265. Special program-related fees: $15–$150 per course for class fees.

Financial Aid Program-specific awards: 1 Skrebineski Fashion Scholarship for full-time freshmen fashion marketing, fashion design, fashion photography majors ($11,600), 1 Pougialis Fine Arts Award for continuing fine arts majors ($2500).

Application Procedures Students admitted directly into the professional program freshman year. Deadline for freshmen and transfers: continuous. Notification date for freshmen and transfers: continuous. Required: essay, high school transcript, college transcript(s) for transfer students, letter of recommendation, students with less than a 2.0 GPA may be required to see an admissions counselor for a personal interview and may be required to attend an intensive remediation program, portfolio for transfer students. Recommended: minimum 2.0 high school GPA, interview, SAT I or ACT test scores. Portfolio reviews held on campus.

Web Site http://www.colum.edu

Undergraduate Contact Mr. Murphy Monroe, Director, Office of Admissions, Columbia College Chicago, 600 South Michigan Avenue, Chicago, Illinois 60605; 312-344-7133, fax: 312-344-8024, e-mail address: admissions@colum.edu

Graduate Contact Keith Cleveland, Dean, Graduate School, Graduate School Admissions, Columbia College Chicago, 600 South Michigan Avenue, Chicago, Illinois 60605; 312-344-7261, fax: 312-344-8047, e-mail address: kcleveland@colum.edu

Columbia College Chicago

Chicago, Illinois

Independent, coed. Urban campus. Total enrollment: 10,842. Art program established 1968.

Degrees Bachelor of Arts in the area of photography; Bachelor of Fine Arts in the area of photography. Majors and concentrations: fine art photography, photojournalism, professional photography. Graduate degrees offered: Master of Fine Arts in the area of photography.

Enrollment 671 total; 645 undergraduate, 26 graduate.

Art Student Profile 67% females, 33% males, 20% minorities, 2% international.

Art Faculty 15 total (full-time), 64 total (part-time). 67% of full-time faculty have terminal degrees. Graduate students teach a few undergraduate courses. Undergraduate student–faculty ratio: 10:1.

Expenses for 2006–2007 Application fee: $35. Comprehensive fee: $26,553 includes full-time tuition ($16,328), mandatory fees ($460), and college room and board ($9765). College room only: $8265. Special program-related fees: $20–$150 per course for class fees.

Financial Aid Program-specific awards: 1 Kodak Scholarship for photography majors ($2000).

Application Procedures Students admitted directly into the professional program freshman year. Deadline for freshmen and transfers: continuous. Notification date for freshmen and transfers: continuous. Required: essay, high school transcript, college transcript(s) for transfer students, letter of recommendation, students with less than a 2.0 GPA may be required to see an admissions counselor for a personal interview and may be required to attend an intensive remediation program, portfolio for transfer students. Recommended: minimum 2.0 high school GPA, interview, SAT I or ACT test scores. Portfolio reviews held on campus.

Web Site http://www.colum.edu

Undergraduate Contact Mr. Murphy Monroe, Director, Office of Admissions, Columbia College Chicago, 600 South Michigan Avenue, Chicago, Illinois 606050; 312-344-7133, fax: 312-344-8024, e-mail address: admissions@colum.edu

Graduate Contact Keith Cleveland, Dean, Graduate School, Graduate School Admissions, Columbia College Chicago, 600 South Michigan Avenue, Chicago, Illinois 60605; 312-344-7261, fax: 312-344-8047, e-mail address: kclevelnad@colum.edu

Columbus College of Art & Design

Columbus, Ohio

Independent, coed. Urban campus. Total enrollment: 1,455. Art program established 1879.

Degrees Bachelor of Fine Arts in the areas of fine art, visual communication, interior design, industrial design, media studies, illustration, fashion design. Majors and concentrations: art/fine arts, fashion design, graphic design, illustration, industrial design, interior design, media studies, visual communication. Cross-registration with Higher Education Council of Columbus. Program accredited by NASAD.

Enrollment 1,374 total; all undergraduate.

Art Student Profile 57% females, 43% males, 18% minorities.

Art Faculty 80 undergraduate (full-time), 105 undergraduate (part-time). 41% of full-time faculty have terminal degrees. Graduate students do not teach undergraduate courses. Undergraduate student–faculty ratio: 10:1.

Student Life Special housing available for art students.

Expenses for 2005–2006 Application fee: $25. Comprehensive fee: $26,728 includes full-time tuition ($19,728), mandatory fees ($550), and college room and board ($6450). Room and board charges vary according to housing facility and student level. Special program-related fees: $25–$160 for lab/studio fees.

Columbus College of Art & Design (continued)

Financial Aid Program-specific awards: 300 International Scholarship Competition Awards for incoming freshmen ($4000–$11,000), 150 art competition award winners for members of National Art Honor Society ($500–$1000).

Application Procedures Students admitted directly into the professional program freshman year. Deadline for freshmen and transfers: continuous. Required: essay, high school transcript, college transcript(s) for transfer students, minimum 2.0 high school GPA, letter of recommendation, portfolio, SAT I or ACT test scores. Recommended: interview. Portfolio reviews held continuously by appointment on campus and off campus; the submission of slides may be substituted for portfolios if a campus visit is impossible.

Web Site http://www.ccad.edu

Undergraduate Contact Thomas E. Green, Director of Admissions, Columbus College of Art & Design, 107 North Ninth Street, Columbus, Ohio 43215; 614-224-9101, fax: 877-869-5897, e-mail address: admissions@ccad.edu

Concordia University

Seward, Nebraska

Independent, coed. Small town campus. Total enrollment: 1,317 (2004). Art program established 1963.

Degrees Bachelor of Fine Arts. Majors and concentrations: art education, graphic design, studio art.

Enrollment 119 total; 83 undergraduate, 36 nonprofessional degree.

Art Student Profile 63% females, 37% males, 2% international.

Art Faculty 6 undergraduate (full-time), 3 undergraduate (part-time). 83% of full-time faculty have terminal degrees. Graduate students do not teach undergraduate courses. Undergraduate student–faculty ratio: 15:1.

Student Life Student groups/activities include theater, music.

Expenses for 2005–2006 Application fee: $25. Comprehensive fee: $22,434 includes full-time tuition ($17,724) and college room and board ($4710). Room and board charges vary according to board plan. Special program-related fees: $40 per course for studio/materials fee.

Financial Aid Program-specific awards: 63 art scholarships for program majors ($2100).

Application Procedures Students apply for admission into the professional program by sophomore year. Deadline for freshmen and transfers: continuous. Notification date for freshmen and transfers: continuous. Required: high school transcript, minimum 2.0 high school GPA, SAT I or ACT test scores, health form, portfolio for scholarship consideration. Recommended: interview, portfolio. Portfolio reviews held as needed on campus; the submission of slides may be substituted for portfolios.

Web Site http://www.cune.edu

Undergraduate Contact Prof. William R. Wolfram, Professor, Art Department, Concordia University, 800 North Columbia Avenue, Seward, Nebraska 68434; 402-643-7499, fax: 402-643-4073, e-mail address: wwolfram@seward.cune.edu

Concordia University

Montreal, Quebec, Canada

Province-supported, coed. Urban campus. Total enrollment: 31,042. Art program established 1975.

Degrees Bachelor of Fine Arts. Majors and concentrations: art education, art history, computer art, design art, digital image/sound and the fine arts, film, studio art. Graduate degrees offered: Master of Arts in the areas of art education, art history, creative art therapies (art therapy/drama therapy), film studies; Master of Fine Arts in the area of studio arts. Doctor of Philosophy in the areas of art education, art history. Cross-registration with any university in Quebec or other approved international institutions.

Enrollment 2,183 total; 1,900 undergraduate, 283 graduate.

Art Student Profile 4% international.

Art Faculty 71 total (full-time), 85 total (part-time). 100% of full-time faculty have terminal degrees. Graduate students teach a few undergraduate courses.

Student Life Student groups/activities include Student-Run Art Gallery, Fine Arts Students Alliance, Art Matters Festival.

Expenses for 2005–2006 Application fee: $50 Canadian dollars. Tuition, fee, and room and board charges are reported in Canadian dollars. Province resident tuition: $1668 full-time. Canadian resident tuition: $4651 full-time. Mandatory fees: $979 full-time. Full-time tuition and fees vary according to program. College room and board: $6905. Room and board charges vary according to housing facility. International student tuition: $11,238 full-time. Special program-related fees: $200–$500 for lab/materials fees.

Financial Aid Program-specific awards: 10 Concordia University Entrance Scholarships for Canadian students ($2000), 1 Anne Savage Memorial Scholarship for art education students ($225), 1 de Sève Anema Scholarship for cinema students ($1000), 1 Phillip Russel George Award for cinema students ($400), 1 Kodak Scholarship for cinema students ($500), 1 Heather Walker Memorial Scholarship for cinema and photography students ($500), 1 Sean Wall Scholarship for cinema students ($420), 2 Cecil Buller-John J. A. Murphy Scholarships in Drawing for student arts students ($1000), 2 Stevenson Colour Scholarships for majors in painting and drawing ($400).

Application Procedures Students admitted directly into the professional program freshman year. Deadline for freshmen and transfers: March 1. Notification date for freshmen and transfers: July 15. Required: high school transcript, college transcript(s) for transfer students, interview, college transcript for transfer students for program in studio arts, letter of intent for programs in art education, design art, computation arts, studio art, ceramics, fibers, art history, portfolio for programs in art education, art history and studio art, design art, computation arts, studio art, ceramics, fibers, painting and drawing, photography, print media, sculpture, film animation, film production, film studies, intermedia and cyber arts. Recommended: minimum 3.0 high school GPA (4.0 scale) for programs in art education, art history. Portfolio reviews held in April for programs in studio arts, art education, design and computation art on campus; the submission of slides may be substituted for portfolios.

Web Site http://www.finearts.concordia.ca

Undergraduate Contact Ms. Jolanta Manowska, Communications Assistant, Office of Student Recruitment, Concordia University, 1455 de Maisonneuve Boulevard West, FB-801,

Montreal, Quebec H3G 1M8, Canada; 514-848-2424 ext. 4772, fax: 514-848-2827, e-mail address: admreg@alcor.concordia.ca

Graduate Contact Ms. Amanda French, Recruitment Officer, Faculty of Fine Arts, Concordia University, 1455 de Maisonneuve Boulevard West, S105, Montreal, Quebec H3G 1M8, Canada; 514-848-2424 ext. 4649, fax: 514-848-7959, e-mail address: amanda.french@concordia.ca

Converse College
Spartanburg, South Carolina
Independent, Total enrollment: 2,176.

Corcoran College of Art and Design
Washington, District of Columbia
Independent, coed. Urban campus. Total enrollment: 590. Art program established 1890.

Degrees Bachelor of Fine Arts in the areas of fine art, graphic design, photography, photojournalism, digital media design; Bachelor of Fine Arts/Master of Arts in Teaching in the area of fine art/teaching. Majors and concentrations: art education, art/fine arts, ceramics, digital art, digital media, drawing, graphic design, painting, photography, photojournalism, printmaking, sculpture. Graduate degrees offered: Master of Arts in the areas of interior design, history of decorative arts, art education. Program accredited by NASAD.

Enrollment 590 total; 520 undergraduate, 70 graduate.

Art Student Profile 69% females, 31% males, 22% minorities, 7% international.

Art Faculty 32 undergraduate (full-time), 223 undergraduate (part-time), 32 graduate (part-time). 30% of full-time faculty have terminal degrees. Graduate students do not teach undergraduate courses. Undergraduate student–faculty ratio: 4:1.

Student Life Student groups/activities include Student Government, Off The Walls Art Sale, student exhibitions, WPA/C. Special housing available for art students.

Expenses for 2005–2006 Application fee: $40. Comprehensive fee: $32,850 includes full-time

Corcoran College of Art and Design (continued)

tuition ($22,700), mandatory fees ($100), and college room and board ($10,050). College room only: $8150. Full-time tuition and fees vary according to degree level.

Financial Aid Program-specific awards: 66 Dean's Scholarships for freshmen and transfers ($1000–$5000), 20 departmental scholarships for continuing students ($1000–$2500), 3 Academic Achievement Awards for entering freshmen ($2000–$9000), 19 President's Awards for freshmen and transfers ($2000–$9000), 8 Delaware College of Art and Design Grants for transfer students from DCAD ($2000–$5500), 8 Faculty Chairs' Grants for entering freshmen ($11,350–$22,700).

Application Procedures Students admitted directly into the professional program freshman year. Deadline for freshmen and transfers: continuous. Required: high school transcript, college transcript(s) for transfer students, minimum 2.0 high school GPA, interview, portfolio, SAT I or ACT test scores. Recommended: essay, minimum 3.0 high school GPA, 3 letters of recommendation. Portfolio reviews held continuously by appointment on campus and off campus in various cities in the U.S.; the submission of slides may be substituted for portfolios for applicants living beyond 200-mile radius.

Web Site http://www.corcoran.edu

Contact Office of Admissions, Corcoran College of Art and Design, 500 17th Street, NW, Washington, District of Columbia 20006-4804; 202-639-1814, fax: 202-639-1830, e-mail address: admissions@corcoran.org

More About the College

The Corcoran College of Art and Design is one of the oldest art schools in the United States and upholds a long tradition of partnership between art schools and museums. Studying at one of the few museum-schools in the country, Corcoran students are surrounded by great art and frequently by the contemporary masters whose work is regularly exhibited. The Corcoran Museum of Art has one of the finest collections of American art in the world, which is supplemented by holdings in European painting and sculpture, classical antiquities, and the decorative arts. As Washington's first museum of art, the Corcoran has played a central role in the development of American culture for more than 125 years. The aspiring young professionals who study

today at the Corcoran College of Art and Design join a great and long tradition of quality and impact on the development of American and international art and design.

Location and Program Facilities Washington is a city of monuments and museums set off by the neoclassical architecture of government buildings, parks, trees, and greenery. With dozens of major colleges and universities in the metropolitan area, there exists a feeling of a giant "campus" in which restaurants, coffee shops, movie theaters, and night spots are intermingled with bookstores, clothing boutiques, and academic facilities. Within a mile of the Corcoran, the city offers numerous museums and galleries, including the National Gallery of Art, the Phillips Collection, the Hirshhorn Museum and Sculpture Garden, and the Smithsonian National Museum of Natural History.

With the exception of the Direct Entry Photography Program, Corcoran undergraduate students take the integrated first-year Foundation program, which includes an introduction to the many art collections of Washington. After their first year, students select a major field of study in fine art, digital media design, graphic design, photography, or photojournalism. Fine Art majors may choose to concentrate in ceramics, digital art, drawing, painting, printmaking, or sculpture. At the graduate studies level, a master's degree is offered in interior design and in the history of decorative arts as well as a five-year combined bachelor's/master's degree program in teaching in the arts.

The Downtown Campus of the Corcoran College of Art and Design is located in the same building as the Corcoran Gallery of Art, one block from the White House, with additional facilities in proximity. The building is one of America's finest examples of Beaux-Arts architecture, with wings designed by Ernest Flagg and Charles Platt.

Freshmen students spend their class time in the downtown and Georgetown buildings. Juniors and seniors in Fine Art have designated studio space as well as generous studio hours.

The Corcoran's nearby Georgetown Campus is home to the Design and Printmaking departments, papermaking and silkscreen facilities, jewelry studio, and state-of-the-art computer laboratories. Georgetown is one of Washington's best-known neighborhoods, with tree-lined streets, historic townhouses, fashionable boutiques, restaurants, and nightlife.

As an appealing alternative to crowded traditional dormitory housing, the College provides new students with attractive, spacious, and furnished supervised apartments. The furnished apartments are subway accessible, close to downtown and Georgetown, and have 24-hour security.

In addition to several nearby museums, a short walk from the business and government district that surrounds the Corcoran takes students to the world-famous Mall and performing arts institutions such as the Kennedy Center, Ford's Theater, and the National Theater. Rock Creek Park, a 1,700-acre public park that has a golf course, bicycle path, picnic area, nature center, playgrounds, tennis center, and Horse Center, is nearby as well. Visitors to the Corcoran who have not experienced Washington, D.C., before should allow a full day or two to explore the city as well as the College and Museum.

Student and Alumni Exhibit Opportunities

Students of all levels have several opportunities to exhibit their work. In the College/Museum space, there are several exhibition areas, including the White Walls Gallery, which is also the site for the annual student sale of art work.

The Corcoran is the only college of art and design that incorporates an exhibition in a prominent museum into its curriculum. For three months of every year, graduating seniors showcase their thesis projects in the Corcoran Museum in a series of weeklong rotating exhibitions. The students are responsible for all aspects of these shows, from exhibition design to installation. These exhibitions culminate, in conjunction with commencement, in a final exhibition featuring at least one work by every graduating senior. Through the formal presentation of their work in the museum, students make the transition to professional artists and designers and are introduced as emerging talents to the public.

The Corcoran Museum also is also the site of the annual juried Corcoran Alumni Association exhibition, presenting works by some of the College's most accomplished alumni, all with extensive lists of exhibitions to their credit and many with gallery affiliations. The Visiting Artists Program also holds its exhibitions in the museum, allowing renowned contemporary artists, scholars, and critics to visit the Corcoran's campus each semester.

The Alumni Gallery, located off the main atrium of the Corcoran Gallery of Art, is dedicated to works by artists and designers who have received their degree from the Corcoran College of Art and Design.

Cornell University

Ithaca, New York

Independent, coed. Small town campus. Total enrollment: 19,447. Art program established 1921.

Degrees Bachelor of Fine Arts. Majors and concentrations: combined media, electronic imaging, painting/drawing, photography, printmaking, sculpture. Graduate degrees offered: Master of Fine Arts.

Enrollment 130 total; 120 undergraduate, 10 graduate.

Art Student Profile 70% females, 30% males, 30% minorities, 8% international.

Art Faculty 10 total (full-time), 6 total (part-time). 100% of full-time faculty have terminal degrees. Graduate students do not teach undergraduate courses. Undergraduate student–faculty ratio: 8:1.

Student Life Student groups/activities include Minority Organization of Architecture, Art, and Planning, Art Majors Organization (AMO). Special housing available for art students.

Expenses for 2005–2006 Application fee: $65. Comprehensive fee: $41,717 includes full-time tuition ($31,300), mandatory fees ($167), and college room and board ($10,250). College

Cornell University (continued)

room only: $6080. Room and board charges vary according to board plan and housing facility. Special program-related fees: $50–$150 for departmental fees.

Application Procedures Students admitted directly into the professional program freshman year. Deadline for freshmen: January 1; transfers: March 15. Notification date for freshmen: April 1; transfers: May 1. Required: essay, high school transcript, college transcript(s) for transfer students, minimum 3.0 high school GPA, 2 letters of recommendation, SAT I or ACT test scores, portfolio containing 15-20 slides. Recommended: interview. Portfolio reviews held by appointment on campus.

Web Site http://www.aap.cornell.edu

Undergraduate Contact Ms. Deborah Durnam, Director of Admissions, College of Architecture, Art and Planning, Cornell University, B-1 West Sibley Hall, Ithaca, New York 14853; 607-255-4376, fax: 607-254-2848, e-mail address: aap_admissions@cornell.edu

Graduate Contact Mr. Buzz Spector, Chair, Department of Art, Cornell University, 224 Olive Tjaden Hall, Ithaca, New York 14853; 607-255-3558, fax: 607-255-3462.

Cornish College of the Arts–Design Department

Seattle, Washington

Independent, coed. Urban campus. Total enrollment: 768. Art program established 1914.

Degrees Bachelor of Fine Arts in the area of design. Majors and concentrations: advertising design, animation, computer animation and interactive media, interior design, visual communication. Program accredited by NASAD.

Enrollment 151 total; all undergraduate.

Art Student Profile 65% females, 35% males, 14% minorities, 4% international.

Art Faculty 10 undergraduate (full-time), 19 undergraduate (part-time). 58% of full-time faculty have terminal degrees. Graduate students do not teach undergraduate courses. Undergraduate student–faculty ratio: 8:1.

Student Life Student groups/activities include American Society of Interior Designers, American Institute of Graphic Arts.

Expenses for 2005–2006 Application fee: $35. Tuition: $21,200 full-time. Mandatory fees: $300 full-time.

Financial Aid Program-specific awards: Nellie Scholarships for new students, departmental scholarships for new and continuing students, Presidential Scholarships for continuing students.

Application Procedures Students admitted directly into the professional program freshman year. Deadline for freshmen and transfers: August 15. Notification date for freshmen and transfers: August 30. Required: essay, high school transcript, college transcript(s) for transfer students, portfolio. Recommended: 2 letters of recommendation, interview, SAT I or ACT test scores. Portfolio reviews held 12 times on campus and off campus at National Portfolio Days (California, Colorado, Oregon, Washington, Illinois, Minnesota, Hawaii); the submission of slides may be substituted for portfolios when distance is prohibitive.

Web Site http://www.cornish.edu

Undergraduate Contact Eric Pederson, Director of Admission, Cornish College of the Arts, 1000 Lenora, Seattle, Washington 98121; 800-726-ARTS, fax: 206-720-1011, e-mail address: epedersen@cornish.edu

Cornish College of the Arts–Art Department

Seattle, Washington

Independent, coed. Urban campus. Total enrollment: 768. Art program established 1914.

Degrees Bachelor of Fine Arts in the area of art. Majors and concentrations: art/fine arts, painting/drawing, photography, printmaking, sculpture, video art. Program accredited by NASAD.

Enrollment 170 total; all undergraduate.

Art Student Profile 65% females, 35% males, 14% minorities, 4% international.

Art Faculty 11 undergraduate (full-time), 5 undergraduate (part-time). 58% of full-time faculty have terminal degrees. Graduate students do not teach undergraduate courses. Undergraduate student–faculty ratio: 8:1.

Student Life Student groups/activities include Film Society.

Expenses for 2005–2006 Application fee: $35. Tuition: $21,200 full-time. Mandatory fees: $300 full-time. Special program-related fees: $250 per semester for lab fees.

Financial Aid Program-specific awards: Nellie Scholarships for new students ($2000–$5000), departmental scholarships for new and continuing students ($500–$7500), Presidential Scholarships for continuing students ($2000–$5000).

Application Procedures Students admitted directly into the professional program freshman year. Deadline for freshmen and transfers: August 15. Notification date for freshmen and transfers: August 30. Required: essay, high school transcript, college transcript(s) for transfer students, minimum 2.0 high school GPA, portfolio. Recommended: 2 letters of recommendation, interview, SAT I or ACT test scores. Portfolio reviews held 20 times and by appointment on campus and off campus in Denver, CO; Portland, OR; Phoenix, AZ; San Francisco, CA; Los Angeles, CA; San Diego, CA; the submission of slides may be substituted for portfolios when distance is prohibitive.

Web Site http://www.cornish.edu

Undergraduate Contact Eric Pedersen, Director of Admission, Cornish College of the Arts, 1000 Lenora, Seattle, Washington 98121; 800-726-ARTS, fax: 206-720-1011, e-mail address: epedersen@cornish.edu

More About the College

For more than ninety years, Cornish College of the Arts has educated students and nurtured artists who, as professionals, have consistently contributed to the culture of society. The Cornish School was founded in 1914 when Nellie Cornish, a woman of profound vision and unlimited energy, realized her vision of a school that offered arts training based on inspirational encouragement and guidance of student self-expression. While Cornish's mission is to "provide students aspiring to become practicing artists with an educational program of the highest quality," its role is far broader. Cornish students, alumni, and faculty members are working artists—theater directors, visual artists, set and lighting designers, dancers, and musicians—making art in and for the community. They are also innovative designers, business leaders, teachers, passionate and supportive audience members, and torchbearers for the arts.

Cornish College of the Arts, one of only three private, nonprofit performing and visual arts colleges in the nation, offers a Bachelor of Music degree and Bachelor of Fine Arts degrees in art, dance, design, music, theater, and performance production. The academic programs are a distinctive blend of visual and performing arts grounded in a core curriculum of humanities and sciences. With more than 140 faculty members and an enrollment of over 750, Cornish has the lowest student-faculty ratio (8:1) in the country for an institution of its kind. Individualized attention and mentoring for every student are emphasized, and students thrive in their chosen artistic disciplines. They are encouraged to exchange ideas, to experiment and find their unique artistic voices, and to share them in both innovative and traditional projects. Cornish challenges artists to broaden their artistic perspectives and engage in creative collaboration by encouraging students to select from a wide range of elective studio courses outside their majors. The educational programs are of the highest possible quality, and the environment at Cornish nurtures creativity and intellectual curiosity and also prepares students to contribute to society as artists, citizens, and innovators.

The Art Department is devoted to realizing the individuality and full potential of each student. The faculty members support artistic play and risk, rigor, and a strong work ethic. Students are challenged to be involved in cross-disciplinary creation and collaboration and to engage with their peers in rich, critical discourse; studio projects; and exhibitions. They become adept at both traditional and contemporary technical approaches to art-making, develop fluency in various visual languages, and learn to understand

Cornish College of the Arts–Art Department (continued)

their work in the context of history and culture and within the larger world of contemporary artistic endeavor.

Campus and Surroundings Seattle has more cultural construction projects in the works than any other urban area in the U.S., with more than $1.2 billion in cultural infrastructure for concert halls, museums, and theaters. The city has 190 galleries, five cultural heritage museums, five art museums, a dance company, a symphony, and twenty-nine professional theater companies and fifty-six fringe theater companies as well as more than eighty clubs with live music. Cornish serves as a focal point for public presentation, artistic criticism, participation, and discussion of the arts in this artistically rich community.

Faculty, Resident Artists, and Alumni The faculty at Cornish represents the largest concentration of practicing artists in the Northwest. They are nationally renowned in their fields and are dedicated to instruction of the arts. Their art can be found in major galleries, theaters, dance troupes, and other prestigious art organizations around the nation. Dedication to Cornish College and the stability of its programs is demonstrated by a faculty retention rate of more than 90 percent.

Since its earliest days, the College has fostered influential artists, arts movements, and arts organizations in the local community and beyond. Prominent members of the Northwest School of Artists, including Mark Tobey, Morris Graves, Guy Anderson, and William Cumming, taught at Cornish College, as did Martha Graham, an inventor of modern dance. Merce Cunningham, the legendary contemporary dancer/choreographer, and broadcast pioneer Chet Huntley were Cornish students. Revolutionary composer John Cage worked and invented the prepared piano at Cornish. In more recent years, the College has nurtured the talents of Heart's Nancy Wilson, Brendan Fraser, and award-winning composer Wendell Yuponce.

Cornish has hosted elite members of the artistic community as artists-in-residence, including Meredith Monk (performance), Mark Morris (dance), Bill Frisell (music), Rinde Eckert (theater), Syvilla Fort (dance), Imogen Cunningham (photography), and Lou Harrison (music). These acclaimed artists provide Cornish students with unique and invaluable educational experiences.

Culver-Stockton College
Canton, Missouri

Independent, coed. Rural campus. Total enrollment: 840. Art program established 1900.

Degrees Bachelor of Fine Arts. Majors and concentrations: graphic design, studio art.

Enrollment 60 total; 42 undergraduate, 18 nonprofessional degree.

Art Student Profile 60% females, 40% males, 8% minorities, 4% international.

Art Faculty 100% of full-time faculty have terminal degrees. Graduate students do not teach undergraduate courses. Undergraduate student–faculty ratio: 12:1.

Student Life Student groups/activities include Images Unlimited (art club).

Expenses for 2006–2007 Application fee: $25. Comprehensive fee: $21,796 includes full-time tuition ($15,250) and college room and board ($6546). College room only: $3030.

Financial Aid Program-specific awards: scholarship awards for program majors ($750–$3000).

Application Procedures Students admitted directly into the professional program freshman year. Deadline for freshmen and transfers: August 31. Required: high school transcript, portfolio, SAT I or ACT test scores. Portfolio reviews held once in November (formally), and as needed from October-April on campus; the submission of slides may be substituted for portfolios.

Web Site http://www.culver.edu

Undergraduate Contact Mr. Joseph E. Jorgensen, Head, Art Department, Culver-Stockton College, Herrick Center, 1 College Hill, Canton, Missouri 63435-1299; 217-231-6368, fax: 217-231-6611, e-mail address: jjorgensen@culver.edu

Daemen College
Amherst, New York

Independent, coed. Suburban campus. Total enrollment: 2,315. Art program established 1948.

Degrees Bachelor of Fine Arts in the areas of applied design, graphic design, fine art. Majors and concentrations: applied design, drawing, graphic design, illustration, painting, printmaking, sculpture. Cross-registration with

17 institutions in the Western New York Consortium of Higher Education.

Enrollment 122 total; 71 undergraduate, 51 nonprofessional degree.

Art Student Profile 67% females, 33% males, 12% minorities.

Art Faculty 4 undergraduate (full-time), 11 undergraduate (part-time). 25% of full-time faculty have terminal degrees. Graduate students do not teach undergraduate courses. Undergraduate student–faculty ratio: 5:1.

Student Life Student groups/activities include Art Club.

Expenses for 2005–2006 Application fee: $25. Comprehensive fee: $24,580 includes full-time tuition ($16,350), mandatory fees ($450), and college room and board ($7780). Room and board charges vary according to board plan and housing facility.

Financial Aid Program-specific awards: 7 Visual Art Scholars Awards for freshmen enrolling in fine arts curriculum ($5000), 8 high school art show scholarships for high school students (award becomes available upon enrollment) ($1813).

Application Procedures Students admitted directly into the professional program freshman year. Deadline for freshmen and transfers: continuous. Notification date for freshmen and transfers: continuous. Required: high school transcript, college transcript(s) for transfer students, portfolio, SAT I or ACT test scores (minimum combined SAT I score of 900, minimum composite ACT score of 16), "C" average in prior college work for transfer students. Recommended: 3 letters of recommendation, interview. Portfolio reviews held continuously on campus; the submission of slides may be substituted for portfolios when distance is prohibitive.

Web Site http://www.daemen.edu/academics/visual_performing_arts/

Undergraduate Contact Admissions Counselor, Admissions Office, Daemen College, 4380 Main Street, Amherst, New York 14226; 716-839-8225, fax: 716-839-8229, e-mail address: admissions@daemen.edu

Delta State University
Cleveland, Mississippi

State-supported, coed. Small town campus. Total enrollment: 3,998. Art program established 1969.

Design Institute of San Diego
San Diego, California

Proprietary, coed. Urban campus. Total enrollment: 450 (2004). Art program established 1977.

Dominican University of California
San Rafael, California

Independent, coed. Suburban campus. Total enrollment: 1,631. Art program established 1982.

Dorothy F. Schmidt College of Arts and Letters

See Florida Atlantic University

Drake University
Des Moines, Iowa

Independent, coed. Suburban campus. Total enrollment: 5,277.

Degrees Bachelor of Arts in the areas of art history, graphic design, studio art; Bachelor of Fine Arts in the areas of studio art, graphic design. Majors and concentrations: art history, drawing, graphic arts, painting, printmaking, sculpture. Cross-registration with The Institute of Italian Studies (Italy). Program accredited by NASAD.

Enrollment 140 total; all undergraduate.

Art Student Profile 75% females, 25% males, 5% minorities, 5% international.

Drake University (continued)

Art Faculty 9 undergraduate (full-time), 5 undergraduate (part-time). 100% of full-time faculty have terminal degrees. Graduate students do not teach undergraduate courses. Undergraduate student–faculty ratio: 12:1.

Student Life Student groups/activities include Art Student Club, American Institute of Graphic Arts (AIGA), Art Directors Association of Iowa.

Expenses for 2005–2006 Application fee: $25. Comprehensive fee: $27,632 includes full-time tuition ($21,100), mandatory fees ($362), and college room and board ($6170). College room only: $3000. Full-time tuition and fees vary according to class time, course load, and student level. Room and board charges vary according to board plan.

Financial Aid Program-specific awards: 25–30 art scholarships for entering freshmen and transfers ($500–$6000).

Application Procedures Students admitted directly into the professional program freshman year. Deadline for freshmen and transfers: continuous. Required: essay, high school transcript, college transcript(s) for transfer students, SAT I or ACT test scores, portfolio for scholarship consideration. Portfolio reviews held as needed on campus and off campus in Denver, CO; St. Louis, MO; Chicago, IL; Minneapolis, MN; Kansas City, KS; the submission of slides may be substituted for portfolios.

Web Site http://www.drake.edu

Undergraduate Contact Robert Craig, Chair, Department of Art and Design, Drake University, 25th and University Avenue, Des Moines, Iowa 50311; 515-271-2863, fax: 515-271-2558, e-mail address: robert.craig@drake.edu

Drexel University

Philadelphia, Pennsylvania

Independent, coed. Urban campus. Total enrollment: 18,466. Art program established 1963.

Degrees Bachelor of Architecture; Bachelor of Science. Majors and concentrations: architecture, digital media, fashion design, fashion design and merchandising, film and video production, graphic design, interior design, music industry, photography, playwriting, screenwriting. Graduate degrees offered: Master of Architecture in the area of architecture; Master of Science in the areas of fashion and interior design, arts administration, digital media, television management. Program accredited by NAAB, FIDER, NASAD.

Enrollment 1,765 total; 1,598 undergraduate, 167 graduate.

Art Student Profile 58% females, 42% males, 3% international.

Art Faculty 70 total (full-time), 170 total (part-time). 90% of full-time faculty have terminal degrees. Graduate students do not teach undergraduate courses. Undergraduate student–faculty ratio: 15:1.

Student Life Student groups/activities include Graphics Group (graphic design students only).

Expenses for 2005–2006 Application fee: $50. Comprehensive fee: $34,795 includes full-time tuition ($22,700), mandatory fees ($1580), and college room and board ($10,515). College room only: $6255. Full-time tuition and fees vary according to course load, program, and student level. Room and board charges vary according to board plan and housing facility. Special program-related fees: $500 per per term for music lessons (private).

Financial Aid Program-specific awards: 2 Suzanne Roberts Awards for graphic and fashion design students financially needy ($15,000).

Application Procedures Students admitted directly into the professional program freshman year. Deadline for freshmen: March 1; transfers: May 1. Notification date for freshmen and transfers: continuous. Required: high school transcript, college transcript(s) for transfer students, minimum 2.0 high school GPA, 2 letters of recommendation, portfolio, SAT I or ACT test scores (minimum combined SAT I score of 1200), essay for architecture applicants, portfolio for fashion design applicants, graphic design, photo, essay for screenwriting, film and video, interior design, design and merchandising. Recommended: minimum 3.0 high school GPA. Portfolio reviews held by appointment on campus; the submission of slides may be substituted for portfolios.

Web Site http://www.drexel.edu/comad

Undergraduate Contact David Miller, Director of Recruitment, Office of the Dean, College of Media Arts and Design, Drexel University, 33rd and Market Streets, Philadelphia, Pennsylvania

19104; 215-895-1675, fax: 215-895-4917, e-mail address: ddm22@drexel.edu

Graduate Contact David Miller, Director of Recruitment, Office of the Dean, Drexel University, Co MAD-33rd and Market Streets, Philadelphia, Pennsylvania 19104; 215-895-1675, fax: 215-895-4917, e-mail address: ddm22@drexel.edu

More About the University

Drexel University, founded in 1891, is a private university comprising seven colleges and three schools. The Antoinette Westphal College of Media Arts and Design is the fourth-largest college in the system, with approximately 1,500 students. There are eleven undergraduate and four graduate programs in a variety of design, media, and performing arts disciplines. Students work closely with faculty members, who are accomplished designers, filmmakers, photographers, animators, artists, and performers, as they study the process and products of their disciplines.

The undergraduate curricula include a liberal arts and science foundation with broad electives; an arts foundation; and professional courses in studio, lab, and classroom formats—providing a thorough understanding of principles and a hands-on approach to learning. Development of the individual student is a fundamental goal of the curricula, and it is achieved through extensive one-to-one interaction between student and teacher.

Program Facilities The facilities are housed in five buildings and include a gallery, two auditoriums, exhibition spaces, drawing and painting studios, a woodshop, and open computer labs. Program-specific facilities and equipment include the following: Architecture (dedicated space for each student, with drafting tables, storage, and a computer lab); Fashion Design (three studios with cutting tables, dress-forms, industrial sewing equipment, a resource library, storage space, computer facilities for pattern/textile design, and an historic costume collection); Design and Merchandising (dedicated classrooms with TeamBoard and a computer lab with Powerbook G4s, Adobe products, and various merchandising software programs); Interior Design (two studios with drafting tables, a resource library, two PC computer labs, AutoCAD, FormZ, and Microstation); Digital Media (two composite stations, two computer labs with Pentium 4/dual processors, a green screen, digital photography and digital audio stations, a gaming lab, a variety of animation software; 3D Studio, Combustion, Maya, Flash, Director, and Adobe products); Dramatic Writing (classrooms with video, DVD, and film projection); Film and Video (a television station, a video production studio, two screening rooms, professional-quality Sony and Panasonic digital cameras, Arri lights, 16mm cameras, DAT recorders, microphones, dollies, c-stands, field monitors, nonlinear editing stations, video, and film projectors); Graphic Design (four digital studios with Macintosh G4s, Quark Express, and Adobe products); Photography (a large shooting studio, two digital photography labs, two large wet labs, six individual senior darkrooms, Nikon digital cameras, Hasselblads, and large format cameras); and Music Industry (three fully equipped digital recording studios; the College's record label, Mad Dragon Records; and two computer labs with mixing boards, electronic keyboards, and practice facilities).

Student Performance/Exhibit Opportunities

Graduating seniors from each discipline in the College of Media Arts and Design are required to exhibit thesis projects. Photography, Interior Design, Graphic Design, Architecture, and Digital Media programs all hold annual exhibitions. Dramatic Writing majors have the option to have their plays produced. Fashion Design seniors and graduate students showcase their collections in a professionally produced and juried fashion show. All Film and Video students compete in the Mad Dragon Film and Video Festival. The Photography senior exhibition takes place at a commercial gallery and has received critical acclaim. In 1999, four students had work acquired by the Princeton University Art Museum. Music Industry students cultivate talent and produce CDs for the College's record label, Mad Dragon Records.

The College's annual AnnX Exhibit is open to all students and faculty and staff members, allowing them to showcase works of painting, drawing, sculpture, film and video, digital media, photography, fashion, interiors, architecture, music, and performance.

Drexel University's Annual Research Day offers all students the opportunity to showcase and exhibit their work while competing for cash prizes.

Career Placement Opportunities Drexel Co-op is the ultimate internship. Drexel University is a leader in career preparation and has long been recognized for its co-operative education programs, through which students alternate periods of full-time professional employment in their fields of interest with classroom studies. Co-op employers have included Liz Claiborne, NBC Television, Disney Studios, Urban Outfitters, Macy's Northeast, Unisys, Cubist Post & Effects, the University of Pennsylvania, G4

Drexel University (continued)

Media, Comcast, Mary Ellen Mark, Andrew Smith Gallery, and National Geographic.

Special Programs The London Program is open to all majors with at least sophomore standing, allowing students to take advantage of London as an international center for fashion, interiors, business, culture, and design and merchandising. Because of its broad focus, students from all majors are encouraged to apply.

The Fashion in London program is open to second-year fashion design students and, by special arrangement, transfer students. The program is offered during the winter term.

The NENE Graphic Design Exchange program in Northampton, United Kingdom, is open to graphic design majors during the fall of their senior year.

Western Landscape is a unique offering that takes students to the canyons of Southern Utah for an intensive landscape photography class.

East Carolina University

Greenville, North Carolina

State-supported, coed. Urban campus. Total enrollment: 23,164. Art program established 1909.

Eastern New Mexico University

Portales, New Mexico

State-supported, coed. Rural campus. Total enrollment: 4,033.

East Tennessee State University

Johnson City, Tennessee

State-supported, coed. Small town campus. Total enrollment: 11,894. Art program established 1911.

Edinboro University of Pennsylvania

Edinboro, Pennsylvania

State-supported, coed. Small town campus. Total enrollment: 7,691. Art program established 1920.

Emmanuel College

Boston, Massachusetts

Independent Roman Catholic, coed. Urban campus. Total enrollment: 2,296. Art program established 1957.

Degrees Bachelor of Fine Arts in the areas of painting and printmaking, visual communications and graphic design. Majors and concentrations: art education, art history, art therapy, graphic arts, painting/drawing, studio art. Cross-registration with Simmons College, Wheelock College, Wentworth Institute of Technology, Massachusetts College of Pharmacy and Allied Health Sciences, Massachusetts College of Art.

Enrollment 103 total.

Art Faculty 4 undergraduate (full-time), 5 undergraduate (part-time). 100% of full-time faculty have terminal degrees. Graduate students do not teach undergraduate courses. Undergraduate student–faculty ratio: 15:1.

Student Life Student groups/activities include professional gallery on campus, membership in Boston Museum of Fine Arts and Gardner Museum.

Expenses for 2005–2006 Application fee: $40. Comprehensive fee: $32,000 includes full-time tuition ($21,900), mandatory fees ($400), and college room and board ($9700). Full-time tuition and fees vary according to course load, degree level, and program. Room and board charges vary according to housing facility. Special program-related fees: $35–$75 per course for materials fee for studio classes.

Financial Aid Program-specific awards available.

Application Procedures Students admitted directly into the professional program freshman year. Deadline for freshmen and transfers: September 1. Notification date for freshmen and transfers: September 16. Required: essay, high school transcript, college transcript(s) for transfer students, minimum 2.0 high school GPA, 2 letters of recommendation, interview, SAT I test score only. Recommended: portfolio. Portfolio reviews held twice on campus; the submission of slides may be substituted for portfolios when time constraints exist.

Web Site http://www.emmanuel.edu

Undergraduate Contact Director of Admissions, Emmanuel College, 400 The Fenway, Boston, Massachusetts 02115; 617-735-9715, fax: 617-735-9877.

Emporia State University

Emporia, Kansas

State-supported, coed. Small town campus. Total enrollment: 6,288. Art program established 1863.

Degrees Bachelor of Fine Arts in the areas of ceramics, painting, photography, printmaking, sculpture and glassforming, graphic design, engraving arts, metals; Bachelor of Science in Education in the area of art. Majors and concentrations: art education, art therapy, ceramics, glassworking, graphic design, painting/drawing, photography, printmaking, sculpture. Program accredited by NASAD.

Enrollment 175 total; 95 undergraduate, 80 nonprofessional degree.

Art Student Profile 60% females, 40% males, 5% minorities, 3% international.

Art Faculty 12 undergraduate (full-time), 2 undergraduate (part-time). 100% of full-time faculty have terminal degrees. Graduate students do not teach undergraduate courses. Undergraduate student–faculty ratio: 13:1.

Student Life Student groups/activities include Alpha Rho Theta, Glass Guild, Kansas Art Education Association Student Chapter.

Expenses for 2005–2006 Application fee: $30. State resident tuition: $2638 full-time. Nonresident tuition: $9990 full-time. Mandatory fees: $668 full-time. Full-time tuition and fees vary according to degree level. College room and board: $4787. College room only: $2363. Room and board charges vary according to board plan and housing facility. Special program-related fees: $10–$120 per class for expendable supplies.

Financial Aid Program-specific awards: 1 Timothy Sharp Memorial Scholarship for art majors ($250), 2 Jerry Ely Awards for art majors ($1000), 1 Hazelrigg Memorial Award for art majors ($250), 3 Art Faculty Awards for art majors ($250), 4 Beulah Holton Memorial Awards for art education majors ($1700), 1 Linda Ball Memorial Award for art majors ($250), 1 Cremer Family Memorial Award for art majors ($500), 1 Jean Hesenbart Memorial Award for art majors ($500), 1 Art 96 Award for art majors ($2000), 4 Ames Family Memorial Awards for art majors ($225).

Application Procedures Students admitted directly into the professional program freshman year. Deadline for freshmen and transfers: continuous. Required: high school transcript, college transcript(s) for transfer students, minimum 3.0 high school GPA, ACT test score only (minimum composite ACT score of 21), portfolio for scholarship consideration. Portfolio reviews held once on campus; the submission of slides may be substituted for portfolios (slides preferred; digital media also accepted).

Web Site http://www.emporia.edu/art/

Undergraduate Contact Elaine O. Henry, Chair, Department of Art, Emporia State University, Campus Box 4015, 1200 Commercial, Emporia, Kansas 66801-5087; 620-341-5246, fax: 620-341-6246, e-mail address: henryela@emporia.edu

Ernest G. Welch School of Art and Design

See Georgia State University

Evangel University

Springfield, Missouri

Independent, coed. Urban campus. Total enrollment: 1,801.

Fashion Institute of Technology

New York, New York

State and locally supported, coed, primarily women. Urban campus. Total enrollment: 10,381. Art program established 1976.

Degrees Bachelor of Fine Arts. Majors and concentrations: accessories design and fabrica-

Fashion Institute of Technology (continued)

tion, art/fine arts, communication design, computer animation and interactive media, fabric styling, fashion design, graphic design, illustration, interior design, packaging design, photography, restoration, textile/surface design, toy design. Graduate degrees offered: Master of Arts in the areas of exhibition design, art market: principles and practice, fashion and textile studies, illustration. Cross-registration with State University of New York System. Program accredited by NASAD, FIDER.

Enrollment 3,094 total; 1,303 undergraduate, 112 graduate, 1,679 nonprofessional degree.

Art Student Profile 80% females, 20% males, 55% minorities, 10% international.

Art Faculty 100 undergraduate (full-time), 4 graduate (full-time), 359 total (part-time). Graduate students do not teach undergraduate courses. Undergraduate student–faculty ratio: 13:1.

Student Life Student groups/activities include literary publications, professional clubs and societies.

Expenses for 2006–2007 Application fee: $40. State resident tuition: $4350 full-time. Nonresident tuition: $10,610 full-time. Mandatory fees: $420 full-time. College room and board: $8409. College room only: $7519.

Application Procedures Students apply for admission into the professional program by junior year. Deadline for freshmen and transfers: continuous. Required: essay, high school transcript, college transcript(s) for transfer students, minimum 2.0 high school GPA, interview, portfolio. Recommended: 3 letters of recommendation. Portfolio reviews held several times on campus; the submission of slides may be substituted for portfolios with permission of the chair.

Web Site http://www.fitnyc.edu

Undergraduate Contact Ms. Dolores Lombardi, Director of Admissions, Fashion Institute of Technology, 7th Avenue at 27th Street, New York, New York 10001-5992; 212-217-7675, fax: 212-217-7481, e-mail address: dolores_lombardi@fitnyc.edu

Graduate Contact Dr. Steven Zucker, Dean, School of Graduate Studies, Fashion Institute of Technology, 7th Avenue at 27th Street, New York, New York 10001-5992; 212-217-5714, fax: 212-217-5156.

More About the College

Known worldwide as the premier institution of fashion education, FIT is also an internationally renowned college of art and design, business, and technology, with more than forty programs leading to A.A.S., B.F.A., B.S., M.A., and M.P.S. degrees. The School of Art and Design's majors span a wide variety of professions—from computer animation and interactive media to toy design, fashion design to fine arts, and packaging design to photography—all based on a solid liberal arts foundation. And as a State University of New York college, tuition is affordable for both in- and out-of-state students.

FIT serves more than 6,500 full-time and 4,000 part-time students who come from New York City, New York State, across the nation, and all over the world. The campus is situated amidst the activity and excitement of New York City, global capital of the arts, fashion, media, and business. This location—where midtown Manhattan, the fashion district, and the galleries of Chelsea converge—permits an exceptional two-way flow between the college and the professions it serves.

The college makes extensive use of the city's creative, cultural, and commercial resources by providing students with unrivaled development and networking opportunities, including internships, professionally sponsored competitions and projects, guest lecturers and industry critics, and field trips. Each academic year, fashion shows of student work are attended and judged by members of the press and industry leaders, and student artwork is regularly displayed in exhibitions on campus and in The Museum at FIT. The college also holds regular job fairs and on-campus recruiting events, and the Career Services department sponsors professional speakers and a career-planning class. More than one third of the college's interns are hired by their sponsor companies into full-time jobs upon graduation, and FIT's career services office reports a 90 percent job-placement rate.

FIT is committed to combining a traditional academic experience with a hands-on studio education and career-focused curricula. Each major is infused with a full liberal arts education, providing students with a global perspective, critical-thinking skills, and the ability to communicate effectively. FIT students graduate with industry-ready skills and a broad-based knowledge, enabling them to achieve notable success.

For the Associate in Applied Science degree, FIT offers eleven majors through the School of Art and Design and four through the Jay and Patty Baker School of Business and Technology. FIT has twenty-two baccalaureate programs: thirteen through the School of Art and Design, eight through the Jay and Patty Baker School of Business and Technology, and one through the School of Liberal Arts. The School of Graduate Studies offers six programs leading to either an M.A. or M.P.S. degree. FIT is an accredited institutional member of the Middle States Association of Colleges and Schools, the National Association of Schools of Art and Design, and the Foundation for Interior Design Education Research.

Program Facilities FIT's nine-building campus comprises an entire city block, with studios and labs that reflect the most advanced educational and industry practices.

The Fred P. Pomerantz Art and Design Center houses photography studios and darkrooms; drawing, painting, printmaking, and sculpture studios; a model-making workshop; and a graphics laboratory. The graphics laboratory is equipped with slide duplication, wire binding, and laminating capabilities and high-resolution, large-format printers to accommodate photography, presentation graphics, overlays and specialty graphics, banners, posters, displays, fine art, textile proofs, and CAD prints.

The Marvin Feldman and Business and Liberal Arts centers offer academic and specialized classrooms, design studios, a professional screen print facility, weaving laboratories, a toy design workshop, and a fragrance development laboratory. The Peter G. Scotese Computer-Aided Design and Communications Center provides students with the opportunity to explore the latest advancements in technology and

their integration in the design of textiles, toys, interiors, fashion, and advertising as well as photography and computer graphics. A state-of-the-art language lab is equipped with twenty-seven individual stations capable of playing and/or recording a variety of audiovisual media, including CDs, DVDs, and video- and audiocassettes. Computer labs, both Mac and PC, are available for both independent student use and class sessions. The Instructional Media Services department provides audiovisual and television support and a complete in-house broadcast studio. The Design/Research Lighting Laboratory, for interior design and display and exhibit design students, features more than 400 commercially available lighting fixtures.

The Shirley Goodman Resource Center houses the Gladys Marcus Library, which contains specialized reference works for history, sociology, technology, art, and literature; international journals and periodicals; sketchbooks and records donated by designers, manufacturers, and merchants; slides, tapes, and periodicals; and more than 290,000 volumes, including books, periodicals, and non-print materials. The Museum at FIT is the repository for one of the most important collections of fashion and textiles in the world, with an emphasis on twentieth-century apparel, and it is used by students, designers, and historians alike for research and inspiration. The museum's galleries provide a showcase for a wide spectrum of exhibitions relevant to fashion and its satellite industries, and the new permanent gallery of fashion and textile history serves as an overview of fashion's past, present, and future. Recent exhibitions of note include *The Corset: Fashioning the Body; London Fashion,* which received the first Richard Martin Award for the Excellence in the Exhibition of Costume from the Costume Society of America, and *Dutch at the Edge of Design: Fashion and Textiles from The Netherlands.* The Student Space gallery regularly exhibits the work of FIT's art and design students, and student work is also displayed throughout the campus.

Also on campus are three venues—the Katie Murphy Amphitheatre, the Morris W. and Fannie B. Haft Auditorium, and the John E. Reeves Great Hall—used for student exhibitions and presentations, industry panels, conferences, and special events.

Student Life Four residence halls house approximately 2,350 students in single-, double-, triple-, and quad-occupancy rooms. Each residence hall has centrally located lounges and laundry facilities. Counselors and student staff members live in the halls to help students adjust to college life and living in New York City. Participation in campus life is

visual

Arts

Fashion Institute of Technology (continued)

encouraged for residential and commuting students through more than sixty campus clubs, numerous organizations, and several athletic teams. Dances, concerts, open markets, films, field trips, and other special and social events are planned by the Student Association and Programming Board and the various FIT clubs throughout the year. Student-run publications include a campus newspaper, a literary and art magazine, and the annual FIT yearbook. The Student Council, the governing body of the Student Association, gives all students the privileges and responsibilities of citizens in a self-governing college community. Many faculty committees include student representatives, and the president of the student government sits on FIT's Board of Trustees.

The eight-story David Dubinsky Student Center offers lounges, a game room, a student radio station, the Style Shop (the FIT student-run boutique), government and club offices, international student advisors, services for students with disabilities, a counseling center, a comprehensive health center, two gyms, a dance studio, and a weight room. FIT has intercollegiate teams in basketball, bowling, cross-country track, dance, tennis, table tennis, and volleyball. In addition, the Athletics and Recreation department sponsors group fitness classes each semester, available at no extra cost to students. Classes include body toning, boxing, dance, soccer, tennis, and yoga. Intramural activities allow students to participate in team and individual sports.

Faculty and Alumni FIT's faculty is drawn from New York City's design and business elite, who provide a hands-on teaching approach and professional acumen. Working experts at the forefront of their respective fields, they offer a curriculum rich in real-world experience, ensuring that programs and schools adapt apace with industry. The college counts among its alumni such iconic luminaries as Calvin Klein and Norma Kamali as well as successful and talented professionals in advertising, packaging, television, the design fields, merchandising, manufacturing, public relations, retailing, and more. This growing network provides unparalleled employment and educational opportunities for both students and graduates through departmental advisory boards, regular guest lectures, and degree-related internships.

Special Programs The Presidential Scholars program, available to academically exceptional students in all disciplines, offers special courses, projects, colloquia, activities, and off-campus visits designed to intellectually stimulate and broaden horizons. Presidential Scholars are given priority course registration, awarded an annual merit stipend of $500, and guaranteed on-campus residence.

Through its Office of International Programs, FIT provides students, chosen on a competitive basis, the opportunity to study abroad for a year, a semester, or in the summer or winter sessions. Study abroad locations include Australia, China, France, Italy, Mexico, and the U.K.

Pre-college programs (Saturday/Summer Live) are available during the fall, spring, and summer. More than forty-five classes offer high school and middle school students the chance to learn in an innovative environment, develop their portfolios, explore a wide range of creative careers, and discover natural talents and abilities.

Finlandia University

Hancock, Michigan

Independent, coed. Small town campus. Total enrollment: 548. Art program established 1996.

Dorothy F. Schmidt College of Arts and Letters
Florida Atlantic University

Boca Raton, Florida

State-supported, coed. Suburban campus. Total enrollment: 25,704. Art program established 1961.

Degrees Bachelor of Arts in the area of art history; Bachelor of Fine Arts in the area of studio art. Majors and concentrations: art history, ceramics, computer art, graphic design, painting, photography, printmaking, sculpture. Graduate degrees offered: Master of Arts in Teaching in the area of art education; Master of Fine Arts in the areas of ceramics, painting, graphic design, computer arts. Cross-registration with Broward Community College, Palm Beach Community College.

Enrollment 166 total; 160 undergraduate, 6 graduate.

Art Student Profile 67% females, 33% males, 13% minorities, 12% international.

Art Faculty 20 total (full-time), 16 total (part-time). 100% of full-time faculty have terminal degrees. Graduate students teach a few undergraduate courses. Undergraduate student–faculty ratio: 18:1.

Student Life Student groups/activities include Potters Guild, juried student show, BFA Show.

Expenses for 2005–2006 Application fee: $30. State resident tuition: $2147 full-time. Nonresident tuition: $14,653 full-time. Mandatory fees: $1112 full-time. Full-time tuition and fees vary according to course load. College room and board: $7962. Room and board charges vary according to board plan and housing facility. Special program-related fees: $15 per course per semester for studio lab fee.

Financial Aid Program-specific awards: 1 Palm Beach Water Color Society Award for art majors, 1 Delray Beach Art League Award for art majors, 1 Dorst Award for seniors, 3 McCoy Awards for ceramics students, 1 American Pen Women Award for female art majors, 2 Women in the Visual Arts Awards for female art majors.

Application Procedures Students admitted directly into the professional program freshman year. Deadline for freshmen and transfers: June 1. Required: high school transcript, college transcript(s) for transfer students, minimum 2.0 high school GPA, SAT I or ACT test scores, minimum 2.0 college GPA for transfer students. Recommended: minimum 3.0 high school GPA, portfolio. Portfolio reviews held by request on campus.

Web Site http://www.fau.edu

Undergraduate Contact Michaela Angela DiCosola, Chair, Department of Visual Arts and Art History, Florida Atlantic University, 777 Glades Road, Boca Raton, Florida 33431; 561-297-3870, fax: 561-297-3078, e-mail address: mdicosol@fau.edu

Graduate Contact Jim Novak, Graduate Advisor/Coordinator/Associate Chair, Department of Visual Arts and Art History, Florida Atlantic University, 777 Glades Road, Boca Raton, Florida 33431; 561-297-3870, fax: 561-297-3078, e-mail address: jnovak@fau.edu

Florida International University

Miami, Florida

State-supported, coed. Urban campus. Total enrollment: 36,904. Art program established 1972.

Degrees Bachelor of Arts in the area of art history; Bachelor of Fine Arts in the area of art. Majors and concentrations: art history, ceramics, drawing, electronic arts, jewelry and metalsmithing, new media, painting, photography, printmaking, sculpture. Graduate degrees offered: Master of Fine Arts in the area of art. Program accredited by NASAD.

Enrollment 265 total; 250 undergraduate, 15 graduate.

Art Student Profile 55% females, 45% males, 50% minorities, 20% international.

Art Faculty 17 undergraduate (full-time), 20 undergraduate (part-time), 4 graduate (full-time), 4 graduate (part-time). 100% of full-time faculty have terminal degrees. Graduate students teach about a quarter of undergraduate courses. Undergraduate student–faculty ratio: 25:1.

Student Life Student groups/activities include Fine Arts Student Association.

Expenses for 2005–2006 Application fee: $25. State resident tuition: $3062 full-time. Nonresident tuition: $15,461 full-time. Mandatory fees: $252 full-time. Full-time tuition and fees vary according to course load. College room and board: $9102. College room only: $5518. Room and board charges vary according to housing facility. Special program-related fees: $15 per course for studio lab fee.

Financial Aid Program-specific awards: 10 Spring Review Scholarships for program majors ($1000).

Application Procedures Students apply for admission into the professional program by sophomore year. Deadline for freshmen and transfers: April 1. Notification date for freshmen and transfers: continuous. Required: high school transcript, college transcript(s) for transfer students, SAT I or ACT test scores, minimum TOEFL score of 550 for international applicants, minimum 2.0 college GPA for transfer students. Recommended: minimum 2.0 high school GPA.

Web Site http://www.fiu.edu/~visart

Undergraduate Contact Mr. William Maguire, Professor, Department of Art and Art History, Florida International University, University Park, Miami, Florida 33199; 305-348-2897, fax: 305-348-6544, e-mail address: maguirew@fiu.edu

Graduate Contact Geoffrey Olsen, Director of Graduate Studies, Department of Art and Art History, Florida International University, Univer-

Florida International University (continued)

sity Park, Miami, Florida 33199; 305-348-2897, e-mail address: olseng@fiu.edu

Florida State University

Tallahassee, Florida

State-supported, coed. Suburban campus. Total enrollment: 39,146. Art program established 1973.

Degrees Bachelor of Fine Arts. Majors and concentrations: graphic design, studio art. Graduate degrees offered: Master of Fine Arts in the area of studio art. Program accredited by NASAD.

Enrollment 544 total; 50 undergraduate, 31 graduate, 463 nonprofessional degree.

Art Student Profile 58% females, 42% males, 28% minorities, 5% international.

Art Faculty 25 total (full-time), 15 total (part-time). 100% of full-time faculty have terminal degrees. Graduate students teach a few undergraduate courses.

Student Life Student groups/activities include Art Student League.

Expenses for 2005–2006 Application fee: $30. State resident tuition: $3208 full-time. Nonresident tuition: $16,340 full-time. Full-time tuition varies according to location. College room and board: $6778. College room only: $3600. Room and board charges vary according to board plan and housing facility. Special program-related fees: $25–$35 per course for lab fee.

Financial Aid Program-specific awards: 3 Andy McLachlin Memorial Endowment Awards for sculpture students ($1000), 5 Ann Kirn Scholarships for graphic design students ($800).

Application Procedures Students apply for admission into the professional program by sophomore year. Deadline for freshmen and transfers: continuous. Required: essay, high school transcript, minimum 2.0 high school GPA, SAT I test score only, portfolio review at end of second year for admission into BFA program. Recommended: minimum 3.0 high school GPA, letter of recommendation. Portfolio reviews held 3 times on campus; the submission of slides may be substituted for portfolios whenever necessary.

Web Site http://art.fsu.edu

Undergraduate Contact Ms. Phyllis Straus, Undergraduate Admissions Coordinator, College of Visual Arts and Dance, Florida State University, 220 FAB, Tallahassee, Florida 32306-1150; 850-644-6474, fax: 850-644-8977.

Graduate Contact Bunnie Hunter, Program Assistant, Department of Art, Florida State University, 220 FAB, Tallahassee, Florida 32306-1150; 850-644-6474, fax: 850-644-8977, e-mail address: hdstripl@mailer.fsu.edu

Fontbonne University

St. Louis, Missouri

Independent Roman Catholic, coed. Suburban campus. Total enrollment: 2,836.

Degrees Bachelor of Fine Arts. Majors and concentrations: ceramics, drawing, graphic design, painting, sculpture, studio art. Graduate degrees offered: Master of Arts/Master of Fine Arts in the area of art. Cross-registration with Webster University, Washington University in St. Louis.

Enrollment 94 total; 22 undergraduate, 21 graduate, 51 nonprofessional degree.

Art Student Profile 40% females, 60% males, 7% minorities, 35% international.

Art Faculty 5 total (full-time), 10 total (part-time). 100% of full-time faculty have terminal degrees. Graduate students do not teach undergraduate courses. Undergraduate student–faculty ratio: 14:1.

Expenses for 2006–2007 Application fee: $25. Comprehensive fee: $24,428 includes full-time tuition ($17,120), mandatory fees ($320), and college room and board ($6988). Special program-related fees: $30–$60 per class for supplies, models, guest speakers.

Financial Aid Program-specific awards: 1–5 Fitzgerald Awards for art majors ($1500).

Application Procedures Students apply for admission into the professional program by junior year. Deadline for freshmen and transfers: continuous. Required: high school transcript, college transcript(s) for transfer students, SAT I or ACT test scores (minimum composite ACT score of 20), minimum 2.5 high school GPA, portfolio for scholarship consideration. Recommended: standing in upper 50% of high school graduating class. Portfolio reviews held continuously on campus; the submission of slides may be substituted for portfolios (slides or CD preferred).

Undergraduate Contact Admissions, Fontbonne University, 6800 Wydown Boulevard, St. Louis, Missouri 63105; 314-889-1400, fax: 314-719-8021, e-mail address: ldoss@fontbonne.edu

Graduate Contact Fine Arts Department, Fontbonne University, 6800 Wydown Boulevard, St. Louis, Missouri 63105; 314-889-1431, fax: 314-889-1451, e-mail address: finearts@fontbonne.edu

Fort Hays State University

Hays, Kansas

State-supported, coed. Small town campus. Total enrollment: 7,373.

Frostburg State University

Frostburg, Maryland

State-supported, coed. Small town campus. Total enrollment: 5,041. Art program established 1993.

Georgia Southern University

Statesboro, Georgia

State-supported, coed. Total enrollment: 16,646. Art program established 1906.

Georgia Southwestern State University

Americus, Georgia

State-supported, coed. Small town campus. Total enrollment: 2,427.

Ernest G. Welch School of Art and Design
Georgia State University

Atlanta, Georgia

State-supported, coed. Urban campus. Total enrollment: 25,945.

Grand Valley State University

Allendale, Michigan

State-supported, coed. Small town campus. Total enrollment: 22,565. Art program established 1961.

Degrees Bachelor of Fine Arts. Majors and concentrations: ceramic art and design, graphic design, illustration, jewelry and metalsmithing, painting/drawing, printmaking, sculpture. Program accredited by NASAD.

Enrollment 526 total; 351 undergraduate, 175 nonprofessional degree.

Art Student Profile 73% females, 27% males, 5% minorities, 1% international.

Art Faculty 30 undergraduate (full-time), 4 undergraduate (part-time). 100% of full-time faculty have terminal degrees. Graduate students do not teach undergraduate courses. Undergraduate student–faculty ratio: 12:1.

Student Life Special housing available for art students.

Expenses for 2005–2006 Application fee: $30. State resident tuition: $6220 full-time. Nonresident tuition: $12,510 full-time. Full-time tuition varies according to course level, program, and student level. College room and board: $6360. Room and board charges vary according to board plan, housing facility, and location. Special program-related fees: $5–$15 per credit for studio maintenance.

Financial Aid Program-specific awards: 6 recruitment awards for freshmen ($1000), 1 Branstrom Award for program majors ($2000), 1 Calder Award for program majors ($1000–$1500), 1 Ox Bow Summer Program Award for program majors ($2000), 1 Margaret Warol Award for art education students ($500), 1 Nedra Otis Smith Award for program majors ($1200), 1 Koeze Award for program majors ($1000).

Grand Valley State University (continued)

Application Procedures Students admitted directly into the professional program freshman year. Deadline for freshmen and transfers: August 1. Notification date for freshmen and transfers: continuous. Required: essay, high school transcript, minimum 3.0 high school GPA, portfolio, ACT test score only (minimum composite ACT score of 21). Portfolio reviews held 8 times on campus and off campus in various cities in Michigan and contiguous states; the submission of slides may be substituted for portfolios.

Web Site http://www.gvsu.edu/art/

Undergraduate Contact Dr. J. David McGee, Chair, Art and Design Department, Grand Valley State University, 1105 CAC, Allendale, Michigan 49401; 616-331-2575, fax: 616-331-3240, e-mail address: mcgeed@gvsu.edu

Green Mountain College

Poultney, Vermont

Independent, coed. Small town campus. Total enrollment: 696. Art program established 1990.

Guilford College

Greensboro, North Carolina

Independent, coed. Suburban campus. Total enrollment: 2,682.

Degrees Bachelor of Fine Arts in the area of studio art. Majors and concentrations: ceramics, painting/drawing, photography, printmaking, sculpture. Cross-registration with University of North Carolina at Greensboro.

Art Faculty 3 undergraduate (full-time), 4 undergraduate (part-time). 100% of full-time faculty have terminal degrees. Graduate students do not teach undergraduate courses.

Student Life Student groups/activities include Annual Student Art Exhibition, senior thesis exhibition.

Expenses for 2006–2007 Application fee: $25. Comprehensive fee: $29,710 includes full-time tuition ($22,690), mandatory fees ($330), and college room and board ($6690).

Financial Aid Program-specific awards: J. S. Laing Art Award for sophomore and junior

program majors, Merry Moore Winette Scholarship for photography majors.

Application Procedures Students apply for admission into the professional program by junior year. Deadline for freshmen: February 1; transfers: May 1. Notification date for freshmen: March 15; transfers: June 1. Required: essay, high school transcript, minimum 2.0 high school GPA, SAT I or ACT test scores. Recommended: letter of recommendation, interview, portfolio. Portfolio reviews held once at end of junior year or by appointment on campus; the submission of slides may be substituted for portfolios whenever necessary.

Undergraduate Contact Roy Nydorf, Chair, Art Department, Guilford College, 5800 West Friendly Avenue, Greensboro, North Carolina 27410; 336-316-2249, fax: 336-316-2467.

Harding University

Searcy, Arkansas

Independent, coed. Small town campus. Total enrollment: 5,744. Art program established 1936.

Harpur College

See State University of New York at Binghamton

Harrington College of Design

Chicago, Illinois

Proprietary, coed, primarily women. Urban campus. Total enrollment: 1,563. Art program established 1931.

Degrees Bachelor of Fine Arts. Majors and concentrations: interior design. Program accredited by NASAD, FIDER.

Enrollment 1,500 total; all undergraduate.

Art Student Profile 98% females, 2% males, 39% minorities.

Art Faculty 15 undergraduate (full-time), 130 undergraduate (part-time). 75% of full-time faculty have terminal degrees. Graduate students do not teach undergraduate courses. Undergraduate student–faculty ratio: 10:1.

Student Life Student groups/activities include American Society of Interior Designers OBD, International Interior Design Association Green Design, Student Government Focus (Digita).

Expenses for 2005–2006 Application fee: $60. Tuition: $6930 full-time. Mandatory fees: $580 full-time. Full-time tuition and fees vary according to course load and program. College room only: $5000. Room charges vary according to housing facility. Special program-related fees: $300 per semester for material fees.

Application Procedures Students admitted directly into the professional program freshman year. Deadline for freshmen and transfers: continuous. Required: high school transcript, college transcript(s) for transfer students, interview. Recommended: essay, minimum 2.0 high school GPA, SAT I or ACT test scores.

Web Site http://www.interiordesign.edu

Undergraduate Contact Wendy Franczyk, Vice President of Admissions, Harrington College of Design, 200 West Madison, Chicago, Illinois 60606; 877-939-4975, fax: 312-697-8115, e-mail address: hiid@interiordesign.edu

Hartford Art School

See University of Hartford

Henry Radford Hope School of Fine Arts

See Indiana University Bloomington

Herron School of Art and Design

See Indiana University–Purdue University Indianapolis

Hope College

Holland, Michigan

Independent, coed. Small town campus. Total enrollment: 3,141. Art program established 1949.

Degrees Bachelor of Arts in the area of fine arts. Majors and concentrations: art history, studio art. Program accredited by NASAD.

Enrollment 51 total; all undergraduate.

Art Student Profile 78% females, 22% males, 10% minorities, 2% international.

Art Faculty 7 undergraduate (full-time), 1 undergraduate (part-time). 85% of full-time faculty have terminal degrees. Graduate students do not teach undergraduate courses. Undergraduate student–faculty ratio: 6:1.

Student Life Student groups/activities include GLCA New York Arts Program, DePree Gallery exhibition program.

Expenses for 2005–2006 Application fee: $35. Comprehensive fee: $28,208 includes full-time tuition ($21,420), mandatory fees ($120), and college room and board ($6668). College room only: $3040. Full-time tuition and fees vary according to course load. Room and board charges vary according to board plan.

Financial Aid Program-specific awards: 10 Distinguished Artist Awards for freshman/transfer art students ($2500).

Application Procedures Students admitted directly into the professional program freshman year. Deadline for freshmen and transfers: continuous. Required: high school transcript, college transcript(s) for transfer students, SAT I or ACT test scores. Recommended: portfolio. Portfolio reviews held once on campus; the submission of slides may be substituted for portfolios.

Web Site http://www.hope.edu/academic/art

Undergraduate Contact Carol Anne Mahsun, Chair, Department of Art and Art History, Hope College, 275 Columbia Avenue, Depree Art Center, Holland, Michigan 49424; 616-395-7500, fax: 616-395-7499, e-mail address: mahsu@hope.edu

Howard University

Washington, District of Columbia

Independent, coed. Urban campus. Total enrollment: 10,623. Art program established 1921.

Visual Arts

Hunter College of the City University of New York

New York, New York

State and locally supported, coed. Urban campus. Total enrollment: 20,843.

Idaho State University

Pocatello, Idaho

State-supported, coed. Small town campus. Total enrollment: 13,977. Art program established 1960.

Degrees Bachelor of Fine Arts in the area of art. Majors and concentrations: ceramics, drawing, jewelry and metalsmithing, painting, printmaking, sculpture, weaving. Graduate degrees offered: Master of Fine Arts in the area of art.

Enrollment 93 total; 80 undergraduate, 13 graduate.

Art Student Profile 71% females, 29% males, 7% minorities.

Art Faculty 5 undergraduate (part-time), 7 graduate (full-time). 100% of full-time faculty have terminal degrees. Graduate students teach a few undergraduate courses. Undergraduate student–faculty ratio: 8:1.

Student Life Student groups/activities include John B. Davis Art Gallery, Art Club.

Expenses for 2006–2007 Application fee: $40. One-time mandatory fee: $660. Nonresident tuition: $7700 full-time. Mandatory fees: $4000 full-time. College room and board: $5030. College room only: $2100. Special program-related fees: $10–$45 per course for lab fees for some studio courses.

Financial Aid Program-specific awards: 1 Robbie Robison Scholarship for art majors ($250–$600), 1 Marky Hinson Scholarship for female art majors ($250–$600), 1 John B. Davis Scholarship for art majors ($250–$600).

Application Procedures Students apply for admission into the professional program by sophomore year. Deadline for freshmen and transfers: August 1. Notification date for freshmen and transfers: August 10. Required: high school transcript, college transcript(s) for transfer students, minimum 2.0 high school GPA, ACT test score only (minimum composite ACT score of 18), 3.0 GPA in Art foundation courses (Art 100, 103, 104, 105 & 106), overall 2.5 GPA. Recommended: minimum 3.0 high school GPA, portfolio.

Web Site http://www.isu.edu/art/

Undergraduate Contact Dr. Miles Friend, Professor, Department of Art and Pre-Architecture, Idaho State University, Box 8004, Pocatello, Idaho 83209-8004; 208-282-2361, fax: 208-282-4741.

Graduate Contact Mr. Robert Granger, Associate Professor of Art, Department of Art and Pre-Architecture, Idaho State University, Box 8004, Pocatello, Idaho 83209-8004; 208-282-3905, fax: 208-282-4741.

The Illinois Institute of Art–Chicago

Chicago, Illinois

Proprietary, coed. Urban campus. Total enrollment: 2,588.

Degrees Bachelor of Arts in the area of fashion marketing and management; Bachelor of Fine Arts in the areas of fashion design, interior design, visual communications, media arts and animation, multimedia and Web design, digital media production, game art and design. Majors and concentrations: digital media production, fashion design, fashion merchandising, game art and design, interior design, media arts/animation, multimedia/ web design, visual communication, Web design.

Art Faculty Graduate students do not teach undergraduate courses.

Student Life Student groups/activities include American Society of Interior Designers, Fashion Group Student Chapter, Center for Design Student Chapter. Special housing available for art students.

Expenses for 2006–2007 Application fee: $150. Tuition: $18,720 full-time. Mandatory fees: $300 full-time. College room only: $8070. Special program-related fees for art supplies.

Financial Aid Program-specific awards: high school scholarships for incoming freshmen, merit scholarships for program students with minimum 2.5 GPA, Excellence Awards for program students with minimum 3.5 GPA.

Application Procedures Students admitted directly into the professional program freshman

year. Deadline for freshmen and transfers: continuous. Notification date for freshmen and transfers: continuous. Required: essay, high school transcript, college transcript(s) for transfer students, interview, high school diploma or GED. Recommended: minimum 2.0 high school GPA, SAT I or ACT test scores.

Web Site http://www.ilic.artinstitutes.edu

Undergraduate Contact Ms. Janis Anton, Director of Admissions, The Illinois Institute of Art–Chicago, 350 North Orleans Street, #136, Chicago, Illinois 60654; 800-351-3450 ext. 6868, fax: 312-280-8562, e-mail address: antonj@aii.edu

More About the Institute

Regardless of which of the nineteen programs a student enrolls, the mission of the faculty is to nurture and stimulate the minds of the students so they are well prepared for the workplace.

The Institute offers programs leading to the Bachelor of Fine Arts in digital media production, fashion design, game art and design, interactive media design, interior design, media arts and animation, visual communications, and visual effects and motion graphics. In addition, the Institute offers a Bachelor of Arts degree in advertising and fashion marketing and management and a Bachelor of Applied Science degree in culinary management. The Institute's associate degree programs include culinary arts, fashion merchandising, fashion production, graphic design, and multimedia production.

In presenting the combination of hands-on training in a student's chosen field, mixed with a base liberal arts curriculum, the Institute prides itself on its aim to be the foundation of many successful careers. Alumni, working for companies ranging from national commercial giants that are familiar to everyday America to the small firm around the corner, have achieved success since the Institute was founded in 1916.

The Institute has a student body that consists of residents of thirty-five states and twenty international countries. The faculty members pull it all together for the students, teaching them to become professionals in the marketplace.

Instruction stresses and aims to stimulate the creative process in students who learn to ask thoughtful questions about what must be conveyed and who the target audience is. In analyzing the parameters of a project, thought must be given to budgetary constraints. This kind of strategic thinking applies to students studying different disciplines, from graphic design to interior design.

Students are given the opportunity, within the framework of their curriculum, to develop their talents and bring reality to their designs. At the Institute, a student is not just sitting in a classroom but is working on deadlines, developing a portfolio, and learning the skills that will pay off when that first job opportunity arrives. The idea is to build the student's confidence and start a career running with a firm base of practical experiences.

Also offered are a full array of student services. Counseling is available, with assistance offered in a wide range of issues. The Career Services Office helps refine the presentation of skills, interests, and qualifications to potential employers, along with providing assistance in finding part-time employment while enrolled. Students are also encouraged to join on-campus and professional organizations related to their interests and fields.

The Institute realizes that affordable and comfortable housing is a concern of every student, especially those coming from a rural environment to a metroplex like Chicago. The housing department makes every effort to respond to such concerns. Multiple units in area apartment complexes are leased by the Institute, and students are assigned to a portion of each, thus providing a campus-style living arrangement.

Campus security is also a high priority. Strict policies pertaining to the possession of drugs and weapons in campus buildings or in off-campus housing are adhered to. Students are urged to take personal responsibility for campus security and crime-awareness issues.

"Chicago is my kind of town" is the famous song lyric. The Institute thinks that it might be yours.

Program Facilities Located in heart of Chicago in the design complex of the Apparel Center/Merchandise Mart Complex on North Orleans Street, the Institute occupies approximately 70,000 square feet. The 50,000-square-foot Loop Campus facility is located at 180 North Wabash Avenue. Classrooms, offices, galleries, and a research center are located in this area. In addition, the Fashion Department contains an array of special equipment, such as power sewing machines, large cutting tables, and steamers. Fashion design classes utilize a walk-in window, mannequins, and other display materials. The Interior Design Resource Center has an extensive collection of fabric and floor-covering samples.

Faculty and Resident Artists The faculty consists of working professionals dedicated to instructing students through a curriculum that will prepare students thoroughly for entry-level positions in their

The Illinois Institute of Art–Chicago (continued)

chosen field. Curricula are reviewed regularly to ensure they meet the needs of a changing marketplace.

Exhibit Opportunities The Institute's students have many opportunities to showcase their work. Students in the fashion studies are offered the opportunity to produce a professional-level fashion show on an annual basis. Interior design students work on projects that simulate on-the-job situations, with media arts and animation students modeling new software creations and applications. For example, student artwork is featured widely in the Institute's catalogs.

Special Programs With the Institute's close ties to the working world, internships in several fields are readily available. International students are welcome and are required to offer proof of a TOEFL score of at least 500, or the completion of a level-109 course at an ELS Language Center.

The Illinois Institute of Art–Schaumburg

Schaumburg, Illinois

Proprietary, coed. Suburban campus. Total enrollment: 1,187. Art program established 1995.

Illinois State University

Normal, Illinois

State-supported, coed. Urban campus. Total enrollment: 20,653. Art program established 1965.

Degrees Bachelor of Fine Arts in the area of art. Majors and concentrations: art/fine arts, ceramics, glass, graphic design, intaglio, jewelry and metalsmithing, lithography, painting/drawing, photography, sculpture, studio art, video art, wood. Graduate degrees offered: Master of Arts/Master of Science in the area of art education; Master of Fine Arts in the area of studio arts. Cross-registration with members of the National Student Exchange Program, University of Wolverhampton (England), University of Sunderland (England), Christ Church University College (England). Program accredited by NASAD.

Enrollment 565 total; 25 undergraduate, 40 graduate, 500 nonprofessional degree.

Art Student Profile 55% females, 45% males, 10% minorities, 1% international.

Art Faculty 40 total (full-time), 4 total (part-time). 100% of full-time faculty have terminal degrees. Graduate students do not teach undergraduate courses. Undergraduate student–faculty ratio: 2:1.

Student Life Student groups/activities include Students in Graphic Design, National Art Education Association Student Chapter, Illinois Art Education Association Student Chapter. Special housing available for art students.

Expenses for 2005–2006 Application fee: $30. State resident tuition: $5400 full-time. Nonresident tuition: $11,280 full-time. Mandatory fees: $1691 full-time. Full-time tuition and fees vary according to course load. College room and board: $5748. College room only: $3010. Room and board charges vary according to board plan. Special program-related fees: $10–$85 per course for studio lab fee.

Financial Aid Program-specific awards: 25–30 departmental scholarships for program majors ($600–$3000).

Application Procedures Students apply for admission into the professional program by sophomore, junior year. Deadline for freshmen and transfers: continuous. Required: essay, high school transcript, college transcript(s) for transfer students, interview, portfolio, SAT I or ACT test scores, minimum 3.0 college GPA for transfers. Portfolio reviews held continuously on campus; the submission of slides may be substituted for portfolios with original work.

Web Site http://www.arts.ilstu.edu/art

Undergraduate Contact Nancy Fewkes, Undergraduate Advisor, School of Art, Illinois State University, Campus Box 5620, Normal, Illinois 61790-5620; 309-438-5621, fax: 309-438-8318.

Graduate Contact William O'Donnell, Graduate Coordinator, School of Art, Illinois State University, Campus Box 5620, Normal, Illinois 61790-5620; 309-438-5621, fax: 309-438-8318.

Illinois Wesleyan University

Bloomington, Illinois

Independent, coed. Suburban campus. Total enrollment: 2,146. Art program established 1850.

Indiana State University

Terre Haute, Indiana

State-supported, coed. Small town campus. Total enrollment: 10,679. Art program established 1870.

Degrees Bachelor of Fine Arts in the area of studio art and design; Bachelor of Science in the area of art education. Majors and concentrations: art education, ceramic art and design, graphic design, painting/drawing, photography, printmaking, sculpture, studio art, wood. Graduate degrees offered: Master of Fine Arts in the area of studio art and design. Program accredited by NASAD.

Enrollment 215 total; 150 undergraduate, 50 graduate, 15 nonprofessional degree.

Art Student Profile 65% females, 35% males, 26% minorities, 8% international.

Art Faculty 13 total (full-time), 2 total (part-time). 92% of full-time faculty have terminal degrees. Graduate students teach a few undergraduate courses. Undergraduate student–faculty ratio: 15:1.

Student Life Student groups/activities include Student Gallery Program, Design Club, Art Club. Special housing available for art students.

Expenses for 2005–2006 Application fee: $25. State resident tuition: $5756 full-time. Nonresident tuition: $12,752 full-time. Mandatory fees: $108 full-time. Full-time tuition and fees vary according to course load. College room and board: $5938. College room only: $3150. Room and board charges vary according to board plan, housing facility, and student level. Special program-related fees: $24 per course for studio lab fee.

Financial Aid Program-specific awards: 1 Hildegard Ping Art and Anthropology Scholarship for program majors ($400), 1 ISU Friends of Art Scholarship for program majors ($500), 10–12 Creative and Performing Arts Scholarships for freshmen ($2000), 1 Indiana Artist-Craftsmen/Talbot Street Art Fair Scholarship for program majors ($350), 1 Violet Helen Rich Scholarship for painting majors ($1500), 1 Elmer J. Porter Scholarship for program majors ($675), 1 Mark Hannig Scholarship for program majors ($1000), 3 Marian J. Frutiger Awards for art majors ($2300).

Application Procedures Students admitted directly into the professional program freshman year. Deadline for freshmen and transfers: August 15. Notification date for freshmen and transfers: continuous. Required: high school transcript, college transcript(s) for transfer students, minimum 2.0 high school GPA, SAT I or ACT test scores, portfolio for scholarship consideration. Portfolio reviews held 6 times on campus and off campus in Vincennes, IN; Fort Wayne, IN; Louisville, KY; Indianapolis, IN; St. Louis, MO; Chicago, IL; the submission of slides may be substituted for portfolios when distance is prohibitive, if original work is unavailable, or for large works of art.

Web Site http://artdept.indstate.edu/

Undergraduate Contact Fran Lattanzio, Undergraduate Advisor, Department of Art, Indiana State University, Fine Arts 108, Terre Haute, Indiana 47809; 812-237-8528, fax: 812-237-4369, e-mail address: artdept@isugw.indstate.edu

Graduate Contact Charles Mayer, Interim Chair, Department of Art, Indiana State University, Fine Arts 108, Terre Haute, Indiana 47809; 812-237-3697, fax: 812-237-4369, e-mail address: artdept@isugw.indstate.edu

Henry Radford Hope School of Fine Arts

Indiana University Bloomington

Bloomington, Indiana

State-supported, coed. Small town campus. Total enrollment: 37,958. Art program established 1896.

Degrees Bachelor of Fine Arts in the areas of ceramics, graphic design, jewelry and metalsmithing, painting, photography, printmaking, sculpture, textiles. Majors and

Indiana University Bloomington (continued)

concentrations: ceramic art and design, digital art, graphic design, jewelry and metalsmithing, painting/drawing, photography, printmaking, sculpture, textile arts. Graduate degrees offered: Master of Arts in the area of art history; Master of Arts in Teaching in the area of art education; Master of Fine Arts in the areas of ceramics, graphic design, jewelry and metalsmithing, painting, photography, printmaking, sculpture, textiles. Doctor of Philosophy in the area of art history. Program accredited by NASAD.

Enrollment 565 total; 60 undergraduate, 165 graduate, 340 nonprofessional degree.

Art Student Profile 60% females, 40% males, 7% minorities, 2% international.

Art Faculty 30 total (full-time), 3 total (part-time). 100% of full-time faculty have terminal degrees. Graduate students teach about a quarter of undergraduate courses. Undergraduate student–faculty ratio: 15:1.

Student Life Student groups/activities include Fine Arts Student Association, Graphic Design Student Association.

Expenses for 2005–2006 Application fee: $50. State resident tuition: $6291 full-time. Nonresident tuition: $18,687 full-time. Mandatory fees: $821 full-time. Full-time tuition and fees vary according to location, program, and student level. College room and board: $6240. College room only: $3760. Room and board charges vary according to board plan and housing facility. Special program-related fees: $23–$100 per course for material fees.

Financial Aid Program-specific awards: 10–15 Hope School of Fine Arts Student Awards for program majors ($150–$2500).

Application Procedures Students apply for admission into the professional program by sophomore, junior year. Deadline for freshmen and transfers: continuous. Notification date for freshmen and transfers: August 29. Required: high school transcript, college transcript(s) for transfer students, SAT I or ACT test scores.

Web Site http://www.fa.indiana.edu/

Undergraduate Contact Nell Weatherwax, Undergraduate Advisor, Henry Radford Hope School of Fine Arts, Indiana University Bloomington, 1201 East 7th Street, Room 123, Bloomington, Indiana 47405; 812-855-1693, fax: 812-855-7498, e-mail address: nweather@indiana.edu

Graduate Contact Elke Pessl, Graduate Services Coordinator, Henry Radford Hope School of Fine Arts, Indiana University Bloomington, 1201 East 7th Street, Room 123, Bloomington, Indiana 47405; 812-855-0188, fax: 812-855-7498, e-mail address: faoffice@indiana.edu

Indiana University of Pennsylvania

Indiana, Pennsylvania

State-supported, coed. Small town campus. Total enrollment: 14,081.

Indiana University–Purdue University Fort Wayne

Fort Wayne, Indiana

State-supported, coed. Urban campus. Total enrollment: 11,795. Art program established 1976.

Herron School of Art and Design

Indiana University–Purdue University Indianapolis

Indianapolis, Indiana

State-supported, coed. Urban campus. Total enrollment: 29,933. Art program established 1902.

Degrees Bachelor of Art Education; Bachelor of Fine Arts in the areas of painting, printmaking, ceramics, sculpture, visual communication, photography, fine arts, furniture design. Majors and concentrations: art education, art/fine arts, ceramic art and design, computer graphics, furniture design, graphic arts, painting/drawing, photography, printmaking, sculpture. Graduate degrees offered: Master of Art Education. Cross-registration with Butler University, University of Indianapolis. Program accredited by NASAD.

Enrollment 785 total; 760 undergraduate, 15 graduate, 10 nonprofessional degree.

Art Student Profile 52% females, 48% males, 10% minorities, 5% international.

Art Faculty 50 undergraduate (full-time), 15 undergraduate (part-time). 100% of full-time faculty have terminal degrees. Graduate students do not teach undergraduate courses. Undergraduate student–faculty ratio: 15:1.

Student Life Student groups/activities include Herron Student Senate, Photography Club, Students in Graphic Design.

Expenses for 2005–2006 Application fee: $50. State resident tuition: $5625 full-time. Nonresident tuition: $15,953 full-time. Mandatory fees: $594 full-time. Full-time tuition and fees vary according to course load and program. College room and board: $4740. College room only: $2340. Room and board charges vary according to board plan and housing facility. Special program-related fees: $150 per year for technology fee.

Financial Aid Program-specific awards: 20 new student awards for program majors ($1500).

Application Procedures Students apply for admission into the professional program by sophomore year. Deadline for freshmen and transfers: May 1. Notification date for freshmen and transfers: July 15. Required: high school transcript, college transcript(s) for transfer students, minimum 2.0 high school GPA, SAT I or ACT test scores (minimum combined SAT I score of 990), portfolio for scholarship consideration. Recommended: minimum 3.0 high school GPA, portfolio. Portfolio reviews held once on campus; the submission of slides may be substituted for portfolios.

Web Site http://www.herron.iupui.edu

Contact Mrs. Beth Spears, Director of Student Services, Herron School of Art and Design, Indiana University–Purdue University Indianapolis, 735 West New York Street, Indianapolis, Indiana 46202; 317-278-9400, fax: 317-278-9401, e-mail address: espears@iupui.edu

International Academy of Design & Technology

Tampa, Florida

Proprietary, coed. Urban campus. Total enrollment: 2,405. Art program established 1984.

Degrees Bachelor of Fine Arts. Majors and concentrations: computer animation, digital photography, digital production, fashion design, graphic design, interactive media, interior design, recording arts. Program accredited by FIDER.

Enrollment 2,000 total.

Art Faculty 13 undergraduate (full-time), 158 undergraduate (part-time). Graduate students do not teach undergraduate courses. Undergraduate student–faculty ratio: 14:1.

Student Life Student groups/activities include American Society of Interior Designers Student Chapter, Fashion Design Club, Siggraph (graphics and animation).

Expenses for 2006–2007 Application fee: $50.

Financial Aid Program-specific awards: 50 Florida High School Partnership Scholarships for entering freshmen ($1000), 15 merit award scholarships for incoming freshmen ($1000–$10,000), Spring Portfolio Review Scholarships for incoming freshmen ($150–$500), International Merit Scholarship ($500–$2500), 1 President's Institutional Scholarship for continuing students ($250–$1000).

Application Procedures Students admitted directly into the professional program freshman year. Deadline for freshmen and transfers: continuous. Required: college transcript(s) for transfer students, high school transcript or GED attestation. Recommended: minimum 2.0 high school GPA, interview, portfolio. Portfolio reviews held on campus.

Web Site http://www.academy.edu

Undergraduate Contact Richard Costa, Vice President, Admissions and Marketing, International Academy of Design & Technology, 5104 Eisenhower Boulevard, Tampa, Florida 33634; 800-ACADEMY ext. 8092, fax: 813-881-0008.

Visual

Arts

International Academy of Design & Technology

Chicago, Illinois

Proprietary, coed. Urban campus. Art program established 1977.

Degrees Bachelor of Arts in the area of merchandising management; Bachelor of Fine Arts in the areas of interior design, fashion design, advertising and design, multimedia production and design. Majors and concentrations: advertising design, computer graphics, fashion design, interactive multimedia, interior design, merchandising management. Program accredited by FIDER.

Enrollment 2,905 total; 2,588 undergraduate, 317 nonprofessional degree.

Art Student Profile 68% females, 32% males, 60% minorities, 1% international.

Art Faculty 26 undergraduate (full-time), 134 undergraduate (part-time). 20% of full-time faculty have terminal degrees. Graduate students do not teach undergraduate courses. Undergraduate student–faculty ratio: 15:1.

Student Life Student groups/activities include American Society of Interior Designers, Fashion Group International, Inc., American Institute of Graphic Arts.

Expenses for 2006–2007 Application fee: $50. Tuition: $22,400 full-time. Mandatory fees: $600 full-time.

Application Procedures Students admitted directly into the professional program freshman year. Deadline for freshmen and transfers: continuous. Required: high school transcript, college transcript(s) for transfer students, interview. Recommended: essay, minimum 2.0 high school GPA, letter of recommendation, portfolio, SAT I or ACT test scores. Portfolio reviews held as needed on campus; the submission of slides may be substituted for portfolios for ease of handling.

Web Site http://www.iadtchicago.com

Undergraduate Contact Doug Lochbaum, Associate Vice President of Admissions, International Academy of Design & Technology, 1 North State Street, Suite 400, Chicago, Illinois 60602-3300; 312-980-9200, fax: 312-541-3929.

Iowa State University of Science and Technology

Ames, Iowa

State-supported, coed. Suburban campus. Total enrollment: 25,741. Art program established 1920.

Degrees Bachelor of Fine Arts in the areas of graphic design, interior design, integrated studio arts. Majors and concentrations: graphic design, integrated studio arts, interior design. Graduate degrees offered: Master of Fine Arts in the areas of graphic design, interior design, integrated visual arts. Program accredited by FIDER.

Enrollment 1,064 total; 600 undergraduate, 65 graduate, 399 nonprofessional degree.

Art Student Profile 60% females, 40% males, 4% minorities, 1% international.

Art Faculty 38 total (full-time), 26 total (part-time). 95% of full-time faculty have terminal degrees. Graduate students teach a few undergraduate courses. Undergraduate student–faculty ratio: 18:1.

Student Life Student groups/activities include Interior Design Student Association, American Institute of Graphic Arts Student Chapter, College of Design Art Club. Special housing available for art students.

Expenses for 2005–2006 Application fee: $30. State resident tuition: $4890 full-time. Nonresident tuition: $14,980 full-time. Mandatory fees: $744 full-time. Full-time tuition and fees vary according to class time, degree level, and program. College room and board: $6197. College room only: $3295. Room and board charges vary according to board plan and housing facility. Special program-related fees: $5–$100 per course for in-studio expenses.

Financial Aid Program-specific awards: 10–12 art and design excellence awards for program majors ($500–$1500), 2 Garfield/Boody Awards for fine arts majors ($1600), 3 Kiser/Beard Awards for interior design majors ($1500), 2–4 art and design minority awards for program majors ($500–$1000), 1–2 graphic design sophomore scholarships for program majors ($500).

Application Procedures Students apply for admission into the professional program by freshman year. Deadline for freshmen and transfers: continuous. Required: high school transcript, college transcript(s) for transfer students, SAT I or ACT test scores, minimum TOEFL score of 550 for international applicants, portfolio for graphic, interior design, and integrated studio arts. Recommended: minimum 2.0 high school GPA, standing in top half of graduating class. Portfolio reviews held once in spring on campus.

Web Site http://www.design.iastate.edu/

Undergraduate Contact Director of Admissions, Iowa State University of Science and Technology, 100 Alumni Hall, Ames, Iowa 50011-2010; 515-294-5836, fax: 515-294-2592, e-mail address: admissions@iastate.edu

Graduate Contact Mona Pett, Secretary, Department of Art and Design, Iowa State University of Science and Technology, 158 College of Design, Ames, Iowa 50011-2010; 515-294-6725, fax: 515-294-2725, e-mail address: grad_admissions@iastate.edu

Ithaca College

Ithaca, New York

Independent, coed. Small town campus. Total enrollment: 6,412. Art program established 1986.

Degrees Bachelor of Fine Arts in the areas of film, photography, visual arts. Majors and concentrations: film, photography, visual arts. Cross-registration with Cornell University, Wells College.

Enrollment 80 total; all undergraduate.

Art Student Profile 40% females, 60% males, 8% minorities, 8% international.

Art Faculty 13 undergraduate (full-time), 4 undergraduate (part-time). 100% of full-time faculty have terminal degrees. Graduate students do not teach undergraduate courses. Undergraduate student–faculty ratio: 6:1.

Student Life Student groups/activities include Television Station, Radio Station, Production Unit.

Expenses for 2005–2006 Application fee: $55. Comprehensive fee: $35,144 includes full-time tuition ($25,194) and college room and board ($9950). College room only: $5120.

Financial Aid Program-specific awards: 2 Kristen Landen Film Scholarships for cinema majors ($1010), 2 Mark Mazura Video Production Scholarships for video production students ($1362), James B. Pendleton Filmmaking Awards for film majors, 18 James B. Pendleton Scholarships for cinema and photography majors ($5665–$7665), 2 Rod Serling Scholarships for video production students ($2158), 1 Mark Wilder Memorial Scholarship for video production students ($1238).

Application Procedures Students admitted directly into the professional program freshman year. Deadline for freshmen: February 1; transfers: March 1. Notification date for freshmen: April 15. Required: essay, high school transcript, college transcript(s) for transfer students, letter of recommendation, SAT I or ACT test scores. Recommended: minimum 3.0 high school GPA, interview.

Web Site http://www.ithaca.edu/rhp.php

Undergraduate Contact Mr. Gerard Turbide, Acting Director, Admission, Ithaca College, 100 Job Hall, Ithaca, New York 14850-7020; 607-274-3124, fax: 607-274-1900, e-mail address: admission@ithaca.edu

Ithaca College

Ithaca, New York

Independent, coed. Small town campus. Total enrollment: 6,412. Art program established 1960.

Degrees Bachelor of Arts in the area of art education; Bachelor of Fine Arts in the area of art. Majors and concentrations: art, art education. Cross-registration with Cornell University, Wells College.

Enrollment 36 total; 14 undergraduate, 22 nonprofessional degree.

Art Student Profile 61% females, 39% males, 11% minorities, 3% international.

Art Faculty 6 undergraduate (full-time), 3 undergraduate (part-time). 100% of full-time faculty have terminal degrees. Graduate students do not teach undergraduate courses. Undergraduate student–faculty ratio: 5:1.

Student Life Student groups/activities include Ithaca College Art Club.

Expenses for 2005–2006 Application fee: $55. Comprehensive fee: $35,144 includes full-time tuition ($25,194) and college room and board ($9950). College room only: $5120. Special program-related fees: $25–$60 per semester for supplies.

Visual Arts

Ithaca College (continued)

Financial Aid Program-specific awards: 1 Donald and Martha Negus Scholarship for program majors ($875).

Application Procedures Students admitted directly into the professional program freshman year. Deadline for freshmen: February 1; transfers: March 1. Notification date for freshmen: April 15. Required: essay, high school transcript, college transcript(s) for transfer students, letter of recommendation, SAT I or ACT test scores. Recommended: minimum 3.0 high school GPA, interview, portfolio. Portfolio reviews held continuously by appointment on campus; the submission of slides may be substituted for portfolios.

Web Site http://www.ithaca.edu/hs.php

Undergraduate Contact Mr. Gerard Turbide, Acting Director, Admission, Ithaca College, 100 Job Hall, Ithaca, New York 14850-7020; 607-274-3124, fax: 607-274-1900, e-mail address: admission@ithaca.edu

Jacksonville State University

Jacksonville, Alabama

State-supported, coed. Small town campus. Total enrollment: 9,110.

Degrees Bachelor of Fine Arts in the area of studio art. Majors and concentrations: ceramics, graphic design, painting/drawing, photography, printmaking. Program accredited by NASAD.

Enrollment 147 total; 94 undergraduate, 53 nonprofessional degree.

Art Student Profile 63% females, 37% males, 12% minorities, 2% international.

Art Faculty 8 undergraduate (full-time), 3 undergraduate (part-time). 100% of full-time faculty have terminal degrees. Graduate students do not teach undergraduate courses. Undergraduate student–faculty ratio: 14:1.

Student Life Student groups/activities include Student Art Alliance, The Potter's Guild.

Expenses for 2005–2006 Application fee: $20. State resident tuition: $4040 full-time. Nonresident tuition: $8080 full-time. College room and board: $3258. College room only: $1680.

Room and board charges vary according to board plan and housing facility.

Financial Aid Program-specific awards: 1 Art Department Award for incoming freshmen ($1000), 2 Art Department Awards for upperclassmen ($1000), 1 Lee Manners Scholarship for junior art majors with 3.0 minimum GPA ($350), 1 Visual Art Society/JSU Scholarship for upperclassmen ($1000).

Application Procedures Students apply for admission into the professional program by sophomore year. Deadline for freshmen and transfers: continuous. Required: high school transcript, portfolio, SAT I or ACT test scores. Recommended: minimum 2.0 high school GPA. Portfolio reviews held twice on campus.

Web Site http://art.jsu.edu

Undergraduate Contact Mr. Charles Groover, Head, Department of Art, Jacksonville State University, 700 Pelham Road North, Jacksonville, Alabama 36265; 256-782-5625, fax: 256-782-5419.

Jacksonville University

Jacksonville, Florida

Independent, coed. Suburban campus. Total enrollment: 2,948. Art program established 1961.

Degrees Bachelor of Fine Arts in the areas of studio art, computer art and design. Majors and concentrations: computer art, studio art.

Enrollment 73 total; all undergraduate.

Art Student Profile 58% females, 42% males, 22% minorities, 3% international.

Art Faculty 7 undergraduate (full-time), 4 undergraduate (part-time). 90% of full-time faculty have terminal degrees. Graduate students do not teach undergraduate courses. Undergraduate student–faculty ratio: 7:1.

Student Life Student groups/activities include Fine Art Society, volunteer city-wide art projects, student group shows.

Expenses for 2005–2006 Application fee: $30. Comprehensive fee: $26,430 includes full-time tuition ($19,970) and college room and board ($6460). College room only: $3030.

Financial Aid Program-specific awards: 2 Phillips Scholarships for those demonstrating exceptional talent ($1500–$6000), 2 Sheldon Bryan

Scholarships for those demonstrating exceptional talent ($1000–$6000).

Application Procedures Students admitted directly into the professional program freshman year. Deadline for freshmen and transfers: continuous. Notification date for freshmen and transfers: continuous. Required: high school transcript, college transcript(s) for transfer students, minimum 2.0 high school GPA, portfolio, SAT I or ACT test scores (minimum combined SAT I score of 800). Recommended: essay, letter of recommendation. Portfolio reviews held 5 times and by appointment on campus and off campus in various high schools in Duval County; the submission of slides may be substituted for portfolios if a campus visit is impossible.

Web Site http://www.ju.edu

Undergraduate Contact Ms. Miriam King, Vice President of Enrollment Management, Jacksonville University, 2800 University Boulevard North, Jacksonville, Florida 32211; 904-256-7000, fax: 904-256-7012, e-mail address: admissions@ju.edu

James Madison University

Harrisonburg, Virginia

State-supported, coed. Small town campus. Total enrollment: 16,938. Art program established 1922.

Johnson State College

Johnson, Vermont

State-supported, coed. Rural campus. Total enrollment: 1,866. Art program established 1982.

J. William Fulbright College of Arts and Sciences

See University of Arkansas

Kansas City Art Institute

Kansas City, Missouri

Independent, coed. Urban campus. Art program established 1885.

Degrees Bachelor of Fine Arts in the areas of ceramics, fiber, painting, printmaking, photography/new media, sculpture, art history, creative writing, animation, graphic design, interdisciplinary arts. Majors and concentrations: animation, art history, ceramics, creative writing, fibers, graphic design, interdisciplinary studies, painting/drawing, photography/new media, printmaking, sculpture. Cross-registration with Kansas City Area Student Exchange. Program accredited by NASAD.

Enrollment 594 total; all undergraduate.

Art Student Profile 56% females, 44% males, 14% minorities, 2% international.

Art Faculty 43 undergraduate (full-time), 36 undergraduate (part-time). 72% of full-time faculty have terminal degrees. Graduate students do not teach undergraduate courses. Undergraduate student–faculty ratio: 12:1.

Student Life Student groups/activities include Student Gallery Committee, Ethnic Student Association, Student Film Series Committee. Special housing available for art students.

Expenses for 2005–2006 Application fee: $35. Comprehensive fee: $29,542 includes full-time tuition ($21,446), mandatory fees ($946), and college room and board ($7150). Full-time tuition and fees vary according to program. Room and board charges vary according to board plan and housing facility. Special program-related fees: $60 per course for sculpture fee, $70 per course for fiber fee, $75 per course for print fee, $140 per course for photo and new media fee, $365 per course for ceramics materials.

Financial Aid Program-specific awards: 300–350 need-based scholarships for program majors ($2000–$8000), 100–125 merit-based scholarships for program majors ($2000–$8000).

Application Procedures Students apply for admission into the professional program by sophomore year. Deadline for freshmen and transfers: continuous. Required: essay, high school transcript, college transcript(s) for transfer students, 2 letters of recommendation, portfolio, SAT I or ACT test scores (minimum

Kansas City Art Institute (continued)

composite ACT score of 20), minimum 2.5 high school GPA. Recommended: interview. Portfolio reviews held continuously on campus and off campus in various locations on National Portfolio Days; the submission of slides may be substituted for portfolios (slides, CD-DVD preferred).

Web Site http://www.kcai.edu

Undergraduate Contact Mr. Larry E. Stone, Vice President for Enrollment Management, Kansas City Art Institute, 4415 Warwick Boulevard, Kansas City, Missouri 64111; 800-522-5224, fax: 816-802-3309, e-mail address: admiss@kcai.edu

More About the Institute

Kansas City Art Institute (KCAI), founded in 1885, is a private and fully accredited distinguished four-year college of art and design. Kansas City Art Institute is accredited by the National Association of Schools of Art and Design (NASAD) and the North

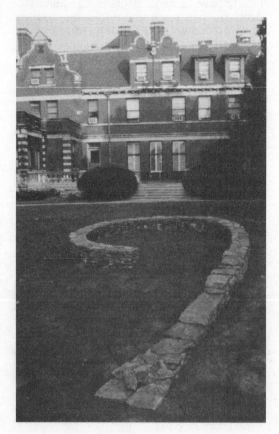

Central Association of Colleges and Secondary Schools. KCAI's 600 students are from thirty-seven states and sixteen nations. Kansas City Art Institute combines intensive time in the classroom, extensive experience in the studio, a broad liberal arts background, focused learning opportunities, and a dynamic campus community. It is this rich combination that develops the "whole" student as an artist and a person.

Kansas City Art Institute is located in the heart of the cultural community of Kansas City. Across the street to the east is the Nelson-Atkins Museum of Art, consistently ranked in the top fifteen general art museums. The Kemper Museum of Contemporary Art is across the street to the west. Galleries and studios, restaurants and cafés, the Country Club Plaza, and other entertainment spots are only a short distance from the campus.

Kansas City Art Institute provides an ideal environment to bring the students' art to life. A scenic 15-acre campus is complete with individual studio space as early as freshman year, cutting-edge technology, wide open spaces, and first-rate facilities that foster creative spirit. The commitment to high-quality resources provides materials that enhance a finished product. The Living Center is a hub of student life and very much the students' space, from the Foundation artwork displayed in the cafeteria to the places, indoors and outdoors, where students gather and talk about their work.

KCAI, consistently recognized for the rigor and diversity of its curriculum, provides quality academic programs that are strengthened by first-rate support services such as the Academic Resource Center, the Computer Graphics Center, the Media Center, the Central Shop, the Career Services Office, and the Library.

KCAI makes it possible for students to study at other schools in the United States and Canada as well as schools in Australia, Ecuador, England, Germany, Hungary, Ireland, Israel, Japan, New Zealand, the Netherlands, and Spain. It is also possible for students to take part in internships at places such as Hallmark Cards, Industrial Light and Magic, Warner Bros., and Bernstein-Rein.

All serious students with a passion for art are encouraged to apply. While it is not mandatory that applicants follow a college preparatory program in high school and take courses in studio and art history, it is highly recommended to assure competitiveness with other applicants. Students are advised to follow a college preparatory curriculum based on the following: four years of English, three years of social sciences, and art courses if possible. Considerable emphasis is placed on abilities in the areas of drawing, color, and design. The criteria for admission requires evaluation of the student's portfolio, academic transcripts, standardized test scores, statement of purpose, letters of recommendation, and other indicators of potential success as a professional artist. Applicants must have successfully completed a recognized secondary school program (high school) or its equivalent, with a good academic record to be eligible for admission to KCAI. KCAI students' backgrounds are diverse, but they share a desire to pursue an education in the arts. The Admissions Committee looks for serious and motivated students who are willing to work hard and take risks. The committee evaluates each application with a great deal of sensitivity and open-mindedness before reaching an admission decision because the Committee knows each student's level of imagination, innovation, and academic achievement is highly individual.

KCAI makes every effort to help students who need financial aid. More than 90 percent of the students attending KCAI receive assistance from one or more financial aid sources. When awarding need-based assistance, KCAI first looks to the financial contribution of the parents and/or student. Students are expected to take an active part in the financing of their education through working, saving, and pursuing scholarships from outside sources. Grants, loans, employment, and monthly payment plans are available. KCAI offers a competitive scholarship competition and KCAI merit awards. The state of Missouri also provides the Charles Gallagher Grant for in-state residents, the A+ Program, and the Bright Flight Program. Applications from students seeking the full range of financial aid opportunities must include the Free Application for Federal Student Aid (FAFSA). For more information, students should contact the admissions office or the financial aid office.

For more information about The Kansas City Art Institute in general, students should call 800-522-5224 (toll-free) or visit KCAI's Web site at http://www.kcai.edu.

Faculty The approximately 75 faculty members at KCAI are a distinguished group. They are recognized scholars, sought-after consultants, talented artists, and professional mentors. They bring impressive degrees from Cranbrook Academy of Art, Pratt Institute, Alfred University, Yale University, and other prestigious programs. Their work has been exhibited all around the world, and it resides in the permanent collections of places such as the Metropolitan Museum of Art, MoMA, The National Museum of Wales, The Nelson-Atkins Museum of Art, and the Smithsonian. They have professional experience through employment and consulting with companies such as Atlantic Records; Hallmark Cards, Inc.; Perry Ellis; and Time/Life Books.

Program Facilities KCAI's ceramics department contains a clay-mixing room, a plaster room, potter's wheels, kilns, and a pitfiring space. There are also various low, mid-range, and high-temperature gas and electric kilns. Students in the painting program have individual studio space as well as studio facilities and resources for a range of painting media and techniques, including oil, acrylic, watercolor, collage, and mixed-media construction as well as art-making innovations in computer technology. Students in the printmaking program work in a well-equipped facility with access at all times to etching, lithography, monoprinting, screen and relief printing, photography, letterpress, digital imaging, and multimedia software. Students in the sculpture program work in both indoor and outdoor areas containing hoists, a forklift, loft studios, and video and slide projection equipment. It is also possible to access ceramic kilns, clay mixing facilities, a complete foundry, and metal fabrication facilities. In all programs, computer hardware and software are available in networked, multiplatform surroundings.

Special Programs In pursuit of the Bachelor of Fine Arts degree, students may complete a comprehensive liberal arts program that complements an emphasis in one of the following majors: animation, art history, ceramics, creative writing, fiber, graphic design, painting, printmaking, photo and new media, sculpture, and interdisciplinary arts.

The School of the Foundation Year provides KCAI's first year studio program. Foundation provides an ideal groundwork for upper-level studies and combines discovery, discipline, and dedication. Studio space is reserved solely for freshmen, giving them an ideal place in which to create.

The School of Liberal Arts offers a curriculum that adds a dimension to a B.F.A. degree that makes a vital difference in the student's education. The liberal arts enhance education by fostering critical-thinking skills and by opening the doors to new subjects in the arts and sciences. At KCAI, it is possible to pursue a major in art history or studio art with an emphasis in creative writing.

The School of Design prepares students to grow with the rapidly developing professional design and animation fields. These programs explore how graphic design and animation create rich communications and tell important stories, emphasizing visual form, process, and "the architecture of experience."

Kansas City Art Institute (continued)

The School of Fine Arts offers majors in the following areas: ceramics, fiber, photo and new media, painting, printmaking, sculpture, and interdisciplinary arts.

The ceramics program at KCAI provides a technical, visual, and conceptual basis for the education of artists. Traditions in ceramic history, pottery, the figure, architecture, and new forms in contemporary sculpture and installation are all explored in the curriculum.

The fiber program at KCAI encompasses not only textile processes, but also experimental techniques and the investigation of materials, issues, ideas, and forms of presentation. Students discover the vast potential of fiber, its history, and its place in contemporary art and design. Internationally prominent faculty members direct an integrated program involving surface design, weaving, papermaking, felting, basketry, clothing and costume construction, and sculptural form-making.

The photography and new media department is divided into three tracks: photography, digital film-making, and new media. Students produce innovative forms of contemporary image-making in a 20,000-square-foot facility with well-designed networked production and post-production equipment. Students are actively engaged in critical, historical, and theoretical discussions examining the interaction of media, art, and society. The program stresses experimentation, collaboration, self-motivation, research, mentoring, and professionalism through curating, exhibitions, and internships.

The painting program at KCAI covers painting's past and present and introduces students to an unusually broad foundation in drawing, painting, and printmaking. The program balances formal and technical experience with intellectual activity, perceptual acumen with conceptual skills, and an awareness of space with attention to effect.

The printmaking program provides a blend of basic studio practice—drawing, painting, collage— with a core of technologies specific to print, such as intaglio, wood block, lithography, letterpress, silkscreen, and book-making. Simultaneously, students learn to utilize digital and Web possibilities, including iMovie, Photoshop, Illustrator, InDesign, Dreamweaver, Flash, and FinalCut Pro.

The sculpture program at KCAI is known among undergraduate programs for providing a strong background in materials, techniques, aesthetics, and ideas. Students learn to carve stone, cast metal, choreograph performance, shoot video, program electronic media, and manipulate sound and light.

The interdisciplinary arts major establishes a dialogue between students and faculty members who are grounded in an established discipline yet are simultaneously investigating ideas and processes that are not easily categorized or defined. Audience, public art, community, ecology, and technology are all explored in order to discover new avenues for art to influence culture and to affect social and political change.

Kean University
Union, New Jersey

State-supported, coed. Urban campus. Total enrollment: 12,958.

Kendall College of Art and Design of Ferris State University
Grand Rapids, Michigan

State-supported, coed. Urban campus. Art program established 1928.

Degrees Bachelor of Fine Arts in the areas of furniture design, industrial design, interior design, illustration, fine arts, metals/jewelry design, art with K-12 art education certificate; Bachelor of Science in the areas of art history-studio, art history-academics. Majors and concentrations: art education, art history, art/fine arts, digital media, furniture design, graphic design, illustration, industrial design, interior design, metals and jewelry, painting, photography, sculpture. Graduate degrees offered: Master of Fine Arts. Program accredited by NASAD, FIDER.

Enrollment 932 total; 909 undergraduate, 23 graduate.

Art Student Profile 50% females, 50% males, 10% minorities, 1% international.

Art Faculty 40 total (full-time), 83 total (part-time). 56% of full-time faculty have terminal degrees. Graduate students do not teach undergraduate courses. Undergraduate student–faculty ratio: 15:1.

Student Life Student groups/activities include Industrial Design Society of America, American Society of Interior Designers, Grand Rapids

Area Furniture Designers, Society of Illustrators, American Center for Design.

Expenses for 2005–2006 Special program-related fees: $140 per semester for studio lab fee, $250 per semester for technology fee.

Financial Aid Program-specific awards: 200 Kendall Scholarships of Merit for program students ($3000).

Application Procedures Students admitted directly into the professional program freshman year. Deadline for freshmen and transfers: continuous. Required: essay, high school transcript, college transcript(s) for transfer students, minimum 2.0 high school GPA, portfolio, ACT test score only (minimum composite ACT score of 17). Recommended: letter of recommendation. Portfolio reviews held continuously on campus and off campus in various high schools, National Portfolio Days; the submission of slides may be substituted for portfolios.

Web Site http://www.kcad.edu

Contact Sandra Britton, Director of Enrollment Services, Kendall College of Art and Design of Ferris State University, 17 Fountain NW, Grand Rapids, Michigan 49503-2003; 616-451-2787, fax: 616-831-9689.

Kent State University

Kent, Ohio

State-supported, coed. Suburban campus. Total enrollment: 23,622.

Degrees Bachelor of Arts in the areas of fine arts, crafts, art history, art education; Bachelor of Fine Arts in the areas of fine arts, crafts. Majors and concentrations: art education, art history, ceramic art and design, glass, jewelry/metalsmithing/enameling, painting/drawing, printmaking, sculpture, textile arts. Graduate degrees offered: Master of Arts in the areas of art history, art education, crafts, fine arts; Master of Fine Arts in the areas of fine arts, crafts. Program accredited by NASAD.

Enrollment 673 total; 605 undergraduate, 68 graduate.

Art Student Profile 58% females, 42% males, 5% minorities, 7% international.

Art Faculty 22 total (full-time), 49 total (part-time). 90% of full-time faculty have terminal degrees. Graduate students teach a few undergraduate courses. Undergraduate student–faculty ratio: 14:1.

Student Life Student groups/activities include Art Education Council, Student Organization of Fine Arts (SOFA), Art History Club. Special housing available for art students.

Expenses for 2005–2006 Application fee: $30. State resident tuition: $7954 full-time. Nonresident tuition: $15,386 full-time. Full-time tuition varies according to course level, course load, degree level, location, program, reciprocity agreements, and student level. College room and board: $6640. College room only: $4040. Room and board charges vary according to board plan and housing facility. Special program-related fees: $10–$45 per credit hour for expendable supplies in selected areas.

Financial Aid Program-specific awards: 16 art scholarships for program majors ($500), 25 Creative Arts Awards for incoming freshmen demonstrating academic achievement ($1000–$2000).

Application Procedures Students admitted directly into the professional program freshman year. Deadline for freshmen and transfers: continuous. Required: high school transcript, college transcript(s) for transfer students, SAT I or ACT test scores. Recommended: minimum 2.0 high school GPA, portfolio. Portfolio reviews held twice on campus.

Web Site http://www.kent.edu/art

Undergraduate Contact Dr. Christine Havice, Associate Professor, School of Art, Kent State University, PO Box 5190, Kent, Ohio 44242-0001; 330-672-2192, fax: 330-672-4729, e-mail address: shavice@kent.edu

Graduate Contact Ms. Janice Lessman-Moss, Coordinator of Graduate Studies, School of Art, Kent State University, PO Box 5190, Kent, Ohio 44242-0001; 330-672-2192, fax: 330-672-4729, e-mail address: jlessman@kent.edu

Kutztown University of Pennsylvania

Kutztown, Pennsylvania

State-supported, coed. Rural campus. Total enrollment: 9,864. Art program established 1924.

Degrees Bachelor of Fine Arts in the areas of fine arts, communication design, crafts; Bach-

Kutztown University of Pennsylvania (continued)

elor of Science in the area of art education. Majors and concentrations: advertising design, art education, ceramics, communication design, craft design, digital design, fibers, graphic design, illustration, metals, painting/drawing, photography, printmaking, sculpture, woodworking design. Graduate degrees offered: Master of Education. Program accredited by NASAD.

Enrollment 1,150 total; 952 undergraduate, 18 graduate, 180 nonprofessional degree.

Art Student Profile 59% females, 41% males, 1% minorities, 1% international.

Art Faculty 60 total (full-time), 30 total (part-time). 95% of full-time faculty have terminal degrees. Graduate students do not teach undergraduate courses. Undergraduate student–faculty ratio: 11:1.

Student Life Student groups/activities include Art Student Association, Art Education Students Association. Special housing available for art students.

Expenses for 2005–2006 Application fee: $35. State resident tuition: $4906 full-time. Nonresident tuition: $12,266 full-time. Mandatory fees: $1519 full-time. College room and board: $5480. College room only: $3900.

Financial Aid Program-specific awards: 1 artistically talented award for talented program majors ($3224–$8198), 1 Morning Call Scholarship for minority students ($800), 1 Karen Anderson Scholarship for those demonstrating need ($500).

Application Procedures Students admitted directly into the professional program freshman year. Deadline for freshmen and transfers: continuous. Required: high school transcript, SAT I or ACT test scores, minimum 2.0 college GPA for transfer applicants, portfolio for fine arts, crafts, and art education applicants, art test for communication design applicants. Portfolio reviews held twice on campus; the submission of slides may be substituted for portfolios.

Web Site http://www.kutztown.edu

Undergraduate Contact Dr. William Stahler, Director of Admissions, Kutztown University of Pennsylvania, 4 Admissions House, Kutztown, Pennsylvania 19530; 610-683-4053, fax: 610-683-1375, e-mail address: wstahler@kutztown.edu

Graduate Contact Dr. Charles Cullum, Dean of Graduate Studies and Extended Learning, Kutztown University of Pennsylvania, Old Main Room 110, Kutztown, Pennsylvania 19530; 610-683-4203, fax: 610-683-1393, e-mail address: ccullum@kutztown.edu

Laguna College of Art & Design

Laguna Beach, California

Independent, coed. Small town campus. Art program established 1961.

Lakehead University

Thunder Bay, Ontario, Canada

Province-supported, coed. Suburban campus. Total enrollment: 7,558. Art program established 1976.

Lamar Dodd School of Art

See University of Georgia

La Roche College

Pittsburgh, Pennsylvania

Independent, coed. Suburban campus. Total enrollment: 1,707.

Degrees Bachelor of Science in the area of graphic and communication design. Majors and concentrations: graphic design and communication, interior design. Cross-registration with Pittsburgh Council on Higher Education. Program accredited by NASAD.

Enrollment 282 total; all undergraduate.

Art Student Profile 53% females, 47% males, 2% minorities, 1% international.

Art Faculty 7 undergraduate (full-time), 15 undergraduate (part-time). Graduate students do not teach undergraduate courses. Undergraduate student–faculty ratio: 23:1.

Student Life Student groups/activities include Pittsburgh Filmmakers.

Expenses for 2005–2006 Application fee: $50. Comprehensive fee: $24,724 includes full-time tuition ($16,780), mandatory fees ($600), and college room and board ($7344). College room only: $4600. Full-time tuition and fees vary according to program. Special program-related fees: $100 for computer lab fee.

Financial Aid Program-specific awards: 1 Sr. Edna Herbst Scholarship for freshmen graphic design majors ($100).

Application Procedures Students admitted directly into the professional program freshman year. Deadline for freshmen and transfers: continuous. Notification date for freshmen and transfers: continuous. Required: essay, high school transcript, college transcript(s) for transfer students, minimum 2.0 high school GPA, 3 letters of recommendation, SAT I or ACT test scores, portfolio for transfer students. Recommended: interview. Portfolio reviews held as needed on campus.

Web Site http://www.laroche.edu

Undergraduate Contact Rosemary E. Gould, MFA, Professor and Department Chair, Graphic and Communication Design, La Roche College, 9000 Babcock Boulevard, Pittsburgh, Pennsylvania 15237; 412-536-1023, fax: 412-536-1093, e-mail address: conwayl1@laroche.edu

La Sierra University

Riverside, California

Independent Seventh-day Adventist, coed. Suburban campus. Total enrollment: 1,941. Art program established 1923.

Degrees Bachelor of Arts in the area of art; Bachelor of Fine Arts in the areas of graphic design, fine art. Majors and concentrations: art education, art/fine arts, graphic design, studio art.

Enrollment 41 total; 28 undergraduate, 13 nonprofessional degree.

Art Student Profile 52% females, 48% males, 40% minorities, 30% international.

Art Faculty 4 undergraduate (full-time), 5 undergraduate (part-time). 75% of full-time faculty have terminal degrees. Graduate students do not teach undergraduate courses. Undergraduate student–faculty ratio: 10:1.

Student Life Student groups/activities include student exhibit in the Brandstater Gallery, internships.

Expenses for 2006–2007 Application fee: $30. Comprehensive fee: $26,507 includes full-time

tuition ($19,908), mandatory fees ($726), and college room and board ($5873). Special program-related fees: $40–$265 per quarter for materials fee, $50 per quarter for model fees.

Financial Aid Program-specific awards: 7 Katchamakoff Scholarships for program majors ($300–$2000).

Application Procedures Students apply for admission into the professional program by sophomore year. Deadline for freshmen and transfers: continuous. Required: high school transcript, college transcript(s) for transfer students, minimum 2.0 high school GPA, 2 letters of recommendation, portfolio. Recommended: minimum 3.0 high school GPA, SAT I or ACT test scores. Portfolio reviews held twice on campus; the submission of slides may be substituted for portfolios at student's discretion.

Web Site http://www.lasierra.edu/art

Undergraduate Contact University Admissions, La Sierra University, 4500 Riverwalk Parkway, Riverside, California 92515-8247; 951-785-2176, e-mail address: admissions@lasierra.edu

Lawrence Technological University

Southfield, Michigan

Independent, coed. Suburban campus. Total enrollment: 4,122. Art program established 1991.

Degrees Bachelor of Fine Arts in the area of imaging; Bachelor of Interior Architecture. Majors and concentrations: digital imaging, graphic design, interior architecture. Graduate degrees offered: Master of Interior Design. Program accredited by FIDER, NASAD.

Enrollment 140 total; 133 undergraduate, 7 graduate.

Art Student Profile 50% females, 50% males, 10% minorities, 10% international.

Art Faculty 6 undergraduate (full-time), 22 undergraduate (part-time). 50% of full-time faculty have terminal degrees. Graduate students do not teach undergraduate courses. Undergraduate student–faculty ratio: 16:1.

Student Life Student groups/activities include International Interior Design Association,

Visual *Arts*

Lawrence Technological University (continued)

American Society of Interior Designers, Illuminating Engineering Society Student Group.

Expenses for 2006–2007 Application fee: $30. Comprehensive fee: $26,709 includes full-time tuition ($19,073), mandatory fees ($370), and college room and board ($7266). College room only: $5286. Special program-related fees: $100 per studio for studio maintenance.

Financial Aid Program-specific awards: 6–7 LTU Scholarships for incoming freshmen ($8000–$8500), 6–7 Trustee Scholarships for incoming freshmen ($1600–$2000).

Application Procedures Students admitted directly into the professional program freshman year. Deadline for freshmen and transfers: continuous. Required: high school transcript, college transcript(s) for transfer students, minimum 2.5 high school GPA. Recommended: essay, 2 letters of recommendation, interview.

Web Site http://www.ltu.edu

Contact Virginia North, Chair, Department of Art and Design, Lawrence Technological University, 21000 West Ten Mile Road, Southfield, Michigan 48075; 248-204-2848, fax: 248-204-2900, e-mail address: north@ltu.edu

Leigh Gerdine College of Fine Arts

See Webster University

Lindenwood University

St. Charles, Missouri

Independent Presbyterian, coed. Suburban campus. Total enrollment: 9,076.

Degrees Bachelor of Arts in the areas of arts administration, art education, fashion design, studio art, art history; Bachelor of Fine Arts in the areas of art, fashion design, graphic design, computer art, multimedia. Majors and concentrations: art education, art history, arts administration, ceramics, computer graphics, design, fashion design, graphic design, multimedia, painting/drawing, photography, printmaking, studio art. Graduate degrees offered: Master of Arts in the area of studio art; Master of Fine Arts in the area of studio art. Cross-registration with Maryville University of Saint Louis, Fontbonne University, Missouri Baptist College, Webster University.

Art Faculty 6 undergraduate (full-time), 3 undergraduate (part-time), 6 graduate (full-time), 3 graduate (part-time). 90% of full-time faculty have terminal degrees. Graduate students do not teach undergraduate courses.

Student Life Student groups/activities include juried art shows, The Pride (Lindenwood magazine), scenic painting.

Expenses for 2006–2007 Application fee: $30. Comprehensive fee: $18,240 includes full-time tuition ($12,000), mandatory fees ($240), and college room and board ($6000). College room only: $3000. Special program-related fees: $25–$80 per class for studio lab fees.

Financial Aid Program-specific awards: art scholarships, talent awards for undergraduates and transfers, talent awards and scholarships for high school students.

Application Procedures Students admitted directly into the professional program freshman year. Deadline for freshmen and transfers: continuous. Required: essay, high school transcript, college transcript(s) for transfer students, minimum 2.0 high school GPA, interview, portfolio, ACT test score only. Recommended: letter of recommendation. Portfolio reviews held continuously on campus and off campus in area high schools; community colleges; art exhibitions; the submission of slides may be substituted for portfolios.

Undergraduate Contact Mr. John Troy, Director, Art Department, Lindenwood University, 209 South Kings Highway, St. Charles, Missouri 63301; 636-949-4856, e-mail address: jtroy@lindenwood.edu

Graduate Contact Dr. Elaine C. Tillinger, Chair, Department of Art, Lindenwood University, 209 South Kings Highway, St. Charles, Missouri 63301; 636-949-4862, fax: 636-949-4910, e-mail address: etillinger@lindenwood.edu

Long Island University, C.W. Post Campus

Brookville, New York

Independent, coed. Suburban campus. Total enrollment: 8,472. Art program established 1954.

Longwood University

Farmville, Virginia

State-supported, coed. Total enrollment: 4,289. Art program established 1920.

Degrees Bachelor of Fine Arts in the area of art. Majors and concentrations: art education, art history, craft design, drawing, graphic design, painting, photography, printmaking.

Enrollment 210 total; all undergraduate.

Art Faculty 12 undergraduate (full-time). 100% of full-time faculty have terminal degrees. Graduate students do not teach undergraduate courses. Undergraduate student–faculty ratio: 17:1.

Student Life Student groups/activities include Kappa Pi.

Expenses for 2005–2006 Application fee: $40. State resident tuition: $3586 full-time. Nonresident tuition: $10,270 full-time. Mandatory fees: $3434 full-time. College room and board: $5586. College room only: $3288. Room and board charges vary according to board plan. Special program-related fees: $10–$70 per class for studio fee.

Financial Aid Program-specific awards: 10 departmental awards for program majors ($500–$1500).

Application Procedures Students admitted directly into the professional program freshman year. Deadline for freshmen and transfers: continuous. Required: essay, high school transcript, college transcript(s) for transfer students, minimum 2.0 high school GPA, SAT I or ACT test scores. Recommended: 3 letters of recommendation.

Web Site http://www.longwood.edu/art

Undergraduate Contact Mr. Chris Register, Chair, Department of Art, Longwood University, 201 High Street, Farmville, Virginia 23909; 434-395-2284, fax: 434-395-2775, e-mail address: registercm@longwood.edu

Louisiana State University and Agricultural and Mechanical College

Baton Rouge, Louisiana

State-supported, coed. Urban campus. Total enrollment: 31,264. Art program established 1930.

Degrees Bachelor of Fine Arts in the area of studio art. Majors and concentrations: ceramics, graphic design, jewelry and metalsmithing, painting/drawing, photography, printmaking, sculpture. Graduate degrees offered: Master of Fine Arts in the area of studio art. Program accredited by NASAD.

Enrollment 763 total; 698 undergraduate, 65 graduate.

Art Student Profile 57% females, 43% males, 3% minorities, 5% international.

Art Faculty 31 total (full-time), 9 total (part-time). 100% of full-time faculty have terminal degrees. Graduate students teach a few undergraduate courses. Undergraduate student–faculty ratio: 20:1.

Student Life Student groups/activities include Exposure (photography club), Ceramic Art Students Association, Graphic Design Student Association.

Expenses for 2005–2006 Application fee: $40. State resident tuition: $2981 full-time. Nonresident tuition: $11,281 full-time. Mandatory fees: $1438 full-time. College room and board: $6330. College room only: $3930. Room and board charges vary according to board plan and housing facility.

Financial Aid Program-specific awards: 4 LSU Scholarships for talented students ($500).

Application Procedures Students admitted directly into the professional program freshman year. Deadline for freshmen and transfers: continuous. Required: high school transcript, college transcript(s) for transfer students, portfolio, SAT I or ACT test scores, minimum 2.5 high school GPA. Portfolio reviews held twice on campus; the submission of slides may be substituted for portfolios if original work is not available.

Web Site http://www.art.lsu.edu

Undergraduate Contact Ms. Melody Guichet, Associate Director, School of Art, Louisiana State University and Agricultural and Mechanical College, 123 Art Building, Baton Rouge, Louisiana 70803; 225-578-5413, fax: 225-578-5424, e-mail address: mguiche@lsu.edu

Graduate Contact Mr. Chris Johns, Graduate Coordinator, School of Art, Louisiana State University and Agricultural and Mechanical College, 123 Art Building, Baton Rouge, Louisiana 70803; 225-578-5411, fax: 225-578-5424.

Visual Arts

Louisiana Tech University

Ruston, Louisiana

State-supported, coed. Small town campus. Total enrollment: 11,691. Art program established 1894.

Degrees Bachelor of Fine Arts in the areas of studio art, photography, communication design. Majors and concentrations: art/fine arts, ceramic art and design, commercial art, computer graphics, painting/drawing, photography, printmaking, sculpture. Graduate degrees offered: Master of Fine Arts in the areas of studio art, photography, interior design, communication design. Cross-registration with Grambling State University. Program accredited by NASAD.

Enrollment 394 total; 386 undergraduate, 8 graduate.

Art Student Profile 55% females, 45% males, 5% minorities, 2% international.

Art Faculty 16 total (full-time), 3 total (part-time). 100% of full-time faculty have terminal degrees. Graduate students teach a few undergraduate courses. Undergraduate student–faculty ratio: 24:1.

Student Life Student groups/activities include Art and Architecture Student Association.

Expenses for 2005–2006 Application fee: $20. State resident tuition: $3914 full-time. Nonresident tuition: $8819 full-time. Mandatory fees: $461 full-time. College room and board: $4035. College room only: $2130. Special program-related fees: $30 per quarter for art and architecture fee and enhancement fee for lecturers, special equipment, and workshops.

Financial Aid Program-specific awards: 8–10 incoming freshmen scholarships for regional high school students ($1000–$2500).

Application Procedures Students admitted directly into the professional program freshman year. Deadline for freshmen and transfers: continuous. Required: high school transcript, college transcript(s) for transfer students, minimum 2.0 high school GPA, SAT I or ACT test scores (minimum combined SAT I score of 1010, minimum composite ACT score of 22). Recommended: interview.

Web Site http://www.art.latech.edu

Undergraduate Contact Ms. Jo Anne Walker, Assistant to the Director, School of Art, Louisiana Tech University, PO Box 3175, Ruston, Louisiana 71272; 318-257-3909, fax: 318-257-4890, e-mail address: jawalker@art.latech.edu

Graduate Contact Mr. Peter Jones, Graduate Coordinator, School of Art, Louisiana Tech University, PO Box 3175, Ruston, Louisiana 71272; 318-257-3909, fax: 318-257-4890, e-mail address: prjones@art.latech.edu

Loyola University New Orleans

New Orleans, Louisiana

Independent Roman Catholic (Jesuit), coed. Urban campus. Total enrollment: 5,423.

Degrees Bachelor of Arts in the areas of graphic design, studio art; Bachelor of Fine Arts. Majors and concentrations: graphic design, studio art.

Enrollment 114 total; all undergraduate.

Art Faculty 12 undergraduate (full-time), 11 undergraduate (part-time). 100% of full-time faculty have terminal degrees. Graduate students do not teach undergraduate courses.

Student Life Student groups/activities include Untitled (art organization), American Institute of Graphic Arts Student Chapter.

Expenses for 2005–2006 Application fee: $20. Comprehensive fee: $33,558 includes full-time tuition ($24,410), mandatory fees ($836), and college room and board ($8312). College room only: $5166. Room and board charges vary according to board plan and housing facility. Special program-related fees: $75 per class for lab fee (selected studio courses).

Financial Aid Program-specific awards: 1 Scully Scholarship for upperclassmen ($500–$1000), 1 Visual Arts Scholarship for entering studio art majors ($3000), 1 Visual Arts Scholarship for entering graphic design majors ($3000).

Application Procedures Students admitted directly into the professional program freshman year. Deadline for freshmen: February 15; transfers: continuous. Notification date for freshmen and transfers: March 15. Required: high school transcript, college transcript(s) for transfer students, minimum 2.0 high school GPA, letter of recommendation, portfolio for scholarship consideration. Portfolio reviews held twice on campus; the submission of slides may be substituted for portfolios.

Undergraduate Contact Chairperson, Department of Visual Arts, Loyola University New Orleans, 6363 Saint Charles Avenue, New Orleans, Louisiana 70118; 504-865-5456, fax: 504-865-5457.

Lyme Academy College of Fine Arts

Old Lyme, Connecticut

Independent, coed. Small town campus. Art program established 1976.

Degrees Bachelor of Fine Arts. Majors and concentrations: painting, sculpture. Program accredited by NASAD.

Enrollment 164 total; 160 undergraduate, 4 graduate.

Art Student Profile 60% females, 40% males, 14% minorities, 2% international.

Art Faculty 11 undergraduate (full-time), 10 undergraduate (part-time). 45% of full-time faculty have terminal degrees. Graduate students do not teach undergraduate courses.

Student Life Student groups/activities include Student Forum, Student Government.

Expenses for 2005–2006 Application fee: $35. Tuition: $16,416 full-time. Mandatory fees: $500 full-time. Special program-related fees: $50 per semester for student activities fee, $95–$330 per semester for model/materials fees.

Financial Aid Program-specific awards: 28 Institutional Awards for program majors ($6000).

Application Procedures Students admitted directly into the professional program freshman year. Deadline for freshmen and transfers: continuous. Required: essay, high school transcript, college transcript(s) for transfer students, minimum 2.0 high school GPA, 2 letters of recommendation, portfolio. Recommended: interview, SAT I or ACT test scores. Portfolio reviews held as needed on campus and off campus at National Portfolio Day Conferences; the submission of slides may be substituted for portfolios if a campus visit is impossible.

Web Site http://www.lymeacademy.edu

Undergraduate Contact Debra A. Sigmon, Director of Admissions, Lyme Academy College of Fine Arts, 84 Lyme Street, Old Lyme, Connecticut 06371; 860-434-5232 ext. 119, fax: 860-434-8725.

More About the Academy

The Lyme Academy College of Fine Art has the unique mission of supporting a contemporary dialogue with classical sources providing an education in the principles, history, techniques, and critical thought processes that have shaped society from the Renaissance to the present.

The College was founded in 1976 by sculptor Elisabeth Gordon Chandler and others dedicated to the belief that serious artists must study the figurative traditions of painting and sculpture, studies that produced the great master artists from Michelangelo to Picasso. The College embraces these disciplines in a rigorous curriculum that places emphasis on life drawing as the foundation for aesthetic development.

Students from across the country seek the College for the education offered, recognizing that their professional future depends on learning the fundamental and basic skills of drawing, painting, and sculpture.

Visual Arts

Lyme Academy College of Fine Arts (continued)

Students and alumni from the College receive honors annually at the Copely Society of Boston, the oldest art association in America. Several have earned the prestigious Robert Brooks Memorial Scholarship. For the past five years, Academy students have earned the four highest awards in the National Arts Club Juried Student Exhibition in New York City. Graduates in the B.F.A. Painting program are eligible to apply for a $5000 Stobart Foundation Fellowship supporting their first year as an emerging artist.

The College offers opportunities for assistantships in area schools and volunteer work for arts groups. The eight-week summer program includes intensive workshops and an eight-week session with a variety of traditional painting, drawing, printmaking, and sculpture courses.

The College's cultural campus extends from New York City to Boston, each just 100 miles away. Additional cultural venues can be found in Connecticut and Rhode Island as well. The College attracts outstanding contemporary, representational, and figurative master teacher/artists to its faculty.

The College encourages its student artists to bring intelligence, passion, and creativity to bear upon each drawing, painting, and sculpture. Emphasizing studio work, the College seeks to create an environment that encourages individual creation and personal responsibility through the profoundly difficult act of making the not-yet-seen and the not-yet-known.

Program Facilities The Lyme Academy College of Fine Art's studios are located adjacent to the Historic Sill House and feature nine spacious well-lit studios and an art supply/book store. The Art History/seminar room and a classroom are located in the Academic Center. Sill House has a professional gallery, administrative offices, and a student kitchen. Campus facilities doubled in 2003 when the Academic Center was completed, bringing individual senior studios on campus along with additional studios, classrooms, galleries, cafe food service, and administrative offices.

Five drawing and painting studios feature north light, air exchange systems, easels, and large storage racks for oversize paintings. Sculpture facilities include two spacious studios with modeling stands, abundant storage shelves, separate storage rooms for works in progress, a carving studio, and a casting room. Student lockers are in the hallways connecting all studios. The Student Commons provides space for exhibitions and student activities. The Academic Center lecture hall hosts visiting artist's lectures, presentations by art dealers and gallery owners, and additional programming. Conversation and counseling is available in the comfortable Student Services office in the Academic Center.

The Krieble Library features Mission Style chairs, study tables, and large windows overlooking the Lieutenant River. The library has nearly 13,000 volumes for Fine Arts and Liberal Arts and Sciences and more than 19,000 slides for research and special projects, fifty-six regular periodical subscriptions, and six computer workstations. The library doubles its size to 46,000 square feet with expansion.

The Art supply/book store has all materials and books necessary for studio and academic programs. Material lists for classes are in the store for reference, which is conveniently open before every class.

Student Exhibit Opportunities Students participate in a Senior Thesis Exhibition before graduation, an annual "All Student Exhibition," and "Faculty Selects Exhibition," and "Student Exhibit" during the holiday season. Freshman-, sophomore-, and junior-level exhibitions are displayed in the Commons and works in progress are shown in the studio hallways. Faculty members recommend students for the National Arts Club Annual Student Exhibition in New York and the Copley Society in Boston. The Academy supports an "Award of Excellence" exhibition fourteen months after graduation.

Special Programs Students may apply for mobility to attend a different college for the first semester of their junior year with an Association of Independent Colleges of Art and Design member school. Frequent trips to New York and Boston take advantage of other cultural opportunities in the area. Precollege life-drawing classes help with portfolio development. The Academy sponsors a Visiting Artist's Lecture series.

Maharishi University of Management

Fairfield, Iowa

Independent, coed. Small town campus. Total enrollment: 741. Art program established 1983.

Degrees Bachelor of Fine Arts in the area of visual arts. Majors and concentrations: art/fine arts, ceramics, digital media, painting/drawing, photography, sculpture, studio art, video art.

Enrollment 40 total; 33 undergraduate, 7 nonprofessional degree.

Art Student Profile 50% females, 50% males, 15% minorities, 30% international.

Art Faculty 5 total (full-time), 6 total (part-time). 65% of full-time faculty have terminal degrees. Graduate students do not teach undergraduate courses. Undergraduate student–faculty ratio: 1:1.

Student Life Student groups/activities include Iowa-wide exhibits.

Expenses for 2006–2007 Application fee: $15. Comprehensive fee: $30,430 includes full-time tuition ($24,000), mandatory fees ($430), and college room and board ($6000). Special program-related fees: $10–$100 per course for lab fees, $150 per course for field trips in Art History courses.

Application Procedures Students apply for admission into the professional program by sophomore, junior year. Deadline for freshmen: continuous. Notification date for freshmen: September 15. Required: essay, high school transcript, college transcript(s) for transfer students, 2 letters of recommendation, SAT I or ACT test scores, minimum 2.5 high school GPA. Recommended: portfolio. Portfolio reviews held twice on campus; the submission of slides may be substituted for portfolios for transfer applicants.

Web Site http://mum.edu/arts

Undergraduate Contact Pat Robinson, Director, Office of Admissions, Maharishi University of Management, 1000 North 4th Street, Fairfield, Iowa 52557; 641-472-1110, fax: 641-472-1179, e-mail address: probinson@mum.edu

Maine College of Art

Portland, Maine

Independent, coed. Urban campus. Total enrollment: 490. Art program established 1882.

Degrees Bachelor of Fine Arts in the areas of ceramics, graphic design, painting, printmaking, photography, sculpture, metalsmithing and jewelry, self-designed studies, illustration, woodworking and furniture design. Majors and concentrations: ceramic art and design, graphic design, illustration, individualized major, jewelry and metalsmithing, new media, painting, photography, printmaking, sculpture, woodworking and furniture design. Graduate degrees offered: Master of Fine Arts in the area of self-designed studio concentrations. Cross-registration with Bowdoin College, Greater Portland Alliance of Colleges and Universities. Program accredited by NASAD.

Enrollment 490 total; 458 undergraduate, 32 graduate.

Art Student Profile 66% females, 34% males, 7% minorities, 1% international.

Art Faculty 32 undergraduate (full-time), 37 undergraduate (part-time), 2 graduate (full-time). 77% of full-time faculty have terminal degrees. Graduate students do not teach undergraduate courses. Undergraduate student–faculty ratio: 10:1.

Student Life Student groups/activities include Creative Community Partnerships, Student Representative Association (SRA). Special housing available for art students.

Expenses for 2006–2007 Application fee: $40. Comprehensive fee: $34,590 includes full-time tuition ($24,670), mandatory fees ($650), and college room and board ($9270). Special program-related fees: $10–$90 per course for studio fees, $150 per year for technology fee.

Financial Aid Program-specific awards: 2 full-tuition scholarships ($24,600), 40 partial-tuition scholarships ($5000–$7500).

Application Procedures Deadline for freshmen and transfers: continuous. Notification date for freshmen and transfers: continuous. Required: essay, high school transcript, college transcript(s) for transfer students, minimum 2.0 high school GPA, 2 letters of recommendation, portfolio, SAT I or ACT test scores. Recommended: interview. Portfolio reviews held continuously on campus and off campus at National Portfolio Days; the submission of slides may be substituted for portfolios when distance is prohibitive.

Web Site http://www.meca.edu

Undergraduate Contact Karen Townsend, Director of Admissions, Maine College of Art, 97 Spring Street, Portland, Maine 04101; 207-775-5157 ext. 254, fax: 207-772-5069, e-mail address: ktownsend@meca.edu

Graduate Contact Ms. Katarina Weslien, Director, MFA in Studio Art, Maine College of Art, 97 Spring Street, Portland, Maine 04101; 207-775-5154 ext. 57, fax: 207-772-5069, e-mail address: kweslien@meca.edu

More About the College

Maine College of Art (MECA) is a dynamic college of art and design where a vibrant student community, world-class faculty, innovative interdisci-

Maine College of Art (continued)

plinary programs, and expansive facilities come together as emerging artists to give fresh vision to Maine's extraordinary legacy in the visual arts. MECA educates artists at all stages of their creative careers, offering both the Bachelor of Fine Arts (B.F.A.) and Master of Fine Arts (M.F.A.) degrees and a wide range of professional institutes and continuing studies classes for individuals of all ages, including a new postbaccalaureate certificate in art education. Founded in 1882, MECA is a fully accredited, independent college with 450 students who come from across the United States and throughout the world. The College offers eleven studio majors and three minors, including art history. In addition to their studio courses, MECA students take a concurrent stream of liberal arts courses, complementing their studio work and offering the broad cultural context critical to an artist's education. Faculty members at Maine College of Art are accomplished, professional artists and dedicated teachers who work closely with their students throughout all four years and beyond. MECA graduates enter the professional world with one of the finest visual arts educations available.

Maine College of Art offers the Bachelor of Fine Arts degree in eleven majors: ceramics, graphic design, illustration, metalsmithing and jewelry, new media, painting, photography, printmaking, sculpture, self-designed, and woodworking and furniture design. Students may also minor in art history, drawing, and illustration. Art education is important to many MECA students, and a postbaccalaureate program in art education offers B.F.A. degree-holders a one-year course of study, as well as hands-on experience in classrooms, museums, and community settings, that leads to certification as K–12 art educators. There is an innovative, low-residency Master of Fine Arts in studio arts program as well.

Located in the heart of Portland's Art's District, amidst galleries, studios, and designer boutiques, MECA's campus consists of two studio and classroom buildings, three residence halls, and a building for administration. First-year students enjoy multiple housing options from traditional dormitories to apartment and family styles. MECA has added a sixty-bed dormitory and an eighty-bed apartment house to its campus in the past year. The beautiful beaux arts Porteous Building, students' primary studio building, is an architectural landmark and one of the finest facilities for art making in the country. Porteous boasts breathtaking views of the Casco Bay Islands to the south and the White Mountains to the north. The Baxter Building also houses classrooms

and studios and is a fine example of Romanesque Revival architecture. Clapp House is the original site of the College and is listed on the National Register of Historic Places. All studios are open to students 24 hours a day, seven days a week.

Portland is a great attraction for students and artists from around the world. MECA is only blocks from the Portland Museum of Art, Portland Symphony Orchestra, Portland Stage Company, and a wealth of other cultural resources. The historic Old Port is home to a wide and eclectic array of restaurants, music venues, and independent retail stores With a bustling, buzzing city scene, Portland draws artists from across the United States and around the world. Over the past two centuries, Maine has played an important and unique role in shaping American art. Renowned artists such as Winslow Homer, Marsden Hartley, Bernice Abbott, Edward Hopper, and Andrew Wyeth have all drawn inspiration from the Maine landscape and people. Currently, MECA students and faculty members are a vital voice in Portland and influence emerging contemporary movements in the visual arts. Hip and comfortable, Portland offers all the advantages of a small city, with easy access to beaches, ski resorts, and Boston.

Student life is busy, and extracurricular activities include exhibition openings, visiting-artist workshops and lectures, a film series, music and cultural events, hiking, outings to the ocean, day trips to Boston galleries, and parties and other celebrations. Students and staff members gather weekly for "Soup and Bread," a popular free lunch held Tuesdays in the College's Student Center. Student life at MECA begins with a weeklong orientation, and peer mentors provide yearlong support for new students. Career services include both individual career counseling sessions and small-group workshops and curatorial and professional internships that prepare students for work in their chosen fields.

Faculty and Visiting Artists Maine College of Art has 38 full-time and 35 part-time faculty members teaching in the B.F.A. program. Faculty members are professional artists, designers, writers, and scholars who are devoted to teaching undergraduate students at all levels of the curriculum. They have been honored by many notable foundations and organizations, including the National Endowment of the Arts, the Getty Foundation, the Mellon Foundation, the New England Foundation of the Arts, and the Haystack Mountain School of Crafts. Their works are featured in galleries and museums throughout the world and in magazines and newspapers like the *New York Times,* the *New Yorker,* and the *Boston Globe.* Faculty members also serve as academic advisers and engage their students in close relationships, actively assisting them in formulating and carrying out their career plans.

Each year, MECA hosts well-known artists, designers, writers, and other scholars who lecture on their work and contemporary issues in the arts. These artists visit classes and work with individual students, providing another rich resource in the creative learning process.

Program Facilities Each department at MECA offers expansive, well-equipped studios that are open to students 24 hours a day. Individual studio space is provided for all students who have declared a major.

The College hosts exhibitions in two of its gallery spaces: the Friedman Student Gallery and the Institute of Contemporary Art (ICA) at Maine College of Art. Works by MECA students as well as regional, national, and international artists are shown in these professional gallery spaces. In addition, students have opportunities to exhibit work in galleries and businesses throughout the city. The College's Joanne Waxman Library is the largest library collection in northern New England that supports teaching and research in the visual arts. The collection consists of approximately 30,000 volumes, ninety current periodical subscriptions, and 52,000 slides. Ideally situated in the Porteous Building, the library's handsome quarters feature tin ceilings and large, Chicago-style windows that overlook historic Congress Street and bathe the reference, study, and reading areas in natural light.

Three computer labs offer more than fifty computers with complete Web, print, and design software; a selection of slide and flatbed scanners; and video production systems. Output capabilities include color laser printing. MECA is committed to incorporating technology across its broad curriculum, from digital life drawing to sound installation, from graphic animation to furniture design, and beyond. MECA graduates are well prepared to thrive in today's artistic world.

Special Programs MECA students take advantage of off-campus study through the Association of Independent Colleges of Art and Design (AICAD) Mobility Program, which provides students with the chance to study for a semester at thirty-five of the member institutions throughout the U.S. and Canada (a complete listing of AICAD schools is included later in this publication). In addition, recent student foreign exchanges have included study in Vietnam, Australia, Ireland, Italy, and South Africa. MECA students also take summer courses at such institutions as the renowned Provincetown Fine Arts Work Center in Massachusetts. The College has a cross-registration

program with Bowdoin College and belongs to a consortium with the University of New England, the University of Southern Maine, Saint Joseph's College, and the Southern Maine Technical Center, allowing cross-registration among the five schools to enrich and expand educational opportunities for all their students.

MECA internships provide ample opportunities for students to apply their expertise while furthering their knowledge of dynamic fields, such as graphic design, animation, and curatorial work. Through MECA's Creative Community Partnerships program, students use art to serve the Greater Portland community, engaging in many social service and education settings that include working with at-risk youth in alternative programs and assisting special-needs children in the local schools. Students are enriched by their active commitment to the community and deeply appreciate the lasting, close-knit relationships with faculty members and peers. This experience of community—engaged, supportive, inspiring, and creative—makes MECA unique.

Manhattanville College

Purchase, New York

Independent, coed. Suburban campus. Total enrollment: 2,806. Art program established 1957.

Marshall University

Huntington, West Virginia

State-supported, coed. Urban campus. Total enrollment: 13,988. Art program established 1984.

Degrees Bachelor of Fine Arts in the area of art studio. Majors and concentrations: ceramics, craft design, graphic design, painting, photography, printmaking, sculpture. Graduate degrees offered: Master of Arts in the areas of art education, art studio. Program accredited by NCATE.

Enrollment 220 total; 200 undergraduate, 20 graduate.

Art Student Profile 52% females, 48% males, 5% minorities, 1% international.

Art Faculty 13 total (full-time), 20 total (part-time). 100% of full-time faculty have terminal degrees. Graduate students teach a

Marshall University (continued)

few undergraduate courses. Undergraduate student–faculty ratio: 17:1.

Student Life Student groups/activities include Sculpture Club, Keramos (Ceramics Club), Graphic Design Club-"Artatak".

Expenses for 2005–2006 Application fee: $25. State resident tuition: $3932 full-time. Nonresident tuition: $10,634 full-time. Full-time tuition varies according to degree level, location, program, and reciprocity agreements. College room and board: $6272. College room only: $3496. Room and board charges vary according to board plan and housing facility. Special program-related fees: $45 per studio course for art supplies .

Financial Aid Program-specific awards: 4–5 art scholarships for program majors ($500), 10 tuition waivers for program majors ($1000), 1 Garth Brown Memorial Scholarship for program majors ($500), 1 Donald Harper Scholarship for program majors ($400), 1 College of Fine Arts Gala Scholarship for program majors ($2000), 1 John Q. Hill Memorial Scholarship for minority program majors ($1000), 1 Stewart Smith Scholarship for program majors ($800).

Application Procedures Students admitted directly into the professional program freshman year. Deadline for freshmen and transfers: August 15. Notification date for freshmen and transfers: continuous. Required: high school transcript, college transcript(s) for transfer students, minimum 2.0 high school GPA, SAT I or ACT test scores. Recommended: 3 letters of recommendation, interview, portfolio. Portfolio reviews held twice on campus; the submission of slides may be substituted for portfolios if a campus visit is impossible.

Web Site http://www.marshall.edu/cofa

Undergraduate Contact Byron Clercx, Chair, Department of Art, Marshall University, 1 John Marshall Drive, Huntington, West Virginia 25755; 304-696-5451, fax: 304-696-6505.

Graduate Contact Byron Clercx, Chair, Department of Art, Marshall University, One John Marshall Drive, Huntington, West Virginia 25755; 304-696-5451, fax: 304-696-6505.

Maryland Institute College of Art

Baltimore, Maryland

Independent, coed. Urban campus. Total enrollment: 1,717. Art program established 1826.

Degrees Bachelor of Fine Arts in the areas of drawing, painting, sculpture, printmaking, general fine arts, ceramics, fibers, photography, illustration, general sculptural studies, graphic design, environmental design, experimental animation, video, interactive media, art history; Bachelor of Fine Arts/Master of Arts in the area of digital arts; Bachelor of Fine Arts/Master of Arts in Teaching. Majors and concentrations: animation, art history, art/fine arts, ceramic art and design, drawing, environmental design, fibers, general sculpture studies, graphic arts, illustration, interactive media, painting, photography, printmaking, sculpture, video art. Graduate degrees offered: Master of Arts in the areas of digital arts, art education, community arts; Master of Fine Arts in the areas of painting, sculpture, art education, photography, mixed media, graphic design. Cross-registration with Johns Hopkins University, University of Baltimore, Goucher College, Loyola College, Peabody Conservatory of Music, Notre Dame College, Association of Independent Colleges of Art and Design, Institute for American Universities (France), Baltimore Collegetown Network. Program accredited by NASAD.

Enrollment 1,711 total; 1,492 undergraduate, 219 graduate.

Art Student Profile 62% females, 38% males, 22% minorities, 5% international.

Art Faculty 104 undergraduate (full-time), 132 undergraduate (part-time), 14 graduate (full-time), 17 graduate (part-time). 86% of full-time faculty have terminal degrees. Graduate students do not teach undergraduate courses. Undergraduate student–faculty ratio: 10:1.

Student Life Student groups/activities include Student Run Forum Group, National Art Educators Association, American Institute of Graphic Arts. Special housing available for art students.

Expenses for 2005–2006 Application fee: $50. Comprehensive fee: $34,450 includes full-time tuition ($26,140), mandatory fees ($780), and college room and board ($7530). College room

only: $5500. Room and board charges vary according to board plan and housing facility.

Financial Aid Program-specific awards: 30 Thalheimer Scholarships for incoming freshmen ($3000–$7500), 15 Academic Excellence Scholarships for incoming freshmen ($5000), 20 C.V. Starr Scholarships for incoming international freshmen or transfers ($2500), 40 Competitive Scholarships for incoming transfers ($1000–$12,000), 150 Competitive Scholarships for incoming freshmen ($1000–$12,000).

Application Procedures Students admitted directly into the professional program freshman year. Deadline for freshmen: February 15; transfers: March 1. Notification date for freshmen: March 15; transfers: April 1. Required: essay, high school transcript, college transcript(s) for transfer students, 3 letters of recommendation, portfolio, SAT I or ACT test scores, minimum TOEFL score of 550 for international applicants. Recommended: minimum 3.0 high school GPA, interview, honors and advanced placement level coursework in English and other humanities subjects. Portfolio reviews held continuously on campus and off campus in various cities; the submission of slides may be substituted for portfolios (slides preferred).

Web Site http://www.mica.edu

Undergraduate Contact Ms. Theresa Lynch Bedoya, Vice President and Dean, Admission and Financial Aid, Maryland Institute College of Art, 1300 Mt. Royal Avenue, Baltimore, Maryland 21217; 410-225-2222, fax: 410-225-2337, e-mail address: admissions@mica.edu

Graduate Contact Scott Kelly, Director of Graduate Admissions, Graduate Studies, Maryland Institute College of Art, 1300 Mt. Royal Avenue, Baltimore, Maryland 21217; 410-225-2256, fax: 410-225-2408.

More About the College

For 180 years, the Maryland Institute College of Art (MICA), has assembled some of the most talented and committed students and faculty members from across the nation and around the world in a creatively energized, intellectually stimulating environment that has been consistently cited as one of the nation's top art colleges. A diverse, 1,800-strong student body comes to this highly selective program from forty-seven states and forty-eight other countries.

Art in the twenty-first century can take the form of object, energy, or expendable materials. Open the

pages of any contemporary art magazine, and one can see oil on canvas, digital collage, net.art, steel fabrication, performance art, multimedia installation, video projection, e-prints, and screenprints. The definition of art is expanding. The boundaries among disciplines and mediums are dissolving. MICA's curriculum has been designed to prepare students for these contemporary approaches to art-making and thinking through a wide choice of studio majors. Students can focus on traditional discipline-based processes, or they can create art that is interactive, uses multiple mediums, or relies on collaboration with other artists—or scientists, writers, or musicians— for its execution. At MICA, painting, sculpture, photography, and other traditional mediums coexist with interdisciplinary, electronic, and multimedia approaches to critical thought. An accomplished faculty includes artists who are pushing the limits of emerging media—as well as those who are masters of traditional media and techniques and others whose work combines the two.

MICA has also taken the position that the quality and rigor of its liberal arts program should equal that of its nationally recognized studio program. This sets MICA apart from other arts colleges, and this commitment is evident in MICA's course offerings and faculty appointments. Each year, students can choose from nearly 200 courses offered in art history, literature, writing, humanities, and sciences. These courses are taught by an exceptional faculty of scholars who have earned advanced degrees from such institutions as Columbia, Harvard, Oxford, Princeton, and the University of Chicago. The faculty members have published widely and have taught at top liberal arts colleges.

Undergraduate study is enriched by the presence of eleven distinctive graduate programs that attract students from the nation's best colleges and universities.

Visual

Arts

Maryland Institute College of Art (continued)

Baltimore, located at the heart of the New York-Washington arts corridor, offers an array of cultural, social, and creative opportunities. MICA's campus of twenty-five buildings is nestled in a charming, historic neighborhood in the midst of the city's cultural center. Two buildings are on the National Register of Historic Places. The area offers the best of urban and town life. Nearby are world-class museums and galleries, the symphony hall and opera house, experimental and community theaters, cafés, bookstores, shops, and art cinemas. The Baltimore Collegetown Network links MICA students with the more than 100,000 college-age men and women who study in the metropolitan region. The MICA campus shuttle system provides transportation throughout the city to parks, museums, other colleges and universities, and entertainment and shopping venues. Weekly trips to New York City and Washington, D.C., are also available.

The Commons and Meyerhoff House housing complexes are designed especially for artists, offering apartment-style living with high-speed Internet access, a fitness center, music room, and dining hall. Students also gather on campus for conversation, coffee, and late fare at the Java Corner and Center Café. Life on campus is enriched by approximately ninety exhibitions a year featuring international, regional, and local artists as well as work by students and faculty members; a weekly film series; lectures by distinguished artists, critics, and scholars; fitness classes and club sports; and excursions into the surrounding countryside.

A highly successful Career Development Center is staffed by professionals dedicated to and specializing in developing art and art-related career opportunities. Students are well prepared for professional arts careers through internships, career counseling and workshops, and connections with the Institute's alumni network—as well as by the example of a faculty of successful artists, published authors, and distinguished scholars.

Strong academic preparation has won students slots in the nation's most prestigious graduate programs. Alumni take out into the world a solid grounding in art-making skills, the ability to continue growing as artists, and the courage to forge paths as entrepreneurs, studio artists, teachers, curators, and designers and in an array of art-related fields limited only by students' ambition and interest.

Facilities The twenty-five buildings on the MICA campus include 430,700 square feet of outstanding instructional facilities dedicated to departments of painting, ceramics, drawing, sculpture, photography, printmaking, fibers, environmental design, graphic design, illustration, video, animation, art education, and liberal arts. There is specialized equipment for work in both traditional and new media in each of these areas. In addition, MICA offers intimately sized liberal arts classrooms; a 550-seat auditorium for film, performance art, theater, poetry readings, and lectures; 24-hour access to studios; independent studio space for seniors; and seven art galleries. The arts-oriented library houses 50,000 volumes, 300 periodicals/media resources, and 250,000 examples of contemporary and historical art in slide, video, CD-ROM, and DVD format. Computers are available for student use in all instructional buildings as well as the twenty-one computer labs and digital classrooms. There are 320 computers for student use; these include Apple G5's, Dell Xeon 3-D animation workstations, digital video editing stations, and computer-controlled looms and sewing machines. Flatbed scanners, high-resolution color laser printers, digital cameras, slide scanners, Epson archival-quality wide-format printers, and CD/DVD recorders are also available. Communication capabilities include e-mail addresses for each student, personalized student portal access, and the campus wireless network system.

Faculty, Resident Artists, and Alumni The faculty of 267 professional artists, designers, and scholars are widely published and represented in public and private collections—from MOMA to the Stedelijk. Faculty members' honors include the Fulbright, Guggenheim, and MacArthur Awards. Nearly 100 percent of the liberal arts faculty members have earned the Ph.D. degree. The student-faculty ratio is 10:1.

There are more than 175 visiting artists, designers, critics, poets, art historians, and filmmakers for residencies or lectures each year. Recent visitors included David Hickey, Manthia Diawara, Joan Fontcuberta, Roberta Smith, William Wegman, and Chipp Kidd. During the past three years, resident artists from Asia, Eastern Europe, and Africa were included.

MICA alumni win international awards, attend prestigious graduate programs, and exhibit in galleries and museums throughout the world. Internationally recognized alumni include Donald Baechler, Mary Miss, Nancy Rubins, Morris Lewis, Jan Staller, and Jeff Koons.

Student Performance/Exhibit Opportunities

MICA has one of the best exhibition programs of art schools in the U.S., with ninety exhibitions per year, many of which are devoted to student work. Students at MICA show their work in the first year. In addition, there are two student-edited and designed publications. Off campus, there is an active local arts scene with numerous galleries and alternative exhibition/ performance spaces.

Special Programs MICA offers a five-year, dual-degree Bachelor of Fine Arts/Master of Arts in Teaching (B.F.A./M.A.T.) program, which combines an undergraduate degree in studio art with teaching certification at the master's level. This dual degree program boasts a 100 percent placement rate. The B.F.A./M.A. degree program in digital arts provides a fifth-year capstone experience. There are also study-abroad opportunities in Canada, England, France, Greece, Ireland, Israel, Japan, Mexico, the Netherlands, Scotland, South Korea, and Turkey, and students can also participate in MICA's New York studio program, MICA in TRIBECA. Cross-enrollment is also possible with The Johns Hopkins University and the Peabody Conservatory of Music. MICA's Career Center lists 1,000 internship opportunities and 1,130 art-related jobs in corporations, cultural institutions, design and architectural firms, and photography studios. The College hosts dozens of corporate recruiters and offers career skills counseling and alumni networking opportunities. Other reality-based programs and courses are offered in topics ranging from promoting oneself as an artist to developing business skills. Job listings and alumni referrals are available nationwide.

Marylhurst University

Marylhurst, Oregon

Independent Roman Catholic, coed. Suburban campus. Total enrollment: 1,268. Art program established 1982.

Degrees Bachelor of Fine Arts in the area of art. Majors and concentrations: art/fine arts, interior design, painting/drawing, photography, sculpture.

Enrollment 180 total; 140 undergraduate, 40 nonprofessional degree.

Art Student Profile 70% females, 30% males, 5% minorities, 2% international.

Art Faculty 27 undergraduate (part-time). Graduate students do not teach undergraduate courses. Undergraduate student–faculty ratio: 7:1.

Student Life Student groups/activities include American Society of Interior Designers Student Chapter.

Expenses for 2005–2006 Application fee: $20. Tuition: $13,860 full-time. Mandatory fees: $360 full-time. Full-time tuition and fees vary according to course load.

Financial Aid Program-specific awards: 20 Mayer Scholarships for program majors ($100).

Application Procedures Students admitted directly into the professional program freshman year. Deadline for freshmen and transfers: continuous. Required: high school transcript.

Web Site http://www.marylhurst.edu/attend/ undergrad/fna-art.html

Undergraduate Contact Mr. Paul Sutinen, Director of Art Programs, Marylhurst University, PO Box 261, Marylhurst, Oregon 97036; 503-699-6242, fax: 503-636-9526, e-mail address: psutinen@marylhurst.edu

Maryville University of Saint Louis

St. Louis, Missouri

Independent, coed. Suburban campus. Total enrollment: 3,223. Art program established 1970.

Degrees Bachelor of Arts in the area of art education K-12; Bachelor of Fine Arts. Majors and concentrations: art education, graphic design, illustration, interior design, studio art. Cross-registration with Webster University, Fontbonne University, Missouri Baptist University, Lindenwood University. Program accredited by NASAD, FIDER, NCATE.

Enrollment 204 total; 183 undergraduate, 19 nonprofessional degree.

Art Student Profile 85% females, 15% males, 8% minorities, 2% international.

Art Faculty 8 undergraduate (full-time), 26 undergraduate (part-time). 100% of full-time faculty have terminal degrees. Graduate students do not teach undergraduate courses. Undergraduate student–faculty ratio: 15:1.

Student Life Student groups/activities include Maryville Chapter of American Society of Interior Design/International Designers Association, Student Life Art Club.

Expenses for 2005–2006 Application fee: $25. Comprehensive fee: $24,670 includes full-time tuition ($17,000), mandatory fees ($320), and college room and board ($7350). College room

Maryville University of Saint Louis (continued)

only: $6425. Full-time tuition and fees vary according to course load. Room and board charges vary according to housing facility. Special program-related fees: $10 per course for audiovisual teaching resources in art history courses, $10–$110 per course for expendable supplies in studio courses.

Financial Aid Program-specific awards: 5–8 art and design scholarships for undergraduates, first time freshmen, and outstanding transfer students ($2500–$4000), 1 The Fine Arts Scholarship for those demonstrating outstanding creative ability in art and design ($1000), 1 The Newman Scholarship for art and design students ($1000).

Application Procedures Students admitted directly into the professional program freshman year. Deadline for freshmen and transfers: continuous. Required: high school transcript, college transcript(s) for transfer students, minimum 2.0 high school GPA, portfolio, SAT I or ACT test scores, writing sample and interview for interior design students. Recommended: letter of recommendation, interview. Portfolio reviews held continuously on campus and off campus in St. Louis, MO; Kansas City, MO; on National Portfolio Days; the submission of slides may be substituted for portfolios if original work is not available, for large works of art, or for three-dimensional pieces.

Web Site http://www.maryville.edu/

Undergraduate Contact Ms. Lynn Jackson, Director, Office of Admissions, Maryville University of Saint Louis, 13550 Conway Road, St. Louis, Missouri 63141-7299; 314-529-9350, fax: 314-529-9927, e-mail address: admissions@maryville.edu

Marywood University

Scranton, Pennsylvania

Independent Roman Catholic, coed. Suburban campus. Total enrollment: 3,127.

Rutgers, The State University of New Jersey
Mason Gross School of the Arts

New Brunswick, New Jersey

State-supported, coed. Small town campus. Art program established 1976.

Degrees Bachelor of Fine Arts in the area of visual arts. Majors and concentrations: ceramics, graphic design, painting/drawing, photography, printmaking, sculpture, video production. Graduate degrees offered: Master of Fine Arts in the area of visual arts.

Enrollment 424 total; 300 undergraduate, 44 graduate, 80 nonprofessional degree.

Art Student Profile 57% females, 43% males, 11% minorities, 5% international.

Art Faculty 20 total (full-time), 11 total (part-time). 98% of full-time faculty have terminal degrees. Graduate students teach a few undergraduate courses. Undergraduate student–faculty ratio: 11:1.

Expenses for 2005–2006 Special program-related fees: $20–$50 per class for supplies/materials.

Financial Aid Program-specific awards: 1 James O. Dumont Award for upperclassmen ($2300), 2–3 Betts Scholarships for upperclassmen ($500).

Application Procedures Students admitted directly into the professional program freshman year. Deadline for freshmen: January 15; transfers: March 15. Notification date for freshmen: June 1; transfers: July 1. Required: high school transcript, college transcript(s) for transfer students, minimum 2.0 high school GPA, portfolio, SAT I or ACT test scores. Recommended: essay. Portfolio reviews held twice on campus and off campus in various cities at College Art Recruitment Fairs; the submission of slides may be substituted for portfolios for out-of-state applicants.

Web Site http://www.masongross.rutgers.edu

Undergraduate Contact Ms. Diane W. Harris, Associate Director, Undergraduate Admissions, Rutgers, The State University of New Jersey, Mason Gross School of the Arts, 65 Davidson Road, Piscataway, New Jersey 08854-8097; 732-932-INFO, fax: 732-445-0237, e-mail address: admissions@asb-ugadm.rutgers.edu

Graduate Contact Ms. Judith A. McCarthy, Associate Director, Graduate and Professional Admissions, Rutgers, The State University of New Jersey, Mason Gross School of the Arts, 18 Bishop Place, New Brunswick, New Jersey 08901; 732-932-7711, fax: 732-932-8231, e-mail address: macvee@rci.rutgers.edu

Massachusetts College of Art

Boston, Massachusetts

State-supported, coed. Urban campus. Total enrollment: 2,130. Art program established 1873.

Degrees Bachelor of Fine Arts in the areas of art education, art history, fine arts, design, media and performing arts. Majors and concentrations: animation, architectural design, art education, art history, art/fine arts, ceramic art and design, fashion design and technology, film studies, glass, graphic arts, illustration, industrial design, interrelated media, jewelry and metalsmithing, painting/drawing, photography, printmaking, sculpture, studio art, textile arts. Graduate degrees offered: Master of Fine Arts in the areas of design, fine arts, media and performing arts; Master of Science in the area of art education. Cross-registration with ProArts Consortium, College Academic Program Sharing, Public College Exchange Program, Colleges of the Fenway. Program accredited by NASAD.

Enrollment 1,637 total; 1,517 undergraduate, 120 graduate.

Art Student Profile 64% females, 36% males, 12% minorities, 5% international.

Art Faculty 74 total (full-time), 124 total (part-time). 78% of full-time faculty have terminal degrees. Graduate students teach a few undergraduate courses. Undergraduate student–faculty ratio: 13:1.

Student Life Student groups/activities include All School Show, visiting artists and professional exhibitions, Christmas Art Sale. Special housing available for art students.

Expenses for 2005–2006 Application fee: $30. State resident tuition: $6850 full-time. Nonresident tuition: $19,200 full-time. College room and board: $9800. Special program-related fees: $25–$250 per course for course lab fees.

Financial Aid Program-specific awards: 44 Presidential Awards for outstanding non-Massachusetts residents ($2500–$15,000), 12 Tsongas Scholarships for outstanding Massachusetts residents ($6850).

Application Procedures Students admitted directly into the professional program freshman year. Deadline for freshmen: February 15; transfers: March 15. Notification date for freshmen: April 15; transfers: May 15. Required: essay, high school transcript, college transcript(s) for transfer students, minimum 3.0 high school GPA, 2 letters of recommendation, portfolio, SAT I or ACT test scores. Portfolio reviews held continuously on campus; the submission of slides may be substituted for portfolios (slides preferred).

Contact Ms. Kay Ransdell, Dean for Admissions and Enrollment Management, Massachusetts College of Art, 621 Huntington Avenue, Boston, Massachusetts 02115-5882; 617-879-7225, fax: 617-879-7250, e-mail address: admissions@massart.edu

Meadows School of the Arts

See Southern Methodist University

Memphis College of Art

Memphis, Tennessee

Independent, coed. Urban campus. Total enrollment: 326. Art program established 1936.

Degrees Bachelor of Fine Arts in the areas of fine arts, design arts. Majors and concentrations: applied art, ceramic art and design, commercial art, computer graphics, graphic arts, illustration, jewelry and metalsmithing, painting/drawing, papermaking, photography, printmaking, sculpture, studio art, textile arts. Graduate degrees offered: Master of Fine Arts in the areas of studio art, computer arts. Cross-registration with Rhodes College, Christian Brothers University, Le Moyne-Owen College. Program accredited by NASAD.

Enrollment 315 total; 294 undergraduate, 21 graduate.

Art Student Profile 52% females, 48% males, 22% minorities, 7% international.

Memphis College of Art (continued)

Art Faculty 20 undergraduate (full-time), 25 undergraduate (part-time). 85% of full-time faculty have terminal degrees. Graduate students teach a few undergraduate courses. Undergraduate student–faculty ratio: 10:1.

Student Life Student groups/activities include Student Government, Arteli (Arts in the Schools), Children's Community Art Classes. Special housing available for art students.

Expenses for 2005–2006 Application fee: $25. Tuition: $17,400 full-time. Mandatory fees: $60 full-time.

Financial Aid Program-specific awards: 300 portfolio scholarships for program majors ($2000–$17,800), 200 work-study awards for program majors ($1000).

Application Procedures Students admitted directly into the professional program freshman year. Deadline for freshmen and transfers: continuous. Required: high school transcript, college transcript(s) for transfer students, portfolio, SAT I or ACT test scores (minimum composite ACT score of 17). Recommended: minimum 2.0 high school GPA, letter of recommendation, interview. Portfolio reviews held weekly on campus and off campus at National Portfolio Days; the submission of slides may be substituted for portfolios whenever needed.

Web Site http://www.mca.edu

Contact Ms. Annette James Moore, Director of Admissions, Memphis College of Art, 1930 Poplar Avenue, Overton Park, Memphis, Tennessee 38104; 800-727-1088, fax: 901-272-5158, e-mail address: info@mca.edu

More About the College

Since 1936, Memphis College of Art (MCA) has been a small, distinctive community of artists. The MCA experience is organized around small classes, independent work, and one-on-one attention and guidance not usually found at a larger institution. Currently students from thirty states and seven countries attend MCA, providing a diversity that is often associated with larger schools.

MCA is located in a 342-acre park in midtown Memphis adjacent to the Memphis Brooks Museum of Art and the Memphis Zoo. Nearby student residences provide living space for new and returning students. Suite-style apartments provide each resident a private room with shared kitchen, laundry, and living room areas. Studio spaces are provided. Other residential options include shared apartments or efficiencies. Two roommates share a furnished apartment with hardwood floors, a sun porch, a kitchen, and studio space. A large variety of affordable housing is also available off-campus to suit all lifestyles and budgets.

Memphis is a great place for an aspiring artist. Known for blues, barbecue, and Elvis, Memphis is also home to Fortune 500 companies, the Grizzlies NBA team, a symphony, an opera, a theater, other colleges and universities, museums, galleries, and almost 1 million residents. Annual festivals on Beale Street and the Mississippi River are popular with students.

MCA is a close-knit community where it's easy to make friends. There are plenty of organized activities to keep students busy, such as Friday night movies, exhibition receptions, community dinners, and an annual ski trip, rafting trip, and Halloween Costume Ball.

Tobey Exhibition Hall hosts numerous shows that expose students to a wide range of contemporary art; the Brode Gallery is a large space dedicated to student art. Students also have the opportunity to learn from visiting artists who provide a constant flow of new creative and intellectual energy. MCA organizes study trips to cities around the world renowned for their culture. In early May, a weeklong workshop is held on Horn Island off the Mississippi coast.

The Career Center offers career assistance for graduating students and part-time job placement for current students. Informative sessions are held to prepare students for career choices and for the job search/interview process. The Job Fair brings regional and national companies to MCA each spring for interviews. Internships and the student-run design agency provide students with professional experience while in school.

Faculty members have been selected for their understanding of the relationship between art and teaching. MCA's Fine Arts faculty members are professional artists who exhibit frequently and regularly execute commissions. The Design Arts faculty members stay on top of the industry through continuing professional design projects. With their knowledge of the job market and galleries at the regional and national levels, faculty members are well qualified to guide students on their career paths. Liberal Studies faculty members are chosen for their impressive credentials and their understanding of the unique nature of MCA students.

MCA is concerned about students whose financial resources are limited. More than 90 percent of the College's students receive some type of financial assistance. Financial aid programs include scholarships, loans, grants, and work-study awards. More than $1 million is awarded by MCA in scholarship and grants each year.

Program Facilities Three fully equipped computer labs feature Macintosh LCD flat-panel desktop computers with high-speed Internet access, laser printers, large-format color ink jet printers, DVD burners, color scanners, and other high-end multimedia peripherals. All stations have the latest graphic design, video, and multimedia software. MCA's shop has 4,400 square feet, with machines for woodworking, metalworking, plastic molding, glass cutting, shrink wrapping, and stretcher and frame construction. The library has more than 16,000 volumes, 120 art journals and periodicals, 36,000 slides, an extensive reproduction collection, audiovisual equipment, a computer writing lab, and an image file. Students have studio spaces provided in their area of study. Conference rooms allow for slide viewing, critiques, and lectures. Sculpture, small metals, and clay have studios with foundry/welding areas for casting and metal work. Clay has wheels, handbuilding, and glazing space as well as a semi-enclosed firing room. Fiber/surface design has three studios, a dye room, manual and computerized looms, washer/dryer, range tops, refrigerators, and sewing machines. Printmaking, papermaking, and book arts studios provide interaction between these media. Printmaking has facilities for lithography, etching, serigraphy, and other processes. Book arts include letter presses and bindery. Papermaking has beaters, hydraulic press, and pulper. Photography has beginning and advanced black and white darkrooms to print 35mm through 4*5 formats. A color lab with a 20-inch color processor and facilities for non-silver and alternative processes and a fully-equipped lighting studio are also available.

Special Programs The New York Studio Program offers students an exciting semester in New York City with artists and students from across the country. The Mobility Program can place a student at another art college for a semester of study. Internships offer experience in fine and design arts fields, such as museum work, art therapy, set design, and advertising. Consortiums with local colleges provide a greater variety of course selection.

Metropolitan State College of Denver

Denver, Colorado

State-supported, coed. Urban campus. Total enrollment: 20,761. Art program established 1965.

Degrees Bachelor of Fine Arts in the area of art. Majors and concentrations: art education, art history, ceramics, communication design, computer imaging, jewelry and metalsmithing, painting/drawing, photography, printmaking, sculpture. Cross-registration with University of Colorado at Denver, Colorado community colleges. Program accredited by NASAD.

Enrollment 800 total; all undergraduate.

Art Student Profile 60% females, 40% males, 20% minorities, 1% international.

Art Faculty 11 undergraduate (full-time), 47 undergraduate (part-time). 99% of full-time faculty have terminal degrees. Graduate students do not teach undergraduate courses. Undergraduate student–faculty ratio: 15:1.

Student Life Student groups/activities include Art Club, Clay Club, Printmaking Club.

Expenses for 2005–2006 Application fee: $25. State resident tuition: $2283 full-time. Nonresident tuition: $9366 full-time. Mandatory fees: $576 full-time. Full-time tuition and fees vary according to course load and location. Special program-related fees: $5–$65 per course for expendable materials and modeling fees.

Application Procedures Students admitted directly into the professional program freshman year. Deadline for freshmen and transfers: continuous. Notification date for freshmen and transfers: continuous. Required: high school transcript, college transcript(s) for transfer students, SAT I or ACT test scores, minimum college GPA of 2.0 for transfer students.

Web Site http://clem.mscd.edu/~art_cs/

Undergraduate Contact Ms. Patricia Yarrow, Program Assistant, Art Department, Metropolitan State College of Denver, Campus Box 59, PO Box 173362, Denver, Colorado 80217-3362; 303-556-3090, fax: 303-556-4094, e-mail address: yarrowp@mscd.edu

Miami International University of Art & Design

Miami, Florida

Proprietary, coed. Urban campus. Total enrollment: 1,406. Art program established 1965.

Degrees Bachelor of Arts in the areas of advertising, fashion merchandising; Bachelor

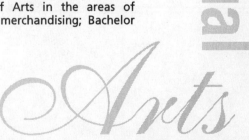

Miami International University of Art & Design (continued)

of Fine Arts. Majors and concentrations: advertising, computer animation, fashion design, fashion merchandising, film, graphic design, interior design, visual arts, visual effects and motion graphics. Graduate degrees offered: Master of Fine Arts in the areas of computer animation, graphic design, visual arts, film, interior design.

Enrollment 1,380 undergraduate, 78 graduate.

Art Student Profile 54% females, 46% males, 65% minorities, 11% international.

Art Faculty 52 total (full-time), 63 total (part-time). Graduate students do not teach undergraduate courses. Undergraduate student–faculty ratio: 18:1.

Student Life Student groups/activities include Siggraph, American Institute of Graphic Arts, American Society of Interior Designers. Special housing available for art students.

Expenses for 2006–2007 Application fee: $50. Tuition: $18,960 full-time. College room only: $6150.

Financial Aid Program-specific awards: 4 President's Scholarships for students in final year of study ($5000), merit scholarships for undergraduates with financial need ($1000).

Application Procedures Students admitted directly into the professional program freshman year. Deadline for freshmen and transfers: continuous. Notification date for freshmen and transfers: continuous. Required: essay, high school transcript, college transcript(s) for transfer students, minimum 2.0 high school GPA, interview, minimum TOEFL score of 500. Recommended: minimum 3.0 high school GPA, 2 letters of recommendation, SAT I or ACT test scores. Portfolio reviews held 4 times on campus and off campus in locations in south Florida; the submission of slides may be substituted for portfolios.

Undergraduate Contact Elsia Suarez, Director of Admission, Miami International University of Art & Design, 1501 Biscayne Boulevard, Miami, Florida 33132; 305-428-5600, fax: 305-374-5933, e-mail address: suareze@aii.edu

Graduate Contact Elisa Suarez, Director of Admission, Miami International University of Art & Design, 1501 Biscayne Boulevard, Miami, Florida 33132; 305-3995-5048, fax: 305-374-5933, e-mail address: suareze@aii.edu

Miami University
Oxford, Ohio

State-related, coed. Small town campus. Total enrollment: 16,338. Art program established 1929.

Degrees Bachelor of Fine Arts in the areas of painting/drawing, jewelry and metalsmithing, printmaking, sculpture, ceramic art and design, graphic arts, photography; Bachelor of Science in the area of art education. Majors and concentrations: art education, art history, ceramic art and design, computer graphics, jewelry and metalsmithing, painting/drawing, photography, printmaking, sculpture. Graduate degrees offered: Master of Arts in the area of art education; Master of Fine Arts in the areas of painting, ceramics, sculpture, jewelry and metalsmithing, printmaking. Cross-registration with John E. Dolibois European Center (Luxembourg). Program accredited by NASAD.

Enrollment 399 total; 380 undergraduate, 19 graduate.

Art Student Profile 68% females, 32% males, 3% minorities.

Art Faculty 12 undergraduate (full-time), 9 undergraduate (part-time), 10 graduate (full-time). 81% of full-time faculty have terminal degrees. Graduate students teach a few undergraduate courses. Undergraduate student–faculty ratio: 15:1.

Student Life Student groups/activities include Art History Association, National Art Education Association Student Chapter, Visual Arts Club.

Expenses for 2005–2006 Application fee: $45. State resident tuition: $19,877 full-time. Nonresident tuition: $19,877 full-time. Mandatory fees: $1610 full-time. College room and board: $7610. College room only: $3860. Room and board charges vary according to board plan and housing facility. Ohio residents receive a minimum of $10,000 in resident scholarships. Special program-related fees: $20–$75 per course for studio supplies.

Financial Aid Program-specific awards: 1 Miami University Scholarship for program majors ($4300), 1 Arthur Damon Art Award for program majors ($1500), 1 School of Fine Arts Award for program majors ($2000), 1 Marston D. Hodgin Award for program majors ($1000), 1 George R. and Galen Glasgow Hoxie Award

($890), 2 Fred and Molly Pye Awards for sophomores and juniors ($475), 1 Barbara Hershey Photo Award for female junior photography majors ($1000), 1 National Woodcarvers Award for upperclass sculpture majors ($1000), 1 Robert Wolfe Printmakers Award for junior and senior printmaking majors ($400).

Application Procedures Students admitted directly into the professional program freshman year. Deadline for freshmen: January 30; transfers: March 1. Notification date for freshmen: March 15. Required: high school transcript, college transcript(s) for transfer students, portfolio, SAT I or ACT test scores. Portfolio reviews held twice on campus; the submission of slides may be substituted for portfolios (slides preferred).

Web Site http://www.fna.muohio.edu/artweb/

Undergraduate Contact Mr. Dennis Tobin, Professor, Department of Art, Miami University, Art Building, Oxford, Ohio 45056; 513-529-1505, fax: 513-529-1532, e-mail address: tobinde@muohio.edu

Graduate Contact Dr. Clive Getty, Associate Professor of Art, Department of Art, Miami University, Art Building, Oxford, Ohio 45056; 513-529-5627, fax: 513-529-1532, e-mail address: gettycf@muohio.edu

Michigan State University

East Lansing, Michigan

State-supported, coed. Suburban campus. Total enrollment: 45,166. Art program established 1931.

Degrees Bachelor of Fine Arts in the areas of studio art, art education. Majors and concentrations: art education, ceramics, graphic design, painting/drawing, photography, printmaking, sculpture. Graduate degrees offered: Master of Fine Arts in the area of studio art.

Enrollment 340 total; 175 undergraduate, 15 graduate, 150 nonprofessional degree.

Art Faculty 24 total (full-time), 5 total (part-time). 100% of full-time faculty have terminal degrees. Graduate students teach a few undergraduate courses. Undergraduate student–faculty ratio: 13:1.

Student Life Student groups/activities include Saturday Art Program, undergraduate exhibit at Kresge Art Museum, Gallery 114 (student exhibition space).

Expenses for 2005–2006 Application fee: $35. State resident tuition: $6705 full-time. Nonresident tuition: $18,458 full-time. Mandatory fees: $882 full-time. Full-time tuition and fees vary according to course load, degree level, program, and student level. College room and board: $5744. College room only: $2488. Room and board charges vary according to board plan and housing facility.

Financial Aid Program-specific awards: 1–4 Creative Arts Scholarships for Michigan resident studio art majors ($500–$3000).

Application Procedures Students admitted directly into the professional program freshman year. Deadline for freshmen and transfers: continuous. Required: high school transcript, college transcript(s) for transfer students, minimum 2.0 high school GPA, SAT I or ACT test scores. Recommended: minimum 3.0 high school GPA.

Web Site http://www.art.msu.edu

Undergraduate Contact Cindy Walter, Academic Advisor, Studio Art Undergraduate Program, Michigan State University, 113 Kresge Art Center, East Lansing, Michigan 48824-1119; 517-432-7033, fax: 517-432-3938, e-mail address: walterc2@msu.edu

Graduate Contact Deborah Ray, Academic Secretary, Studio Art Graduate Program, Michigan State University, 113 Kresge Art Center, East Lansing, Michigan 48824-1119; 517-355-7611, fax: 517-432-3938, e-mail address: raydeb@msu.edu

Middle Tennessee State University

Murfreesboro, Tennessee

State-supported, coed. Total enrollment: 22,554. Art program established 1954.

Midge Karr Fine Art Department

See New York Institute of Technology

Midwestern State University

Wichita Falls, Texas

State-supported, coed. Urban campus. Total enrollment: 6,279.

Degrees Bachelor of Fine Arts in the area of studio art. Majors and concentrations: ceramics, commercial art, jewelry and metalsmithing, painting, photography, printmaking, sculpture.

Art Faculty 5 total (full-time), 1 total (part-time). 100% of full-time faculty have terminal degrees. Graduate students do not teach undergraduate courses.

Student Life Student groups/activities include off-campus exhibitions.

Expenses for 2006–2007 Application fee: $25. State resident tuition: $1500 full-time. Nonresident tuition: $9750 full-time. Mandatory fees: $3066 full-time. College room and board: $5220. College room only: $2660. Special program-related fees: $75–$250 per course for supplies and materials.

Financial Aid Program-specific awards: endowed scholarships for academically qualified/talented applicants.

Application Procedures Students admitted directly into the professional program freshman year. Deadline for freshmen and transfers: August 1. Required: high school transcript, college transcript(s) for transfer students, SAT I or ACT test scores. Recommended: minimum 2.0 high school GPA.

Undergraduate Contact Nancy Steele-Hamme, Chair, Art Department, Midwestern State University, 3410 Taft Boulevard, Fain Fine Arts Center, Wichita Falls, Texas 76308; 940-397-4606, fax: 940-397-4369, e-mail address: nancy.steele@mwsu.edu

Millikin University

Decatur, Illinois

Independent, coed. Suburban campus. Total enrollment: 2,641. Art program established 1903.

Degrees Bachelor of Fine Arts. Majors and concentrations: art education, art therapy, art/fine arts, commercial art, computer graphics, studio art.

Enrollment 137 total; all undergraduate.

Art Student Profile 50% females, 50% males, 4% minorities.

Art Faculty 5 undergraduate (full-time), 3 undergraduate (part-time). 100% of full-time faculty have terminal degrees. Graduate students do not teach undergraduate courses. Undergraduate student–faculty ratio: 16:1.

Student Life Student groups/activities include Art Club, AIGA.

Expenses for 2005–2006 Application fee: $0. One-time mandatory fee: $75. Comprehensive fee: $27,834 includes full-time tuition ($20,696), mandatory fees ($425), and college room and board ($6713). College room only: $3763. Full-time tuition and fees vary according to course load. Room and board charges vary according to board plan and housing facility. Special program-related fees: $10–$50 per semester for lab fees.

Financial Aid Program-specific awards: 20–30 talent awards for incoming students ($500–$3000).

Application Procedures Students apply for admission into the professional program by sophomore year. Deadline for freshmen and transfers: continuous. Required: high school transcript, college transcript(s) for transfer students, letter of recommendation, interview, portfolio, SAT I or ACT test scores. Portfolio reviews held by appointment on campus and off campus in St. Louis, MO; Indianapolis, IN; the submission of slides may be substituted for portfolios for large works of art.

Web Site http://www.millikin.edu

Undergraduate Contact Mr. Ed Walker, Chairman, Art Department, Millikin University, 1184 West Main Street, Decatur, Illinois 62522; 217-424-6228, fax: 217-424-3993, e-mail address: ewalker@mail.millikin.edu

Milwaukee Institute of Art and Design

Milwaukee, Wisconsin

Independent, coed. Total enrollment: 645. Art program established 1974.

Degrees Bachelor of Fine Arts. Majors and concentrations: communication design, computer animation and interactive media, drawing, fine art studio, illustration, industrial design, interior architecture and design, painting, photography, printmaking, sculpture. Cross-registration with Marquette University. Program accredited by NASAD.

Enrollment 636 total; all undergraduate.

Art Student Profile 53% females, 47% males, 18% minorities, 1% international.

Art Faculty 33 undergraduate (full-time), 60 undergraduate (part-time). 88% of full-time faculty have terminal degrees. Graduate students do not teach undergraduate courses. Undergraduate student–faculty ratio: 14:1.

Student Life Student groups/activities include student exhibitions, Student Government, student publication. Special housing available for art students.

Expenses for 2006–2007 Application fee: $25. Comprehensive fee: $30,400 includes full-time tuition ($23,100), mandatory fees ($300), and college room and board ($7000). Special program-related fees: $5–$95 per course for supplies/models.

Financial Aid Program-specific awards: 22–35 MIAD Scholarships for continuing students ($2000–$2200), 125 MIAD Admissions Scholarships for incoming students ($5500–$22,200).

Application Procedures Students admitted directly into the professional program freshman year. Deadline for freshmen and transfers: continuous. Required: essay, high school transcript, college transcript(s) for transfer students, minimum 2.0 high school GPA, interview, portfolio. Recommended: minimum 3.0 high school GPA, 2 letters of recommendation, SAT I or ACT test scores, minimum 3.0 GPA in high school art classes. Portfolio reviews held continuously on campus and off campus; the submission of slides may be substituted for portfolios when distance is prohibitive.

Web Site http://www.miad.edu

Undergraduate Contact Mr. Mark Fetherston, Director of Admissions, Milwaukee Institute of Art and Design, 273 East Erie Street, Milwaukee, Wisconsin 53202; 414-291-8070, fax: 414-291-8077, e-mail address: miadadm@miad.edu

More About the Institute

The Milwaukee Institute of Art and Design (MIAD) is Wisconsin's only four-year independent professional art and design college. Founded in 1974 as a successor to the Layton School of Art, MIAD offers a Bachelor of Fine Arts (B.F.A.) degree in eleven majors: communication design, drawing, illustration, industrial design, integrated fine-arts studio, interior architecture and design, painting, photography, printmaking, sculpture, and time-based media. Minors can be earned in all eleven disciplines as well as in advertising, animation, art history, business, video, and writing. The curricula reflect the latest in professional needs, techniques, trends, and innovations. The ongoing emphasis is on problem solving within a rapidly changing world. MIAD is a place where students learn to achieve their goals and do not merely replicate the theories and processes of others.

All MIAD faculty members are practicing professionals recognized in their field of instruction. They share their knowledge and experience with talented, motivated students. Attention to individual students and their work is ensured through a small student-faculty ratio.

MIAD studios and classrooms are in a state-of-the-art, multiwindowed, renovated, five-story building. It has the light necessary to artists and wide-open spaces for creating oversized paintings and sculptures and full-size industrial prototypes. The ventilation system provides a safe environment, and the studio space per student is one of the largest in the country.

Computer labs offer the most current software and hardware for animation; graphic, industrial, and interior/architectural design; and video editing as well as fine-art imaging. A fully equipped sculpture department, a 3-D lab, extensive printmaking facilities, and digital photography facilities offer artists wide choices and venues for expressing themselves.

The college is located in Milwaukee's historic Third Ward near Lake Michigan. This safe neighborhood of turn-of-the-century buildings is home to artists' lofts, galleries, specialty shops, restaurants, and a live theater complex. Student housing and a Student Center are in historic buildings that offer comfort, security, and convenience in unique, artistic settings.

MIAD students have a wide range of exhibition and internship opportunities each year. These include an ongoing series of shows in the MIAD Student Gallery, as well as the annual Graduate Exhibition and internships with many of the area's most prestigious design, architectural, and photographic studios and several of the city's professional performing art troupes. Also, MIAD students are

Milwaukee Institute of Art and Design (continued)

regularly invited by local galleries to submit work for local and regional exhibitions.

Alumni own or are affiliated with local and national advertising agencies, design studios, and publishers, and many design for industries throughout the world. Their fine art is in private and corporate collections; they operate their own galleries; and, thanks to their education, they pursue myriad other satisfying and rewarding careers.

Special Programs Extended academic opportunities are available to students through an affiliation with nearby Marquette University. MIAD students can choose from a wide variety of liberal studies courses, plus, they may use that school's excellent Recreation Center and access its full range of health services.

A mobility program allows MIAD students to study at more than thirty affiliated U.S. art and design schools, including an internship/study program in New York City. MIAD offers a unique blend of international-study experiences. These include trips to major European cities as part of course offerings in liberal studies. MIAD maintains exchange opportunities for students to study with other notable art and design colleges in France, Germany, Japan, Korea, and Poland.

Minneapolis College of Art and Design

Minneapolis, Minnesota

Independent, coed. Urban campus. Total enrollment: 722. Art program established 1886.

Degrees Bachelor of Fine Arts in the areas of design, fine arts, media arts; Bachelor of Science in the area of visualization. Majors and concentrations: advertising design, animation, comic art, drawing, filmmaking, fine art studio, furniture design, graphic design, illustration, interactive media, painting, photography, printmaking, sculpture, visualization. Graduate degrees offered: Master of Fine Arts in the area of visual studies. Cross-registration with Macalester College. Program accredited by NASAD.

Enrollment 718 total; 662 undergraduate, 56 graduate.

Art Student Profile 43% females, 57% males, 18% minorities, 7% international.

Art Faculty 36 total (full-time), 70 total (part-time). 80% of full-time faculty have terminal degrees. Graduate students do not teach undergraduate courses. Undergraduate student–faculty ratio: 14:1.

Student Life Student groups/activities include Friday Film Series, International Association of Graphic Arts Student Chapter (IAGA), Lingo Club. Special housing available for art students.

Expenses for 2005–2006 Application fee: $35. Comprehensive fee: $31,010 includes full-time tuition ($24,800), mandatory fees ($240), and college room and board ($5970). College room only: $3770. Room and board charges vary according to housing facility. Special program-related fees: $20–$215 per semester for resource fee.

Financial Aid Program-specific awards: MCAD Visual Scholarships for incoming students ($7500), Friends of MCAD Awards for incoming students ($6000).

Application Procedures Students admitted directly into the professional program freshman year. Deadline for freshmen and transfers: continuous. Required: high school transcript, college transcript(s) for transfer students, letter of recommendation, portfolio, SAT I or ACT test scores, statement of interest, essay for visualization majors. Recommended: minimum 2.0 high school GPA, interview. Portfolio reviews held as needed on campus and off campus at National Portfolio Days; the submission of slides may be substituted for portfolios for large works of art or when distance is prohibitive.

Web Site http://www.mcad.edu/

Contact William Mullen, Director of Admissions, Minneapolis College of Art and Design, 2501 Stevens Avenue South, Minneapolis, Minnesota 55404; 612-874-3762, fax: 612-874-3701, e-mail address: william_mullen@mcad.edu

Minnesota State University Mankato

Mankato, Minnesota

State-supported, coed. Small town campus. Total enrollment: 14,335.

Degrees Bachelor of Fine Arts in the area of art. Majors and concentrations: ceramics, drawing, fibers, graphic arts, painting, photography, printmaking, sculpture. Graduate degrees offered: Master of Arts in the area of studio art. Cross-registration with Gustavus Adolphus College. Program accredited by NASAD.

Enrollment 312 total; 243 undergraduate, 12 graduate, 57 nonprofessional degree.

Art Student Profile 55% females, 45% males, 2% minorities, 5% international.

Art Faculty 14 undergraduate (full-time), 6 total (part-time). 100% of full-time faculty have terminal degrees. Graduate students teach a few undergraduate courses. Undergraduate student–faculty ratio: 20:1.

Student Life Student groups/activities include Art League, Photography Club, Mudworks Ceramics Student Organization, AIGA Student Chapter.

Expenses for 2005–2006 Application fee: $20. State resident tuition: $5104 full-time. Nonresident tuition: $10,932 full-time. Mandatory fees: $742 full-time. Full-time tuition and fees vary according to course load and reciprocity agreements. College room and board: $5083. Room and board charges vary according to board plan. Special program-related fees: $15–$90 per semester for art supplies.

Financial Aid Program-specific awards: 6–8 Faculty Nominated Awards for program majors ($500).

Application Procedures Students apply for admission into the professional program by sophomore, junior year. Deadline for freshmen: March 15; transfers: continuous. Notification date for freshmen and transfers: continuous. Required: high school transcript, college transcript(s) for transfer students, SAT I or ACT test scores.

Web Site http://www.mnsu.edu/dept/artdept

Contact Mr. James Johnson, Chair, Art Department, Minnesota State University Mankato, Nelson Hall 136, Mankato, Minnesota 56001; 507-389-6412, fax: 507-389-2816, e-mail address: james.johnson@mnsu.edu

Roland Dille Center for the Arts
Minnesota State University Moorhead
Moorhead, Minnesota

State-supported, coed. Urban campus. Total enrollment: 7,652.

Mississippi State University
Mississippi State, Mississippi

State-supported, coed. Total enrollment: 16,101. Art program established 1968.

Mississippi University for Women
Columbus, Mississippi

State-supported, coed, primarily women. Small town campus. Total enrollment: 2,328. Art program established 1941.

Degrees Bachelor of Fine Arts in the areas of fine arts, art education. Majors and concentrations: art education, art/fine arts, graphic arts, interior design, studio art. Cross-registration with Mississippi State University. Program accredited by NASAD.

Enrollment 102 total; 70 undergraduate, 32 nonprofessional degree.

Art Student Profile 75% females, 25% males, 5% minorities, 5% international.

Art Faculty 7 undergraduate (full-time), 1 undergraduate (part-time). 100% of full-time faculty have terminal degrees. Graduate students do not teach undergraduate courses. Undergraduate student–faculty ratio: 12:1.

Student Life Student groups/activities include Art Student League, American Society of Interior Designers, Kappa Pi.

Expenses for 2005–2006 Special program-related fees: $20 per course for graphic design, interior design supplies, $40 per course for fiber art, clay arts, metal arts, sculpture supplies.

Visual *Arts*

Mississippi University for Women (continued)

Financial Aid Program-specific awards: 5–7 specified scholarships for program majors ($250–$1800), 10–12 division scholarships for program majors ($250–$500).

Application Procedures Students apply for admission into the professional program by sophomore year. Deadline for freshmen and transfers: continuous. Required: high school transcript, college transcript(s) for transfer students, minimum 2.0 high school GPA, ACT test score only. Recommended: interview, portfolio. Portfolio reviews held once and by appointment on campus.

Web Site http://www.muw.edu/fine_arts

Undergraduate Contact Terri Heath, Director of Admissions, Enrollment Management/Admissions, Mississippi University for Women, Box W-1613, Columbus, Mississippi 39701; 662-329-7106, fax: 662-241-7481, e-mail address: theath@muw.edu

Missouri State University

Springfield, Missouri

State-supported, coed. Suburban campus. Total enrollment: 18,928. Art program established 1945.

Degrees Bachelor of Fine Arts in the areas of design, art, digital animation; Bachelor of Science in the area of electronic art; Bachelor of Science in Education. Majors and concentrations: art education, ceramics, computer animation, drawing, electronic arts, graphic design, illustration, image production, jewelry and metalsmithing, painting, photography, printmaking, sculpture. Graduate degrees offered: Master of Science in the area of art education.

Enrollment 572 total; 490 undergraduate, 12 graduate, 70 nonprofessional degree.

Art Faculty 29 total (full-time), 14 total (part-time). 100% of full-time faculty have terminal degrees. Graduate students do not teach undergraduate courses. Undergraduate student–faculty ratio: 15:1.

Student Life Student groups/activities include Design Student Club, Student Artist Association, clubs in various areas of emphasis.

Expenses for 2006–2007 Application fee: $30. State resident tuition: $4920 full-time. Nonresi-

dent tuition: $9840 full-time. Mandatory fees: $534 full-time. College room and board: $5294. College room only: $3462.

Financial Aid Program-specific awards: 10 departmental awards for program majors ($500–$800).

Application Procedures Students apply for admission into the professional program by sophomore year. Deadline for freshmen and transfers: July 30. Notification date for freshmen and transfers: continuous. Required: high school transcript, college transcript(s) for transfer students, minimum 2.0 high school GPA, portfolio, SAT I or ACT test scores. Portfolio reviews held twice on campus; the submission of slides may be substituted for portfolios.

Web Site http://www.smsu.edu/contrib/art/index.html

Undergraduate Contact Prof. Andrew L. Cohen, Department Head, Art and Design Department, Missouri State University, 901 South National, Springfield, Missouri 65804; 417-836-5110, fax: 417-836-6055.

Graduate Contact Dr. Steve Willis, Coordinator, Art Education Department, Missouri State University, 901 South National, Springfield, Missouri 65804; 417-836-6693, fax: 417-836-6055.

Montserrat College of Art

Beverly, Massachusetts

Independent, coed. Suburban campus. Total enrollment: 299. Art program established 1970.

Degrees Bachelor of Fine Arts. Majors and concentrations: art/fine arts, graphic design, illustration, painting/drawing, photography, printmaking, sculpture. Cross-registration with Northeast Consortium of Colleges and Universities in Massachusetts, Association of Independent Colleges of Art and Design. Program accredited by NASAD.

Enrollment 299 total; all undergraduate.

Art Student Profile 64% females, 36% males, 5% minorities.

Art Faculty 24 undergraduate (full-time), 38 undergraduate (part-time). 67% of full-time faculty have terminal degrees. Graduate students do not teach undergraduate courses. Undergraduate student–faculty ratio: 7:1.

Student Life Student groups/activities include Student Government, Meals-on-the-Cheap Committee, Coffee House Organization. Special housing available for art students.

Expenses for 2005–2006 Application fee: $40. One-time mandatory fee: $725. Tuition: $19,934 full-time. Mandatory fees: $745 full-time. Full-time tuition and fees vary according to course load. College room only: $5300. Room charges vary according to housing facility.

Financial Aid Program-specific awards: 185 Montserrat Grants for those demonstrating need ($2477), 2 Presidential Awards for program majors ($15,250), 178 talent awards for those demonstrating merit ($2498), 2 Beverly Scholarships for residents of Beverly demonstrating need ($5625).

Application Procedures Students admitted directly into the professional program freshman year. Deadline for freshmen and transfers: August 1. Notification date for freshmen and transfers: August 15. Required: essay, high school transcript, college transcript(s) for transfer students, minimum 2.0 high school GPA, 2 letters of recommendation, portfolio, SAT I or ACT test scores, minimum TOEFL score of 550 for international students. Recommended: minimum 3.0 high school GPA, interview. Portfolio reviews held continuously on campus and off campus in nationally; the submission of slides may be substituted for portfolios if a campus visit is impossible.

Web Site http://www.montserrat.edu

Undergraduate Contact Ms. Jessica Sarin-Perry, Dean of Admissions and Enrollment Management, Admissions, Montserrat College of Art, 23 Essex Street, Box 26, Beverly, Massachusetts 01915; 800-836-0487, fax: 978-921-4241, e-mail address: admiss@montserrat.edu

More About the College

Montserrat College of Art takes a highly personal approach to teaching, valuing above all else the combination of strong individual support and challenging creative instruction. Located on Boston's North Shore, it is a place where students feel inspired, encouraged, and at home.

Students come to Montserrat to gain professional competence, to develop their own unique abilities, and to engage in new areas of experience in pursuit of their Bachelor of Fine Arts (B.F.A.) degree. With an enrollment of approximately 300 students of diverse cultural and artistic backgrounds, the College is large

enough to offer the wide array of courses and concentrations that compose a strong visual arts curriculum, yet small enough to provide the personal attention that is often difficult to find in larger educational environments. Small classes encourage intensive, individualized instruction by a faculty of professional artists and designers and accomplished scholars.

The first year of foundation studies is a carefully crafted sequence of complementary courses emphasizing the visual, technical, written, and verbal skills essential to a successful art college experience. After foundation, a student may choose to major in fine arts, graphic design, illustration, new media, painting and drawing, photography, printmaking, or sculpture, or combine any one of the studio majors with a second major in art education. The Montserrat curriculum allows students to explore a wide range of studio electives not necessarily related to their concentration, encouraging the development of a truly unique, artistic voice.

Experiential learning provides a unique opportunity for students to gain professional practice. During

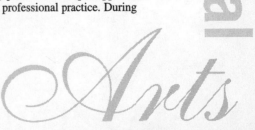

Montserrat College of Art (continued)

the junior year, internships and apprenticeships provide students with opportunities to experience the world of work and to integrate classroom learning with the realities of the workplace.

Entry into the Senior Seminar is determined by a faculty panel. Here, students have the opportunity to delve independently into a significant, coherent body of work and exhibit seminar work. This revelatory experience helps the artist and designer to mature and ultimately make the transition into professional life.

Montserrat is a residential college with apartment-style housing nestled among the homes of downtown Beverly, located on Boston's North Shore. Boston and Cambridge are easily accessible by car or commuter train. World-class museums, such as the Boston Museum of Fine Arts; galleries; libraries; shopping; sports; and a variety of entertainment options provide a stimulating intellectual, cultural, and social environment in which to live and learn.

Program Facilities The Montserrat campus has five galleries that feature exciting exhibitions by professional artists of national and international note and artists within the College community. The Visiting Artist and Lectures Series programs expose students to a wide range of viewpoints and aesthetics.

Montserrat's main building, the historic Hardie Building, houses four floors of studios, classrooms, exhibition spaces, and the Paul Scott Library. Specially equipped studios for printmaking, photography, and painting, as well as video and computer labs are located here. The library contains a collection of more than 13,000 books, numerous art and related periodicals, videos, CD-ROMs, and other resources. The library offers Internet access and houses a comprehensive slide collection.

Montserrat's Cabot Studio Building offers facilities for sculpture and semi-private studios for seniors concentrating in painting, photography, printmaking, sculpture, and mixed-media. Across Cabot Street are the newly renovated studios for the Illustration and Graphic Design Departments, including a gallery and semi-private studio spaces for seniors. Adjacent to the studios are reproduction equipment and an extensive collection of research materials for nature and costume studies. Graphic Design students work in an environment similar to a professional design studio with computers, access to the Internet, and a meeting area.

All students are entitled to free admission to Boston's Museum of Fine Arts, one of the finest collections of art in the world. The museum houses permanent exhibits of art and artifacts representing virtually all periods and civilizations as well as changing exhibitions of art.

Special Programs Montserrat offers students a variety of opportunities to broaden their horizons and earn credit towards their degree through local, national, and international study. The College is a member of the Northeast Consortium of Colleges and Universities in Massachusetts. Students may take classes and use the library facilities of member colleges. Through Montserrat's membership in the Association of Independent Colleges of Art and Design (AICAD), students may spend a semester or year in comparable studies at a member institution. The AICAD New York Studio Program offers third-year students the opportunity to spend a summer in New York City.

Students may spend a month in the walled, papal city of Viterbo in Italy while attending Montserrat's summer, residential program. Intensive courses in painting, drawing, photography, art history, and writing are offered.

High school students can experience life at Montserrat through the summer Pre-College program, which takes place in July on the College's campus. This four-week program is primarily for students entering their junior or senior year of high school and is designed to help young artists evaluate a career in the arts and develop a portfolio suitable for college admission. Students participate in assignments and critiques led by top instructors from Montserrat and other Boston-area colleges and, upon completion of the program, earn 3 college credits.

Moore College of Art & Design

Philadelphia, Pennsylvania

Independent, women only. Urban campus. Total enrollment: 491. Art program established 1848.

Degrees Bachelor of Fine Arts in the areas of art education, art history. Majors and concentrations: art education, art history, curatorial studies, fashion design, graphic design, illustration, interior design, photography/digital arts, textile arts, three-dimensional studies, two-dimensional studies. Program accredited by NASAD, FIDER.

Enrollment 491 total; all undergraduate.

Art Student Profile 99% females, 1% males, 23% minorities, 2% international.

Art Faculty 32 undergraduate (full-time), 74 undergraduate (part-time). 66% of full-time faculty have terminal degrees. Graduate students do not teach undergraduate courses. Undergraduate student–faculty ratio: 8:1.

Student Life Student groups/activities include senior show/student show, fashion show, Moore Magazine. Special housing available for art students.

Expenses for 2006–2007 Application fee: $40. Comprehensive fee: $32,256 includes full-time tuition ($22,846), mandatory fees ($756), and college room and board ($8654). College room only: $5227.

Financial Aid Program-specific awards: 1 Evelyn A. Whittaker Award for those demonstrating need and talent ($15,000), 100 Moore College of Art and Design Presidential and Merit Awards for academically and artistically talented students ($500–$4000), 10 W. W. Smith Awards for those demonstrating talent and academic achievement ($2000), 1 Moore College of Art and Design Partnership Award for Philadelphia public school applicants demonstrating need ($15,000), 8 Sarah Peters Awards for talented freshmen ($500), 2–4 Appleman Awards for adult students demonstrating need/talent ($10,000–$12,500), 8 Fred and Naomi Hazell Awards for oil painters demonstrating need/talent ($16,000), 1 Charming Shops Scholarship for fashion/textile design juniors and seniors ($2000), 1 Kristen McCabe Memorial Award for talented junior or senior graphic design majors ($500).

Application Procedures Students apply for admission into the professional program by sophomore year. Deadline for freshmen and transfers: continuous. Notification date for freshmen and transfers: August 15. Required: high school transcript, college transcript(s) for transfer students, minimum 2.0 high school GPA, letter of recommendation, portfolio, SAT I or ACT test scores (minimum combined SAT I score of 850, minimum composite ACT score of 17). Recommended: essay, interview. Portfolio reviews held continuously on campus and off campus at National Portfolio Days; the submission of slides may be substituted for portfolios when distance is prohibitive.

Web Site http://www.moore.edu

Undergraduate Contact Ms. Heeseung Lee, Director of Admissions, Moore College of Art & Design, 20th and The Parkway, Philadelphia, Pennsylvania 19103-1179; 215-568-4515 ext. 1107, fax: 215-568-3547, e-mail address: admiss@moore.edu

More About the College

Moore College of Art & Design sets the standard of excellence in educating women for careers in art and design. As the first and only women's college of the visual arts in the nation, founded in 1848, Moore students enjoy an accessible, supportive small college community and learn from a dedicated faculty of award-winning artists, designers, and scholars.

With an average of 500 students and a 9:1 student-to-faculty member ratio, Moore offers eleven Bachelor of Fine Arts majors in art education, art history, curatorial studies, fashion design, 2-D and 3-D fine arts, graphic design, illustration, interior design, photography and digital arts, and textile design. Career and leadership skills are emphasized throughout the academic programs, with each major providing extensive career preparation for their respective fields.

The Locks Career Center for Women in the Arts facilitates internships for students to gain practical professional experience. The Locks Career Center also provides a broad range of career resources for students and alumnae, such as one-on-one career counseling, mentoring, job bulletins, and workshops on topics from networking to resume writing.

On-campus leadership organizations provide the chance to learn about and utilize leadership skills, and to develop self-confidence. Leadership fellowship opportunities provide financial support for students to work, either with an individual leader in the arts community or within an innovative organization. Other experiences are available through community service or study abroad.

Moore's size creates a community experience where students live and learn in a comfortable, supportive environment—one where students from different majors, backgrounds, cultures, and lifestyles can learn from each other. The campus includes Sarah Peter Hall, Wilson Hall, Main Residence, and Sartain Hall. The main campus includes expansive studios and classrooms, technology centers, two auditoriums, Fox Commons, MAC and PC computer labs, a professional woodshop, ferrous and nonferrous metal workshops, ceramic studios with indoor and outdoor kilns, abundant student exhibition space, two contemporary art galleries, several outdoor courtyards, and the dining café. The Connolly Library's holdings feature 40,000 monographs, Internet access, 185 art journals, a slide collection of more than 123,000 images, and picture files of 300,000 images.

Moore College of Art & Design (continued)

The support system and friendships formed by living in college housing often help ease first-year students' transition into the college setting. Approximately 70 percent of first-year students live in College housing, which includes Main Residence Hall and Sartain Hall. Other students choose to live off campus. There are numerous apartments in Philadelphia's neighboring residential areas.

Moore graduates become part of and have access to a broad network of fellow alumnae of accomplished artists, designers, and creative leaders in a wide variety of industries. Among Moore's notable graduates are fashion designer and business icon Adrienne Vittadini; renowned twentieth-century portraitist Alice Neel; award-winning interior designer Karon Daroff; and Pulitzer Prize-winning photojournalist Sharon J. Wohlmuth.

Moore College of Art & Design is accredited by the Commission on Higher Education of the Middle States Association of Colleges and Schools, 3624 Market Street, Philadelphia, Pennsylvania 19104-2680, 215-662-5606. The Commission on Higher Education is an institutional accrediting agency recognized by the U.S. Secretary of Education and the Commission on Recognition of Postsecondary Accreditation; by the National Association of Schools of Art and Design, 11250 Roger Bacon Drive, Suite 21, Reston, Virginia 20190, 703-437-0700; by the Commonwealth of Pennsylvania, Department of Education, 333 Market Street, Harrisburg, Pennsylvania 17126-0333, 717-787-5820; and by the Foundation for Interior Design Education Research, 146 Monroe Center NW, #1318, Grand Rapids, Michigan 49503-2822, 616-458-0400.

Mount Allison University

Sackville, New Brunswick, Canada

Province-supported, coed. Small town campus. Total enrollment: 2,369. Art program established 1941.

Degrees Bachelor of Fine Arts. Majors and concentrations: open media, painting/drawing, photography, printmaking, sculpture. Cross-registration with Université de Strasbourg (France), Universitöt Tubingen (Germany).

Enrollment 121 total; all undergraduate.

Art Student Profile 85% females, 15% males, 2% international.

Art Faculty 7 undergraduate (full-time), 3 undergraduate (part-time). 86% of full-time

faculty have terminal degrees. Graduate students do not teach undergraduate courses. Undergraduate student–faculty ratio: 18:1.

Student Life Student groups/activities include Fine Arts Society.

Expenses for 2005–2006 Application fee: $50 Canadian dollars. Tuition, fee, and room and board charges are reported in Canadian dollars. Province resident tuition: $6100 full-time. Mandatory fees: $242 full-time. Full-time tuition and fees vary according to course load. College room and board: $6630. College room only: $3430. Room and board charges vary according to board plan. International student tuition: $12,200 full-time.

Financial Aid Program-specific awards: 1 Pulford Award for freshmen program majors ($1000), 1–2 Chang Awards for senior program majors ($500–$1000), 1 Crake Award for graduating students ($500), 2 Gairdner Awards for top program majors ($1000), University Scholarships for those in top 10% of program ($750).

Application Procedures Students admitted directly into the professional program freshman year. Deadline for freshmen: April 5; transfers: July 5. Notification date for freshmen and transfers: continuous. Required: high school transcript, college transcript(s) for transfer students, minimum 3.0 high school GPA, 2 letters of recommendation, portfolio. Portfolio reviews held once on campus; the submission of slides may be substituted for portfolios at student's discretion.

Web Site http://www.mta.ca/faculty/arts-letters/finearts/

Undergraduate Contact Heather Patterson, Manager of Admissions, Scholarships and Financial Aid, Student Administrative Services, Mount Allison University, 65 York Street, Sackville, New Brunswick E4L 1E4, Canada; 506-364-2266, fax: 506-364-2272.

Murray State University

Murray, Kentucky

State-supported, coed. Small town campus. Total enrollment: 10,266. Art program established 1926.

Degrees Bachelor of Fine Arts in the areas of studio art, art education. Majors and concentrations: art education, ceramics, graphic design, jewelry and metalsmithing, painting/

drawing, photography, printmaking, sculpture, wood. Program accredited by NASAD, NCATE.

Enrollment 215 total; 50 undergraduate, 165 nonprofessional degree.

Art Student Profile 46% females, 54% males, 3% minorities, 5% international.

Art Faculty 14 undergraduate (full-time), 2 undergraduate (part-time). 100% of full-time faculty have terminal degrees. Graduate students do not teach undergraduate courses. Undergraduate student–faculty ratio: 14:1.

Student Life Student groups/activities include Organization of Murray Art Students.

Expenses for 2005–2006 Application fee: $30. State resident tuition: $3792 full-time. Nonresident tuition: $5464 full-time. Mandatory fees: $636 full-time. Full-time tuition and fees vary according to reciprocity agreements. College room and board: $4472. College room only: $2366. Room and board charges vary according to board plan. Special program-related fees: $13 per credit hour for supplies and equipment.

Financial Aid Program-specific awards: 15–20 Department of Art Scholarships for program majors ($500–$2500).

Application Procedures Students admitted directly into the professional program freshman year. Deadline for freshmen and transfers: continuous. Required: high school transcript, college transcript(s) for transfer students, ACT test score only.

Web Site http://www.murraystate.edu

Undergraduate Contact Mr. Dick Dougherty, Chair, Department of Art, Murray State University, 604 Fine Arts Building, Murray, Kentucky 42071-3342; 270-762-3784, fax: 270-762-3920, e-mail address: dick.dougherty@murray state.edu

Myers School of Art

See The University of Akron

The New England School of Art & Design

See Suffolk University

New Jersey City University

Jersey City, New Jersey

State-supported, coed. Urban campus. Total enrollment: 8,464. Art program established 1961.

New Mexico Highlands University

Las Vegas, New Mexico

State-supported, coed. Small town campus. Total enrollment: 3,750.

New Mexico State University

Las Cruces, New Mexico

State-supported, coed. Suburban campus. Total enrollment: 16,072. Art program established 1948.

Degrees Bachelor of Fine Arts in the area of studio art. Majors and concentrations: ceramic art and design, graphic design, jewelry and metalsmithing, painting/drawing, photography, printmaking, sculpture. Graduate degrees offered: Master of Arts in the areas of studio art, art history; Master of Fine Arts in the area of studio art.

Enrollment 275 total; 247 undergraduate, 28 graduate.

Art Student Profile 55% females, 45% males, 30% minorities.

Art Faculty 12 total (full-time), 2 total (part-time). 100% of full-time faculty have terminal degrees. Graduate students teach a few undergraduate courses. Undergraduate student–faculty ratio: 15:1.

Expenses for 2005–2006 Application fee: $15. State resident tuition: $2868 full-time. Nonresident tuition: $12,156 full-time. Mandatory fees: $1050 full-time. College room and board: $5332. College room only: $3072. Room and board charges vary according to board plan and gender.

Visual Arts

New Mexico State University (continued)

Application Procedures Students apply for admission into the professional program by freshman year. Deadline for freshmen and transfers: August 14. Required: high school transcript, college transcript(s) for transfer students, SAT I or ACT test scores.

Web Site http://www.nmsu.edu/~artdept

Contact Mr. Spencer Fidler, Head, Art Department, New Mexico State University, Box 30001, Department 3572, Las Cruces, New Mexico 88003-0001; 505-646-1705, fax: 505-646-8036, e-mail address: artdept@nmsu.edu

The New School: A University

See Parsons The New School for Design

New World School of the Arts

Miami, Florida

State-supported, coed. Urban campus. Total enrollment: 371. Art program established 1988.

Degrees Bachelor of Fine Arts. Majors and concentrations: drawing, electronic intermedia, graphic design, painting, photography, printmaking, sculpture. Mandatory cross-registration with University of Florida, Miami-Dade College. Program accredited by NASAD.

Enrollment 145 total; all undergraduate.

Art Student Profile 50% females, 50% males, 81% minorities, 2% international.

Art Faculty 5 undergraduate (full-time), 13 undergraduate (part-time). 100% of full-time faculty have terminal degrees. Graduate students do not teach undergraduate courses. Undergraduate student–faculty ratio: 11:1.

Student Life Student groups/activities include Art Club, Student Government, juried art shows.

Expenses for 2005–2006 Application fee: $0. State resident tuition: $12,000 full-time. Nonresident tuition: $17,000 full-time.

Financial Aid Program-specific awards: 4 Nation's Bank Merit Scholarships for program

majors ($2000), 6 Ronnie Bogaev Merit Scholarships for female in-state program majors ($2000), 18 Frances Wolfson Merit Scholarships for program majors ($2000), 15 Miami-Dade College Scholarships for program majors ($1000).

Application Procedures Students admitted directly into the professional program freshman year. Deadline for freshmen and transfers: continuous. Notification date for freshmen and transfers: continuous. Required: essay, high school transcript, college transcript(s) for transfer students, 2 letters of recommendation, portfolio. Recommended: minimum 2.0 high school GPA, interview, SAT I or ACT test scores. Auditions held on campus and off campus in Sarasota, FL. Portfolio reviews held continuously on campus and off campus in various locations in Florida; the submission of slides may be substituted for portfolios when distance is prohibitive.

Web Site http://www.mdc.edu/nwsa

Undergraduate Contact Pamela Neumann, Recruitment and Admissions Coordinator, Student Services, New World School of the Arts, 300 Northeast 2nd Avenue, Miami, Florida 33132; 305-237-7007, fax: 305-237-3794, e-mail address: nwsaadm@mdc.edu

Midge Karr Fine Art Department
New York Institute of Technology

Old Westbury, New York

Independent, coed. Suburban campus. Total enrollment: 11,141. Art program established 1960.

Degrees Bachelor of Fine Arts. Majors and concentrations: art education, computer graphics, graphic design.

Enrollment 250 total; all undergraduate.

Art Student Profile 55% females, 45% males, 25% minorities, 20% international.

Art Faculty 8 undergraduate (full-time), 30 undergraduate (part-time). 80% of full-time faculty have terminal degrees. Graduate students teach about a quarter of undergraduate courses. Undergraduate student–faculty ratio: 7:1.

Student Life Student groups/activities include American Society of Interior Designers, Digital Sculpture Club, Computer Graphics Club.

Expenses for 2005–2006 Application fee: $50. Comprehensive fee: $30,040 includes full-time tuition ($18,696), mandatory fees ($540), and college room and board ($10,804). College room only: $5600. Full-time tuition and fees vary according to course load and program. Room and board charges vary according to board plan, housing facility, and location. Special program-related fees: $10–$40 per course for studio supplies.

Financial Aid Program-specific awards: Presidential Awards for academically qualified applicants ($2200–$2600), academic achievement awards for academically qualified applicants ($1200–$1800), academic incentive awards for academically qualified applicants ($600).

Application Procedures Students admitted directly into the professional program freshman year. Deadline for freshmen and transfers: continuous. Required: essay, high school transcript, college transcript(s) for transfer students, minimum 2.0 high school GPA, interview, portfolio, SAT I or ACT test scores. Recommended: 2 letters of recommendation. Portfolio reviews held continuously on campus and off campus in New York, NY; the submission of slides may be substituted for portfolios for out-of-state applicants.

Web Site http://www.nyit.edu

Undergraduate Contact Mr. Emanuel Saladino, Administrative Assistant, Midge Karr Fine Art Department, New York Institute of Technology, PO Box 8000, Old Westbury, New York 11568-8000; 516-686-7542, fax: 516-686-7428, e-mail address: esaladin@nyit.edu

New York School of Interior Design

New York, New York

Independent, coed, primarily women. Urban campus. Total enrollment: 739. Art program established 1916.

Degrees Bachelor of Fine Arts in the area of interior design. Majors and concentrations: interior design. Graduate degrees offered: Master of Fine Arts in the area of interior design. Program accredited by NASAD, FIDER.

Enrollment 726 total; 160 undergraduate, 15 graduate, 551 nonprofessional degree.

Art Student Profile 80% females, 20% males, 10% minorities, 10% international.

Art Faculty 4 total (full-time), 71 total (part-time). 35% of full-time faculty have terminal degrees. Graduate students do not teach undergraduate courses. Undergraduate student–faculty ratio: 10:1.

Student Life Student groups/activities include American Society of Interior Designers Student Chapter.

Expenses for 2006–2007 Application fee: $50. Tuition: $18,600 full-time. Mandatory fees: $220 full-time.

Financial Aid Program-specific awards: 50 Institutional and Endowed Scholarships for program majors ($1000–$10,000).

Application Procedures Students admitted directly into the professional program freshman year. Deadline for freshmen and transfers: continuous. Required: essay, high school transcript, college transcript(s) for transfer students, minimum 2.0 high school GPA, 2 letters of recommendation, portfolio, SAT I or ACT test scores (minimum combined SAT I score of 1000, minimum composite ACT score of 20). Recommended: minimum 3.0 high school GPA, interview. Portfolio reviews held continuously on campus and off campus in various college fairs; the submission of slides may be substituted for portfolios when distance is prohibitive.

Web Site http://www.nysid.edu

Contact Mr. David T. Sprouls, Director of Admissions, New York School of Interior Design, 170 East 70th Street, New York, New York 10021; 212-472-1500 ext. 202, fax: 212-472-1867, e-mail address: admissions@nysid.edu

More About the School

Throughout its history, the New York School of Interior Design (NYSID) has devoted all of its resources to a single field of study—interior design. NYSID is specifically designed for those who wish to pursue a career in one or more of the various fields of interior design and wish to do so under the guidance of a faculty consisting of practicing designers, architects, and art and architectural historians. The various academic programs comprise an integrated curriculum covering architecture, design problem solving, history of art, interior design concepts, interiors and furniture, materials and methods,

New York School of Interior Design (continued)

philosophy and theory, professional design procedures, and technical and communication skills.

Because of its select faculty and established reputation, the School continues to maintain a close relationship with the interior design industry. This provides an excellent means for students to develop associations that offer opportunities to move into the profession after completing their degree program at NYSID.

Many of the world's most important museums, galleries, and showrooms are within walking distance. The city is world-renowned for its cultural activities, architecture, historic districts, and cosmopolitan urban experience.

NYSID is located on a quiet, tree-lined street in Manhattan's landmark Upper East Side Historic District. The School has two auditorium spaces, light-filled studios and classrooms, a CAD lab, and a lighting design lab. NYSID also has a library containing a comprehensive collection of books, journals, periodicals, and trade and auction catalogs specifically devoted to the interior design field and related fine arts; a materials library; an atelier; two galleries; a rooftop terrace; and a café, bookstore, and student lounge.

NYSID has an active student chapter of the American Society of Interior Designers (ASID). ASID organizes lectures, tours, workshops, and other events throughout the school year, providing an inside view of the interior design industry.

One of the strengths of NYSID is its gallery exhibitions relating to architecture and design. Open to both students and the public, the gallery has mounted such acclaimed shows as *Designers Salute Edith Wharton and The Mount; Albert Hadley: Drawings and the Design Process;* and *Bob the Roman: Heroic Antiquity and the Architecture of Robert Adam.* The School also sponsors lectures and symposia. Guest lecturers have included Mario Buatta, Charlotte Moss, Albert Hadley, Eric Cohler, John Saladino, Clodagh, and David Garrard Lowe. Students are encouraged to attend the lecture series.

The School maintains an active placement service for graduates and current students. Many students find work while still at NYSID. Because of its reputation in the design field, many NYSID graduates are employed in the best design, architectural, and industry-related firms in New York City, across the United States, and around the world.

Tisch School of the Arts - Department of Photography and Imaging
New York University
New York, New York

Independent, coed. Urban campus. Total enrollment: 40,004. Art program established 1965.

Degrees Bachelor of Fine Arts. Majors and concentrations: photography and imaging.

Enrollment 134 total; all undergraduate.

Art Student Profile 63% females, 37% males, 20% minorities, 5% international.

Art Faculty 11 undergraduate (full-time), 15 undergraduate (part-time). 73% of full-time faculty have terminal degrees. Graduate students do not teach undergraduate courses. Undergraduate student–faculty ratio: 8:1.

Student Life Student groups/activities include Community Connections, The Collective, Tisch Talent Guild.

Expenses for 2005–2006 Application fee: $65. Comprehensive fee: $43,170 includes full-time tuition ($29,890), mandatory fees ($1800), and college room and board ($11,480). Full-time tuition and fees vary according to program. Room and board charges vary according to board plan and housing facility. Special program-related fees: $255 per course for photo lab fee.

Application Procedures Students admitted directly into the professional program freshman year. Deadline for freshmen: January 15; transfers: April 1. Notification date for freshmen: April 1; transfers: May 15. Required: essay, high school transcript, college transcript(s) for transfer students, 2 letters of recommendation, portfolio, SAT I or ACT test scores, resume, department questionnaire. Recommended: minimum 3.0 high school GPA.

Web Site http://photo.tisch.nyu.edu

Undergraduate Contact Mr. Andrew I. Uriarte, Director of Recruitment and Student Affairs, Tisch School of the Arts, New York University, 721 Broadway, 8th Floor, New York, New York 10003-6807; 212-998-1900, fax: 212-995-4060.

New York University Steinhardt School

New York University

New York, New York

Independent, coed. Urban campus. Total enrollment: 40,004.

Degrees Bachelor of Fine Arts in the area of studio art. Majors and concentrations: studio art. Graduate degrees offered: Master of Arts in the areas of studio art (3-summer program), studio art: art in media, visual culture: theory, visual culture: costume studies, art education, visual arts administration, art therapy; Master of Fine Arts in the area of studio art. Doctor of Philosophy in the area of visual culture and education.

Enrollment 469 total; 202 undergraduate, 267 graduate.

Art Student Profile 80% females, 20% males, 27% minorities, 10% international.

Art Faculty 11 total (full-time), 114 total (part-time). 64% of full-time faculty have terminal degrees. Graduate students teach a few undergraduate courses. Undergraduate student–faculty ratio: 1:1.

Expenses for 2005–2006 Application fee: $65. Comprehensive fee: $43,170 includes full-time tuition ($29,890), mandatory fees ($1800), and college room and board ($11,480). Full-time tuition and fees vary according to program. Room and board charges vary according to board plan and housing facility. Special program-related fees: $250 per semester for lab fees.

Application Procedures Students admitted directly into the professional program freshman year. Deadline for freshmen: January 15; transfers: April 1. Notification date for freshmen: April 1; transfers: September 1. Required: essay, high school transcript, college transcript(s) for transfer students, 3 letters of recommendation, portfolio, SAT I or ACT test scores, TOEFL score for non-native English speakers, strong high school GPA. Portfolio reviews held continuously on campus and off campus in venues in New York State; the submission of slides may be substituted for portfolios.

Web Site http://www.steinhardt.nyu.edu/gonow

Undergraduate Contact Ms. Candice MacLusky, Assistant Director of Undergraduate Admissions, New York University, 22 Washington Square North, New York, New York 10011-9191; 212-998-4500, fax: 212-995-4902.

Graduate Contact Mr. John Myers, Director of Enrollment Services, Office of Graduate Admissions, The Steinhardt School of Education, New York University, 82 Washington Square East, 2nd Floor, New York, New York 10003-6680; 212-998-5030, fax: 212-995-4328, e-mail address: ed.gradadmissions@nyu.edu

New York University Steinhardt School

See New York University

North Carolina School of the Arts

Winston-Salem, North Carolina

State-supported, coed. Urban campus. Total enrollment: 827. Art program established 1965.

Degrees Bachelor of Fine Arts in the area of filmmaking. Majors and concentrations: cinematography, directing, editing and sound, production, production/design, screenwriting. Graduate degrees offered: Master of Fine Arts in the area of film music composition.

Enrollment 243 total; 204 undergraduate, 39 nonprofessional degree.

Art Student Profile 29% females, 71% males, 11% minorities, 2% international.

Art Faculty 25 undergraduate (full-time), 2 undergraduate (part-time), 2 graduate (full-time). 42% of full-time faculty have terminal degrees. Graduate students do not teach undergraduate courses. Undergraduate student–faculty ratio: 10:1.

Student Life Special housing available for art students.

Expenses for 2005–2006 Application fee: $50. State resident tuition: $2755 full-time. Nonresident tuition: $14,035 full-time. Mandatory fees: $1551 full-time. Full-time tuition and fees vary according to program. College room and board: $5700. College room only: $3035. Room

North Carolina School of the Arts (continued)

and board charges vary according to board plan and housing facility. Special program-related fees: $750 per year for School of Filmmaking (supplies).

Financial Aid Program-specific awards: 100 talent/need scholarships ($1879).

Application Procedures Students admitted directly into the professional program freshman year. Deadline for freshmen and transfers: March 1. Required: essay, high school transcript, college transcript(s) for transfer students, 2 letters of recommendation, interview, audition, on-site writing exercise. Recommended: SAT I or ACT test scores. Auditions held by appointment on campus.

Undergraduate Contact Ms. Sheeler Lawson, Director of Admissions, North Carolina School of the Arts, 1533 South Main Street, Winston-Salem, North Carolina 27117; 336-770-3291, fax: 336-770-3370, e-mail address: admissions@ncarts.edu

Northern Illinois University

De Kalb, Illinois

State-supported, coed. Small town campus. Total enrollment: 25,208.

Degrees Bachelor of Arts in the areas of art history, art; Bachelor of Fine Arts in the area of studio and design; Bachelor of Science in the area of art education. Majors and concentrations: animation, art education, art history, art/fine arts, ceramics, fibers, illustration, jewelry and metalsmithing, painting/drawing, photography, printmaking, sculpture, video art, visual communication. Graduate degrees offered: Master of Arts in the area of studio art and design; Master of Fine Arts in the area of studio and design; Master of Science in Education in the area of art education. Cross-registration with twelve Illinois community colleges. Program accredited by NASAD.

Enrollment 1,004 total; 679 undergraduate, 58 graduate, 267 nonprofessional degree.

Art Student Profile 59% females, 41% males, 6% minorities, 1% international.

Art Faculty 41 total (full-time), 21 total (part-time). 90% of full-time faculty have terminal degrees. Graduate students teach a few undergraduate courses. Undergraduate student–faculty ratio: 16:1.

Student Life Student groups/activities include National Art Education Association Student Chapter, American Institute of Graphic Arts Student Chapter, Ars Nova Student Group. Special housing available for art students.

Expenses for 2005–2006 State resident tuition: $5061 full-time. Nonresident tuition: $10,123 full-time. Mandatory fees: $1378 full-time. Full-time tuition and fees vary according to course load. College room and board: $5950. Room and board charges vary according to board plan and housing facility. Special program-related fees: $5–$126 per course for lab/materials fees/visiting artists and scholars/technology.

Financial Aid Program-specific awards: 6–12 tuition waivers for high school seniors ($2362–$3148).

Application Procedures Students admitted directly into the professional program freshman year. Deadline for freshmen and transfers: continuous. Notification date for freshmen and transfers: continuous. Required: high school transcript, college transcript(s) for transfer students, minimum 2.0 high school GPA, SAT I or ACT test scores (minimum composite ACT score of 19), standing in top half of graduating class, completion of college preparatory courses.

Web Site http://www.vpa.niu.edu/art/

Undergraduate Contact Office of Admissions, Northern Illinois University, Williston Hall Room 101, De Kalb, Illinois 60115; 815-753-0446, fax: 815-753-1783, e-mail address: admissions-info@niu.edu

Graduate Contact Yale Factor, Coordinator of Graduate Program, School of Art, Northern Illinois University, De Kalb, Illinois 60115-2883; 815-753-0292.

Northern Kentucky University

Highland Heights, Kentucky

State-supported, coed. Suburban campus. Total enrollment: 13,908. Art program established 1968.

Degrees Bachelor of Fine Arts in the areas of graphic design, intermedia, art history with studio. Majors and concentrations: applied photography, art education, art history, ceramics, graphic design, intermedia, painting/drawing, photography, printmaking, sculpture. Cross-registration with Northern Kentucky/Greater Cincinnati Consortium of Colleges and Universities.

Enrollment 410 total; 60 undergraduate, 350 nonprofessional degree.

Art Student Profile 60% females, 40% males, 2% minorities, 1% international.

Art Faculty 19 undergraduate (full-time), 7 undergraduate (part-time). 90% of full-time faculty have terminal degrees. Graduate students do not teach undergraduate courses. Undergraduate student–faculty ratio: 17:1.

Student Life Student groups/activities include Students in Design, Mudd Club, Photography Club.

Expenses for 2005–2006 Application fee: $30. State resident tuition: $4968 full-time. Nonresident tuition: $9696 full-time. Full-time tuition varies according to location. College room and board: $4660. College room only: $2580. Room and board charges vary according to board plan, housing facility, and location. Special program-related fees: $20–$200 per semester for incidental fee, technology fee, and support of learning surcharge.

Financial Aid Program-specific awards: 1–2 Friends of Fine Arts Awards for continuing students ($2500), 6 University Art Awards for continuing students ($2500), 1 Schiff Scholarship for continuing students ($2500).

Application Procedures Students apply for admission into the professional program by sophomore, junior year. Deadline for freshmen and transfers: August 1. Required: high school transcript, college transcript(s) for transfer students, minimum 2.0 high school GPA, ACT test score only, minimum 2.5 college GPA with a 3.0 art major GPA.

Web Site http://www.nku.edu/~art

Undergraduate Contact Thomas McGovern, Chairman, Department of Art, Northern Kentucky University, Fine Arts Center 312, Highland Heights, Kentucky 41099; 859-572-5421, fax: 859-572-6501, e-mail address: mcgovern@nku.edu

Northwestern State University of Louisiana
Natchitoches, Louisiana

State-supported, coed. Small town campus. Total enrollment: 9,847.

Degrees Bachelor of Fine Arts in the area of fine and graphic arts; Bachelor of Science. Majors and concentrations: graphic communication, studio art. Program accredited by NASAD.

Enrollment 112 total; all undergraduate.

Art Student Profile 60% females, 40% males, 20% minorities, 5% international.

Art Faculty 7 total (full-time), 1 total (part-time). 83% of full-time faculty have terminal degrees. Graduate students teach a few undergraduate courses. Undergraduate student–faculty ratio: 16:1.

Student Life Student groups/activities include Student Art Society, Student Art Show. Special housing available for art students.

Expenses for 2005–2006 Application fee: $20. State resident tuition: $2240 full-time. Nonresident tuition: $8318 full-time. Mandatory fees: $1153 full-time. Full-time tuition and fees vary according to course load. College room and board: $3626. College room only: $2050. Room and board charges vary according to board plan, housing facility, and location. Special program-related fees: $25–$50 for supplies.

Financial Aid Program-specific awards: 10 art scholarships ($500).

Application Procedures Students admitted directly into the professional program freshman year. Deadline for freshmen and transfers: continuous. Required: high school transcript, college transcript(s) for transfer students, minimum 2.0 high school GPA, SAT I or ACT test scores (minimum combined SAT I score of 950, minimum composite ACT score of 20), 16.5 Units of Regents' High School core curriculum (T.O.P.S.). Portfolio reviews held continuously on campus; the submission of slides may be substituted for portfolios.

Web Site http://www.nsula.edu/capa

Undergraduate Contact Dr. Roger A. Chandler, Associate Professor/Coordinator of Fine and Graphic Art, Fine and Graphic Arts, Northwestern State University of Louisiana, NSU College

Northwestern State University of Louisiana (continued)

Avenue, Natchitoches, Louisiana 71497; 318-357-6176, fax: 318-357-5906, e-mail address: chandlerr@nsula.edu

Notre Dame de Namur University

Belmont, California

Independent Roman Catholic, coed. Suburban campus. Total enrollment: 1,588. Art program established 1851.

Degrees Bachelor of Arts; Bachelor of Fine Arts. Majors and concentrations: art, art history, graphic design, painting/drawing, printmaking, studio art. Cross-registration with Trinity College, Emmanuel College.

Enrollment 35 total; all undergraduate.

Art Student Profile 70% females, 30% males, 40% minorities, 10% international.

Art Faculty 2 undergraduate (full-time), 7 undergraduate (part-time). 100% of full-time faculty have terminal degrees. Graduate students do not teach undergraduate courses. Undergraduate student–faculty ratio: 7:1.

Student Life Student groups/activities include College Art Association, American Institute of Graphic Arts.

Expenses for 2006–2007 Application fee: $40. Comprehensive fee: $34,230 includes full-time tuition ($23,650), mandatory fees ($200), and college room and board ($10,380). College room only: $7000.

Financial Aid Program-specific awards: 8 Emerging Artist Talent Scholarships for program students ($7500–$9500).

Application Procedures Students admitted directly into the professional program freshman year. Deadline for freshmen and transfers: continuous. Notification date for freshmen and transfers: continuous. Required: essay, high school transcript, college transcript(s) for transfer students, letter of recommendation, SAT I or ACT test scores, minimum 2.0 college GPA for transfers. Recommended: portfolio. Portfolio reviews held 24 times on campus; the submission of slides may be substituted for portfolios.

Web Site http://www.ndnu.edu

Undergraduate Contact Betty Friedman, Chair, Department of Art, Notre Dame de Namur University, 1500 Ralston Avenue, Belmont, California 94002-1997; 650-508-3631, fax: 650-508-3488, e-mail address: bfriedman@ndnu.edu

NSCAD University

Halifax, Nova Scotia, Canada

Province-supported, coed. Urban campus. Total enrollment: 1,011. Art program established 1887.

Degrees Bachelor of Arts in the area of visual arts; Bachelor of Design; Bachelor of Fine Arts in the area of fine arts. Majors and concentrations: art history, art/fine arts, ceramics, communication design, film, graphic design, international graphic design, jewelry and metalsmithing, media arts, photography, textiles. Graduate degrees offered: Master of Arts in the area of art education; Master of Fine Arts in the areas of fine arts, design, craft. Cross-registration with Dalhousie University, St. Mary's University, Mount St. Vincent University.

Enrollment 887 total; 872 undergraduate, 15 graduate.

Art Student Profile 69% females, 31% males, 6% international.

Art Faculty 42 total (full-time), 38 total (part-time). 95% of full-time faculty have terminal degrees. Graduate students teach a few undergraduate courses. Undergraduate student–faculty ratio: 12:1.

Student Life Student groups/activities include "SOTA" (college publication), Women's Collective, Mosaic (minority ethnic group).

Expenses for 2006–2007 Application fee: $35 Canadian dollars. Province resident tuition: $5501 full-time. Canadian resident tuition: $5501 full-time. College room and board: $8022. International student tuition: $12,125 full-time.

Financial Aid Program-specific awards: 85 merit scholarships for those demonstrating talent and academic achievement ($800), 6 Joseph Beuys Memorial Scholarships for those demonstrating talent and academic achievement ($1500), 5 Harrison McCain Scholarships for those demonstrating talent and academic achievement ($13,500).

Application Procedures Students admitted directly into the professional program freshman year. Deadline for freshmen: March 15; transfers: February 15. Notification date for freshmen and transfers: June 20. Required: essay, high school transcript, college transcript(s) for transfer students, portfolio, minimum TOEFL score of 577 for non-English speaking applicants, 2 letters of recommendation for mature applicants. Recommended: interview. Portfolio reviews held twice on campus; the submission of slides may be substituted for portfolios for large or fragile works of art.

Web Site http://www.nscad.ns.ca

Contact Mr. Terrence Bailey, Director, Admissions, Office of Student and Academic Services, NSCAD University, 5163 Duke Street, Halifax, Nova Scotia B3J 3J6, Canada; 902-494-8129, fax: 902-425-2987, e-mail address: admissions@nscad.ca

Ohio Northern University
Ada, Ohio

Independent, coed. Small town campus. Total enrollment: 3,542. Art program established 1961.

Degrees Bachelor of Fine Arts. Majors and concentrations: graphic design, studio art. Cross-registration with University of Ulster (UK), Burren College of Art (Ireland), Studio Art Centers International (Italy).

Enrollment 41 total.

Art Student Profile 51% females, 49% males, 3% minorities, 1% international.

Art Faculty 4 undergraduate (full-time), 4 undergraduate (part-time). 100% of full-time faculty have terminal degrees. Graduate students do not teach undergraduate courses. Undergraduate student–faculty ratio: 7:1.

Student Life Student groups/activities include Kappa Pi/Alpha Epsilon Rho, Theta Alpha Phi, American Institute of Graphic Arts.

Expenses for 2006–2007 Application fee: $30. Comprehensive fee: $35,340 includes full-time tuition ($28,050), mandatory fees ($210), and college room and board ($7080). College room only: $3540.

Financial Aid Program-specific awards: art talent awards for art majors ($2500–$8000).

Application Procedures Students admitted directly into the professional program freshman year. Deadline for freshmen and transfers: continuous. Notification date for freshmen and transfers: August 15. Required: high school transcript, college transcript(s) for transfer students, minimum 2.0 high school GPA, SAT I or ACT test scores, minimum 2.5 high school GPA, portfolio for scholarship consideration. Recommended: essay, minimum 3.0 high school GPA, interview, portfolio. Portfolio reviews held by request on campus; the submission of slides may be substituted for portfolios with approval from the department.

Web Site http://www.onu.edu

Undergraduate Contact Ms. Karen Condeni, Vice President and Dean of Admissions, Ohio Northern University, 525 South Main Street, Ada, Ohio 45810; 419-772-2260, fax: 419-772-2313, e-mail address: admissions-ug@onu.edu

The Ohio State University
Columbus, Ohio

State-supported, coed. Total enrollment: 50,504.

Degrees Bachelor of Fine Arts. Majors and concentrations: art and technology, ceramics, glass, painting/drawing, photography, printmaking, sculpture. Graduate degrees offered: Master of Fine Arts in the areas of ceramics, glass, sculpture, painting/drawing, printmaking, photography, art and technology. Cross-registration with Columbus College of Art and Design. Program accredited by NASAD.

Enrollment 345 total; 158 undergraduate, 54 graduate, 133 nonprofessional degree.

Art Student Profile 40% females, 60% males, 3% minorities, 20% international.

Art Faculty 22 total (full-time), 15 total (part-time). 100% of full-time faculty have terminal degrees. Graduate students teach more than half of undergraduate courses. Undergraduate student–faculty ratio: 7:1.

Student Life Student groups/activities include Student League of Independent Potters, Student Printmakers Association, Undergraduate Student Art League. Special housing available for art students.

Expenses for 2005–2006 Application fee: $40. State resident tuition: $7929 full-time. Nonresi-

The Ohio State University (continued)

dent tuition: $19,152 full-time. Mandatory fees: $153 full-time. Full-time tuition and fees vary according to course load, program, reciprocity agreements, and student level. College room and board: $7275. Room and board charges vary according to board plan and housing facility. Special program-related fees: $3 per credit hour for technology fee.

Financial Aid Program-specific awards: 1 Hoylt L. Sherman Scholarship for art majors ($1500), 2–5 Arthur E. Baggs Memorial Scholarships for ceramic majors ($750), 1–3 Robert and Marion Gatrell Scholarships for art majors ($900), 1–5 Edith Fergus Gilmore Awards for art majors ($400).

Application Procedures Students apply for admission into the professional program by sophomore, junior year. Deadline for freshmen and transfers: continuous. Required: high school transcript, college transcript(s) for transfer students, SAT I or ACT test scores, portfolio upon completion of foundation courses. Portfolio reviews held twice a year on campus; the submission of slides may be substituted for portfolios for transfer applicants when original work is no longer available or for large works of art and three-dimensional pieces.

Web Site http://art.osu.edu/index_flash.html

Undergraduate Contact University Admissions, The Ohio State University, 1800 Cannon Drive, 3rd Floor Lincoln Tower, Columbus, Ohio 43210; 614-292-3980, fax: 614-292-4818.

Graduate Contact Ms. Cathy Ellis, Assistant to Chair, Department of Art, The Ohio State University, 146 Hopkins Hall, 128 North Oval Mall, Columbus, Ohio 43210; 614-292-5072, fax: 614-292-1674, e-mail address: ellis.11@osu.edu

Ohio University

Athens, Ohio

State-supported, coed. Small town campus. Total enrollment: 20,396.

Ohio Wesleyan University

Delaware, Ohio

Independent United Methodist, coed. Small town campus. Total enrollment: 1,976. Art program established 1864.

Oklahoma Baptist University

Shawnee, Oklahoma

Independent Southern Baptist, coed. Total enrollment: 1,883 (2004). Art program established 1980.

Degrees Bachelor of Fine Arts. Majors and concentrations: studio art. Cross-registration with St. Gregory's University.

Enrollment 43 total; 10 undergraduate, 33 nonprofessional degree.

Art Student Profile 55% females, 45% males, 8% minorities, 2% international.

Art Faculty 3 undergraduate (full-time), 3 undergraduate (part-time). 33% of full-time faculty have terminal degrees. Graduate students do not teach undergraduate courses. Undergraduate student–faculty ratio: 8:1.

Student Life Student groups/activities include Art Club.

Expenses for 2005–2006 Application fee: $25. Comprehensive fee: $17,986 includes full-time tuition ($12,924), mandatory fees ($922), and college room and board ($4140). College room only: $1840. Full-time tuition and fees vary according to course load. Room and board charges vary according to board plan and housing facility. Special program-related fees: $25 per course for material fees.

Financial Aid Program-specific awards: 24 art scholarships for program majors ($1117).

Application Procedures Students admitted directly into the professional program freshman year. Deadline for freshmen and transfers: continuous. Required: high school transcript, college transcript(s) for transfer students, minimum 2.0 high school GPA, SAT I or ACT test scores. Recommended: portfolio. Portfolio reviews held continuously on campus; the submission of slides may be substituted for portfolios when distance is prohibitive.

Web Site http://www.okbu.edu

Undergraduate Contact Mr. Trent Argo, Dean of Admissions, Oklahoma Baptist University, Box 61174, 500 West University, Shawnee, Oklahoma 74804; 800-654-3285, fax: 405-878-2046, e-mail address: trent.argo@okbu.edu

Oklahoma State University

Stillwater, Oklahoma

State-supported, coed. Small town campus. Total enrollment: 23,461. Art program established 1924.

Degrees Bachelor of Fine Arts in the areas of graphic design, studio art. Majors and concentrations: ceramics, electronic media, graphic arts, illustration, jewelry and metalsmithing, painting/drawing, printmaking, sculpture.

Enrollment 232 total; 182 undergraduate, 50 nonprofessional degree.

Art Student Profile 58% females, 42% males, 8% minorities, 5% international.

Art Faculty 14 undergraduate (full-time), 6 undergraduate (part-time). 100% of full-time faculty have terminal degrees. Graduate students do not teach undergraduate courses. Undergraduate student–faculty ratio: 20:1.

Student Life Student groups/activities include Annual Juried Student Art Exhibition, Annual Interdesign Competition, Graduating Senior Portfolio Exhibition.

Expenses for 2005–2006 Application fee: $40. State resident tuition: $3099 full-time. Nonresident tuition: $11,122 full-time. Mandatory fees: $1266 full-time. Full-time tuition and fees vary according to program and student level. College room and board: $5848. College room only: $2848. Room and board charges vary according to board plan, housing facility, and location. Special program-related fees: $5–$85 per course for expendable materials, $25 per course for model fees.

Financial Aid Program-specific awards: 9 freshmen/transfer scholarships for freshmen and transfer students ($1000), 5 Medical Heritage Gallery Scholarships for continuing students ($1500).

Application Procedures Students apply for admission into the professional program by sophomore year. Deadline for freshmen and transfers: continuous. Required: high school transcript, college transcript(s) for transfer students, minimum 2.0 high school GPA, SAT I or ACT test scores (minimum composite ACT score of 22), portfolio for scholarship consideration. Portfolio reviews held once on campus and off campus in Tulsa, OK; the submission of slides may be substituted for portfolios for large works of art and three-dimensional pieces and for out-of-state applicants.

Web Site http://art.okstate.edu/

Undergraduate Contact Ms. Sallie McCorkle, Head, Department of Art, Oklahoma State University, 108 Bartlett Center, Stillwater, Oklahoma 74078-4085; 405-744-6016, fax: 405-744-5767.

Old Dominion University

Norfolk, Virginia

State-supported, coed. Urban campus. Total enrollment: 21,274. Art program established 1963.

O'More College of Design

Franklin, Tennessee

Independent, coed, primarily women. Small town campus. Art program established 1970.

Degrees Bachelor of Fine Arts in the areas of interior design, fashion design, visual communications. Majors and concentrations: fashion design and merchandising, interior design, visual communication. Cross-registration with Belmont University. Program accredited by FIDER.

Enrollment 160 total; all undergraduate.

Art Student Profile 89% females, 11% males, 4% minorities, 1% international.

Art Faculty 5 undergraduate (full-time), 40 undergraduate (part-time). 30% of full-time faculty have terminal degrees. Graduate students do not teach undergraduate courses. Undergraduate student–faculty ratio: 3:1.

Student Life Student groups/activities include O'More Fashion and Merchandising Association, American Society of Interior Designers, International Interior Design Association.

Expenses for 2005–200 Special program-related fees: $30–$100 per course for studio art courses.

Financial Aid Program-specific awards: 20–30 need-based scholarships for those demonstrating need ($1500), Presidential Merit Scholarships for those demonstrating academic achievement ($1500–$6500).

Visual Arts

O'More College of Design (continued)

Application Procedures Students admitted directly into the professional program freshman year. Deadline for freshmen and transfers: continuous. Required: high school transcript, college transcript(s) for transfer students, minimum 2.0 high school GPA, SAT I or ACT test scores. Recommended: interview, portfolio, portfolio of artwork or completion of departmental home exam. Portfolio reviews held once on campus; the submission of slides may be substituted for portfolios if original work is not available.

Web Site http://www.omorecollege.edu

Undergraduate Contact Chris Lee, Dean of Enrollment, O'More College of Design, 423 South Margin Street, Franklin, Tennessee 37064; 615-794-4254 ext. 32, fax: 615-790-1662, e-mail address: clee@omorecollege.edu

Oregon College of Art & Craft

Portland, Oregon

Independent, coed. Urban campus. Total enrollment: 147. Art program established 1994.

Degrees Bachelor of Fine Arts in the area of crafts. Majors and concentrations: book arts, ceramics, fibers, metals, painting/drawing, photography, wood. Cross-registration with Pacific Northwest College of Art. Program accredited by NASAD.

Enrollment 147 total; 142 undergraduate, 5 nonprofessional degree.

Art Student Profile 65% females, 35% males, 8% minorities, 2% international.

Art Faculty 8 undergraduate (full-time), 13 undergraduate (part-time). 90% of full-time faculty have terminal degrees. Graduate students do not teach undergraduate courses. Undergraduate student–faculty ratio: 8:1.

Student Life Student groups/activities include teaching summer children's classes, Annual Juried Student Show, Student Lecture Series. Special housing available for art students.

Expenses for 2006–2007 Application fee: $35. Tuition: $16,900 full-time. Mandatory fees: $982 full-time. College room only: $3600. Special program-related fees: $1000 per year for studio fees.

Financial Aid Program-specific awards: 85 tuition grants for those demonstrating need ($1500), 52 tuition work-study awards for those demonstrating need ($2300), 5 merit scholarships for talented incoming students ($5000), 2 May Georges Fibers Scholarships for first, second, and third-year students ($500–$3000), 1 Jean Vollum Metals Scholarship for first, second, and third-year students ($500–$1000), 2 Oregon Guild of Woodworkers Scholarships for first, second, and third-year students ($250).

Application Procedures Students admitted directly into the professional program freshman year. Deadline for freshmen and transfers: continuous. Required: essay, high school transcript, college transcript(s) for transfer students, 2 letters of recommendation, interview, portfolio, minimum 2.5 high school GPA for applicants direct from high school, minimum 2.0 college GPA for transfer students. Recommended: minimum 3.0 high school GPA, SAT I or ACT test scores. Portfolio reviews held as needed on campus and off campus at National Portfolio Days; the submission of slides may be substituted for portfolios (slides preferred).

Web Site http://www.ocac.edu

Undergraduate Contact Barry A. Beach, Director of Admissions, Oregon College of Art & Craft, 8245 Southwest Barnes Road, Portland, Oregon 97225; 800-390-0632 ext. 141, fax: 503-297-9651, e-mail address: admissions@ocac.edu

Otis College of Art and Design

Los Angeles, California

Independent, coed. Urban campus. Total enrollment: 1,098. Art program established 1918.

Degrees Bachelor of Fine Arts in the areas of fine arts, architecture/landscape/interiors, communication arts, digital media, fashion design, interactive product design, toy design. Majors and concentrations: advertising design, architecture, art/fine arts, digital multi-media, drawing, fashion design and technology, graphic design, illustration, interior design, landscape architecture, new genres, painting, photography, printmaking, product design, sculpture, toy design, video art. Graduate degrees offered: Master of Fine Arts in the areas of painting, photography, sculpture, new media, writing. Program accredited by NASAD.

Enrollment 1,098 total; 1,040 undergraduate, 58 graduate.

Art Student Profile 66% females, 34% males, 55% minorities, 12% international.

Art Faculty 51 total (full-time), 226 total (part-time). 71% of full-time faculty have terminal degrees. Graduate students teach a few undergraduate courses. Undergraduate student–faculty ratio: 9:1.

Student Life Student groups/activities include Wash Magazine, SIGGRAPH, Cultural and Social Network Groups. Special housing available for art students.

Expenses for 2006–2007 Application fee: $50. Tuition: $26,996 full-time. Mandatory fees: $550 full-time. Special program-related fees: $25 per semester for general college materials fee, $75 per semester for technology fee, $200 per semester for registration fee.

Financial Aid Program-specific awards: Otis Institutional Grants for program students, international student scholarships for international students, transfer student scholarships for transfer students.

Application Procedures Students admitted directly into the professional program freshman year. Deadline for freshmen and transfers: continuous. Notification date for freshmen and transfers: continuous. Required: essay, high school transcript, college transcript(s) for transfer students, portfolio, SAT I or ACT test scores, minimum TOEFL score of 550 (paper-based), 213 (computer-based) for international applicants, minimum 2.5 high school GPA/college GPA. Recommended: minimum 3.0 high school GPA, 2 letters of recommendation, interview. Portfolio reviews held continuously on campus and off campus at National Portfolio Days; the submission of slides may be substituted for portfolios (slides preferred, CD's or DVD's accepted).

Web Site http://www.otis.edu

Undergraduate Contact Mr. Marc D. Meredith, Dean of Admissions, Admissions Office, Otis College of Art and Design, 9045 Lincoln Boulevard, Los Angeles, California 90045; 310-665-6820, fax: 310-665-6821, e-mail address: admissions@otis.edu

Graduate Contact Graduate Studies, Otis College of Art and Design, 9045 Lincoln Boule-vard, Los Angeles, California 90045; 310-665-6892, fax: 310-665-6890, e-mail address: grads@otis.edu

More About the School

Otis prepares diverse students of art and design to enrich the world through their creativity, their skills, and their vision.

A four-year education at Otis begins with Foundation year, during which students from all majors take core studio classes: drawing and composition, figure-drawing, and two- and three-dimensional design. The philosophy is that all artists and designers need well-developed hand-eye skills and sophisticated creative-thinking skills in order to succeed. As they move into the second year, students begin to make their skills more specialized according to their intended major. Top-level studio training in all disciplines is enhanced by a liberal arts and sciences curriculum (LAS) that emphasizes cultural curiosity and intellectual rigor. The LAS classes are intended to complement and expand students' critical thinking as they prepare for the workplaces of the future.

Faculty members who are working professionals, along with visiting artists, designers, lecturers, and writers, share a wealth of expertise and new perspectives with the diverse student population. Lectures, hands-on instruction, studio visits, and personal critiques facilitate dynamic teacher/student and student/student interactions. As part of the commitment to giving students every opportunity to succeed, Otis offers a new Learning Resource Center. Otis also offers an Honors program in liberal studies and art history.

A network of alumni includes individuals who have created such cultural icons as the first Walt Disney animated cartoons; the Academy Award–

Arts

Otis College of Art and Design (continued)

winning special effects for *Lord of the Rings;* products and promotional materials for Columbia, A&M, and Virgin Records; editorial illustrations and cover art for the *Los Angeles Times, Time, Omni, The New Yorker, Buzz,* and *American Film*; costumes for the *Titanic,* Bram Stoker's *Dracula,* and *Harry Potter* and numerous Academy Award–winning films costumed by alumna Edith Head; production design for Spike Lee; and the fashion-forward imagery of such industry leaders as NIKE, Guess?, Richard Tyler, Isaac Mizrahi, Mossimo, and Anne Cole. Otis alumni are featured in major museums, such as the Whitney Museum of American Art; Museum of Modern Art, New York; Guggenheim Museum; Art Institute of Chicago; Corcoran Gallery of Art; Los Angeles County Museum of Art; and Museum of Contemporary Art, Los Angeles, and in galleries around the world.

Otis College of Art and Design, founded in 1918, stands as one of LA's oldest and most important cultural institutions. Otis is proud of its long traditions. Its growth and dynamic character demonstrate the long-term commitment of the College, its faculty members, and its administration as well as the solid support of the art, design, and philanthropic communities. Today's Otis students are artists and designers dedicated to developing technical, critical, and creative skills that can lead them into the future.

Program Facilities The new Galef Center for Fine Arts houses painting and sculpture studios, photo/video studios, and individual student spaces. Other facilities include wood/metal/plastic shops; expanded industry-standard Mac/Windows lab and scanning, large-scale output, and 3-D laser modeling; video/sound editing; lithography/etching presses; the city's oldest, most renowned college fine arts press; extensive library holdings in fine art, design, art history, humanities, critical studies, and periodicals; visual resources center; and Graduate Studios.

Faculty and Visiting Artists Professional faculty members include fashion, toy, digital, and product designers; architects; photographers; and fine artists, among them Roy Dowell, Annette Kapon, Suzanne Lacy, Linda Pollari, Harry Mott, Martin Caveza, Steve McAdam, Ave Pildas, Rosemary Brantley, Scott Grieger, Holly Tempo, Carole Caroompas, Linda Burnham, Judie Bamber, Meg Cranston, Dana Duff, Linda Hudson, Larry Johnson, Debra Ballard, Parme Giutini, Heather Joseph-Witham, and Paul Vangelisti. Guest lecturers and visiting artists/designers include Dave Hickey, Alexis Smith, Barbara Kruger, Dan Graham, Rod Beatty, Bob Mackie, Jeremy Scott, Eduardo Lucero, and Isabel Toldeo.

Student Exhibit Opportunities Students have the opportunity to exhibit their work at numerous locations and functions, such as the Abe and Helen Bolsky Gallery, extensive informal exhibit space in the Galef Center, the annual senior show in all departments, the MFA exhibition, local and national competitions, juried fashion shows, the annual literary magazine, and the Otis Design and Illustration Groups.

Special Programs Special Programs include the Summer of Art precollege program; summer study in Pont-Aven, France; the Spring Paris trip for Foundation students; internship opportunities in all departments; OTIS-LA, an intensive language and acculturation program designed for incoming international students; and community outreach through Otis Evening College. A new fine arts program, ACT (Artists, Community, and Teaching), gives students an introduction to teaching art as a social practice and as a career path.

Housing The College recently added Otis Housing, which is based in a nearby luxury apartment complex and overseen by the Student Affairs Office. Geared toward first-year students, the apartments are two-bedroom/two-bath units that are shared by 4 students. Paid utilities, secure parking, T1 access, and full kitchens, along with a pool, spa, and recreation facilities, make Otis Housing attractive and comfortable. Residence Life staff members live in the complex.

Campuses Otis College of Art and Design's Goldsmith Campus consists of the Galef Center for Fine Arts (housing the School of Fine Arts) and Kathleen Ahmanson Hall (housing Architecture/Landscape/Interiors, Communication Arts, Digital Media, Interactive Product Design, and Toy Design). The campus is located on Los Angeles' Westside. Nearby are the communities of Venice and Santa Monica, home to many prominent fine arts studios and galleries. The location of the Goldsmith campus and the nearby Graduate Studios places students in the center of the vital, international artistic/design community that fuels the Los Angeles fine arts, toy, digital media, and product design worlds.

Otis School of Fashion is located in LA's downtown fashion district within the California Mart Center that is headquarters for many fashion collections and vendors. This places students' day-to-day activities in a unique relationship to an industry that is in need of talented and well-educated designers. The program's structure brings in top designers to work as mentors with junior and senior students on projects from children's sports and swimwear categories to finely tailored men's and glamorous women's evening wear. The annual Otis Scholarship Benefit Fashion Show is an important fashion industry and celebrity event that showcases the best work created by students.

Pacific Lutheran University

Tacoma, Washington

Independent, coed. Suburban campus. Total enrollment: 3,680. Art program established 1947.

Pacific Northwest College of Art

Portland, Oregon

Independent, coed. Urban campus. Art program established 1909.

Degrees Bachelor of Fine Arts. Majors and concentrations: communication design, illustration, intermedia, painting, photography, printmaking, sculpture. Cross-registration with Oregon Independent Colleges Association. Program accredited by NASAD.

Enrollment 303 total; all undergraduate.

Art Student Profile 55% females, 45% males, 10% minorities, 2% international.

Art Faculty 13 undergraduate (full-time), 38 undergraduate (part-time). 85% of full-time faculty have terminal degrees. Graduate students do not teach undergraduate courses. Undergraduate student–faculty ratio: 12:1.

Student Life Student groups/activities include in-house art gallery, public art gallery. Special housing available for art students.

Expenses for 2006–2007 Application fee: $35. Tuition: $17,480 full-time. Mandatory fees: $692 full-time. College room only: $5200. Special program-related fees: $235 per course for private studio rental for third- and fourth-year students.

Financial Aid Program-specific awards: 1 Robert Wiener Travel Award for seniors ($1200), 1 Gamblin Painting Award for juniors ($500), 4 Nancy Tonkin Memorial Scholarships for sophomores/juniors/seniors ($6000), 4 Leta Kennedy Scholarships for freshmen ($3000), 2 Robert C. Lee Printmaking Scholarships for sophomores and juniors ($4000), 1 Ed and Sandy Martin Award for sophomores/juniors/seniors ($1000), 2 Jane Chase Memorial Scholarships for sophomores/juniors/seniors ($1000), 3 William Jamison Scholarships for sophomores/juniors/seniors ($2500), 2 Hearst Foundation Scholarships for transfers ($3000), 1 Dorothy Lemelson Scholarship for freshmen ($25,000).

Application Procedures Students admitted directly into the professional program freshman year. Deadline for freshmen and transfers: continuous. Required: essay, high school transcript, college transcript(s) for transfer students, minimum 2.0 high school GPA, portfolio, documentation of high school graduation. Recommended: minimum 3.0 high school GPA, interview, SAT I or ACT test scores. Portfolio reviews held continuously (student need not be present) on campus and off campus at National Portfolio Days; the submission of slides may be substituted for portfolios.

Web Site http://www.pnca.edu

Undergraduate Contact Rebecca Haas, Admissions Office, Pacific Northwest College of Art, 1241 NW Johnson Street, Portland, Oregon 97209; 503-521-8972, fax: 503-821-8978, e-mail address: admissions@pnca.edu

Paier College of Art, Inc.

Hamden, Connecticut

Proprietary, coed. Suburban campus. Art program established 1946.

The New School: A University
Parsons The New School for Design

New York, New York

Independent, coed. Urban campus. Total enrollment: 3,502. Art program established 1896.

Degrees Bachelor of Fine Arts in the areas of fine art, illustration, communication design, fashion design, product design, architectural design, interior design, photography, integrated design curriculum, design and technology; Bachelor of Business Administration in

Parsons The New School for Design (continued)

the area of design and management. Majors and concentrations: architectural design, art/fine arts, communication design, design and management, design technology, fashion design, graphic arts, illustration, integrated design curriculum, interior design, photography, product design. Graduate degrees offered: Master of Arts in the area of history of decorative arts; Master of Fine Arts in the areas of design and technology, fine arts, lighting design, photography; Master of Architecture. Cross-registration with Eugene Lang College-New School University. Program accredited by NASAD.

Enrollment 3,502 total; 3,072 undergraduate, 430 graduate.

Art Student Profile 78% females, 22% males, 36% minorities, 33% international.

Art Faculty 72 total (full-time), 879 total (part-time). Graduate students do not teach undergraduate courses. Undergraduate student–faculty ratio: 8:1.

Student Life Student groups/activities include Student Gallery, Student Government. Special housing available for art students.

Expenses for 2005–2006 Application fee: $50. Comprehensive fee: $40,930 includes full-time tuition ($28,560), mandatory fees ($620), and college room and board ($11,750). College room only: $8750. Room and board charges vary according to board plan and housing facility.

Financial Aid Program-specific awards: Parsons Scholarships for those demonstrating need, University Scholars Scholarships for African-American and Latino students demonstrating need, Parsons Restricted Scholarships for those demonstrating need and academic achievement.

Application Procedures Students admitted directly into the professional program freshman year. Deadline for freshmen and transfers: continuous. Notification date for freshmen and transfers: July 1. Required: high school transcript, college transcript(s) for transfer students, minimum 2.0 high school GPA, portfolio, SAT I or ACT test scores, home examination, minimum TOEFL score of 550 (paper-based) for all non-native speakers of English. Recommended: minimum 3.0 high school GPA, interview. Portfolio reviews held continuously by appointment on campus; the submission of slides may be substituted for portfolios when distance is prohibitive.

Web Site http://www.parsons.edu

Undergraduate Contact Jim Stillwell, Assistant Director of Admissions, Parsons The New School for Design, 66 Fifth Avenue, New York, New York 10011-8878; 212-229-5150, fax: 212-229-8975, e-mail address: parsadm@newschool.edu

Graduate Contact Director of Admissions, Parsons The New School for Design, 66 Fifth Avenue, New York, New York 10011-8878; 212-229-5150, fax: 212-229-8975, e-mail address: parsadm@newschool.edu

More About the School

At Parsons The New School for Design, students not only learn about art and design—they redefine it. Successful alumni have paved the way for future graduates for a century, and both current students and recent graduates find that a Parsons education resonates in this competitive industry. From the latest in technology design to fashion, product design, and architecture, the School takes pride in staying on the cutting edge and emphasizes the need to design innovative solutions to real-world issues. Students explore new ways to use art and design to help meet society's evolving needs, including using green technology in architecture projects, developing educational video games, and building portable, low-cost dwellings. The faculty members, many of whom are working artists and designers in New York City, bring their professional expertise into the classroom and challenge and encourage students to realize their artistic and professional goals.

Campus and Surroundings Parsons' New York City location provides students with perhaps their most important resource. An international center for art, entertainment, and commerce, the city is an exceptional place to live and study design. The School's main campus is located in Greenwich Village, and the Fashion Design Department is located in midtown, in the heart of the Fashion District. For Parsons' students, the city becomes their home away from home as well as the source of their ideas. Parsons' faculty members use New York City as an urban design laboratory, visiting institutions such as the Metropolitan Museum of Art, Cooper-Hewitt National Design Museum, the Museum of Modern Art, and about eighty other museums. Although every art school organizes student exhibitions, Parsons students have the opportunity to show their work in some of the major galleries and design fairs in New York and internationally. In the past, student work has appeared in Chelsea galleries and museums, the International Contemporary Furniture Fair, the Art Director's Club, and Saks Fifth Avenue.

Program Facilities Since 1970, Parsons The New School for Design has been part of The New School, one of the most diverse educational establishments in the nation, and students benefit from being part of a university community. Campuswide liberal arts programs give Parsons students the opportunity to study with other New School faculty members and share classes with students in liberal studies, social and political science, and performing arts programs. The New School offers students access to more than 1,000 computer workstations and several libraries. The Adam & Sophie Gimbel Design Library includes new and rare books and special collections books on art and design as well as mounted plates, slide collections, and periodicals. The Gimbel Library also stores a digital image collection with online access and is home to the world-renowned Anna-Maria and Stephen Kellen Archives Center. A citywide consortium links the libraries of Parsons, The New School, New York University, and Cooper Union, providing unparalleled access to information. The new Angelo Donghia Materials Library and Study Center houses a computer lab, gallery, lecture hall, and library that put state-of-the-art materials at students' fingertips.

Faculty, Resident Artists, and Alumni Alumni are an important part of the Parsons community and make up an unparalleled network of designers and artists. Notable graduates include Mark Badgley and James Mischka, fashion designers; Sheila Bridges, interior designer; Bridget de Socio, graphic designer; Peter de Seve, illustrator; Sue de Beer, artist; Angelo Donghia, interior designer; Jamie Drake, interior designer; Bea Feitler , graphic designer; Tom Ford, fashion designer; Albert Hadley, interior designer; Edward Hopper, artist; Marc Jacobs, fashion de-

signer; Jasper Johns, artist; Donna Karan, fashion designer; Reed Krakoff , CEO of Coach; Alex Lee, product designer and president of OXO; Ryan McGinley, photographer; Lazaro Hernandez and Jack McCollough, fashion designers (Proenza Schouler); Norman Rockwell, illustrator; Joel Schumacher, filmmaker; Richard Silverstein, graphic designer; Anna Sui, fashion designer; and Brian Tolle, artist.

Student Performance Opportunities The School has also worked hard to create relationships with New York's impressive art and design community. It organizes its own public exhibitions and programs, which gives students access to top professionals. Panels and lectures with leading artists and designers, such as Donna Karen, Chuck Close, and Frank Gehry supplement studio and class work. There are also a number of internships and job opportunities available to through the School's office of career services. In fact, many of the alumni who interned as students with businesses, such as galleries, private studios, design houses, and e-commerce and technology start-ups, have gone on to have successful careers in those industries.

Special Programs Parsons has been a forerunner in the field of art and design since the school's founding in 1896. By locating visual beauty in the ordinary things of middle-class American life, Parsons virtually invented the modern concept of design in America. In 2006, Parsons celebrated the centennial of its Fashion Design, Interior Design, and Communication Design programs, which were the first of their kind in the nation. Internationalism has also always been an essential ingredient of Parsons' success. In 1920, Parsons was the first art and design school in America to found a campus abroad. Today, Parsons has affiliate schools in Paris; Kanazawa, Japan; Seoul, South Korea; and Altos de Chavon in the Dominican Republic. Parsons' rigorous programs and distinguished faculty members embrace curricular innovation, pioneer new uses of technology, and instill in students a global perspective in design.

Peck School of the Arts
See University of Wisconsin–Milwaukee

Pennsylvania Academy of the Fine Arts
Philadelphia, Pennsylvania
Independent, coed. Urban campus. Art program established 1805.

Pennsylvania Academy of the Fine Arts (continued)

Degrees Bachelor of Fine Arts in the areas of painting, printmaking, sculpture, drawing. Majors and concentrations: drawing, painting, printmaking, sculpture. Graduate degrees offered: Master of Fine Arts in the areas of painting, sculpture, printmaking, drawing. Cross-registration with University of Pennsylvania. Program accredited by NASAD.

Enrollment 241 total; 190 undergraduate, 51 graduate.

Art Student Profile 50% females, 50% males, 16% minorities, 5% international.

Art Faculty 31 total (full-time), 32 total (part-time). 40% of full-time faculty have terminal degrees. Graduate students do not teach undergraduate courses. Undergraduate student–faculty ratio: 6:1.

Student Life Student groups/activities include visiting artists lectures, sculpture competitions, drawing marathon. Special housing available for art students.

Expenses for 2005–2006 Special program-related fees: $20 for locker fee, $20 for technology fee, $40 for student activity fee, $150 for general fee, $200 for studio deposit (3rd and 4th year).

Financial Aid Program-specific awards: travel scholarships for juniors and seniors, Institutional Scholarships for those demonstrating need and merit.

Application Procedures Students admitted directly into the professional program freshman year. Deadline for freshmen and transfers: continuous. Required: essay, high school transcript, college transcript(s) for transfer students, 2 letters of recommendation, portfolio, TOEFL score and affidavit of support for international applicants. Recommended: minimum 3.0 high school GPA, interview. Portfolio reviews held as needed on campus; the submission of slides may be substituted for portfolios for large works of art or when distance is prohibitive.

Web Site http://www.pafa.edu

Contact Stan Greidus, Vice President of Admissions and Financial Aid, Pennsylvania Academy of the Fine Arts, 128 North Broad Street, Philadelphia, Pennsylvania 19102; 215-972-7625, fax: 215-569-0153, e-mail address: admissions@pafa.edu

More About the Academy

The Pennsylvania Academy has been training America's best artists for more than 200 years. Steeped in history, the Academy has a long list of famous alumni and a current faculty of working professional artists who form a continuous tradition of excellence in the studio arts of painting, drawing, sculpture, and printmaking. Students at the Academy are passionate about their craft and their future as artists. The Academy teaches technique and imparts knowledge and skills to enable students to become the artists they want to be. The Academy is a unique community of working artists combined with a world-class collection of American art, located in one of the largest and liveliest art communities in the country.

The Academy offers a two-year Master of Fine Arts (M.F.A.) Program, a one-year Post-Baccalaureate Program, a four-year Certificate Program, and a coordinated Bachelor of Fine Arts (B.F.A.) program with the University of Pennsylvania, with studio-based majors in painting, drawing, printmaking, and sculpture. Students work closely with a large faculty of resident and visiting artist-critics. The range of styles and approaches represented by both students and faculty members is diverse and supportive of the many directions in contemporary art making. Students at the Academy come from all walks of life, age groups, and widely varying backgrounds. This creates a high-energy community, bound together by a passion for making art and being artists.

The four-year Certificate Program is the most historic of the academic programs at the Pennsylvania Academy. In the first two years, students receive a thorough training in traditional and contemporary techniques of painting, drawing, sculpture, and printmaking. Under the mentorship of master artists, students take classes in cast drawing, life drawing and painting, anatomy, color, still life, figure modeling, perspective, etching, woodcut, and art history. In their second year, students choose to focus their study in the majors of drawing, painting, sculpture, or printmaking. Third- and fourth-year students receive private studios while continuing an intensive mentoring relationship with critics chosen from a large faculty of professional working artists who represent a wide range of aesthetic viewpoints.

The Certificate program emphasizes excellence in studio art–making skills and abilities, and drawing is emphasized at all levels of the curriculum. All students attend critiques and lectures given by visiting artists and critics and are in daily contact with the Academy's outstanding collection of American art. At the conclusion of their studies, students mount a thesis exhibition within the galleries of the Samuel M.V. Hamilton Building.

Academy students can also obtain a Bachelor of Fine Arts (B.F.A.) degree through the coordinated program with the University of Pennsylvania. For more than seventy years, Pennsylvania Academy of the Fine Arts and the University of Pennsylvania have cooperatively offered a unique educational combination of nationally renowned studio art training and Ivy League academics.

Students admitted to the B.F.A. program may begin studies at Penn after completing their first year of study at the Academy. This self-paced program offers students maximum flexibility in their academic pursuits.

The Master of Fine Arts (M.F.A.) program is an intensive, two-year studio art–making experience that involves daily interaction with an outstanding faculty of resident and visiting artists, regular private and group critiques, seminars in critical readings, a written thesis component, exposure to an outstanding visiting-artist program, and participation in graduate drawing and painting—reflecting the Pennsylvania Academy's emphasis on achieving a high degree of skill in drawing and studio art–making practice. Students are expected to possess an unusually strong work ethic and to be highly productive and able to work independently.

The master's degree program is centered in the studio arts of painting, drawing, printmaking, and sculpture, but within these disciplines, it displays considerable diversity in its approach. All students are provided a private studio in the new Samuel M.V. Hamilton Building, with proper ventilation and 24-hour secure access to facilities.

During both years of study, every M.F.A. student must enroll in drawing and seminar classes that meet once a week at scheduled times. Students may also elect to take classes within the Academy's Certificate Program, with its emphasis on working from life and the acquisition of traditional art-making skills. This, in conjunction with extensive access to the private studio, provides an open schedule that allows flexibility within the program. The Studio Critique system allows the student to choose three faculty critics from a large faculty representing a wide range of studio practice.

The Post-Baccalaureate Program is designed to address the needs of a wide range of students: those with an undergraduate degree who have substantial studio experience but need an additional year of studio work to develop a strong, cohesive, and competitive body of work; students requiring a year of intensive studio work prior to beginning a graduate-level program, or individuals with a degree in art who wish to pursue work in a different medium. It combines an advanced academic program of foundation and techniques with an upper-level, independent studio/critique system and seminars designed to develop personal vision through exposure to trends in contemporary art issues.

Pennsylvania College of Art & Design

Lancaster, Pennsylvania

Independent, coed. Urban campus. Total enrollment: 225. Art program established 1982.

Degrees Bachelor of Fine Arts in the areas of communication arts, fine art, photography. Majors and concentrations: art/fine arts, graphic design, illustration, photography. Program accredited by NASAD.

Enrollment 225 total; all undergraduate.

Art Student Profile 61% females, 39% males, 14% minorities.

Art Faculty 11 undergraduate (full-time), 40 undergraduate (part-time). 70% of full-time faculty have terminal degrees. Graduate students do not teach undergraduate courses. Undergraduate student–faculty ratio: 9:1.

Student Life Student groups/activities include Society of Illustrators Student Competition, Lancaster Museum of Art Annual Open Art Award Exhibition, client-based projects resulting in printed work (for designers and illustrators).

Pennsylvania College of Art & Design (continued)

Expenses for 2006–2007 Application fee: $40. Tuition: $13,607 full-time. Mandatory fees: $450 full-time.

Financial Aid Program-specific awards: 3 PSA&D Foundation Scholarships for incoming foundation students demonstrating artistic merit and academic achievement ($3500), 1 Brenda Swain Memorial Scholarship for juniors demonstrating academic and artistic achievement ($500), 1 UPS Scholarship for current students demonstrating academic achievement ($1375), 1 UPS Minority Scholarship for current students of Hispanic or African-American descent demonstrating academic achievement ($1375), 1 Susquehanna Pfaltzgraff Scholarship for incoming foundation students from York County, PA demonstrating academic achievement ($1000).

Application Procedures Students admitted directly into the professional program freshman year. Deadline for freshmen and transfers: continuous. Required: essay, high school transcript, college transcript(s) for transfer students, interview, portfolio. Recommended: minimum 2.0 high school GPA, 2 letters of recommendation. Portfolio reviews held on campus and off campus in Baltimore, MD; Philadelphia, PA; the submission of slides may be substituted for portfolios when distance is prohibitive.

Web Site http://www.pcad.edu

Undergraduate Contact Susan P. Matson, Director of Enrollment Management and Marketing, Pennsylvania College of Art & Design, 204 North Prince Street, Lancaster, Pennsylvania 17608-0059; 717-396-7833, fax: 717-396-1339, e-mail address: admissions@pcad.edu

More About the College

Pennsylvania College of Art and Design (PCA&D) began as the dream of a handful of dedicated artists and their supporters in the spring of 1982. Two decades later, PCA&D has grown into a professional art college recognized as a leader in central Pennsylvania's visual arts community. While the school has grown and the curriculum has been enhanced, PCA&D's mission has remained the same—to provide a professional education in the visual arts that allows students to pursue art as a life's work and gives them the breadth of knowledge needed to live a life that is personally meaningful and contributes to the cultural and economic aspects of the community.

Accredited by the National Association of Schools of Art and Design, and a candidate for accreditation by the Middle States Association of Colleges and Schools, PCA&D offers four-year Bachelor of Fine Arts (B.F.A.) degree programs in fine arts, graphic design, illustration, and photography. The College also offers continuing education opportunities with certificate programs in print design, Web design, home interiors, and mural painting. In addition, a wide variety of credit and noncredit studio and computer courses for adults and youths are available.

Providing a complementary balance to the program's studio work, the College has carefully developed specific liberal arts requirements and electives with a relevance to the education and life of an artist. Another feature of the curriculum is the internship program for all B.F.A. students, which provides them with professional experiences and opportunities. PCA&D students have produced work for or interned at numerous companies on the East Coast, including advertising agencies, design studios, art galleries, publishing companies, and museums.

PCA&D prides itself on maintaining a professionally relevant curriculum and providing students with a good educational value. The College is pleased to offer its program at a tuition that is considerably less expensive than other professional art colleges. Coupling that with the fact that PCA&D is located in historic downtown Lancaster, Pennsylvania, a city where living expenses are much lower than its metropolitan counterparts, further alleviates the impact of financing a college education.

Another attribute of PCA&D's programs is the low teacher-student ratio (1:10). With individualized attention from faculty members, who are all working artists and designers, PCA&D students have a first-hand view of an artist's lifestyle, challenges, and rewards. Gaining such insight is critical to sustaining a career in the visual arts.

PCA&D salutes its alumni who are making their mark in the field of art and design. Whether they are exhibiting fine artists, creative directors in advertising agencies, designers for international corporations, or illustrators for national publications, the College's graduates are sharing their talents with industry giants. These successes are evidence of the high-quality education and invaluable real-life experiences the College provides its students.

The College facility has more than 62,000 square feet of well-maintained and highly-functional work and study space, with numerous art and design studios, computer imaging labs, printmaking studios, darkrooms, woodshop, photo labs, plug-n-play labs, and galleries. The College also houses its own library on-site, with Access Pennsylvania (AccessPA) privileges.

Pennsylvania College of Art & Design's Lancaster, Pennsylvania, location offers both the advantages of a city and the comfort and safety of a small town. The city's tree-lined streets provide a beautiful setting for many galleries, shops, restaurants, and clubs. In addition, Lancaster is centrally located and only a few hours from some of the East Coast's most important cultural centers—Baltimore, New York City, Philadelphia, and Washington, D.C.

PCA&D is proud of the quality and strength of its programs, curriculum, and faculty, and encourages prospective students to visit the College and learn more about the PCA&D experience.

For more information, students should contact: Pennsylvania College of Art and Design, 204 N. Prince Street, P.O. Box 59, Lancaster, Pennsylvania 17608-0059; Phone: (717) 396-7833; E-mail: admissions@pcad.edu; Web site: http://www.pcad.edu.

The Pennsylvania State University University Park Campus

University Park, Pennsylvania

State-related, coed. Small town campus. Total enrollment: 40,709. Art program established 1964.

Degrees Bachelor of Fine Arts in the area of studio art; Bachelor of Science in the area of studio art. Majors and concentrations: ceramic art and design, painting/drawing, photography, printmaking, sculpture. Graduate degrees offered: Master of Fine Arts in the area of studio art. Program accredited by NASAD.

Enrollment 485 total; 84 undergraduate, 18 graduate, 383 nonprofessional degree.

Art Student Profile 59% females, 41% males, 10% minorities, 20% international.

Art Faculty 25 total (full-time), 1 total (part-time). 100% of full-time faculty have terminal degrees. Graduate students do not teach undergraduate courses. Undergraduate student–faculty ratio: 17:1.

Student Life Student groups/activities include Schreyers Honors College. Special housing available for art students.

Expenses for 2005–2006 Application fee: $50. State resident tuition: $11,024 full-time. Non-resident tuition: $21,260 full-time. Mandatory fees: $484 full-time. College room and board: $6530. College room only: $3430.

Financial Aid Program-specific awards: 1 Gallu Scholarship for incoming freshmen ($1000).

Application Procedures Students apply for admission into the professional program by sophomore year. Deadline for freshmen: November 30; transfers: March 1. Notification date for freshmen and transfers: continuous. Required: essay, high school transcript, college transcript(s) for transfer students, minimum 2.0 high school GPA, portfolio, SAT I or ACT test scores, portfolio (15-20 colored slides). Portfolio reviews held twice on campus.

Web Site http://www.sva.psu.edu/

Contact Ms. Kitty Haupt, Staff Assistant, School of Visual Arts, The Pennsylvania State University University Park Campus, 210 Paterson Building, University Park, Pennsylvania 16802; 814-865-0444, fax: 814-865-1158, e-mail address: kjh1@psu.edu

Pittsburg State University

Pittsburg, Kansas

State-supported, coed. Small town campus. Total enrollment: 6,628.

Degrees Bachelor of Fine Arts in the area of art; Bachelor of Science in Education in the area of art education. Majors and concentrations: art education, ceramic art and design, electronic arts, jewelry and metalsmithing, painting/drawing. Graduate degrees offered: Master of Arts in the area of art.

Enrollment 74 total; 67 undergraduate, 7 graduate.

Pittsburg State University (continued)

Art Student Profile 55% females, 45% males, 1% minorities, 1% international.

Art Faculty 7 undergraduate (full-time), 1 undergraduate (part-time), 7 graduate (full-time). 100% of full-time faculty have terminal degrees. Graduate students teach a few undergraduate courses. Undergraduate student–faculty ratio: 20:1.

Student Life Student groups/activities include senior and graduate exhibits, judging of art exhibits.

Expenses for 2005–2006 Application fee: $30. State resident tuition: $2850 full-time. Nonresident tuition: $9732 full-time. Mandatory fees: $712 full-time. College room and board: $4550. Room and board charges vary according to board plan and housing facility.

Financial Aid Program-specific awards: 1 Bertha Spencer Scholarship for program majors, 1 Laurence A. Wooster Scholarship for program majors, 1 University Arts Association Scholarship for program majors, 1 E. V. and F. B. Baxter Scholarship for program majors, 1 Bert and Lilly Keeney Scholarship for program majors.

Application Procedures Students admitted directly into the professional program freshman year. Deadline for freshmen and transfers: August 15. Required: high school transcript, minimum 2.0 high school GPA, GED (if applicable).

Web Site http://www.pittstate.edu/art/

Undergraduate Contact Dr. Larrie Moody, Chairperson, Art Department, Pittsburg State University, 1701 South Broadway, Pittsburg, Kansas 66762-7512; 620-235-4302, fax: 620-235-4303, e-mail address: art@pittstate.edu

Graduate Contact Dr. Peggy Snyder, Dean, Graduate Studies, Pittsburg State University, 1701 South Broadway, Pittsburg, Kansas 66762; 620-235-4223, fax: 620-235-4219, e-mail address: psnyder@pittstate.edu

Plymouth State University
Plymouth, New Hampshire

State-supported, coed. Total enrollment: 5,264. Art program established 1960.

Point Park University
Pittsburgh, Pennsylvania

Independent, coed. Urban campus. Total enrollment: 3,407. Art program established 2003.

Degrees Bachelor of Arts in the area of cinema and digital arts. Majors and concentrations: cinema and digital arts. Cross-registration with Carnegie Mellon University, University of Pittsburgh, Chatham College, Robert Morris University, Duquesne University, Carlow University.

Enrollment 150 total; all undergraduate.

Art Student Profile 40% females, 60% males, 10% minorities, 10% international.

Art Faculty 4 undergraduate (full-time), 10 undergraduate (part-time). 90% of full-time faculty have terminal degrees. Graduate students do not teach undergraduate courses. Undergraduate student–faculty ratio: 18:1.

Expenses for 2005–2006 Application fee: $40. Comprehensive fee: $24,160 includes full-time tuition ($16,280), mandatory fees ($460), and college room and board ($7420). College room only: $3500. Full-time tuition and fees vary according to program. Room and board charges vary according to board plan.

Financial Aid Program-specific awards: Cinema Scholarship for those demonstrating talent and academic achievement ($1500–$5000), Cinema Apprenticeship for those demonstrating talent ($1500–$5000), Academic Scholarship for those demonstrating talent and academic achievement ($1000–$5000).

Application Procedures Students admitted directly into the professional program freshman year. Deadline for freshmen and transfers: May 1. Required: essay, high school transcript, minimum 2.0 high school GPA, 2 letters of recommendation, interview, portfolio, SAT I or ACT test scores. Portfolio reviews held 10 times on campus and off campus in by telephone.

Web Site http://www.pointpark.edu

Undergraduate Contact Bonnie Sampson, Administrative Assistant, Cinema & Digital Arts, Conservatory of Performing Arts, Point Park University, 201 Wood Street, Pittsburgh, Pennsylvania 15222-1988; 412-392-3450.

More About the University

Point Park University offers students real-world experiences in an exciting campus environment, the chance to meet and learn with students from thirty-five states and fifty countries, and the excitement and culture of the vibrant city surrounding the University.

The Cinema and Digital Arts Program is offered through the Media Production Program, which is part of the Conservatory of Performing Arts. As one of the top programs of its kind in the nation, the Conservatory of Performing Arts combines hands-on experience and rigorous training with internationally recognized master teachers, so students develop their craft working with professional artists who are involved in their professions outside of the University as well as in the classroom.

Cinema and Digital Arts is an innovatively designed program, with an emphasis on professional education and liberal arts, both in theory and in practice. Exploring the integration of media and the arts in society as well as the impact of technology on culture, the curriculum provides practical, professional training while developing a sound foundation in the arts and humanities. Theory and aesthetics are taught as an integral part of developing communication and production skills. The degree offered is a four-year, 120-credit Bachelor of Arts (B.A.).

The program consists of a combination of courses, workshops, productions, and crew assignments, and students have opportunities to earn credit for real-world experience through the internship program. There is a strong emphasis on collaboration. While the teachers demand professionalism and discipline, they go out of their way to mentor and evaluate the students as they develop as artists.

During the first two years, students are trained in all the fundamental crafts of cinema production. Then, in the junior and senior years, students select a concentration in producing, directing, editing, screenwriting, or cinematography for advanced study and practice. Each year, students make films using professional digital video cameras and nonlinear editing systems. This approach allows each student to develop a specific set of skills and to produce a reel that showcases their talents in their specializations. Furthermore, by shooting primarily on digital formats, students do not have the extra expense of film, processing, and video transfers. So, instead of worrying about the budget, they can focus on the creative challenges of bringing their stories to the screen. Students graduate with several great pieces and all the technical skills they need to take the world by storm.

The University's downtown location provides convenient access to numerous theaters, restaurants, parks, sports venues, museums, and movie theaters. Through the philanthropic efforts of such financial entrepreneurs as Carnegie and Frick, Pittsburgh has had a long tradition as a cultural center. The city has an excellent symphony and ballet company, and the Pittsburgh Opera gives performances regularly. Legitimate theater, ethnic festivals, and top nightclub attractions fill out the entertainment spectrum. In addition, the nation's first educational TV station, WQED, provides a wealth of stimulating offerings. PNC Park, Heinz Field, and Mellon Arena are sites of professional sporting events and frequent entertainment spectacles and are within walking distance of the University. A short bus ride away is the Oakland section of Pittsburgh, the location of several renowned museums.

Program Facilities The Cinema and Digital Arts Program has new, state-of-the-art facilities, including ten nonlinear editing suites, a sound mixing studio, a Foley/audio recording studio, and a professionally equipped soundstage. With western Pennsylvania as its back lot, the creative possibilities are limitless.

The recent construction of the television studio in the University Center marks the start of a two-year period of exciting capital projects. The state-of-the-art television studio and editing suites, together with the GRW Theater that is already there, will provide cutting-edge experiences for students in the Cinema and Digital Arts Program.

Exhibit Opportunities The campus offers a student-run cinema society, the Sprocket Guild, and frequent movie screenings that include open showings of student work. The Cinema and Digital Arts Program culminates with the annual Point Park Digital Film Festival, presented to showcase graduating senior thesis production projects.

Special Programs Characterized by a willingness to innovate, the University has been active since its inception in establishing internship possibilities with the many resources for career preparation in Pittsburgh, including internship programs with local broadcasting stations.

Potter College of Arts, Humanities, and Social Sciences

See Western Kentucky University

Pratt Institute

Brooklyn, New York

Independent, coed. Urban campus. Total enrollment: 4,588. Art program established 1887.

Pratt Institute (continued)

Degrees Bachelor of Architecture; Bachelor of Fine Arts in the areas of communications design, fine arts, fashion design, interior design, art and design education, computer graphics, criticism and history of art, media arts, writing for publication, performance and media; Bachelor of Industrial Design; Bachelor of Science in the area of visual and critical studies. Majors and concentrations: animation, art direction, art education, art history, ceramic art and design, critical studies, digital art, fashion design, film, graphic design, illustration, industrial design, interior design, jewelry and metalsmithing, painting/drawing, photography, printmaking, sculpture, visual studies, writing for publication/performance/media. Graduate degrees offered: Master of Architecture; Master of Fine Arts in the areas of fine arts, digital arts; Master of Industrial Design; Master of Professional Studies in the areas of art therapy, design management, arts and cultural management, creative development and special education; Master of Science in the areas of communication and package design, interior design, art and design education, art history and criticism, urban design, library science. Program accredited by NASAD, FIDER.

Enrollment 4,585 total; 3,023 undergraduate, 1,518 graduate, 44 nonprofessional degree.

Art Student Profile 63% females, 37% males, 39% minorities, 14% international.

Art Faculty 121 total (full-time), 778 total (part-time). 62% of full-time faculty have terminal degrees. Graduate students do not teach undergraduate courses. Undergraduate student–faculty ratio: 11:1.

Student Life Student groups/activities include Industrial Design Society of America, American Society of Interior Designers, American Institute of Graphic Arts. Special housing available for art students.

Expenses for 2006–2007 Application fee: $40. Comprehensive fee: $38,082 includes full-time tuition ($28,100), mandatory fees ($1130), and college room and board ($8852). College room only: $5552.

Financial Aid Program-specific awards: Presidential Pratt Merit Awards for freshmen and transfer students ($1000–$15,000).

Application Procedures Students admitted directly into the professional program freshman year. Deadline for freshmen: February 1; transfers: continuous. Required: essay, high school transcript, college transcript(s) for transfer students, letter of recommendation, portfolio, SAT I or ACT test scores, writing sample for some majors. Recommended: minimum 3.0 high school GPA, interview. Portfolio reviews held continuously on campus and off campus in various locations on National Portfolio Days; the submission of slides may be substituted for portfolios when distance is prohibitive (beyond a 100-mile radius).

Web Site http://www.pratt.edu/ad/fineart/index.html

Undergraduate Contact Ms. Judith Aaron, Vice President for Enrollment, Admissions Department, Pratt Institute, 200 Willoughby Avenue, Brooklyn, New York 11205; 718-636-3669, fax: 718-399-4242, e-mail address: admissions@pratt.edu

Graduate Contact Ms. Young Hah, Director of Graduate and International Admissions, Admissions Department, Pratt Institute, 200 Willoughby Avenue, Brooklyn, New York 11205; 718-636-3669, fax: 718-399-4242, e-mail address: admissions@pratt.edu

More About the Institute

Pratt Institute is located on a 25-acre tree-lined campus, with twenty-seven buildings, including landmarked Romanesque- and Renaissance Revival–style structures, in Brooklyn's historic Clinton Hill section. Approximately 94 percent of freshmen live in one of Pratt's six residence halls. On-campus parking is available for residents and commuters. Pratt's proximity to New York City, which offers a vast array of professional, cultural, and recreational opportunities, is a distinct advantage to students. Through Pratt's optional internship program, qualified students are offered challenging on-the-job experience in Manhattan's top galleries and design firms, giving them firsthand work experience as well as credit toward their professional degree. This extension of the classroom into the professional world adds a practical dimension to their education.

Pratt is one of the largest undergraduate and graduate schools for art, design, and architecture in the United States, offering a wide range of cross-disciplinary study options, dual degrees, and major concentrations. Pratt offers undergraduate degrees in architecture, art history and criticism, art and design education, communication design (advertising art direction, graphic design, and illustration), computer graphics and interactive media, critical and visual studies, fine arts (ceramics, jewelry design, painting/drawing, printmaking, and sculpture), fashion design, industrial design, interior design, media arts (film/video and photography), and writing for publication, performance, and media. Graduate degrees are offered in architecture, art history and criticism, art and design education, art therapy, dance therapy, city and regional planning, computer graphics and interactive media, communication design (graphic and packaging design), facilities management, fine art (painting/drawing, printmaking, photography, sculpture, and new forms), arts and cultural management, design management, industrial design, interior design, historic preservation, and urban design.

Student services include academic advisement, career planning and placement, counseling, and academic skills development. There are more than sixty student-run organizations, including fraternities, sororities, professional societies, and clubs. Pratt participates in NCAA and ECAA men's and women's varsity competitions and has intramural sports teams as well.

Pratt Institute has educated professionals for productive careers in artistic and technical fields since its founding in 1887. By employing seasoned professionals as instructors; supporting its innovative programming with an extensive array of art- and design-related studios, workshops, computer labs, and galleries; and providing a rigorous liberal arts core curriculum (mandatory for all students), Pratt Institute offers students an outstanding professional as well as an academically well-rounded education. The fact that Pratt has one of the highest student retention rates in the country among schools of its kind confirms the satisfaction students and their families report about the quality of the education they receive here.

Pratt's faculty members, all practicing professionals, bring to the classroom a "real-world" expertise, a strong theoretical base, and the high standards of their professional work. Pratt faculty members enjoy overwhelming success and critical acclaim in their prospective fields. They have garnered prestigious academic and professional awards, including Tiffany, Fulbright, and Guggenheim grants, and have been provided with publishing contracts, travel and research scholarships, and exhibition opportunities. This intimate acquaintance with "real-world" success and high critical standards has a significant impact on Pratt students, leading them to rewarding and lucrative careers in the fields of art and design.

For more than 100 years, the Institute has produced great artists and designers. The following are just a few of Pratt's alumni and their outstanding accomplishments: Bob Giraldi, director of award-winning TV commercials, including the Michael Jackson Pepsi commercials; Morris Cousins, industrial designer and founder of Tupperware; Betsey Johnson, fashion designer; Ellsworth Kelly, painter; Robert Wilson, performance artist; Bruce Hannah, Knoll furniture designer; Paul Rand, graphic designer of IBM, Westinghouse, and NEXT computer logos; and William Boyer, automobile designer of the classic Thunderbird.

Pratt is the only school for art and design in New York that has a traditional college campus containing spacious lawns and tree-lined plazas. Its numerous buildings offer an abundance of light, air, and open space—highly conducive to focused, serious studio work—and house a wealth of art and design support facilities that include exhibition galleries; printmaking, woodworking, and metalworking shops; casting forges; sculpture and ceramic studios; photo printing darkrooms; film studios; projection and editing rooms; animation stands; and computer labs.

The educational goal of the School of Art and Design is to educate whole artists, writers, and designers. A Pratt education focuses primarily on two objectives: professional training—emphasizing the learning of skills, techniques, and the methodology necessary for students to perform in the professional community as productive artists, writers, or designers—and building students' critical awareness through exposure to a strong liberal arts curriculum. Pratt students are encouraged to enroll in courses outside their major and explore the interconnectedness of art, design, writing, technology, and human need.

At Pratt, future art teachers discover themselves by teaching classes in the Department of Art and Design Education's Saturday Art School. For almost a century, this laboratory school has provided New York City children, adolescents, and, more recently, adults and senior citizens with a high-quality art program.

Visual Arts

Pratt Institute (continued)

By educating more than four generations of students to be creative, technically skilled, and adaptable professionals, Pratt has earned an international reputation that attracts more than 4,500 undergraduate and graduate students annually from more than forty-seven states and forty countries.

Purchase College, State University of New York

Purchase, New York

State-supported, coed. Small town campus. Total enrollment: 3,826. Art program established 1972.

Degrees Bachelor of Fine Arts in the areas of painting/drawing, printmaking, photography, design, sculpture, art of the book. Majors and concentrations: art/fine arts, book arts, graphic design, painting/drawing, photography, printmaking, sculpture, studio art. Graduate degrees offered: Master of Fine Arts in the areas of painting/drawing, printmaking, sculpture, art of the book. Program accredited by NASAD.

Enrollment 402 total; 393 undergraduate, 9 graduate.

Art Student Profile 59% females, 41% males, 19% minorities, 4% international.

Art Faculty 19 total (full-time), 23 total (part-time). 88% of full-time faculty have terminal degrees. Graduate students teach a few undergraduate courses. Undergraduate student–faculty ratio: 16:1.

Student Life Student groups/activities include Visual Artists for Visual Arts, Sonodanza (interdisciplinary performing arts/visual arts group), senior show.

Expenses for 2006–2007 Application fee: $40. State resident tuition: $4350 full-time. Nonresident tuition: $10,610 full-time. Mandatory fees: $1258 full-time. College room and board: $8466. College room only: $5378. Special program-related fees: $35–$165 per course for materials fee for studio courses.

Financial Aid Program-specific awards: 70 art and design scholarships/awards ($1500).

Application Procedures Students admitted directly into the professional program freshman year. Deadline for freshmen and transfers: March 15. Notification date for freshmen and transfers: April 15. Required: essay, high school transcript, college transcript(s) for transfer students, minimum 2.0 high school GPA, 2 letters of recommendation, portfolio, SAT I or ACT test scores, minimum TOEFL score of 550 for international applicants. Recommended: minimum 3.0 high school GPA, interview. Portfolio reviews held twice on campus at National Portfolio Day Association events; the submission of slides may be substituted for portfolios whenever needed.

Web Site http://www.purchase.edu

Undergraduate Contact Mr. Simone Varadian, Counselor, Admissions Department, Purchase College, State University of New York, 735 Anderson Hill Road, Purchase, New York 10577-1400; 914-251-6307, fax: 914-251-6314, e-mail address: simone.varadian@purchase.edu

Graduate Contact Ms. Sabrina Johnston, Counselor, Admissions Department, Purchase College, State University of New York, 735 Anderson Hill Road, Purchase, New York 10577-1400; 914-251-6479, fax: 914-251-6314.

More About the College

Purchase College is fulfilling its mission that "artists and scholars are indispensable both to each other and to an enlightened society." Unique in the history of postsecondary education, professional and conservatory programs in visual and performing arts coexist and interact with a small and selective liberal arts college. Philosophically as well as pragmatically, the purpose of the Visual Arts program is to provide an educational atmosphere in which students and artists work together, engage in critical dialogue, experiment, test their ideas, and learn. The School of Art+Design at Purchase College offers professional programs that prepare students for careers in the visual arts by honoring tradition, encouraging experimentation, and embracing new concepts, materials, and technologies. A faculty of working artists and designers is committed to creating a supportive climate in which students are passionate about learning to see, to think, to create, and to reflect. The internationally renowned Neuberger Museum, located next door to the Art+Design Building, enhances learning through its collections and exhibitions and access to curators, artists, designers, and educators.

The School of Art+Design offers a four-year curriculum, which culminates in the Bachelor of Fine Arts (B.F.A.) degree.

Each student works closely with a faculty adviser to establish a program of study that allows the student to develop particular areas of interest and to prepare for professional status in art and design. In the professional art school program, the student investigates introductory courses in different visual arts disciplines and, in the course of four years, specializes in one area of study, including graphic design, painting and drawing, photography, printmaking/art of the book, video and time-based media, and sculpture/3-D media. Some students may wish to pursue an interdisciplinary course of study where several media areas are investigated with an emphasis on synthesis and juxtaposition.

Performing arts students and faculty members from the three other conservatories on campus: Dance, Music, and Theater Arts and Film, as well as the Performing Arts Center, add to the scope of the critical and aesthetic discourse at the College. Study in the visual and performing arts is enhanced by a strong liberal arts curriculum, which informs the work and expands the interests of art students to better prepare them to not only make art, but to excel and to contribute to the field in significant ways.

This ability is evidenced in the professional achievement of recent alumni in exhibiting in such venues as the Museum of Modern Art, the Los Angeles County Museum of Art, and the Whitney Museum of American Art and a wide range of noted galleries nationally and in other countries. Alumni of the School hold a variety of positions in the design field, including those of art director at Rolling Stone magazine, Atlantic Records, and Coach, Inc. Accolades for the School's alumni/ae include selection as the United States' representative to the prestigious Venice Biennale, a coveted honor, and such significant and highly regarded fellowships and grants as the Fulbright, Guggenheim, MacArthur, Prix de Rome, and New York Foundation for the Arts.

The interaction of artists in conservatory programs and scholars in the liberal arts and sciences creates a cross-fertilization that is mutually beneficial. This, then, is the premise and promise of Purchase College, and the culture of the campus reflects it. On any given day, one can attend a lecture on music, a dance rehearsal, a gallery opening, and more. This environment is stimulating and a springboard for the individual imagination.

Queen's University at Kingston

Kingston, Ontario, Canada

Province-supported, coed. Urban campus. Total enrollment: 20,783. Art program established 1969.

Degrees Bachelor of Fine Arts in the area of studio art with an art history component (general and honours). Majors and concentrations: media arts, painting, printmaking, sculpture.

Enrollment 120 total; all undergraduate.

Art Student Profile 80% females, 20% males, 20% minorities, 1% international.

Art Faculty 2 undergraduate (full-time), 10 undergraduate (part-time). 50% of full-time faculty have terminal degrees. Graduate students do not teach undergraduate courses. Undergraduate student–faculty ratio: 20:1.

Student Life Student groups/activities include Docents of Agnes Etherington Art Centre, shows at student-run Union Gallery, shows at local galleries.

Expenses for 2005–2006 Application fee: $90 Canadian dollars. Special program-related fees: $75 per trip for Montreal, Toronto, Ottawa trips, $300 per trip for gallery tour to New York City, $500–$1000 per year for materials (fine art students).

Financial Aid Program-specific awards: 1 Robert Shotton Memorial Entrance Scholarship for freshmen art students demonstrating talent ($500), 1 The Alfred Bader Scholarship for art history students ($600), 1 The Janet Braicle Book Prize for art history students ($70), 1 The Harold and Helen Cave Scholarship for art history students ($2500), 1 The Milada Svaton Neumann Award for art history students ($800), 1 The Wallace Near Prize for art history students ($3200), 1 The Margaret Craig Scholarship in Fine Art for 4th year studio students, 1 The Helen Nininger Memorial Scholarship in Fine Art for full-time 2nd, 3rd or 4th year painter.

Application Procedures Students admitted directly into the professional program freshman year. Deadline for freshmen and transfers: March 30. Required: high school transcript, college transcript(s) for transfer students, minimum 3.0 high school GPA, portfolio.

Queen's University at Kingston (continued)

Portfolio reviews held in the spring on campus; the submission of slides may be substituted for portfolios (preferred).

Web Site http://www.queensu.ca/art

Undergraduate Contact Jan Winton, BFA Coordinator, Department of Art, Queen's University at Kingston, Ontario Hall, Kingston, Ontario K7L 3N6, Canada; 613-533-6000 ext. 77353, fax: 613-533-6891, e-mail address: jw5@post.queensu.ca

Quincy University

Quincy, Illinois

Independent Roman Catholic, coed. Small town campus. Total enrollment: 1,359.

Degrees Bachelor of Fine Arts. Majors and concentrations: art.

Enrollment 8 total; all undergraduate.

Art Student Profile 54% females, 46% males, 10% minorities, 2% international.

Art Faculty 2 undergraduate (full-time), 3 undergraduate (part-time). 100% of full-time faculty have terminal degrees. Graduate students do not teach undergraduate courses. Undergraduate student–faculty ratio: 2:1.

Student Life Student groups/activities include student show, senior show.

Expenses for 2006–2007 Application fee: $25. Comprehensive fee: $25,970 includes full-time tuition ($18,450), mandatory fees ($560), and college room and board ($6960). College room only: $3740. Special program-related fees: $10–$25 per course for lab fees.

Financial Aid Program-specific awards: 12 de Mero Scholarships for program majors ($1000–$2000), 1–2 Helmer Fine Arts Scholarships for program majors ($500–$1000), 1 Mejer Visual Arts Scholarship for program majors ($100), 1 Tom Brown Art Scholarship for program majors ($800).

Application Procedures Students admitted directly into the professional program freshman year. Deadline for freshmen and transfers: continuous. Required: essay, high school transcript, college transcript(s) for transfer students, minimum 2.0 high school GPA, letter of recommendation, portfolio, SAT I or ACT test scores (minimum combined SAT I score of 964, minimum composite ACT score of 20). Recom-

mended: interview. Portfolio reviews held continuously on campus; the submission of slides may be substituted for portfolios if a campus visit is impossible, with permission of the chair.

Web Site http://www.quincy.edu

Undergraduate Contact Mr. Mark P. Clynes, Vice President of Enrollment, Quincy University, 1800 College Avenue, Quincy, Illinois 62301-2699; 217-228-5215, fax: 217-228-5479, e-mail address: admissions@quincy.edu

Radford University

Radford, Virginia

State-supported, coed. Small town campus. Total enrollment: 9,552.

Rhode Island College

Providence, Rhode Island

State-supported, coed. Suburban campus. Total enrollment: 8,871.

Degrees Bachelor of Arts in the areas of studio art, art history; Bachelor of Fine Arts in the area of studio art; Bachelor of Science in the area of art education. Majors and concentrations: art education, art history, ceramics, graphic design, jewelry and metalsmithing, painting, photography, printmaking, sculpture. Graduate degrees offered: Master of Arts in Teaching in the area of art education. Program accredited by NASAD.

Enrollment 391 total; 341 undergraduate, 50 graduate.

Art Student Profile 57% females, 43% males, 1% minorities, 2% international.

Art Faculty 15 total (full-time), 20 total (part-time). 100% of full-time faculty have terminal degrees. Graduate students do not teach undergraduate courses. Undergraduate student–faculty ratio: 10:1.

Student Life Student groups/activities include Art Club, Artist Cooperative, National Art Education Association-Student Chapter.

Expenses for 2005–2006 Application fee: $50. State resident tuition: $3888 full-time. Nonresident tuition: $11,200 full-time. Mandatory fees: $788 full-time. College room and board: $7010. College room only: $3740. Room and board charges vary according to board plan and housing facility. Special program-related fees: $10 per studio course for supplies.

Financial Aid Program-specific awards: 15 Special Talent Awards for art majors ($600).

Application Procedures Students apply for admission into the professional program by sophomore year. Deadline for freshmen and transfers: April 1. Required: essay, high school transcript, college transcript(s) for transfer students, SAT I or ACT test scores, portfolio for transfer applicants and for scholarship consideration. Recommended: interview. Portfolio reviews held twice on campus; the submission of slides may be substituted for portfolios for large works of art or when distance is prohibitive.

Web Site http://www.ric.edu

Undergraduate Contact Heemong Kim, Chairperson, Art Department, Rhode Island College, 600 Mount Pleasant Avenue, Providence, Rhode Island 02908; 401-456-8054, fax: 401-456-4755, e-mail address: hkim@ric.edu

Graduate Contact Dr. Donna Darling Kelly, Coordinator, Art Education Program, Rhode Island College, 600 Mount Pleasant Avenue, Providence, Rhode Island 02908; 401-456-8054, fax: 401-456-4755.

Rhode Island School of Design

Providence, Rhode Island

Independent, coed. Urban campus. Total enrollment: 2,258. Art program established 1877.

Degrees Bachelor of Fine Arts; Bachelor of Industrial Design. Majors and concentrations: apparel design, architecture, ceramics, film/animation/video, furniture design, glass, graphic design, illustration, industrial design, interior architecture, jewelry and metalsmithing, painting, photography, printmaking, sculpture, textiles. Graduate degrees offered: Master of Arts in the area of art education; Master of Architecture; Master of Arts in Teaching in the area of art education; Master of Fine Arts in the areas of ceramics, furniture design, graphic design, glass, jewelry and metals, painting, printmaking, photography, sculpture, textiles, digital media; Master of Interior Architecture; Master of Industrial Design; Master of Landscape Architecture.

Cross-registration with Brown University. Program accredited by NASAD, ASLA, NAAB.

Enrollment 2,258 total; 1,878 undergraduate, 380 graduate.

Art Student Profile 70% females, 30% males, 23% minorities, 16% international.

Art Faculty 139 total (full-time), 355 total (part-time). 73% of full-time faculty have terminal degrees. Graduate students teach a few undergraduate courses. Undergraduate student–faculty ratio: 9:1.

Student Life Student groups/activities include Film Society, Performance Club. Special housing available for art students.

Expenses for 2006–2007 Application fee: $50. Comprehensive fee: $40,740 includes full-time tuition ($31,145), mandatory fees ($235), and college room and board ($9360). College room only: $5260. Special program-related fees: $10–$100 per course for lab fees for certain courses.

Financial Aid Program-specific awards: 600 RISD Scholarships for those demonstrating financial need ($12,141), 5–7 Trustees Scholarships for above-average students with exceptional artistic ability ($5000).

Application Procedures Students admitted directly into the professional program freshman year. Deadline for freshmen: February 15; transfers: March 31. Notification date for freshmen: April 1; transfers: May 1. Required: essay, high school transcript, college transcript(s) for transfer students, portfolio, SAT I or ACT test scores, 3 original drawings. Recommended: minimum 3.0 high school GPA, 3 letters of recommendation. the submission of slides may be substituted for portfolios (slides or prints required).

Web Site http://www.risd.edu

Contact Admissions Office, Rhode Island School of Design, 2 College Street, Providence, Rhode Island 02903; 401-454-6300, fax: 401-454-6309, e-mail address: admissions@risd.edu

More About the School

Students who come to Rhode Island School of Design (RISD, pronounced riz-dee) join an intense creative artists' community that has been internationally respected for its excellent education for more than 125 years. This dynamic atmosphere—created among people with similar interests, talents, and focus—is frequently noted by many sources as a

Rhode Island School of Design (continued)

distinguishing feature of RISD, which has been cited consistently as a leading visual arts college in numerous college guides and surveys.

RISD's 2,200 students, coming from more than fifty nations around the world, find an extensive range of sixteen majors in areas of architecture, design, and the fine arts. This diverse choice of disciplines creates an enriched environment of ideas and personal directions. Students find balance in the curriculum between focus on their major interest, experimentation in related studios, and innovative cross-disciplinary study. It is a frequent happening at RISD for a student in one studio major to work jointly with a classmate from another department on a single project, broadening understanding of the creative opportunities between disciplines. Digital technology continues to expand the range of tools available to artists and designers, and RISD now has more than 400 computer systems and related equipment available in twenty departmental and specialized labs. A number of departments now assign each student a powerful laptop computer with specialized software, running on a wireless campus network. There are a number of real-world connections to industry at RISD, involving research design studios sponsored by NASA, Sikorsky, Rubbermaid, and Nissan and innovative courses taught jointly with other colleges, such as the product development collaboration between RISD's Industrial Design Department and M.B.A. students from MIT.

The environment of the college is greatly enhanced by seventeen graduate programs, including a recently established program in digital media. RISD's graduate programs are widely respected and frequently cited in surveys as leaders in their visual disciplines.

RISD's 280 studio faculty members are among the leaders in the visual arts, passionate about the fulfillment that the arts bring to the individual and the role of the arts and design in society. They include designers of products found in most homes, award-winning authors and illustrators, painters and sculptors whose work can be seen in major museums and galleries, and acclaimed architects, filmmakers, and textile artists.

Liberal arts form an important component of each student's study as well, and RISD invests notably in the quality of its academic course offerings. There are 25 full-time faculty members in liberal arts departments, all holding the highest degree in their discipline, and 55 part-time faculty members who specialize in certain areas; this number and quality of academic faculty members is unusual for a visual arts college and results in a varied selection of more than 210 courses yearly. Students may choose to enrich the basic liberal arts requirements by pursuing a concentration in art history; English; or history, philosophy, and social sciences.

RISD is located in Providence, described in numerous media stories as a "Renaissance City" and chronicled recently in *Money* magazine as "the best place to live in the eastern United States." Home to students from a number of colleges, Providence offers numerous social and cultural opportunities and an active visual and performing arts community.

Comprehensive career planning support is available to all students and alumni in the Alumni and Career Services Office. Seminars on a wide array of topics that are critical to artists and their career development, individual career counseling, on-campus recruiting, and online listings of available jobs, internships, and fellowships are among the services available. Students are encouraged to participate in professional internships and, on average, more than 60 percent of graduates have experienced at least one internship opportunity. Students have interned recently at WGBE, Cannondale, Walt Disney, Pixar, and Pentagram.

RISD alumni consistently win major competitions, prestigious awards, and recognition for their works in the arts, industry, and education. David Weisner and Chris van Allsburg have won the nationally acclaimed Caldecott Medal for their children's books. Designer Nicole Miller is noted for her collections of women's apparel and men's accessories. Roz Chast's books of her own cartoons (featured often in *The New Yorker*), Henry Horenstein's photography books, and Ken Druse's books on plants and landscape design have won numerous awards. Architect Deborah Berke is recognized for her work in a variety of residential and commercial settings. Glass artists Toots Zynsky and Howard Ben Tre, painter Kara Walker, and filmmakers Martha Coolidge and Gus van Sant are but a few of the successes among RISD's 16,000 alumni. Profiles of many others are available on RISD's Web site at http://www.risd.edu.

Program Facilities RISD's facilities consist of forty buildings with more than 1,000,000 square feet of space, including specialized studio spaces and equipment; access to studio spaces, with upperclass students often having a private studio space; sixteen residence halls offering a variety of living environments; the Museum of Art, with more than 80,000 objects frequently used for study purposes by faculty members and students; a library with more than 100,000 volumes, including artist's and rare books, an image research collection of 470,000 clippings and photographs and 160,000 slides; and the Nature Lab with 80,000 objects available for study and research.

Faculty and Resident Artists RISD has 360 faculty members, 140 of them full-time and readily available to students on campus. More than 200 artists and guest critics visit the campus on average each year. Among recent visitors were Janine Antoni, sculptor; Philip Glass, composer/musician; Bill Ivey, Chairman of the National Endowment for the Arts; Pat Olezko, performance artist; David Byrne, musician; Todd Oldham, designer; David Hickey, art critic; and Dale Chihuly, glass artist.

Student Exhibit Opportunities Exhibition opportunities for students include two college-wide galleries and eight departmental exhibition spaces on campus, with an average of 125 shows staged each year.

Special Programs The European Honors Program allows students to study in Rome for their junior or senior year. Study-abroad exchange agreements are in place with forty-four other art and design colleges around the world. Wintersession term provides unique study opportunities each year, including travel-abroad courses (recently to Italy, Switzerland, Paris, Cuba, Ghana, New Zealand, and Mexico). Mobility program are available with thirty-two other arts colleges. RISD also offers a Summer Studies Program, with courses designed to meet the needs of beginning to advanced students. These courses run from two to six weeks, many offer college credit, and all are taught by distinguished teachers drawn from the School's regular faculty members or visiting experts. Summer Studies also offers a study-abroad option.

Rice University

Houston, Texas

Independent, coed. Urban campus. Total enrollment: 5,258.

Ringling School of Art and Design

Sarasota, Florida

Independent, coed. Small town campus. Total enrollment: 1,088. Art program established 1931.

Degrees Bachelor of Fine Arts. Majors and concentrations: art/fine arts, computer animation, graphic and interactive communication, illustration, interior design, photography and digital imaging. Cross-registration with members of Association of Independent Colleges of Art and Design. Program accredited by NASAD, FIDER.

Enrollment 1,008 total; all undergraduate.

Art Student Profile 49% females, 51% males, 18% minorities, 5% international.

Art Faculty 60 undergraduate (full-time), 59 undergraduate (part-time). 72% of full-time faculty have terminal degrees. Graduate students do not teach undergraduate courses. Undergraduate student–faculty ratio: 13:1.

Student Life Student groups/activities include Campus Activities Board, Phi Delta Theta/Sigma Sigma Sigma, preprofessional organizations. Special housing available for art students.

Expenses for 2005–2006 Application fee: $35. Comprehensive fee: $30,565 includes full-time tuition ($21,200), mandatory fees ($200), and college room and board ($9165). College room only: $4917. Full-time tuition and fees vary according to course load, program, and student level. Room and board charges vary according to board plan and housing facility. Special program-related fees: $1100 per year for Core Studio Program Technology fee.

Financial Aid Program-specific awards: 5 Presidential Scholarships for incoming students ($7000), 73 need/merit scholarships for incoming students ($2870).

Application Procedures Students admitted directly into the professional program freshman year. Deadline for freshmen and transfers: continuous. Notification date for freshmen and transfers: continuous. Required: essay, high school transcript, college transcript(s) for transfer students, minimum 2.0 high school GPA, 2 letters of recommendation, portfolio. Recommended: interview, SAT I or ACT test scores. Portfolio reviews held continuously on campus and off campus at National Portfolio Days; the submission of slides may be substituted for portfolios.

Web Site http://www.ringling.edu

Undergraduate Contact Mr. James H. Dean, Dean of Admissions, Admissions, Ringling School of Art and Design, 2700 North Tamiami Trail, Sarasota, Florida 34234; 941-351-5100 ext. 7523, fax: 941-359-7517, e-mail address: admissions@ringling.edu

Ringling School of Art and Design (continued)

More About the School

For nearly 75 years, Ringling School of Art and Design has cultivated the creative spirit in art and design students from around the globe . . . transforming our visual world. Founded in 1931 by noted art collector, real estate magnate, and circus impresario John Ringling, the private, not-for-profit college is fully accredited by the National Association of Schools of Art and Design (NASAD; http://nasad.arts-accredit.org) and the Southern Association of Colleges and Schools (SACS; www.sacscoc.org).

Located on the Gulf Coast of Florida, the picturesque 35-acre campus today includes seventy-eight buildings and enrolls more than 1,000 students from forty-three states and twenty-eight other countries—more than half of whom reside on the pedestrian-friendly residential campus. The School's 130 faculty members are all professional artists, designers, and scholars who actively pursue their own work outside the classroom.

The School's rigorous curriculum engages innovation and tradition through a strong, well-rounded first-year Core Studio Program and a deep focus on the liberal arts. Students pursue one of eight majors leading to their B.F.A. degrees: computer animation, digital film, fine arts, game art and design, graphic and interactive communication, illustration, interior design, or photography and digital imaging.

The academic emphasis on professional portfolio development and career preparation provides students with a well-rounded education. This is backed up by the extensive career-related services available during a student's time at the School and throughout their professional life.

The Center for Career Services lists nearly 1,000 employment opportunities and internships each year, available 24 hours a day at http://www.collegecentral.com/ringling. The center offers workshops and seminars on professional skills, such as portfolio preparation, resume writing, and interviewing, and can assist students in researching opportunities for additional training and graduate education. Nearly four dozen nationally recognized recruiters visit Ringling School's campus each year to interview students and to make employment and internship offers. Among the most outstanding organizations recruiting at Ringling School are Hallmark Cards, CNN Headline News, Sony Pictures ImageWorks, DreamWorks Animation SKG, Disney, Electronic Arts (EA), American Greetings, and even the Central Intelligence Agency (CIA).

The College believes passionately in the development and support of the whole student by preparing each graduate to be successful in their chosen careers as well as socially responsible artist-citizens. As a testament to the educational principles instilled in them, students donate hours upon hours of their personal time to volunteering on myriad local community public service projects and participating in student organizations. Clubs on campus provide a well-balanced calendar of cocurricular events, leadership opportunities, and social activities. Organizations include the Student Government Association and many diverse clubs focusing on artistic development, recreation, special interests, theater and dance, social and community service, Greek and spiritual life, and more. Students are recognized for their contributions through awards and honors and a comprehensive cocurricular transcript reflecting their participation in these areas.

Ringling School traditions include Family Weekend, Latino Heritage Month, National Collegiate Alcohol Awareness Week, National Coming Out Day, Black History Month, and Women's History Month.

Other celebrations include beach parties, holiday parties, and a President's reception for graduates and their families.

More than half of Ringling School students live on campus in one of ten different, modern, and well-equipped residence halls and apartments. In addition to the convenience of campus living, residents benefit from a variety of programs, residence hall support staff, and campus food service. To enhance the campus experience and create a hub for student activities, a dynamic, 80,000-square-foot five-story Student Center is scheduled to open in fall 2006. The building includes a fitness center and exercise studio, student activity center and meeting spaces, Outtakes Café, classrooms, an exhibition hall, and two floors of student residences.

To begin the school year, a New Student Orientation program is held for all new students and their parents during the week prior to the start of the fall semester. Orientation includes opportunities to meet other students, hear from key faculty members and administrators, attend presentations on academic expectations and campus resources, and to enjoy a number of relaxing, social activities with family members and classmates.

Ringling School of Art and Design welcomes applications from students with a serious commitment to the visual arts. Admission is based on a review of the student's portfolio, academic record, essay, and teacher recommendations. All applicants are reviewed individually, with special consideration given to creative ability and potential for success in college-level studies.

Program/Academic Facilities At Ringling School, facilities include the Verman Kimbrough Memorial Library, with 55,000 volumes, including more than 6,100 videos, CDs, and DVDs, 350 periodical subscriptions, hand-made artist's books, and a separate collection of more than 127,000 slides; Selby Gallery, with international and nationally recognized shows, annual juried student and faculty exhibitions; specialized studios for painting, printmaking, sculpture, wood, graphic design, computer animation, illustration, figure drawing, interior design, and CAD; and the Deborah M. Cooley Photography Center, with studios, darkrooms, and digital labs.

The computer-student ratio is greater than 1:2. Computer facilities include four high-end visual 3-D workstation laboratories, twelve high-end Macintosh workstation laboratories, three Intel-Xeon-based class workstation laboratories, three audio and video editing laboratories, and several digital photography labs. Labs are equipped with high-end workstations, peripherals (scanners, printers, etc.), and numerous general-purpose software packages and tools, including desktop publishing, editors, file-transfer tools, spreadsheets, Web tools, imaging tools, utility applications, and graphics-generation equipment. All personal computers, workstations, and printers are connected to the campus network.

A rich collection of discipline-specific software packages is also available in the computer labs, including Alias Maya; 2d3 Boujou; Shake; Pixar Rendering Tools; Apple Computer: Compressor, Cinema Tools, FinalCut Pro, DVD Studio Pro, iDVD, iPhoto, iMovie, iTunes, LiveType, Safari, Soundtrack, Pro Kit, and Ableton; Crater: CTP; Reel Smart: Motion Blur and Stop Motion Pro; Maxon: Body Paint 3D, Auto*des*sys, and FormZ; AutoDesk: Architectural Desktop, Autocad, and Autodesk Viz; Adobe Creative Suite; Acrobat Pro; After Effects; Audition; GoLive; Encore; ImageReady; FontFolio; Premiere; Dreamweaver and Flash; Microsoft: Office, Front Page, Access, Project, and Implementation Tools; and Corel: Painter, BareBones, and BBEdit.

All on-campus residence halls allow students direct access to on-campus computing resources and the Internet with a blazing DS3 speed from the comfort and convenience of their own rooms.

Rochester Institute of Technology

Rochester, New York

Independent, coed. Suburban campus. Total enrollment: 15,200. Art program established 1885.

Rockford College

Rockford, Illinois

Independent, coed. Suburban campus. Total enrollment: 1,376.

Rocky Mountain College of Art & Design

Denver, Colorado

Proprietary, coed. Suburban campus. Art program established 1963.

Degrees Bachelor of Fine Arts. Majors and concentrations: animation, art education, art/fine arts, graphic design and interactive

Rocky Mountain College of Art & Design (continued)

media, illustration, interior design. Program accredited by FIDER, NASAD.

Enrollment 451 total; all undergraduate.

Art Student Profile 51% females, 49% males, 5% minorities, 4% international.

Art Faculty 24 undergraduate (full-time), 48 undergraduate (part-time). 80% of full-time faculty have terminal degrees. Graduate students do not teach undergraduate courses. Undergraduate student–faculty ratio: 19:1.

Student Life Student groups/activities include ASIFA (International animated film society), American Society of Interior Designers, American Institute of Graphic Arts.

Expenses for 2005–2006 Application fee: $35. Tuition: $17,880 full-time. College room only: $3840.

Financial Aid Program-specific awards: RMCAD portfolio merit award for incoming students ($12,000).

Application Procedures Students admitted directly into the professional program freshman year. Deadline for freshmen and transfers: continuous. Notification date for freshmen and transfers: continuous. Required: essay, high school transcript, college transcript(s) for transfer students, minimum 2.0 high school GPA, interview, portfolio, SAT I or ACT test scores. Portfolio reviews held continuously on campus; the submission of slides may be substituted for portfolios.

Web Site http://www.rmcad.edu

Undergraduate Contact Ms. Angela Carlson, Director of Admissions, Rocky Mountain College of Art & Design, 1600 Pierce Street, Denver, Colorado 80214; 800-888-2787, fax: 303-759-4970, e-mail address: admissions@rmcad.edu

Roger Williams University

Bristol, Rhode Island

Independent, coed. Total enrollment: 5,214. Art program established 1972.

Degrees Bachelor of Arts in the area of visual art studies. Majors and concentrations: art, ceramics, drawing, painting, photography.

Enrollment 37 total; all undergraduate.

Art Student Profile 51% females, 49% males, 6% minorities, 2% international.

Art Faculty 4 undergraduate (full-time), 14 undergraduate (part-time). Graduate students do not teach undergraduate courses. Undergraduate student–faculty ratio: 3:1.

Student Life Student groups/activities include Art Society.

Expenses for 2006–2007 Application fee: $50. Comprehensive fee: $34,759 includes full-time tuition ($22,932), mandatory fees ($1134), and college room and board ($10,693). College room only: $5569.

Application Procedures Students admitted directly into the professional program freshman year. Deadline for freshmen and transfers: continuous. Required: essay, high school transcript, college transcript(s) for transfer students, 2 letters of recommendation, portfolio, SAT I or ACT test scores. Portfolio reviews held on campus; the submission of slides may be substituted for portfolios.

Web Site http://www.rwu.edu

Undergraduate Contact Michelle L. Beauregard, Director of Freshman Admissions, Roger Williams University, 1 Old Ferry Road, Bristol, Rhode Island 02809; 401-254-3500, fax: 401-254-3557, e-mail address: admit@rwu.edu

Graduate Contact Matthew McDonough, Director of Graduate Admissions, Roger Williams University, 1 Old Ferry Road, Bristol, Rhode Island 02809; 401-254-3500, fax: 401-254-3557, e-mail address: mmcdonough@rwu.edu

Roland Dille Center for the Arts

See Minnesota State University Moorhead

Rosemont College

Rosemont, Pennsylvania

Independent Roman Catholic, Suburban campus. Total enrollment: 1,048. Art program established 1969.

Russell Sage College

Troy, New York

Independent, women only. Urban campus. Total enrollment: 838. Art program established 1916.

Degrees Bachelor of Arts. Majors and concentrations: creative arts and therapy. Program accredited by NASAD.

Enrollment 30 total; all undergraduate.

Art Student Profile 100% females, 7% minorities.

Art Faculty 5 undergraduate (full-time), 2 undergraduate (part-time). 71% of full-time faculty have terminal degrees. Graduate students do not teach undergraduate courses. Undergraduate student–faculty ratio: 12:1.

Expenses for 2005–2006 Application fee: $30. Comprehensive fee: $31,060 includes full-time tuition ($22,650), mandatory fees ($870), and college room and board ($7540). College room only: $3650.

Application Procedures Students admitted directly into the professional program freshman year. Deadline for freshmen: August 1; transfers: continuous. Required: essay, high school transcript, college transcript(s) for transfer students, minimum 2.0 high school GPA, 2 letters of recommendation, SAT I or ACT test scores. Recommended: interview, portfolio. Auditions held on individual basis on campus. Portfolio reviews held on individual basis on campus; the submission of slides may be substituted for portfolios.

Web Site http://www.sage.edu

Undergraduate Contact Kathy Rusch, Director of Admissions, Admissions, Russell Sage College, 45 Ferry Street, Troy, New York 12180; 518-244-2217, fax: 518-244-6880, e-mail address: ruschk@sage.edu

Rutgers, The State University of New Jersey

See Mason Gross School of the Arts

St. Cloud State University

St. Cloud, Minnesota

State-supported, coed. Suburban campus. Total enrollment: 15,964. Art program established 1973.

St. John's University

Jamaica, New York

Independent, coed. Urban campus. Total enrollment: 20,346.

Saint Mary's College

Notre Dame, Indiana

Independent Roman Catholic, women only. Suburban campus. Total enrollment: 1,397.

Degrees Bachelor of Arts/Bachelor of Fine Arts. Majors and concentrations: art history, art/fine arts, ceramic art and design, fibers, painting/drawing, photography, printmaking, sculpture, studio art. Cross-registration with University of Notre Dame, Indiana Technical College, Indiana University South Bend, Goshen College, Bethel College. Program accredited by NASAD.

Enrollment 50 total; all undergraduate.

Art Student Profile 100% females, 10% minorities, 10% international.

Art Faculty 6 undergraduate (full-time), 3 undergraduate (part-time). 100% of full-time faculty have terminal degrees. Graduate students do not teach undergraduate courses. Undergraduate student–faculty ratio: 10:1.

Student Life Student groups/activities include Art Club, National Association of Schools of Art and Design.

Expenses for 2006–2007 Application fee: $30. Comprehensive fee: $34,005 includes full-time tuition ($25,030), mandatory fees ($550), and college room and board ($8425). College room only: $5190.

Financial Aid Program-specific awards: art talent awards for art majors demonstrating need ($500), 1 Theresa McLaughlin Award for freshmen art majors demonstrating need ($1000).

Application Procedures Students admitted directly into the professional program freshman year. Deadline for freshmen: March 1; transfers: April 15. Notification date for freshmen and transfers: continuous. Required: essay, high school transcript, minimum 3.0 high school GPA, letter of recommendation, SAT I or ACT test scores. Recommended: interview, portfolio. Portfolio reviews held twice on campus; the submission of slides may be

Saint Mary's College (continued)

substituted for portfolios for large works of art and three-dimensional pieces.

Web Site http://www.saintmarys.edu

Undergraduate Contact Admissions Office, Saint Mary's College, Notre Dame, Indiana 46556; 219-284-4587, fax: 219-284-4716.

Sam Houston State University

Huntsville, Texas

State-supported, coed. Small town campus. Total enrollment: 15,000. Art program established 1940.

San Francisco Art Institute

San Francisco, California

Independent, coed. Urban campus. Total enrollment: 595. Art program established 1871.

Degrees Bachelor of Arts in the areas of history and theory of contemporary art, urban studies; Bachelor of Fine Arts in the areas of design and technology, film, new genres, painting, photography, printmaking, sculpture. Majors and concentrations: design and technology, film, new genres, painting, photography, printmaking, sculpture, urban studies. Graduate degrees offered: Master of Arts in the areas of exhibition and museum studies, history and theory of contemporary art, urban studies; Master of Fine Arts in the areas of design and technology, film, new genres, painting, photography, printmaking, sculpture. Cross-registration with . Program accredited by NASAD.

Enrollment 584 total; 369 undergraduate, 215 graduate.

Art Student Profile 55% females, 45% males, 31% minorities, 9% international.

Art Faculty 145 total. 95% of full-time faculty have terminal degrees. Graduate students do not teach undergraduate courses. Undergraduate student–faculty ratio: 4:1.

Student Life Student groups/activities include student-run galleries, exhibitions, and lectures, Student Union Events, internships. Special housing available for art students.

Expenses for 2006–2007 Application fee: $65. Tuition: $27,400 full-time. College room only: $6540.

Financial Aid Program-specific awards: 35 Community College Scholarships for outstanding transfer students from community colleges ($5979), 153 merit-based scholarships for all undergraduate students ($6515), 307 Competitive Scholarships for all undergraduate students ($5717).

Application Procedures Students apply for admission into the professional program by sophomore year. Deadline for freshmen and transfers: continuous. Required: essay, high school transcript, college transcript(s) for transfer students, portfolio, SAT I or ACT test scores, TOEFL score of 580 for international students, English translation of transcripts for international students. Recommended: minimum 2.0 high school GPA, letter of recommendation, interview. Portfolio reviews held continuously on campus and off campus in locations nationwide; the submission of slides may be substituted for portfolios for out-of-state or international applicants.

Web Site http://www.sfai.edu

Contact Paula Farmer, Director of Admissions, San Francisco Art Institute, 800 Chestnut Street, San Francisco, California 94133; 415-749-4500, fax: 415-749-4592, e-mail address: admissions@sfai.edu

More About the Institute

As artists become greater participants in all aspects of contemporary society, it is crucial that they acquire the tools, technical skills, and self-confidence to engage fully in these vital new roles. Small enough for students and faculty members to work closely together and develop important relationships, yet large enough so that students are exposed to a great variety of work and artists, the San Francisco Art Institute provides an intensive environment for focused art making. The Art Institute emphasizes vision, skill, imagination, intellectual development, hands-on experience, and engagement with the world. Interdisciplinary courses recognize that contemporary art encompasses a broad spectrum of forms, philosophies, and aesthetic approaches, and does not presume separations between fine and applied arts, or the arts and other disciplines. While studio practice is at the core of the curriculum, an institute-wide

Alcatraz, Golden Gate Bridge, and a large portion of San Francisco Bay; and is adjacent to North Beach and Chinatown, two major cultural centers of the city. Downtown galleries and museums are within walking distance, and the variety of public transportation provides easy access to all of the Bay Area's many cultural and recreational resources. The 70,000-square foot Graduate Center is located near the waterfront in an area of artists' lofts and has electric rail and bus lines connecting it to the rest of the city. The San Francisco Bay Area is one of the most culturally diverse populations in the world as well as a center for advanced research and technology.

The undergraduate campus has numerous individual and group studios, as well as facilities for photographic processing and printing and film editing (both film-based and digital); video and sound editing and production; large-scale ceramic sculpture; a wood shop; painting studios with north-facing windows and color-balanced lighting; lithography, etching, and silkscreening studios; four digital media classrooms equipped with Macintosh G5 computers and flat-screen monitors; a large-format (up to 44 inches wide) digital printing center; performance studios; a large auditorium with DV and 16mm film projection; numerous gallery spaces on campus for showing student work, including an outdoor amphitheater; two galleries for curated exhibitions of contemporary art organized to support academic programs; and the Anne Bremer Memorial Library, with more than 30,000 volumes, subscriptions to more than 200 general-interest and fine-arts periodicals, as well as films, videos, audiotapes, and more than 100,000 slides.

The Graduate Center houses more than 250 individual and group studios for graduate students and visiting artists; classrooms, seminar rooms, a digital media and sound studio, film and photography studios, a wood shop, student lounge, critique spaces, and an exhibition space for work by both students and faculty members. Graduate students have access to all the facilities of both campuses.

The San Francisco Art Institute is a laboratory for artists at all stages of their careers, where research and development are supported and encouraged. The Art Institute's public programs provide a forum for a wide range of contemporary art and theories through exhibitions, lectures, panel discussions, and symposia. Integrated scheduling, which combines semester-long classes with two-week intensive courses, offers variety, flexibility, and the opportunity to focus on specific areas of studio practice or to develop projects in a concentrated period of time. The Mobility Exchange Program (travel/study) offers students an opportunity to participate in a one-semester exchange

emphasis on critique and courses in art history, liberal arts, and critical studies foster and challenge critical-thinking skills and strengthen students' ability to speak and write confidently about their work. Thinking, like drawing or any other discipline in art making, requires practice. The critique animates both the studio and liberal arts programs, emphasizing the development of the individual and their own line of reasoning—what motivates them and their work. In the critique process, students are charged not only with examining other students' artwork, but also with creating an environment where artists learn to support their colleagues through criticism and encouragement, and to push each other beyond their current abilities.

The San Francisco Art Institute undergraduate campus is located on Russian Hill, with views of

San Francisco Art Institute (continued)

program at other schools in the United States. Courses are also available during summer and winter breaks. Semester-long international exchange programs are also available. The Center for Individual Learning provides support in the development of language and writing skills. Through internships, residencies, apprenticeships, teaching opportunities, and academic classes that involve community interaction, students expand their artistic and social vocabularies and become effective, creative agents of change.

For more information, prospective students should contact the Institute at 800-345-SFAI (toll-free), e-mail admissions@sfai.edu, or visit the Web site at http://www.sfai.edu.

San Jose State University

San Jose, California

State-supported, coed. Urban campus. Total enrollment: 29,975. Art program established 1911.

Degrees Bachelor of Fine Arts in the areas of graphic design, interior design, animation/illustration, digital media art, photography, spatial art, pictorial art; Bachelor of Science in the area of industrial design. Majors and concentrations: animation, art education, art history, digital media art, graphic design, illustration, industrial design, interior design, photography, pictorial arts, spatial arts. Graduate degrees offered: Master of Arts in the area of art (art history); Master of Fine Arts in the areas of art (pictorial, spatial, photography, digital media). Cross-registration with California State University System and California community colleges. Program accredited by NASAD.

Enrollment 2,000 total; 1,900 undergraduate, 100 graduate.

Art Student Profile 55% females, 45% males, 55% minorities, 5% international.

Art Faculty 32 total (full-time), 62 total (part-time). 92% of full-time faculty have terminal degrees. Graduate students teach a few undergraduate courses. Undergraduate student–faculty ratio: 17:1.

Student Life Student groups/activities include American Society of Interior Designers, Industrial Design Society of America, American Institute of Graphic Arts.

Expenses for 2005–2006 Application fee: $55. Nonresident tuition: $10,170 full-time. Mandatory fees: $3292 full-time. Full-time tuition and fees vary according to course load. College room and board: $8718. College room only: $5412. Room and board charges vary according to board plan and housing facility. Special program-related fees: $25–$40 per course for materials fee.

Financial Aid Program-specific awards: 10–15 Speddy Urban Awards for program students ($500–$1000), 5–10 Dooley Awards for program students ($500–$1000), 15–25 art scholarships for artistically talented program majors ($300).

Application Procedures Students apply for admission into the professional program by sophomore year. Deadline for freshmen and transfers: August 1. Required: high school transcript, college transcript(s) for transfer students, minimum 3.0 high school GPA, portfolio, SAT I or ACT test scores, standing in upper 30% of graduating class, minimum SAT I or ACT score dependent on high school grade point average. Portfolio reviews held twice on campus; the submission of slides may be substituted for portfolios whenever needed.

Web Site http://ad.sjsu.edu

Undergraduate Contact Office of Admissions and Records, San Jose State University, One Washington Square, San Jose, California 95192-0009; 408-924-2080.

Graduate Contact Deborah Wijas, Graduate Office, School of Art and Design, San Jose State University, 1 Washington Square, San Jose, California 95192-0089; 408-924-4346, fax: 408-924-4326, e-mail address: dwijas@email.jsu.edu

Savannah College of Art and Design

Savannah, Georgia

Independent, coed. Urban campus. Total enrollment: 7,356. Art program established 1978.

Degrees Bachelor of Fine Arts. Majors and concentrations: advertising design, animation, architectural history, architecture, art history, broadcast design, fashion design, fibers, film and television, furniture design, graphic design, historical preservation, illustration, industrial design, interactive design and game development, interior design, media and performing arts, metals and jewelry, painting, photography, production/design, sequential art, sound design, visual effects. Graduate degrees offered: Master of Arts; Master of Fine Arts; Master of Architecture in the area of architecture. Program accredited by NAAB.

Enrollment 7,356 total; 6,136 undergraduate, 1,220 graduate.

Art Student Profile 50% females, 50% males, 10% minorities, 9% international.

Art Faculty 366 total (full-time), 53 total (part-time). 80% of full-time faculty have terminal degrees. Graduate students do not teach undergraduate courses. Undergraduate student–faculty ratio: 18:1.

Student Life Student groups/activities include Industrial Design Society of America, American Institute of Graphic Arts, American Institute of Architecture Students. Special housing available for art students.

Expenses for 2006–2007 Application fee: $50. Comprehensive fee: $33,045 includes full-time tuition ($22,950), mandatory fees ($500), and college room and board ($9595). College room only: $6250.

Financial Aid Program-specific awards: May and Paul Poetter Scholarships for National Merit Finalists and high school valedictorians/salutatorians (minimum 1450 SAT/minimum 33 ACT) ($10,000), Academic Honors Scholarship for National Merit Semifinalists or minimum 1100 SAT/minimum 24 ACT ($1500–$15,000), Frances Larkin McCommon Scholarship for those with superior portfolio ($15,000), Artistic Honors Scholarship for Congressional Art Competition first-place recipients and Governor's Honors Scholars ($1500–$15,000), Combined Honors Scholarships for undergraduate students who have demonstrated outstanding ability in both academic and artistic endeavors ($3000–$10,000), SCAD Scholars Awards for those with minimum 3.5 high school GPA and minimum SAT/ACT 1220/27 demonstrating superior leadership ($15,000), Transfer Scholars Awards for those with 45 quarter or 27 semester hours with 3.50 GPA and outstanding talent in visual or performing arts ($15,000).

Application Procedures Students admitted directly into the professional program freshman year. Deadline for freshmen and transfers: continuous. Notification date for freshmen and transfers: continuous. Required: high school transcript, college transcript(s) for transfer students, 3 letters of recommendation, SAT I or ACT test scores, For scholarship consideration, a portfolio is required for some studio majors and an audition is required for media and performing arts majors. Recommended: interview, portfolio. Auditions held monthly on campus and off campus in various cities; videotaped performances are permissible as a substitute for live auditions when distance is prohibitive and for international applicants. Portfolio reviews held monthly on campus and off campus in various cities; the submission of slides may be substituted for portfolios when distance is prohibitive and for international applicants.

Web Site http://www.scad.edu

Undergraduate Contact Ginger Hansen, Executive Director of Recruitment, Admission, Savannah College of Art and Design, PO Box 2072, Savannah, Georgia 31402-3146; 912-525-5964, fax: 912-525-5983, e-mail address: ghunt@scad.edu

Graduate Contact Darrell Tutchton, Director of Graduate Enrollment, Admission, Savannah College of Art and Design, PO Box 2072, Savannah, Georgia 31402-3146; 912-525-5961, fax: 912-525-5985, e-mail address: dtutchto@scad.edu

School of the Art Institute of Chicago

Chicago, Illinois

Independent, coed. Urban campus. Total enrollment: 2,679. Art program established 1866.

Degrees Bachelor of Arts in the area of visual and critical studies; Bachelor of Fine Arts in the areas of studio with emphasis in art history, theory and criticism, with emphasis in art education, or emphasis in writing; Bachelor of Interior Architecture. Majors and concentrations: art and technology, art education, ceramic art and design, fashion design and technology, fibers, film/video/new media, graphic arts, interior architecture, painting/drawing, performance art, photography, printmaking, sculpture, sound design, textile arts, video art, writing. Graduate degrees offered: Master of Arts in the areas of art education, arts administration, modern art

School of the Art Institute of Chicago (continued)

history and criticism, art therapy, teaching, visual and critical studies; Master of Fine Arts in the areas of studio, writing; Master of Science in the area of historic preservation; Master of Architecture; Master of Design in Designed Objects; Master of Interior Architecture. Cross-registration with Roosevelt University, member schools of Association of Independent Colleges of Art and Design. Program accredited by NASAD.

Enrollment 2,679 total; 2,008 undergraduate, 580 graduate, 91 nonprofessional degree.

Art Student Profile 66% females, 34% males, 35% minorities, 17% international.

Art Faculty 89% of full-time faculty have terminal degrees. Graduate students teach a few undergraduate courses. Undergraduate student–faculty ratio: 11:1.

Student Life Student groups/activities include Student Government, "F" Student Newspaper, SAIC TV. Special housing available for art students.

Expenses for 2006–2007 Application fee: $65. Tuition: $28,950 full-time. Mandatory fees: $250 full-time. College room only: $8600.

Financial Aid Program-specific awards: 3 Chairman's Awards for qualified applicants ($28,950), 913 SAIC Grants for those demonstrating need ($10,962), 30 Presidential Scholarships for qualified applicants ($12,000), 42 Recognition Scholarships for qualified applicants ($6000), 69 Incentive Scholarships for qualified applicants ($3000), 144 Enrichment Scholars Grants for qualified applicants ($2000), 350 Academic Scholarships for qualified applicants ($2000).

Application Procedures Students admitted directly into the professional program freshman year. Deadline for freshmen and transfers: continuous. Required: essay, high school transcript, college transcript(s) for transfer students, letter of recommendation, portfolio, SAT I or ACT test scores. Recommended: minimum 3.0 high school GPA, interview. Portfolio reviews held continuously on campus and off campus; the submission of slides may be substituted for portfolios required for transfer credit evaluation.

Web Site http://www.artic.edu/saic

Undergraduate Contact Scott Ramon, Director, Undergraduate Admissions, School of the Art Institute of Chicago, 36 South Wabash Avenue, Suite 1201, Chicago, Illinois 60603; 312-629-6100, fax: 312-629-6101, e-mail address: admiss@artic.edu

Graduate Contact Andre Van De Putte, Associate Director, Graduate Admissions, School of the Art Institute of Chicago, 36 South Wabash Avenue, Suite 1201, Chicago, Illinois 60603; 312-629-6100, fax: 312-629-6101, e-mail address: admiss@artic.edu

More About the School

Since its founding in 1866, the School of the Art Institute of Chicago (SAIC) has been providing a leading global vision for the education of artists, designers, and others who shape contemporary art practice. SAIC's primary purpose is to foster the conceptual and technical education of artists, designers, and scholars in a highly professional, studio-oriented, and academically rigorous environment, encouraging excellence, critical inquiry, and experimentation. In 2002, the School was recognized as "the most influential art school in the nation" by a poll conducted by Columbia University and a panel of national art critics. *U.S. News & World Report* has consistently ranked SAIC's Master of Fine Arts program as number one in the nation.

The 2,000 undergraduates, 570 graduate students, and faculty consisting of artists, designers, and scholars work in an environment that facilitates the exchange of ideas, the sharing of resources, and the critiquing and refining of technical abilities and conceptual issues.

SAIC is distinguished from other art and design schools in the breadth and depth of its curriculum, with more than 900 courses offered each semester. SAIC is committed to interdisciplinary exploration and the awareness that the boundaries between artistic fields are not always easily defined. Students do not declare a major but are free to design a path of study that best suits their creative development. A student may choose to do all their course work in one area of study or amongst multiple department areas. SAIC's credit/no-credit grading system encourages students to think creatively and to develop the self-motivation necessary for life as a practicing artist, designer, and scholar in the twenty-first century. The School enriches its strong studio program with a first-rate, nationally and regionally accredited liberal arts education, and it has one of the largest art history departments in the nation. SAIC is the only college in the country that offers a systematic series of courses on the history, theory, and philosophical bases of art criticism.

SAIC is located in the heart of downtown Chicago, home to the nation's second-largest art scene that includes world-class museums, galleries, alternative spaces, and arts organizations. Chicago itself is a vital part of SAIC, as a source of social and cultural activities and the stimulus for ideas and attitudes ultimately expressed through art. Peter Frank, art critic and curator says, "Of all American cities, Chicago has contributed the most solid and distinctive artwork and art thinking. The School of the Art Institute of Chicago is at the nucleus of this longstanding distinction."

Millennium Park, located across the street from SAIC, is a twenty-first-century marvel, and SAIC, its faculty members, and its students played a key role in its realization. One of the signature pieces of public art in the park, the Crown Fountain by Spanish artist Jaume Plensa, was created with the assistance of both SAIC students and faculty members, who collaborated with Plensa in producing the 1,000 video portraits that are screened continuously on the fountain's twin video towers. The park, with its unique mix of art, architecture, and nature, has become an urban oasis for SAIC students.

SAIC maintains two distinctive residence halls with loft-style rooms—each with their own bathroom, kitchen, voicemail, and Internet access. The residence halls offer 24-hour security and controlled access as well as spacious, well-lit studios; lounge rooms with big screen TVs; computer labs; and laundry facilities. Students can immerse themselves in a community of fellow artists, live in the heart of Chicago's loop, and enjoy conveniences unavailable in most student apartments.

SAIC offers a wide variety of unique resources, beginning with the collection of its sister institution, the Art Institute of Chicago, and its Ryerson Library and Burnham Library of Architecture, the largest art and architecture research libraries in the country. The Gene Siskel Film Center presents significant programs of world cinema and presentations by an international array of film and video artists. SAIC's Video Data Bank houses more than 1,800 titles and is the leading resource in the country for videotapes by and about contemporary artists. The Poetry Center brings renowned poets and writers to Chicago to share their work with the public.

Additional services include an international student office, a multicultural affairs office, health and counseling services, a learning center (offering support services for students with learning disabilities), and an extensive program for academic advising. SAIC is home to the largest and most successful arts-related Cooperative Education program in the country, providing employment opportu-

nities worldwide. The Career Development Center assists in researching job and grant opportunities, preparing portfolios and artist statements, exploring exhibition possibilities, and understanding the legal aspects of entrepreneurship. The center maintains an online database that lists local and national positions, including freelance, part-time, and full-time employment.

Program Facilities SAIC's campus encompasses five buildings in downtown Chicago, including a 40,000-square-foot permanent exhibition space. There are fully equipped studios for each area of concentration, and the School's policy allows 24-hour access to facilities.

The Painting and Drawing department has many well-lit studio classrooms, individual space for select undergraduate and graduate students, and space for critiques. Facilities in the sculpture department include a complete woodshop, a welding shop, a bronze and aluminum foundry, a plaster room, and both indoor and outdoor exhibition spaces. A well-equipped metals shop allows for forging, forming, joining, and casting of nonferrous metals. Design students can take advantage of a computer-controlled CNC router. The Printmedia department has etching presses, stone lithography presses, a screen-printing studio, a Heidelberg Kord and Chief offset press, a process camera, a large-format camera, a professional photomechanical darkroom, artists' books studio, a computer lab, and a Novajet printer.

The Art and Technology department supports several computer labs, including Macintosh-based labs equipped with Maya systems. The department also maintains a multimedia authoring suite, an electronics construction shop, a microcontroller development and programming area, a kinetics shop, neon and holography studios, installation space, and MIDI and digital sound systems. The Film, Video, and New Media department has equipment ranging from a unique hand-built image processor to the latest prosumer, professional, and industrial video equipment. Digital editing systems support current digital, tape, and disk output. Equipment available to students includes digital cameras, projectors, switchers, light kits, and microphones. Film equipment includes sync and nonsync film cameras, sound equipment, optical printers, a wet lab for image processing, and animation stands, cameras, and editing software. In addition, the department facilities also include a sixty-seat theater, a 25-foot shooting set, work studios for 3-D and 2-D animation, and a professional interlock sound suite.

The Photography department has large printing labs, an alternative process darkroom, individual

School of the Art Institute of Chicago (continued)

color-exposing rooms, mural printing rooms, 30-inch by 50-inch processors for color negative and positive printing, a shooting studio, a computer classroom with multiple stations, a computer peripheral area with a flatbed and a variety of film scanners, a 4-by-5 film recorder, various printers, Durst-Lambda digital laser, and large format capability. The Sound department offers studios and workstations equipped with digital editing systems, multitracks and digital recorders, and several digital and rare vintage analog synthesizers and samplers. A larger configurable space is equipped with a multichannel sound system and ceiling grid that makes it suitable for performances and installations.

The Ceramics department's facilities include clay mixers, an extruder, a slab roller, complete moldmaking and casting facilities, and several styles of wheels. Diverse firing options in various kiln styles include high- and low-fire oxidation and reduction, soda, and raku. The Visual Communication department's facilities include state-of-the-art computer labs with color scanners, a copy stand, and spacious studios. Students in the Fashion Design department study design and construction in a spacious facility with industrial-grade equipment. The department houses a Fashion Resource Center, with a collection of worldwide designer garments and a research library with rare books, videotapes, and international publications. The Fiber and Material Studies department has a computer programmable loom, more than thirty traditional looms, a large area for hand construction, full facilities for screenprinting on fabric that includes a darkroom for photo-screeners, a computer lab, a computer loom, and a kitchen with industrial washers and dryers used for the setting of dyes.

Three general-access Media Centers lend thousands of pieces of audiovisual equipment to students. General-access computer labs are equipped with Macintosh workstations that have the latest versions of digital video, desktop publishing, 3-D rendering, Web-site authoring, animation, multimedia, graphic, and audio software applications. The workstations are equipped with various flatbed, negative and slide scanners, film recorders, CD/DVD authoring, and editing peripherals. The lab offers 24-hour access and weekly instructional workshops on specialized equipment. SAIC also has a full-service color digital output Service Bureau, which specializes in laser printing and large-format ink-jet printing.

The John M. Flaxman Library collections include 60,000 volumes on art and the liberal arts and sciences, 360 periodical subscriptions, films, videos, audiotapes, CDs, microforms, and picture files. The Joan Flasch Artists' Book Collection contains more than 3,000 artists' books, along with a research collection of exhibition catalogs and other related material. The MacLean Visual Resource Center maintains a noncirculating collection of more than 500,000 slides.

Faculty, Resident Artists, and Alumni Faculty members are selected for their skills, insight, and dedication as teachers and for their professional accomplishments as artists, designers, and scholars. There are currently 470 full- and part-time faculty members, among them 70 NEA grant recipients, 11 Louis Comfort Tiffany Foundation Fellowship recipients, and 9 Rockefeller Foundation grant recipients. SAIC faculty members have their work exhibited in museums, galleries, and festivals nationally and internationally. They publish books, plays, poetry, and criticism; organize and curate exhibitions; and design, build, and preserve buildings throughout the world. Each year, 100 or more well-known visiting artists, including poets, political activists, designers, and visual artists, present workshops and provide individual student critiques through the Visiting Artists Program. Notable alumni include Claes Oldenburg, Ivan Albright, Georgia O'Keefe, David Sedaris, Cynthia Rowley, and Vincente Minnelli.

Student Performance/Exhibit Opportunities The School's exhibition spaces include the Betty Rymer Gallery, which highlights work from departments and presents special exhibitions, and Gallery 2, with exhibition space, a performance space, and a space designed for site-specific installations. In addition, Gallery X and the Lounge Gallery, sponsored by the Student Union Galleries, provide exhibition space for currently enrolled students. The Fashion department hosts a fashion show in late spring for students in their second, third, and fourth year. The First-Year Program sponsors ArtBash in the spring of each year, highlighting the work produced in its program.

Off-Campus Arrangements SAIC's Mobility Program allows students to attend partner schools within the United States and Canada and includes the New York Studio semester. The School also maintains semester exchange agreements with more than twenty schools in Europe, Asia, and South America, and students may develop their own individual programs. SAIC faculty members also lead study trips during each summer and winter interim to such destinations as Cuba, Czech Republic, Italy, Japan, Los Angeles, Puerto Rico, and Vietnam.

School of the Museum of Fine Arts, Boston

Boston, Massachusetts

Independent, coed. Urban campus. Total enrollment: 773. Art program established 1876.

Degrees Bachelor of Arts/Bachelor of Fine Arts. Majors and concentrations: animation, art education, art/fine arts, ceramics, drawing, film, illustration, jewelry and metalsmithing, painting, papermaking, performance, photography, printmaking, sculpture, self-designed art, sound art, stained glass, studio art, text and image art, textile arts, video art. Graduate degrees offered: Master of Arts in Teaching; Master of Fine Arts. Cross-registration with ProArts Consortium, Association of Independent Colleges of Art and Design, Wheaton College, Tufts University, Massachusetts Institute of Technology. Program accredited by NASAD.

Enrollment 773 total; 677 undergraduate, 96 graduate.

Art Student Profile 67% females, 33% males, 11% minorities, 6% international.

Art Faculty 51 total (full-time), 129 total (part-time). 46% of full-time faculty have terminal degrees. Graduate students teach a few undergraduate courses. Undergraduate student–faculty ratio: 9:1.

Student Life Student groups/activities include Film Club, Infra Sculpture, Gay/Lesbian/Transgender and Supporters (Outloud!). Special housing available for art students.

Expenses for 2005–2006 Application fee: $65. Tuition: $23,850 full-time. Mandatory fees: $910 full-time. Full-time tuition and fees vary according to course load, degree level, and program. College room only: $10,795. Room charges vary according to housing facility. Special program-related fees: $482 per semester for comprehensive fee, $1895 per year for health insurance.

Financial Aid Program-specific awards: art merit scholarships, 434 School of the Museum of Fine Arts Grants for those demonstrating need ($15,500).

Application Procedures Students admitted directly into the professional program freshman year. Deadline for freshmen: February 1; transfers: March 1. Notification date for freshmen and transfers: continuous. Required: essay, high school transcript, college transcript(s) for transfer students, 2 letters of recommendation, portfolio, SAT or ACT (for some applicants). Recommended: minimum 2.0 high school GPA, minimum 3.0 high school GPA, interview. Portfolio reviews held weekly on campus and off campus at National Portfolio Days; the submission of slides may be substituted for portfolios.

Web Site http://www.smfa.edu

Undergraduate Contact Susan Clain, Dean of Admissions, School of the Museum of Fine Arts, Boston, 230 The Fenway, Boston, Massachusetts 02115; 617-369-3626, fax: 617-369-4264, e-mail address: admissions@smfa.edu

Graduate Contact Veronique Latimer, Assistant Dean of Admissions, School of the Museum of Fine Arts, Boston, 230 The Fenway, Boston, Massachusetts 02115; 617-369-3626, fax: 617-369-4264, e-mail address: admissions@smfa.edu

More About the School

The School of the Museum of Fine Arts, Boston (SMFA), is a unique institution dedicated to educating artists and focused on fostering creative investigation, risk-taking, and individual vision. Everyone at the SMFA recognizes that disciplines converge and influence each other and that contemporary art is truly interdisciplinary. The School does not have a mandatory foundations program nor does it have majors. Instead, all students are encouraged to build solid foundations and acquire skill sets in numerous disciplines in order to create new possibilities and forms of artmaking. Students are given the freedom to design a program of study that best suits their needs and goals. This freedom comes with strong support and guidance from faculty advisers.

In partnership with Tufts University, the School offers the following degree programs: the Bachelor of Fine Arts, the Bachelor of Fine Arts in Art Education, the five-year Combined-Degree program (B.A./B.F.A. or B.S./B.F.A.), the Master of Fine Arts, and the Master of Arts in Teaching in Art Education. All students in degree programs are fully enrolled at the SMFA and Tufts University and graduate with a Tufts degree. The School also offers the all-studio diploma program and one-year Fifth Year and Post-Baccalaureate Certificate programs. The School is a division of the Museum of Fine Arts, Boston, which is located across the street from the School.

The diversity of the faculty members and the range of facilities allow the student to develop a very personal and individual means of expression. Course

School of the Museum of Fine Arts, Boston (continued)

teaching methods range from structured classes, with regular attendance, to individual instruction for work done independently outside the School. Class sizes are generally small, and every area of study is supported by accomplished, professional faculty members; extensive programs with visiting artists; and an energetic schedule of exhibitions. At the end of each semester, the student presents a body of art work to a review board consisting of faculty members and students. There is a discussion of the total semester experience, and suggestions are made for future study. A block of credits is awarded, appropriate to the term's accomplishments, and a written evaluation is made.

Boston is home to many educational and cultural institutions. The Museum School is a vital member of the art community, presenting a dynamic schedule of exhibitions, lectures, and panel discussions throughout the academic year. As a division of the Museum of Fine Arts, students also have special access to the educational resources, collections, curatorial departments, and special programs of one of the most comprehensive and outstanding collections of art in the world.

Program Facilities The SMFA campus features several buildings with 24-hour security and extensive access for students. The two main buildings house classrooms, studios, state-of-the-art equipment, exhibition spaces, computer and video labs, the Writing Center, the W. Van Alan Clark Jr. Library, and Café des Arts, which serves breakfast, lunch, and dinner.

The School provides a limited number of individual studio spaces for undergraduate degree students and diploma students. Students have 24-hour access to most studio spaces and facilities. Students may apply for studio space in the summer months.

There is a limited amount of residential housing in the Artists' Residence Hall at Massachusetts College of Art. The majority of students choose to live in nearby off-campus apartments, and the SMFA Student Affairs Office can help find the right location and the right roommate.

Faculty, Visiting Artists, and Alumni All studio faculty members are practicing professional artists with regional, national, and international reputations. The Visiting Artists Program encourages students to interact with prominent artists.

Exhibition Opportunities The Museum School provides students with more than 8,000 square feet of exhibition space in six galleries. These excellent sites are in addition to contemporary gallery space at the Museum of Fine Arts, Boston, where winners of the prestigious Traveling Scholars awards exhibit every year. Student-curated exhibitions are also on view at the museum throughout the year. The School also sponsors a number of special prize funds, offering students the chance to win travel grants, cash awards, and exhibition opportunities.

Special Programs The School is a division of the Museum of Fine Arts and is in partnership with Tufts University; special mobility programs are available with Massachusetts Institute of Technology. As a member of the ProArts Consortium in Boston and the Association of Independent Colleges of Art and Design (AICAD), students have the opportunity to study at colleges throughout the United States and abroad.

School of Visual Arts

New York, New York

Proprietary, coed. Urban campus. Total enrollment: 3,575. Art program established 1947.

Degrees Bachelor of Fine Arts in the areas of advertising, animation, cartooning, computer art, film and video, fine arts, graphic design, illustration, interior design, photography, visual and critical studies. Majors and concentrations: advertising design, animation, art/fine arts, cartooning, computer art, film and video production, graphic design, illustration, interior design, painting/drawing, photography, printmaking, sculpture, studio art, visual studies. Graduate degrees offered: Master of Arts in Teaching in the area of art education; Master of Fine Arts in the areas of computer art, design, fine arts, illustration as visual essay, photography and related media, art criticism and writing; Master of Professional Studies in the area of art therapy. Program accredited by NASAD, FIDER.

Enrollment 3,350 total; 2,900 undergraduate, 392 graduate.

Art Student Profile 53% females, 47% males, 26% minorities, 11% international.

Art Faculty 700 total (part-time). Graduate students do not teach undergraduate courses. Undergraduate student–faculty ratio: 9:1.

Student Life Student groups/activities include Visual Arts Students Association, Visual Opinion (campus literary magazine), WSVA campus radio station.

Expenses for 2005–2006 Application fee: $50. Comprehensive fee: $32,580 includes full-time tuition ($20,080), mandatory fees ($1000), and college room and board ($11,500). College room only: $9000. Full-time tuition and fees vary according to program. Room and board charges vary according to board plan, gender, housing facility, and location. Special program-related fees: $150–$1100 per semester for departmental fee.

Financial Aid Program-specific awards: Silas H. Rhodes Scholarship ($10,000).

Application Procedures Students admitted directly into the professional program freshman year. Deadline for freshmen and transfers: continuous. Required: essay, high school transcript, college transcript(s) for transfer students, portfolio, SAT I or ACT test scores, 2-part essay for film applicants, TOEFL score for applicants whose primary language is not English. Recommended: interview, minimum 2.5 high school GPA. Portfolio reviews held by appointment year-round on campus and off campus in various locations throughout the U.S. on National Portfolio Days; the submission of slides may be substituted for portfolios (required for transfers, scholarship applicants, and students not attending an in-person portfolio review).

Web Site http://www.schoolofvisualarts.edu

Contact Terese Nehra, Director of Admissions, School of Visual Arts, 209 East 23rd Street, New York, New York 10010; 212-592-2100, fax: 212-592-2116, e-mail address: admissions@sva.edu

More About the School

The School of Visual Arts (SVA), well-positioned in the heart of New York City, offers students the opportunity to become involved in one of America's largest and most vibrant cities, the art capital of the world. The energy, spirit, and desire to be the best that characterizes New York is embodied in SVA's renowned faculty of more than 700 working professionals who challenge and inspire their students.

The four-year curriculum remains responsive to the needs and demands of the industry and is designed to allow students a greater freedom of choice in electives and requirements with each succeeding year. The first year of each program, a foundation year, ensures the mastery of basic skills in each chosen discipline as well as in writing and art history. After the first year, students focus on specific areas of concentration and, under the guidance of academic advisers and faculty members, pursue their own individual goals.

In addition, SVA's Internship for Credit Program gives students the chance to work alongside top art directors, photographers, painters, and illustrators and in film and animation studios. SVA has a very high job placement rate—89 percent of SVA's students are employed within a year of graduation.

Program Facilities SVA provides students with studios that continually mirror the standards of the professional art world and has one of the largest and most well-equipped computer art campuses in the country. Studio space and equipment are offered in different departments, varying in availability depending on such factors as the student's class seniority and major of study. The SVA library's holdings include distinctive multimedia collections, over 65,000 books, more than 260 periodicals subscriptions, and special collections of pictures, color slides, film scripts, comics, videotapes, exhibition catalogs, CD-ROMs, and recordings.

Faculty, Resident Artists, and Alumni The School of Visual Arts is proud of its illustrious faculty of more than 700 professional artists and designers who represent an array of fields in the fine and applied arts. Each faculty member has chosen to commit to the professional art world as well as to teaching the next generation of artists. The SVA community is enthusiastic about the faculty's ability to balance the life of a dynamic artist with the vivaciousness that only a dedicated teacher can provide to his or her students. The School of Visual Arts has some of the world's greatest artists among its alumni. Many of them live and work in New York City; others can be found throughout the United States and in more than thirty countries around the world. They work at advertising agencies, television networks, publishing houses, film studios, recording companies, design firms, art galleries, and major museums. Others do freelance work or run their own start-up companies. Still others extend SVA's tradition of educating artists by becoming teachers and therapists themselves.

Exhibit Opportunities The College operates three campus galleries as well as a Chelsea gallery space, affording SVA students the opportunity to exhibit their work twelve months a year. Students are encouraged to show their work outside of SVA's framework by participating in exhibits and competitions held in New York City and throughout the United States.

Special Programs SVA students have the opportunity to participate in art programs abroad during the summer semester. SVA offers Painting in Barcelona, Painting in Florence, Digital Photography in Florence, and the Art, Myths, and History of Ancient Greece.

School of Visual Arts (continued)

Third-year students in film and video, fine arts, graphic design, illustration, interior design, and photography have the opportunity to study abroad for one semester at an AIAS (Association of Independent Art Schools) affiliate in Europe.

Seton Hall University

South Orange, New Jersey

Independent Roman Catholic, coed. Suburban campus. Total enrollment: 9,637. Art program established 1968.

Degrees Bachelor of Arts in the areas of art history, fine arts, graphic design/advertising art; Bachelor of Science in the area of art education. Majors and concentrations: advertising, art education, art history, art/fine arts, graphic design, interactive design and game development. Graduate degrees offered: Master of Arts in the area of museum professions.

Enrollment 130 total; 60 undergraduate, 70 graduate.

Art Student Profile 60% females, 40% males, 15% minorities, 5% international.

Art Faculty 7 undergraduate (full-time), 2 graduate (full-time), 13 total (part-time). 100% of full-time faculty have terminal degrees. Graduate students do not teach undergraduate courses. Undergraduate student–faculty ratio: 15:1.

Student Life Student groups/activities include student exhibitions, gallery exhibitions.

Expenses for 2006–2007 Application fee: $55. Comprehensive fee: $35,186 includes full-time tuition ($22,770), mandatory fees ($1950), and college room and board ($10,466). College room only: $6664.

Financial Aid Program-specific awards: 1 Henry Gasser Scholarship for art majors demonstrating talent and/or academic achievement ($1800).

Application Procedures Students admitted directly into the professional program freshman year. Deadline for freshmen and transfers: continuous. Required: essay, high school transcript, college transcript(s) for transfer students, minimum 2.0 high school GPA, 3 letters of recommendation, SAT I or ACT test scores. Recommended: minimum 3.0 high school GPA, interview, portfolio. Portfolio reviews held as needed on campus; the submission of slides may be substituted for portfolios for large works of art.

Web Site http://www.shu.edu

Undergraduate Contact Admissions Office, Seton Hall University, 400 South Orange Avenue, South Orange, New Jersey 07079-2696; 973-761-9000 ext. 9332.

Graduate Contact Dr. Petra Chu, Director, MA Program in Museum Professions, Department of Art and Music, Seton Hall University, 400 South Orange Avenue, South Orange, New Jersey 07079-2696; 973-761-7966, fax: 973-275-2368, e-mail address: chupetra@shu.edu

Seton Hill University

Greensburg, Pennsylvania

Independent Roman Catholic, coed. Small town campus. Total enrollment: 1,863. Art program established 1955.

Degrees Bachelor of Fine Arts in the areas of graphic design, 2-D media, 3-D media, art and technology. Majors and concentrations: art and technology, art education, art history, art therapy, art/fine arts, arts management, graphic design, sculpture, self-designed art, studio art, three-dimensional studies, two-dimensional studies. Graduate degrees offered: Master of Arts in the area of art therapy. Cross-registration with Saint Vincent College, Pittsburgh Filmmakers.

Enrollment 110 total; 53 undergraduate, 27 graduate, 30 nonprofessional degree.

Art Student Profile 80% females, 20% males, 10% minorities, 10% international.

Art Faculty 6 undergraduate (full-time), 5 undergraduate (part-time), 1 graduate (full-time), 2 graduate (part-time). 85% of full-time faculty have terminal degrees. Graduate students do not teach undergraduate courses. Undergraduate student–faculty ratio: 8:1.

Student Life Student groups/activities include Student In The Arts (SITA), American Institute of Graphic Arts, Student Art Therapy Association.

Expenses for 2005–2006 Application fee: $35. Comprehensive fee: $29,020 includes full-time tuition ($21,870), mandatory fees ($120), and college room and board ($7030). Room and board charges vary according to board plan and housing facility. Special program-related fees: $10–$100 per course for supplies.

Financial Aid Program-specific awards: 1–2 Hensler-Irwin Scholarships for freshmen program majors ($750), 1 Josefa Filkosky Scholarship for juniors ($700).

Application Procedures Students admitted directly into the professional program freshman year. Deadline for freshmen and transfers: July 30. Notification date for freshmen and transfers: continuous. Required: high school transcript, college transcript(s) for transfer students, minimum 2.0 high school GPA, 3 letters of recommendation, portfolio, SAT I or ACT test scores. Recommended: essay, minimum 3.0 high school GPA, interview. Portfolio reviews held continuously on campus; the submission of slides may be substituted for portfolios when distance is prohibitive.

Web Site http://www.setonhill.edu

Undergraduate Contact Mary Kay Cooper, Director, Admissions Office, Seton Hill University, College Avenue, Greensburg, Pennsylvania 15601; 724-830-4639, fax: 724-830-4611, e-mail address: mcooper@setonhill.edu

Graduate Contact Ms. Nina Denninger, Director, Graduate Program in Art Therapy, Seton Hill University, Seton Hill Drive, Greensburg, Pennsylvania 15601; 724-830-1047, fax: 724-830-4611, e-mail address: dennib7@setonhill.edu

Shepherd University

Shepherdstown, West Virginia

State-supported, coed. Small town campus. Total enrollment: 3,901. Art program established 1950.

Degrees Bachelor of Fine Arts in the areas of graphic design, photography/computer digital imagery, painting, printmaking, sculpture. Majors and concentrations: art/fine arts, digital imaging, graphic design, illustration, painting/drawing, photography, printmaking, sculpture.

Enrollment 250 total; 225 undergraduate, 25 nonprofessional degree.

Art Student Profile 55% females, 45% males, 9% minorities, 5% international.

Art Faculty 10 undergraduate (full-time), 10 undergraduate (part-time). 100% of full-time faculty have terminal degrees. Graduate students do not teach undergraduate courses. Undergraduate student–faculty ratio: 15:1.

Student Life Student groups/activities include Art Alliance Exhibits, Performing and Visual Arts Series, American Institute of Graphic Arts.

Expenses for 2005–2006 Application fee: $35. State resident tuition: $4046 full-time. Nonresident tuition: $10,618 full-time. Full-time tuition varies according to degree level, program, and reciprocity agreements. College room and board: $6020. Room and board charges vary according to board plan and housing facility. Special program-related fees: $25 per course for studio fee.

Financial Aid Program-specific awards: 12 art scholarships for West Virginia resident program majors ($2000), 2 Blundell Awards for first-year students ($700), 2 Bridgeforth Awards for photography/computer imaging students ($500–$1000), 2 Hendricks Scholarships for art majors ($600).

Application Procedures Students admitted directly into the professional program freshman year. Deadline for freshmen and transfers: February 1. Notification date for freshmen and transfers: April 1. Required: high school transcript, college transcript(s) for transfer students, minimum 2.0 high school GPA, interview, portfolio, SAT I or ACT test scores. Portfolio reviews held 6 times on campus; the submission of slides may be substituted for portfolios (slides/CD preferred).

Web Site http://www.shepherd.edu

Undergraduate Contact Ms. Kimberly Scranage, Director of Admissions, Shepherd University, PO Box 3210, Shepherdstown, West Virginia 25443; 304-876-5212, fax: 304-876-3101, e-mail address: kscranag@shepherd.edu

Shorter College

Rome, Georgia

Independent Baptist, coed. Small town campus. Total enrollment: 967. Art program established 1994.

Simon Fraser University

Burnaby, British Columbia, Canada

Province-supported, coed. Suburban campus. Total enrollment: 20,187. Art program established 1992.

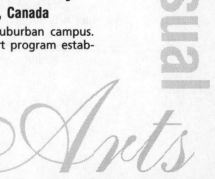

Simon Fraser University (continued)

Degrees Bachelor of Fine Arts. Majors and concentrations: visual arts. Graduate degrees offered: Master of Fine Arts in the area of interdisciplinary studies.

Enrollment 78 total.

Art Faculty 4 total (full-time). 100% of full-time faculty have terminal degrees. Graduate students teach a few undergraduate courses. Undergraduate student–faculty ratio: 26:1.

Expenses for 2006–2007 Application fee: $100 Canadian dollars. Tuition and fee charges are reported in Canadian dollars. Special program-related fees: $50–$100 per semester for studio lab fee.

Financial Aid Program-specific awards: 1 Murray Farr Scholarship for program majors ($500), 1 Adaline May Clark Scholarship for program majors ($500), 1 SCA Scholarship for program majors ($1000), 1 Helen Pitt Award for program majors ($1000), 3 Bice Caple Awards for students in SCA ($1000), 2 SFU Service Awards for students in SCA ($250), 1 F.W. Sullivan Visual Arts Award for program majors ($650), 1 Volunteers of Burnaby Art Gallery Award in Visual Art for program majors ($690).

Application Procedures Students admitted directly into the professional program freshman year. Deadline for freshmen and transfers: April 30. Required: high school transcript, college transcript(s) for transfer students, minimum 3.0 high school GPA, interview, portfolio. Portfolio reviews held twice on campus or portfolio may be sent by mail on campus; the submission of slides may be substituted for portfolios for international applicants and for large works of art.

Web Site http://www.sfu.ca/sca

Undergraduate Contact Linda Hegland, Undergraduate Advisor, School for the Contemporary Arts, Simon Fraser University, 8888 University Drive, Burnaby, British Columbia V5A 1S6, Canada; 604-291-3363, fax: 604-291-5907, e-mail address: ca@sfu.ca

Graduate Contact Noni Fidler, Graduate Secretary, MFA Program, School for the Contemporary Arts, Simon Fraser University, 8888 University Drive, Burnaby, British Columbia V5A 1S6, Canada; 604-291-3724, fax: 604-291-5907, e-mail address: mfagrad@sfu.ca

Slippery Rock University of Pennsylvania

Slippery Rock, Pennsylvania

State-supported, coed. Rural campus. Total enrollment: 8,105.

Sonoma State University

Rohnert Park, California

State-supported, coed. Small town campus. Total enrollment: 7,749. Art program established 1967.

Degrees Bachelor of Fine Arts in the areas of painting, printmaking, sculpture, photography. Majors and concentrations: art/fine arts, painting/drawing, photography, printmaking, sculpture. Cross-registration with San Francisco State University. Program accredited by NASAD.

Enrollment 15 total; all undergraduate.

Art Student Profile 47% females, 53% males.

Art Faculty 5 undergraduate (full-time), 2 undergraduate (part-time). 100% of full-time faculty have terminal degrees. Graduate students do not teach undergraduate courses. Undergraduate student–faculty ratio: 19:1.

Student Life Student groups/activities include BFA Student Exhibition, student art exhibition.

Expenses for 2005–2006 Application fee: $55. State resident tuition: $0 full-time. Nonresident tuition: $10,170 full-time. Mandatory fees: $3616 full-time. Full-time tuition and fees vary according to course load. College room and board: $8890. College room only: $6052. Room and board charges vary according to board plan and housing facility. Special program-related fees: $10–$68 per course for supplies.

Financial Aid Program-specific awards: 1 William Smith Award for ceramics majors ($500), 1 William Smith Award for studio art majors ($500), 1 Brooks Award for art history majors ($400), 1 John Bolles Scholarship for program majors ($750), 2 Art Department Scholarships for program majors ($300), 2 Edward Boyle Scholarships for program majors ($250), 1 Hendrickson Family Scholarship for painting majors ($750).

visual

Arts

Application Procedures Students apply for admission into the professional program by sophomore, junior year. Deadline for freshmen and transfers: May 31. Required: essay, college transcript(s) for transfer students, minimum 3.0 high school GPA, 2 letters of recommendation, portfolio. Portfolio reviews held twice on campus; the submission of slides may be substituted for portfolios (slides preferred).

Web Site http://www.sonoma.edu/art/

Undergraduate Contact Mr. Stephen Galloway, Department of Art and Art History, Sonoma State University, 1801 East Cotati Avenue, Rohnert Park, California 94928; 707-664-2364, fax: 707-664-4333, e-mail address: stephen.galloway@sonoma.edu

Southeast Missouri State University

Cape Girardeau, Missouri

State-supported, coed. Small town campus. Total enrollment: 10,292. Art program established 1874.

Southern California Institute of Architecture

Los Angeles, California

Independent, coed. Urban campus. Total enrollment: 447 (2004).

Southern Illinois University Carbondale

Carbondale, Illinois

State-supported, coed. Rural campus. Total enrollment: 21,441. Art program established 1931.

Degrees Bachelor of Fine Arts in the area of art. Majors and concentrations: art education, ceramic art and design, communication design, glass, industrial design, jewelry and metalsmithing, painting/drawing, printmaking,

sculpture. Graduate degrees offered: Master of Fine Arts in the area of art. Program accredited by NASAD.

Enrollment 541 total; 142 undergraduate, 58 graduate, 341 nonprofessional degree.

Art Student Profile 50% females, 50% males, 4% minorities, 6% international.

Art Faculty 25 total (full-time), 6 total (part-time). 100% of full-time faculty have terminal degrees. Graduate students teach about a quarter of undergraduate courses. Undergraduate student–faculty ratio: 5:1.

Student Life Student groups/activities include League of Art and Design, Industrial Design Society of America Student Chapter, American Center for Design. Special housing available for art students.

Expenses for 2005–2006 Application fee: $30. State resident tuition: $5310 full-time. Nonresident tuition: $13,275 full-time. Mandatory fees: $1521 full-time. Full-time tuition and fees vary according to course load and student level. College room and board: $5560. College room only: $3058. Room and board charges vary according to board plan and housing facility. Special program-related fees: $3–$75 per course for studio materials, $50 per course for model fees.

Financial Aid Program-specific awards: 5–7 talent scholarships for incoming students ($1000), 2 Mitchell Scholarships for incoming students from southern Illinois ($1000), 2–4 Celine A. Chu Memorial Scholarships for junior and senior painting, drawing, printmaking majors ($500), 2–10 Rickert Ziebold Trust Awards for graduating seniors ($2000–$10,000).

Application Procedures Students apply for admission into the professional program by sophomore year. Deadline for freshmen and transfers: continuous. Notification date for freshmen and transfers: continuous. Required: high school transcript, college transcript(s) for transfer students, portfolio, SAT I or ACT test scores (minimum composite ACT score of 20), minimum 2.0 college GPA for transfer students. Portfolio reviews held twice on campus.

Web Site http://www.artanddesign.siu.edu

Undergraduate Contact Ms. Joyce Jolliff, Academic Advisor, School of Art and Design, Southern Illinois University Carbondale, Carbondale, Illinois 62901-4301; 618-453-4313, fax: 618-453-7710, e-mail address: jjolliff@siu.edu

Southern Illinois University Carbondale (continued)

Graduate Contact Mr. Edward Shay, Graduate Program Head, School of Art and Design, Southern Illinois University Carbondale, Carbondale, Illinois 62901-4301; 618-453-8635, fax: 618-453-7710, e-mail address: shay@siu.edu

Southern Illinois University Edwardsville

Edwardsville, Illinois

State-supported, coed. Suburban campus. Total enrollment: 13,460. Art program established 1958.

Meadows School of the Arts
Southern Methodist University

Dallas, Texas

Independent, coed. Suburban campus. Total enrollment: 11,152. Art program established 1939.

Degrees Bachelor of Fine Arts in the area of art. Majors and concentrations: ceramics, drawing, painting, photography, printmaking, sculpture. Graduate degrees offered: Master of Fine Arts in the area of art. Program accredited by NASAD.

Enrollment 85 total; 75 undergraduate, 10 graduate.

Art Student Profile 59% females, 41% males, 22% minorities, 5% international.

Art Faculty 12 total (full-time), 4 total (part-time). 90% of full-time faculty have terminal degrees. Graduate students do not teach undergraduate courses. Undergraduate student–faculty ratio: 6:1.

Student Life Student groups/activities include Student Art Association, Meadows Graduate Council, Pollock Gallery. Special housing available for art students.

Expenses for 2006–2007 Application fee: $50. Comprehensive fee: $38,325 includes full-time tuition ($25,400), mandatory fees ($3230), and college room and board ($9695). College room

only: $5775. Special program-related fees: $30 per credit hour for model and supply fees.

Financial Aid Program-specific awards: 10–15 Meadows Artistic Scholarships for talented program majors ($1000–$6000).

Application Procedures Students apply for admission into the professional program by sophomore year. Deadline for freshmen and transfers: continuous. Required: essay, high school transcript, college transcript(s) for transfer students, letter of recommendation, SAT I or ACT test scores. Recommended: interview, portfolio. Portfolio reviews held once on campus; the submission of slides may be substituted for portfolios (slides preferred).

Web Site http://smu.edu/meadows/art/

Undergraduate Contact Tommy Newton, Director of Recruitment, Meadows School of the Arts, Southern Methodist University, PO Box 750356, Dallas, Texas 75275-0356; 214-768-4067, fax: 214-768-3272, e-mail address: tnewton@smu.edu

Graduate Contact Ms. Jean Cherry, Director of Graduate Admissions, Meadows School of the Arts, Southern Methodist University, PO Box 750356, Dallas, Texas 75275-0356; 214-768-3765, fax: 214-768-3272, e-mail address: jcherry@smu.edu

Southern Oregon University

Ashland, Oregon

State-supported, coed. Small town campus. Total enrollment: 4,977. Art program established 1983.

Degrees Bachelor of Fine Arts. Majors and concentrations: ceramics, digital art and design, painting/drawing, photography, printmaking, sculpture. Cross-registration with members of the National Student Exchange Program.

Enrollment 271 total; 21 undergraduate, 250 nonprofessional degree.

Art Student Profile 50% females, 50% males, 10% minorities, 10% international.

Art Faculty 10 undergraduate (full-time), 6 undergraduate (part-time). 90% of full-time faculty have terminal degrees. Graduate students do not teach undergraduate courses. Undergraduate student–faculty ratio: 2:1.

Student Life Student groups/activities include Schneider Museum of Art, student gallery management programs, Southern Oregon Fine Art Students.

Expenses for 2006–2007 Application fee: $50. State resident tuition: $4986 full-time. Nonresident tuition: $14,691 full-time. College room and board: $6468. Special program-related fees: $5–$100 per course for lab/materials fees.

Financial Aid Program-specific awards: 1 Mulling Award in Art for art majors demonstrating artistic ability ($500), 1 Schneider Merit Award in Art for art majors demonstrating artistic ability ($1000), 1–4 John Humbird Dickey Memorial Scholarships for art majors demonstrating artistic ability and financial need ($1000), 1 anonymous art award for art majors demonstrating artistic ability ($100), 1 Sam and Helen Bernstein Award for artistically talented students ($200).

Application Procedures Students apply for admission into the professional program by sophomore year. Deadline for freshmen and transfers: continuous. Notification date for freshmen and transfers: continuous. Required: high school transcript, college transcript(s) for transfer students, minimum 3.0 high school GPA, portfolio, SAT I or ACT test scores. Portfolio reviews held twice on campus; the submission of slides may be substituted for portfolios for transfer applicants.

Web Site http://www.sou.edu/art/

Undergraduate Contact Mara Affre, Director, Admissions and Records Department, Southern Oregon University, 1250 Siskiyou Boulevard, Ashland, Oregon 97520; 541-552-6411, fax: 541-552-6614.

State University of New York at Buffalo

Buffalo, New York

State-supported, coed. Total enrollment: 27,220. Art program established 1954.

Degrees Bachelor of Fine Arts in the area of fine art. Majors and concentrations: communication design, computer art, painting/drawing, photography, printmaking, sculpture. Graduate degrees offered: Master of Fine Arts in the area of fine art. Cross-registration with State University of New York College at Buffalo. Program accredited by NASAD.

Enrollment 257 total; 196 undergraduate, 22 graduate, 39 nonprofessional degree.

Art Student Profile 61% females, 39% males, 18% minorities, 6% international.

Art Faculty 15 total (full-time), 20 total (part-time). 86% of full-time faculty have terminal degrees. Graduate students teach a few undergraduate courses. Undergraduate student–faculty ratio: 19:1.

Student Life Student groups/activities include Art Department Gallery exhibits, University Gallery exhibits, Student Visual Art Organization.

Expenses for 2005–2006 Application fee: $40. State resident tuition: $4350 full-time. Nonresident tuition: $10,610 full-time. Mandatory fees: $1718 full-time. College room and board: $7626. College room only: $4636. Room and board charges vary according to board plan and housing facility. Special program-related fees: $20–$100 per course for lab fees, supplies, models.

Financial Aid Program-specific awards: 1 Julius Bloom Memorial Scholarship for graphic arts or graphic design students ($350), 1 Dennis Domkowski Memorial Scholarship for communication design program students ($350), 1 Rumsey Summer Scholarship for junior art majors ($2000), 8 Morrison Scholarships for art majors demonstrating financial need ($1500), 1 Elliott Painting Scholarship for painting juniors ($500–$600), 1 Sentz Award for art major ($450), 2 Eugene L. Gaier Excellence in Printmaking Awards for students in printmaking ($250), 1 Eugene L. Gaier Excellence in Drawing Award for drawing students ($500), 1 Sentz Award for art majors ($450), 1 Cober Award for drawing students ($500), 1 Townsend Award for photo students ($500).

Application Procedures Students admitted directly into the professional program freshman year. Deadline for freshmen: April 15; transfers: October 30. Notification date for freshmen: May 1; transfers: November 15. Required: college transcript(s) for transfer students, portfolio, SAT I or ACT test scores, portfolio review after freshman year for admission to department. Recommended: essay. Portfolio reviews held 5 times on campus and off campus at National Portfolio Days;

State University of New York at Buffalo (continued)

Rochester or Syracuse NY; Toronto, CAN; Cleveland, OH; Sarasota, FL; the submission of slides may be substituted for portfolios if a campus visit is impossible.

Web Site http://www.art.buffalo.edu

Undergraduate Contact Mr. Kim James Yarwood, Academic Advisor, Department of Art, State University of New York at Buffalo, 202 Center for the Arts, Buffalo, New York 14260-6010; 716-645-6000 ext. 1371, fax: 716-645-6970, e-mail address: yarwood@acsu.buffalo.edu

Graduate Contact Mr. Reinhard Reitzestein, Director of Graduate Studies, Department of Art, State University of New York at Buffalo, 202 Center for the Arts, Buffalo, New York 14260-6010; 716-645-6878 ext. 1353, fax: 716-645-6970.

State University of New York at New Paltz

New Paltz, New York

State-supported, coed. Small town campus. Total enrollment: 7,825. Art program established 1960.

State University of New York at Plattsburgh

Plattsburgh, New York

State-supported, coed. Small town campus. Total enrollment: 6,044.

Degrees Bachelor of Fine Arts in the area of art. Majors and concentrations: studio art. Cross-registration with Clinton Community College, State University of New York Empire State College.

Enrollment 246 total; all undergraduate.

Art Student Profile 61% females, 39% males, 7% minorities, 5% international.

Art Faculty 10 undergraduate (full-time), 5 undergraduate (part-time). 100% of full-time faculty have terminal degrees. Graduate students do not teach undergraduate courses. Undergraduate student–faculty ratio: 20:1.

Student Life Student groups/activities include campus student exhibits, on-campus workshops presented by renowned artists, critics, and historians, off-campus field trips.

Expenses for 2006–2007 Application fee: $40. State resident tuition: $4350 full-time. Nonresident tuition: $10,610 full-time. Mandatory fees: $946 full-time. College room and board: $7066. College room only: $4400. Special program-related fees: $15–$35 per studio course for specialized lab/equipment fees.

Financial Aid Program-specific awards: 15 Winkel Awards for art students ($200–$1000), 1 Glauhinger Award for sculpture students ($3400), 1 Parnass Award for photography students ($2000).

Application Procedures Students admitted directly into the professional program freshman year. Deadline for freshmen and transfers: continuous. Required: high school transcript, college transcript(s) for transfer students, minimum 3.0 high school GPA, portfolio, SAT I or ACT test scores (minimum combined SAT I score of 900, minimum composite ACT score of 19). Recommended: essay, interview, 2-3 letters of recommendation. Portfolio reviews held continuously on campus; the submission of slides may be substituted for portfolios.

Web Site http://www.plattsburgh.edu/art

Undergraduate Contact Richard J. Higgins, Director, Admissions, State University of New York at Plattsburgh, 101 Broad Street, Kehoe Administration Building, Plattsburgh, New York 12901; 518-564-2040, e-mail address: higginrj@plattsburgh.edu

State University of New York, Fredonia

Fredonia, New York

State-supported, coed. Small town campus. Total enrollment: 5,432. Art program established 1968.

Degrees Bachelor of Fine Arts in the areas of drawing, painting, sculpture, ceramics, illustration, photography, graphic design, media arts. Majors and concentrations: ceramics, drawing, graphic design, illustration, media arts, painting, photography, sculpture.

Enrollment 260 total; 55 undergraduate, 205 nonprofessional degree.

Art Student Profile 55% females, 45% males, 1% minorities, 2% international.

Art Faculty 13 undergraduate (full-time), 7 undergraduate (part-time). 100% of full-time faculty have terminal degrees. Graduate students do not teach undergraduate courses. Undergraduate student–faculty ratio: 14:1.

Student Life Student groups/activities include Art Forum, AIGA, Media Arts.

Expenses for 2005–2006 Application fee: $40. State resident tuition: $4350 full-time. Nonresident tuition: $10,610 full-time. Mandatory fees: $1091 full-time. College room and board: $6940. College room only: $4350. Room and board charges vary according to board plan and housing facility. Special program-related fees: $10–$70 per course for lab fees.

Financial Aid Program-specific awards: 5 departmental scholarships for talented students ($350), 1 George W. Booth Award for incoming freshmen ($2000).

Application Procedures Students apply for admission into the professional program by junior year. Deadline for freshmen and transfers: continuous. Required: essay, high school transcript, college transcript(s) for transfer students, portfolio, SAT I or ACT test scores. Recommended: minimum 3.0 high school GPA, 3 letters of recommendation, interview. Portfolio reviews held by appointment on campus; the submission of slides may be substituted for portfolios (slides preferred).

Web Site http://www.fredonia.edu/department/art/

Undergraduate Contact Ms. Elizabeth Lee, Chair, Department of Visual Arts and New Media, State University of New York, Fredonia, Rockefeller Center, Fredonia, New York 14063; 716-673-3537, fax: 716-673-4990, e-mail address: elizabeth.lee@fredonia.edu

Stephen F. Austin State University

Nacogdoches, Texas

State-supported, coed. Small town campus. Total enrollment: 11,435. Art program established 1923.

Degrees Bachelor of Fine Arts in the area of art. Majors and concentrations: advertising design, art education, ceramics, digital media, drawing, film, metals and jewelry, painting, photography, printmaking, sculpture, studio art. Graduate degrees offered: Master of Fine Arts in the area of art. Program accredited by NASAD.

Enrollment 301 total; 258 undergraduate, 32 graduate, 11 nonprofessional degree.

Art Student Profile 45% females, 55% males, 5% minorities.

Art Faculty 17 total (full-time), 4 total (part-time). 100% of full-time faculty have terminal degrees. Graduate students teach a few undergraduate courses. Undergraduate student–faculty ratio: 18:1.

Student Life Student groups/activities include Art Alliance (student art group), Ad Hoc Student Advertising Design Group, Art Metal Jewelry Society, The F-Stops Here (Photography).

Expenses for 2005–2006 Application fee: $25. State resident tuition: $4718 full-time. Nonresident tuition: $12,998 full-time. Full-time tuition varies according to course load. College room and board: $5459. Room and board charges vary according to board plan and housing facility. Special program-related fees: $19–$157 per course for supplies, instrumental support (lab monitors, etc.).

Financial Aid Program-specific awards: 8–12 art scholarships for program majors ($250–$1000).

Application Procedures Students admitted directly into the professional program freshman year. Deadline for freshmen and transfers: August 15. Required: high school transcript, college transcript(s) for transfer students, SAT I or ACT test scores. Recommended: minimum 3.0 high school GPA, portfolio. Portfolio reviews held 6 times on campus and off campus in Dallas, TX; Houston, TX; the submission of slides may be substituted for portfolios if originals or CDs are not available.

Web Site http://www.art.sfasu.edu

Contact Dr. David A. Lewis, Chairman, Department of Art, Stephen F. Austin State University, Box 13001 SFA Station, Nacogdoches, Texas 75962-3001; 936-468-4804, fax: 936-468-4041, e-mail address: dlewis@sfasu.edu

Stephens College

Columbia, Missouri

Independent, Urban campus. Total enrollment: 824. Art program established 1954.

Degrees Bachelor of Fine Arts. Majors and concentrations: fashion design, graphic design, interior design. Cross-registration with Mid-Missouri Associated Colleges and Universities.

Enrollment 155 total; all undergraduate.

Art Student Profile 100% females, 17% minorities.

Art Faculty 5 undergraduate (full-time), 5 undergraduate (part-time). 80% of full-time faculty have terminal degrees. Graduate students do not teach undergraduate courses. Undergraduate student–faculty ratio: 12:1.

Student Life Student groups/activities include Pi Phi Rho (fashion honorary society), Innovative Fashion Association (all fashion majors).

Expenses for 2006–2007 Application fee: $25. Comprehensive fee: $28,475 includes full-time tuition ($20,500) and college room and board ($7975). College room only: $4760. Special program-related fees: $20–$150 per course for lab fee.

Financial Aid Program-specific awards: 1 Gardner Nettleton Endowed Scholarship for outstanding art and graphic students ($3500).

Application Procedures Students admitted directly into the professional program freshman year. Deadline for freshmen and transfers: July 31. Notification date for freshmen and transfers: continuous. Required: essay, high school transcript, college transcript(s) for transfer students, minimum 2.0 high school GPA, letter of recommendation, SAT I or ACT test scores (minimum combined SAT I score of 1090, minimum composite ACT score of 21). Recommended: minimum 3.0 high school GPA, interview, portfolio. Portfolio reviews held as needed for advanced placement on campus; the submission of slides may be substituted for portfolios if original work is not available.

Web Site http://www.stephens.edu

Undergraduate Contact Office of Admission, Stephens College, Campus Box 2121, Columbia, Missouri 65215; 800-876-7207, fax: 573-876-7237, e-mail address: apply@stephens.edu

The New England School of Art & Design
Suffolk University

Boston, Massachusetts

Independent, coed. Urban campus. Total enrollment: 8,474. Art program established 1923.

Degrees Bachelor of Fine Arts in the areas of fine arts, graphic design, interior design. Majors and concentrations: art/fine arts, graphic design, interior design. Graduate degrees offered: Master of Arts in the areas of interior design, graphic design. Program accredited by NASAD, FIDER.

Enrollment 311 total; 176 undergraduate, 103 graduate, 32 nonprofessional degree.

Art Student Profile 72% females, 28% males, 5% minorities, 18% international.

Art Faculty 16 undergraduate (full-time), 48 undergraduate (part-time), 2 graduate (full-time), 6 graduate (part-time). 91% of full-time faculty have terminal degrees. Graduate students do not teach undergraduate courses. Undergraduate student–faculty ratio: 8:1.

Student Life Student groups/activities include American Society of Interior Designers Student Chapter, International Interior Design Association Student Chapter, American Institute of Graphic Arts (AIGA).

Expenses for 2005–2006 Application fee: $50. Comprehensive fee: $33,160 includes full-time tuition ($21,140), mandatory fees ($80), and college room and board ($11,940). College room only: $10,020. Room and board charges vary according to board plan and housing facility. Special program-related fees: $140 per course for studio fee.

Financial Aid Program-specific awards: 2–4 J.W.S. Cox Scholarships for those demonstrating talent ($1000–$2000), 1–2 Peter and Gretchen Paige Scholarships for those demonstrating talent ($4000–$5000), 2–4 Schrafft Scholarships Program for Boston residents ($2000–$3000).

Application Procedures Students admitted directly into the professional program freshman year. Deadline for freshmen and transfers: continuous. Required: essay, high school transcript, college transcript(s) for transfer students, minimum 2.0 high school GPA, 2 letters of recommendation, portfolio, SAT I or ACT test scores. Recommended: interview. Portfolio reviews held continuously on campus and off campus at National Portfolio Days; the submission of slides may be substituted for portfolios whenever needed.

Web Site http://www.suffolk.edu/nesad

Undergraduate Contact Ms. Yvette Velez, Associate Director of Admission, Undergraduate Admission, Suffolk University, 8 Ashburton Place, Boston, Massachusetts 02108; 617-573-8460, fax: 617-742-4291, e-mail address: yvelez@suffolk.edu

Graduate Contact Ms. Judith Reynolds, Director of Admission, Graduate Admission, Suffolk University, 8 Ashburton Place, Boston, Massachusetts 02108; 617-573-8302, fax: 617-523-0116, e-mail address: jreynold@suffolk.edu

Sul Ross State University

Alpine, Texas

State-supported, coed. Small town campus. Total enrollment: 1,954 (2003). Art program established 1923.

Degrees Bachelor of Fine Arts in the areas of art, art education. Majors and concentrations: art education, art history, art/fine arts, ceramic art and design, glass, painting/drawing, photography, printmaking, rock art studies, sculpture, studio art. Graduate degrees offered: Master of Arts in the areas of art, art education; Master of Education in the areas of art, art education. Cross-registration with University of Texas at El Paso, University of Texas of the Permian Basin, Odessa College, South Plains College, El Paso Community College, Midland College.

Enrollment 39 total; 24 undergraduate, 15 graduate.

Art Student Profile 47% females, 53% males, 45% minorities, 1% international.

Art Faculty 3 total (full-time), 2 total (part-time). 100% of full-time faculty have terminal degrees. Graduate students do not teach undergraduate courses. Undergraduate student–faculty ratio: 12:1.

Student Life Student groups/activities include Art Club, student art show, Kappa Pi (art fraternity).

Expenses for 2005–2006 Special program-related fees: $35 per 3 credits for plaster and clay for sculpture classes, $35 per 3 credits for

clay and glazes for ceramics classes, $40 per 3 credits for welding supplies, $40 per 3 credits for bronze, wax, and ceramic shell for casting.

Financial Aid Program-specific awards: 6 Boatright Scholarships for program students ($150–$300), 3 art excellence awards for program students ($300), 2 Sarah Milfia Hill Memorial Scholarship Fund Awards for program students ($200), 1 Mary E. Thain Award for program students ($150).

Application Procedures Students admitted directly into the professional program freshman year. Deadline for freshmen and transfers: continuous. Required: high school transcript, college transcript(s) for transfer students, minimum 2.0 high school GPA, portfolio, SAT I or ACT test scores (minimum combined SAT I score of 800, minimum composite ACT score of 20). Recommended: interview. Portfolio reviews held once on campus; the submission of slides may be substituted for portfolios with some original work.

Web Site http://www.sulross.edu/

Undergraduate Contact Robert C. Cullins, Director of Admissions, Sul Ross State University, Box C-2, Alpine, Texas 79832; 915-837-8050.

Graduate Contact Linda Coleman, Director of Graduate Admissions, Sul Ross State University, Box C-2, Alpine, Texas 79832; 915-837-8050.

Syracuse University

Syracuse, New York

Independent, coed. Urban campus. Total enrollment: 17,266. Art program established 1873.

Degrees Bachelor of Fine Arts in the areas of advertising design, art education, ceramics, computer art, communication design, fiber structure/interlocking, history of art, interior design, jewelry/metalsmithing, painting, photography, printmaking, sculpture, surface pattern design, illustration, film; Bachelor of Industrial Design in the area of industrial and interaction design; Bachelor of Science in the area of environmental design. Majors and concentrations: advertising design, art education, art history, ceramics, communication design, computer art, environmental design, fashion design, fibers, film, illustration, industrial design, interior design, jewelry and

Syracuse University (continued)

metalsmithing, painting/drawing, photography, printmaking, sculpture, surface design, textile design, video art. Graduate degrees offered: Master of Fine Arts in the areas of advertising design, ceramics, computer arts, fiber structure and interlocking, film, illustration, interior design, jewelry and metalsmithing, museum studies, painting, photography, printmaking, sculpture, surface pattern design, video; Master of Industrial Design. Program accredited by NASAD, FIDER.

Enrollment 1,403 total; 1,259 undergraduate, 144 graduate.

Art Student Profile 66% females, 34% males, 13% minorities.

Art Faculty 67 total (full-time), 43 total (part-time). 88% of full-time faculty have terminal degrees. Graduate students teach a few undergraduate courses. Undergraduate student–faculty ratio: 18:1.

Student Life Student groups/activities include American Society of Interior Designers, Industrial Design Society of America, New York Society of Illustrators.

Expenses for 2005–2006 Application fee: $60. Comprehensive fee: $38,655 includes full-time tuition ($27,210), mandatory fees ($1075), and college room and board ($10,370). College room only: $5620. Room and board charges vary according to board plan and housing facility. Special program-related fees: $10–$150 per semester for lab fees to cover costs of models and special supplies.

Financial Aid Program-specific awards: art merit scholarships for incoming freshmen ($4000), 1 National Scholastic Award for Art National Scholarship winners ($2000).

Application Procedures Students admitted directly into the professional program freshman year. Deadline for freshmen and transfers: January 1. Notification date for freshmen: March 1; transfers: August 15. Required: essay, high school transcript, college transcript(s) for transfer students, minimum 3.0 high school GPA, 2 letters of recommendation, portfolio, SAT I or ACT test scores, high school counselor evaluation. Recommended: interview. Portfolio reviews held continuously on campus and off campus in New York, NY; Boston, MA; Philadelphia, PA; Baltimore, MD; Hartford, CT;

Chicago, IL; the submission of slides may be substituted for portfolios when distance is prohibited.

Web Site http://vpa.syr.edu/

Undergraduate Contact Director, CVPA Recruitment and Admissions, College of Visual and Performing Arts, Syracuse University, 202P Crouse College, Syracuse, New York 13244-1010; 315-443-2769, fax: 315-443-1935, e-mail address: admissu@syr.edu

Graduate Contact Graduate School, Syracuse University, Suite 303 Bowne Hall, Syracuse, New York 13244; 315-443-3028, fax: 315-443-3423, e-mail address: gradschl@syr.edu

More About the School

The School of Art and Design has a tradition of excellence that goes back more than 100 years. In fact, Syracuse University was the first university in the country to grant a Bachelor of Fine Arts (B.F.A.) degree. The School of Art and Design and Department of Transmedia encourage students to reach their creative and intellectual potential and prepare them as professional artists, designers, and educators. All students in the Bachelor of Fine Arts and Bachelor of Industrial Design (B.I.D.) degree programs start with a one-year foundation program that offers studio work and academic courses in art and design history and writing, plus an academic and/or studio elective. In the sophomore year, students begin specialization toward their major; typically, each semester, they take studio courses in their major, studio electives, and/or academic electives or requirements. The studio electives allow them to experiment in disciplines and media outside the major. The academic electives may be selected from the broad range of courses offered by the University.

The School of Art and Design includes a program in environmental design that leads to a B.S. degree and requires a portfolio for entry.

Students benefit from a faculty of practicing professionals whose work is included in the permanent collections of the Smithsonian; the Art Institute of Chicago; the International Polaroid Collection in Cambridge, Massachusetts; the Museum of Fine Art in Houston; the Museum of Modern Art in New York City; the National Gallery of Canada in Ottawa, Ontario; the Gallerie Degli Uffici in Florence, Italy; and the Museo Nacional Centro de Arte Reina Sofia in Madrid, Spain. Faculty members have also contributed to such publications as *Time*, *Esquire*, *Life*, the *New York Times*, the *Washington Post*, *Audubon Magazine*, and *National Lampoon*. Their

Our world can be your stage.

 Roger Williams University
Learning to Bridge the World

 50TH 1956 2006 **ANNIVERSARY**

Office of Undergraduate Admission
One Old Ferry Road
Bristol, RI 02809-2921

1-866-570-8173
admit@rwu.edu
www.rwu.edu

Creativity flourishes at Roger Williams University, a leading liberal arts university in New England.

Refine your writing, visual arts skills and performance techniques, energized by our beautiful 140-acre waterfront campus in historic Bristol, Rhode Island, easily accessible from Boston and New York.

Accredited by the New England Association of Schools and Colleges, Roger Williams University draws 3,650 full-time undergraduates who benefit from a dedicated faculty and an ideal academic setting with excellent facilities, recreation, athletics, and social opportunities. The Roger Williams education produces well-rounded students who successfully bridge transitions to a rewarding career and gratifying life.

The Theatre Program
The Roger Williams Theatre Program is unique in the range and breadth of its areas of study, offering you the opportunity to major in Theatre, leading to a Bachelor of Arts degree.

Creative Writing Program
Roger Williams University is one of the few colleges and universities in the United States to offer an undergraduate major in Creative Writing, leading to a Bachelor of Fine Arts degree.

Dance Performance Studies
The University offers courses in technique, choreography, history, pedagogy, movement analysis, performance techniques, and movement theatre (we are the only dance-based university program in the country to offer this training).

Graphic Design Communications
This program consists of a contemporary blend of a liberal arts education and applied technology. Students draw on their complete educational experience to create images and visual messages that are thought-provoking, well-researched, and technically excellent.

Visual Arts Studies
Our School of Architecture, Art and Historic Preservation offers the Bachelor of Arts degree in Visual Arts Studies. You can develop your talents in one of the following disciplines: Painting/Drawing/Printmaking, Sculpture, or Photography/Digital Media.

work is commissioned by clients in the United States and abroad, and many publish and exhibit in Europe and Asia.

An extensive network of active and successful alumni, comprehensive visiting artist programs, well-known faculty members, and University programs and organizations all contribute to the internship and professional opportunities for students.

The city of Syracuse itself offers a rich culture of its own. The Everson Museum of Art houses one of the foremost ceramic collections in the United States and offers a diverse exhibition schedule. The Syracuse Symphony Orchestra, the Syracuse Opera, and the Society for New Music, as well as nationally known comedians, rock groups, and dance companies, perform frequently. Nestled between the Finger Lakes and the Adirondacks, Syracuse is within a day's drive of New York City, Boston, Philadelphia, Toronto, and Montreal.

Program Facilities Comstock Art Facility: studios for ceramics, fibers, jewelry and metalsmithing, printmaking, and sculpture and three-dimensional design studios; Crouse College: drawing and design studios and classrooms; Dorothea Ilgen Shaffer Art Building: Joe and Emily Lowe Art Gallery; Shemin auditorium (300 seats); Green & Seifter Lecture Hall (60 seats); facilities for fashion design, textile design, surface pattern design, illustration, art photography, art video, computer art, film, drawing, and painting; and individual painting studios for undergraduates; Smith Hall (Center for Design): studios for industrial and interaction design, interior design, and environmental design; Lyman Hall: studios for fashion design; M-17 Skytop Building: art education program facilities; the Warehouse: facilities for advertising design and communications design.

Faculty, Resident Artists, and Alumni Faculty members are well-established professional artists and designers who are active locally, nationally, and internationally; several are Guggenheim, Pulitzer, and Fulbright fellows and recipients of grants from the National Endowment for the Arts, Ford Foundation, and the Rockefeller Foundation. Alumni are prestigious figures in the museum and gallery world who exhibit locally, nationally, and internationally as well as professionals and executives in prominent agencies, firms, and corporations.

Student Exhibit Opportunities Exhibit space is in the Joe and Emily Lowe Art Gallery, the Comstock Art Facility, Smith Hall, the Shaffer Art Building, Crouse College, and the Schine Student Center.

Special Programs Weekly visiting artist programs in studio arts and visual communication feature lectures and critiques of student work and are open to all. Students may study abroad in Florence, Barcelona, or London, through SU Abroad. Internships are available through the Syracuse University Internship Program and the Career Services Center at galleries, museums, newspapers and magazines, design agencies, and local television stations. An honors program is available for students who desire a rigorous academic challenge.

Temple University, Tyler School of Art

See Tyler School of Art of Temple University

Tennessee Technological University

See Appalachian Center for Craft

Texas A&M University–Commerce

Commerce, Texas

State-supported, coed. Small town campus. Total enrollment: 8,787.

Degrees Bachelor of Arts; Bachelor of Fine Arts in the areas of design communications, new media, art direction, studio art; Bachelor of Science. Majors and concentrations: art, art direction, art education, ceramics, design communication, experimental studies, illustration, new media, painting, photography, printmaking, sculpture, studio art. Graduate degrees offered: Master of Fine Arts in the areas of sculpture, painting, ceramics, illustration, experimental studies, photography. Cross-registration with University of North Texas, Texas Woman's University.

Enrollment 359 total; 335 undergraduate, 24 graduate.

Art Student Profile 65% females, 35% males, 4% minorities, 5% international.

Art Faculty 18 undergraduate (part-time), 9 total (full-time). 98% of full-time faculty have terminal degrees. Graduate students do not teach undergraduate courses. Undergraduate student–faculty ratio: 14:1.

Texas A&M University–Commerce (continued)

Student Life Student groups/activities include Students Art Association, Photo Society, Clay Club.

Expenses for 2005–2006 Application fee: 25. State resident tuition: $3834 full-time. Nonresident tuition: $11,574 full-time. Mandatory fees: $990 full-time. Full-time tuition and fees vary according to course load. College room and board: $5740. Room and board charges vary according to board plan and housing facility. Special program-related fees: $5–$50 per semester for instruction and curriculum fee.

Financial Aid Program-specific awards: 7–12 endowed scholarships for program majors ($200–$500).

Application Procedures Students apply for admission into the professional program by sophomore year. Deadline for freshmen: August 15; transfers: August 19. Required: high school transcript, college transcript(s) for transfer students, SAT I or ACT test scores, portfolio for transfer students. Portfolio reviews held by request on campus; the submission of slides may be substituted for portfolios if of good quality.

Web Site http://www.tamu-commerce.edu/art

Undergraduate Contact Stan Godwin, Head, Department of Art, Texas A&M University–Commerce, PO Box 3011, Commerce, Texas 75429-3011; 903-886-5234, fax: 903-886-5987, e-mail address: stan_godwin@tamu-commerce.edu

Graduate Contact Mr. Michael Miller, Graduate Coordinator, Department of Art, Texas A&M University–Commerce, PO Box 3011, Commerce, Texas 75429-3011; 903-886-5208, fax: 903-886-5987, e-mail address: michael_miller@tamu-commerce.edu

Texas A&M University– Corpus Christi

Corpus Christi, Texas

State-supported, coed. Suburban campus. Total enrollment: 8,227.

Degrees Bachelor of Fine Arts. Majors and concentrations: art education, studio art.

Graduate degrees offered: Master of Fine Arts in the area of studio art.

Art Faculty 10 total (full-time), 10 total (part-time). 90% of full-time faculty have terminal degrees. Graduate students do not teach undergraduate courses.

Student Life Student groups/activities include Student Art Association.

Expenses for 2005–2006 Application fee: $20. State resident tuition: $3348 full-time. Nonresident tuition: $11,628 full-time. Mandatory fees: $1168 full-time. Full-time tuition and fees vary according to course load. College room and board: $7800. College room only: $5400. Room and board charges vary according to housing facility. Special program-related fees: $25–$65 per course for art material fees.

Financial Aid Program-specific awards: Fine Arts Studio Scholarships for program majors ($500–$2000).

Application Procedures Students apply for admission into the professional program by junior year. Required: essay, high school transcript, college transcript(s) for transfer students, minimum 2.0 high school GPA, portfolio, SAT I or ACT test scores, completion of college preparatory courses. Recommended: minimum 3.0 high school GPA, letter of recommendation. Portfolio reviews held twice on campus; the submission of slides may be substituted for portfolios if accompanied by a slide list and descriptions.

Web Site http://www.tamucc.edu

Undergraduate Contact Prof. Jack Gron, Chair, Department of Art, Texas A&M University–Corpus Christi, 6300 Ocean Drive, Unit 5721, Corpus Christi, Texas 78412-5721; 361-825-2317, fax: 361-825-6097.

Graduate Contact Dr. Carey Rote, Graduate Program Coordinator, Professor, Department of Art, Texas A&M University–Corpus Christi, 6300 Ocean Drive, Unit 5721, Corpus Christi, Texas 78412-5721; 361-825-2372, fax: 361-825-6097, e-mail address: carey.rote@mail.tamucc.edu

Texas A&M University–Kingsville

Kingsville, Texas

State-supported, coed. Small town campus. Total enrollment: 7,126. Art program established 1959.

Texas Christian University

Fort Worth, Texas

Independent, coed. Suburban campus. Total enrollment: 8,749. Art program established 1884.

Texas Southern University

Houston, Texas

State-supported, coed. Urban campus. Total enrollment: 11,903. Art program established 1948.

Texas State University-San Marcos

San Marcos, Texas

State-supported, coed. Suburban campus. Total enrollment: 27,129. Art program established 1940.

Degrees Bachelor of Fine Arts in the areas of studio art, communication design, art education, art history, digital photographic imaging. Majors and concentrations: art education, art history, ceramics, communication design, digital imaging, drawing, fibers, metals, painting, photography, printmaking, sculpture, watercolors.

Enrollment 1,000 total; 850 undergraduate, 150 nonprofessional degree.

Art Student Profile 54% females, 46% males, 27% minorities, 1% international.

Art Faculty 25 undergraduate (full-time), 28 undergraduate (part-time). 89% of full-time faculty have terminal degrees. Graduate students do not teach undergraduate courses. Undergraduate student–faculty ratio: 20:1.

Student Life Student groups/activities include Metals Guild, CASA-Ceramics Organization, AIGA-National Communication Design Organization, In Focus (photography), Art Education Association, FASA (Fine Art Student Association).

Expenses for 2005–2006 Application fee: $40. State resident tuition: $3780 full-time. Nonresident tuition: $12,060 full-time. Mandatory fees: $1472 full-time. Full-time tuition and fees vary according to course load. College room and board: $5610. College room only: $3524. Room and board charges vary according to board plan and housing facility. Special program-related fees: $15–$55 per course for material fees.

Financial Aid Program-specific awards: 2 Dr. Francis Henry Scholarships for art education majors ($500), 1 Louise Eckerd McGehee Scholarship for program majors ($500), 8–12 student services fee scholarships for program majors ($200–$400), 1 Presidential Upper-Level Scholarship for program majors ($1200), 1 Turner Endowed Scholarship for painting majors ($500), 1 Department of Art and Design Scholarship for program majors ($500), 1 Barbara Shimkus Endowed Scholarship for communication design majors ($500), 1 Art History Scholarship ($500).

Application Procedures Students admitted directly into the professional program freshman year. Deadline for freshmen and transfers: July 1. Required: high school transcript, college transcript(s) for transfer students, minimum 3.0 high school GPA, SAT I or ACT test scores.

Web Site http://www.finearts.swt.edu/finearts.html

Undergraduate Contact Veronica Fernandez, Academic Advisor, Department of Art and Design, Texas State University-San Marcos, 601 University Drive, San Marcos, Texas 78666; 512-245-2611, fax: 512-245-7969, e-mail address: km31@swt.edu

Texas Tech University

Lubbock, Texas

State-supported, coed. Urban campus. Total enrollment: 28,001. Art program established 1967.

Texas Tech University (continued)

Degrees Bachelor of Fine Arts in the areas of studio art, design communication, visual studies. Majors and concentrations: ceramics, communication design, jewelry and metalsmithing, painting/drawing, photography, printmaking, sculpture, visual studies. Graduate degrees offered: Master of Fine Arts in the area of art. Doctor of Arts in the area of fine arts. Program accredited by NASAD.

Enrollment 452 total; 400 undergraduate, 32 graduate, 20 nonprofessional degree.

Art Student Profile 54% females, 46% males, 18% minorities, 1% international.

Art Faculty 29 total (full-time), 14 total (part-time). 93% of full-time faculty have terminal degrees. Graduate students teach a few undergraduate courses. Undergraduate student–faculty ratio: 11:1.

Student Life Student groups/activities include National Art Education Association Student Chapter, Design Communication Association, Metalsmithing Club.

Expenses for 2005–2006 Application fee: $50. State resident tuition: $3870 full-time. Nonresident tuition: $12,150 full-time. Mandatory fees: $2282 full-time. Full-time tuition and fees vary according to course load, program, and reciprocity agreements. College room and board: $6875. College room only: $3663. Room and board charges vary according to board plan and housing facility. Special program-related fees: $8–$150 per course for art supplies.

Financial Aid Program-specific awards: 20–25 art scholarships for program students ($200–$500), 3–5 H.Y. Price Scholarships for program students ($3000).

Application Procedures Students admitted directly into the professional program freshman year. Deadline for freshmen and transfers: continuous. Notification date for freshmen and transfers: continuous. Required: essay, high school transcript, minimum 2.0 high school GPA, SAT I or ACT test scores, minimum TOEFL score of 550 for international applicants, slides or videotape of portfolio. Portfolio reviews held 4 times on campus and off campus in Junction, TX.

Web Site http://www.art.ttu.edu

Undergraduate Contact Djuana Young, Director, Undergraduate Admissions, Texas Tech University, Box 45005, Lubbock, Texas 79409-5005; 806-742-1482.

Graduate Contact Ann McGlynn, Assistant Dean, Graduate Admissions, Texas Tech University, Box 41030, Lubbock, Texas 79409-1030; 806-742-2787, fax: 806-742-4038.

Texas Woman's University

Denton, Texas

State-supported, coed, primarily women. Suburban campus. Total enrollment: 11,344. Art program established 1903.

Degrees Bachelor of Fine Arts in the areas of painting, photography, ceramics, sculpture, graphic design. Majors and concentrations: art history, ceramic art and design, graphic design, painting/drawing, photography, sculpture. Graduate degrees offered: Master of Arts in the areas of art education, graphic design, art history; Master of Fine Arts in the areas of painting, photography, ceramics, sculpture. Cross-registration with University of North Texas, Texas A&M University-Commerce.

Enrollment 217 total; 120 undergraduate, 65 graduate, 32 nonprofessional degree.

Art Student Profile 85% females, 15% males, 11% minorities, 15% international.

Art Faculty 8 total (full-time), 4 total (part-time). 100% of full-time faculty have terminal degrees. Graduate students teach a few undergraduate courses. Undergraduate student–faculty ratio: 13:1.

Student Life Student groups/activities include Delta Phi Delta, Clay Underground, Photographic Artists Coalition. Special housing available for art students.

Expenses for 2006–2007 Application fee: $30. State resident tuition: $3690 full-time. Nonresident tuition: $11,970 full-time. Mandatory fees: $1320 full-time. College room and board: $5598. College room only: $2804. Special program-related fees: $20–$60 per semester for studio courses.

Financial Aid Program-specific awards: 2–5 Marie Delleney Awards for art majors ($200–$500), 2 Helen Thomas Perry Awards for junior or senior art majors ($1000), 1–3 Hazel

Snodgrass Awards for art majors ($200–$300), 1–2 Ludie Clark Thompson Awards for art majors ($200–$300), 2–4 Noreen Kitsinger Awards for art education majors ($200–$300), 2–5 Sue Comer Awards for art majors ($200–$300), 1–3 Dorothy Laselle Awards for freshmen or sophomore art majors ($300–$400), 6–12 Coreen Spellman Awards for Delta Phi Delta members ($100–$200), 1 J. Brough Miller Scholarship for art majors ($400), 1–2 Rowena Caldwell Elkin Scholarships for art majors ($500–$1000).

Application Procedures Students admitted directly into the professional program freshman year. Deadline for freshmen and transfers: July 15. Notification date for freshmen and transfers: August 1. Required: high school transcript, college transcript(s) for transfer students, minimum 2.0 high school GPA, SAT I or ACT test scores. Recommended: 3 letters of recommendation, interview.

Web Site http://www.twu.edu/as/va

Contact Mr. John Weinkein, Chair, Department of Visual Arts, Texas Woman's University, PO Box 425469, TWU Station, Denton, Texas 76204; 940-898-2530, fax: 940-898-2496, e-mail address: visualarts@twu.edu

Tisch School of the Arts - Department of Photography and Imaging

See New York University

Truman State University

Kirksville, Missouri

State-supported, coed. Small town campus. Total enrollment: 5,803.

Degrees Bachelor of Fine Arts in the areas of studio art, visual communications. Majors and concentrations: art history, ceramic art and design, painting, printmaking, sculpture, textile arts, visual communication. Graduate degrees offered: Master of Art Education.

Enrollment 163 total; 162 undergraduate, 1 graduate.

Art Student Profile 67% females, 33% males, 1% minorities.

Art Faculty 12 total (full-time). 100% of full-time faculty have terminal degrees. Graduate students do not teach undergraduate courses. Undergraduate student–faculty ratio: 14:1.

Student Life Student groups/activities include Student Art History Society, Missouri Art Education Association, Art Club.

Expenses for 2005–2006 Application fee: $0. One-time mandatory fee: $150. State resident tuition: $5740 full-time. Nonresident tuition: $9920 full-time. Mandatory fees: $72 full-time. College room and board: $5380. Room and board charges vary according to housing facility. Special program-related fees: $10–$30 per semester for art supplies.

Financial Aid Program-specific awards: 8 endowed scholarships for outstanding program majors ($500–$1500), 14 service scholarships for program majors ($400–$700).

Application Procedures Students admitted directly into the professional program freshman year. Deadline for freshmen and transfers: May 1. Notification date for freshmen: December 15. Required: essay, high school transcript, college transcript(s) for transfer students, minimum 3.0 high school GPA, portfolio, SAT I or ACT test scores. Portfolio reviews held twice on campus; the submission of slides may be substituted for portfolios when distance is prohibitive.

Web Site http://www.truman.edu

Undergraduate Contact Mr. Robert L. Jones, Head, Division of Fine Arts, Truman State University, 100 East Normal, Ophelia Parrish 1101, Kirksville, Missouri 63501; 660-785-4417, fax: 660-785-7463, e-mail address: finearts@truman.edu

Graduate Contact Prof. Wynne Wilbur, MAE Program Coordinator, Division of Fine Arts, Truman State University, 100 East Normal, Ophelia Parrish 1101, Kirksville, Missouri 63501; 660-785-4417, fax: 660-785-7463, e-mail address: wwilbur@truman.edu

Temple University, Tyler School of Art
Tyler School of Art of Temple University

Philadelphia, Pennsylvania

State-related, coed. Urban campus. Total enrollment: 33,693. Art program established 1935.

Tyler School of Art of Temple University (continued)

Degrees Bachelor of Architecture in the area of architecture; Bachelor of Fine Arts in the areas of ceramics/glass, fibers, graphic and interactive design, painting/drawing, photography, printmaking, sculpture, art education, metals/jewelry/CAD-CAM. Majors and concentrations: architecture, art education, art history, CAD/CAM, ceramic art and design, commercial art, computer graphics, digital imaging, fibers, glass, graphic arts, graphic design, illustration, jewelry and metalsmithing, painting/drawing, photography, printmaking, sculpture, visual studies. Graduate degrees offered: Master of Arts in the area of art history; Master of Education in the area of art education; Master of Fine Arts in the areas of ceramics/glass, fibers, jewelry/metals, painting/drawing, photography, printmaking, sculpture, graphic and interactive design. Doctor of Philosophy in the area of art history. Program accredited by NASAD, NAAB.

Enrollment 885 total; 700 undergraduate, 76 graduate, 109 nonprofessional degree.

Art Student Profile 52% females, 48% males, 14% minorities, 4% international.

Art Faculty 54 total (full-time), 32 total (part-time). 95% of full-time faculty have terminal degrees. Graduate students teach a few undergraduate courses. Undergraduate student–faculty ratio: 11:1.

Student Life Student groups/activities include Student Alliance, Intellectual Heritage Society, Art Honor Society. Special housing available for art students.

Expenses for 2005–2006 Application fee: $35. State resident tuition: $9140 full-time. Nonresident tuition: $16,736 full-time. Mandatory fees: $500 full-time. Full-time tuition and fees vary according to course load, location, program, and reciprocity agreements. College room and board: $7794. College room only: $5054. Room and board charges vary according to board plan and housing facility. Special program-related fees: $25–$300 per course for lab fees.

Financial Aid Program-specific awards: 10–25 merit scholarships for program students ($1000–$10,500), 10–100 academic scholarships for program students ($1000–$10,500).

Application Procedures Students admitted directly into the professional program freshman year. Deadline for freshmen: April 1; transfers: June 1. Notification date for freshmen and transfers: continuous. Required: essay, high school transcript, college transcript(s) for transfer students, portfolio, SAT I or ACT test scores (minimum combined SAT I score of 1100, minimum composite ACT score of 23), slides for transfer applicants (or CD ROM), self-portrait. Recommended: minimum 3.0 high school GPA, interview. Portfolio reviews held 27 times on campus and off campus at National Portfolio Day Association venues and selected high schools; the submission of slides may be substituted for portfolios for freshmen applicants, for large works of art, or if distance is prohibitive.

Web Site http://www.temple.edu/tyler

Undergraduate Contact Ms. Carmina Cianciulli, Assistant Dean for Admissions, Tyler School of Art, Temple University, 7725 Penrose Avenue, Elkins Park, Pennsylvania 19027; 215-782-2875, fax: 215-782-2711, e-mail address: tylerart@temple.edu

Graduate Contact Ms. Carmina Cianciulli, Assistant Dean for Admissions, Tyler School of Art of Temple University, Temple University, 7725 Penrose Avenue, Elkins Park, Pennsylvania 19027; 215-782-2875, fax: 215-782-2711, e-mail address: tylerart@temple.edu

Myers School of Art
The University of Akron
Akron, Ohio

State-supported, coed. Urban campus. Total enrollment: 21,049. Art program established 1970.

Degrees Bachelor of Arts in the areas of art studio, art history, art education; Bachelor of Fine Arts in the areas of photography, printmaking, metalsmithing, graphics, sculpture, ceramics, painting and drawing. Majors and concentrations: art education, art history, ceramic art and design, graphic design, jewelry and metalsmithing, painting/drawing, photography, printmaking, sculpture, studio art. Program accredited by NASAD.

Enrollment 868 total; 498 undergraduate, 370 nonprofessional degree.

Art Student Profile 50% females, 50% males, 8% minorities, 1% international.

Art Faculty 23 undergraduate (full-time), 23 undergraduate (part-time). 100% of full-time faculty have terminal degrees. Graduate students do not teach undergraduate courses. Undergraduate student–faculty ratio: 14:1.

Student Life Student groups/activities include Student Art League.

Expenses for 2005–2006 Application fee: $30. State resident tuition: $6810 full-time. Nonresident tuition: $15,535 full-time. Mandatory fees: $1148 full-time. Full-time tuition and fees vary according to course load, degree level, and location. College room and board: $7208. College room only: $4494. Room and board charges vary according to board plan and housing facility. Special program-related fees: $35 per semester for metalsmithing materials, $35 per semester for printmaking materials, $35 per semester for photography supplies, $50 per semester for computer materials, $65 per semester for ceramics supplies.

Financial Aid Program-specific awards: 1–4 Scholastics Art and Writing Awards for incoming freshmen program majors ($2000), 1–4 Governor's Art Youth Awards for Ohio resident program majors ($2000), 3–7 incoming freshmen awards for incoming freshmen program majors ($1200), 13–20 School of Art Scholarships for continuing program majors based on portfolio and GPA ($1500), 25 funded travel awards for current students ($1000), 10 tools and materials awards for current students ($500).

Application Procedures Students apply for admission into the professional program by sophomore year. Deadline for freshmen: June 30; transfers: July 30. Required: high school transcript, college transcript(s) for transfer students, minimum 2.0 high school GPA, SAT I or ACT test scores, portfolio for transfer students, minimum 3.0 college GPA in art courses for transfer students, letters of recommendation and portfolio for scholarship consideration. Recommended: portfolio. Portfolio reviews held 2 scheduled dates and as needed on campus; the submission of slides may be substituted for portfolios for out-of-state applicants.

Web Site http://www.uakron.edu/art/

Undergraduate Contact Office of Admissions, The University of Akron, 381 Buchtel Common, Akron, Ohio 44325-2001; 330-972-7100, fax: 330-972-7022, e-mail address: admissions@uakron.edu

The University of Alabama

Tuscaloosa, Alabama

State-supported, coed. Suburban campus. Total enrollment: 21,835. Art program established 1946.

Degrees Bachelor of Fine Arts in the area of studio art. Majors and concentrations: art/fine arts, ceramic art and design, painting/drawing, photography, printmaking, sculpture. Graduate degrees offered: Master of Fine Arts in the areas of painting, printmaking, ceramics, sculpture, photography, studio art. Program accredited by NASAD.

Enrollment 255 total; 42 undergraduate, 29 graduate, 184 nonprofessional degree.

Art Student Profile 63% females, 37% males, 13% minorities, 2% international.

Art Faculty 14 total (full-time), 4 total (part-time). 93% of full-time faculty have terminal degrees. Graduate students teach a few undergraduate courses. Undergraduate student–faculty ratio: 2:1.

Student Life Student groups/activities include Art Student League.

Expenses for 2005–2006 Application fee: $30. State resident tuition: $4864 full-time. Nonresident tuition: $13,516 full-time. Full-time tuition varies according to course load. College room and board: $5024. College room only: $3120. Room and board charges vary according to board plan and housing facility. Special program-related fees: $25–$55 per semester for studio fees for classes.

Financial Aid Program-specific awards: 3 Mary M. Morgan Scholarships for program students ($9000), 3 Bradley Endowed Scholarships for program students ($4330), 1 Ruth K. Larcom Society for the Fine Arts Scholarship for competition ($4400), 5 Julie Peake Holaday Memorial Scholarships for program students ($7228), 2 Art Students Endowed Scholarships for program students ($1462), 1 Richard Zollner Scholarship for program students ($1542), 2 Alvin C. Sella and Joseph Sella Endowed Scholarships for program students ($1338).

Application Procedures Students apply for admission into the professional program by sophomore year. Deadline for freshmen and

The University of Alabama (continued)

transfers: continuous. Required: high school transcript, college transcript(s) for transfer students, minimum 2.0 high school GPA, portfolio, SAT I or ACT test scores (minimum combined SAT I score of 1030, minimum composite ACT score of 22), high school transcript for transfer applicants with fewer than 24 semester hours. Portfolio reviews held twice on campus; the submission of slides may be substituted for portfolios contact department for details.

Web Site http://www.as.ua.edu/art

Undergraduate Contact Ms. Mary K. Spiegel, Director, Undergraduate Admissions, The University of Alabama, Box 870132, Tuscaloosa, Alabama 35487; 205-348-8197, fax: 205-348-9046, e-mail address: mary.spiegel@ua.edu

Graduate Contact Dr. Carl F. Williams, Director, Graduate Admissions and Recruitment, The University of Alabama, PO Box 870118, Tuscaloosa, Alabama 35487; 205-348-5921, fax: 205-348-0400, e-mail address: cwilliam@aalan.ua.edu

The University of Alabama at Birmingham

Birmingham, Alabama

State-supported, coed. Urban campus. Total enrollment: 16,572. Art program established 1972.

University of Alaska Anchorage

Anchorage, Alaska

State-supported, coed. Urban campus. Total enrollment: 16,261. Art program established 1988.

The University of Arizona

Tucson, Arizona

State-supported, coed. Urban campus. Total enrollment: 37,036.

Degrees Bachelor of Fine Arts in the areas of art education, studio art. Majors and concen-

trations: art education, art history, ceramic art and design, computer graphics, new genres, painting/drawing, photography, printmaking, sculpture, studio art, textile arts, visual communication. Graduate degrees offered: Master of Arts in the areas of art education, art history; Master of Fine Arts in the area of studio art. Doctor of Philosophy in the area of art history. Cross-registration with Pima Community College. Program accredited by NASAD.

Enrollment 1,108 total; 900 undergraduate, 98 graduate, 110 nonprofessional degree.

Art Student Profile 67% females, 33% males, 17% minorities.

Art Faculty 40 total (full-time), 7 total (part-time). 97% of full-time faculty have terminal degrees. Graduate students teach about a quarter of undergraduate courses. Undergraduate student–faculty ratio: 17:1.

Student Life Student groups/activities include Art Club/Photo Club, Committee for Advancement of Art Students, American Institute of Graphic Arts.

Expenses for 2005–2006 Application fee: $25. State resident tuition: $4394 full-time. Nonresident tuition: $13,578 full-time. Mandatory fees: $104 full-time. Full-time tuition and fees vary according to course load. College room and board: $7460. College room only: $4100. Room and board charges vary according to board plan and housing facility. Special program-related fees: $10–$50 per semester for supplies for some studio courses.

Financial Aid Program-specific awards: 1 Robert C. Brown Memorial Scholarship for program majors ($750), Edward Francis Dunn Scholarships for program majors ($4600), Albert and Kathryn Haldeman Scholarships for program majors ($3600), 1 Hudson Foundation Scholarship for program majors ($1200), Samuel Latta Kingan Scholarships for program majors ($2300), 1 Stephen Langmade Scholarship for program majors ($950), 8 Regents In-State Registration Scholarships for state resident program majors ($1700), 5 Regents In-State Registration Scholarships for state resident program majors demonstrating need ($1700), 10 Regents Non-Resident Tuition Scholarships for out-of-state program majors ($4000), 1 Sandy Truett Memorial Scholarship for program majors ($1050).

Application Procedures Students apply for admission into the professional program by sophomore year. Deadline for freshmen: March 5; transfers: May 5. Required: high school transcript, college transcript(s) for transfer students, portfolio, SAT I or ACT test scores (minimum combined SAT I score of 1040, minimum composite ACT score of 22), minimum 2.5 high school GPA for state residents, minimum 3.0 high school GPA for out-of-state residents, slides of portfolio for visual communications majors. Portfolio reviews held twice on campus.

Web Site http://www.arts.arizona.edu/art

Undergraduate Contact Ms. Lisa Kreamer, Undergraduate Advising Coordinator, School of Art, The University of Arizona, Art Building, Room 138, PO Box 210002, Tucson, Arizona 85721-0002; 520-621-2618, fax: 520-621-2353, e-mail address: kreamer@u.arizona.edu

Graduate Contact Ms. Debra Lesko, Graduate Specialist, School of Art, The University of Arizona, Art Building, Room 101D, PO Box 210002, Tucson, Arizona 85721-0002; 520-621-8518, fax: 520-621-2955, e-mail address: dlesko@email.arizona.edu

J. William Fulbright College of Arts and Sciences
University of Arkansas
Fayetteville, Arkansas

State-supported, coed. Suburban campus. Total enrollment: 17,821. Art program established 1874.

Degrees Bachelor of Fine Arts in the areas of studio art, art education. Majors and concentrations: art education, ceramics, drawing, graphic design, jewelry, painting, photography, printmaking, sculpture, visual design. Graduate degrees offered: Master of Fine Arts in the area of art.

Enrollment 58 total; 43 undergraduate, 15 graduate.

Art Faculty 10 total (full-time), 4 total (part-time). 98% of full-time faculty have terminal degrees. Graduate students do not teach undergraduate courses.

Student Life Student groups/activities include Fine Arts League, University Union Programs Fine Arts Committee.

Expenses for 2005–2006 Application fee: $40. State resident tuition: $4361 full-time. Nonresident tuition: $12,089 full-time. Mandatory fees: $1133 full-time. College room and board: $6365. College room only: $3782. Room and board charges vary according to board plan and housing facility. Special program-related fees: $4 per credit hour for teaching equipment.

Financial Aid Program-specific awards: David Durst Award for program students, Blanche Elliot Awards for sophomores, juniors, and seniors, Tom Turpin Award for freshmen, Neppie Conner Award for sophomores, Collier Photo Award for juniors and seniors, Bedford Camera Award for juniors and seniors, Charles Okerbloom Scholarships for program majors, Mountain Lake Estates Photography Award for program majors, Nina Erikson Awards for program majors.

Application Procedures Students apply for admission into the professional program by sophomore year. Deadline for freshmen: February 15. Notification date for freshmen and transfers: August 15. Required: essay, high school transcript, college transcript(s) for transfer students, SAT I or ACT test scores (minimum composite ACT score of 30), minimum 2.0 college GPA for transfers.

Web Site http://www.uark.edu/~artinfo/art.html

Undergraduate Contact Chair, Art Department, University of Arkansas, 116 Fine Arts Center, Fayetteville, Arkansas 72701; 501-575-5202, fax: 501-575-2062.

Graduate Contact Prof. Michael Peven, MFA Coordinator, Art Department, University of Arkansas, 116 Fine Arts Center, Fayetteville, Arkansas 72701; 501-575-5202, fax: 501-575-2062, e-mail address: mpeven@uark.edu

University of Bridgeport
Bridgeport, Connecticut

Independent, coed. Urban campus. Total enrollment: 3,626.

Degrees Bachelor of Arts in the areas of graphic design, illustration; Bachelor of Fine Arts in the areas of graphic design, illustration; Bachelor of Science in the areas of interior design, industrial design, graphic design, illustration. Majors and concentra-

Visual

Arts

University of Bridgeport (continued)

tions: graphic design, illustration, industrial design, interior design. Program accredited by NASAD.

Enrollment 98 total; all undergraduate.

Art Student Profile 45% females, 55% males, 30% minorities, 18% international.

Art Faculty 4 undergraduate (full-time), 10 undergraduate (part-time). 100% of full-time faculty have terminal degrees. Graduate students do not teach undergraduate courses. Undergraduate student–faculty ratio: 10:1.

Student Life Student groups/activities include art shows.

Expenses for 2005–2006 Application fee: $25. Comprehensive fee: $29,595 includes full-time tuition ($19,200), mandatory fees ($1395), and college room and board ($9000). College room only: $4600. Full-time tuition and fees vary according to program. Room and board charges vary according to board plan and student level.

Application Procedures Students admitted directly into the professional program freshman year. Deadline for freshmen and transfers: continuous. Required: essay, high school transcript, college transcript(s) for transfer students, portfolio, SAT I or ACT test scores. Recommended: minimum 2.0 high school GPA, 2 letters of recommendation, interview. Portfolio reviews held as needed on campus; the submission of slides may be substituted for portfolios for international applicants.

Web Site http://www.bridgeport.edu

Undergraduate Contact Ms. Barbara L. Maryak, Dean of Admissions, University of Bridgeport, 126 Park Avenue, Bridgeport, Connecticut 06604; 800-EXCEL-UB, fax: 203-576-4941, e-mail address: admit@bridgeport.edu

The University of British Columbia

Vancouver, British Columbia, Canada

Province-supported, coed. Urban campus. Total enrollment: 42,427. Art program established 1955.

Degrees Bachelor of Arts in the areas of art history, studio art; Bachelor of Fine Arts in the area of visual arts. Majors and concentrations: art history, studio art. Graduate degrees offered: Master of Arts in the areas of art history, critical curatorial studies; Master of Fine Arts in the area of studio art. Doctor of Philosophy in the area of art history.

Enrollment 296 total; 209 undergraduate, 53 graduate, 34 nonprofessional degree.

Art Student Profile 20% international.

Art Faculty 20 total (full-time), 13 total (part-time). Graduate students teach a few undergraduate courses. Undergraduate student–faculty ratio: 9:1.

Student Life Student groups/activities include Graduate Student Art History Symposium, Fine Art Gallery student exhibitions, MFA Open Studios.

Financial Aid Program-specific awards: 1 Faculty Women's Club Ida Green Award for academically qualified applicants ($2500), 1 Florence Muriel Meltzer Scholarship for academically qualified applicants ($2000), 1 Helen Pitt Graduating Award for academically qualified applicants ($1000), 1 IODE Fine Arts Foundation Scholarship for academically qualified applicants ($1000), 1 Sharon Yacawer Frohlinger Memorial Scholarship for academically qualified applicants ($325), 1 Koerner Memorial Scholarship for academically qualified applicants ($1650).

Application Procedures Students apply for admission into the professional program by junior year. Deadline for freshmen and transfers: March 31. Required: college transcript(s) for transfer students, minimum 3.0 high school GPA, portfolio and interview to enter third-year studio program. Recommended: high school transcript. Portfolio reviews held once in April on campus; the submission of slides may be substituted for portfolios for out-of-town applicants.

Web Site http://www.finearts.ubc.ca

Undergraduate Contact Ms. Lorra Ward, Undergraduate Secretary, Department of Art History, Visual Art, and Theory, The University of British Columbia, 6333 Memorial Road #403, Vancouver, British Columbia V6T 1Z2, Canada; 604-822-2757, fax: 604-822-9003, e-mail address: finearts@interchange.ubc.ca

Graduate Contact Ms. Whitney Friesen, Graduate Secretary and Secretary to the Head, Department of Art History, Visual Art, and Theory, The University of British Columbia, 6333 Memorial Road #403, Vancouver, British

Columbia V6T 1Z2, Canada; 604-822-5650, fax: 604-822-9003, e-mail address: whitneyf@ interchange.ubc.ca

University of Calgary

Calgary, Alberta, Canada

Province-supported, coed. Urban campus. Total enrollment: 27,928. Art program established 1967.

Degrees Bachelor of Fine Arts in the areas of art, developmental art. Majors and concentrations: developmental art, painting/drawing, photography, printmaking, sculpture. Graduate degrees offered: Master of Fine Arts in the area of art.

Enrollment 326 total; 237 undergraduate, 14 graduate, 75 nonprofessional degree.

Art Student Profile 66% females, 34% males, 4% international.

Art Faculty 16 total (full-time), 12 total (part-time). 100% of full-time faculty have terminal degrees. Graduate students teach a few undergraduate courses. Undergraduate student–faculty ratio: 14:1.

Student Life Student groups/activities include on-campus exhibitions in two venues, BFA and MFA shows, Art Students Society.

Expenses for 2005–2006 Application fee: $130 Canadian dollars. Tuition and fee charges are reported in Canadian dollars.

Financial Aid Program-specific awards: 1 Alberta Printmakers Society Award for printmakers ($100), 1 Continuing Arts Association Travel Scholarship for those demonstrating academic achievement ($900), 1 Bow Fort Chapter I.O.D.E. Bursary for those demonstrating academic achievement ($250), 2 Heinz Jordan Memorial Scholarships for those demonstrating academic achievement ($500), 2 Santo Mignosa Awards for printmakers ($500), 1 Sadie M. Nelson Bursary in Art for those demonstrating need and academic merit ($500), 1 Western Silk Screen Prize for silk screen majors ($300), 1 BFA Graduation Committee Prize for those entering final year in visual arts program ($250), 1 Jack Wise Award for Excellence in Painting for continuing students who have completed Art 451 and 453 ($300), 2 25th Anniversary Scholarships for those demonstrating academic merit ($1000), 1 Stadelbauer Award for developmental art students ($1250).

Application Procedures Students admitted directly into the professional program freshman year. Deadline for freshmen and transfers: April 1. Required: high school transcript, portfolio, standing in top 75% of graduating class. Recommended: SAT I test score only. Portfolio reviews held once on campus; the submission of slides may be substituted for portfolios.

Web Site http://www.ucalgary.ca

Contact Ms. Karen Lyons, Student Advisor, Faculty of Fine Arts Student Success Team (FASST), University of Calgary, 2500 University Drive, NW, Calgary, Alberta T2N 1N4, Canada; 403-220-5384, fax: 403-282-6925, e-mail address: lyons@ucalgary.ca

University of Central Arkansas

Conway, Arkansas

State-supported, coed. Small town campus. Total enrollment: 11,375. Art program established 1927.

Degrees Bachelor of Fine Arts. Majors and concentrations: studio art. Program accredited by NASAD.

Enrollment 181 total; 23 undergraduate, 158 nonprofessional degree.

Art Student Profile 61% females, 39% males, 13% minorities, 3% international.

Art Faculty 13 undergraduate (full-time), 1 undergraduate (part-time). 100% of full-time faculty have terminal degrees. Graduate students do not teach undergraduate courses. Undergraduate student–faculty ratio: 15:1.

Student Life Student groups/activities include Student Studio Art Guild, Student Art Education Association, Student Art History Association.

Expenses for 2005–2006 Application fee: $0. State resident tuition: $4500 full-time. Nonresident tuition: $9000 full-time. Mandatory fees: $1164 full-time. College room and board: $4320. College room only: $1940. Room and board charges vary according to board plan and housing facility.

University of Central Arkansas (continued)

Financial Aid Program-specific awards: 15 Performance in Art Scholarships for art majors ($1000–$2000), 1 Disterheft Scholarship for art majors ($1000), 1 Curtis Scholarship for art majors ($600).

Application Procedures Students apply for admission into the professional program by sophomore year. Deadline for freshmen and transfers: continuous. Required: high school transcript, college transcript(s) for transfer students, ACT test score only, portfolio review for transfer students. Recommended: minimum 3.0 high school GPA.

Web Site http://www.uca.edu/cfac/art

Undergraduate Contact Dr. Jeffrey R. Young, Chair, Department of Art, University of Central Arkansas, Conway, Arkansas 72035; 501-450-3113, fax: 501-450-5788, e-mail address: jyoung@uca.edu

University of Central Florida

Orlando, Florida

State-supported, coed. Suburban campus. Total enrollment: 44,953.

Degrees Bachelor of Fine Arts in the area of art. Majors and concentrations: animation, art history, ceramic art and design, graphic design, painting/drawing, photography, printmaking, sculpture. Graduate degrees offered: Master of Fine Arts in the area of computer art. Cross-registration with Florida community colleges.

Enrollment 528 total; 90 undergraduate, 9 graduate, 429 nonprofessional degree.

Art Student Profile 51% females, 49% males, 27% minorities, 1% international.

Art Faculty 25 undergraduate (full-time), 4 undergraduate (part-time), 3 graduate (full-time). 95% of full-time faculty have terminal degrees. Graduate students teach a few undergraduate courses. Undergraduate student–faculty ratio: 20:1.

Student Life Student groups/activities include Arts Alliance, Pottery Guild, Animation Club.

Expenses for 2005–2006 Application fee: $30. State resident tuition: $3141 full-time. Nonresident tuition: $16,272 full-time. Mandatory fees: $198 full-time. Full-time tuition and fees vary according to course load. College room and board: $7400. College room only: $4300. Room and board charges vary according to board plan and housing facility. Special program-related fees: $45 per course for materials.

Financial Aid Program-specific awards: 1 Altrusa Award for studio art majors ($500), 3 Escher Animation Awards for animation majors ($50–$200), 2 Juror 1 and Juror 2 Awards for photography majors ($100–$200).

Application Procedures Students apply for admission into the professional program by sophomore year. Deadline for freshmen and transfers: July 15. Notification date for freshmen and transfers: continuous. Required: high school transcript, college transcript(s) for transfer students, minimum 2.0 high school GPA, portfolio, SAT I or ACT test scores, minimum 2.0 college GPA for transfer students, TOEFL score for international applicants. Portfolio reviews held once on campus; the submission of slides may be substituted for portfolios whenever needed.

Web Site http://www.art.ucf.edu

Undergraduate Contact Prof. Jagdish Chavda, Advisor, Art Department, University of Central Florida, VAB117, Orlando, Florida 32816; 407-823-2676, fax: 407-823-6470, e-mail address: jchavda@mail.ucf.edu

Graduate Contact Prof. Scott Hall, Assistant Professor, Art, University of Central Florida, VAB117, Orlando, Florida 32816; 407-823-2676, fax: 407-823-6470, e-mail address: shall@mail.ucf.edu

University of Cincinnati

Cincinnati, Ohio

State-supported, coed. Urban campus. Total enrollment: 27,932. Art program established 1967.

Degrees Bachelor of Fine Arts in the area of art education. Majors and concentrations: media arts, three-dimensional studies, two-dimensional studies. Graduate degrees offered: Master of Arts in the areas of art history, art education; Master of Fine Arts in the area of fine arts. Cross-registration with The Ohio Valley Consortium of Colleges and Universities. Program accredited by NASAD.

Enrollment 340 total; 247 undergraduate, 93 graduate.

Art Student Profile 55% females, 45% males, 2% minorities, 5% international.

Art Faculty 25 total (full-time), 5 total (part-time). 100% of full-time faculty have terminal degrees. Graduate students teach a few undergraduate courses. Undergraduate student–faculty ratio: 13:1.

Student Life Student groups/activities include Fine Arts Association, National Art Education Associate-UC Chapter, Graduate Student Association-Fine Arts Chapter.

Expenses for 2005–2006 Application fee: $40. State resident tuition: $7458 full-time. Nonresident tuition: $21,210 full-time. Mandatory fees: $1425 full-time. Full-time tuition and fees vary according to course load, degree level, location, program, and reciprocity agreements. College room and board: $7890. College room only: $4680. Room and board charges vary according to board plan and housing facility. Special program-related fees: $45 per course for lab fee-art supplies.

Financial Aid Program-specific awards: 3–7 Wolf Stein Travel Fellowships for upper-level undergraduates ($1500–$2500), 1 Rockwood Production Grant for electronic art majors ($1000), 1 Dean Tatgenhorst Conrad Scholarship for art/art history majors ($1000), 6 art scholarships for art majors ($1500).

Application Procedures Students admitted directly into the professional program freshman year. Deadline for freshmen and transfers: continuous. Notification date for freshmen: September 20. Required: high school transcript, college transcript(s) for transfer students, portfolio, SAT I or ACT test scores (minimum combined SAT I score of 980, minimum composite ACT score of 21), minimum 2.5 high school GPA for transfer students, standing in top third of graduating class. Recommended: interview. Portfolio reviews held 15 times on campus and off campus in Cincinnati, OH; Louisville, KY; the submission of slides may be substituted for portfolios.

Web Site http://www.daap.uc.edu

Undergraduate Contact Prof. Denise Burge, Undergraduate Advisor, School of Art, University of Cincinnati, Mail Location 0016, Cincinnati, Ohio 45221; 513-556-2426, fax: 513-556-2887, e-mail address: dburge@cinci.rr.com

Graduate Contact Ms. Kimberly Burleigh, Director of Graduate Studies in Fine Arts, School of Art, University of Cincinnati, Mail Location 0016, Cincinnati, Ohio 45221; 513-556-2075, fax: 513-556-2887, e-mail address: kimberly.burleigh@uc.edu

University of Colorado at Boulder

Boulder, Colorado

State-supported, coed. Small town campus. Total enrollment: 31,068. Art program established 1932.

Degrees Bachelor of Arts in the area of art history; Bachelor of Fine Arts in the area of studio art. Majors and concentrations: art history, studio art. Graduate degrees offered: Master of Arts in the area of art history; Master of Fine Arts in the area of studio art.

Enrollment 1,157 total; 1,100 undergraduate, 57 graduate.

Art Student Profile 69% females, 31% males, 7% minorities, 4% international.

Art Faculty 31 total (full-time), 10 total (part-time). 100% of full-time faculty have terminal degrees. Graduate students teach about a quarter of undergraduate courses. Undergraduate student–faculty ratio: 35:1.

Student Life Student groups/activities include Art Student League.

Expenses for 2005–2006 Application fee: $50. One-time mandatory fee: $108. State resident tuition: $4446 full-time. Nonresident tuition: $21,900 full-time. Mandatory fees: $926 full-time. Full-time tuition and fees vary according to program. College room and board: $7980. Room and board charges vary according to board plan, location, and student level. Special program-related fees: $50 per course for non-studio course, $50 per credit hour for studio course.

Financial Aid Program-specific awards: 20 scholarships for program majors ($500–$2000).

Application Procedures Deadline for freshmen and transfers: continuous. Required: high school transcript, college transcript(s) for transfer students, minimum 2.0 high school GPA, SAT I or ACT test scores, portfolio upon completion of foundation courses (slides permissible) for BFA. Portfolio reviews held once

University of Colorado at Boulder (continued)

on campus; the submission of slides may be substituted for portfolios.

Web Site http://www.colorado.edu/arts

Undergraduate Contact Admissions, University of Colorado at Boulder, Campus Box 552, Boulder, Colorado 80309; 303-492-6301.

Graduate Contact Alexei Bogdanov, Graduate Coordinator, Department of Fine Arts, University of Colorado at Boulder, Campus Box 318, Boulder, Colorado 80309-0318; 303-492-2419, fax: 303-492-4886, e-mail address: alexei.bogdanov@colorado.edu

University of Colorado at Denver and Health Sciences Center - Downtown Denver Campus

Denver, Colorado

State-supported, coed. Urban campus. Total enrollment: 19,755. Art program established 1980.

University of Connecticut

Storrs, Connecticut

State-supported, coed. Rural campus. Total enrollment: 23,185.

Degrees Bachelor of Fine Arts in the area of art. Majors and concentrations: art/fine arts, communication design, illustration, painting/drawing, photography, printmaking, sculpture. Graduate degrees offered: Master of Fine Arts in the area of art. Program accredited by NASAD.

Enrollment 250 total; 240 undergraduate, 10 graduate.

Art Student Profile 58% females, 42% males, 7% minorities, 3% international.

Art Faculty 18 total (full-time), 14 total (part-time). 100% of full-time faculty have terminal degrees. Graduate students teach a few undergraduate courses. Undergraduate student–faculty ratio: 15:1.

Student Life Special housing available for art students.

Expenses for 2006–2007 Application fee: $70. State resident tuition: $6456 full-time. Nonresident tuition: $19,656 full-time. Mandatory fees: $1906 full-time. College room and board: $8266. College room only: $4350. Special program-related fees: $15–$75 per course for expendable supplies in studio courses.

Financial Aid Program-specific awards: 1 Victor Borge Scholarship for incoming freshmen ($1000), 8 Fine Arts Talent Scholarships for program students ($3000), 1 anniversary scholarship for program students ($1400), 1 Alaimo Scholarship for program students ($1000), 2 Fine Arts Talent Scholarships for incoming freshmen ($3000), 1 Fine Arts Talent Scholarship for incoming freshmen ($1000).

Application Procedures Students admitted directly into the professional program freshman year. Deadline for freshmen: April 1; transfers: May 1. Required: essay, high school transcript, college transcript(s) for transfer students, minimum 2.0 high school GPA, portfolio, SAT I or ACT test scores. Recommended: minimum 3.0 high school GPA, 3 letters of recommendation, interview. Portfolio reviews held 3 times on campus and off campus in Boston, MA; Hartford, CT; the submission of slides may be substituted for portfolios at student's discretion.

Web Site http://www.art.uconn.edu

Undergraduate Contact Ray DiCapua, Associate Head and Associate Professor, Department of Art and Art History, University of Connecticut, 830 Bolton Road, U-1099, Storrs, Connecticut 06269-1099; 860-486-3930, fax: 860-486-3869, e-mail address: ralph.dicapua@uconn.edu

Graduate Contact Charles Hogen, Graduate Program Coordinator and Associate Professor, Department of Art and Art History, University of Connecticut, 830 Bolton Road, U-1099, Storrs, Connecticut 06269-1099; 860-486-3930, fax: 860-486-3869, e-mail address: charles.hagen@uconn.edu

University of Dayton

Dayton, Ohio

Independent Roman Catholic, coed. Suburban campus. Total enrollment: 10,572. Art program established 1960.

Degrees Bachelor of Fine Arts in the areas of art education, studio art, visual communication design, photography. Majors and concentrations: art education, art/fine arts, computer graphics, graphic arts, illustration, photography, studio art. Cross-registration with Miami Valley Consortium.

Enrollment 226 total; 177 undergraduate, 49 nonprofessional degree.

Art Student Profile 70% females, 30% males, 5% minorities, 2% international.

Art Faculty 15 undergraduate (full-time), 20 undergraduate (part-time). 100% of full-time faculty have terminal degrees. Graduate students do not teach undergraduate courses. Undergraduate student–faculty ratio: 5:1.

Student Life Student groups/activities include Horvath Student Art Show, Stander Symposium, student organization in design, fine art, and photography.

Expenses for 2005–2006 Application fee: $0. Comprehensive fee: $29,626 includes full-time tuition ($22,046), mandatory fees ($800), and college room and board ($6780). College room only: $4000. Full-time tuition and fees vary according to program. Room and board charges vary according to board plan, housing facility, and student level. Special program-related fees: $20–$75 per semester for studio/lab fees.

Financial Aid Program-specific awards: 5–10 Visual Arts Scholarships for freshmen ($2500), 1 Gordon Richardson Scholarship for juniors ($2000), 3 Horvath Scholarships for sophomores ($1000), 1 Anne Perman Scholarship for upperclassmen ($2000).

Application Procedures Students admitted directly into the professional program freshman year. Deadline for freshmen: continuous; transfers: August 5. Required: essay, high school transcript, college transcript(s) for transfer students, minimum 2.0 high school GPA, letter of recommendation, SAT I or ACT test scores, record of leadership and service. Recommended: interview, portfolio. Portfolio reviews held as needed on campus and off campus in various cities in Indiana, Ohio, Kentucky; the submission of slides may be substituted for portfolios if original work is not available.

Web Site http://www.as.udayton.edu/visualarts/

Undergraduate Contact Office of Admission, University of Dayton, 300 College Park, Dayton, Ohio 45469-1611; 937-229-4411.

University of Delaware

Newark, Delaware

State-related, coed. Small town campus. Total enrollment: 20,373.

University of Denver

Denver, Colorado

Independent, coed. Total enrollment: 10,374. Art program established 1929.

Degrees Bachelor of Fine Arts in the areas of electronic media arts design, art education, studio art. Majors and concentrations: art education, ceramic art and design, electronic media, painting/drawing, photography, preconservation, printmaking, sculpture. Graduate degrees offered: Master of Arts in the area of art history; Master of Fine Arts in the area of electronic media arts design. Program accredited by NASAD.

Enrollment 176 total; 23 undergraduate, 40 graduate, 113 nonprofessional degree.

Art Student Profile 77% females, 23% males, 15% minorities, 10% international.

Art Faculty 17 total (full-time), 5 total (part-time). 100% of full-time faculty have terminal degrees. Graduate students teach a few undergraduate courses.

Student Life Student groups/activities include ...isms (student art organization), Gallery 023 (student run exhibition space), DU AIGA (DU student group of the American Institute of Graphic Arts).

Expenses for 2005–2006 Application fee: $50. Comprehensive fee: $37,159 includes full-time tuition ($27,756), mandatory fees ($654), and college room and board ($8749). College room only: $5355. Full-time tuition and fees vary according to class time, course load, and program. Room and board charges vary according to board plan and housing facility. Special program-related fees: $10–$80 per course for lab fees, course materials.

Financial Aid Program-specific awards: 5 Harrison Scholarships for those demonstrating talent and need ($5000–$20,000), 20 art scholarships for those demonstrating talent and academic achievement ($500–$20,000).

Application Procedures Students admitted directly into the professional program freshman

University of Denver (continued)

year. Deadline for freshmen: February 1; transfers: continuous. Notification date for freshmen and transfers: continuous. Required: essay, high school transcript, college transcript(s) for transfer students, 2 letters of recommendation, interview, portfolio, SAT I or ACT test scores. Portfolio reviews held as needed on campus; the submission of slides may be substituted for portfolios (slides preferred).

Web Site http://www.du.edu/art/

Undergraduate Contact Ms. Margret Korzus, Associate Dean, Office of Admissions, University of Denver, University Hall, 2197 South University Boulevard, Denver, Colorado 80208; 303-871-2794, fax: 303-871-3301, e-mail address: mkorzus@du.edu

Graduate Contact Dr. M. E. Warlick, Graduate Advisor, School of Art and Art History, University of Denver, 2121 East Asbury Avenue, Denver, Colorado 80208; 303-871-2846, fax: 303-871-4112, e-mail address: mwarlick@du.edu

University of Evansville

Evansville, Indiana

Independent, coed. Suburban campus. Total enrollment: 2,836. Art program established 1960.

Degrees Bachelor of Fine Arts. Majors and concentrations: ceramics, painting, sculpture.

Enrollment 80 total; all undergraduate.

Art Student Profile 62% females, 38% males, 1% minorities, 15% international.

Art Faculty 3 undergraduate (full-time), 6 undergraduate (part-time). 100% of full-time faculty have terminal degrees. Graduate students do not teach undergraduate courses. Undergraduate student–faculty ratio: 11:1.

Student Life Student groups/activities include Clay Club, Kappa Pi.

Expenses for 2005–2006 Application fee: $35. Comprehensive fee: $28,320 includes full-time tuition ($21,120), mandatory fees ($540), and college room and board ($6660). College room only: $3280. Room and board charges vary according to board plan and housing facility. Special program-related fees: $25–$50 per semester for ceramics, photography, printmaking, metals, sculpture.

Financial Aid Program-specific awards: 25 art and academic scholarships for freshmen program majors ($500–$10,000), art and academic scholarships for transfer program majors.

Application Procedures Students apply for admission into the professional program by sophomore, junior year. Deadline for freshmen: May 1; transfers: June 1. Notification date for freshmen and transfers: continuous. Required: essay, high school transcript, college transcript(s) for transfer students, minimum 2.0 high school GPA, SAT I or ACT test scores (minimum combined SAT I score of 920, minimum composite ACT score of 19). Recommended: minimum 3.0 high school GPA, 2 letters of recommendation, interview, portfolio. Portfolio reviews held continuously on campus and off campus in Louisville, KY; the submission of slides may be substituted for portfolios whenever needed.

Web Site http://www.evansville.edu

Undergraduate Contact Mr. William F. Brown, Chairman, Department of Art, University of Evansville, 1800 Lincoln Avenue, Evansville, Indiana 47722; 812-479-2043, fax: 812-479-2320, e-mail address: bb32@evansville.edu

University of Florida

Gainesville, Florida

State-supported, coed. Suburban campus. Total enrollment: 49,693. Art program established 1929.

Degrees Bachelor of Arts in the areas of art history, art education, general visual art studies, digital arts and sciences; Bachelor of Fine Arts in the areas of ceramics, drawing, graphic design, painting, creative photography, printmaking, sculpture, electronic intermedia. Majors and concentrations: art education, art history, ceramics, digital arts and sciences, electronic intermedia, general visual arts studies, graphic design, painting/drawing, photography, printmaking, sculpture. Graduate degrees offered: Master of Arts in the areas of digital arts and sciences, museum studies, art education, art history; Master of Fine Arts in the areas of ceramics, drawing, graphic design, painting, creative photography, printmaking, sculpture, electronic intermedia. Cross-registration with Penland School of Crafts, New World School for the Arts. Program accredited by NASAD, NCATE.

Enrollment 612 total; 506 undergraduate, 106 graduate.

Art Student Profile 63% females, 37% males, 23% minorities, 2% international.

Art Faculty 31 total (full-time), 4 total (part-time). 100% of full-time faculty have terminal degrees. Graduate students teach about a quarter of undergraduate courses. Undergraduate student–faculty ratio: 18:1.

Student Life Student groups/activities include Departure: GNV publication, Fine Arts College Council, Annual Juried Student Exhibition. Special housing available for art students.

Expenses for 2005–2006 Application fee: $30. State resident tuition: $3,094 full-time. Nonresident tuition: $17,222 full-time. College room and board: $6260. College room only: $3940. Room and board charges vary according to board plan and housing facility. Special program-related fees: $15–$45 per course for lab fee for studio courses.

Financial Aid Program-specific awards: 2 Amy DeGrove Scholarships for freshmen and juniors ($2500), 1 Ann Marston Scholarship for juniors and seniors ($500), 2 James J. Rizzi Scholarships for studio majors ($3000).

Application Procedures Students apply for admission into the professional program by sophomore year. Deadline for freshmen: January 30; transfers: February 15. Notification date for freshmen: continuous; transfers: March 29. Required: essay, high school transcript, college transcript(s) for transfer students, minimum 3.0 high school GPA, letter of recommendation, SAT I or ACT test scores (minimum combined SAT I score of 970, minimum composite ACT score of 20), completion of pre-professional courses Drawing I and II, Design I and II, Survey Art History I and II, portfolio for transfers. Portfolio reviews held twice on campus; the submission of slides may be substituted for portfolios.

Web Site http://www.arts.ufl.edu/art

Undergraduate Contact Trisha Suggs, Undergraduate Coordinator/Academic Advisor, School of Art and Art History, University of Florida, FAC 101, PO Box 115801, Gainesville, Florida 32611-5801; 352-392-0201, fax: 352-392-8453, e-mail address: trimax23@ufl.edu

Graduate Contact Kristin Flierl, Graduate Program Assistant, School of Art and Art History, University of Florida, FAC 101, PO Box 115801, Gainesville, Florida 32611-5801; 352-392-0201 ext. 201, fax: 352-392-8453, e-mail address: kflierl@ufl.edu

Lamar Dodd School of Art
University of Georgia
Athens, Georgia

State-supported, coed. Suburban campus. Total enrollment: 33,660. Art program established 1937.

Degrees Bachelor of Fine Arts in the area of art. Majors and concentrations: art education, ceramics, digital media, fabric design, graphic design, interior design, jewelry and metalsmithing, painting/drawing, photography, printmaking, scientific illustration, sculpture. Graduate degrees offered: Master of Arts in the areas of art history, art education; Master of Fine Arts in the area of art. Doctor of Philosophy in the areas of art history, art education. Cross-registration with 19 area institutions. Program accredited by NASAD, FIDER.

Enrollment 1,072 total; 296 undergraduate, 96 graduate, 680 nonprofessional degree.

Art Student Profile 68% females, 32% males, 12% minorities, 4% international.

Art Faculty 57 total (full-time), 20 total (part-time). 98% of full-time faculty have terminal degrees. Graduate students teach a few undergraduate courses. Undergraduate student–faculty ratio: 15:1.

Student Life Student groups/activities include American Society of Interior Designers Student Chapter, National Art Education Association Student Chapter.

Expenses for 2005–2006 Application fee: $50. State resident tuition: $3638 full-time. Nonresident tuition: $15,858 full-time. Mandatory fees: $990 full-time. Full-time tuition and fees vary according to course load, location, program, and reciprocity agreements. College room and board: $6376. College room only: $3436. Room and board charges vary according to board plan and housing facility. Special program-related fees: $10–$100 per course for supplies.

Visual *Arts*

University of Georgia (continued)

Financial Aid Program-specific awards: 30 art awards for program students ($500–$1000).

Application Procedures Students apply for admission into the professional program by freshman year. Deadline for freshmen: March 1; transfers: July 1. Notification date for freshmen: March 31. Required: high school transcript, minimum 3.0 high school GPA, SAT I or ACT test scores (minimum combined SAT I score of 1100), portfolio after the first semester.

Web Site http://www.art.uga.edu

Undergraduate Contact Dr. Nancy G. McDuff, Director of Admissions, University of Georgia, 114 Academic Building, Athens, Georgia 30602; 706-542-8776, fax: 706-542-1466.

Graduate Contact Ms. Andra Corvin, Degree Program Specialist, Lamar Dodd School of Art, University of Georgia, Visual Arts Building, Athens, Georgia 30602; 706-542-1636, fax: 706-542-0226.

Hartford Art School
University of Hartford
West Hartford, Connecticut

Independent, coed. Suburban campus. Total enrollment: 7,260. Art program established 1877.

Degrees Bachelor of Fine Arts in the area of art. Majors and concentrations: ceramics, drawing, illustration, media arts, painting, photography, printmaking, sculpture, visual communication design. Graduate degrees offered: Master of Fine Arts in the area of art. Cross-registration with Trinity College, Saint Joseph College, Hartford Seminary. Program accredited by NASAD.

Enrollment 360 total; 345 undergraduate, 15 graduate.

Art Student Profile 55% females, 45% males, 5% minorities, 2% international.

Art Faculty 20 total (full-time), 21 total (part-time). 96% of full-time faculty have terminal degrees. Graduate students do not teach undergraduate courses. Undergraduate student–faculty ratio: 13:1.

Student Life Student groups/activities include Student Association, student newspaper and yearbook staff, professional fraternities and sororities. Special housing available for art students.

Expenses for 2006–2007 Application fee: $35. Comprehensive fee: $35,688 includes full-time tuition ($24,576), mandatory fees ($1190), and college room and board ($9922). College room only: $6118.

Financial Aid Program-specific awards: 45 endowed scholarships for those demonstrating need ($2500), 15–20 artistic merit awards for artistically talented students ($5000–$16,000), 15–25 academic talent awards for those with high SAT scores, high GPA, in top 10% of class ($9000–$15,000).

Application Procedures Students admitted directly into the professional program freshman year. Deadline for freshmen and transfers: continuous. Notification date for freshmen and transfers: continuous. Required: high school transcript, college transcript(s) for transfer students, minimum 2.0 high school GPA, 2 letters of recommendation, portfolio, SAT I or ACT test scores. Recommended: essay, interview. Portfolio reviews held by appointment on campus and off campus in Hartford, CT; Philadelphia, PA; Miami, FL; New York, NY; Boston, MA; Syracuse, NY; Washington, DC; Baltimore, MD on National Portfolio Days; the submission of slides may be substituted for portfolios when distance is prohibitive.

Web Site http://www.hartfordartschool.org

Undergraduate Contact Mr. Robert Calafiore, Assistant Dean, Hartford Art School, University of Hartford, 200 Bloomfield Avenue, West Hartford, Connecticut 06117; 860-768-4827, fax: 860-768-5296.

Graduate Contact Mr. Stephen Brown, Associate Professor, Graduate Director, Hartford Art School, University of Hartford, 200 Bloomfield Avenue, West Hartford, Connecticut 06117; 860-768-4393, fax: 860-768-5296.

University of Hawaii at Manoa
Honolulu, Hawaii

State-supported, coed. Urban campus. Total enrollment: 20,644. Art program established 1907.

University of Houston

Houston, Texas

State-supported, coed. Urban campus. Total enrollment: 35,344. Art program established 1962.

Degrees Bachelor of Fine Arts in the areas of graphic communication, interior design, photography/digital media, sculpture, painting. Majors and concentrations: digital imaging, graphic design, interior design, painting/drawing, photography, photography/digital media, sculpture. Graduate degrees offered: Master of Fine Arts in the areas of graphic communication, interior design, photography/digital media, painting, sculpture.

Enrollment 965 total; 670 undergraduate, 40 graduate, 255 nonprofessional degree.

Art Student Profile 70% females, 30% males, 44% minorities, 5% international.

Art Faculty 25 total (full-time), 13 total (part-time). 100% of full-time faculty have terminal degrees. Graduate students teach a few undergraduate courses. Undergraduate student–faculty ratio: 22:1.

Student Life Student groups/activities include Graphic Communication Student Association, American Society of Interior Designers Student Chapter, Clayworks (ceramics student association).

Expenses for 2005–2006 Application fee: $50. State resident tuition: $3920 full-time. Nonresident tuition: $12,200 full-time. Mandatory fees: $2566 full-time. Full-time tuition and fees vary according to course level, course load, degree level, location, program, reciprocity agreements, and student level. College room and board: $6058. College room only: $3492. Room and board charges vary according to board plan and housing facility. Special program-related fees: $20–$100 per course for equipment maintenance and supplies fee.

Financial Aid Program-specific awards: 15 Flaxman Scholarships for seniors ($500–$1400), 2 George Bunker Scholarships for program majors ($2500), 2–4 LaRuth Blaine Scholarships for interior design majors ($1000–$2000), 1–4 Choate/Palmer Scholarships for program majors demonstrating need ($1000).

Application Procedures Students admitted directly into the professional program freshman year. Deadline for freshmen: April 1; transfers: May 1. Notification date for freshmen and transfers: continuous. Required: high school transcript, college transcript(s) for transfer students, SAT I or ACT test scores, GPA requirement varies according to test scores and class rank.

Web Site http://www.art.uh.edu/

Undergraduate Contact Admission Office, University of Houston, 129 Ezekiel Cullen Building, Houston, Texas 77204-2023; 713-743-1010.

Graduate Contact Cathy Hunt, Graduate Advisor, School of Art, University of Houston, Fine Arts Building, Room 100, Houston, Texas 77204-4019; 713-743-2830, fax: 713-743-2823, e-mail address: chunt@uh.edu

University of Idaho

Moscow, Idaho

State-supported, coed. Small town campus. Total enrollment: 12,476.

University of Illinois at Chicago

Chicago, Illinois

State-supported, coed. Total enrollment: 24,812. Art program established 1966.

Degrees Bachelor of Fine Arts in the areas of studio arts, graphic design, industrial design, photo/film/electronic media, art education. Majors and concentrations: art education, electronic arts, film, graphic arts, industrial design, painting/drawing, photography, sculpture, studio art, video art. Graduate degrees offered: Master of Fine Arts in the areas of studio arts, photography, graphic design, industrial design, film/animation/video, electronic visualization. Program accredited by NASAD.

Enrollment 697 total; 607 undergraduate, 90 graduate.

Art Student Profile 60% females, 40% males, 20% minorities, 10% international.

Art Faculty 27 total (full-time), 9 total (part-time). 100% of full-time faculty have terminal degrees. Graduate students teach a few undergraduate courses. Undergraduate student–faculty ratio: 25:1.

University of Illinois at Chicago (continued)

Student Life Student groups/activities include American Center for Design Student Chapter, Industrial Design Society of America Student Chapter.

Expenses for 2005–2006 Application fee: $40. State resident tuition: $6194 full-time. Nonresident tuition: $18,584 full-time. Mandatory fees: $2108 full-time. College room and board: $7954. Special program-related fees: $15–$150 per class for models, equipment, darkroom facilities.

Financial Aid Program-specific awards: 10–12 talent/tuition waivers for academically qualified program majors ($2722–$6052).

Application Procedures Students apply for admission into the professional program by sophomore year. Deadline for freshmen: May 1; transfers: June 1. Notification date for freshmen and transfers: continuous. Required: high school transcript, college transcript(s) for transfer students, minimum 2.0 high school GPA, SAT I or ACT test scores (minimum composite ACT score of 21), minimum TOEFL score of 520 for international applicants, minimum 2.5 (4.0 scale) or 3.75 (5.0 scale) college GPA for transfer students, portfolio for graphic design and art education majors and transfers in certain areas, standing in upper 50% of graduating class. Recommended: essay, letter of recommendation, interview. Portfolio reviews held by arrangement on campus; the submission of slides may be substituted for portfolios (slides preferred).

Web Site http://www.uic.edu/aa/artd/

Undergraduate Contact Erin Brady, Academic Advisor, Undergraduate, School of Art and Design, University of Illinois at Chicago, 929 West Harrison Street, 106 Jefferson Hall, M/C 036, Chicago, Illinois 60607-7038; 312-996-3337, fax: 312-413-2333, e-mail address: ebrady@uic.edu

Graduate Contact Mara Kruger, Academic Advisor, Graduate, School of Art and Design, University of Illinois at Chicago, 929 West Harrison Street, 106 Jefferson Hall M/C 036, Chicago, Illinois 60607-7038; 312-996-3337, fax: 312-413-2333, e-mail address: marak@uic.edu

University of Illinois at Urbana–Champaign

Champaign, Illinois

State-supported, coed. Small town campus. Total enrollment: 41,938.

Degrees Bachelor of Fine Arts. Majors and concentrations: art education, art history, ceramics, graphic design, industrial design, metals, painting, photography, sculpture. Graduate degrees offered: Master of Arts in the areas of art education, art history; Master of Fine Arts in the areas of ceramics, graphic design, industrial design, metals, painting, photography, sculpture. Doctor of Education in the area of art education; Doctor of Philosophy in the area of art history. Program accredited by NASAD.

Enrollment 650 total; 550 undergraduate, 100 graduate.

Art Student Profile 60% females, 40% males, 1% minorities, 2% international.

Art Faculty 64 total (full-time), 3 total (part-time). 99% of full-time faculty have terminal degrees. Graduate students teach a few undergraduate courses. Undergraduate student–faculty ratio: 10:1.

Student Life Student groups/activities include organizations for all major areas, Industrial Design Society of America, National Art Education Association.

Expenses for 2005–2006 Application fee: $40. State resident tuition: $7042 full-time. Nonresident tuition: $21,128 full-time. Mandatory fees: $1582 full-time. Full-time tuition and fees vary according to course load, program, and student level. College room and board: $7176. College room only: $2970. Room and board charges vary according to board plan and housing facility. Special program-related fees: $200–$300 per semester for equipment and materials fees.

Financial Aid Program-specific awards: 60–70 tuition support awards for program majors ($800–$3000).

Application Procedures Students apply for admission into the professional program by freshman year. Deadline for freshmen: January 1; transfers: March 1. Required: essay, high school transcript, college transcript(s) for transfer students, SAT I or ACT test scores, CD or slide portfolio for all studio programs, writing sample for art history transfers, ITBS for transfer into art education. Portfolio reviews held once for freshmen, once for transfer students on campus; the submission of slides may be substituted for portfolios.

Web Site http://www.art.uiuc.edu

Undergraduate Contact Mark Avery, Undergraduate Specialist, School of Art and Design, University of Illinois at Urbana–Champaign, 408 East Peabody Drive, Champaign, Illinois 61820; 217-333-6632, fax: 217-244-7688.

Graduate Contact Ms. Marsha Biddle, Graduate Specialist, School of Art and Design, University of Illinois at Urbana–Champaign, 408 East Peabody Drive, Champaign, Illinois 61820; 217-333-0642, fax: 217-244-7688.

University of Indianapolis

Indianapolis, Indiana

Independent, coed. Suburban campus. Total enrollment: 4,462. Art program established 1904.

Degrees Bachelor of Fine Arts in the areas of studio art, visual communication design. Majors and concentrations: ceramics, painting/drawing. Cross-registration with Consortium for Urban Education. Program accredited by NASAD.

Enrollment 107 total; 13 undergraduate, 94 nonprofessional degree.

Art Student Profile 60% females, 40% males, 5% minorities, 15% international.

Art Faculty 6 undergraduate (full-time), 6 total (part-time). 100% of full-time faculty have terminal degrees. Graduate students do not teach undergraduate courses. Undergraduate student–faculty ratio: 6:1.

Student Life Student groups/activities include Indianapolis Student Art Association.

Expenses for 2005–2006 Application fee: $20. Comprehensive fee: $24,990 includes full-time tuition ($17,980) and college room and board ($7010). Full-time tuition varies according to program. Room and board charges vary according to board plan and housing facility.

Financial Aid Program-specific awards: 1 Gerald Boyce Scholarship for art majors ($3000), 6–8 departmental scholarships for incoming Fresh-

men ($3000), 1 A. E. Gott Award for art majors ($1000), 1 M. E. Gott Award for art majors ($600).

Application Procedures Students apply for admission into the professional program by sophomore year. Deadline for freshmen and transfers: continuous. Required: essay, high school transcript, college transcript(s) for transfer students, minimum 2.0 high school GPA, SAT I or ACT test scores, interview and portfolio for scholarship consideration. Portfolio reviews held once in January, February, and June on campus; the submission of slides may be substituted for portfolios when distance in prohibitive.

Web Site http://art.uindy.edu

Undergraduate Contact Ronald Wilks, Director of Admissions, University of Indianapolis, 1400 East Hanna Avenue, Indianapolis, Indiana 46227-3697; 317-788-3216, fax: 317-788-6105, e-mail address: cambridge@uindy.edu

The University of Iowa

Iowa City, Iowa

State-supported, coed. Small town campus. Total enrollment: 28,426. Art program established 1936.

Degrees Bachelor of Fine Arts in the area of studio arts. Majors and concentrations: art education, art history, art/fine arts, ceramics, design, intermedia, jewelry and metalsmithing, painting/drawing, photography, printmaking, sculpture, studio art, video art. Graduate degrees offered: Master of Arts in the areas of art history, studio arts; Master of Fine Arts in the area of studio arts. Doctor of Philosophy in the area of art history.

Enrollment 917 total; 767 undergraduate, 150 graduate.

Art Student Profile 60% females, 40% males, 8% minorities, 4% international.

Art Faculty 36 total (full-time), 9 total (part-time). 94% of full-time faculty have terminal degrees. Graduate students do not teach undergraduate courses. Undergraduate student–faculty ratio: 17:1.

Student Life Student groups/activities include Art History Society, College Art Association, art exhibitions.

Expenses for 2006–2007 Application fee: $40. State resident tuition: $5110 full-time. Nonresi-

The University of Iowa (continued)

dent tuition: $17,334 full-time. Mandatory fees: $825 full-time. College room and board: $6912. Special program-related fees: $10–$200 per course for model/lab fees.

Financial Aid Program-specific awards: 1 Iowa Center for Art Scholarship for freshmen program majors ($3000), 1 Mary Sue Miller Memorial Award for freshmen program majors ($600–$1000), 1 Emma McAllister Novel Award for minority program majors ($1000), 1–3 Schumacher Awards for program majors ($1600–$1800).

Application Procedures Students admitted directly into the professional program freshman year. Deadline for freshmen and transfers: continuous. Required: high school transcript, college transcript(s) for transfer students, SAT I or ACT test scores, minimum 2.25 high school GPA. Recommended: interview, portfolio for transfer students. Portfolio reviews held twice on campus; the submission of slides may be substituted for portfolios for three-dimensional works of art.

Web Site http://www.uiowa.edu/~art/

Undergraduate Contact Evelyn Acosta-Weirich, Undergraduate Advisor, School of Art and Art History, The University of Iowa, E100 Art Building, Iowa City, Iowa 52242; 319-335-1779, fax: 319-335-1774, e-mail address: evelyn-weirich@uiowa.edu

Graduate Contact Ms. Laura Jorgensen, Graduate Secretary, School of Art and Art History, The University of Iowa, E100 Art Building, Iowa City, Iowa 52242; 319-335-1758, fax: 319-335-1774, e-mail address: laura-jorgensen@uiowa.edu

University of Kansas

Lawrence, Kansas

State-supported, coed. Total enrollment: 28,949.

Degrees Bachelor of Fine Arts in the areas of paqinting, sculpture, printmaking, expanded media. Majors and concentrations: painting, printmaking, sculpture. Graduate degrees offered: Master of Fine Arts in the areas of painting, sculpture, printmaking, expanded media. Program accredited by NASAD.

Enrollment 174 total; 156 undergraduate, 17 graduate, 1 nonprofessional degree.

Art Faculty 15 total (full-time), 5 total (part-time). 100% of full-time faculty have terminal degrees. Graduate students teach a few undergraduate courses. Undergraduate student–faculty ratio: 9:1.

Expenses for 2005–2006 Application fee: $30. State resident tuition: $4824 full-time. Nonresident tuition: $13,277 full-time. Mandatory fees: $589 full-time. Full-time tuition and fees vary according to program and reciprocity agreements. College room and board: $5502. College room only: $2752. Room and board charges vary according to board plan and housing facility.

Financial Aid Program-specific awards: 7 Creative and Performing Arts Scholarships for incoming freshmen ($4100), 6 Basic Studies Scholarships for sophomores ($1500), 50 departmental scholarships and awards for program majors ($3100), 13 Hollander Foundation Scholarships and Awards for program majors ($2700).

Application Procedures Students apply for admission into the professional program by freshman year. Deadline for freshmen: April 1; transfers: June 1. Notification date for freshmen and transfers: January 19. Required: high school transcript, SAT I or ACT test scores. Recommended: portfolio for transfer applicants. Portfolio reviews held 3 times in Chicago, IL; St. Louis, MO; Kansas City, MO; the submission of slides may be substituted for portfolios for large works of art.

Web Site http://www.ku.edu/~sfa/

Undergraduate Contact Ms. Judith McCrea, Chair, Department of Art, University of Kansas, 1467 Jayhawk Boulevard, Lawrence, Kansas 66045-7531; 785-864-4401, fax: 785-864-4404, e-mail address: jmccrea@ku.edu

Graduate Contact Gina Westergard, Graduate Director, Department of Art, University of Kansas, 1467 Jayhawk Boulevard, Lawrence, Kansas 66045-7531; 785-864-4401, fax: 785-864-4404, e-mail address: ginaw@ku.edu

University of Louisiana at Lafayette

Lafayette, Louisiana

State-supported, coed. Urban campus. Total enrollment: 17,075. Art program established 1957.

Degrees Bachelor of Interior Design. Majors and concentrations: interior design. Program accredited by FIDER, NASAD.

Enrollment 123 total; all undergraduate.

Art Student Profile 99% females, 1% males, 2% minorities.

Art Faculty 4 undergraduate (full-time), 1 undergraduate (part-time). 100% of full-time faculty have terminal degrees. Graduate students do not teach undergraduate courses. Undergraduate student–faculty ratio: 18:1.

Student Life Student groups/activities include American Society of Interior Designers, American Institute of Architects.

Expenses for 2005–2006 Application fee: $25. State resident tuition: $3324 full-time. Nonresident tuition: $9504 full-time. Full-time tuition varies according to course load. College room and board: $3478. Room and board charges vary according to board plan and housing facility.

Financial Aid Program-specific awards: 1 ASID Scholarship for third- or fourth- year program majors ($1000), 1 Clay Breauy Scholarship for first year architecture, interior design, or industrial design majors ($600).

Application Procedures Students admitted directly into the professional program freshman year. Deadline for freshmen and transfers: continuous. Notification date for freshmen and transfers: continuous. Required: high school transcript, college transcript(s) for transfer students, minimum 2.0 high school GPA, ACT test score only, portfolio for transfer applicants. Portfolio reviews held by appointment on campus; the submission of slides may be substituted for portfolios.

Web Site http://arts.louisiana.edu

Undergraduate Contact M. Jean Edwards, Coordinator, Interior Design Program, School of Architecture, University of Louisiana at Lafayette, College of the Arts, Box 43850, Lafayette, Louisiana 70504-3850; 337-482-5020, fax: 337-482-1128.

Allen R. Hite Art Institute
University of Louisville
Louisville, Kentucky

State-supported, coed. Urban campus. Total enrollment: 20,734. Art program established 1936.

Degrees Bachelor of Fine Arts in the areas of interior architecture, communication arts and design, 2-D studios, 3-D studios. Majors and concentrations: ceramics, glass, graphic arts, interior design, painting/drawing, photography, printmaking, sculpture, textile arts, three-dimensional studies, two-dimensional studies. Graduate degrees offered: Master of Arts in the areas of art, art history, critical and curatorial studies; Master of Arts in Teaching in the area of art education. Doctor of Philosophy in the area of art history. Cross-registration with Metroversity/University Exchange Consortium. Program accredited by FIDER.

Enrollment 537 total; 146 undergraduate, 59 graduate, 332 nonprofessional degree.

Art Student Profile 69% females, 31% males, 9% minorities, 2% international.

Art Faculty 22 total (full-time), 12 total (part-time). 100% of full-time faculty have terminal degrees. Graduate students do not teach undergraduate courses. Undergraduate student–faculty ratio: 7:1.

Student Life Student groups/activities include Student Art League, American Society of Interior Designers, Louisville Graphic Design Association.

Expenses for 2005–2006 Application fee: $30. State resident tuition: $5532 full-time. Nonresident tuition: $15,092 full-time. Full-time tuition varies according to reciprocity agreements. College room and board: $6036. College room only: $4490. Room and board charges vary according to board plan and housing facility. Special program-related fees: $13–$25 per course for supplies.

Financial Aid Program-specific awards: 24 Hite Scholarships for enrolled students ($1000–$5500), 4 Hendershot Scholarships for incoming freshmen ($6000), 1 Nay Scholarship for incoming freshmen ($5500), 1 Kaden Scholarship for enrolled students ($1000–$3000).

Application Procedures Students apply for admission into the professional program by sophomore year. Deadline for freshmen and transfers: continuous. Required: essay, high school transcript, college transcript(s) for transfer students, minimum 2.0 high school GPA, portfolio, SAT I or ACT test scores. Recommended: interview, minimum 3.0 high school GPA in major area. Portfolio reviews held as needed on campus; the submission of slides

University of Louisville (continued)

may be substituted for portfolios (slides or digital images preferred).

Web Site http://art.louisville.edu

Undergraduate Contact Theresa Berbet, Administrative Assistant, Fine Arts Department, University of Louisville, 104 Schneider Hall, Louisville, Kentucky 40292; 502-852-6794, fax: 502-852-6791.

Graduate Contact Ms. Janice Blair, Program Assistant, Fine Arts Department, University of Louisville, Lutz Hall, Louisville, Kentucky 40292; 502-852-5914, fax: 502-852-6791, e-mail address: jablai01@gwise.louisville.edu

University of Mary Hardin-Baylor

Belton, Texas

Independent Southern Baptist, coed. Small town campus. Total enrollment: 2,727. Art program established 1930.

University of Massachusetts Amherst

Amherst, Massachusetts

State-supported, coed. Total enrollment: 25,093. Art program established 1958.

Degrees Bachelor of Fine Arts in the areas of studio art, art education, design and architecture. Majors and concentrations: art education, art history, ceramics, computer art, interior architecture and design, painting, photography, printmaking, sculpture. Graduate degrees offered: Master of Arts in the areas of art education, art history; Master of Fine Arts in the area of studio art; Master of Science in the area of interior design; Master of Architecture in the area of architecture. Cross-registration with Smith College, Amherst College, Mount Holyoke College, Hampshire College. Program accredited by NAAB.

Enrollment 346 total; 264 undergraduate, 68 graduate, 14 nonprofessional degree.

Art Faculty 32 total (full-time), 12 total (part-time). 100% of full-time faculty have terminal degrees. Graduate students teach

about a quarter of undergraduate courses. Undergraduate student–faculty ratio: 12:1.

Student Life Student groups/activities include Design Students Organization, American Society of Interior Designers Student Chapter.

Expenses for 2006–2007 Application fee: $40. State resident tuition: $2031 full-time. Nonresident tuition: $10,857 full-time. Mandatory fees: $7564 full-time.

Financial Aid Program-specific awards: Chancellor Talent Awards for in-state students showing academic and artistic merit.

Application Procedures Students admitted directly into the professional program freshman year. Deadline for freshmen: February 1; transfers: May 1. Required: essay, high school transcript, college transcript(s) for transfer students, minimum 3.0 high school GPA, portfolio, SAT I or ACT test scores. Recommended: letter of recommendation. Portfolio reviews held continuously on campus; the submission of slides may be substituted for portfolios (slides preferred).

Web Site http://www.umass.edu/art/

Undergraduate Contact Patricia Galvis-Assmus, Undergraduate Program Director, Department of Art, University of Massachusetts Amherst, 151 Presidents Drive, Room 357, Fine Arts Center, Amherst, Massachusetts 01003; 413-545-0866, fax: 413-545-3929.

Graduate Contact Mr. Max Page, Graduate Program Director, Department of Art, University of Massachusetts Amherst, 151 Presidents Drive, Room 362, Fine Arts Center, Amherst, Massachusetts 01003; 413-545-6940, fax: 413-545-3929.

University of Massachusetts Dartmouth

North Dartmouth, Massachusetts

State-supported, coed. Suburban campus. Total enrollment: 8,549. Art program established 1964.

Degrees Bachelor of Arts in the area of art history; Bachelor of Fine Arts in the areas of visual design, painting, sculpture, textile design/fiber arts, art education. Majors and concentrations: art education, art history, art/fine arts, ceramics, fiber arts, graphic design/letterform, illustration, jewelry and metalsmithing, multimedia, painting/drawing, photographic/electronic imaging, sculpture, textile design, visual design. Graduate degrees offered: Master of Art Education in the area of art education; Master of Fine Arts in the areas of visual design, artisanry, fine arts. Cross-registration with University of Massachusetts System, Southeastern Association for Cooperation in Higher Education in Massachusetts. Program accredited by NASAD.

Enrollment 674 total; 572 undergraduate, 102 graduate.

Art Student Profile 65% females, 35% males, 9% minorities, 2% international.

Art Faculty 42 total (full-time), 22 total (part-time). 90% of full-time faculty have terminal degrees. Graduate students teach a few undergraduate courses. Undergraduate student–faculty ratio: 11:1.

Student Life Student groups/activities include Metals Guild, Sculpture Club, Communicatus.

Expenses for 2005–2006 Application fee: $35, $55 for nonresidents. State resident tuition: $1417 full-time. Nonresident tuition: $8099 full-time. Mandatory fees: $6619 full-time. Full-time tuition and fees vary according to reciprocity agreements. College room and board: $7634. College room only: $4460. Room and board charges vary according to board plan and housing facility. Special program-related fees: $243 per semester for CVPA fee.

Financial Aid Program-specific awards: Clement Yeager Scholarships for visual or performing art students ($700–$2500), 1 Barbara Eckhardt Memorial Scholarship for fiber arts students ($1500–$2000), 1 Emil "Smokey" Ameen Endowment Scholarship for CVPA students ($200), 1 David and Alfrede Myerson Scholarship for CVPA students ($600), 1 Alda Alves and Bruce Yenawine Scholarship for CVPA students ($1000), 4 Ayuko Ito Scholarships for CVPA students ($1000), 1 Lillian Telles Jenkins Scholarship for CVPA students ($400), 1 Samuel Gamburd Memorial Art Scholarship for design or fine arts students ($750).

Application Procedures Students admitted directly into the professional program freshman year. Deadline for freshmen and transfers: continuous. Notification date for freshmen and transfers: continuous. Required: high school transcript, college transcript(s) for transfer students, minimum 2.0 high school GPA, portfolio, SAT I or ACT test scores, slides of portfolio. Recommended: essay, minimum 3.0 high school GPA, 3 letters of recommendation. Portfolio reviews held continuously on campus; the submission of slides may be substituted for portfolios (required).

Web Site http://www.umassd.edu/CVPA

Undergraduate Contact Mr. Steven T. Briggs, Director of Admissions, University of Massachusetts Dartmouth, 285 Old Westport Road, North Dartmouth, Massachusetts 02747-2300; 508-999-8606, fax: 508-999-8755, e-mail address: admissions@umassd.edu

Graduate Contact Ms. Carol Novo, Staff Assistant, Graduate Admissions, University of Massachusetts Dartmouth, 285 Old Westport Road, North Dartmouth, Massachusetts 02747-2300; 508-999-8604, fax: 508-999-8183, e-mail address: graduate@umassd.edu

More About the College

The College of Visual and Performing Arts (CVPA) is a fully accredited, comprehensive arts college, with bachelor's and master's degree programs that prepare students for careers in the arts. Unlike most professional art schools, which are independent, CVPA is an active component of a comprehensive university, with all of the educational resources that implies.

CVPA offers a breadth of high-level programs. Students can study art education, art history, illustration, graphic design/letterform, photographic/electronic imaging, ceramics, jewelry/metals, textile design, fiber arts, painting/2-D studies, sculpture/3-D studies, and music—which includes Western music, world music, technology, jazz studies, music education, and composition. The visual arts Foundation Program introduces students to visual concepts and practices and is required of all first-year studio majors.

The Campus Noted architect Paul Rudolf created a dramatic design for UMass Dartmouth's 710-acre main campus. CVPA's studios and classrooms are located there and in the exciting new Star Store. Formerly a department store in nearby downtown New Bedford, the Star Store has been converted into a modern urban arts complex with spacious studios, galleries, and state-of-the-art equipment. CVPA is located just minutes from the Atlantic Ocean; about 30 minutes from Cape Cod or Providence, Rhode Island; and 1 hour from Boston.

Facilities Located on both the North Dartmouth and New Bedford campuses of the University, the facilities and equipment available to students in the College of Visual and Performing Arts are among the finest in New England. CVPA encourages applicants

University of Massachusetts Dartmouth (continued)

to attend its Open House or to schedule a campus visit to tour the College's artist studios, ample classroom spaces, state-of-the-art computer labs, artisanry workshops, photography and printmaking studios, music practice rooms, recital hall, and the many additional features the University has to offer.

Faculty CVPA faculty members are artists, musicians, composers, and educators—each distinguished in his or her field. Many are recipients of such prestigious awards as the National Endowment for the Arts, Massachusetts Cultural Council grants, Fulbright fellows, and national and international arts fellowships. Faculty members exhibit in galleries and museums regionally and nationally and perform on concert stages and smaller venues both in the United States and abroad.

Exhibition Opportunities CVPA's significant contribution to the regional arts scene is evident in its dynamic presence within the southcoast communities. The College is active in downtown New Bedford, participating in the monthly AHA! Night venues and exhibiting work in local storefronts. The College's galleries maintain a high caliber of exhibitions on the Dartmouth campus in the Campus Gallery and Gallery One and in New Bedford at the University Art Gallery and Gallery 244.

The University Art Gallery is devoted to showing the work of international and national artists. The CVPA Campus Gallery and Gallery One feature frequently changing exhibitions of CVPA student and faculty work that is curated by college faculty members. Gallery 244 is a student-run gallery, featuring work by graduate students—emerging artists in their own right.

Special Programs Study abroad is encouraged; current programs in Scotland, Portugal, and Sicily offer excellent opportunities to expand a student's experience. Internships and experiential learning are also encouraged; recent placements have included Graphics Express; WGBH; the Museum of Fine Arts, Boston; the Smithsonian; Guilford of Maine; and the Walt Disney Studios.

University of Massachusetts Lowell

Lowell, Massachusetts

State-supported, coed. Urban campus. Total enrollment: 10,666. Art program established 1982.

Degrees Bachelor of Fine Arts in the areas of fine arts, graphic design. Majors and concentrations: animation, drawing, graphic design, illustration, interactive media, painting, photography, sculpture, Web design. Cross-registration with the 15 Massachusetts community colleges. Program accredited by NASAD.

Enrollment 275 total; all undergraduate.

Art Student Profile 48% females, 52% males, 7% minorities, 2% international.

Art Faculty 8 undergraduate (full-time), 15 undergraduate (part-time). 100% of full-time faculty have terminal degrees. Graduate students do not teach undergraduate courses. Undergraduate student–faculty ratio: 15:1.

Student Life Student groups/activities include Art History Club, Art Co-Op Club.

Expenses for 2005–2006 Application fee: $20. State resident tuition: $1454 full-time. Nonresident tuition: $8567 full-time. Mandatory fees: $6712 full-time. College room and board: $6311. College room only: $3810. Room and board charges vary according to board plan and housing facility.

Financial Aid Program-specific awards: 5 Fine Art Scholarships ($500).

Application Procedures Students admitted directly into the professional program freshman year. Deadline for freshmen and transfers: continuous. Required: high school transcript, college transcript(s) for transfer students, minimum 2.0 high school GPA, 2 letters of recommendation, SAT I test score only (minimum combined SAT I score of 960), portfolio for transfer students. Portfolio reviews held twice on campus; the submission of slides may be substituted for portfolios when distance is prohibitive.

Web Site http://www.uml.edu/Dept/Art/

Undergraduate Contact Jim Coates, Chairperson, Art Department, University of Massachusetts Lowell, 71 Wilder Street, Suite 8, McGauvran Student Union Building, Room 126, Lowell, Massachusetts 01854; 978-934-3494, fax: 978-934-4050, e-mail address: art@uml.edu

University of Memphis

Memphis, Tennessee

State-supported, coed. Urban campus. Total enrollment: 20,465.

University of Miami

Coral Gables, Florida

Independent, coed. Suburban campus. Total enrollment: 15,674. Art program established 1954.

University of Michigan

Ann Arbor, Michigan

State-supported, coed. Suburban campus. Total enrollment: 39,993. Art program established 1954.

Degrees Bachelor of Fine Arts in the area of art and design. Majors and concentrations: art, ceramics, electronic media, fibers, graphic design, industrial design, installation art, jewelry and metalsmithing, painting/drawing, performance art, photography, printmaking, scientific illustration, sculpture, sound art. Graduate degrees offered: Master of Fine Arts in the area of art and design. Program accredited by NASAD.

Enrollment 489 total; 470 undergraduate, 19 graduate.

Art Student Profile 65% females, 35% males, 14% minorities, 3% international.

Art Faculty 34 total (full-time), 40 total (part-time). 95% of full-time faculty have terminal degrees. Graduate students do not teach undergraduate courses. Undergraduate student–faculty ratio: 18:1.

Student Life Student groups/activities include Society of Art Students, Industrial Design Society of America Student Chapter, American Institute of Graphic Arts. Special housing available for art students.

Expenses for 2005–2006 Application fee: $40. State resident tuition: $9213 full-time. Nonresident tuition: $27,602 full-time. Mandatory fees: $187 full-time. Full-time tuition and fees vary according to course load, degree level, location, program, and student level. College room and board: $7374. Room and board charges vary according to board plan and housing facility. Special program-related fees: $250–$500 per semester for materials fee.

Financial Aid Program-specific awards: 1 Shipman Scholarship for those demonstrating academic achievement and artistic ability.

Application Procedures Students admitted directly into the professional program freshman year. Deadline for freshmen and transfers: February 1. Notification date for freshmen and transfers: May 1. Required: essay, high school transcript, college transcript(s) for transfer students, minimum 3.0 high school GPA, portfolio, SAT I or ACT test scores (minimum combined SAT I score of 1150, minimum composite ACT score of 25). Recommended: interview. Portfolio reviews held 3 times plus ad hoc on campus; the submission of slides may be substituted for portfolios if accompanied by an index sheet detailing each piece and sufficient return postage.

Web Site http://www.art-design.umich.edu

Undergraduate Contact Joann McDaniel, Director of Undergraduate Academic Services, School of Art and Design, University of Michigan, 2000 Bonisteel Boulevard, Ann Arbor, Michigan 48109-2069; 734-764-0397, fax: 734-936-0469, e-mail address: ad@umich.edu

Graduate Contact Wendy Dignan, Director of Graduate Academic Services, School of Art and Design, University of Michigan, 2000 Bonisteel Boulevard, Ann Arbor, Michigan 48109-2069; 734-764-0397, fax: 734-936-0469, e-mail address: adgradinfo@umich.edu

University of Minnesota, Duluth

Duluth, Minnesota

State-supported, coed. Suburban campus. Total enrollment: 10,496. Art program established 1947.

Degrees Bachelor of Fine Arts in the areas of general studio art, pre-graduate studio art, graphic design, art education, pre-graduate art and technology. Majors and concentrations: art and technology, art education, graphic design, studio art. Graduate degrees offered: Master of Fine Arts in the area of graphic design. Cross-registration with University of Wisconsin-Superior, College of St. Scholastica.

Enrollment 398 total; 396 undergraduate, 2 graduate.

Art Student Profile 58% females, 42% males, 3% minorities, 1% international.

Visual

Arts

University of Minnesota, Duluth (continued)

Art Faculty 19 undergraduate (full-time), 5 undergraduate (part-time). 95% of full-time faculty have terminal degrees. Graduate students teach a few undergraduate courses. Undergraduate student–faculty ratio: 17:1.

Student Life Student groups/activities include American Institute of Graphic Arts, Portfolio One-on-One.

Expenses for 2005–2006 Application fee: $35. State resident tuition: $7170 full-time. Nonresident tuition: $18,270 full-time. Mandatory fees: $1758 full-time. Full-time tuition and fees vary according to course load, degree level, program, and reciprocity agreements. College room and board: $5546. Special program-related fees: $62 per semester for computer lab fees, $200 per semester for technology fees, technology equipment, acquisition.

Financial Aid Program-specific awards: 1 Art Gift Fund for program majors ($500), 1 Jaros Photography Fund for photography minors ($550), 10–15 Raymond W. Darland Art Awards for program majors ($1000), 2 Gershgol Awards for program majors ($1900), 1–2 Mitchell and Schissell Awards for program majors ($1000), 1 Edith M. Nelson Award for program majors ($800), 1–2 Cheng-Khee Chee Art Scholarships for program majors ($650), 1–2 Skolmars Family Scholarships for program majors ($500), 3 Howard W. Lyons Scholarships for program majors ($600), 3 AIGA Scholarships for graphic design majors ($500).

Application Procedures Students apply for admission into the professional program by freshman year. Deadline for freshmen: March 1; transfers: June 15. Required: high school transcript, college transcript(s) for transfer students, SAT I or ACT test scores (minimum composite ACT score of 19), high school rank at or above 65th percentile, portfolio in spring of freshman year. Portfolio reviews held on campus.

Web Site http://www.d.umn.edu/art/

Undergraduate Contact Director, Admissions, University of Minnesota, Duluth, 184 Darland Administration Building, Duluth, Minnesota 55812; 218-726-7171, e-mail address: admis@d.umn.edu

Graduate Contact Robert Appleton, Director of Graduate Studies, Art and Design Department, University of Minnesota, Duluth, H317, 1201 Ordean Court, Duluth, Minnesota 55812; 218-726-6141, fax: 218-726-6532, e-mail address: rappleto@d.umn.edu

University of Minnesota, Twin Cities Campus

Minneapolis, Minnesota

State-supported, coed. Urban campus. Total enrollment: 51,175. Art program established 1950.

Degrees Bachelor of Fine Arts in the area of art. Majors and concentrations: ceramics, painting/drawing, photography, printmaking, sculpture. Graduate degrees offered: Master of Fine Arts in the area of art.

Enrollment 590 total; 50 undergraduate, 40 graduate, 500 nonprofessional degree.

Art Student Profile 52% females, 48% males, 18% minorities, 6% international.

Art Faculty 23 undergraduate (full-time), 15 undergraduate (part-time), 23 graduate (full-time). 94% of full-time faculty have terminal degrees. Graduate students teach a few undergraduate courses. Undergraduate student–faculty ratio: 2:1.

Student Life Student groups/activities include Arts Collective. Special housing available for art students.

Expenses for 2005–2006 Application fee: $45. State resident tuition: $7140 full-time. Nonresident tuition: $19,670 full-time. Mandatory fees: $1482 full-time. Full-time tuition and fees vary according to program and reciprocity agreements. College room and board: $6722. College room only: $3886. Room and board charges vary according to board plan, housing facility, and location. Special program-related fees: $15–$250 per class for materials fees.

Application Procedures Students apply for admission into the professional program by junior year. Deadline for freshmen: December 15; transfers: June 1. Notification date for freshmen: January 15; transfers: July 15. Required: high school transcript, college transcript(s) for transfer students, SAT I or ACT test scores, minimum 2.8 high school GPA.

Web Site http://artdept.umn.edu

Undergraduate Contact Office of Admissions, University of Minnesota, Twin Cities Campus,

240 Williamson, 231 Pillsbury Avenue SE, Minneapolis, Minnesota 55455; 800-752-1000.

Graduate Contact Director of Graduate Studies, Department of Art, University of Minnesota, Twin Cities Campus, 405 21st Avenue South, Minneapolis, Minnesota 55455; 612-625-8096, fax: 612-625-7881, e-mail address: artdept@umn.edu

University of Mississippi

University, Mississippi

State-supported, coed. Small town campus. Total enrollment: 14,901. Art program established 1948.

Degrees Bachelor of Fine Arts in the area of art. Majors and concentrations: art history, studio art. Graduate degrees offered: Master of Arts; Master of Fine Arts in the area of art. Program accredited by NASAD.

Enrollment 279 total; 38 undergraduate, 11 graduate, 230 nonprofessional degree.

Art Student Profile 43% females, 57% males, 13% minorities, 3% international.

Art Faculty 9 total (full-time), 13 total (part-time). 100% of full-time faculty have terminal degrees. Graduate students teach a few undergraduate courses. Undergraduate student–faculty ratio: 4:1.

Student Life Student groups/activities include Student Art Association, Mud Daubers, American Institute of Graphic Arts, Vasari Society (art history student organization), Kappa Pi.

Expenses for 2005–2006 Application fee: $25, $40 for nonresidents. State resident tuition: $4320 full-time. Nonresident tuition: $9744 full-time. College room and board: $5762. College room only: $2972. Room and board charges vary according to board plan and housing facility. Special program-related fees: $20 per credit hour for materials fees.

Financial Aid Program-specific awards: 10–15 art merit scholarships for portfolio students ($200–$800).

Application Procedures Students apply for admission into the professional program by sophomore, junior year. Deadline for freshmen and transfers: July 25. Notification date for freshmen and transfers: continuous. Required: high school transcript, college transcript(s) for transfer students, minimum 2.0 high school GPA, ACT test score only (mini-mum composite ACT score of 18), portfolio for transfer applicants and for acceptance into the BFA program upon completion of 18 semester hours in studio art. Portfolio reviews held once on campus; the submission of slides may be substituted for portfolios.

Web Site http://www.olemiss.edu/depts/art

Undergraduate Contact Dr. Nancy L. Wicker, Chair, Art Department, University of Mississippi, 116 Meek Hall, University, Mississippi 38677; 662-915-7193, fax: 662-915-5013, e-mail address: art@olemiss.edu

Graduate Contact Dr. Nancy L. Wicker, Graduate Coordinator, Art Department, University of Mississippi, 116 Meek Hall, University, Mississippi 38677; 662-915-7193, fax: 662-915-5013, e-mail address: art@olemiss.edu

University of Missouri–Columbia

Columbia, Missouri

State-supported, coed. Small town campus. Total enrollment: 27,985. Art program established 1979.

Degrees Bachelor of Fine Arts in the area of art. Majors and concentrations: ceramics, digital art, drawing, fibers, graphic design, painting, photography, printmaking, sculpture, three-dimensional studies, two-dimensional studies, watercolors. Graduate degrees offered: Master of Fine Arts in the area of art. Cross-registration with Mid-Missouri Associated Colleges and Universities.

Enrollment 127 undergraduate, 16 graduate, 116 nonprofessional degree.

Art Student Profile 57% females, 43% males, 5% minorities, 2% international.

Art Faculty 17 total (full-time), 8 total (part-time). 90% of full-time faculty have terminal degrees. Graduate students teach about a quarter of undergraduate courses. Undergraduate student–faculty ratio: 10:1.

Student Life Student groups/activities include Imprint (graphics club), Muck (ceramics club), Student Art Community. Special housing available for art students.

Expenses for 2005–2006 Application fee: $35. State resident tuition: $6495 full-time. Nonresident tuition: $16,272 full-time. Mandatory fees: $1250 full-time. Full-time tuition and fees

University of Missouri–Columbia (continued)

vary according to course load, program, and reciprocity agreements. College room and board: $6245. Room and board charges vary according to board plan and housing facility. Special program-related fees: $40–$100 per course for lab fees.

Financial Aid Program-specific awards: 1 Hennessey Scholarship for program majors demonstrating financial need ($2500), 1 William Ittner Award for program majors ($500), 1 Cox Scholarship for ceramics students ($500), 1 McNair Fellowship for program majors demonstrating financial need, 1 Radford Michael Perrine Scholarship for program majors, 1 Hazel (Pat) Steele Burney Endowment for program majors–undergraduate and graduate.

Application Procedures Students admitted directly into the professional program freshman year. Deadline for freshmen: May 1; transfers: July 1. Notification date for freshmen and transfers: continuous. Required: high school transcript, college transcript(s) for transfer students, SAT I or ACT test scores, minimum 3.0 high school GPA in studio art courses.

Web Site http://web.missouri.edu/~artwww

Undergraduate Contact Deborah Huelsbergen, Director of Undergraduate Studies, Department of Art, University of Missouri–Columbia, A 126 Fine Arts, Columbia, Missouri 65211-6090; 573-882-9444, fax: 573-884-6807, e-mail address: huelsbergend@missouri.edu

Graduate Contact Josephine M. Stealey, Director of Graduate Studies, Department of Art, University of Missouri–Columbia, A 126 Fine Arts, Columbia, Missouri 65211-6090; 573-882-9435, fax: 573-884-6807, e-mail address: stealeyj@missouri.edu

University of Missouri–St. Louis

St. Louis, Missouri

State-supported, coed. Suburban campus. Total enrollment: 15,561. Art program established 1996.

The University of Montana–Missoula

Missoula, Montana

State-supported, coed. Total enrollment: 13,602. Art program established 1957.

Degrees Bachelor of Fine Arts in the area of art. Majors and concentrations: art education, art/fine arts, ceramics, painting/drawing, photography, printmaking, sculpture. Graduate degrees offered: Master of Arts in the area of art history; Master of Fine Arts in the area of art. Program accredited by NASAD.

Enrollment 424 total; 306 undergraduate, 14 graduate, 104 nonprofessional degree.

Art Student Profile 53% females, 47% males, 1% minorities, 1% international.

Art Faculty 13 total (full-time), 11 total (part-time). 100% of full-time faculty have terminal degrees. Graduate students teach a few undergraduate courses. Undergraduate student–faculty ratio: 20:1.

Student Life Student groups/activities include Artists' Collective, Gallery of Visual Arts, Montana Museum of Arts and Culture.

Expenses for 2006–2007 Application fee: $30. State resident tuition: $3739 full-time. Nonresident tuition: $13,246 full-time. Mandatory fees: $1291 full-time. College room and board: $5860. College room only: $2660. Special program-related fees: $18–$65 per course for materials and supplies.

Financial Aid Program-specific awards: 2 Wallace Awards for sophomore or junior program majors ($1000), 1 Pat Williams Scholarship for sophomore or junior program majors ($500), 1 Walter Hook Scholarship for sophomore or junior program majors ($1000), 1 Diggs Scholarship for sophomore or junior program majors ($500), 1 Thomas Wickes Award for sophomore or junior art majors ($2500).

Application Procedures Students apply for admission into the professional program by sophomore year. Deadline for freshmen and transfers: continuous. Required: high school transcript, SAT I or ACT test scores (minimum combined SAT I score of 920), minimum 2.5 high school GPA. Recommended: portfolio. Portfolio reviews held twice on campus; the submission of slides may be substituted for portfolios.

Web Site http://www.sfa.umt.edu

Undergraduate Contact New Student Services, The University of Montana–Missoula, Lommasson Center #103, Missoula, Montana 59812; 406-243-6266, fax: 406-243-4087.

Graduate Contact Graduate School, The University of Montana–Missoula, Lommasson Center, Missoula, Montana 59812; 406-243-2572, fax: 406-243-4593, e-mail address: gradschl@ mso.umt.edu

University of Montevallo

Montevallo, Alabama

State-supported, coed. Small town campus. Total enrollment: 2,999.

University of Nebraska–Lincoln

Lincoln, Nebraska

State-supported, coed. Urban campus. Total enrollment: 21,675. Art program established 1918.

Degrees Bachelor of Fine Arts in the area of studio art. Majors and concentrations: art history, ceramics, drawing, graphic design, illustration, painting, photography, printmaking, sculpture, studio art. Graduate degrees offered: Master of Fine Arts in the area of studio art. Cross-registration with University of Nebraska at Omaha, University of Nebraska at Kearney. Program accredited by NASAD.

Enrollment 337 total; 250 undergraduate, 33 graduate, 54 nonprofessional degree.

Art Student Profile 58% females, 42% males, 8% minorities, 2% international.

Art Faculty 18 total (full-time), 3 total (part-time). 100% of full-time faculty have terminal degrees. Graduate students teach a few undergraduate courses.

Student Life Student groups/activities include Annual Juried Undergraduate Exhibition.

Expenses for 2005–2006 Application fee: $45. State resident tuition: $4530 full-time. Nonresident tuition: $13,440 full-time. Mandatory fees: $1010 full-time. Full-time tuition and fees vary according to course load. College room and board: $6008. College room only: $3239.

Room and board charges vary according to board plan and housing facility. Special program-related fees: $15–$150 per semester for lab fees.

Financial Aid Program-specific awards: 38 endowed scholarships for program majors ($760).

Application Procedures Students admitted directly into the professional program freshman year. Deadline for freshmen and transfers: June 30. Required: high school transcript, college transcript(s) for transfer students, minimum 2.0 high school GPA, SAT I or ACT test scores (minimum combined SAT I score of 1050, minimum composite ACT score of 22). Recommended: interview.

Web Site http://www.unl.edu

Undergraduate Contact Admission Office, University of Nebraska–Lincoln, Alexander Building, 1410 O Street, Lincoln, Nebraska 68588-0417; 402-472-2023, fax: 402-472-0670.

Graduate Contact Prof. Santiago Cal, Chairperson, Graduate Committee, Department of Art and Art History, University of Nebraska–Lincoln, 120 Richards Hall, Lincoln, Nebraska 68588-0114; 402-472-2102, fax: 402-472-9746.

University of Nevada, Las Vegas

Las Vegas, Nevada

State-supported, coed. Urban campus. Total enrollment: 27,344. Art program established 1964.

University of New Hampshire

Durham, New Hampshire

State-supported, coed. Small town campus. Total enrollment: 14,564.

University of New Mexico

Albuquerque, New Mexico

State-supported, coed. Urban campus. Total enrollment: 26,172.

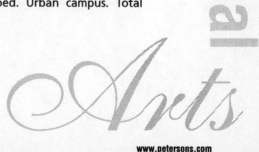

University of New Mexico (continued)

Degrees Bachelor of Fine Arts in the area of studio art. Majors and concentrations: art/fine arts, studio art. Graduate degrees offered: Master of Arts in the area of art history; Master of Fine Arts in the area of studio art. Doctor of Philosophy in the area of art history.

Enrollment 394 total; 185 undergraduate, 85 graduate, 124 nonprofessional degree.

Art Student Profile 63% females, 37% males, 28% minorities.

Art Faculty 30 total (full-time), 15 total (part-time). 100% of full-time faculty have terminal degrees. Graduate students teach about a quarter of undergraduate courses. Undergraduate student–faculty ratio: 35:1.

Student Life Student groups/activities include Art Student Association Gallery.

Expenses for 2005–2006 Application fee: $20. State resident tuition: $4108 full-time. Nonresident tuition: $13,438 full-time. College room and board: $6518. College room only: $3818. Room and board charges vary according to board plan and housing facility. Special program-related fees: $18–$130 for studio/art history courses for materials/technology fee.

Financial Aid Program-specific awards: 12 art scholarships for juniors in College of Fine Arts ($500).

Application Procedures Students apply for admission into the professional program by junior year. Deadline for freshmen and transfers: June 15. Required: high school transcript, SAT I or ACT test scores, minimum 2.5 high school GPA, portfolio for transfer students. Recommended: essay. Videotaped performances are permissible as a substitute for live auditions. Portfolio reviews held continuously by appointment on campus; the submission of slides may be substituted for portfolios.

Web Site http://www.unm.edu/~artdept2/

Undergraduate Contact Office of Admissions, University of New Mexico, Albuquerque, New Mexico 87131; 505-277-2446.

Graduate Contact Ms. Kristie Chung, Graduate Advisor, Department of Art and Art History, University of New Mexico, Albuquerque, New Mexico 87131; 505-277-6672, fax: 505-277-5955.

University of North Alabama

Florence, Alabama

State-supported, coed. Urban campus. Total enrollment: 6,415. Art program established 1930.

Degrees Bachelor of Fine Arts in the area of art. Majors and concentrations: ceramics, graphic design, painting, photography, sculpture. Cross-registration with other institutions in Alabama (specific courses only). Program accredited by NASAD.

Enrollment 104 total; 48 undergraduate, 56 nonprofessional degree.

Art Student Profile 60% females, 40% males, 5% minorities, 2% international.

Art Faculty 8 undergraduate (full-time). 100% of full-time faculty have terminal degrees. Graduate students do not teach undergraduate courses. Undergraduate student–faculty ratio: 6:1.

Student Life Student groups/activities include Student Art Association, FLORALA (student newspaper) and Diorama (yearbook), Lights and Shadows "Magazine".

Expenses for 2005–2006 Application fee: $25. State resident tuition: $3648 full-time. Nonresident tuition: $7296 full-time. Mandatory fees: $718 full-time. College room and board: $4170. College room only: $1960. Room and board charges vary according to board plan and housing facility. Special program-related fees: $30 per semester for studio lab fee.

Financial Aid Program-specific awards: 1 endowed scholarship for program majors ($500), 2 academic scholarships (visual arts) for talented freshmen or transfer program majors ($1000).

Application Procedures Students apply for admission into the professional program by sophomore year. Deadline for freshmen and transfers: August 30. Notification date for freshmen and transfers: continuous. Required: high school transcript, college transcript(s) for transfer students, SAT I or ACT test scores, portfolio after 45 hours for entry into BFA program. Recommended: minimum 2.0 high school GPA. Portfolio reviews held twice on campus.

Web Site http://www.una.edu

Undergraduate Contact Dr. Sue Wilson, Dean of Enrollment Management, Admissions Office, University of North Alabama, Box 5058, Florence, Alabama 35632-0001; 256-765-4680, fax: 256-765-4329, e-mail address: swilson@unanov.una.edu

The University of North Carolina at Asheville

Asheville, North Carolina

State-supported, coed. Suburban campus. Total enrollment: 3,513. Art program established 1966.

The University of North Carolina at Charlotte

Charlotte, North Carolina

State-supported, coed. Suburban campus. Total enrollment: 20,772. Art program established 1965.

Degrees Bachelor of Fine Arts in the area of art. Majors and concentrations: art history, ceramics, cross-discipline studies, fibers, graphic design, illustration, painting, photography, printmaking/drawing, sculpture.

Enrollment 419 total; all undergraduate.

Art Student Profile 54% females, 46% males, 11% minorities, 2% international.

Art Faculty 23 undergraduate (full-time), 15 undergraduate (part-time). 100% of full-time faculty have terminal degrees. Graduate students do not teach undergraduate courses. Undergraduate student–faculty ratio: 16:1.

Student Life Student groups/activities include National Art Education Association Student Chapter, Art Student Association.

Expenses for 2005–2006 Application fee: $50. State resident tuition: $2129 full-time. Nonresident tuition: $12,541 full-time. Mandatory fees: $1420 full-time. Full-time tuition and fees vary according to course load. College room and board: $5550. College room only: $2840. Room and board charges vary according to board plan and housing facility.

Financial Aid Program-specific awards: 4 art scholarships for freshmen and transfers ($2000).

Application Procedures Students admitted directly into the professional program freshman year. Deadline for freshmen and transfers: continuous. Required: high school transcript, college transcript(s) for transfer students, minimum 3.0 high school GPA, interview, portfolio, SAT I or ACT test scores. Portfolio reviews held on campus; the submission of slides may be substituted for portfolios for freshmen and transfers.

Web Site http://www.uncc.edu/art/

Undergraduate Contact Department of Art, The University of North Carolina at Charlotte, 173 Rowe Building, Charlotte, North Carolina 28223; 704-687-2473, fax: 704-687-2591.

The University of North Carolina at Greensboro

Greensboro, North Carolina

State-supported, coed. Urban campus. Total enrollment: 16,060. Art program established 1936.

Degrees Bachelor of Arts in the area of studio art; Bachelor of Fine Arts in the areas of studio art, art education. Majors and concentrations: art education, art history and museum studies, design, museum studies, painting/drawing, sculpture, studio art. Graduate degrees offered: Master of Fine Arts in the area of studio art. Cross-registration with Guilford College, Greensboro College, North Carolina Agricultural and Technical State University.

Art Faculty 16 total (full-time), 4 total (part-time). 100% of full-time faculty have terminal degrees. Graduate students do not teach undergraduate courses.

Student Life Student groups/activities include Student Art Alliance, Coraddi Art Magazine. Special housing available for art students.

Expenses for 2006–2007 Application fee: $45. State resident tuition: $2308 full-time. Nonresident tuition: $13,576 full-time. Mandatory fees: $1505 full-time. College room and board: $5706. College room only: $3232.

Financial Aid Program-specific awards: Falk Scholarships for those demonstrating need and merit, Pierce Memorial Scholarship for North Carolina residents, Peter Agostini and Andrew Martin Scholarship for art majors with financial need, Reeves Scholarship for art

The University of North Carolina at Greensboro (continued)

majors, Mary Cochrane Austin Scholarships for North Carolina art majors, Elizabeth Jastrow Scholarship for junior art history majors.

Application Procedures Students admitted directly into the professional program freshman year. Deadline for freshmen and transfers: March 1. Required: high school transcript, college transcript(s) for transfer students, SAT I or ACT test scores (minimum combined SAT I score of 1000), portfolio for transfer students and for scholarship consideration, minimum 2.9 high school GPA. Portfolio reviews held continuously by appointment on campus; the submission of slides may be substituted for portfolios.

Web Site http://www.uncg.edu/art

Undergraduate Contact Robert Gerhart, Undergraduate Advisor, Department of Art, The University of North Carolina at Greensboro, PO Box 26170, Greensboro, North Carolina 27402-6170; 336-334-5909, fax: 336-334-5270, e-mail address: rrgerhar@uncg.edu

Graduate Contact Patricia Wasserboehr, Head, Department of Art, The University of North Carolina at Greensboro, PO Box 26170, Greensboro, North Carolina 27402-6170; 336-334-5248, fax: 336-334-5270, e-mail address: p_wasser@uncg.edu

University of North Dakota

Grand Forks, North Dakota

State-supported, coed. Small town campus. Total enrollment: 12,954. Art program established 1978.

Degrees Bachelor of Fine Arts in the area of visual arts. Majors and concentrations: ceramic art and design, fibers, jewelry and metalsmithing, new media, painting/drawing, photography, printmaking, sculpture. Graduate degrees offered: Master of Fine Arts in the area of visual arts. Program accredited by NASAD.

Enrollment 114 total; 65 undergraduate, 14 graduate, 35 nonprofessional degree.

Art Student Profile 60% females, 40% males, 3% minorities, 1% international.

Art Faculty 11 undergraduate (full-time), 8 undergraduate (part-time), 11 graduate (full-time). 100% of full-time faculty have terminal degrees. Graduate students teach a few undergraduate courses. Undergraduate student–faculty ratio: 6:1.

Student Life Student groups/activities include Ceramic Arts Organization, Art Student Collective, League of Metalsmiths.

Expenses for 2005–2006 Application fee: $35. State resident tuition: $4390 full-time. Nonresident tuition: $11,722 full-time. Mandatory fees: $937 full-time. Full-time tuition and fees vary according to degree level, program, and reciprocity agreements. College room and board: $4787. College room only: $1979. Room and board charges vary according to board plan and housing facility.

Financial Aid Program-specific awards: 2 Beverly Bushaw Gulmon Scholarships ($750), 2 Stephanie Prepioria Memorial Scholarships ($600), 1 M. Anderson Scholarship ($600), 2 Friedmen Scholarships ($300–$500), 1 Mary Ellen Rogers Scholarship for sculpture students ($300), 1 Alma Anderson Scholarship ($500), 2 Haugen Scholarships ($650), 2 Rod and Carmen Gergstrom Thorpe Scholarships ($1000).

Application Procedures Students apply for admission into the professional program by sophomore year. Deadline for freshmen and transfers: continuous. Required: high school transcript, college transcript(s) for transfer students, portfolio, ACT test score only. Portfolio reviews held by appointment on campus; the submission of slides may be substituted for portfolios for large works of art or when distance is prohibitive.

Web Site http://www.und.edu/dept/arts2000

Undergraduate Contact Dr. Arthur F. Jones, Chair, Department of Art, University of North Dakota, Box 7099, Grand Forks, North Dakota 58202; 701-777-2257, fax: 701-777-2903, e-mail address: anita_monsebroten@und.nodak.edu

Graduate Contact Mr. Kim Fink, Assistant Professor, Department of Art, University of North Dakota, Box 7099, Grand Forks, North Dakota 58202; 701-777-2257 ext. 2905, fax: 701-777-2903, e-mail address: kim_fink@und.nodak.edu

University of Northern Iowa

Cedar Falls, Iowa

State-supported, coed. Small town campus. Total enrollment: 12,622. Art program established 1895.

Degrees Bachelor of Fine Arts in the area of studio arts. Majors and concentrations: ceramics, drawing, graphic design, jewelry and metalsmithing, painting, photography, printmaking, sculpture. Graduate degrees offered: Master of Arts. Cross-registration with institutions of the International Student Exchange Program and National Student Exchange Program. Program accredited by NASAD.

Enrollment 405 total; 26 undergraduate, 3 graduate, 376 nonprofessional degree.

Art Faculty 17 total (full-time), 5 total (part-time). 82% of full-time faculty have terminal degrees. Graduate students do not teach undergraduate courses. Undergraduate student–faculty ratio: 3:1.

Student Life Student groups/activities include ARTS-UNI, Student Art Education Association.

Expenses for 2005–2006 Application fee: $30. State resident tuition: $4890 full-time. Nonresident tuition: $12,502 full-time. Mandatory fees: $712 full-time. Full-time tuition and fees vary according to course load. College room and board: $5531. College room only: $2588. Room and board charges vary according to board plan and housing facility. Special program-related fees: $10–$50 per course for lab fee.

Financial Aid Program-specific awards: Art Department Scholarships for incoming program students ($1000–$3500), Tostlebe Ray Scholarships for undergraduate art majors ($2445).

Application Procedures Students apply for admission into the professional program by sophomore, junior year. Deadline for freshmen and transfers: continuous. Required: high school transcript, college transcript(s) for transfer students, portfolio, SAT I or ACT test scores, TOEFL score for international applicants. Portfolio reviews held twice on campus; the submission of slides may be substituted for portfolios whenever needed.

Web Site http://www.uni.edu/artdept

Undergraduate Contact Stephen W. Taft, Acting Head, Department of Art, University of Northern Iowa, 104 Kamerick Building, Cedar Falls, Iowa 50614-0362; 319-273-2077, fax: 319-273-7333, e-mail address: nancy.sheerer@uni.edu

Graduate Contact Prof. Jean Petsch, Graduate Coordinator, Department of Art, University of Northern Iowa, 104 Kamerick Building, Cedar Falls, Iowa 50614-0362; 319-273-2077, fax: 319-273-7333, e-mail address: jean.petsch@uni.edu

University of North Florida

Jacksonville, Florida

State-supported, coed. Urban campus. Total enrollment: 15,234. Art program established 1972.

Degrees Bachelor of Fine Arts. Majors and concentrations: ceramics, drawing, graphic design, multimedia, painting, photography, sculpture. Cross-registration with state-supported campuses in Florida.

Enrollment 401 total; 175 undergraduate, 226 nonprofessional degree.

Art Student Profile 64% females, 36% males, 15% minorities, 5% international.

Art Faculty 27 undergraduate (full-time), 3 undergraduate (part-time). 100% of full-time faculty have terminal degrees. Graduate students do not teach undergraduate courses. Undergraduate student–faculty ratio: 18:1.

Student Life Student groups/activities include American Institute of Graphic Arts.

Expenses for 2005–2006 Application fee: $30. State resident tuition: $3269 full-time. Nonresident tuition: $14,911 full-time. College room and board: $6640. College room only: $3810. Room and board charges vary according to board plan and housing facility. Special program-related fees: $40 per course for materials.

Financial Aid Program-specific awards: 1–4 Neil Gray Scholarships for junior and senior program majors ($1500), 1 St. Johns and Partners Scholarship for senior program majors ($1500).

University of North Florida (continued)

Application Procedures Students apply for admission into the professional program by junior year. Deadline for freshmen and transfers: July 2. Notification date for freshmen and transfers: continuous. Required: high school transcript, college transcript(s) for transfer students, minimum 2.0 high school GPA, SAT I or ACT test scores (minimum combined SAT I score of 1140, minimum composite ACT score of 25), portfolio for graphic design and multimedia applicants. Portfolio reviews held twice on campus; the submission of slides may be substituted for portfolios for large works of art and when the slides are of adequate quality.

Web Site http://www.unf.edu/coas/cva/visarts. swf

Undergraduate Contact Registrar, University of North Florida, 4567 St. Johns Bluff Road South, Jacksonville, Florida 32224; 904-620-2624.

University of North Texas

Denton, Texas

State-supported, coed. Suburban campus. Total enrollment: 32,047. Art program established 1894.

University of Notre Dame

Notre Dame, Indiana

Independent Roman Catholic, coed. Suburban campus. Total enrollment: 11,417. Art program established 1842.

Degrees Bachelor of Fine Arts in the areas of studio art, design. Majors and concentrations: art/fine arts, ceramic art and design, computer graphics, graphic arts, industrial design, painting/drawing, photography, printmaking, sculpture, studio art. Graduate degrees offered: Master of Arts in the area of art history; Master of Fine Arts in the areas of studio art, design. Program accredited by NASD.

Enrollment 226 total; 39 undergraduate, 21 graduate, 166 nonprofessional degree.

Art Student Profile 75% females, 25% males, 20% minorities, 30% international.

Art Faculty 20 total (full-time), 6 total (part-time). 100% of full-time faculty have terminal degrees. Graduate students teach about a quarter of undergraduate courses.

Student Life Student groups/activities include student exhibitions.

Expenses for 2006–2007 Application fee: $50. Comprehensive fee: $42,172 includes full-time tuition ($32,900), mandatory fees ($542), and college room and board ($8730). Special program-related fees: $15–$100 per course for studio materials.

Application Procedures Students apply for admission into the professional program by sophomore year. Deadline for freshmen and transfers: January 4. Notification date for freshmen and transfers: April 10. Required: essay, high school transcript, minimum 3.0 high school GPA, 2 letters of recommendation. Recommended: interview, slide portfolio. Portfolio reviews held by request on campus; the submission of slides may be substituted for portfolios (slides preferred).

Web Site http://www.nd.edu/~art

Undergraduate Contact Admissions Office, University of Notre Dame, 113 Main Building, Notre Dame, Indiana 46556; 574-631-7505.

Graduate Contact Ms. Jean A. Dibble, Graduate Director, Department of Art, Art History, and Design, University of Notre Dame, 306 Riley Hall of Art, Notre Dame, Indiana 46556; 574-631-4272, fax: 574-631-6312, e-mail address: dibble.1@nd.edu

University of Oklahoma

Norman, Oklahoma

State-supported, coed. Suburban campus. Total enrollment: 26,968. Art program established 1903.

University of Oregon

Eugene, Oregon

State-supported, coed. Urban campus. Total enrollment: 20,347. Art program established 1929.

Degrees Bachelor of Fine Arts in the areas of painting, sculpture, ceramics, fibers, metalsmithing and jewelry, printmaking, photography, multimedia design, digital arts. Majors and concentrations: animation, ceramics, computer graphics, digital art, fibers, jewelry and metalsmithing, multimedia, painting/drawing, photography, printmaking, sculpture. Graduate degrees offered: Master of Fine Arts in the areas of painting, sculpture, ceramics, fibers, metalsmithing and jewelry, printmaking, photography, multimedia design, digital arts. Program accredited by NASAD.

Enrollment 645 total; 150 undergraduate, 45 graduate, 450 nonprofessional degree.

Art Student Profile 50% females, 50% males, 10% minorities, 3% international.

Art Faculty 20 total (full-time), 20 total (part-time). 90% of full-time faculty have terminal degrees. Graduate students teach a few undergraduate courses. Undergraduate student–faculty ratio: 10:1.

Student Life Special housing available for art students.

Expenses for 2005–2006 Application fee: $50. State resident tuition: $4164 full-time. Nonresident tuition: $15,996 full-time. Mandatory fees: $1449 full-time. Full-time tuition and fees vary according to class time, course level, course load, degree level, program, and reciprocity agreements. College room and board: $7496. Room and board charges vary according to board plan and housing facility. Special program-related fees: $5–$80 per course for material fees, $25 per course for studio fees, $50 per term for digital arts program fee.

Financial Aid Program-specific awards: 1 Eugene Weavers' Guild Scholarship for continuing weaving students ($150), 4 Phillip Johnson Scholarships for continuing painting and printmaking students ($200–$400), 1 LaVerne Krause Scholarship for continuing printmaking students ($300–$750), 4 David McCosh Painting Scholarships for continuing painting students ($200–$400), 1 Jack Wilkinson Paint Award for continuing painting students ($200–$400), 1 Molly Muntzel Award for continuing painting students ($200–$400).

Application Procedures Students apply for admission into the professional program by junior year. Deadline for freshmen and transfers: March 1. Notification date for freshmen and transfers: April 1. Required: letter of recommendation, portfolio, statement of interest, college transcript(s) for 2nd degree students. Portfolio reviews held once (digital arts), 3 times (all others) on campus; the submission of slides may be substituted for portfolios (slides preferred).

Web Site http://art-uo.uoregon.edu

Undergraduate Contact Ms. Heidi Howes, Admissions, Department of Art, University of Oregon, 5232 University of Oregon, Eugene, Oregon 97403-5232; 541-346-3610, fax: 541-346-3626, e-mail address: hhowes@uoregon.edu

Graduate Contact Ms. Bonnie Lawrence, Graduate Program Coordinator, Department of Art, University of Oregon, 5232 University of Oregon, Eugene, Oregon 97403-5232; 541-346-3618, fax: 541-346-3626, e-mail address: blawrenc@uoregon.edu

University of Regina

Regina, Saskatchewan, Canada

Province-supported, coed. Urban campus. Total enrollment: 12,670. Art program established 1915.

Degrees Bachelor of Fine Arts. Majors and concentrations: ceramics, drawing, intermedia, painting, printmaking, sculpture. Graduate degrees offered: Master of Fine Arts in the areas of drawing, painting, sculpture, ceramics, printmaking, intermedia.

Enrollment 100 total; 91 undergraduate, 9 graduate.

Art Student Profile 55% females, 45% males, 2% minorities, 5% international.

Art Faculty 11 total (full-time), 6 total (part-time). 90% of full-time faculty have terminal degrees. Graduate students teach a few undergraduate courses. Undergraduate student–faculty ratio: 15:1.

Student Life Student groups/activities include The 5th Parallel Gallery (student-run gallery), Visual Arts Association (VASA), U of R Ceramic Students Society.

Expenses for 2005–2006 Application fee: $60 Canadian dollars. Tuition, fee, and room and board charges are reported in Canadian dollars. Canadian resident tuition: $4551 full-time. Mandatory fees: $412 full-time. Full-time tuition and fees vary according to course load and program. College room and board: $5767. College room only: $3960. Room and board charges vary according to board plan and housing facility. International student tuition: $8627 full-time.

University of Regina (continued)

Financial Aid Program-specific awards: 3 endowed scholarships for program majors ($50–$250), 4 funded scholarships for program majors ($250–$1000).

Application Procedures Students admitted directly into the professional program freshman year. Deadline for freshmen and transfers: continuous. Notification date for freshmen and transfers: August 15. Required: high school transcript, college transcript(s) for transfer students, minimum 2.0 high school GPA, portfolio. Recommended: letter of recommendation, interview. Portfolio reviews held twice on campus; the submission of slides may be substituted for portfolios for large works of art or when distance is prohibitive.

Web Site http://www.uregina.ca/finearts/visual/index.html

Undergraduate Contact Mr. David Garneau, Head, Department of Visual Arts, University of Regina, University Center, Room 247, Regina, Saskatchewan S4S 0A2, Canada; 306-585-5552, fax: 306-585-5526.

Graduate Contact Leesa Streifler, Graduate Program Coordinator, Department of Visual Arts, University of Regina, University Center, Room 247, Regina, Saskatchewan S4S 0A2, Canada; 306-585-5529, fax: 306-585-5526.

University of South Alabama

Mobile, Alabama

State-supported, coed. Suburban campus. Total enrollment: 13,122. Art program established 1964.

University of South Carolina

Columbia, South Carolina

State-supported, coed. Total enrollment: 27,065.

Degrees Bachelor of Fine Arts in the areas of studio art, art education, art history. Majors and concentrations: art education, art history, ceramics, drawing, graphic design, painting, photography, printmaking, three-dimensional studies. Graduate degrees offered: Master of Fine Arts in the area of studio art.

Enrollment 314 total; 100 undergraduate, 14 graduate, 200 nonprofessional degree.

Art Faculty 33 total (full-time), 14 total (part-time). 100% of full-time faculty have terminal degrees. Graduate students teach a few undergraduate courses. Undergraduate student–faculty ratio: 10:1.

Expenses for 2005–2006 Application fee: $50. State resident tuition: $6914 full-time. Nonresident tuition: $18,556 full-time. Full-time tuition varies according to program. College room and board: $6080. Room and board charges vary according to board plan, housing facility, and location. Special program-related fees: $50 per class for lab fees (supplies).

Financial Aid Program-specific awards: 4 Katherine Heyward Scholarships for academically qualified entering and continuing students ($800), 2 Delores Cauthen Scholarships for academically qualified entering and continuing students ($800), 4 Yaghjian Chair in Painting Awards for academically qualified entering and continuing students ($800).

Application Procedures Students admitted directly into the professional program freshman year. Deadline for freshmen and transfers: continuous. Required: college transcript(s) for transfer students, minimum 3.0 high school GPA.

Contact Jodi Salter, Student Services Coordinator, Art Department, University of South Carolina, Columbia, South Carolina 29208; 803-777-8179, fax: 803-777-0535, e-mail address: jodi.salter@sc.edu

The University of South Dakota

Vermillion, South Dakota

State-supported, coed. Small town campus. Total enrollment: 8,641. Art program established 1882.

University of Southern California

Los Angeles, California

Independent, coed. Urban campus. Total enrollment: 32,836. Art program established 1895.

Degrees Bachelor of Fine Arts in the area of studio arts. Majors and concentrations: art/fine arts, ceramic art and design, communication design, computer imaging, digital media, new genres, painting/drawing, photography, printmaking, public art studies, sculpture, studio art. Graduate degrees offered: Master of Fine Arts in the area of studio arts; Master of Public Art Studies.

Enrollment 340 total; 100 undergraduate, 40 graduate, 200 nonprofessional degree.

Art Student Profile 50% females, 50% males, 20% minorities, 16% international.

Art Faculty 17 total (full-time), 51 total (part-time). 85% of full-time faculty have terminal degrees. Graduate students do not teach undergraduate courses. Undergraduate student–faculty ratio: 6:1.

Student Life Student groups/activities include Annual Student Art Exhibition, Animation Club, Fine Art Students Association.

Expenses for 2005–2006 Application fee: $65. Comprehensive fee: $41,618 includes full-time tuition ($31,458), mandatory fees ($550), and college room and board ($9610). College room only: $5260. Full-time tuition and fees vary according to program. Room and board charges vary according to board plan and housing facility. Special program-related fees: $55 per course for lab/studio materials fee.

Financial Aid Program-specific awards: 30 Fine Art Scholarships for program majors ($2000).

Application Procedures Students admitted directly into the professional program freshman year. Deadline for freshmen: January 10; transfers: February 1. Notification date for freshmen: May 1; transfers: June 1. Required: essay, high school transcript, college transcript(s) for transfer students, portfolio, SAT I or ACT test scores, slides for transfer applicants, minimum 3.3 college GPA for transfer applicants. Recommended: interview, minimum 3.5 high school GPA. Portfolio reviews held continuously on campus; the submission of slides may be substituted for portfolios.

Web Site http://finearts.usc.edu

Contact Ms. Penelope Jones, Director of Admissions, School of Fine Arts, University of Southern California, Watt Hall 104, Los Angeles, California 90089-0292; 213-740-9153, fax: 213-740-8938, e-mail address: finearts@usc.edu

University of Southern Maine

Portland, Maine

State-supported, coed. Suburban campus. Total enrollment: 10,944. Art program established 1976.

Degrees Bachelor of Fine Arts in the areas of studio art, art education. Majors and concentrations: art education, ceramics, digital art, drawing, painting, photography, printmaking, sculpture. Cross-registration with Maine College of Art, University of New England, St. Joseph's College, Westbrook College, Southern Maine Technical College. Program accredited by NASAD.

Enrollment 290 total; all undergraduate.

Art Faculty 12 undergraduate (full-time), 12 undergraduate (part-time). 100% of full-time faculty have terminal degrees. Graduate students do not teach undergraduate courses. Undergraduate student–faculty ratio: 13:1.

Student Life Student groups/activities include Union of the Visual Arts.

Expenses for 2005–2006 Application fee: $40. State resident tuition: $4980 full-time. Nonresident tuition: $13,800 full-time. Mandatory fees: $926 full-time. Full-time tuition and fees vary according to course load, degree level, and reciprocity agreements. College room and board: $6755. College room only: $3586. Room and board charges vary according to board plan, housing facility, and location. Special program-related fees: $10–$120 per semester for supplies for some studio and lecture courses.

Application Procedures Students apply for admission into the professional program by freshman year. Deadline for freshmen: August 1; transfers: continuous. Notification date for freshmen and transfers: July 15. Required:

Visual

Arts

University of Southern Maine (continued)

essay, high school transcript, college transcript(s) for transfer students, letter of recommendation, portfolio, SAT I or ACT test scores. Recommended: minimum 2.0 high school GPA, interview. Portfolio reviews held twice on campus.

Web Site http://www.usm.maine.edu

Undergraduate Contact Dee Gardner, Director of Admissions, University of Southern Maine, 37 College Avenue, Gorham, Maine 04038; 207-780-5670, fax: 207-780-5640.

The University of Tennessee

Knoxville, Tennessee

State-supported, coed. Urban campus. Total enrollment: 31,157. Art program established 1947.

Degrees Bachelor of Fine Arts in the areas of studio art, graphic design. Majors and concentrations: art history, ceramics, drawing, graphic design, media arts, painting, printmaking, sculpture, watercolors. Graduate degrees offered: Master of Fine Arts in the area of studio art. Cross-registration with Arrowmont School of Art and Crafts. Program accredited by NASAD.

Enrollment 635 total; 450 undergraduate, 35 graduate, 150 nonprofessional degree.

Art Student Profile 58% females, 42% males, 2% minorities, 2% international.

Art Faculty 27 total (full-time), 12 total (part-time). 100% of full-time faculty have terminal degrees. Graduate students teach a few undergraduate courses. Undergraduate student–faculty ratio: 17:1.

Student Life Student groups/activities include University of Tennessee Potters, Student Art History Association, Sculpture Club, University of Tennessee Print Club.

Expenses for 2005–2006 Application fee: $30. State resident tuition: $5290 full-time. Nonresident tuition: $16,360 full-time. Mandatory fees: $336 full-time. Full-time tuition and fees vary according to location and program. College room and board: $5560. College room only: $2890. Room and board charges vary

according to board plan and housing facility. Special program-related fees: $10–$100 per course for lab fees.

Financial Aid Program-specific awards: 1–3 Orin B. and Erma G. Graff Scholarship for freshmen ($2000), 1 Buck Ewing Undergraduate Scholarship for juniors and seniors ($2000), Mary Louise Seilaz Awards for program students ($1000), T. H. Jeanette Gillespie Awards for juniors and seniors ($500), 1 Mary Lynn Glustoff Memorial Scholarship for program students ($1000), 1 Rod Norman Memorial Scholarship for program students ($500), 1–3 Dorothy Dille Materials/Travel Awards ($1000), 1–2 freshmen scholarships ($2000), 1 Art History Award ($500).

Application Procedures Students apply for admission into the professional program by freshman year. Deadline for freshmen and transfers: June 2. Required: high school transcript, college transcript(s) for transfer students, minimum 3.0 high school GPA, SAT I or ACT test scores.

Web Site http://art.utk.edu

Undergraduate Contact Dr. Timothy W. Hiles, Associate Director, School of Art, The University of Tennessee, 1715 Volunteer Boulevard, Knoxville, Tennessee 37996-2410; 865-974-3407, fax: 865-974-3198, e-mail address: thiles@utk.edu

Graduate Contact Tom Riesing, Graduate Coordinator, School of Art, The University of Tennessee, 1715 Volunteer Boulevard, Knoxville, Tennessee 37996-2410; 865-974-3407, fax: 865-974-3198, e-mail address: triesing@utk.edu

The University of Tennessee at Chattanooga

Chattanooga, Tennessee

State-supported, coed. Urban campus. Total enrollment: 8,656. Art program established 1952.

The University of Tennessee at Martin

Martin, Tennessee

State-supported, coed. Small town campus. Total enrollment: 6,484. Art program established 1999.

The University of Texas at Arlington

Arlington, Texas

State-supported, coed. Urban campus. Total enrollment: 25,432.

The University of Texas at Austin

Austin, Texas

State-supported, coed. Urban campus. Total enrollment: 49,696. Art program established 1938.

Degrees Bachelor of Fine Arts. Majors and concentrations: design, studio art, visual arts. Graduate degrees offered: Master of Fine Arts in the areas of studio art, design. Program accredited by NASAD.

Enrollment 784 total; 371 undergraduate, 44 graduate, 369 nonprofessional degree.

Art Student Profile 70% females, 30% males, 28% minorities, 3% international.

Art Faculty 61 total (full-time), 5 total (part-time). 97% of full-time faculty have terminal degrees. Graduate students teach a few undergraduate courses. Undergraduate student–faculty ratio: 18:1.

Student Life Student groups/activities include Fine Arts Student Council, Art Students Association, Undergraduate Art History Association.

Expenses for 2005–2006 Application fee: $60. State resident tuition: $6972 full-time. Nonresident tuition: $16,310 full-time. Full-time tuition varies according to course load and program. College room and board: $7638. Room and board charges vary according to

board plan, housing facility, and location. Special program-related fees: $84–$210 per course for lab fees.

Financial Aid Program-specific awards: 6 department scholarships for currently enrolled students ($1000).

Application Procedures Deadline for freshmen: February 1; transfers: March 1. Notification date for freshmen and transfers: April 15. Required: essay, high school transcript, college transcript(s) for transfer students, SAT I or ACT test scores, portfolio for transfer applicants. Recommended: 3 letters of recommendation.

Web Site http://www.utexas.edu/cofa/a_ah/

Undergraduate Contact Mr. Shane Sullivan, Academic Advisor II, Department of Art and Art History, The University of Texas at Austin, Art 3.342, Austin, Texas 78712-1285; 512-475-7718, fax: 512-471-7801, e-mail address: shanesullivan@mail.utexas.edu

Graduate Contact Judy Clack, Graduate Coordinator, Department of Art and Art History, The University of Texas at Austin, Art 3.328, Austin, Texas 78712-1285; 512-471-3377, fax: 512-471-7801, e-mail address: jclack@mail.utexas.edu

The University of Texas at El Paso

El Paso, Texas

State-supported, coed. Urban campus. Total enrollment: 19,268. Art program established 1958.

Degrees Bachelor of Fine Arts in the areas of painting, sculpture, ceramics, drawing, metals, graphic design, printmaking. Majors and concentrations: ceramics, drawing, graphic design, metals, painting, printmaking, sculpture.

Enrollment 400 total; 300 undergraduate, 100 nonprofessional degree.

Art Student Profile 50% females, 50% males, 80% minorities, 10% international.

Art Faculty 15 undergraduate (full-time), 16 undergraduate (part-time), 11 graduate (full-time). 80% of full-time faculty have terminal degrees. Graduate students teach a few undergraduate courses. Undergraduate student–faculty ratio: 10:1.

Expenses for 2005–2006 Application fee: $0. State resident tuition: $3930 full-time. Nonresi-

Visual Arts

The University of Texas at El Paso (continued)

dent tuition: $12,210 full-time. Mandatory fees: $1134 full-time. College room only: $4095. Room charges vary according to housing facility. Special program-related fees: $2–$40 per course for lab fees.

Financial Aid Program-specific awards: endowed awards for program majors.

Application Procedures Students admitted directly into the professional program freshman year. Deadline for freshmen and transfers: continuous. Required: high school transcript, college transcript(s) for transfer students, minimum 2.0 high school GPA, SAT I or ACT test scores.

Web Site http://www.utep.edu/arts/

Contact Mr. Vincent Burke, Advisor, Department of Art, The University of Texas at El Paso, 500 West University Avenue, Fox Fine Arts Center, #350, El Paso, Texas 79968-0548; 915-747-7842, fax: 915-747-6749, e-mail address: vburke@utep.edu

The University of Texas at San Antonio

San Antonio, Texas

State-supported, coed. Suburban campus. Total enrollment: 27,337. Art program established 1974.

The University of Texas at Tyler

Tyler, Texas

State-supported, coed. Urban campus. Total enrollment: 5,748. Art program established 1970.

The University of Texas–Pan American

Edinburg, Texas

State-supported, coed. Small town campus. Total enrollment: 17,048. Art program established 1970.

The University of the Arts

Philadelphia, Pennsylvania

Independent, coed. Total enrollment: 2,277. Art program established 1876.

Degrees Bachelor of Fine Arts in the areas of graphic design, painting, printmaking, sculpture, illustration, photography, animation, ceramics, wood, multimedia, writing for film and television; Bachelor of Science in the areas of industrial design, communication. Majors and concentrations: animation, digital art, film and video production, film studies, graphic design, illustration, industrial design, multimedia, painting, painting/drawing, photography, printmaking, sculpture. Graduate degrees offered: Master of Arts in the areas of art education, museum education, museum communication; Master of Arts in Teaching in the area of visual art; Master of Fine Arts in the areas of museum exhibition planning and design, book arts/printmaking, painting, sculpture, ceramics; Master of Industrial Design in the area of industrial design. Cross-registration with schools sponsored by American Independent Colleges of Art and Design. Program accredited by NASAD, IDSA.

Enrollment 1,327 total; 1,146 undergraduate, 181 graduate.

Art Student Profile 56% females, 44% males, 18% minorities, 3% international.

Art Faculty 36 undergraduate (full-time), 118 undergraduate (part-time), 20 graduate (full-time), 25 graduate (part-time). 82% of full-time faculty have terminal degrees. Graduate students do not teach undergraduate courses. Undergraduate student–faculty ratio: 7:1.

Student Life Student groups/activities include Student Government. Special housing available for art students.

Expenses for 2006–2007 Application fee: $60. Tuition: $24,730 full-time. Mandatory fees: $950 full-time. College room only: $6300. Special program-related fees for various lab fees (depending on the curriculum).

Financial Aid Program-specific awards: 50 merit scholarships for program students ($500–$10,000).

Application Procedures Students apply for admission into the professional program by sophomore year. Deadline for freshmen and transfers: continuous. Notification date for freshmen and transfers: September 1. Required: essay, high school transcript, college transcript(s) for transfer students, minimum 2.0 high school GPA, letter of recommendation, portfolio, SAT I or ACT test scores. Recommended: minimum 3.0 high school GPA, interview. Portfolio reviews held continuously by appointment on campus and off campus at National Portfolio Days; the submission of slides may be substituted for portfolios when distance is prohibitive.

Web Site http://www.uarts.edu

Contact Susan Gandy, Director of Admission, The University of the Arts, 320 South Broad Street, Philadelphia, Pennsylvania 19102; 800-616-ARTS ext. 6049, fax: 215-717-6045, e-mail address: admissions@uarts.edu

More About the University

The University of the Arts (UArts) is unique among the nation's leading colleges and universities. Located in Center City Philadelphia, UArts is the only school in the country devoted to all the arts and communication. Composed of the College of Art and Design, the College of Performing Arts, and the College of Media and Communication, UArts offers intensive concentration within each major as well as other creative opportunities for further artistic exploration and growth.

More than 2,200 undergraduate and graduate students from forty states and thirty countries are enrolled. UArts educates professional artists, performers, and communicators—people who make their living creating, designing, communicating, and performing. The active Internship Program offers students opportunities to gain hands-on experience in their field during the academic year.

The College of Art and Design offers a full range of programs in the visual arts. It includes dynamic programs in animation, crafts, films/digital video, graphic design, illustration, industrial design, painting/drawing, photography, printmaking/book arts, and sculpture. These programs share both exceptionally high standards and a supportive, personal environment to explore and grow as a creative individual.

The College of Performing Arts combines both the exhilaration of performance and the diligent commitment to practice and rehearsal to sharpen technique and shape vision. It includes the Schools of Dance, Music, and Theater. The College offers outstanding opportunities to perform as well as the chance to grow as an artist through rigorous training.

The College of Media and Communications explores new ideas and concepts in a changing world.

Video games, the Internet, CD-ROM technology, interactive television, and virtual reality are just a few examples of the emerging forms that are featured in the challenging and exciting curriculum. Offering majors in writing for film and television, multimedia, and communication, the College celebrates the interdisciplinary nature of these new forms of creative expression. Now, students who want to learn more about media and communication before choosing a major can enroll in the UArts Discovery Year, giving them time to explore where their passions lie.

Program Facilities UArts offers excellent facilities to support all of its programs in an environment rich with opportunities to encounter art and artistic inspiration. The studios, shops, theaters, recital halls, labs, galleries, and libraries are housed nearby in Hamilton Hall, the Terra Building, the Merriam Theater, the Arts Bank, and Anderson Hall, the nine-story studio building.

The facilities in the College of Art and Design include a broad range of studios and equipment: woodworking and metal shops, including a foundry; printmaking shops and digital pre-press labs; fine arts, crafts, design, and film/animation studios; and digital imaging labs. Four gas and several electric kilns are available for work in ceramics, as is a forge for sculpture. A large weaving shop offers dozens of looms and a dyeing room. Facilities supporting work in film, video, photography, and animation are extensive and first-class. UArts is one of the first academic institutions to acquire a 3-D printer and scanner for student use. It is used primarily by industrial design and jewelry design students to develop mock-ups of their ideas faster and less expensively than the traditional way of hand molding wax or foam.

The School of Dance offers a rigorous studio experience, and its home is the newly-renovated Terra Building. Dance studios are bright, well-lit, and fully equipped with barres and mirrors, responsive suspension floors, beautiful windows, ceiling fans, pianos, and audio systems. Visiting artists, including Mikhail Baryshnikov and members of the Twyla Tharp Company, teach master classes and meet informally with students. In addition to the 1,600-seat Merriam Theater, student performances are held in the 240-seat UArts Dance Theater. The Alfred M. Greenfield Library houses an extensive collection of dance books and video tapes.

The School of Music at UArts has three big bands, thirty-five small jazz ensembles, seven vocal ensembles, and ten traditional ensembles. In addition to performance opportunities in recital halls and theaters, facilities include fully equipped music studios,

The University of the Arts (continued)

practice rooms, and a class piano laboratory. The MIDI and Recording Studio is a modern recording and music technology facility with a complete 32-input recording studio, MIDI and computer labs, computer and synthesizer work-station labs, and an audio-for-video dubbing and editing room. Most practice rooms are equipped with grand pianos, and a suite of fully equipped percussion studios is also available for student practice.

Students in the College of Media and Communication have ready access to state-of-the-art audio and video systems; highly portable equipment; preproduction and postproduction studios; PC-, MAC-, and Unix-based systems; and industry-standard software used for audio, video, and Web work. The College supports a student-run Webzine and Web radio and hosts a number of student- and alumni-produced Web sites. UArts is a member of the New Media Centers (NMC), an organization of leading universities and corporations dedicated to innovative uses of technology.

Faculty, Residential Artists, and Alumni Numbering 476 full- and part-time members, the faculty is the driving force of the UArts programs. They are practicing professionals, most with advanced degrees, who are committed to both their own creative expression and to the development of their students. The student-faculty ratio is 10:1, so students can be assured of individual attention and guidance.

Visiting artists have included these fine professionals: Dance: Suzanne Farrell, Edward Villelo, Mikhail Baryshnikov, Donna McKechnie, Oleg Eriansky, Gabriella Darvash, James Truitt, Meredith Monk, and Ronnie Favors. Music: Andre Watts, Jack Elliott, Wynton Marsalis, Pierre Boulez, Bill Joel, George Crumb, Eddie Gomez, Placido Domingo, Klaus Tennstedt, Ricardo Muti, Thad Jones, Mel Lewis, Peter Erskine, and Stanley Clarke. Theater: Elizabeth Ashley, Laurie Anderson, Tommy Hicks, and David Henry Hwang.

Proud alumni include Philadelphia Orchestra violinist Michael Ludwig; Alvin Ailey Dance member Antonio Carlos Scott; artist Sidney Goodman; Tony Award-nominated dancer/actress Rhonda LaChanze Sapp; illustrator Arnold Roth; jazz artist/composer Stanley Clarke; director Joe Dante; illustrator Charles Santore; dancer/choreographer Judith Jamison; actress Irene Bodard; concert pianist Lydia Artymiw; children's book authors/illustrators Jan and Stan Berenstain; and the Quay Brothers.

Student Performance/Exhibit Opportunities Events include exhibitions in UArts galleries, ensemble productions, student composition concerts featuring original choreography, repertory concerts, an annual freshmen inter-arts project, recitals, and appearances with visiting artists.

Special Programs Programs include student exchanges with other schools and colleges, foreign and summer studies, pre-College Summer Institute for talented and motivated high school students, career planning and placement, personal counseling, academic support, professional and peer tutoring, services for students with disabilities, and international student services. This year students in the UArts Colleges of Performing Arts and Media and Communication celebrated the inauguration of an exciting partnership with the Liverpool Institute for the Performing Arts (LIPA) in England. Initiatives between the schools include class-abroad opportunities, student exchanges, recordings, performance workshops, and joint master's degree programs.

University of the Pacific
Stockton, California

Independent, coed. Suburban campus. Total enrollment: 6,196. Art program established 1980.

Degrees Bachelor of Fine Arts. Majors and concentrations: graphic design, studio art. Program accredited by NASAD.

Enrollment 90 total; 65 undergraduate, 25 nonprofessional degree.

Art Student Profile 65% females, 35% males, 45% minorities, 5% international.

Art Faculty 8 undergraduate (full-time), 3 undergraduate (part-time). 100% of full-time faculty have terminal degrees. Graduate students do not teach undergraduate courses. Undergraduate student–faculty ratio: 8:1.

Expenses for 2005–2006 Application fee: $60. Comprehensive fee: $34,566 includes full-time tuition ($25,658), mandatory fees ($430), and college room and board ($8478). College room only: $5760. Room and board charges vary according to board plan and housing facility. Special program-related fees: $10–$75 per course for studio materials.

Financial Aid Program-specific awards: 10–20 endowed scholarships for art majors ($2000–$5000).

Application Procedures Students admitted directly into the professional program freshman year. Deadline for freshmen: March 1. Notification date for freshmen: April 15. Required:

essay, high school transcript, minimum 2.0 high school GPA, letter of recommendation, SAT I or ACT test scores. Recommended: minimum 3.0 high school GPA, portfolio.

Web Site http://www1.uop.edu/cop/art/index.html

Undergraduate Contact Office of Admissions, University of the Pacific, 3601 Pacific Avenue, Stockton, California 95211-0197; 800-959-2867, fax: 209-946-2413, e-mail address: admissions@uop.edu

University of Utah

Salt Lake City, Utah

State-supported, coed. Urban campus. Total enrollment: 29,012. Art program established 1890.

Degrees Bachelor of Fine Arts in the area of art. Majors and concentrations: art education, ceramics, digital imaging, graphic design, illustration, intermedia, painting/drawing, photography, printmaking, sculpture. Graduate degrees offered: Master of Fine Arts in the area of art.

Enrollment 675 total; 540 undergraduate, 25 graduate, 110 nonprofessional degree.

Art Student Profile 50% females, 50% males, 12% minorities, 10% international.

Art Faculty 19 total (full-time), 20 total (part-time). 100% of full-time faculty have terminal degrees. Graduate students do not teach undergraduate courses. Undergraduate student–faculty ratio: 13:1.

Student Life Student groups/activities include student exhibitions/associations, intercollegiate exhibitions, interdepartmental collaborative classes. Special housing available for art students.

Expenses for 2005–2006 Application fee: $35. State resident tuition: $3672 full-time. Nonresident tuition: $12,860 full-time. Mandatory fees: $670 full-time. Full-time tuition and fees vary according to course level, course load, degree level, and student level. College room and board: $5422. College room only: $2704. Room and board charges vary according to board plan and housing facility. Special program-related fees: $30–$75 per course for tools and equipment maintenance, materials.

Financial Aid Program-specific awards: 4 departmental tuition scholarships for freshmen and continuing students ($4000), 2 Ann Cannon Scholarships for continuing students ($1000), 1 Ethel A. Rolapp Award for graduating students ($2000), 1 William & Anna Spiess Scholarship for continuing students ($1000), 14 C. M. Cristensen Scholarships for freshmen and continuing students ($1800), 1 Florence Ware Scholarship for continuing students ($1500), 1 freshman tuition scholarship for freshmen ($4000), 1 Grace Durkee Meldrum Scholarship for continuing students ($2500), 1 Paul Davis Travel Award for continuing students ($500), 1 outstanding high school award for incoming high school students ($500).

Application Procedures Students apply for admission into the professional program by freshman year. Deadline for freshmen and transfers: continuous. Notification date for freshmen and transfers: continuous. Required: high school transcript, college transcript(s) for transfer students, minimum 2.0 high school GPA, SAT I or ACT test scores (minimum combined SAT I score of 860, minimum composite ACT score of 18), portfolio for transfer students and for scholarship consideration. Recommended: minimum 3.0 high school GPA. Portfolio reviews held as needed on campus; the submission of slides may be substituted for portfolios for large works of art.

Web Site http://www.art.utah.edu/

Undergraduate Contact Ms. Nevon Bruschke, Undergraduate Advisor, Department of Art and Art History, University of Utah, 375 South 1530 E Room 161, Salt Lake City, Utah 84112-0380; 801-581-8677, fax: 801-585-6171, e-mail address: nevon.bruschke@utah.edu

Graduate Contact Prof. Brian Snapp, Graduate Director of MFA Program, Department of Art and Art History, University of Utah, 375 South 1530 E Room 161, Salt Lake City, Utah 84112-0380; 801-581-8677, fax: 801-585-6171, e-mail address: fireart@xmission.com

University of Washington

Seattle, Washington

State-supported, coed. Urban campus. Total enrollment: 39,251. Art program established 1867.

Degrees Bachelor of Fine Arts in the area of art. Majors and concentrations: ceramics, fi-

University of Washington (continued)

bers, industrial design, metals, painting/drawing, photography, printmaking, sculpture, visual communication design. Graduate degrees offered: Master of Fine Arts in the area of art.

Enrollment 1,300 total; 700 undergraduate, 50 graduate, 550 nonprofessional degree.

Art Student Profile 65% females, 35% males, 10% minorities, 10% international.

Art Faculty 36 total (full-time), 4 total (part-time). 94% of full-time faculty have terminal degrees. Graduate students teach a few undergraduate courses. Undergraduate student–faculty ratio: 14:1.

Student Life Student groups/activities include School of Art Open House, Art on Loan.

Expenses for 2005–2006 Application fee: $50. State resident tuition: $5532 full-time. Nonresident tuition: $19,830 full-time. Special program-related fees: $35–$110 per course for materials fee.

Financial Aid Program-specific awards: 56 School of Art Scholarships for program majors ($1000).

Application Procedures Students apply for admission into the professional program by freshman, sophomore, junior year. Deadline for freshmen: February 1; transfers: April 1. Notification date for freshmen: March 15. Required: essay, high school transcript, college transcript(s) for transfer students, SAT I or ACT test scores, portfolio for transfer applicants. Portfolio reviews held continuously on campus; the submission of slides may be substituted for portfolios whenever needed.

Web Site http://art.washington.edu

Undergraduate Contact Admissions Office, University of Washington, Box 355840, Seattle, Washington 98195-5840; 206-543-9686.

Graduate Contact Katherine Reeves Bagley, Administrative Coordinator, School of Art, University of Washington, Box 353440, Seattle, Washington 98195-3440; 206-543-0646, fax: 206-685-1657, e-mail address: gradart@u.washington.edu

University of West Florida

Pensacola, Florida

State-supported, coed. Suburban campus. Total enrollment: 9,632. Art program established 1980.

Degrees Bachelor of Arts in the areas of art education, studio arts, art history; Bachelor of Fine Arts in the area of studio arts. Majors and concentrations: art history, art/fine arts, digital media, studio art.

Enrollment 210 total; 190 undergraduate, 20 nonprofessional degree.

Art Student Profile 75% females, 25% males, 4% minorities, 3% international.

Art Faculty 9 undergraduate (full-time), 10 undergraduate (part-time). 100% of full-time faculty have terminal degrees. Graduate students do not teach undergraduate courses. Undergraduate student–faculty ratio: 13:1.

Student Life Student groups/activities include S.M.A.S.H. (Students Make Art Stuff Happen).

Expenses for 2005–2006 Application fee: $30. State resident tuition: $2147 full-time. Nonresident tuition: $14,654 full-time. Mandatory fees: $1050 full-time. Full-time tuition and fees vary according to location. College room and board: $6600. Room and board charges vary according to housing facility. Special program-related fees: $15–$48 per course for materials and lab fees.

Financial Aid Program-specific awards: 6 talent scholarships for incoming students ($1000).

Application Procedures Students apply for admission into the professional program by junior year. Deadline for freshmen and transfers: June 1. Required: high school transcript, college transcript(s) for transfer students, minimum 2.0 high school GPA, SAT I or ACT test scores.

Web Site http://uwf.edu/art/art.cfm?p=1

Undergraduate Contact Dr. Suzette Doyon, Chair, Department of Art, University of West Florida, 11000 University Parkway, Pensacola, Florida 32514; 850-474-2045, fax: 850-474-2043, e-mail address: sdoyon@uwf.edu

University of West Georgia

Carrollton, Georgia

State-supported, coed. Small town campus. Total enrollment: 10,155. Art program established 1972.

University of Wisconsin–Eau Claire

Eau Claire, Wisconsin

State-supported, coed. Urban campus. Total enrollment: 10,566. Art program established 1969.

University of Wisconsin–Madison

Madison, Wisconsin

State-supported, coed. Urban campus. Total enrollment: 41,480.

Degrees Bachelor of Fine Arts in the area of art; Bachelor of Science in the area of art. Majors and concentrations: art education, art/fine arts, graphic design. Graduate degrees offered: Master of Arts in the areas of art, art education; Master of Fine Arts in the area of art. Program accredited by NASAD.

Enrollment 569 total; 439 undergraduate, 130 graduate.

Art Student Profile 60% females, 40% males, 10% minorities, 1% international.

Art Faculty 32 total (full-time), 4 total (part-time). 100% of full-time faculty have terminal degrees. Graduate students teach a few undergraduate courses. Undergraduate student–faculty ratio: 23:1.

Expenses for 2005–2006 Application fee: $35. State resident tuition: $6284 full-time. Nonresident tuition: $20,284 full-time. Mandatory fees: $333 full-time. Full-time tuition and fees vary according to degree level and reciprocity agreements. College room and board: $6500. Room and board charges vary according to board plan, housing facility, and location. Special program-related fees: $10–$300 per course for expendable supplies.

Financial Aid Program-specific awards: 4 Edith Gilbertson Scholarships for continuing program students ($1000), 2 Ethel Odegaard Scholarships for continuing program students ($1250), 1 Carrie Jones Cady Scholarship for continuing program students ($350).

Application Procedures Students admitted directly into the professional program freshman year. Deadline for freshmen and transfers: February 1. Required: high school transcript, college transcript(s) for transfer students, minimum 3.0 high school GPA, SAT I test score only.

Web Site http://www.education.wisc.edu

Undergraduate Contact Mr. Keith White, Assistant Director, Undergraduate Admissions, University of Wisconsin–Madison, 750 University Avenue, Madison, Wisconsin 53706; 608-262-3961, e-mail address: keith.white@mail.admin.wisc.edu

Graduate Contact Ms. Carla Leskinen, Secretary, Art Department, University of Wisconsin–Madison, 455 North Park Street, 6241 Humanities Building, Madison, Wisconsin 53706; 608-262-1660.

Peck School of the Arts
University of Wisconsin–Milwaukee

Milwaukee, Wisconsin

State-supported, coed. Urban campus. Total enrollment: 27,502. Art program established 1961.

University of Wisconsin–Oshkosh

Oshkosh, Wisconsin

State-supported, coed. Suburban campus. Total enrollment: 10,997.

Degrees Bachelor of Fine Arts in the areas of art education, studio/fine arts, graphic communications. Majors and concentrations: applied design, art education, ceramics, drawing, fibers, graphic communication, metals, painting, photography, printmaking, sculpture.

Enrollment 370 total.

Art Faculty 14 total (full-time), 6 total (part-time). 100% of full-time faculty have terminal degrees. Graduate students do not teach undergraduate courses. Undergraduate student–faculty ratio: 20:1.

Expenses for 2005–2006 Application fee: $35. State resident tuition: $4,981 full-time. Nonresident tuition: $15,027 full-time. Full-time tuition varies according to reciprocity agree-

Visual Arts

University of Wisconsin–Oshkosh (continued)

ments. College room and board: $4884. College room only: $2784. Room and board charges vary according to board plan and housing facility. Special program-related fees: $10–$30 per course per semester for lab fees.

Financial Aid Program-specific awards: Charles Charonis Scholarship for junior or senior art education majors, Milton Gardener Sculpture Scholarship for junior or senior sculpture students, Bill Neiderberger Scholarship for junior or senior art students, Willcockson Scholarships for incoming freshmen, William Leffin Scholarship for program majors.

Application Procedures Students admitted directly into the professional program freshman year. Deadline for freshmen and transfers: continuous. Notification date for freshmen and transfers: continuous. Required: high school transcript, college transcript(s) for transfer students, standing in top half of graduating class or minimum ACT score of 22.

Web Site http://www.uwosh.edu

Undergraduate Contact Chair, Department of Art, University of Wisconsin–Oshkosh, 900 Algoma Boulevard, Oshkosh, Wisconsin 54901; 920-424-0492, fax: 920-424-1738.

University of Wisconsin–Stevens Point

Stevens Point, Wisconsin

State-supported, coed. Small town campus. Total enrollment: 8,577.

Degrees Bachelor of Fine Arts in the area of art. Majors and concentrations: graphic design, three-dimensional studies, two-dimensional studies. Program accredited by NASAD.

Enrollment 300 total; 240 undergraduate, 60 nonprofessional degree.

Art Student Profile 60% females, 40% males, 6% minorities, 5% international.

Art Faculty 15 undergraduate (full-time), 5 undergraduate (part-time). 100% of full-time faculty have terminal degrees. Graduate students do not teach undergraduate courses. Undergraduate student–faculty ratio: 20:1.

Student Life Student groups/activities include Student Art League, American Institute of Graphic Design Student Chapter, Carlsten Gallery Advisory Committee.

Expenses for 2005–2006 Application fee: $35. State resident tuition: $4277 full-time. Nonresident tuition: $14,323 full-time. Mandatory fees: $785 full-time. Full-time tuition and fees vary according to course load and reciprocity agreements. College room and board: $4322. College room only: $2574. Room and board charges vary according to housing facility. Special program-related fees: $15–$50 per course for studio fees (course materials).

Financial Aid Program-specific awards: 2 Arts Bash Scholarships for those demonstrating financial need ($1250).

Application Procedures Students apply for admission into the professional program by sophomore year. Deadline for freshmen and transfers: continuous. Required: high school transcript, college transcript(s) for transfer students, SAT I or ACT test scores, portfolio for transfers students. Recommended: interview, portfolio. Portfolio reviews held 2 times on campus; the submission of slides may be substituted for portfolios if original work is not available.

Web Site http://www.uwsp.edu/art-design/

Undergraduate Contact Mr. Jeffrey Morin, Chair, Department of Art and Design, University of Wisconsin–Stevens Point, College of Fine Arts and Communication, Stevens Point, Wisconsin 54481; 715-346-2669, fax: 715-346-4072.

University of Wisconsin–Stout

Menomonie, Wisconsin

State-supported, coed. Small town campus. Total enrollment: 7,891.

Degrees Bachelor of Fine Arts in the area of art; Bachelor of Science in the area of art education. Majors and concentrations: art education, graphic design, industrial design, interior design, multimedia design, studio art. Program accredited by NASAD, FIDER.

Enrollment 785 total; all undergraduate.

Art Student Profile 61% females, 39% males, 5% minorities, 1% international.

Art Faculty 28 undergraduate (full-time), 8 undergraduate (part-time). 95% of full-time faculty have terminal degrees. Graduate students do not teach undergraduate courses. Undergraduate student–faculty ratio: 15:1.

Student Life Student groups/activities include Industrial Design Society of America Student Chapter (IDSA), American Society of Interior Designers Student Chapter (ASID), Graphic Design Association Student Chapter (GDA).

Expenses for 2005–2006 Application fee: $35. State resident tuition: $4745 full-time. Nonresident tuition: $15,078 full-time. Mandatory fees: $1847 full-time. Full-time tuition and fees vary according to reciprocity agreements. College room and board: $4572. College room only: $2814. Room and board charges vary according to board plan and housing facility.

Financial Aid Program-specific awards: 1 John and Frances Furlong Art Scholarship for art/art education majors ($1000), 2 Bud and Betty Micheels Student Artist-in-Residence Grants for undergraduates ($1500), 1 Larsen Design Scholarship for art/graphic design or multimedia design major ($1000).

Application Procedures Students admitted directly into the professional program freshman year. Deadline for freshmen and transfers: continuous. Notification date for freshmen and transfers: continuous. Required: high school transcript, college transcript(s) for transfer students, ACT test score only. Recommended: letter of recommendation.

Web Site http://www.uwstout.edu/programs/bfaa

Undergraduate Contact Dr. Cynthia Gilberts, Director of Admissions, University of Wisconsin–Stout, 124 Bowman Hall, Menomonie, Wisconsin 54751; 715-232-1232, fax: 715-232-1667, e-mail address: gilbertsc@uwstout.edu

University of Wisconsin–Superior

Superior, Wisconsin

State-supported, coed. Small town campus. Total enrollment: 2,872. Art program established 1922.

Degrees Bachelor of Fine Arts in the area of art; Bachelor of Science in the areas of art therapy, art education, art history. Majors and concentrations: art education, art history, art therapy, ceramics, fibers, individualized major, painting, photography, printmaking, sculp-

ture. Graduate degrees offered: Master of Arts in the areas of art therapy, art education, studio art, art history. Cross-registration with University of Minnesota-Duluth.

Enrollment 124 total; 100 undergraduate, 24 graduate.

Art Student Profile 65% females, 35% males, 3% minorities, 3% international.

Art Faculty 4 undergraduate (full-time), 2 undergraduate (part-time), 3 graduate (full-time). 100% of full-time faculty have terminal degrees. Graduate students do not teach undergraduate courses. Undergraduate student–faculty ratio: 17:1.

Student Life Student groups/activities include Art Student Club, Ceramic Invitational Golf Tournament.

Expenses for 2005–2006 Application fee: $35. State resident tuition: $4,427 full-time. Nonresident tuition: $14,473 full-time. Mandatory fees: $761 full-time. College room and board: $4422. College room only: $2552. Special program-related fees: $15–$50 per course for lab fees for expendable materials.

Financial Aid Program-specific awards: 10 departmental awards for program majors ($1000).

Application Procedures Students apply for admission into the professional program by sophomore year. Deadline for freshmen and transfers: continuous. Required: high school transcript, college transcript(s) for transfer students, minimum 3.0 high school GPA, SAT I or ACT test scores, standing in top 50% of graduating class. Recommended: interview. Portfolio reviews held on campus; the submission of slides may be substituted for portfolios.

Undergraduate Contact Mr. James Grittner, Chair, Visual Arts Department, University of Wisconsin–Superior, 1800 Grand Avenue, Superior, Wisconsin 54880; 715-394-8391, e-mail address: jgrittne@staff.uwsuper.edu

Graduate Contact Mr. Mel Olsen, Dean of Graduate School, University of Wisconsin–Superior, 1800 Grand Avenue, Superior, Wisconsin 54880; 715-394-6504.

Visual Arts

University of Wisconsin–Whitewater

Whitewater, Wisconsin

State-supported, coed. Small town campus. Total enrollment: 10,750. Art program established 1963.

Utah State University

Logan, Utah

State-supported, coed. Urban campus. Total enrollment: 14,458. Art program established 1908.

Degrees Bachelor of Fine Arts in the area of art. Majors and concentrations: art education, art history, ceramics, graphic design, painting/drawing, photography, printmaking, sculpture. Graduate degrees offered: Master of Fine Arts in the area of art.

Enrollment 530 total; 400 undergraduate, 30 graduate, 100 nonprofessional degree.

Art Faculty 15 total (full-time), 2 total (part-time). 100% of full-time faculty have terminal degrees. Graduate students teach a few undergraduate courses. Undergraduate student–faculty ratio: 22:1.

Student Life Student groups/activities include Printmaking Guild, Student Art Guild, Ceramics Guild.

Expenses for 2005–2006 Application fee: $40. State resident tuition: $3128 full-time. Nonresident tuition: $10,072 full-time. Mandatory fees: $544 full-time. Full-time tuition and fees vary according to course load and student level. College room and board: $4330. College room only: $1550. Room and board charges vary according to board plan and housing facility. Special program-related fees: $15–$75 per semester for lab fees.

Financial Aid Program-specific awards: 8 endowed scholarships for studio art or art education majors, 5 University Scholarships for incoming freshmen ($1100).

Application Procedures Students apply for admission into the professional program by sophomore year. Deadline for freshmen and transfers: continuous. Required: essay, high school transcript, college transcript(s) for transfer students, minimum 2.0 high school GPA, 3 letters of recommendation, portfolio, SAT I or ACT test scores. Portfolio reviews held once on campus; the submission of slides may be substituted for portfolios.

Web Site http://www.usu.edu

Undergraduate Contact Director of Undergraduate Curriculum, Department of Art, Utah State University, 4000 Old Main Hill, Logan, Utah 84322-4000; 435-797-3460, fax: 435-797-3412.

Graduate Contact Prof. Christopher Terry, Director of Graduate Curriculum, Department of Art, Utah State University, 400 Old Main Hill, Logan, Utah 84322-4000; 435-797-3340, fax: 435-797-3412.

Valdosta State University

Valdosta, Georgia

State-supported, coed. Small town campus. Total enrollment: 10,503.

Degrees Bachelor of Fine Arts in the areas of art, art education, interior design. Majors and concentrations: art education, art/fine arts, interior design. Graduate degrees offered: Master of Art Education. Program accredited by NASAD.

Enrollment 266 total; 246 undergraduate, 20 nonprofessional degree.

Art Student Profile 74% females, 26% males, 19% minorities, 3% international.

Art Faculty 16 undergraduate (full-time), 5 undergraduate (part-time), 4 graduate (full-time). 100% of full-time faculty have terminal degrees. Graduate students do not teach undergraduate courses. Undergraduate student–faculty ratio: 16:1.

Student Life Student groups/activities include Art Student League, National Art Education Association Student Chapter, ASID (American Society of Interior Designers).

Expenses for 2005–2006 Application fee: $20. State resident tuition: $2438 full-time. Nonresident tuition: $9754 full-time. Mandatory fees: $840 full-time. College room and board: $5524. College room only: $2904. Room and board charges vary according to board plan and housing facility. Special program-related fees: $20 per course for materials purchase in lab classes.

Financial Aid Program-specific awards: 3 freshman art scholarships for incoming majors

Visual Arts

($700–$1000), 2 Fortner Scholarships for continuing majors ($1275), 1–5 Art Department Assistantships for program majors, 1 Lee Bennet Scholarship for continuing majors ($2800).

Application Procedures Students admitted directly into the professional program freshman year. Deadline for freshmen and transfers: continuous. Required: high school transcript, college transcript(s) for transfer students, SAT I or ACT test scores, completion of college preparatory curriculum or equivalent, minimum re-centered SAT I scores of 440 verbal and 410 math or ACT English 18 and ACT Math 17. Recommended: minimum 2.0 high school GPA, portfolio. Portfolio reviews held once on campus; the submission of slides may be substituted for portfolios whenever needed.

Web Site http://www.valdosta.edu/art/

Undergraduate Contact Mr. Walter Peacock, Director, Admissions Office, Valdosta State University, 1500 North Patterson Street, Valdosta, Georgia 31698; 229-333-5791, e-mail address: wpeacock@valdosta.edu

Graduate Contact Dr. J. Stephen Lahr, Professor/ Art Education, Department of Art, Valdosta State University, 1500 North Patterson Street, Valdosta, Georgia 31698; 229-333-5835, fax: 229-245-3799, e-mail address: jslahr@ valdosta.edu

Virginia Commonwealth University

Richmond, Virginia

State-supported, coed. Urban campus. Total enrollment: 29,349. Art program established 1928.

Degrees Bachelor of Arts in the area of fashion merchandising; Bachelor of Fine Arts in the areas of film, art education, communication arts, crafts, fashion, interior design, painting/ printmaking, sculpture, photography, graphic design, kinetic imaging. Majors and concentrations: animation, art education, art history, communication design, crafts, digital imaging, fashion design, fashion merchandising, film, furniture design, glassworking, graphic arts, illustration, interior design, jewelry and metalsmithing, kinetic imaging, medical illustration, painting/drawing, photography, printmaking, sculpture, textile arts, video art, woodworking design. Graduate degrees offered: Master of Art Education; Master of Fine Arts in the areas of art education, crafts, interior design, painting/printmaking, photography, sculpture, graphic design, film, kinetic imaging. Doctor of Philosophy in the area of art history. Program accredited by NASAD, NCATE, CIDA.

Enrollment 3,279 total; 2,968 undergraduate, 311 graduate.

Art Student Profile 66% females, 34% males, 26% minorities, 17% international.

Art Faculty 80 total (full-time), 145 total (part-time). 97% of full-time faculty have terminal degrees. Graduate students teach a few undergraduate courses. Undergraduate student–faculty ratio: 13:1.

Student Life Student groups/activities include Annual Juried Student Exhibitions at the Anderson Gallery. Special housing available for art students.

Expenses for 2005–2006 Application fee: $30. State resident tuition: $5385 full-time. Nonresident tuition: $17,440 full-time. College room and board: $7042. College room only: $4102. Room and board charges vary according to board plan. Special program-related fees: $257 per semester for comprehensive arts fee.

Financial Aid Program-specific awards: 15–16 Dean's Scholarships for current students ($2000), 1–2 Doris Lansing Scholarship for entering freshmen ($1000–$2500), university scholarship for entering freshmen ($2000– $12,000).

Application Procedures Students apply for admission into the professional program by freshman year. Deadline for freshmen and transfers: February 1. Notification date for freshmen and transfers: continuous. Required: essay, high school transcript, college transcript(s) for transfer students, letter of recommendation, portfolio, SAT I or ACT test scores, slide portfolio of 12 to 16 works, or digital images of 12 to 16 works, or portfolio of 10 drawing/design exercises. Recommended: minimum 2.0 high school GPA. Portfolio reviews held continuously on campus and off campus; the submission of slides may be substituted for portfolios.

Web Site http://www.vcu.edu/artweb/

Undergraduate Contact Ms. Carolyn Henne, Assistant Dean for Student Affairs, School of

Virginia Commonwealth University (continued)

the Arts, Virginia Commonwealth University, PO Box 842519, Richmond, Virginia 23284-2519; 866-534-3201, fax: 804-828-6469, e-mail address: chenne@vcu.edu

Graduate Contact Mr. Joseph Seipel, Senior Associate Dean for Academic Affairs and Director of Graduate Studies, School of the Arts, Virginia Commonwealth University, PO Box 842519, Richmond, Virginia 23284-2519; 804-225-4295, fax: 804-828-6469, e-mail address: jseipel@vcu.edu

More About the School

With approximately 3,200 full-time students, the School of the Arts at Virginia Commonwealth University (VCUarts) is one of the largest art schools in the nation. VCUarts hosts more than 300 on-campus performances and exhibitions each year at the W.E. Singleton Center for the Performing Arts, the Grace Street Theatre, the Anderson Gallery, the Fine Arts Building Gallery, Solvent Space Gallery, and the Student Commons Gallery. Faculty members and students are also involved in hundreds of exhibitions and performances throughout the United States and the world.

VCUarts has fourteen degree-awarding departments. The performing arts departments are Dance and Choreography, Music, and Theatre. Fine arts and design students are required to complete the yearlong Art Foundation Program prior to declaring a major in one of the following departments: Art Education; Communication Arts; Craft/Material Studies (students specialize in one of five material areas: fiber, metal, wood, glass, or ceramics); Fashion Design and Merchandising; Graphic Design; Interior Design; Kinetic Imaging (video, animation, and sound); Painting and Printmaking (facilities include lithography, etching, and screen printing studios); Photography and Film; and Sculpture. The Art History department and the Fashion Merchandising tract do not require completion of the Art Foundation Program.

U.S. News & World Report ranks the School of the Arts sixth in the nation among schools of art and design and the highest ranking public university art school in the nation. Individual departments recognized in the report include Sculpture (first), Graphic Design (fourth), and Painting and Printmaking (tenth). *Interior Design* magazine has recognized VCU's Interior Design program as one of the top five in the nation. In 2002, W. E. Singleton committed $2 million to the VCU Jazz Studies Program (Depart-

ment of Music), the largest gift ever made to a university-level jazz education program.

"The true measure of our reputation is how we are recognized outside of the school. In the past four years our alumni and faculty have received three Guggenheim Fellowships, two awards from the American Academy of Arts and letters, and two MacArthur Fellows "Genius" awards, among many others. This kind of achievement surpasses that of most universities, let alone individual art schools."
——Dean Richard Toscan

The school's outstanding faculty members have published numerous books, including *Alice Aycock: Sculpture and Projects* by Dr. Robert C. Hobbs (2005), *A History of Graphic Design* by Phillip Meggs (1998), *Attention's Loop* by Elizabeth King (1999), *Hypergraphics* by Roy McKelvey (1998), *Milton Avery: The Late Paintings* by Robert Hobbs (2001), and *Type in Motion 2* by Matthew Woolman (2005). VCUarts also has an extensive schedule of visiting artists and professors each semester. For up-to-date information about speakers, visiting artists, and exhibitions, students should visit http://www.vcu.edu.

The Anderson Gallery, located in the heart of the academic campus, is recognized internationally as a major exhibitor of contemporary art. It has a record of grants from the National Endowment for the Arts and the Institute of Museum Services. Recent exhibitions at the Anderson Gallery included prints by Francesco Clemente, drawings by David Hockney, electronic sculptures by Jim Campbell, and kinetic sculptures by Gregory Barsamian. The Gallery has a permanent collection of more than 2,500 objects, including an impression of the only known etching by Vincent Van Gogh and prints by Durer, Rembrandt, Homer, Renoir, William Wegman, and Andy Warhol.

The School of Arts has cooperative educational agreements and/or on-site study in Russia, Germany, Italy, England, China, Africa, and Latin America. The VCU School of the Arts in Qatar was established in 1998 and offers B.F.A. degree programs in fashion design and merchandising, graphic arts, and interior design.

The School of the Arts is a part of Virginia Commonwealth University, one of eighty-four Research I universities in the nation with more than 26,000 students. In addition to completing the arts and general education curricula, students at VCUarts have an opportunity to study in the University's other academic programs: business, dentistry, education, engineering, humanities and sciences, mass communication, medicine, nursing, pharmacy, and social work.

The University guarantees on-campus housing to all incoming freshmen; there are additional housing opportunities throughout the historic Fan residential district, which borders the campus.

The city of Richmond has a great number of art galleries and clubs, museums, and music and theater performance groups, including ballet, symphony, and opera. Richmond is a 2-hour drive from Washington, D.C., and is 1 hour from historic Williamsburg.

Virginia Intermont College

Bristol, Virginia

Independent, coed. Small town campus. Total enrollment: 1,138.

Degrees Bachelor of Fine Arts. Majors and concentrations: art/fine arts, graphic arts, photography and imaging. Cross-registration with King College.

Enrollment 107 total; all undergraduate.

Art Student Profile 71% females, 29% males, 4% minorities, 3% international.

Art Faculty 8 undergraduate (full-time), 3 undergraduate (part-time). 60% of full-time faculty have terminal degrees. Graduate students do not teach undergraduate courses. Undergraduate student–faculty ratio: 10:1.

Student Life Student groups/activities include Society for Photographic Arts, Society for Photographic Education, Collegiate Arts Association.

Expenses for 2005–2006 Application fee: $15. Comprehensive fee: $22,200 includes full-time tuition ($15,500), mandatory fees ($950), and college room and board ($5750). College room only: $2750. Full-time tuition and fees vary according to class time and program. Room and board charges vary according to housing facility. Special program-related fees: $45–$50 per course for computer lab use, $50 per course for lab fees, $70 per course for advanced color and professional courses, $100 for photography workshop fee.

Financial Aid Program-specific awards: 60 departmental awards for program majors ($1200).

Application Procedures Students admitted directly into the professional program freshman year. Deadline for freshmen and transfers: continuous. Notification date for freshmen

and transfers: continuous. Required: high school transcript, college transcript(s) for transfer students, minimum 2.0 high school GPA, SAT I or ACT test scores, portfolio for scholarship consideration. Recommended: interview, portfolio. Portfolio reviews held by request on campus; the submission of slides may be substituted for portfolios for large works of art or when a campus visit is impossible.

Undergraduate Contact Mr. Craig Wesley, Vice President for Enrollment Management, Virginia Intermont College, Box D-460, Bristol, Virginia 24201; 276-466-7856, fax: 276-466-7855, e-mail address: viadmit@vic.edu

Virginia State University

Petersburg, Virginia

State-supported, coed. Suburban campus. Total enrollment: 5,055.

Washburn University

Topeka, Kansas

City-supported, coed. Urban campus. Total enrollment: 7,261. Art program established 1897.

Degrees Bachelor of Fine Arts. Majors and concentrations: art education, visual arts. Program accredited by NASAD.

Enrollment 110 total; 50 undergraduate, 60 nonprofessional degree.

Art Student Profile 56% females, 44% males, 2% minorities, 2% international.

Art Faculty 6 undergraduate (full-time), 7 undergraduate (part-time). 100% of full-time faculty have terminal degrees. Graduate students do not teach undergraduate courses. Undergraduate student–faculty ratio: 9:1.

Student Life Student groups/activities include Washburn Art Student Association, Mulvane Art Museum. Special housing available for art students.

Expenses for 2005–2006 Application fee: $20. State resident tuition: $4920 full-time. Nonresident tuition: $11,130 full-time. Mandatory fees: $62 full-time. College room and board: $4752. College room only: $2772.

Financial Aid Program-specific awards: 20 Art Department Scholarship Awards for art majors

Washburn University (continued)

($1200–$1800), 1 Pollak Art Purchase Award for junior or senior art majors ($1300).

Application Procedures Students apply for admission into the professional program by sophomore year. Deadline for freshmen and transfers: continuous. Required: high school transcript, college transcript(s) for transfer students, ACT test score only (minimum composite ACT score of 17), minimum 2.0 high school GPA for out-of-state applicants. Recommended: portfolio for transfer applicants. Portfolio reviews held twice during sophomore year on campus; the submission of slides may be substituted for portfolios for transfer applicants.

Web Site http://www.washburn.edu/cas/art/index.html

Undergraduate Contact Ms. Glenda Taylor, Chair, Department of Art, Washburn University, 1700 College Street, Topeka, Kansas 66621; 785-231-1010 ext. 2238, fax: 785-231-1089, e-mail address: glenda.taylor@washburn.edu

Washington State University

Pullman, Washington

State-supported, coed. Rural campus. Total enrollment: 23,544. Art program established 1910.

Washington University in St. Louis

St. Louis, Missouri

Independent, coed. Suburban campus. Total enrollment: 13,383.

Degrees Bachelor of Fine Arts. Majors and concentrations: advertising design, fashion design, graphic design, illustration, painting, photography, photography/digital media, printmaking/drawing, sculpture. Graduate degrees offered: Master of Fine Arts in the areas of studio art: ceramics, painting, photography, sculpture, printmaking/drawing, digital imaging. Program accredited by NASAD.

Enrollment 376 total; 349 undergraduate, 21 graduate, 6 nonprofessional degree.

Art Student Profile 76% females, 24% males, 14% minorities, 1% international.

Art Faculty 32 total (full-time), 19 total (part-time). 92% of full-time faculty have terminal degrees. Graduate students teach a few undergraduate courses. Undergraduate student–faculty ratio: 11:1.

Student Life Student groups/activities include American Institute of Graphic Arts Student Chapter, Mid-America College Art Association.

Expenses for 2006–2007 Application fee: $55. Comprehensive fee: $44,240 includes full-time tuition ($32,800), mandatory fees ($988), and college room and board ($10,452). College room only: $6402. Special program-related fees: $25–$250 per semester for material fees/lab fees.

Financial Aid Program-specific awards: 1 Conway/Proetz Award for high academic and artistic achievement ($31,000).

Application Procedures Students admitted directly into the professional program freshman year. Deadline for freshmen: January 15; transfers: June 1. Notification date for freshmen: April 1; transfers: August 1. Required: essay, high school transcript, college transcript(s) for transfer students, minimum 3.0 high school GPA, 2 letters of recommendation, SAT I or ACT test scores, portfolio for transfer students. Recommended: portfolio. Portfolio reviews held once on campus and off campus; the submission of slides may be substituted for portfolios.

Web Site http://art.wustl.edu

Undergraduate Contact Undergraduate Admissions, Washington University in St. Louis, Campus Box 1089, 1 Brookings Drive, St. Louis, Missouri 63130; 314-935-6000, fax: 314-935-4949.

Graduate Contact Mr. Eric Troffkin, Director of Graduate Studies, School of Art, Washington University in St. Louis, Campus Box 1031, 1 Brookings Drive, St. Louis, Missouri 63130; 314-935-5884, fax: 314-935-6462, e-mail address: troffkin@art.wustl.edu

Wayne State University

Detroit, Michigan

State-supported, coed. Urban campus. Total enrollment: 33,137.

Degrees Bachelor of Arts in the areas of fashion design and merchandising, art history, art; Bachelor of Fine Arts in the area of art; Bachelor of Science in the area of fashion design and merchandising. Majors and concentrations: apparel design, art history, ceramic art and design, drawing, electronic arts, fashion design, fashion merchandising, fibers, graphic design, industrial design, interior design, jewelry and metalsmithing, painting, painting/drawing, photography, printmaking, sculpture. Graduate degrees offered: Master of Arts in the areas of fine arts, art history, fashion design and merchandising; Master of Fine Arts in the area of art. Cross-registration with University of Windsor (Canada).

Enrollment 926 total; 875 undergraduate, 51 graduate.

Art Student Profile 60% females, 40% males, 25% minorities, 5% international.

Art Faculty 32 total (full-time), 39 total (part-time). 100% of full-time faculty have terminal degrees. Graduate students teach a few undergraduate courses. Undergraduate student–faculty ratio: 23:1.

Student Life Student groups/activities include Fashion Design and Merchandising Club, Art Student Art Organization.

Expenses for 2005–2006 Application fee: $30. State resident tuition: $5682 full-time. Nonresident tuition: $13,014 full-time. Mandatory fees: $757 full-time. Full-time tuition and fees vary according to student level. College room and board: $5350. Room and board charges vary according to housing facility. Special program-related fees: $15–$75 per course for materials, model fees, special course expenses.

Financial Aid Program-specific awards: 4 talent awards for program majors ($1600), 1 Becker Award for program majors ($1500), 10 endowed scholarships for program majors ($1300), 2 endowed travel scholarships for program majors ($2000).

Application Procedures Students admitted directly into the professional program freshman year. Deadline for freshmen and transfers: continuous. Required: high school transcript, college transcript(s) for transfer students, minimum 2.0 high school GPA, SAT I or ACT test scores (minimum combined SAT I score of 970, minimum composite ACT score of 21), possible portfolio review for graphic design, interior design, or industrial design for transfer students.

Web Site http://www.art.wayne.edu

Undergraduate Contact Michele Porter, Academic Services Officer II, Department of Art and Art History, Wayne State University, 150 Art Building, Detroit, Michigan 48202; 313-577-2980, fax: 313-577-3491, e-mail address: aa2961@wayne.edu

Graduate Contact John Richardson, Graduate Advisor, Department of Art and Art History, Wayne State University, 150 Art Building, Detroit, Michigan 48202; 313-577-2980, fax: 313-577-3491.

Weber State University
Ogden, Utah

State-supported, coed. Urban campus. Total enrollment: 18,142. Art program established 1965.

Degrees Bachelor of Fine Arts in the areas of two-dimensional art, three-dimensional art, photography, visual communication/design, art teaching, general art. Majors and concentrations: art education, photography, three-dimensional studies, two-dimensional studies, visual communication.

Enrollment 300 total; 125 undergraduate, 175 nonprofessional degree.

Art Student Profile 51% females, 49% males, 6% minorities, 5% international.

Art Faculty 12 undergraduate (full-time), 19 undergraduate (part-time). 100% of full-time faculty have terminal degrees. Graduate students teach a few undergraduate courses. Undergraduate student–faculty ratio: 17:1.

Student Life Student groups/activities include Student Art Guild, American Institute of Graphic Arts.

Expenses for 2005–2006 Application fee: $30. State resident tuition: $2547 full-time. Nonresident tuition: $9008 full-time. Mandatory fees: $591 full-time. College room and board: $6500. College room only: $3300. Room and board charges vary according to board plan and housing facility. Special program-related fees: $10 per class for painting supplies, $40 per class for sculpture supplies, $40 per class for metals/jewelry supplies, $40 per class for weaving supplies, $45 per class for visual communication lab fee, $60 per class for

Weber State University (continued)

printmaking supplies, $60 per class for ceramics supplies, $125 per class for photography supplies.

Financial Aid Program-specific awards: 10 University Academic Scholarships for visual arts students, 5 State Activity Scholarships for incoming and continuing art majors ($1500), 7 Sponsor Scholarships for incoming and continuing art majors ($2100).

Application Procedures Students apply for admission into the professional program by sophomore, junior year. Deadline for freshmen and transfers: continuous. Notification date for freshmen and transfers: continuous. Required: college transcript(s) for transfer students, interview, portfolio. Recommended: SAT I or ACT test scores. Portfolio reviews held twice on campus.

Web Site http://departments.weber.edu/dova/

Undergraduate Contact Mr. Drex Brooks, Chairman, Department of Visual Arts, Weber State University, 2001 University Circle, Ogden, Utah 84408-2001; 801-626-6455, fax: 801-626-6976, e-mail address: dbrooks1@weber.edu

Leigh Gerdine College of Fine Arts
Webster University
St. Louis, Missouri

Independent, coed. Suburban campus. Total enrollment: 7,327. Art program established 1960.

Degrees Bachelor of Arts in the areas of studio art, art history and criticism, art education K-12 certification; Bachelor of Fine Arts in the areas of studio art, graphic design. Majors and concentrations: art education, art history, art therapy, ceramic art and design, ceramics, graphic design, media arts, media performance, painting/drawing, photography, printmaking, sculpture. Graduate degrees offered: Master of Arts in the areas of studio art, art history and criticism. Cross-registration with various colleges in St. Louis.

Enrollment 195 total; 180 undergraduate, 15 graduate.

Art Student Profile 60% females, 40% males, 11% minorities, 4% international.

Art Faculty 10 total (full-time), 21 total (part-time). 100% of full-time faculty have terminal degrees. Graduate students do not teach undergraduate courses. Undergraduate student–faculty ratio: 10:1.

Student Life Student groups/activities include Art Council, Graduate Art Council.

Expenses for 2005–2006 Application fee: $25. Comprehensive fee: $23,947 includes full-time tuition ($17,210) and college room and board ($6737). College room only: $3586. Full-time tuition varies according to program. Room and board charges vary according to board plan and housing facility. Special program-related fees: $50–$150 per course for studio lab fee.

Financial Aid Program-specific awards: 1 Sr. Gabriel Mary Hoare Scholarship for visual arts students ($15,000).

Application Procedures Students apply for admission into the professional program by junior year. Notification date for freshmen and transfers: July 15. Required: essay, high school transcript, college transcript(s) for transfer students, minimum 2.0 high school GPA, 2 letters of recommendation, interview, portfolio, SAT I or ACT test scores (minimum composite ACT score of 21), minimum combined SAT Reasoning Score of 1400. Recommended: minimum 3.0 high school GPA. Portfolio reviews held 10 times on campus and off campus in Vienna, Austria; the submission of slides may be substituted for portfolios when distance is prohibitive.

Web Site http://www.webster.edu/depts/finearts/art

Undergraduate Contact Jennifer Andonoff, Portfolio Review Coordinator, Office of Admissions, Webster University, 470 East Lockwood Avenue, St. Louis, Missouri 63119-3194; 314-968-7001, fax: 314-968-7115, e-mail address: andronoff@webster.edu

Graduate Contact Dr. Jeffrey A. Hughes, Graduate Program Coordinator, Department of Art, Webster University, 470 East Lockwood Avenue, St. Louis, Missouri 63119-3194; 314-968-7159, fax: 314-968-7139, e-mail address: hughes@webster.edu

West Chester University of Pennsylvania
West Chester, Pennsylvania

State-supported, coed. Suburban campus. Total enrollment: 12,988.

Degrees Bachelor of Arts in the area of art; Bachelor of Fine Arts in the area of studio art. Majors and concentrations: art/fine arts, ceramics, computer graphics, painting/drawing, sculpture.

Enrollment 225 total; all undergraduate.

Art Student Profile 60% females, 40% males.

Art Faculty 12 undergraduate (full-time), 3 undergraduate (part-time). 100% of full-time faculty have terminal degrees. Graduate students do not teach undergraduate courses. Undergraduate student–faculty ratio: 10:1.

Student Life Student groups/activities include Print Club, Art Association, American Institute of Graphic Arts.

Expenses for 2006–2007 Application fee: $35. State resident tuition: $4906 full-time. Nonresident tuition: $12,266 full-time. Mandatory fees: $1241 full-time. College room and board: $6208. College room only: $4140.

Financial Aid Program-specific awards: 2 McKinney Scholarships for junior painting majors ($1000), 1 Bessie Grubb Scholarship for junior graphic design majors ($1000), 1 Hawthorne Scholarship for painting majors ($1000).

Application Procedures Students admitted directly into the professional program freshman year. Deadline for freshmen and transfers: continuous. Required: essay, high school transcript, college transcript(s) for transfer students, minimum 2.0 high school GPA, SAT I or ACT test scores (minimum combined SAT I score of 1000). Recommended: minimum 3.0 high school GPA.

Undergraduate Contact Mr. John Baker, Chair, Art Department, West Chester University of Pennsylvania, Mitchell Hall, West Chester, Pennsylvania 19383; 610-436-2755, e-mail address: jbaker@wcupa.edu

Western Carolina University

Cullowhee, North Carolina

State-supported, coed. Rural campus. Total enrollment: 8,665. Art program established 1964.

Degrees Bachelor of Fine Arts in the areas of studio art, graphic design. Majors and concentrations: book arts, ceramic art and design, graphic design, painting/drawing, photography, printmaking, sculpture. Graduate degrees offered: Master of Art in Education; Master of Arts in Teaching; Master of Fine Arts in the area of fine arts. Cross-registration with Penland School of Crafts.

Enrollment 167 total; 150 undergraduate, 4 graduate, 13 nonprofessional degree.

Art Student Profile 50% females, 50% males, 3% minorities, 1% international.

Art Faculty 12 total (full-time), 13 total (part-time). 100% of full-time faculty have terminal degrees. Graduate students do not teach undergraduate courses. Undergraduate student–faculty ratio: 15:1.

Student Life Student groups/activities include Annual Student Exhibition, Nomad (student art and literature publication), Art Students League.

Expenses for 2006–2007 Application fee: $40.

Financial Aid Program-specific awards: 1 Lorraine Stone Scholarship for non-traditional students ($1000), 4 departmental scholarships for program students ($500), 1 Macon County Art Scholarship for program students from Macon County ($1000).

Application Procedures Students admitted directly into the professional program freshman year. Deadline for freshmen and transfers: continuous. Notification date for freshmen and transfers: August 1. Required: high school transcript, college transcript(s) for transfer students, minimum 2.0 high school GPA, 3 letters of recommendation, SAT I or ACT test scores. Recommended: interview, portfolio. Portfolio reviews held continuously on campus; the submission of slides may be substituted for portfolios (slides preferred).

Web Site http://www.wcu.edu/as/

Undergraduate Contact Mr. Matt Liddle, Acting Head, Department of Art, Western Carolina University, Cullowhee, North Carolina 28723; 828-227-7210 ext. 3590, fax: 828-227-7505, e-mail address: wcuart@wcu.edu

Western Illinois University

Macomb, Illinois

State-supported, coed. Small town campus. Total enrollment: 13,404. Art program established 1938.

Potter College of Arts, Humanities, and Social Sciences

Western Kentucky University

Bowling Green, Kentucky

State-supported, coed. Suburban campus. Total enrollment: 18,634. Art program established 1960.

Western Michigan University

Kalamazoo, Michigan

State-supported, coed. Urban campus. Total enrollment: 26,239.

Degrees Bachelor of Fine Arts in the areas of painting, ceramics, sculpture, photography, graphic design, printmaking. Majors and concentrations: art education, art history, art/fine arts, ceramics, graphic design, metals and jewelry, painting, photography, printmaking, sculpture. Graduate degrees offered: Master of Arts in the area of art education; Master of Fine Arts in the areas of painting, printmaking, graphic design, sculpture, ceramics, photography. Cross-registration with Michigan colleges and universities and community colleges. Program accredited by NASAD.

Enrollment 668 total; 385 undergraduate, 8 graduate, 275 nonprofessional degree.

Art Faculty 21 total (full-time), 18 total (part-time). 100% of full-time faculty have terminal degrees. Graduate students teach a few undergraduate courses. Undergraduate student–faculty ratio: 25:1.

Student Life Student groups/activities include Students in Design, Michigan Art Education Association.

Expenses for 2005–2006 Application fee: $35. State resident tuition: $5826 full-time. Nonresident tuition: $15,204 full-time. Mandatory fees: $652 full-time. Full-time tuition and fees vary according to course load, location, and student level. College room and board: $6651. College room only: $3518. Room and board charges vary according to board plan. Special program-related fees: $25–$150 per class for studio fees.

Financial Aid Program-specific awards: 1 departmental scholarship for freshmen with outstanding portfolios ($500), 5 James Kerr and Rose Netzorg Kerr Awards for outstanding students ($400), 9 Art Star Awards for junior/senior art majors ($200), 2 Elizabeth Smutz Awards for outstanding art education majors ($600), 2 Haig and Janette Tashjian Scholarships for outstanding art education majors demonstrating need ($1100), 2 Walter F. Enz Memorial Awards for outstanding art students ($1000), 7 Angie Gayman Carmer Art Scholarships for art students with minimum 3.5 GPA demonstrating financial need ($1400), 4 foundation scholarships for outstanding students in foundation courses ($375), 20 enrichment grants for full-time art students ($600).

Application Procedures Students apply for admission into the professional program by freshman, sophomore year. Deadline for freshmen and transfers: March 14. Notification date for freshmen and transfers: April 1. Required: essay, high school transcript, college transcript(s) for transfer students, minimum 2.0 high school GPA, letter of recommendation, portfolio, ACT test score only. Recommended: minimum 3.0 high school GPA. Portfolio reviews held once for graphic design majors and 2 times for other program majors on campus; the submission of slides may be substituted for portfolios on a case-by-case basis.

Web Site http://www.wmich.edu/art

Undergraduate Contact John Kollig, Academic Advisor, Department of Art, Western Michigan University, 1201 Oliver Street, Kalamazoo, Michigan 49008; 269-387-2440, fax: 269-387-2477, e-mail address: john.kollig@wmich.edu

Graduate Contact Ellen Armstrong, Academic Advisor, Department of Art, Western Michigan University, 1201 Oliver Street, Kalamazoo, Michigan 49008; 269-387-2440, fax: 269-387-2477, e-mail address: ellen.armstrong@wmich.edu

West Texas A&M University

Canyon, Texas

State-supported, coed. Small town campus. Total enrollment: 8,667. Art program established 1953.

Degrees Bachelor of Fine Arts in the areas of studio art, graphic design. Majors and concentrations: ceramics, computer art, glassworking, graphic design, jewelry and metalsmithing, painting/drawing, printmaking, sculpture. Graduate degrees offered: Master of Arts in the area of art; Master of Fine Arts in the area of studio art.

Enrollment 106 total; 80 undergraduate, 21 graduate, 5 nonprofessional degree.

Art Student Profile 48% females, 52% males, 10% minorities, 3% international.

Art Faculty 5 total (full-time), 3 total (part-time). 100% of full-time faculty have terminal degrees. Graduate students teach a few undergraduate courses. Undergraduate student–faculty ratio: 16:1.

Student Life Student groups/activities include Art This.

Expenses for 2005–2006 Application fee: $25. State resident tuition: $2760 full-time. Nonresident tuition: $11,040 full-time. Mandatory fees: $996 full-time. College room and board: $4916. College room only: $2300. Special program-related fees: $7–$30 per course for lab fees.

Financial Aid Program-specific awards: 2 Levi Margaret Cole Endowment Awards for program majors ($200–$500), 1 Charles Hohmann Endowment Award for graphic design majors ($400), 1 Mary Moody Northen Endowment Award for program majors ($200–$500), 1 Isabel Robinson Scholarship for program majors ($200–$500), 1 Emmit Smith Art Scholarship for studio art students ($200–$500), 12 Foundation for Fine Arts Awards for program majors ($200–$500), 6 Sybil Harrington Scholarships for program majors ($500–$1000), 4 Harrington Bequest Awards for program majors ($200–$500), 1 Georgia O'Keefe Scholarship for program majors ($500–$600).

Application Procedures Students admitted directly into the professional program freshman year. Deadline for freshmen and transfers: continuous. Required: high school transcript, college transcript(s) for transfer students, SAT I or ACT test scores. Recommended: 2 letters of recommendation, interview, portfolio. Portfolio reviews held once and as needed on campus; the submission of slides may be substituted for portfolios when distance is prohibitive.

Web Site http://www.wtamu.edu

Undergraduate Contact Mr. Royal Brantley, Head, Department of Art, Communication and Theater, West Texas A&M University, WTAMU Box 60747, Canyon, Texas 79016; 806-651-2799, fax: 806-651-2818, e-mail address: rbrantley@mail.wtamu.edu

Graduate Contact Mr. David Rindlisbacher, Graduate Program Coordinator, Department of Art, Communication and Theater, West Texas A&M University, WTAMU Box 60747, Canyon, Texas 79016; 806-651-2792, fax: 806-651-2818, e-mail address: drindlisbacher@mail.wtamu.edu

West Virginia University

Morgantown, West Virginia

State-supported, coed. Small town campus. Total enrollment: 26,051. Art program established 1897.

Degrees Bachelor of Fine Arts. Majors and concentrations: art education, ceramics, graphic design, intermedia, painting/drawing, printmaking, sculpture. Graduate degrees offered: Master of Arts in the areas of art education, studio art; Master of Fine Arts in the areas of painting, printmaking, sculpture, ceramics, new forms (experimental). Program accredited by NASAD.

Enrollment 328 total; 310 undergraduate, 18 graduate.

Art Student Profile 55% females, 45% males, 6% minorities, 4% international.

Art Faculty 16 total (full-time), 3 total (part-time). 98% of full-time faculty have terminal degrees. Graduate students teach a few undergraduate courses. Undergraduate student–faculty ratio: 17:1.

Student Life Student groups/activities include Student Art Association, National Association of Art Education student chapter. Special housing available for art students.

Expenses for 2005–2006 Application fee: $25. State resident tuition: $4164 full-time. Nonresident tuition: $12,874 full-time. Full-time tuition varies according to location, program, and reciprocity agreements. College room and board: $6342. College room only: $3348. Room and board charges vary according to board plan, housing facility, and location. Special program-related fees: $75 per 3 credit hours for expendable supplies for studio courses.

West Virginia University (continued)

Financial Aid Program-specific awards: 12 Fine Arts Awards for program students ($2000–$6000), 3 Loyalty Permanent Endowment Awards for state residents ($1000), 1 Gabriel Fellowship for state residents ($1000), 6 Mesaros Scholarships for junior and senior art majors ($500–$2000).

Application Procedures Students apply for admission into the professional program by sophomore year. Deadline for freshmen and transfers: February 1. Notification date for freshmen and transfers: March 1. Required: high school transcript, college transcript(s) for transfer students, minimum 2.0 high school GPA, letter of recommendation, portfolio, SAT I or ACT test scores. Recommended: interview. Portfolio reviews held 3 times on campus; the submission of slides may be substituted for portfolios if original work is not available or distance is prohibitive.

Web Site http://www.wvu.edu/~ccarts

Undergraduate Contact Ms. Kristina Olson, Undergraduate Advisor, Division of Art, West Virginia University, College of Creative Arts, PO Box 6111, Morgantown, West Virginia 26506-6111; 304-293-4841 ext. 3210, fax: 304-293-5731, e-mail address: kristina.olson2@mail.wvu.edu

Graduate Contact Mr. Sergio Soave, Chair, Division of Art, West Virginia University, College of Creative Arts, PO Box 6111, Morgantown, West Virginia 26506-6111; 304-293-4841 ext. 3138, fax: 304-293-5731, e-mail address: sergio.soave@mail.wvu.edu

Williams Baptist College

Walnut Ridge, Arkansas

Independent Southern Baptist, coed. Rural campus. Total enrollment: 653 (2004). Art program established 1994.

Degrees Bachelor of Fine Arts in the area of studio art. Majors and concentrations: ceramics, painting, printmaking.

Art Faculty 1 undergraduate (full-time), 1 undergraduate (part-time). Graduate students do not teach undergraduate courses.

Student Life Student groups/activities include Art Club.

Expenses for 2005–2006 Special program-related fees: $75 per course for studio fee.

Financial Aid Program-specific awards: art scholarship for program majors.

Application Procedures Students admitted directly into the professional program freshman year. Deadline for freshmen and transfers: continuous. Required: high school transcript, college transcript(s) for transfer students, portfolio, SAT I or ACT test scores. Recommended: interview, minimum 2.5 high school GPA. Portfolio reviews held once per semester after completion of foundation courses on campus; the submission of slides may be substituted for portfolios when distance is prohibitive.

Web Site http://www.wbcoll.edu

Undergraduate Contact Dr. David Midkiff, Chairman, Department of Art, Williams Baptist College, PO Box 3536 WBC, Walnut Ridge, Arkansas 72476; 870-759-4141, fax: 870-886-3924, e-mail address: dmidkiff@wbcoll.edu

Winthrop University

Rock Hill, South Carolina

State-supported, coed. Suburban campus. Total enrollment: 6,480. Art program established 1984.

Wright State University

Dayton, Ohio

State-supported, coed. Suburban campus. Total enrollment: 16,207. Art program established 1964.

Degrees Bachelor of Fine Arts in the areas of art education, fine arts. Majors and concentrations: art education, painting, photography, printmaking, sculpture.

Enrollment 231 total; 158 undergraduate, 73 nonprofessional degree.

Art Student Profile 70% females, 30% males, 21% minorities, 4% international.

Art Faculty 10 undergraduate (full-time), 7 undergraduate (part-time). 100% of full-time faculty have terminal degrees. Graduate students do not teach undergraduate courses. Undergraduate student–faculty ratio: 9:1.

Expenses for 2006–2007 Application fee: $30. State resident tuition: $7278 full-time. Nonresident tuition: $14,004 full-time. College room and board: $7180. Special program-related fees: $35–$120 per course for materials fee.

Financial Aid Program-specific awards: 10–20 Art Department Merit Scholarships for program majors ($1800), 2–4 Arts Gala Scholarships for entering program majors ($5000).

Application Procedures Students apply for admission into the professional program by sophomore year. Deadline for freshmen and transfers: continuous. Required: high school transcript, college transcript(s) for transfer students, SAT I or ACT test scores.

Web Site http://www.wright.edu

Undergraduate Contact Dr. Linda Caron, Chair, Department of Art and Art History, Wright State University, Creative Arts Center A-226, Colonel Glenn Highway, Dayton, Ohio 45435; 937-775-2896, fax: 937-775-3049, e-mail address: linda.caron@wright.edu

Xavier University

Cincinnati, Ohio

Independent Roman Catholic, coed. Suburban campus. Total enrollment: 6,665. Art program established 1980.

York University

Toronto, Ontario, Canada

Province-supported, coed. Urban campus. Total enrollment: 49,496. Art program established 1969.

Degrees Bachelor of Design in the area of communications design; Bachelor of Fine Arts in the area of visual arts. Majors and concentrations: design, drawing, new media, painting, photography, printmaking, sculpture. Graduate degrees offered: Master of Design in the areas of graphic, communications design; Master of Fine Arts in the area of visual arts. Mandatory cross-registration with Sheridan College (BDes program only).

Enrollment 1,167 total; 1,019 undergraduate, 19 graduate, 129 nonprofessional degree.

Art Student Profile 74% females, 26% males, 4% international.

Art Faculty 35 total (full-time), 31 total (part-time). 88% of full-time faculty have terminal degrees. Graduate students teach a few undergraduate courses. Undergraduate student–faculty ratio: 12:1.

Student Life Student groups/activities include Visual Arts Student Council, Creative Arts Students Association.

Expenses for 2005–2006 Application fee: $90 Canadian dollars. Comprehensive fee: $10,981 includes full-time tuition ($4862) and college room and board ($6119). College room only: $3719. Full-time tuition varies according to course load, degree level, and program. Room and board charges vary according to board plan and housing facility. International student tuition: $14,862 full-time. Special program-related fees: $15–$150 per semester for lab fees for photography, sculpture, printmaking, and new media.

Financial Aid Program-specific awards: 6 talent awards for applicants with outstanding portfolios ($1000), 2 international talent awards for international applicants with outstanding portfolios ($2000), 5 Harry Rowe Bursaries for those demonstrating achievement or potential in artistic or scholarly work ($2000), 20 Fine Arts Bursaries for academically qualified applicants demonstrating financial need ($200–$700), 5 Jack Bush Scholarships for those demonstrating merit in studio work ($800), 6 L.L. Odette Sculpture Scholarships for juniors or seniors showing excellence in sculpture ($500), 2 Nirvan Bhavan Foundation Scholarships for juniors or seniors in Indian studies demonstrating need ($3000), 2 Michael Plexhan Awards for juniors or seniors demonstrating creative innovation and need ($2000), 1 Department of Visual Arts Award for those demonstrating financial need and with B average ($1000), 1 Joseph Drapell Award for those demonstrating financial need and academic and artistic excellence ($850).

Application Procedures Students admitted directly into the professional program freshman year. Deadline for freshmen and transfers: March 1. Notification date for freshmen: June 30; transfers: July 15. Required: high school transcript, college transcript(s) for transfer students, minimum 3.0 high school GPA, portfolio, SAT I, ACT or Canadian equivalent, interview for applicants within a reasonable distance, questionnaire. Recommended: interview. Portfolio reviews held 15 times on

York University (continued)

campus; the submission of slides may be substituted for portfolios when distance is prohibitive or for large works of art.

Web Site http://www.yorku.ca/finearts/visa/

Undergraduate Contact Mary Riccardi, Advisor, Student and Academic Services, York University, 201 Goldfarb Centre of Fine Arts, Toronto, Ontario M3J 1P3, Canada; 416-736-2100 ext. 77345, fax: 416-736-5447, e-mail address: mriccardi@yorku.ca

Graduate Contact Yvonne Singer, Graduate Director, Department of Visual Arts, York University, 232 CFA, 4700 Keele Street, Toronto, Ontario M3J 1P3, Canada; 416-736-5533, fax: 416-736-5875.

Youngstown State University

Youngstown, Ohio

State-supported, coed. Urban campus. Total enrollment: 12,809. Art program established 1927.

Degrees Bachelor of Arts in the area of art history; Bachelor of Fine Arts in the area of studio art; Bachelor of Science in the area of art education. Majors and concentrations: art and technology, art education, art history, general studio, graphic design, individualized major, painting, photography, printmaking, spatial arts. Program accredited by NASAD.

Enrollment 313 total; 307 undergraduate, 6 graduate.

Art Student Profile 55% females, 45% males, 9% minorities, 2% international.

Art Faculty 16 undergraduate (full-time), 20 undergraduate (part-time). 95% of full-time faculty have terminal degrees. Graduate students do not teach undergraduate courses. Undergraduate student–faculty ratio: 13:1.

Student Life Student groups/activities include Student Art Association, American Institute of Graphic Arts Student Organization, Spatial Arts Alliance.

Expenses for 2005–2006 Application fee: $30. State resident tuition: $6104 full-time. Nonresident tuition: $11,312 full-time. Mandatory fees: $229 full-time. Full-time tuition and fees vary according to course load. College room and board: $6280. Room and board charges vary according to board plan and housing facility. Special program-related fees: $45 per course for art history classes, $60 per course for studio lab fees.

Financial Aid Program-specific awards: Beecher Talent Scholarships for freshmen (renewable) ($1000), Scholastics Portfolio Award for freshmen (renewable) ($2000), Trumbull County Scholarship for freshmen (renewable) ($300), Cubbison Painting Award for freshmen ($2500).

Application Procedures Students apply for admission into the professional program by sophomore year. Deadline for freshmen and transfers: continuous. Required: high school transcript, college transcript(s) for transfer students, portfolio for scholarship consideration. Recommended: SAT I or ACT test scores. Portfolio reviews held twice on campus; the submission of slides may be substituted for portfolios.

Web Site http://www.fpa.ysu.edu/art/index. html

Undergraduate Contact Chair, Department of Art, Youngstown State University, 1 University Plaza, Youngstown, Ohio 44555; 330-941-3627, fax: 330-941-7183, e-mail address: art@cc.ysu.edu

Appendixes

Summer Programs in Art

ABBEY ROAD OVERSEAS PROGRAMS

Abbey Road Overseas Programs–Pre-College: Art History, Studio Art, and Italian–Florence

Dr. Arthur Kian
Managing Director
8904 Rangely Avenue
West Hollywood, CA 90048
Phone: 888-462-2239
Fax: 866-488-4642
E-mail: info@goabbeyroad.com
Web site: www.goabbeyroad.com/florence.htm

APPEL FARM ARTS AND MUSIC CENTER

Appel Farm Summer Arts Camp

Ms. Jennie Quinn
Camp Director
PO Box 888
Elmer, NJ 08318-0888
Phone: 856-358-2472
Fax: 856-358-6513
E-mail: appelcamp@aol.com
Web site: www.appelfarm.org

ATELIER DES ARTS

Francia Tobacman
Director
55 Bethune Street, B645
New York, NY 10014
Phone: 212-727-1756
Fax: 212-691-0631
E-mail: info@atelierdesarts.org
Web site: www.atelierdesarts.org

BELVOIR TERRACE

Summer Contact: Ms. Nancy S. Goldberg
Director
80 Cliffwood Street
Lenox, MA 01240
Phone: 413-637-0555
Fax: 413-637-4651
E-mail: belvoirt@aol.com
Web site: www.belvoirterrace.com

Winter Contact: Ms. Nancy S. Goldberg
Director
101 West 79th Street
New York, NY 10024
Phone: 212-580-3398
Fax: 212-579-7282
E-mail: info@belvoirterrace.com
Web site: www.belvoirterrace.com

CALIFORNIA STATE SUMMER SCHOOL FOR THE ARTS/INNER SPARK

Summer Contact: Shelly Reyes
Office Assistant
1010 Hurley
Suite 185
Sacramento, CA 95825
Phone: 916-274-5815
Fax: 916-274-5814
E-mail: shelly@innerspark.us
Web site: www.innerspark.us

Winter Contact: Shelly Reyes
Office Assistant
PO Box 1077
Sacramento, CA 95812-1077
Phone: 916-274-5815
Fax: 916-274-5814
E-mail: shelly@innerspark.us
Web site: www.innerspark.us

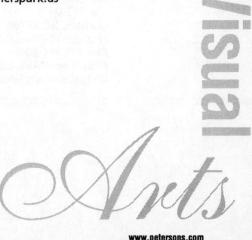

Visual *Arts*

CAPITOL REGION EDUCATION COUNCIL

Center for Creative Youth

Nancy Wolfe
Director
Wesleyan University
350 High Street
Middletown, CT 06459
Phone: 860-685-3307
Fax: 860-685-3311
E-mail: ccy@wesleyan.edu
Web site: www.crec.org/ccy

CARNEGIE MELLON UNIVERSITY

Carnegie Mellon University Pre-College Program in the Fine Arts

Mr. Joel Ripka
Office of Admission, Pre-College Programs
5000 Forbes Avenue
Pittsburgh, PA 15213-3890
Phone: 412-268-2082
Fax: 412-268-7838
E-mail: precollege@andrew.cmu.edu
Web site: www.cmu.edu/enrollment/pre-college

CHOATE ROSEMARY HALL

Choate Rosemary Hall Summer Arts Conservatory–Visual Arts Program

Mrs. Randi J. Brandt
Admissions Director, Arts Conservatory
Paul Mellon Arts Center
333 Christian Street
Wallingford, CT 06492
Phone: 203-697-2423
Fax: 203-697-2396
E-mail: rbrandt@choate.edu
Web site: www.choate.edu/summerprograms

DUKE YOUTH PROGRAMS–DUKE UNIVERSITY CONTINUING STUDIES

EXPRESSIONS! Duke Fine Arts Camp

Youth Program Director
203 Bishop's House
Box 90702
Durham, NC 27708
Phone: 919-684-6259
Fax: 919-681-8235
E-mail: youth@duke.edu
Web site: www.learnmore.duke.edu/youth

THE EXPERIMENT IN INTERNATIONAL LIVING

The Experiment in International Living–France, Five-Week Art and Adventure in Provence

Annie Thompson
Enrollment Director
Summer Abroad, Kipling Road
PO Box 676
Brattleboro, VT 05302-0676
Phone: 800-345-2929
Fax: 802-258-3428
E-mail: eil@worldlearning.org
Web site: www.usexperiment.org

THE EXPERIMENT IN INTERNATIONAL LIVING

The Experiment in International Living–United Kingdom Filmmaking Program and Homestay

Annie Thompson
Enrollment Director
Summer Abroad, Kipling Road
PO Box 676
Brattleboro, VT 05302-0676
Phone: 800-345-2929
Fax: 802-258-3428
E-mail: eil@worldlearning.org
Web site: www.usexperiment.org

FLS INTERNATIONAL

Study Tours and Cinema Program in the USA–Oxnard College

Ms. Veronica Perez
Director of Admissions
101 East Green Street #14
Pasadena, CA 91105
Phone: 626-795-2912
Fax: 626-795-5564
E-mail: veronica@fls.net
Web site: www.fls.net

HOLLINS UNIVERSITY

Hollinsummer

Ms. Julie Aavatsmark
Associate Director of Admissions
PO Box 9707
Roanoke, VA 24020
Phone: 800-456-9595
Fax: 540-362-6218
E-mail: jaavatsmark@hollins.edu
Web site: www.hollins.edu/

THE HOTCHKISS SCHOOL

Hotchkiss School Summer Music Studies

Christie Gurney Rawlings
Admission and Student Life Director
PO Box 800
Lakeville, CT 06039
Phone: 860-435-3173
Fax: 860-435-4413
E-mail: crawling@hotchkiss.org
Web site: www.hotchkiss.org/AboutHotchkiss/
SummerProg.asp

IDYLLWILD ARTS FOUNDATION

Idyllwild Arts Summer Program–Youth Arts Center

Diane Dennis
Registrar, Summer Program
PO Box 38
Idyllwild, CA 92549
Phone: 951-659-2171 ext. 2365
Fax: 951-659-4552
E-mail: summer@idyllwildarts.org
Web site: www.idyllwildarts.org

INTERLOCHEN CENTER FOR THE ARTS

Interlochen Arts Camp

Ms. Amy Packard
Director of Admissions
PO Box 199
Interlochen, MI 49643
Phone: 231-276-7472
Fax: 231-276-7464
E-mail: admissions@interlochen.org
Web site: www.interlochen.org/

INTERN EXCHANGE INTERNATIONAL, LTD.

IEI–Digital Media Plus Programme

Nina Miller Glickman
Director
1858 Mallard Lane
Villanova, PA 19085
Phone: 610-527-6066
Fax: 610-527-5499
E-mail: info@internexchange.com
Web site: www.internexchange.com

INTERN EXCHANGE INTERNATIONAL, LTD.

IEI–Fashion and Design Plus Programme

Nina Miller Glickman
Director
1858 Mallard Lane
Villanova, PA 19085
Phone: 610-527-6066
Fax: 610-527-5499
E-mail: info@internexchange.com
Web site: www.internexchange.com

INTERN EXCHANGE INTERNATIONAL, LTD.

IEI–Fine Arts Plus Programme

Nina Miller Glickman
Director
1858 Mallard Lane
Villanova, PA 19085
Phone: 610-527-6066
Fax: 610-527-5499
E-mail: info@internexchange.com
Web site: www.internexchange.com

INTERN EXCHANGE INTERNATIONAL, LTD.

IEI–Photography Plus Programme

Nina Miller Glickman
Director
1858 Mallard Lane
Villanova, PA 19085
Phone: 610-527-6066
Fax: 610-527-5499
E-mail: info@internexchange.com
Web site: www.internexchange.com

INTERN EXCHANGE INTERNATIONAL, LTD.

IEI–Theatre Plus Programme

Nina Miller Glickman
Director
1858 Mallard Lane
Villanova, PA 19085
Phone: 610-527-6066
Fax: 610-527-5499
E-mail: info@internexchange.com
Web site: www.internexchange.com

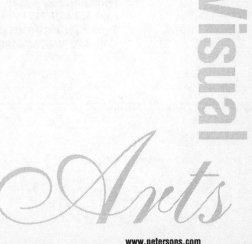

Visual Arts

KNOWLEDGE EXCHANGE INSTITUTE

Knowledge Exchange Institute–Artist Abroad Program in Italy

Mr. Alex Von
KEI Program Manager
111 John Street
Suite 800
New York, NY 10038
Phone: 800-831-5095
Fax: 212-528-2095
E-mail: info@knowledgeexchange.org
Web site: www.KnowledgeExchange.org

LEYSIN AMERICAN SCHOOL IN SWITZERLAND

Summer in Switzerland

Mr. Paul E. Dyer
US Director of Admissions
PO Box 7154
Portsmouth, NH 03802
Phone: 603-431-7654
Fax: 603-431-1280
E-mail: admissions@las.ch
Web site: www.las.ch/summer

MASSACHUSETTS COLLEGE OF ART

Massachusetts College of Art/Creative Vacation

Lin Lufkin
Program Administrative Assistant
621 Huntington Avenue
Boston, MA 02115
Phone: 617-879-7170
Fax: 617-879-7171
E-mail: llufkin@massart.edu
Web site: www.massartplus.org

MASSACHUSETTS COLLEGE OF ART

Massachusetts College of Art/Summer Studios

Lin Lufkin
Program Administrative Assistant
621 Huntington Avenue
Boston, MA 02115
Phone: 617-879-7170
Fax: 617-879-7171
E-mail: llufkin@massart.edu
Web site: www.massartplus.org

NEW YORK FILM ACADEMY

The New York Film Academy, Disney-MGM Studios, FL

Admissions
100 East 17th Street
New York, NY 10003
Phone: 212-674-4300
Fax: 212-477-1414
E-mail: film@nyfa.com
Web site: www.nyfa.com

NEW YORK FILM ACADEMY

The New York Film Academy, Harvard University, Cambridge, MA

Admissions
100 East 17th Street
New York, NY 10003
Phone: 212-674-4300
Fax: 212-477-1414
E-mail: film@nyfa.com
Web site: www.nyfa.com

NEW YORK FILM ACADEMY

The New York Film Academy in Florence, Italy

Admissions
100 East 17th Street
New York, NY 10003
Phone: 212-674-4300
Fax: 212-477-1414
E-mail: film@nyfa.com
Web site: www.nyfa.com

NEW YORK FILM ACADEMY

The New York Film Academy/Saint Catherine's College at Oxford University

Admissions
100 East 17th Street
New York, NY 10003
Phone: 212-674-4300
Fax: 212-477-1414
E-mail: film@nyfa.com
Web site: www.nyfa.com

Visual *Arts*

NEW YORK FILM ACADEMY

The New York Film Academy in Paris

Admissions
100 East 17th Street
New York, NY 10003
Phone: 212-674-4300
Fax: 212-477-1414
E-mail: film@nyfa.com
Web site: www.nyfa.com

NEW YORK FILM ACADEMY

The New York Film Academy, Princeton University, Princeton, NJ

Admissions
100 East 17th Street
New York, NY 10003
Phone: 212-674-4300
Fax: 212-477-1414
E-mail: film@nyfa.com
Web site: www.nyfa.com

NEW YORK FILM ACADEMY

The New York Film Academy, The Dalton School, New York, NY

Admissions
100 East 17th Street
New York, NY 10003
Phone: 212-674-4300
Fax: 212-477-1414
E-mail: film@nyfa.com
Web site: www.nyfa.com

NEW YORK FILM ACADEMY

The New York Film Academy, Universal Studios, Hollywood, Ca

Admissions
100 East 17th Street
New York, NY 10003
Phone: 212-674-4300
Fax: 212-477-1414
E-mail: film@nyfa.com
Web site: www.nyfa.com

NEW YORK UNIVERSITY, TISCH SCHOOL OF THE ARTS

Tisch School of the Arts–International High School Program–Dublin

Mr. Josh Murray
Assistant Director of Recruitment
Special Programs
721 Broadway
12th Floor
New York, NY 10003
Phone: 212-998-1500
Fax: 212-995-4610
E-mail: tisch.special.info@nyu.edu
Web site: specialprograms.tisch.nyu.edu

NEW YORK UNIVERSITY, TISCH SCHOOL OF THE ARTS

Tisch School of the Arts–International High School Program–Paris

Josh Murray
Assistant Director of Recruitment
Special Programs
721 Broadway
12th Floor
New York, NY 10003
Phone: 212-998-1500
Fax: 212-995-4610
E-mail: tisch.special.info@nyu.edu
Web site: specialprograms.tisch.nyu.edu

NEW YORK UNIVERSITY, TISCH SCHOOL OF THE ARTS

Tisch School of the Arts–Summer High School Programs

Josh Murray
Assistant Director of Recruitment
721 Broadway
New York, NY 10003
Phone: 212-998-1500
Fax: 212-995-4578
E-mail: tisch.special.info@nyu.edu
Web site: specialprograms.tisch.nyu.edu

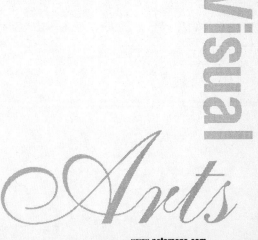

Visual Arts

OXFORD MEDIA SCHOOL

Oxford Media School–Film

Mr. Desmond Smith
Director
110 Pricefield Road
Toronto, ON M4W 1Z9, Canada
Phone: 416-964-0746
Fax: 416-929-4230
E-mail: newsco@sympatico.ca
Web site: www.oxfordmediaschool.com

OXFORD MEDIA SCHOOL

Oxford Media School–Film Master Class

Mr. Desmond Smith
Director
110 Pricefield Road
Toronto, ON M4W 1Z9, Canada
Phone: 416-964-0746
Fax: 416-929-4230
E-mail: newsco@sympatico.ca
Web site: www.oxfordmediaschool.com

PARSONS SCHOOL OF DESIGN

Parsons Pre-College Academy

Charlotte Rice
Director, Pre-Enrollment Programs
66 Fifth Avenue
New York, NY 10011
Phone: 212-229-8925
Fax: 212-229-8975
E-mail: summer@newschool.edu
Web site: www.parsons.edu/summer

PARSONS SCHOOL OF DESIGN

Parsons Summer Intensive Studies–New York

Charlotte Rice
Director, Pre-Enrollment Programs
66 Fifth Avenue
New York, NY 10011
Phone: 212-229-8925
Fax: 212-229-8975
E-mail: summer@newschool.edu
Web site: www.parsons.edu/summer

PARSONS SCHOOL OF DESIGN

Parsons Summer Intensive Studies–Paris

Mr. Roland Schneider
Program Coordinator
Paris, France
Phone: 212-229-8925
Fax: 212-229-8975
E-mail: summer@newschool.edu
Web site: www.parsons.edu/summer

PRATT INSTITUTE

Pratt Institute Summer Pre-College Program for High School Students

Ms. Johndell Wilson
Program Assistant
200 Willoughby Avenue
113 Engineering Building
Brooklyn, NY 11205
Phone: 718-636-3453
Fax: 718-399-4410
E-mail: precollege@pratt.edu
Web site: www.pratt.edu/precollege/

THE PUTNEY SCHOOL

The Putney School Summer Arts Program

Maria Ogden
Administrative Coordinator
Elm Lea Farm
418 Houghton Brook Road
Putney, VT 05346
Phone: 802-387-6297
Fax: 802-387-6216
E-mail: summer@putneyschool.org
Web site: www.putneyschool.org/summer

PUTNEY STUDENT TRAVEL

Excel at Amherst College and Williams College

Summer Contact: Patrick Noyes
Director
345 Hickory Ridge Road
Putney, VT 05346
Phone: 802-387-5000
Fax: 802-387-4276
E-mail: excel@goputney.com
Web site: www.goputney.com

Winter Contact: Patrick Noyes
Amherst College
Amherst, MA 01002
E-mail:
Web site: www.goputney.com

PUTNEY STUDENT TRAVEL

Putney Student Travel–Cultural Exploration–Studio Art in Rome

Jeffrey Shumlin
Director
345 Hickory Ridge Road
Putney, VT 05346
Phone: 802-387-5000
Fax: 802-387-4276
E-mail: info@goputney.com
Web site: www.goputney.com

RHODE ISLAND SCHOOL OF DESIGN

Rhode Island School of Design Pre-College Program

Mr. Marc Torick
Continuing Education Office/Summer
    Programs
2 College Street
Providence, RI 02903-2787
Phone: 401-454-6200
Fax: 401-454-6218
E-mail: cemail@risd.edu
Web site: www.risd.edu/precollege.cfm

RINGLING SCHOOL OF ART AND DESIGN

Ringling School of Art and Design Pre-College Perspective

Nancee Clark
Director of Continuing Studies and Special
    Programs
2700 North Tamiami Trail
Sarasota, FL 34234
Phone: 941-955-8866
Fax: 941-955-8801
E-mail: cpe@ringling.edu
Web site: www.ringling.edu/precollege

SARAH LAWRENCE COLLEGE

Sarah Lawrence College Summer High School Programs

Liz Irmiter
Director of Special Programs
1 Mead Way
Bronxville, NY 10708
Phone: 914-395-2693
Fax: 914-395-2694
E-mail:
    specialprograms@sarahlawrence.edu
Web site: www.sarahlawrence.edu/summer

SAVANNAH COLLEGE OF ART AND DESIGN

Savannah College of Art and Design Rising Star

Admission Department
PO Box 2072
Savannah, GA 31402-2072
Phone: 800-869-7223
Fax: 912-525-5986
E-mail: admission@scad.edu
Web site: www.scad.edu/summer

SAVANNAH COLLEGE OF ART AND DESIGN

Savannah College of Art and Design SCAD Summer Seminars

Admission Department
PO Box 2072
Savannah, GA 31402-2072
Phone: 800-869-7223
Fax: 912-525-5986
E-mail: admission@scad.edu
Web site: www.scad.edu/summer

SCHOOL OF THE MUSEUM OF FINE ARTS, BOSTON

School of the Museum of Fine Arts, Boston–Pre-College Summer Studio

Debra Samdperil
Director of Continuing Education and the
    Artist's Resource Center
230 The Fenway
Boston, MA 02115
Phone: 617-267-1219
Fax: 617-369-3679
E-mail: coned@smfa.edu
Web site: www.smfa.edu/precollege

SKIDMORE COLLEGE

Skidmore College–Acceleration Program in Art for High School Students

Ms. Marianne Needham
Coordinator
815 North Broadway
Saratoga Springs, NY 12866
Phone: 518-580-5052
Fax: 518-580-5029
E-mail: mneedham@skidmore.edu
Web site: www.skidmore.edu/academics/art/
    summersix/

Visual *Arts*

SUFFIELD ACADEMY

The Summer Academy at Suffield

Tony O'Shaughnessy
Director, Summer Academy Admissions
185 North Main Street
Suffield, CT 06078
Phone: 860-386-4475
Fax: 860-386-4476
E-mail: summer@suffieldacademy.org
Web site: www.suffieldsummer.org

SYRACUSE UNIVERSITY

Syracuse University Summer College

Jolynn Parker
Program Manager
111 Waverly Avenue
Suite 240
Syracuse, NY 13244-1270
Phone: 315-443-5297
Fax: 315-443-3976
E-mail: sumcoll@syr.edu
Web site: www.summercollege.syr.edu/

UCLA SUMMER SESSIONS AND SPECIAL PROGRAMS

UCLA Summer Experience: Institutes

Dr. Susan Pertel Jain
Director of Academic Program
   Development
Box 951418
Los Angeles, CA 90095
Phone: 310-825-4101
Fax: 310-825-1528
E-mail: spjain@summer.ucla.edu
Web site: www.summer.ucla.edu

THE UNIVERSITY OF IOWA

Iowa Young Writers' Studio

Ms. Trish Walsh
Director
C215 Seashore Hall
Iowa City, IA 52242-1402
Phone: 319-335-4209
Fax: 319-335-4743
E-mail: iyws@uiowa.edu
Web site: www.uiowa.edu/~iyws

UNIVERSITY OF MARYLAND, OFFICE OF SUMMER AND WINTER TERMS

The Arts! at Maryland

Terrie Hruzd
Program Manager, Office of Summer and
   Winter Terms
2103 Reckord Armory
College Park, MD 20742
Phone: 301-405-8588
Fax: 301-314-9572
E-mail: hruzd@umd.edu
Web site: www.summer.umd.edu/arts

UNIVERSITY OF PENNSYLVANIA

University of Pennsylvania–Penn Summer Art Studio

Mr. Matthew Palmer
Summer Sessions Assistant
3440 Market Street, Suite 100
Philadelphia, PA 19104-3335
Phone: 215-746-6901
Fax: 215-573-2053
E-mail: hsprogs@sas.upenn.edu
Web site: www.upenn.edu/summer

THE UNIVERSITY OF THE ARTS

Pre-College Summer Institute, The University of the Arts

Erin Elman
Director, Pre-College Programs
320 South Broad Street
Philadelphia, PA 19102
Phone: 215-717-6430
Fax: 215-717-6433
E-mail: precollege@uarts.edu
Web site: www.uarts.edu/precollege

Visual

Arts

WASHINGTON UNIVERSITY IN ST. LOUIS, SCHOOL OF ART

Washington University in St. Louis, School of Art–Portfolio Plus

Katerina Papageorgio
Assistant Dean of Undergraduate
    Programs
Washington University in St. Louis, School
    of Art
Box 1031
One Brookings Drive
St. Louis, MO 63130
Phone: 314-935-6500
Fax: 314-935-4643
E-mail: cpapageo@art.wustl.edu
Web site: www.artsci.wustl.edu/~artweb/
    washUSoa/

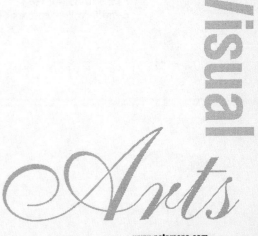

Scholarships for Artists

AACE INTERNATIONAL
http://www.aacei.org

AACE International Competitive Scholarship

Charla Miller, Staff Director-Education and Administration
AACE International
209 Prairie Avenue, Suite 100
Morgantown, WV 26501
Phone: 304-296-8444 Ext. 113
Fax: 304-291-5728
E-mail: cmiller@aacei.org

ACADEMY FOUNDATION OF THE ACADEMY OF MOTION PICTURE ARTS AND SCIENCES
http://www.oscars.org/saa

Academy of Motion Picture Student Academy Award-Honorary Foreign Film

Richard Miller, Awards Administration Director
Academy Foundation of the Academy of Motion Picture Arts and Sciences
8949 Wilshire Boulevard
Beverly Hills, CA 90211-1972
Phone: 310-247-3000
Fax: 310-859-9619
E-mail: rmiller@oscars.org

Academy of Motion Pictures Student Academy Awards

Richard Miller, Awards Administration Director
Academy Foundation of the Academy of Motion Picture Arts and Sciences
8949 Wilshire Boulevard
Beverly Hills, CA 90211-1972
Phone: 310-247-3000 Ext. 129
Fax: 310-859-9619
E-mail: rmiller@oscars.org

ACADEMY OF TELEVISION ARTS AND SCIENCES FOUNDATION
http://www.emmys.tv/foundation

Academy of Television Arts and Sciences College Television Awards

Nancy Robinson, Programs Coordinator
Academy of Television Arts and Sciences Foundation
5220 Lankershim Boulevard
North Hollywood, CA 91601
Phone: 818-754-2839
Fax: 818-761-8524
E-mail: collegeawards@emmys.org

ACI INTERNATIONAL/CONCRETE RESEARCH AND EDUCATION FOUNDATION (CONREF)
http://www.concrete.org

Kumar Mehta Scholarship

Jessie Bournay, Fundraising and Scholarship Assistant
ACI International/Concrete Research and Education Foundation (CONREF)
38800 Country Club Drive
Farmington Hills, MI 48331
Phone: 248-848-3832
Fax: 248-848-3740
E-mail: scholarships@concrete.org

Peter D. Courtois Concrete Construction Scholarship

Jessie Bournay, Fundraising and Scholarship Assistant
ACI International/Concrete Research and Education Foundation (CONREF)
38800 Country Club Drive
Farmington Hills, MI 48331
Phone: 248-848-3832
Fax: 248-848-3740
E-mail: scholarships@concrete.org

V. Mohan Malhotra Scholarship

Jessie Bournay, Fundraising and
Scholarship Assistant
ACI International/Concrete Research and
Education Foundation (CONREF)
38800 Country Club Drive
Farmington Hills, MI 48331
Phone: 248-848-3832
Fax: 248-848-3740
E-mail: scholarships@concrete.org

W.R. Grace Scholarship Award

Jessie Bournay, Fundraising and
Scholarship Assistant
ACI International/Concrete Research and
Education Foundation (CONREF)
38800 Country Club Drive
Farmington Hills, MI 48331
Phone: 248-848-3832
Fax: 248-848-3740
E-mail: scholarships@concrete.org

ADC RESEARCH INSTITUTE
http://www.adc.org

**Jack Shaheen Mass Communications
Scholarship Award**

Marvin Wingfield, Director of Education
and Outreach
ADC Research Institute
4201 Connecticut Avenue, NW Suite 300
Washington, DC 20008
Phone: 202-244-2990
Fax: 202-244-3196
E-mail: marvinw@adc.org

**ADVERTISING FEDERATION OF FORT
WAYNE, INC.**
http://www.adfedfortwayne.org

**Advertising Federation of Fort Wayne, Inc.,
Scholarship**

Scholarship Committee
Advertising Federation of Fort Wayne, Inc.
PO Box 10066
Fort Wayne, IN 46850
Phone: 260-427-9106

**ALLIANCE FOR YOUNG ARTISTS AND
WRITERS, INC.**
http://www.artandwriting.org

**Scholastic Art and Writing Awards-Art
Section**

Alliance for Young Artists and Writers, Inc.
557 Broadway
New York, NY 10012-1396
Phone: 212-343-6493

ALPHA DELTA KAPPA FOUNDATION
http://www.alphadeltakappa.org

**Apha Delta Kappa Foundation Fine Arts
Grants**

Dee Frost, Scholarships and Grants
Coordinator
Alpha Delta Kappa Foundation
1615 West 92nd Street
Kansas City, MO 64114-3296
Phone: 816-363-5525
Fax: 816-363-4010
E-mail: headquarters@alphadeltakappa.org

AMERICAN ARCHITECTURAL FOUNDATION
http://www.archfoundation.org

**American Institute of Architects Minority/
Disadvantaged Scholarship**

Mary Felber, Director of Scholarship
Programs
American Architectural Foundation
1735 New York Avenue, NW
Washington, DC 20006-5292
Phone: 202-626-7511
Fax: 202-626-7509
E-mail: mfelber@archfoundation.org

AMERICAN INSTITUTE OF ARCHITECTS
http://www.aia.org

**American Institute of Architects/American
Architectural Foundation
Minority/Disadvantaged Scholarships**

Mary Felber, Scholarship Chair
American Institute of Architects
1735 New York Avenue, NW
Washington, DC 20006-5292
Phone: 202-626-7511
Fax: 202-626-7509
E-mail: mfelber@aia.org

visual Arts

AMERICAN INSTITUTE OF ARCHITECTS, NEW YORK CHAPTER
http://www.aiany.org

The Douglas Haskell Award for Student Journalism

Marcus Bleyer
American Institute of Architects, New York Chapter
536 LaGuardia Place
New York, NY 10012
Phone: 212-358-6117
E-mail: mbleyer@aiany.org

Women's Architectural Auxiliary Eleanor Allwork Scholarship Grants

Marcus Bleyer
American Institute of Architects, New York Chapter
536 LaGuardia Place
New York, NY 10012
Phone: 212-358-6117
E-mail: mbleyer@aiany.org

AMERICAN INSTITUTE OF ARCHITECTS, WEST VIRGINIA CHAPTER
http://www.aiawv.org

AIA West Virginia Scholarship Program

Roberta Guffey, Executive Director
American Institute of Architects, West Virginia Chapter
PO Box 813
Charleston, WV 25323
Phone: 304-344-9872
Fax: 304-343-0205
E-mail: roberta.guffey@aiawv.org

AMERICAN LEGION AUXILIARY, DEPARTMENT OF WASHINGTON
http://www.walegion-aux.org

Florence Lemcke Memorial Scholarship in Fine Arts

Crystal Lawrence, Department Secretary
American Legion Auxiliary, Department of Washington
3600 Ruddell Road
Lacey, WA 98503
Phone: 360-456-5995
Fax: 360-491-7442
E-mail: alawash@qwest.net

AMERICAN LEGION, PRESS CLUB OF NEW JERSEY

American Legion Press Club of New Jersey and Post 170 Arthur Dehardt Memorial Scholarship

Jack W. Kuepfer, Scholarship Chairman ALPC of NJ
American Legion, Press Club of New Jersey
68 Merrill Road
Clifton, NJ 07012-1622
Phone: 973-473-5176

AMERICAN PHILOLOGICAL ASSOCIATION
http://www.apaclassics.org

Minority Student Summer Scholarship

Adam Blistein, Executive Director
American Philological Association
University of Pennsylvania, 292 Logan Hall, 249 South 36th Street
Philadelphia, PA 19104-6304
Phone: 215-898-4975
Fax: 215-573-7874
E-mail: apaclassics@sas.upenn.edu

AMERICAN SCHOOL OF CLASSICAL STUDIES AT ATHENS
http://www.ascsa.edu.gr

ASCSA Summer Sessions Open Scholarships

Timothy F Winters, Chair, Committee of Summer Sessions
American School of Classical Studies at Athens
6-8 Charlton Street
Princeton, NJ 08540
Phone: 609-683-0800
Fax: 609-924-0578
E-mail: ascsa@ascsa.org

AMERICAN SOCIETY OF INTERIOR DESIGNERS (ASID) EDUCATION FOUNDATION, INC.
http://www.asid.org

ASID Educational Foundation/Irene Winifred Eno Grant

American Society of Interior Designers (ASID) Education Foundation, Inc.
608 Massachusetts Avenue, NE
Washington, DC 20002-6006
Phone: 202-546-3480
Fax: 202-546-3240
E-mail: education@asid.org

ASID Educational Foundation/Joel Polsky Academic Achievement Award

American Society of Interior Designers (ASID) Education Foundation, Inc.
608 Massachusetts Avenue, NE
Washington, DC 20002-6006
Phone: 202-546-3480
Fax: 202-546-3240
E-mail: education@asid.org

ASID Educational Foundation/Yale R. Burge Competition

American Society of Interior Designers (ASID) Education Foundation, Inc.
608 Massachusetts Avenue, NE
Washington, DC 20002-6006
Phone: 202-546-3480
Fax: 202-546-3240
E-mail: education@asid.org

ANGELUS AWARDS STUDENT FILM FESTIVAL
http://www.angelus.org

Angelus Awards Student Film Festival

Monika Moreno, Director, Angelus Awards
Angelus Awards Student Film Festival
7201 Sunset Boulevard
Los Angeles, CA 90046
Phone: 323-874-6633 Ext. 24
Fax: 323-874-1168
E-mail: monika@angelus.org

ART INSTITUTES
http://www.artinstitutes.edu

National Art Honor Society Scholarship

Bill McAnulty, National Art Honor Society Scholarship
Art Institutes
c/o The Art Institute of Pittsburgh, 420 Boulevard of the Allies
Pittsburgh, PA 15219-1328
Phone: 800-275-2470

National Poster Design Contest

Michael Maki, Vice President for Academic Affairs
Art Institutes
210 Sixth Ave, 32nd Floor
Pittsburgh, PA 15222-2598
Phone: 888-624-0300

ARTIST-BLACKSMITH'S ASSOCIATION OF NORTH AMERICA, INC.
http://www.abana.org

Artist's- Blacksmith's Association of North America, Inc. Scholarship Program

Lee Ann Mitchell, Central Office Administrator
Artist-Blacksmith's Association of North America, Inc.
PO Box 816
Farmington, GA 30638-0816
Phone: 706-310-1030
Fax: 706-769-7147
E-mail: abana@abana.org

Artist's-Blacksmith's Association of North America, Inc. Affiliate Visiting Artist Grant Program

Lee Ann Mitchell, Central Office Administrator
Artist-Blacksmith's Association of North America, Inc.
PO Box 816
Farmington, GA 30638-0816
Phone: 706-310-1030
Fax: 706-769-7147
E-mail: abana@abana.org

ARTIST'S MAGAZINE
http://www.artistsmagazine.com

Artist's Magazine's Annual Art Competition

Terri Boes, Customer Service Representative
Artist's Magazine
4700 East Galbraith Road
Cincinnati, OH 45236
Phone: 513-531-2690 Ext. 1328
Fax: 513-531-0798
E-mail: arts-competition@fwpubs.com

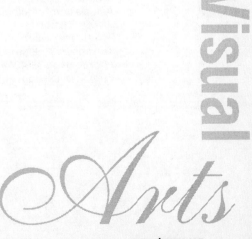

Visual Arts

ASIAN AMERICAN JOURNALISTS ASSOCIATION
http://www.aaja.org

Asian-American Journalists Association Scholarship

Brandon Sugiyama, Student Programs
    Coordinator
Asian American Journalists Association
1182 Market Street, Suite 320
San Francisco, CA 94102
Phone: 415-346-2051 Ext. 102
Fax: 415-346-6343
E-mail: programs@aaja.org

ASPRS, THE IMAGING AND GEOSPATIAL INFORMATION SOCIETY
http://www.asprs.org

Robert E. Altenhofen Memorial Scholarship

Jesse Winch, Program Manager
ASPRS, The Imaging and Geospatial
    Information Society
5410 Grosvenor Lane, Suite 210
Bethesda, MD 20814-2160
Phone: 301-493-0290 Ext. 101
Fax: 301-493-0208
E-mail: scholarships@asprs.org

Space Imaging Award for Application of High Resolution Digital Satellite Imagery

Jesse Winch, Program Manager
ASPRS, The Imaging and Geospatial
    Information Society
5410 Grosvenor Lane, Suite 210
Bethesda, MD 20814-2160
Phone: 301-493-0290 Ext. 101
Fax: 301-493-0208
E-mail: scholarships@asprs.org

ASSOCIATION FOR WOMEN IN ARCHITECTURE FOUNDATION
http://www.awa-la.org

Association for Women in Architecture Scholarship

Nina Briggs, Scholarship Chair
Association for Women in Architecture
    Foundation
386 Beech Avenue, Unit B4
Torrance, CA 90501-6203
Phone: 310-533-4042
E-mail: ninabriggs@earthlink.net

AUTHOR SERVICES, INC.
http://www.writersofthefuture.com

L. Ron Hubbard's Illustrators of the Future Contest

Judy Young, Contest Administrator
Author Services, Inc.
PO Box 3190
Los Angeles, CA 90078
Phone: 323-466-3310
Fax: 323-466-6474
E-mail: contests@authorservicesinc.com

BEINECKE SCHOLARSHIP PROGRAM
http://www.beineckescholarship.org/

Beinecke Scholarship for Graduate Study

Thomas Parkinson, Program Director
Beinecke Scholarship Program
PO Box 125
Fogelsville, PA 18051-0125
Phone: 610-395-5560
Fax: 610-625-7919
E-mail: beineckescholarship@earthlink.net

BMI FOUNDATION, INC.
http://www.bmi.com

BMI Student Composer Awards

Mr. Ralph N. Jackson, Director, BMI
    Student Composer Awards
BMI Foundation, Inc.
320 West 57th Street
New York, NY 10019
Phone: 212-586-2000
Fax: 212-245-8986
E-mail: classical@bmi.com

CALIFORNIA ALLIANCE FOR ARTS EDUCATION (CAAE)
http://www.artsed411.org

Emerging Young Artist Awards

Peggy Burt, Project Manager
California Alliance for Arts Education
    (CAAE)
495 East Colorado Boulevard
Pasadena, CA 91101
Phone: 626-578-9315 Ext. 102
Fax: 626-578-9894
E-mail: peggy@artsed411.org

CALIFORNIA CHICANO NEWS MEDIA ASSOCIATION (CCNMA)
http://www.ccnma.org

Joel Garcia Memorial Scholarship

Julio Moran, Executive Director
California Chicano News Media Association (CCNMA)
300 South Grand Avenue, Suite 3950
Los Angeles, CA 90071-8110
Phone: 213-437-4408
Fax: 213-437-4423
E-mail: ccnmainfo@ccnma.org

CENTRAL INTELLIGENCE AGENCY
http://www.cia.gov

Central Intelligence Agency Undergraduate Scholarship Program

Van Patrick, Chief, College Relations
Central Intelligence Agency
Recruitment Center
L 100 LF7
Washington, DC 20505
Phone: 703-613-8388
Fax: 703-613-7676
E-mail: ivanilp0@ucia.gov

CHARLES & LUCILLE KING FAMILY FOUNDATION, INC.
http://www.kingfoundation.org/

Charles and Lucille King Family Foundation Scholarships

Michael Donovan, Educational Director
Charles & Lucille King Family Foundation, Inc.
366 Madison Avenue, 10th Floor
New York, NY 10017
Phone: 212-682-2913
Fax: 212-949-0728
E-mail: info@kingfoundation.org

CIRI FOUNDATION
http://www.thecirifoundation.org

CIRI Foundation Susie Qimmiqsak Bevins Endowment Scholarship Fund

Phone: 907-263-5582
Fax: 907-263-5588

COLLEGEBOUND FOUNDATION
http://www.collegeboundfoundation.org

Janet B. Sondheim Scholarship

April Bell, Associate Program Director
CollegeBound Foundation
300 Water Street, Suite 300
Baltimore, MD 21202
Phone: 410-783-2905 Ext. 208
Fax: 410-727-5786
E-mail: abell@collegeboundfoundation.org

CONNECTICUT CHAPTER OF SOCIETY OF PROFESSIONAL JOURNALISTS
http://www.ctspj.org

Connecticut SPJ Bob Eddy Scholarship Program

Debra Estock, Scholarship Committee Chairman
Connecticut Chapter of Society of Professional Journalists
71 Kenwood Avenue
Fairfield, CT 06430
Phone: 203-255-2127
E-mail: destock963@aol.com

COSTUME SOCIETY OF AMERICA
http://www.costumesocietyamerica.com

Adele Filene Travel Award

Kim Righi, Program Contact
Costume Society of America
203 Towne Center Drive, PO Box 73
Hillsborough, NJ 08844
Phone: 800-272-9447
E-mail:
national.office@costumesocietyamerica.com

Stella Blum Research Grant

Kim Righi, Program Contact
Costume Society of America
203 Towne Center Drive, PO Box 73
Hillsborough, NJ 08844
Phone: 800-272-9447
E-mail:
national.office@costumesocietyamerica.com

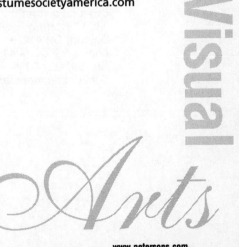

Visual *Arts*

CULTURE CONNECTION
http://www.thecultureconnection.com

Culture Connection Foundation Scholarship

Anna Leis, National Program Director
Culture Connection
8888 Keystone Crossing, Suite 1300
Indianapolis, IN 46240
Phone: 317-547-7055
E-mail:
   annaleis@thecultureconnection.com

**DALLAS ARCHITECTURAL FOUNDATION-HKS/
JOHN HUMPHRIES MINORITY SCHOLARSHIP**
http://www.dallasfoundation.org

**Dallas Architectural Foundation - Harrell and
Hamilton Scholarship Fund**

Dallas Architectural Foundation-HKS/John
   Humphries Minority Scholarship
1444 Oak Lawn Avenue, Suite 600
Dallas, TX 75207
Phone: 214-742-3242

**DALLAS-FORT WORTH ASSOCIATION OF
BLACK COMMUNICATORS**
http://www.dfwabc.org

Future Journalists Scholarship Program

Ira Hadnot, DFW/ABC Scholarship Chair
Phone: 469-330-9696

DAYTON FOUNDATION
http://www.daytonfoundation.org

**American Institute of Architecture (AIA)
Dayton Architectural Scholarship Fund**

Diane Timmons, Director Grants and
   Programs
Dayton Foundation
2300 Kettering Tower
Dayton, OH 45423
E-mail: dtimmons@daytonfoundation.org

Larry Fullerton Photojournalism Scholarship

Diane Timmons, Director of Grants and
   Programs
Dayton Foundation
2300 Kettering Tower
Dayton, OH 45423
Phone: 937-222-0410
Fax: 937-222-0636
E-mail: dtimmons@daytonfoundation.org

**ELECTRONIC DOCUMENT SYSTEMS
FOUNDATION**
http://www.edsf.org

**Electronic Document Systems Foundation
Scholarship Awards**

Jeanne Mowlds, Executive Director
Electronic Document Systems Foundation
24238 Hawthorne Boulevard
608 Silver Spur Road, Suite 280
Rolling Hills Estates, CA 90274-3616
Phone: 310-265-5510
Fax: 310-265-5588
E-mail: jcmowlds@aol.com

ELIZABETH GREENSHIELDS FOUNDATION

Elizabeth Greenshields Award/Grant

Diane Pitcher, Applications Coordinator
Elizabeth Greenshields Foundation
1814 Sherbrooke Street West, Suite 1
Montreal, QC H3H IE4
Canada
Phone: 514-937-9225
Fax: 514-937-0141
E-mail: greenshields@bellnet.ca

FISHER BROADCASTING COMPANY
http://www.fisherbroadcasting.com

**Fisher Broadcasting, Inc., Scholarship for
Minorities**

Annnarie Hitchcock, Human Resources
   Administrator
Fisher Broadcasting Company
100 4th Avenue North, Suite 510
Seattle, WA 98109
Phone: 206-404-6050
Fax: 206-404-6760

**FLORIDA EDUCATIONAL FACILITIES
PLANNERS' ASSOCIATION**
http://www.fefpa.org

FEFPA Assistantship

Bob Griffith, FEFPA Assistantship, Selection
   Committee Chair
Florida Educational Facilities Planners'
   Association
Florida International University, University
   Park, CSC 236
Miami, FL 33199

GENERAL FEDERATION OF WOMEN'S CLUBS OF MASSACHUSETTS
http://www.gfwcma.org/

General Federation of Women's Clubs of Massachusetts Pennies For Art

Kay Doody, Art Chairman
General Federation of Women's Clubs of Massachusetts
PO Box 679
Sudbury, MA 01776-0679
Phone: 978-443-4569
E-mail: kdoody1890@aol.com

GEORGE BIRD GRINNELL AMERICAN INDIAN FUND
http://www.grinnellfund.org/

Al Qoyawayma Award

Paula Mintzies, President
George Bird Grinnell American Indian Fund
PO Box 59033
Potomac, MD 20859
Phone: 301-424-2440
Fax: 301-424-8281

GETTY GRANT PROGRAM
http://www.getty.edu/grants

Library Research Grants

Kathleen Johnson, Program Associate
Getty Grant Program
1200 Getty Center Drive, Suite 800
Los Angeles, CA 90049-1685
Phone: 310-440-7320
Fax: 310-440-7703
E-mail: researchgrants@getty.edu

GOLDEN KEY INTERNATIONAL HONOUR SOCIETY
http://www.goldenkey.org

Visual and Performing Arts Achievement Awards

Scholarship Program Administrators
Golden Key International Honour Society
PO Box 23737
Nashville, TN 37202
Phone: 800-377-2401

GREAT LAKES COMMISSION
http://www.glc.org

Carol A. Ratza Memorial Scholarship

Christine Manninen, Program Manager
Great Lakes Commission
Eisenhower Corporate Park, 2805 South Industrial Highway, Suite 100
Ann Arbor, MI 48104-6791
Phone: 734-971-9135
Fax: 734-971-9150
E-mail: manninen@glc.org

HALLMARK GRAPHIC ARTS SCHOLARSHIP

Hallmark Graphic Arts Scholarship

Laura Wayland-Smith Hatch, Director
Hallmark Graphic Arts Scholarship
c/o Gravure Education Foundation
107 East Sutton Place
Wilmington, DE 19810
Phone: 315-589-8879
E-mail: lwshatch@gaa.org

HAWAIIAN LODGE, F.& A. M.
http://www.hawaiianlodge.org/

Hawaiian Lodge Scholarships

Chairman, Scholarship Committee
Hawaiian Lodge, F.& A. M.
1227 Makiki Street
Honolulu, HI 96814
Phone: 808-979-7809
E-mail: secretary@hawaiianlodge.org

HELLENIC UNIVERSITY CLUB OF PHILADELPHIA
http://www.hucphila.org

The Dimitri J. Ververelli Memorial Scholarship for Architecture and/or Engineering

Zoe Tripolitis, Scholarship Chairman
Hellenic University Club of Philadelphia
PO Box 42199
Philadelphia, PA 19101
Phone: 215-483-7440
E-mail: zoe.tripolitis@arkemagroup.com

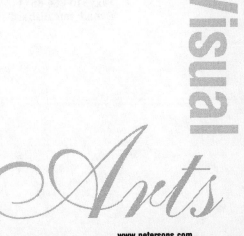

Visual Arts

HERB SOCIETY OF AMERICA
http://www.herbsociety.org

Herb Society Research Grants

The Herb Society of America, Inc. Research
    Grant
Herb Society of America
9019 Kirtland-Chardon Road
Kirtland, OH 44094
Phone: 440-256-0514
Fax: 440-256-0541
E-mail: herbs@herbsociety.org

HISPANIC COLLEGE FUND, INC.
http://www.hispanicfund.org

Denny's/Hispanic College Fund Scholarship

Stina Augustsson, Program Manager
Hispanic College Fund, Inc.
1717 Pennsylvania Avenue, NW, Suite 460
Washington, DC 20006
Phone: 202-296-5400
Fax: 202-296-3774
E-mail: hcf-info@hispanicfund.org

El Nuevo Constructor Scholarship Program

Stina Augustsson, Program Manager
Hispanic College Fund, Inc.
1717 Pennsylvania Avenue, NW, Suite 460
Washington, DC 20006
Phone: 202-296-5400
Fax: 202-296-3774
E-mail: hcf-info@hispanicfund.org

**ILLUMINATING ENGINEERING SOCIETY OF
NORTH AMERICA**
http://www.iesna.org

Robert W. Thunen Memorial Scholarships

Chairperson (Thunen Scholarship
    Committee)
Illuminating Engineering Society of North
    America
IESNA Golden Gate Section, 1514 Gibbons
    Drive
Alameda, CA 94501-4001
Phone: 510-864-0204
Fax: 510-864-8511
E-mail: mrcatisbac@aol.com

**ILLUMINATING ENGINEERING SOCIETY OF
NORTH AMERICA–GOLDEN GATE SECTION**
http://www.iesgg.org

Alan Lucas Memorial Educational Scholarship

Phil Hall, Coordinator
Illuminating Engineering Society of North
    America–Golden Gate Section
1514 Gibbons Drive
Alameda, CA 94501
Phone: 510-208-5005 Ext. 3030
E-mail: information@iesgg.org

Robert W. Thunen Memorial Scholarships

Phil Hall, Coordinator
Illuminating Engineering Society of North
    America–Golden Gate Section
1514 Gibbons Drive
Alameda, CA 94501
Phone: 510-208-5005 Ext. 3030
E-mail: information@iesgg.org

**INDIANAPOLIS ASSOCIATION OF BLACK
JOURNALISTS**
http://www.iabj.net

Lynn Dean Ford IABJ Scholarship Awards

Courtenay Edelhart, Scholarship
    Committee Chair
Indianapolis Association of Black
    Journalists
PO Box 441795
Indianapolis, IN 46244-1795
Phone: 317-388-8163
E-mail: courtenay.edelhart@indystar.com

INSTITUTE FOR HUMANE STUDIES
http://www.theihs.org

Film and Fiction Scholarship

Institute for Humane Studies
3301 North Fairfax Drive, Suite 440
Arlington, VA 22201-4432
Phone: 703-993-4880
Fax: 703-993-4890
E-mail: ihs@gmu.edu

INTERNATIONAL COMMUNICATIONS INDUSTRIES FOUNDATION
http://www.infocomm.org/foundation

ICIF Scholarship for Dependents of Member Organizations

Duffy Wilbert, Vice President, Membership
International Communications Industries
   Foundation
11242 Waples Mill Road, Suite 200
Fairfax, VA 22030
Phone: 703-273-7200 Ext. 3470
Fax: 703-278-8082
E-mail: dwilbert@infocomm.org

International Communications Industries Foundation AV Scholarship

Duffy Wilbert, Vice President, Membership
International Communications Industries
   Foundation
11242 Waples Mill Road, Suite 200
Fairfax, VA 22030
Phone: 703-273-7200 Ext. 3470
Fax: 703-278-8082
E-mail: dwilbert@infocomm.org

INTERNATIONAL FACILITY MANAGEMENT ASSOCIATION FOUNDATION
http://www.ifmafoundation.org

IFMA Foundation Scholarships

Mr. William Rub, Foundation Manager
International Facility Management
   Association Foundation
1 East Greenway Plaza
Suite 1100
Houston, TX 77046-0194
Phone: 713-623-4362 Ext. 158
Fax: 713-623-6124
E-mail: william.rub@ifma.org

INTERNATIONAL FOODSERVICE EDITORIAL COUNCIL
http://www.ifec-is-us.com

International Foodservice Editorial Council Communications Scholarship

Carol Lally, Executive Director
International Foodservice Editorial Council
PO Box 491
Hyde Park, NY 12538-0491
Phone: 845-229-6973
Fax: 845-229-6993
E-mail: ifec@aol.com

INTERNATIONAL FURNISHINGS AND DESIGN ASSOCIATION
http://www.ifdaef.org

Charles D. Mayo Scholarship

Joan Long, Director of Grants
International Furnishings and Design
   Association
191 Clarksville Road
Princeton Junction, NJ 08550
Phone: 919-847-3064
Fax: 919-847-3064
E-mail: jlongdesigns@yahoo.com

IFDA Student Scholarship

Joan Long, Director of Grants
International Furnishings and Design
   Association
191 Clarksville Road
Princeton Junction, NJ 08550
Phone: 919-847-3064
Fax: 919-847-3064
E-mail: jlongdesigns@yahoo.com

Ruth Clark Scholarship

Joan Long, Director of Grants
International Furnishings and Design
   Association
191 Clarksville Road
Princeton Junction, NJ 08550
Phone: 919-847-3064
Fax: 919-847-3064
E-mail: jlongdesigns@yahoo.com

JACK J. ISGUR FOUNDATION

Jack J. Isgur Foundation Scholarship

Charles Jensen, Attorney at Law
Jack J. Isgur Foundation
c/o Charles F. Jensen, Stinson, Morrison,
   Hecker LLP
1201 Walnut Street, 28th Floor
Kansas City, MO 64106
Phone: 816-691-2760
Fax: 816-691-3495
E-mail: cjensen@stinsonmoheck.com

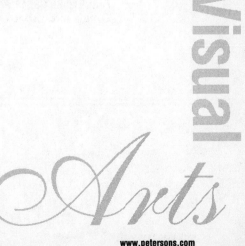

Visual *Arts*

JOHN C. SANTISTEVAN MEMORIAL SCHOLARSHIP
http://www.santistevanart.org

John C. Santistevan Memorial Scholarship

Ivan Houston, President
John C. Santistevan Memorial Scholarship
419 North Larch Mont Boulevard, Number 98
Los Angeles, CA 90004

JOHN F. AND ANNA LEE STACEY SCHOLARSHIP FUND
http://www.nationalcowboymuseum.org

John F. and Anna Lee Stacey Scholarship Fund

Ed Muno, Art Curator
John F. and Anna Lee Stacey Scholarship Fund
1700 Northeast 63rd Street
Oklahoma City, OK 73111
Phone: 405-478-2250
Fax: 405-478-4714

JUNIOR ACHIEVEMENT
http://www.ja.org

Walt Disney Company Foundation Scholarship

Scholarship Coordinator
Junior Achievement
1 Education Way
Colorado Springs, CO 80906
Phone: 719-535-2954
Fax: 719-540-6175

LA KELLEY COMMUNICATIONS
http://www.kelleycom.com

Artistic Endeavors Scholarship

Sandy Aultman
LA Kelley Communications
1405 W. Pinhook Road, Suite 101
Lafayette, LA 70503
Phone: 337-261-9787
Fax: 337-261-1787

LINCOLN COMMUNITY FOUNDATION
http://www.lcf.org

Haymarket Gallery Emerging Artists Scholarship

Debra Shoemaker, Director of Program and Distribution
Lincoln Community Foundation
215 Centennial Mall South, Suite 200
Lincoln, NE 68508
Phone: 402-474-2345
Fax: 402-476-8532
E-mail: debs@lcf.org

LIQUITEX ARTIST MATERIALS PURCHASE AWARD PROGRAM
http://www.liquitex.com

Liquitex Excellence in Art Purchase Award Program

Application available at Web site.

MAINE GRAPHICS ARTS ASSOCIATION

Maine Graphics Art Association

Angie Dougherty, Director
Maine Graphics Arts Association
PO Box 874
Auburn, ME 04212-0874
Phone: 207-883-3083
Fax: 207-883-3158
E-mail: edpougher@maine.rr.com

MEDIA ACTION NETWORK FOR ASIAN AMERICANS
http://www.manaa.org

MANAA Media Scholarships for Asian American Students

MANAA Scholarship
Media Action Network for Asian Americans
PO Box 11105
Burbank, CA 91510
E-mail: manaaletters@yahoo.com.

METAVUE CORPORATION
http://www.metavue.com

The FW Rausch Arts and Humanities Paper Contest

Michael Rufflo
Metavue Corporation
1110 Surrey Drive
Sun Prairie, WI 53590
Phone: 608-577-0642
Fax: 512-685-4074
E-mail: rufflo@metavue.com

MIDWEST ROOFING CONTRACTORS ASSOCIATION
http://www.mrca.org

MRCA Foundation Scholarship Program

MRCA Foundation
Midwest Roofing Contractors Association
4840 Bob Billings Parkway, Suite 1000
Lawrence, KS 66049-3862

NATIONAL ART MATERIALS TRADE ASSOCIATION
http://www.namta.org

National Art Materials Trade Association Art Major Scholarship

Katharine Coffey, Scholarship Coordinator
National Art Materials Trade Association
15806 Brookway Drive, Suite 300
Huntersville, NC 28078
Phone: 704-892-6244
Fax: 704-892-6247
E-mail: kcoffey@namta.org

NATIONAL ASSOCIATION OF BLACK JOURNALISTS
http://www.nabj.org

National Association of Black Journalists Non-Sustaining Scholarship Awards

Ryan Williams, Program and Exposition
  Coordinator
National Association of Black Journalists
8701-A Adelphi Road
Adelphi, MD 20783-1716
Phone: 301-445-7100 Ext. 109
Fax: 301-445-7101

Visual Task Force Scholarship

Program and Exposition Coordinator
National Association of Black Journalists
8701-A Adelphi Road
Adelphi, MD 20783-1716
Phone: 301-445-7100
Fax: 301-445-7101

NATIONAL ASSOCIATION OF WOMEN IN CONSTRUCTION
http://nawic.org

NAWIC Undergraduate Scholarships

Scholarship Administrator
National Association of Women in
  Construction
327 South Adams Street
Fort Worth, TX 76104
E-mail: nawic@nawic.org

NATIONAL FEDERATION OF THE BLIND
http://www.nfb.org

Howard Brown Rickard Scholarship

Peggy Elliot, Chairman, Scholarship
  Committee
National Federation of the Blind
805 5th Avenue
Grinnell, IA 50112
Phone: 641-236-3366

NATIONAL FOUNDATION FOR ADVANCEMENT IN THE ARTS
http://www.artsawards.org

Arts Recognition and Talent Search (ARTS)

Programs Department
National Foundation for Advancement in
  the Arts
444 Brickell Avenue, Suite R14
Miami, FL 33133
Phone: 800-970-2787
Fax: 305-377-1149
E-mail: nfaa@nfaa.org

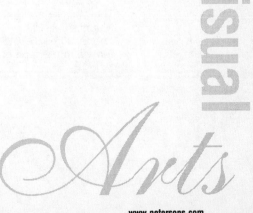

NATIONAL INSTITUTE OF BUILDING SCIENCES, MULTIHAZARD MITIGATION COUNCIL
http://www.nibs.org

Architecture, Construction, and Engineering Mentor Program Scholarships

Pamela Mullender, Acting Executive
  Director, ACE Mentor Program
National Institute of Building Sciences,
  Multihazard Mitigation Council
National Institute of Building Sciences,
  1090 Vermont Avenue, NW, Suite 700
Washington, DC 20005
Phone: 202-898-6396
Fax: 202-289-1092

NATIONAL LEAGUE OF AMERICAN PEN WOMEN, INC.
http://www.americanpenwomen.org

NLAPW Virginia Liebeler Biennial Grants for Mature Women (Arts)

NLAPW Virginia Liebeler Biennial Grants
  for Women
National League of American Pen
  Women, Inc.
1300 17th Street, NW
Washington, DC 20036-1973

NATIONAL OPERA ASSOCIATION
http://www.noa.org

NOA Vocal Competition/ Legacy Award Program

Robert Hansen, Executive Secretary
National Opera Association
PO Box 60869
Canyon, TX 79016-0869
Phone: 806-651-2857
Fax: 806-651-2958
E-mail: hansen@mail.wtamu.edu

NATIONAL PRESS PHOTOGRAPHERS FOUNDATION, INC.
http://www.nppa.org

Bob East Scholarship

Chuck Fadely
National Press Photographers
  Foundation, Inc.
The Miami Herald, One Herald Plaza
Miami, FL 33132
Phone: 305-376-2015
E-mail: info@nppa.org

National Press Photographers Foundation Still Photographer Scholarship

Bill Sanders, Photo Editor
E-mail: wsanders@citizen-times.com

National Press Photographers Foundation Television News Scholarship

Ed Dooks
National Press Photographers
  Foundation, Inc.
5 Mohawk Drive
Lexington, MA 02421-6217
E-mail: dooks@verizon.net

Reid Blackburn Scholarship

Jeremiah Coughlan, Staff Photographer
National Press Photographers
  Foundation, Inc.
The Columbian, 701 West 8th Street
Vancouver, WA 98660
Phone: 360-694-3391
E-mail: coughlan@attbi.com

NATIONAL SCULPTURE SOCIETY
http://www.nationalsculpture.org

National Sculpture Competition for Young Sculptors

Gwen Pier, Executive Director
National Sculpture Society
237 Park Avenue
New York, NY 10017
Phone: 212-764-5645 Ext. 15
Fax: 212-764-5651
E-mail: gwen@nationalsculpture.org

National Sculpture Society Scholarships

Gwen Pier, Executive Director
National Sculpture Society
237 Park Avenue
New York, NY 10017
Phone: 212-764-5645
Fax: 212-764-5651
E-mail: gwen@nationalsculpture.org

Visual

Arts

NATIONAL WRITERS ASSOCIATION FOUNDATION
http://www.nationalwriters.com

National Writers Association Foundation Scholarships

Sandy Welchel, Executive Director
National Writers Association Foundation
10940 South Parker Road, Suite 508
Parker, CO 80134
Phone: 303-841-0246
Fax: 303-841-2607
E-mail: info@nationalwriters.com

NEBRASKA PRESS ASSOCIATION
http://www.nebpress.com

Nebraska Press Association Foundation, Inc., Scholarship

Allen Beermann, Executive Director
Nebraska Press Association
845 S Street
Lincoln, NE 68508-1226
Phone: 402-476-2851
Fax: 402-476-2942
E-mail: nebpress@nebpress.com

NETWORK OF EXECUTIVE WOMEN IN HOSPITALITY
http://www.newh.org

Network of Executive Women in Hospitality, Inc. Scholarship

Rebecca Folkerts, local NEWH Chapter
Phone: 800-593-6394

NEW ENGLAND FILM AND VIDEO FESTIVAL

New England Film and Video Festival Awards

Sandra Sullivan, Festival Co-director
New England Film and Video Festival
119 Braintree Street, Box 159, Suite 104
Boston, MA 02134
Phone: 617-783-9241 Ext. 12
Fax: 617-783-4368
E-mail: festival@bfvf.org

NEW ENGLAND PRINTING AND PUBLISHING COUNCIL
http://www.ppcne.org

New England Graphic Arts Scholarship

Kurt Drescher, Scholarship Chair
New England Printing and Publishing Council
PO Box 593
Reading, MA 01867-0218
Phone: 781-944-1116
Fax: 781-944-3905

NEW JERSEY SOCIETY OF ARCHITECTS/AIA NEW JERSEY SCHOLARSHIP FOUNDATION
http://www.aia-nj.org/about/scholarship.shtml

New Jersey Society of Architects Scholarship

Robert Zaccone, President
New Jersey Society of Architects/AIA New Jersey Scholarship Foundation
212 White Avenue
Old Tappan, NJ 07675
Phone: 201-767-9575
Fax: 201-767-5541

NEW YORK STATE EDUCATION DEPARTMENT
http://www.highered.nysed.gov

Regents Professional Opportunity Scholarship

Lewis J. Hall, Coordinator
New York State Education Department
Room 1078 EBA
Albany, NY 12234
Phone: 518-486-1319
Fax: 518-486-5346

ORANGE COUNTY COMMUNITY FOUNDATION
http://www.heef.org

Architecture and Engineering Scholarship Program

Rose Garris, Hispanic Education Endowment Fund
Orange County Community Foundation
30 Corporate Park, Suite 410
Irvine, CA 92606
Phone: 949-543-4202 Ext. 23
Fax: 949-553-4211

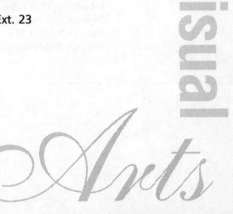

Visual Arts

Arts Scholarship Program

Rose Garris, Hispanic Education
Endowment Fund
Orange County Community Foundation
30 Corporate Park, Suite 410
Irvine, CA 92606
Phone: 949-543-4202 Ext. 23
Fax: 949-553-4211

**OREGON STUDENT ASSISTANCE
COMMISSION**
http://www.osac.state.or.us

Glenn R. and Juanita B. Struble Scholarship II

Director of Grant Programs
Oregon Student Assistance Commission
1500 Valley River Drive, Suite 100
Eugene, OR 97401-7020
Phone: 800-452-8807 Ext. 7395

Homestead Capital Housing Scholarship

Director of Grant Programs
Oregon Student Assistance Commission
1500 Valley River Drive, Suite 100
Eugene, OR 97401-7020
Phone: 800-452-8807 Ext. 7395

**OUTDOOR WRITERS ASSOCIATION OF
AMERICA**
http://www.owaa.org/

**Outdoor Writers Association of America
Bodie McDowell Scholarship Award**

Executive Director
Outdoor Writers Association of America
121 Hickory Street, Suite 1
Missoula, MT 59801
Phone: 406-728-7434
Fax: 406-728-7445
E-mail: owaa@montana.com

PARK PEOPLE
http://www.parkpeople.org

The Park People $2000 Scholarship

Scholarship Chair
Park People
3015 Richmond, Suite 210
Houston, TX 77098
Phone: 713-942-8429
Fax: 713-942-7275
E-mail: annem@parkpeople.org

**PHI DELTA THETA EDUCATIONAL
FOUNDATION**
http://phideltatheta.org

Francis D. Lyon Scholarships

Carmalieta Jenkins, Assistant to the
President
Phi Delta Theta Educational Foundation
2 South Campus Avenue
Oxford, OH 45056-1801
Phone: 513-523-6966
Fax: 513-523-9200
E-mail: carmalieta@phideltatheta.org

**PLUMBING-HEATING-COOLING
CONTRACTORS ASSOCIATION EDUCATION
FOUNDATION**
http://www.phccweb.org

Bradford White Corporation Scholarship

Program Assistant
Plumbing-Heating-Cooling Contractors
Association Education Foundation
PO Box 6808
Falls Church, VA 22040
Phone: 703-237-8100

Delta Faucet Company Scholarship Program

Scholarship Administrator
Plumbing-Heating-Cooling Contractors
Association Education Foundation
PO Box 6808
Falls Church, VA 22040
Phone: 800-533-7694
Fax: 703-237-7442
E-mail: naphcc@naphcc.org

**PHCC Educational Foundation Need-Based
Scholarship**

Scholarship Administrator
Plumbing-Heating-Cooling Contractors
Association Education Foundation
PO Box 6808
Falls Church, VA 22040

visual

Arts

PHCC Educational Foundation Scholarship Program

Scholarship Administrator
Plumbing-Heating-Cooling Contractors Association Education Foundation
PO Box 6808
Falls Church, VA 22040
Phone: 800-533-7694
Fax: 703-237-7442
E-mail: naphcc@naphcc.org

POLISH ARTS CLUB OF BUFFALO SCHOLARSHIP FOUNDATION
http://pacb.bfn.org/about/constitution.html

Polish Arts Club of Buffalo Scholarship Foundation Trust

Ann Flansburg, Selection Chair
Polish Arts Club of Buffalo Scholarship Foundation
PO Box 1362
Williamsville, NY 14231-1362
Phone: 716-626-9083
E-mail: donflans123@aol.com

PRINT AND GRAPHIC SCHOLARSHIP FOUNDATION
http://www.gain.net

Print and Graphics Scholarships

Bernadine Eckert, Program Administrator
Print and Graphic Scholarship Foundation
Printing Industries of America/Graphic Arts Technical Foundation
200 Deer Run Road
Sewickley, PA 15143-2600
Phone: 412-741-6860
Fax: 412-741-2311
E-mail: pgsf@gatf.org

PRINTING AND IMAGING ASSOCIATION OF MIDAMERICA
http://www.piamidam.org

Clampitt Paper/Henry Phillips Memorial Scholarship

Clampitt Paper/Henry Phillips Memorial Scholarship
Printing and Imaging Association of MidAmerica
c/o PIA-MidAmerica, 8828 North Stemmons, Suite 505
Dallas, TX 75247
Phone: 214-630-8871 Ext. 205
E-mail: dodier@piamidam.org

PRINTING INDUSTRIES OF MICHIGAN, INC. SCHOLARSHIP
http://www.print.org

Printing Industries of Michigan Scholarship Fund

Scholarship Committee
Printing Industries of Michigan, Inc. Scholarship
23815 Northwestern Highway, Suite 2700
Southfield, MI 48075-7713

PRINTING INDUSTRIES OF WISCONSIN EDUCATION FOUNDATION SCHOLARSHIPS
http://www.piw.org

Madison Area Club of Printing House Craftsmen Scholarship

Doug Mackenzie
Printing Industries of Wisconsin Education Foundation Scholarships
Stoughton High School, 600 Llincoln Avenue
Stoughton, WI 53589
Phone: 608-877-5781
Fax: 608-877-5619
E-mail: mackedo@mail.stoughton.k12.wi.us

PRINTING INDUSTRY OF MINNESOTA EDUCATION FOUNDATION
http://www.pimn.org

Printing Industry of Minnesota Education Foundation Scholarship Fund

Carla Steuck, Director of Education Services
Printing Industry of Minnesota Education Foundation
2829 University Avenue SE, Suite 750
Minneapolis, MN 55414-3248
Phone: 612-379-6012
Fax: 612-379-6030
E-mail: csteuck@pimn.org

QUILL AND SCROLL FOUNDATION
http://www.uiowa.edu/~quill-sc

Edward J. Nell Memorial Scholarship in Journalism

Richard Johns, Executive Director
Quill and Scroll Foundation
312 WSSH, School of Journalism
Iowa City, IA 52242-1528
Phone: 319-335-3321
Fax: 319-335-5210
E-mail: quill-scroll@uiowa.edu

Visual Arts

Quill and Scroll International Writing/Photo Contest

Richard Johns, Executive Director
Quill and Scroll Foundation
312 WSSH, School of Journalism
Iowa City, IA 52242-1528
Phone: 319-335-3321
Fax: 319-335-5210
E-mail: quill-scroll@uiowa.edu

RADIO-TELEVISION NEWS DIRECTORS ASSOCIATION AND FOUNDATION
http://www.rtndf.org/

Carole Simpson Scholarship

Karen Jackson-Bullitt, Project Coordinator
Radio-Television News Directors
    Association and Foundation
1600 K Street, NW, Suite 700
Washington, DC 20006
Phone: 202-467-5218
Fax: 202-223-4007
E-mail: karenb@rtndf.org

RHODE ISLAND FOUNDATION
http://www.rifoundation.org

Constant Memorial Scholarship for Aquidneck Island Residents

Libby Monahan, Scholarship Coordinator
Rhode Island Foundation
1 Union Station
Providence, RI 02903
Phone: 401-274-4564
Fax: 401-272-1359
E-mail: libbym@rifoundation.org

Rhode Island Edsal Advertising Scholarship

Scholarship Coordinator
Rhode Island Foundation
1 Union Station
Providence, RI 02903
Phone: 401-274-4564
Fax: 401-272-1359

ROBERT H. MOLLOHAN FAMILY CHARITABLE FOUNDATION, INC.
http://www.mollohanfoundation.org

Mary Olive Eddy Jones Art Scholarship

Teah Bayless, Program Manager
Robert H. Mollohan Family Charitable
    Foundation, Inc.
1000 Technology Drive, Suite 2000
Fairmont, WV 26554
Phone: 304-333-2251
Fax: 304-333-3900
E-mail: tmbayless@wvhtf.org

SAN FRANCISCO FOUNDATION
http://www.sff.org

Phelan Art Award in Filmmaking

Art Awards Coordinator
San Francisco Foundation
225 Bush Street, Suite 500
San Francisco, CA 94104
Phone: 415-733-8500

Phelan Art Award in Video

Art Awards Coordinator
San Francisco Foundation
225 Bush Street, Suite 500
San Francisco, CA 94104
Phone: 415-733-8500

SISTER KENNY REHABILITATION INSTITUTE
http://www.allina.com/

International Art Show for Artists with Disabilities

Laura Swift, Administrative Assistant
Sister Kenny Rehabilitation Institute
800 East 28th Street
Minneapolis, MN 55407-3799
Phone: 612-863-4466
Fax: 612-863-8942
E-mail: laura.swift@allina.com

SOCIETY OF AMERICAN MILITARY ENGINEERS—VIRGINIA PENINSULA POST
http://posts.same.org/vapeninsula/

The Virginia Peninsula Post of the Society of American Military Engineers (S.A.M.E.) Scholarship

Jeffrey B. Merz, Scholarship Chair
Society of American Military Engineers—
Virginia Peninsula Post
Society of American Military Engineers,
129 Andrews Street, Suite 102
Langley AFB, VA 23665-2769
Phone: 757-764-6579
E-mail: jeffrey.merz@langley.af.mil

SOCIETY OF AMERICAN REGISTERED ARCHITECTS
http://www.sara-national.org

SARA Student Design Competition

Cathie Moscato, Program Administrator
Society of American Registered Architects
PO Box 280
Cosby, TN 37822
Phone: 423-487-0365
Fax: 423-487-0365
E-mail: cathiemoscato@hotmail.com

SOCIETY OF MOTION PICTURE AND TELEVISION ENGINEERS
http://www.smpte.org

Lou Wolf Memorial Scholarship

Sally-Ann D'Amato, Society of Motion
Picture and Television Engineers
Society of Motion Picture and Television
Engineers
3 Barker Avenue
White Plains, NY 10601
Phone: 914-761-1100
E-mail: sdamato@smpte.org

Student Paper Award

Sally-Ann D'Amato, Society of Motion
Picture and Television Engineers
Society of Motion Picture and Television
Engineers
3 Barker Avenue
White Plains, NY 10601
Phone: 914-761-1100
E-mail: sdamato@smpte.org

SOUTH DAKOTA RETAILERS ASSOCIATION
http://www.sdra.org

South Dakota Retailers Association Scholarship Program

Donna Leslie, Communications Director
South Dakota Retailers Association
PO Box 638
Pierre, SD 57501
Phone: 800-658-5545
Fax: 605-224-2059
E-mail: dleslie@sdra.org

TAG AND LABEL MANUFACTURERS INSTITUTE, INC.
http://www.tlmi.com

TLMI 4 Year Colleges/Full-Time Students Scholarship

Karen Planz
Tag and Label Manufacturers Institute, Inc.
40 Shuman Boulevard, Suite 295
Naperville, IL 60563
Phone: 800-533-8564
E-mail: office@tlmi.com

TELETOON
http://www.teletoon.com

Teletoon Animation Scholarship Award Competition

Denise Vaughan, Senior Coordinator,
Public Relations
Teletoon
BCE Place
181 Bay Street, PO Box 787
Toronto M5J 2T3
Canada
Phone: 416-956-2060
Fax: 416-956-2070
E-mail: scholarship@teletoon.com

TEXAS ARTS AND CRAFTS EDUCATIONAL FOUNDATION
http://www.tacef.org

Emerging Texas Artist Scholarship

Texas Arts and Crafts Educational
Foundation
PO Box 291527
Kerrville, TX 78029-1527
Phone: 830-896-5711
E-mail: info@tacef.org

TEXAS GRAPHIC ARTS EDUCATIONAL FOUNDATION SCHOLARSHIPS

Texas Graphic Arts Educational Foundation Scholarships

Jim Weinstein, Director, Texas Graphic Arts Educational Foundation
Texas Graphic Arts Educational Foundation Scholarships
1720 Regal Row, Suite 150
Dallas, TX 75235
Phone: 214-630-8277
Fax: 214-637-1508

TEXAS GRIDIRON CLUB, INC.
http://www.spjfw.org

Texas Gridiron Club Scholarships

Angie Summers, Scholarships Coordinator
Texas Gridiron Club, Inc.
709 Houston Street
Arlington, TX 76012

TURNER CONSTRUCTION COMPANY
http://www.turnerconstruction.com

YouthForce 2020 Scholarship Program

Stephanie V. Ansari, Community Affairs Coordinator
Turner Construction Company
375 Hudson Street, 6th Floor
New York, NY 10014

U.S. FISH AND WILDLIFE SERVICE
http://duckstamps.fws.gov

Federal Junior Duck Stamp Conservation and Design Competition

Pat Fisher, Submit entry to State Coordinator, see Web site.
U.S. Fish and Wildlife Service
Federal Duck Stamp Office, 4401 North Fairfax Drive, Suite 4073
Arlington, VA 22203-1622
Phone: 703-358-2007

UNICO NATIONAL, INC
http://www.unico.org

Theodore Mazza Scholarship

UNICO National, Inc
UNICO National, Inc
271 US Highway 46 West, Suite A-108
Fairfield, NJ 07004
Phone: 973-808-0035
Fax: 973-808-0043

UNITED METHODIST COMMUNICATIONS
http://www.umcom.org/

Leonard M. Perryman Communications Scholarship for Ethnic Minority Students

Amelia Tucker-Shaw, Coordinator
United Methodist Communications
810 12th Avenue, South
Nashville, TN 37202-4744
Phone: 888-278-4862
E-mail: atucker-shaw@umcom.org

UNITED NEGRO COLLEGE FUND
http://www.uncf.org

Houston Symphony/ Top Ladies Scholarship

Rebecca Bennett, Director, Program Services
United Negro College Fund
8260 Willow Oaks Corporate Drive
Fairfax, VA 22031-8044
Phone: 800-331-2244
E-mail: rbennett@uncf.org

UNIVERSITY FILM AND VIDEO ASSOCIATION
http://www.ufva.org

University Film and Video Association Carole Fielding Student Grants

Prof. Robert Johnson, Jr., Chair, Carole Fielding Grants
University Film and Video Association
Framingham State College, 100 State Street
Framingham, MA 01701-9101
Phone: 508-626-4684
Fax: 508-626-4847
E-mail: rjohnso@frc.mass.edu

VALLEY PRESS CLUB
http://www.valleypressclub.com/

Valley Press Club Scholarships, The Republican Scholarship; Photojournalism Scholarship, Channel 22 Scholarship

Robert McClellan, Scholarship committee chair
Valley Press Club
PO Box 5475
Springfield, MA 01101
Phone: 413-783-3355

VARIAZIONE MIXED MEDIA ARTISTS' COLLECTIVE
http://www.zneart.com

Learning Scholarship

Zen Learning Scholarship
VariaZioNE Mixed Media Artists' Collective
1152 Crellin Road
Pleasanton, CA 94566

W. EUGENE SMITH MEMORIAL FUND, INC.
http://www.smithfund.org

W. Eugene Smith Grant in Humanistic Photography

Suzanne Nicholas, c/o ICP
W. Eugene Smith Memorial Fund, Inc.
1133 Avenue of Americas
New York, NY 10036
Phone: 212-857-9720

WATERBURY FOUNDATION
http://www.conncf.org/

Lois McMillen Memorial Scholarship Fund

Josh Carey, Program Officer
Waterbury Foundation
43 Field Street
Waterbury, CT 06702-1216
Phone: 203-753-1315
Fax: 203-756-3054
E-mail: jcarey@conncf.org

WAVERLY COMMUNITY HOUSE, INC.
http://www.waverlycomm.com

F. Lammot Belin Arts Scholarship

Chairperson
Waverly Community House, Inc.
1115 North Abington Road
PO Box 142
Waverly, PA 18471
Phone: 570-586-8191
Fax: 570-586-0185
E-mail: info@waverlycomm.com

WEST VIRGINIA SOCIETY OF ARCHITECTS/AIA
http://www.aiawv.org

West Virginia Society of Architects/AIA Scholarship

Roberta Guffey, Executive Director
West Virginia Society of Architects/AIA
223 Hale Street
Charleston, WV 25323
Phone: 304-344-9872
Fax: 304-343-0205
E-mail: Roberta.Guffey@aiawv.org

WOMEN IN FILM AND TELEVISION (WIFT)
http://www.wif.org

WIF Foundation Scholarship

Gayle Nachlix, WIF Foundation Scholarship
    Coordinator
Women in Film and Television (WIFT)
8857 West Olympic Boulevard, Suite 201
Beverly Hills, CA 90211
Phone: 310-657-5144

WORLDFEST INTERNATIONAL FILM AND VIDEO FESTIVAL
http://www.worldfest.org

Worldfest Student Film Award

Hunter Todd, Executive Director
Worldfest International Film and Video
    Festival
PO Box 56566
Houston, TX 77256-6566
Phone: 713-965-9955
Fax: 713-965-9960
E-mail: mail@worldfest.org

WORLDSTUDIO FOUNDATION
http://www.worldstudio.org

Worldstudio AIGA Scholarships

Scholarship Coordinator
Worldstudio Foundation
200 Varick Street, Suite 507
New York, NY 10014
Phone: 212-366-1317 Ext. 18
Fax: 212-807-0024
E-mail: scholarships@worldstudio.org

Worldstudio Foundation Scholarship Program

Scholarship Coordinator
Worldstudio Foundation
200 Varick Street, Suite 507
New York, NY 10014
Phone: 212-366-1317 Ext. 18
Fax: 212-807-0024
E-mail: scholarships@worldstudio.org

Visual Arts

Additional Resources

AMERICAN SOCIETY OF INTERIOR DESIGNERS (ASID)
608 Massachusetts Ave., NE
Washington, DC 20002-6006
Phone: 202-546-3480
Fax: (202) 546-3240
www.asid.org

FOUNDATION FOR INTERIOR DESIGN EDUCATION RESEARCH (FIDER)
146 Monroe Center NW, Suite 1318
Grand Rapids, MI 49503-2822
Phone: 616-458-0400
Fax: 616-458-0460
fider@fider.org

NATIONAL ART HONOR SOCIETIES
A Program of the National Art Education Association
1916 Association Drive
Reston, VA 20191-1590
Phone: 703-860-8000
Fax: 703-860-2960
www.naea-reston.org

NATIONAL ASSOCIATION OF SCHOOLS OF ART AND DESIGN (NASAD)
11250 Roger Bacon Drive, Suite 21
Reston, VA 20190-5248
Phone: 703-437-0700
Fax: 703-437-6312
E-mail: info@arts-accredit.org

NATIONAL FOUNDATION FOR ADVANCEMENT IN THE ARTS (NFAA)
Arts Recognition and Talent Search® (ARTS)
444 Brickell Avenue, P-14
Miami, FL 33131
Phone: 305-377-1140
Fax: 305-377-1149

NATIONAL PORTFOLIO DAY ASSOCIATION (NPDA)
www.npda.org

THE SOCIETY OF ILLUSTRATORS
128 East 63rd Street (between Park and Lexington Avenues)
New York, NY 10021-7303
Phone: 212-838-2560
Fax: 212-838-2561
E-mail: info@societyillustrators.org
www.societyillustrators.org

VISUAL AND PERFORMING ARTS COLLEGE FAIRS
National Association for College Admission Counseling (NACAC)
1631 Prince Street
Alexandria, Virginia, 22314
Phone: 703-836-2222
Fax: 703-836-8015

Visual *Arts*

Indexes

Majors and Concentrations

Visual

Arts

Visual *Arts*

Drawing *(continued)*

Editing

Editing and sound

Editorial illustration

Electronic arts

Electronic imaging

Electronic intermedia

Electronic media

Enameling

Entertainment art/animation

Environmental design

Experimental studies

Fabric design

Fabric styling

Fashion design

Fashion design and merchandising

Visual *Arts*

Visual Arts

Visual *Arts*

Painting/drawing

Academy of Art University *113*
Alberta College of Art & Design *115*
Alfred University *117*
American University *118*
Arcadia University *121*
Arkansas State University *122*
Brenau University *136*
Brigham Young University *136*
Brooklyn College of the City University of New York *137*
California College of the Arts *138*
California State University, Chico *142*
California State University, Fullerton *143*
California State University, Long Beach *144*
Central Michigan University *147*
College for Creative Studies *150*
Columbia College *156*
Cornell University *163*
Cornish College of the Arts *164*
Emmanuel College *170*
Emporia State University *171*
Grand Valley State University *177*
Guilford College *178*
Illinois State University *182*
Indiana State University *183*
Indiana University Bloomington *183*
Indiana University–Purdue University Indianapolis *184*
Jacksonville State University *188*
Kansas City Art Institute *189*
Kent State University *193*
Kutztown University of Pennsylvania *193*
Lindenwood University *196*
Louisiana State University and Agricultural and Mechanical College *197*
Louisiana Tech University *198*
Maharishi University of Management *200*
Marylhurst University *207*
Massachusetts College of Art *209*
Memphis College of Art *209*
Metropolitan State College of Denver *211*
Miami University *212*
Michigan State University *213*
Montserrat College of Art *218*
Mount Allison University *222*
Murray State University *222*
New Mexico State University *223*
Northern Illinois University *228*
Northern Kentucky University *228*
Notre Dame de Namur University *230*
The Ohio State University *231*
Oklahoma State University *233*
Oregon College of Art & Craft *234*
The Pennsylvania State University University Park Campus *243*

Pittsburg State University *243*
Pratt Institute *245*
Purchase College, State University of New York *248*
Rutgers, The State University of New Jersey, Mason Gross School of the Arts *208*
Saint Mary's College *257*
School of the Art Institute of Chicago *261*
School of Visual Arts *266*
Shepherd University *269*
Sonoma State University *270*
Southern Illinois University Carbondale *271*
Southern Oregon University *272*
State University of New York at Buffalo *273*
Sul Ross State University *277*
Syracuse University *277*
Temple University *283*
Texas Tech University *281*
Texas Woman's University *282*
The University of Akron *284*
The University of Alabama *285*
The University of Arizona *286*
University of Calgary *289*
University of Central Florida *290*
University of Connecticut *292*
University of Denver *293*
University of Florida *294*
University of Georgia *295*
University of Houston *297*
University of Illinois at Chicago *297*
University of Indianapolis *299*
The University of Iowa *299*
University of Louisville *301*
University of Massachusetts Dartmouth *302*
University of Michigan *305*
University of Minnesota, Twin Cities Campus *306*
The University of Montana–Missoula *308*
The University of North Carolina at Greensboro *311*
University of North Dakota *312*
University of Notre Dame *314*
University of Oregon *314*
University of Southern California *317*
The University of the Arts *320*
University of Utah *323*
University of Washington *323*
Utah State University *328*
Virginia Commonwealth University *329*
Wayne State University *332*
Webster University *334*
West Chester University of Pennsylvania *334*
Western Carolina University *335*
West Texas A&M University *336*
West Virginia University *337*

Photography (continued)

Savannah College of Art and Design *260*
School of the Art Institute of Chicago *261*
School of the Museum of Fine Arts, Boston *265*
School of Visual Arts *266*
Shepherd University *269*
Sonoma State University *270*
Southern Methodist University *272*
Southern Oregon University *272*
State University of New York at Buffalo *273*
State University of New York, Fredonia *274*
Stephen F. Austin State University *275*
Sul Ross State University *277*
Syracuse University *277*
Temple University *283*
Texas A&M University–Commerce *279*
Texas State University-San Marcos *281*
Texas Tech University *281*
Texas Woman's University *282*
The University of Akron *284*
The University of Alabama *285*
The University of Arizona *286*
University of Arkansas *287*
University of Calgary *289*
University of Central Florida *290*
University of Connecticut *292*
University of Dayton *292*
University of Denver *293*
University of Florida *294*
University of Georgia *295*
University of Hartford *296*
University of Houston *297*
University of Illinois at Chicago *297*
University of Illinois at Urbana–Champaign *298*
The University of Iowa *299*
University of Louisville *301*
University of Massachusetts Amherst *302*
University of Massachusetts Lowell *304*
University of Michigan *305*
University of Minnesota, Twin Cities Campus *306*
University of Missouri–Columbia *307*
The University of Montana–Missoula *308*
University of Nebraska–Lincoln *309*
University of North Alabama *310*
The University of North Carolina at Charlotte *311*
University of North Dakota *312*
University of Northern Iowa *313*
University of North Florida *313*
University of Notre Dame *314*
University of Oregon *314*
University of South Carolina *316*
University of Southern California *317*
University of Southern Maine *317*
The University of the Arts *320*

University of Utah *323*
University of Washington *323*
University of Wisconsin–Oshkosh *325*
University of Wisconsin–Superior *327*
Utah State University *328*
Virginia Commonwealth University *329*
Washington University in St. Louis *332*
Wayne State University *332*
Weber State University *333*
Webster University *334*
Western Carolina University *335*
Western Michigan University *336*
Wright State University *338*
York University *339*
Youngstown State University *340*

Photography and digital imaging
Ringling School of Art and Design *253*

Photography and imaging
New York University *226*
Virginia Intermont College *331*

Photography/digital arts
Moore College of Art & Design *220*

Photography/digital media
University of Houston *297*
Washington University in St. Louis *332*

Photography/new media
Kansas City Art Institute *189*

Photojournalism
Columbia College Chicago *159*
Corcoran College of Art and Design *161*

Pictorial arts
San Jose State University *260*

Playwriting
Drexel University *168*

Pottery
Colorado State University *155*

Pre-architecture
Adrian College *115*

Pre-art therapy
Adrian College *115*
Alfred University *117*
Arcadia University *121*

Pre-conservation
University of Denver *293*

Print media
Alfred University *117*

Printmaking

Printmaking (continued)
University of Calgary *289*
University of Central Florida *290*
University of Connecticut *292*
University of Denver *293*
University of Florida *294*
University of Georgia *295*
University of Hartford *296*
The University of Iowa *299*
University of Kansas *300*
University of Louisville *301*
University of Massachusetts Amherst *302*
University of Michigan *305*
University of Minnesota, Twin Cities Campus *306*
University of Missouri–Columbia *307*
The University of Montana–Missoula *308*
University of Nebraska–Lincoln *309*
University of North Dakota *312*
University of Northern Iowa *313*
University of Notre Dame *314*
University of Oregon *314*
University of Regina *315*
University of South Carolina *316*
University of Southern California *317*
University of Southern Maine *317*
The University of Tennessee *318*
The University of Texas at El Paso *319*
The University of the Arts *320*
University of Utah *323*
University of Washington *323*
University of Wisconsin–Oshkosh *325*
University of Wisconsin–Superior *327*
Utah State University *328*
Virginia Commonwealth University *329*
Wayne State University *332*
Webster University *334*
Western Carolina University *335*
Western Michigan University *336*
West Texas A&M University *336*
West Virginia University *337*
Williams Baptist College *338*
Wright State University *338*
York University *339*
Youngstown State University *340*

Printmaking/drawing
The University of North Carolina at Charlotte *311*
Washington University in St. Louis *332*

Product design
Art Center College of Design *124*
College for Creative Studies *150*
Columbia College Chicago *158*
Otis College of Art and Design *234*
Parsons The New School for Design *237*

Production
Columbia College Chicago *156*
North Carolina School of the Arts *227*

Production/design
North Carolina School of the Arts *227*
Savannah College of Art and Design *260*

Professional photography
Columbia College Chicago *159*

Public art studies
California College of the Arts *138*
University of Southern California *317*

Recording arts
International Academy of Design & Technology *185*

Restoration
Fashion Institute of Technology *171*

Rock art studies
Sul Ross State University *277*

Scientific illustration
Arcadia University *121*
University of Georgia *295*
University of Michigan *305*

Screenwriting
Columbia College Chicago *156*
Drexel University *168*
North Carolina School of the Arts *227*

Sculpture
Academy of Art University *113*
Alberta College of Art & Design *115*
Alfred University *117*
American University *118*
Arkansas State University *122*
Art Academy of Cincinnati *122*
The Art Institute of Boston at Lesley University *126*
Ball State University *130*
Baylor University *131*
Birmingham-Southern College *133*
Boston University *133*
Bowling Green State University *135*
Brenau University *136*
Brigham Young University *136*
Brooklyn College of the City University of New York *137*
California College of the Arts *138*
California State University, Chico *142*
California State University, Fullerton *143*
California State University, Long Beach *144*
Central Michigan University *147*
Clarke College *148*
The Cleveland Institute of Art *148*

Visual Arts

Visual Arts

University of Colorado at Boulder *291*
University of Dayton *292*
University of Illinois at Chicago *297*
The University of Iowa *299*
University of Minnesota, Duluth *305*
University of Mississippi *307*
University of Nebraska–Lincoln *309*
University of New Mexico *309*
The University of North Carolina at Greensboro *311*
University of Notre Dame *314*
University of Southern California *317*
The University of Texas at Austin *319*
University of the Pacific *322*
University of West Florida *324*
University of Wisconsin–Stout *326*

Surface design
Syracuse University *277*
Tennessee Technological University *119*

Text and image art
School of the Museum of Fine Arts, Boston *265*

Textile arts
California College of the Arts *138*
College for Creative Studies *150*
Indiana University Bloomington *183*
Kent State University *193*
Massachusetts College of Art *209*
Memphis College of Art *209*
Moore College of Art & Design *220*
School of the Art Institute of Chicago *261*
School of the Museum of Fine Arts, Boston *265*
Tennessee Technological University *119*
Truman State University *283*
The University of Arizona *286*
University of Louisville *301*
Virginia Commonwealth University *329*

Textile design
Syracuse University *277*
University of Massachusetts Dartmouth *302*

Textile/surface design
Fashion Institute of Technology *171*

Textiles
NSCAD University *230*
Rhode Island School of Design *251*

Three-dimensional studies
Bowling Green State University *135*
Moore College of Art & Design *220*
Seton Hill University *268*
University of Cincinnati *290*
University of Louisville *301*
University of Missouri–Columbia *307*

University of South Carolina *316*
University of Wisconsin–Stevens Point *326*
Weber State University *333*

Toy design
Fashion Institute of Technology *171*
Otis College of Art and Design *234*

Traditional animation
Columbia College Chicago *156*

Transportation design
Academy of Art University *113*
Art Center College of Design *124*
College for Creative Studies *150*

Two-dimensional studies
Bowling Green State University *135*
Moore College of Art & Design *220*
Seton Hill University *268*
University of Cincinnati *290*
University of Louisville *301*
University of Missouri–Columbia *307*
University of Wisconsin–Stevens Point *326*
Weber State University *333*

Urban studies
San Francisco Art Institute *258*

Video and sonic arts
Alfred University *117*

Video art
Cornish College of the Arts *164*
Illinois State University *182*
Maharishi University of Management *200*
Maryland Institute College of Art *204*
Northern Illinois University *228*
Otis College of Art and Design *234*
School of the Art Institute of Chicago *261*
School of the Museum of Fine Arts, Boston *265*
Syracuse University *277*
University of Illinois at Chicago *297*
The University of Iowa *299*
Virginia Commonwealth University *329*

Video production
Rutgers, The State University of New Jersey, Mason Gross School of the Arts *208*

Visual and game programming
The Art Institute of California–San Francisco *128*
The Art Institute of Phoenix *129*

Visual arts
Albion College *116*
Ithaca College *187*
Miami International University of Art & Design *211*
Simon Fraser University *269*

Visual

Arts

Alphabetical Listing of Schools

Visual

Arts

Visual *Arts*

Tyler School of Art of Temple University, Philadelphia, PA *283*

U

The University of Akron, Akron, OH *284*
The University of Alabama, Tuscaloosa, AL *285*
The University of Alabama at Birmingham, Birmingham, AL *286*
University of Alaska Anchorage, Anchorage, AK *286*
The University of Arizona, Tucson, AZ *286*
University of Arkansas, Fayetteville, AR *287*
University of Bridgeport, Bridgeport, CT *287*
The University of British Columbia, Vancouver, BC, Canada *288*
University of Calgary, Calgary, AB, Canada *289*
University of Central Arkansas, Conway, AR *289*
University of Central Florida, Orlando, FL *290*
University of Cincinnati, Cincinnati, OH *290*
University of Colorado at Boulder, Boulder, CO *291*
University of Colorado at Denver and Health Sciences Center - Downtown Denver Campus, Denver, CO *292*
University of Connecticut, Storrs, CT *292*
University of Dayton, Dayton, OH *292*
University of Delaware, Newark, DE *293*
University of Denver, Denver, CO *293*
University of Evansville, Evansville, IN *294*
University of Florida, Gainesville, FL *294*
University of Georgia, Athens, GA *295*
University of Hartford, West Hartford, CT *296*
University of Hawaii at Manoa, Honolulu, HI *296*
University of Houston, Houston, TX *297*
University of Idaho, Moscow, ID *297*
University of Illinois at Chicago, Chicago, IL *297*
University of Illinois at Urbana–Champaign, Champaign, IL *298*
University of Indianapolis, Indianapolis, IN *299*
The University of Iowa, Iowa City, IA *299*
University of Kansas, Lawrence, KS *300*
University of Louisiana at Lafayette, Lafayette, LA *300*
University of Louisville, Louisville, KY *301*
University of Mary Hardin-Baylor, Belton, TX *302*
University of Massachusetts Amherst, Amherst, MA *302*
University of Massachusetts Dartmouth, North Dartmouth, MA *302*
University of Massachusetts Lowell, Lowell, MA *304*
University of Memphis, Memphis, TN *304*
University of Miami, Coral Gables, FL *305*
University of Michigan, Ann Arbor, MI *305*
University of Minnesota, Duluth, Duluth, MN *305*
University of Minnesota, Twin Cities Campus, Minneapolis, MN *306*
University of Mississippi, University, MS *307*

University of Missouri–Columbia, Columbia, MO *307*
University of Missouri–St. Louis, St. Louis, MO *308*
The University of Montana–Missoula, Missoula, MT *308*
University of Montevallo, Montevallo, AL *309*
University of Nebraska–Lincoln, Lincoln, NE *309*
University of Nevada, Las Vegas, Las Vegas, NV *309*
University of New Hampshire, Durham, NH *309*
University of New Mexico, Albuquerque, NM *309*
University of North Alabama, Florence, AL *310*
The University of North Carolina at Asheville, Asheville, NC *311*
The University of North Carolina at Charlotte, Charlotte, NC *311*
The University of North Carolina at Greensboro, Greensboro, NC *311*
University of North Dakota, Grand Forks, ND *312*
University of Northern Iowa, Cedar Falls, IA *313*
University of North Florida, Jacksonville, FL *313*
University of North Texas, Denton, TX *314*
University of Notre Dame, Notre Dame, IN *314*
University of Oklahoma, Norman, OK *314*
University of Oregon, Eugene, OR *314*
University of Regina, Regina, SK, Canada *315*
University of South Alabama, Mobile, AL *316*
University of South Carolina, Columbia, SC *316*
The University of South Dakota, Vermillion, SD *316*
University of Southern California, Los Angeles, CA *317*
University of Southern Maine, Portland, ME *317*
The University of Tennessee, Knoxville, TN *318*
The University of Tennessee at Chattanooga, Chattanooga, TN *318*
The University of Tennessee at Martin, Martin, TN *319*
The University of Texas at Arlington, Arlington, TX *319*
The University of Texas at Austin, Austin, TX *319*
The University of Texas at El Paso, El Paso, TX *319*
The University of Texas at San Antonio, San Antonio, TX *320*
The University of Texas at Tyler, Tyler, TX *320*
The University of Texas–Pan American, Edinburg, TX *320*
The University of the Arts, Philadelphia, PA *320*
University of the Pacific, Stockton, CA *322*
University of Utah, Salt Lake City, UT *323*
University of Washington, Seattle, WA *323*
University of West Florida, Pensacola, FL *324*
University of West Georgia, Carrollton, GA *324*
University of Wisconsin–Eau Claire, Eau Claire, WI *325*
University of Wisconsin–Madison, Madison, WI *325*
University of Wisconsin–Milwaukee, Milwaukee, WI *325*
University of Wisconsin–Oshkosh, Oshkosh, WI *325*

Visual

Arts

Visual

Arts

Peterson's
Book Satisfaction Survey

Give Us Your Feedback

Thank you for choosing Peterson's as your source for personalized solutions for your education and career achievement. Please take a few minutes to answer the following questions. Your answers will go a long way in helping us to produce the most user-friendly and comprehensive resources to meet your individual needs.

When completed, please tear out this page and mail it to us at:

> Publishing Department
> PETERSON'S, A Nelnet Company
> 2000 Lenox Drive
> Lawrenceville, NJ 08648

You can also complete this survey online at **www.petersons.com/booksurvey.**

1. **What is the ISBN of the book you have purchased? (The ISBN can be found on the book's back cover in the lower right-hand corner.)** _____

2. **Where did you purchase this book?**
   - ❑ Retailer, such as Barnes & Noble
   - ❑ Online reseller, such as Amazon.com
   - ❑ Petersons.com
   - ❑ Other (please specify) _____

3. **If you purchased this book on Petersons.com, please rate the following aspects of your online purchasing experience on a scale of 4 to 1**
   (4 = Excellent and 1 = Poor).

	4	3	2	1
Comprehensiveness of Peterson's Online Bookstore page	❑	❑	❑	❑
Overall online customer experience	❑	❑	❑	❑

4. **Which category best describes you?**
   - ❑ High school student
   - ❑ Parent of high school student
   - ❑ College student
   - ❑ Graduate/professional student
   - ❑ Returning adult student
   - ❑ Teacher
   - ❑ Counselor
   - ❑ Working professional/military
   - ❑ Other (please specify) _____

5. **Rate your overall satisfaction with this book.**

Extremely Satisfied	Satisfied	Not Satisfied
❑	❑	❑

6. Rate each of the following aspects of this book on a scale of 4 to 1 (4 = Excellent and 1 = Poor).

	4	3	2	1
Comprehensiveness of the information	❑	❑	❑	❑
Accuracy of the information	❑	❑	❑	❑
Usability	❑	❑	❑	❑
Cover design	❑	❑	❑	❑
Book layout	❑	❑	❑	❑
Special features (e.g., CD, flashcards, charts, etc.)	❑	❑	❑	❑
Value for the money	❑	❑	❑	❑

7. This book was recommended by:

❑ Guidance counselor
❑ Parent/guardian
❑ Family member/relative
❑ Friend
❑ Teacher
❑ Not recommended by anyone—I found the book on my own
❑ Other (please specify) _____

8. Would you recommend this book to others?

Yes	Not Sure	No
❑	❑	❑

9. Please provide any additional comments.

_____

_____

_____

_____

Remember, you can tear out this page and mail it to us at:

Publishing Department
PETERSON'S, A Nelnet Company
2000 Lenox Drive
Lawrenceville, NJ 08648

or you can complete the survey online at **www.petersons.com/booksurvey.**

Your feedback is important to us at Peterson's, and we thank you for your time!

If you would like us to keep in touch with you about new products and services, please include your e-mail here: _____